TRADE RULES
IN THE MAKING

TRADE RULES
IN THE MAKING

Challenges in Regional and

Multilateral Negotiations

Miguel Rodríguez Mendoza

Patrick Low

Barbara Kotschwar

Editors

ORGANIZATION OF AMERICAN STATES

BROOKINGS INSTITUTION PRESS

Washington, D.C.

ABOUT BROOKINGS

The Brookings Institution is a private nonprofit organization devoted to research, education, and publication on important issues of domestic and foreign policy. Its principal purpose is to bring knowledge to bear on current and emerging policy problems. The Institution maintains a position of neutrality on issues of public policy. Interpretations or conclusions in publications of the Brookings Institution Press should be understood to be solely those of the authors.

Library of Congress Cataloging-in-Publication data

Trade rules in the making : challenges in regional and
multilateral negotiations / Miguel Rodríguez Mendoza, Patrick Low,
and Barbara Kotschwar, editors
p.   cm.
Includes bibliographical references and index.
ISBN 0-8157-5679-8 (alk. paper)
1. Free trade—America.   2. America—Economic integration.
3. Regionalism—America.   I. Rodríguez Mendoza, Miguel.
II. Low, Patrick, 1949–   .   III. Kotschwar, Barbara.
HF1745.T73   1999   99-6279
382′.71′097—dc21   CIP

9 8 7 6 5 4 3 2 1

The paper used in this publication meets the minimum requirements of the American
National Standard for Information Sciences—Permanence of Paper for Printed
Library Materials: ANSI Z39.48-1984.

Typeset in Times Roman

Composition by Princeton Editorial Associates
Scottsdale, Arizona, and Roosevelt, New Jersey

Printed by R. R. Donnelley and Sons Co.
Harrisonburg, Virginia

Foreword

This volume arose out of a series of papers prepared for a joint project undertaken by the Organization of American States (OAS), Georgetown University, and the World Trade Organization (WTO). The aim of this undertaking is to support the countries in the Western Hemisphere, particularly the smaller economies, as they move toward open trade and investment relations.

The chapters presented in this volume were first discussed at a conference, held at the OAS headquarters in Washington, D.C., in May 1998. The book targets the key trade issues on the agenda at both the regional and multilateral levels and will serve as a textbook for a training course for government officials from the smaller countries of the Americas. The volume is timely for the countries of the Western Hemisphere, as they are currently negotiating a Free Trade Area of the Americas (FTAA) and preparing for a potential new round of multilateral trade negotiations.

One of the primary principles guiding the FTAA negotiations is that of WTO consistency. Although the need for consistency should be self-evident, as nearly all FTAA participants are members of the WTO, the formal recognition of this principle from the outset of the negotiations is significant—and will have an important impact on the content of the FTAA agreement. In order to comply with the GATT/WTO rules on regionalism, the FTAA will have to encompass "substantially all" trade among its members, may not raise barriers to trade with outside sources, and must be fully operational within ten years of the signing of the agreement.

The FTAA will address traditional as well as many nontraditional trade issues. In the traditional arena of border measures, the FTAA seeks the removal of all tariffs and other barriers to trade among the participants—a goal not yet achieved in the multilateral arena. Together with issues such as tariff and nontariff barrier reductions, rules of origin, and customs procedures, the negotiators will tackle such new trade issues as competition policy, which has never been the subject of a multilateral agreement, and for which only the European countries have implemented a common regional approach. The difficulties in negotiating an investment agreement should not be underestimated, and issues such as government procurement, while covered in a plurilateral WTO agreement, will pose distinct challenges to the countries of this region. By including new issues and aiming to *eliminate* barriers to trade and investment, the FTAA is designed not only to be WTO consistent but to go beyond the WTO Agreement.

An important element of the FTAA is its recognition of the different size and levels of development of its members—and its intent to address this. The FTAA will be a unique endeavor to eliminate barriers to trade and investment among the economies of thirty-four countries that vary greatly in terms of size and territory, population, and natural resource endowments. Although reciprocal agreements between large and small countries, almost unheard of in the past, are becoming more and more common, the underlying challenges to ensure the full participation of the smaller economies in the negotiations, as well as the implementation of the agreements, remain.

To facilitate the participation of these small countries in the FTAA process, the OAS, through its Trade Unit and with the financial support of the OAS Inter-American Council for Integral Development (CIDI), has come together with Georgetown University to develop a comprehensive seminar on regional and multilateral trade issues. We hope that the discussions in this book will help clarify the issues that will be negotiated and be a useful resource for the countries as they move toward their goal of trade and investment liberalization.

César Gaviria   Arturo Valenzuela
Secretary General   Director, Center for Latin American Studies
Organization of American States   Georgetown University

Acknowledgments

Although three names are listed on the cover of this book, a much larger number of people have contributed to the construction of this volume.

First we must recognize the tireless efforts and enduring patience of Veronica Luckow, without whose research assistance and management skills this book would not have been possible. Jane Thery coordinated the overall project and offered support and advice throughout the process. A special word of gratitude is also due Sam Laird, whose help at various phases of this project was absolutely invaluable. Many others offered ideas, suggestions, comments, and inspiration to this project. We especially acknowledge the contributions of William Berensen, Gonzalo Capriles, Murray Gibbs, Henry Gill, Gustavo Guzmán, Pamela Hamilton, Gary Hufbauer, Robin King, Donald Mackay, César Parga, Sarath Rajapatirana, José Manuel Salazar, Jeffrey Schott, and Ernesto Stein, as well as the many anonymous reviewers who offered useful comments on the manuscripts.

Adriana Perez-Mina and Antonio Gago offered able assistance with both the book and the conference at which the papers that later became chapters of the book were presented. Nancy Davidson and Janet Walker of the Brookings Institution ably managed the editing process. We are grateful to Ivonne Zuniga, Francisco Coves, and Pedro Perez for their invaluable assistance in putting the conference together and making sure that the meeting ran smoothly.

The Organization of American States and Georgetown University must be thanked for funding and housing the project. Neither these institutions nor the people mentioned above are held accountable for any errors, omissions, or overstatements made in the work. This responsibility lies with the editors and the authors of the chapters.

Contents

PART TWO   PREFERENTIAL TRADE AND REGIONAL AGREEMENTS

PART THREE   ENHANCING TRADE RULES

PART FOUR   THE NEWEST TRADE POLICY ISSUES

Tables

Figures

Trade Rules in the Making: An Overview

Miguel Rodríguez Mendoza,
Patrick Low, and Barbara Kotschwar

Three unremitting trends over the last few decades have fundamentally changed the nature of the debate about regionalism and the way that analysts and policymakers think about the relationship between regional trade agreements and the multilateral trading system. First, trade policy is no longer primarily about trade measures at the border. Deepening economic integration and the increasing fusion of national economies into a global whole make international cooperation across a far broader spectrum of policies more essential than ever before.

Second, the number of countries that have become players in the world economy has increased enormously. Great disparity exists among these countries, adding further to the challenges of securing shared benefits from international cooperation. The increase in the number of countries participating in the world economy is about numbers only in a trivial sense. What has really counted is the changed policy stance of many countries, such that greater openness and continuing liberalization have raised the stakes of dozens of countries in the nature and functioning of the international economy.

Third, more and more countries have entered into regional integration agreements, which can now be counted in dozens and involve all but very few countries in one sort or another of preferential trading arrangement. Some countries, especially in Latin America, are members of several agreements that cover a significant proportion of their international trade relationships.

1

Many would argue that the first two trends in the international economy noted here—an expanding policy agenda of growing complexity and heightened but disparate national interests in a progressively integrating world—help to explain the third trend, that of growing regionalism. And herein lies the core policy challenge of regionalism and of defining the appropriate relationship between regionalism and multilateralism. Piecemeal economic integration may be seen, at least in part, as an attempt to render economic integration more manageable. It may also be seen as a recipe for securing more rapid results. But because of its geographically exclusionary nature, it also runs the risk of complicating or even frustrating the attainment of the true benefits of economic integration on a global scale. Countless writers on regionalism have inevitably focused on this potential contradiction—that in reaching for the benefits of integration, badly conceived regional approaches may attenuate those very benefits. Therein lies the importance of securing the appropriate balance of emphasis between regional agreements and the multilateral trading system. It is clear that outward-looking regional agreements based on trade liberalization commitments are much more likely to be positive from a multilateral perspective than some earlier regional integration efforts that placed emphasis on enlarging the import substitution base rather than competing in world markets.

Much analysis, both old and new, of the economic effects and political economy implications of regional integration initiatives fails to draw a priori welfare conclusions. The theory of second best finds a prominent place in this discourse, and the theory's baseline conclusion about the welfare effects of partial liberalization scenarios is that "it all depends"; the specificity of circumstances, the details of particular arrangements, and even the political motivation for pursuing them can all be determinants of welfare outcomes. It is for this reason that empirical work has become so important in helping us to understand the likely consequences of particular trade policy arrangements.

It is easy for governments to pay verbal homage to the primacy of their commitment to the multilateral trading system while they focus their efforts on their regional priorities. It is equally easy for defenders of multilateralism to fall into the trap of seeking perfection at the expense of progress. At the same time protagonists of regional arrangements may sometimes succumb to the fallacy of presenting any liberalization, however narrowly drawn in geographical terms, as better than no liberalization. The right balance of emphasis and priorities—the balance that will promote welfare through a judicious mix of emphasis on the regional and the multilateral—requires careful analysis of the many policy issues at stake. Consistency and complementarity are crucial.

The collection of chapters that make up this volume seeks to contribute to our understanding of economic integration issues, entering into considerable detail on an eclectic set of policy questions. These chapters have been written for policymakers, for practitioners—for those who must deal directly with the reality that both regionalism and multilateralism are with us, and they are here to stay for the foreseeable future. The challenge, therefore, is to manage trade relations within these different frameworks in the collective interest, not to question the basic legitimacy of particular types of trade arrangements. Neither do the chapters purport to address theoretical questions that have attracted growing attention among analysts as regionalism has burgeoned.

The chapters are unusually wide-ranging in their scope for a single volume, addressing trade and trade-related policy issues that are relevant in both the regional and the multilateral context, as well as such matters as nonreciprocal preference schemes. No effort has been made to fashion a set of chapters that are in agreement on all issues. It will be readily apparent that the views of authors differ on a number of points, some more fundamentally than others, but such divergence can only enrich the debate. What follows is a brief summary of the main points made in the chapters of the volume, and it must be emphasized that this summary is a poor substitute for reading the chapters themselves.

Part I: Regionalism and Multilateral Rules

Robert Z. Lawrence reviews the tensions between regional and multilateral agreements by tracing the evolution of international trade policy over the last few decades. Taking the perspective of developing countries, he examines historical shifts in the focus of trade policy and the role of regional and multilateral arrangements in achieving trade liberalization. Lawrence sees the current trend toward deeper international integration as a result of the changing realities of trade policy. Whereas the emphasis in the period immediately after World War II was on dismantling at-the-border barriers, leaving countries free to pursue domestic policies in areas such as investment, competition policy, and regulatory standards, there is now a drive for the harmonization and reconciliation of domestic policies at the world level.

There are political as well as functional reasons for this trend. As foreign trade and foreign investment have become increasingly complementary, trade policymakers have sought to cover the regulatory conditions under which foreign investors operate. Already present at the multilateral level, particularly since the agreements reached during the Uruguay Round, the new regulatory orientation of trade policy is also permeating regional arrangements, including those concluded among developing countries. As these countries try to attract foreign investment, they tailor their agreements to meet the regulatory concerns of foreign firms. Lawrence thinks that trade agreements "are motivated by the desire to facilitate international investment and the operations of multinational firms as much as by the desire to promote trade. Although liberalization to permit trade requires the removal of border barriers—a relatively shallow form of integration—the development of regional production systems and the promotion of investment in services requires deeper forms of international integration of national regulatory systems and policies."

Seen in this light, regionalism in developing countries is a result of their increasing participation in the global economy. Still the question as to the relevance of regionalism vis-à-vis multilateralism remains. Lawrence sees no cause for concern. Historically regional trade arrangements and the international system have coexisted and complemented each other, as both have allowed countries to move toward free trade. In Lawrence's view it would be erroneous to consider regional arrangements as "second best" alternatives and thus inferior to the multilateral approach, as traditional analyses do. In fact, some issues are better dealt with at the regional level. For issues of "deeper" integration, which involve domestic regulatory concerns, regional arrangements could well be the "first best." After all, a results-oriented approach—with the ultimate end of trade liberalization—need not be biased by predetermined value judgments about the means.

Still, the debate continues. Robert E. Hudec and James D. Southwick examine the implementation problems posed by Article XXIV of the General Agreement on Tariffs and Trade (GATT)—the legal instrument by which the multilateral system addresses regional arrangements—and the extent to which those have been addressed by the Uruguay Round understanding on this provision. These authors see Article XXIV as reflecting a basic tension in the world trading system. It recognizes the desire and right of countries to enter into regional agreements—customs unions and free trade areas. At the same time it seeks to prevent the trade diversion that could result from allowing "members of a regional trade agreement to treat each other more favorably than they treat other WTO [World Trade Organization] members."

The two basic requirements of Article XXIV—not to raise duties and other trade barriers to third countries and to eliminate trade restrictions on "substantially all" trade—have been subject to different interpretations. The Uruguay Round Understanding on Article XXIV helped to clarify some of the issues, such as the methodology for estimating the overall incidence of duties of customs unions on third countries. On other issues such as rules of origin, limited progress was made in spite of the widely held view that rules of origin could have a detrimental effect on multilateral trade relations. Neither was progress made toward clarifying the "substantially all" trade requirement, leaving open the question of whether the exclusion from the agreements of entire economic sectors, such as agriculture, would make them fail the test of Article XXIV.

A related issue is that of the right of members of a regional agreement to exclude other members from restrictions—quantitative restrictions, tariffs, and other measures—that they can apply under various GATT provisions. In some cases excluding partners from the measures could impose additional burdens on nonmembers. For example, in a balance of payments crisis the exclusion of partner countries from the restrictions imposed to cope with the crisis might make those restrictions more severe or of a longer duration, thus affecting the trade of nonmembers beyond what would be necessary had members also been included. The same principle applies to safeguards—an area in which the tendency in modern regional agreements is to exclude members—and to anti-dumping and countervailing duties. These are certainly issues not yet satisfactorily resolved. They may be tackled in future WTO negotiations or further clarified by recourse to dispute settlement procedures.

Closing the section on regionalism and multilateralism, Miguel Rodríguez Mendoza focuses on two of the most dynamic Latin American regional agreements, those of the Southern Common Market (Mercosur) and the Andean Community. He seeks to assess the impact of these regional agreements both on members' trade with one another and on their trade with third countries using a number of analytical tools. He points out that these agreements have had a positive impact on members' trade liberalization efforts and on trade growth among their member countries. At the same time, trade with the rest of the world has not suffered as the agreements have moved forward in accomplishing their objectives. He attributes this to the greater market orientation of the arrangements and to the trade liberalization measures implemented by their member countries in the late 1980s.

The Mercosur and the Andean Community have moved well beyond what previous Latin American agreements achieved. They have effected a significant reduction of barriers to trade among their members and implemented common external tariffs whose levels are comparable to the lower tariff rates achieved through the members' trade liberalization. Although exemptions still exist, they are in the process of being phased out. Both agreements have weathered crises, financial as well as political. The agreements have been kept open to the outside world, thus benefiting other countries as well, and are being implemented with due regard to the multilateral commitments of their member countries.

Part II: Preferential Trade and Regional Agreements

In the first chapter of this section Bonapas Onguglo analyzes in depth existing unilateral trade preference schemes and speculates as to their future. Barbara Kotschwar then sets forth the challenges facing smaller economies integrating into reciprocal trade agreements and discusses some policy options to address these issues. Next Jean-Marie Grether and Marcelo Olarreaga measure the magnitude of preferential trade in relation to world trade. Finally Roberto Bouzas draws parallels between today's preferential trade agreements and earlier ones.

In his chapter Bonapas Onguglo looks at a number of preferential schemes, including the Generalized System of Preferences (GSP), the Caribbean Basin Initiative (CBI), the Andean Trade Preference Act (ATPA), the South Pacific Regional Trade and Economic Cooperation Agreement (SPARTECA), and the Lomé Convention. He explores these kinds of trade relationships, explains the evolution away from preferential arrangements, and speculates on future trade relationships between developed and developing countries. Onguglo thinks these schemes have been "resilient and durable instruments of development cooperation." The GSP, for one, has been in operation for over twenty-seven years and in 1996 covered about 24 percent of U.S. imports from beneficiary countries. In the European Union GSP preferences covered 37 percent of imports from beneficiary countries for the same year. Preferential trade arrangements have allowed some countries to diversify their exports and develop new export industries.

Despite these benefits, Onguglo recognizes a number of constraints. For example, while product coverage includes most agricultural and industrial exports, there are always a few notable exceptions. In order to benefit from these schemes, countries must meet certain noneconomic conditions. At the same time, the tariff decreases and increases in bound duty-free treatment of goods in developed countries have greatly reduced the margin of preference available to beneficiaries of special and differential treatment, and thus may decrease the desirability of these preferences.

The participation of smaller economies in the process of negotiating the proposed Free Trade Area of the Americas (FTAA) is the focus of Barbara Kotschwar's chapter. A debate between theory and practice is at issue. Although conventional trade theory points unequivocally to the gains from trade that accrue to small countries as they open their economies or enter into trade agreements with larger countries, the real world may not be quite so tidy. As Kotschwar writes, "Although smaller size may net unequivocal gains in the simple classical trade model, this same factor of smallness is associated with market and resource constraints that . . . may weigh quite heavily on the consciousness of policymakers while deciding whether to engage in trade and integration arrangements."

The countries involved in negotiating the FTAA vary widely in size, territory, population, natural resource endowments, and levels of economic development. One illustration of this disparity is the case of Jamaica, a country that is not the smallest of the FTAA participants, but could fit 250 times into the territory of Argentina, not by any stretch the largest FTAA participant. This asymmetry explains why the participation of the smaller economies has been an important topic in the FTAA negotiation process.

Kotschwar's chapter considers some of the characteristics that make the smaller countries "different" from the other countries participating in the negotiations—and that require consideration by the architects of the FTAA framework. At stake is how to ensure the fullest participation of these countries in the FTAA while taking due account of their basic needs and concerns. As the FTAA will be a reciprocal agreement, this will involve allowing the smaller economies the greatest flexibility in meeting their obligations. Measures include extended time frames for the phasing out of tariff and nontariff barriers; flexibility in the implementation of the agreements, including joint implementation of some measures; and provision of technical assistance in the negotiating process as well as the implementation phase.

For most of the smaller economies in the Western Hemisphere the cost of nonparticipation in the FTAA would outweigh that of participation in the agreement, as they would be isolated from the markets that now constitute a large part of their trade. By participating fully in the FTAA, Caribbean and Central American countries will be legally entitled to enter their most important markets—those of the United States and Canada—by means of a binding agreement rather than by relying on the fragile unilateral preferential arrangements now in place. Therefore, the FTAA process, through its participatory, consensual principles, gives the small countries the opportunity to shape the framework in which they will conduct trade with their hemispheric partners.

As Grether and Olarreaga show, preferential trade agreements have proliferated in recent years. The authors estimate that the share of world trade represented by preferential trade is about 42 percent for the period from 1993 through 1997. This proportion varies across regions; Europe is the most concentrated participant, with a 70 percent share. In the Western Hemisphere the share of total trade represented by preferential trade is about 25 percent. Disaggregating these figures to see the impact of unilateral preferences and taking the GSP as a proxy for unilateral preferential trade, the authors find that trade under the GSP has declined over the two periods studied—roughly the first and second halves of the 1990s—from 7 percent to 3 percent of preferential trade. This suggests that developing countries rely less than previously on the GSP as a means of integrating into the world economy than previously and more on other means of integration—for example, on preferential trade agreements with developed countries.

Grether and Olarreaga also find that the move toward preferential trade seems to depend on country size and level of GDP per capita. This, they speculate, may be due to factors such as bargaining power incentives and financial constraints. Another observation is that countries that have entered into regional arrangements in the latter half of the 1990s have tended to be the most open economies, supporting the notion that the rise in regionalism can be an engine for the multilateral system rather than an impediment to it.

Roberto Bouzas examines past regional arrangements and assesses the elements that have made them successful—or not. An essential element, according to Bouzas, is political commitment. The strength of this political commitment is determined by broader governance questions and the economic policy environment. To date, all success stories examined involve developed countries with mature governance institutions, stable macroeconomic environments, and relatively common values and objectives.

The institutional designs of successful regional arrangements differ. At one extreme is the European Union with its highly structured institutions and supranational decisionmaking bodies. Other successful initiatives have adopted alternative frameworks. Considering the multitude of failed regional integration experiences, institutional design does not appear to be a major explanatory factor. Whatever the institutional framework, Bouzas finds that successful arrangements aim toward a "deepening and leveling of the playing field." As market integration develops, the demand for a more stable and predictable environment increases, thus stimulating a deepening of the scope of regional preferential agreements. Similarly, as market integration grows, demands for a level playing field mount.

Regional arrangements are the result of a variety of motives, which include political, strategic, bargaining, and trade policy considerations. These arrangements have rarely resulted from a careful, objective examination of economic costs and benefits. But the existence of net economic benefits and the issue of their distribution among member countries have turned into important factors as agreements have been implemented.

Part III: Enhancing Trade Rules

This section examines the heart of the matter—improving market access through trade liberalization. Although at both the regional and the multilateral level trade policy has become increasingly complex and topics on the trade agenda broader, barriers at nations' borders continue to be significant. As the agenda increasingly involves disciplines, many posit that traditional market access issues have lost importance. In many elements of interest to developing countries this is not yet the case.

A "traditional" issue, but one that remains central to market access negotiations, is that of reducing tariffs and nontariff measures. The main focus of negotiations in the first seven rounds of multilateral negotiations, border measures lately have been eclipsed as complex disciplines have taken their place on the international trade agenda and as countries have undertaken unilateral trade liberalization initiatives. Average tariffs have fallen considerably over the last fifty years, and developing countries, especially those in the Western Hemisphere, have dramatically liberalized their trade regimes. The reduction of tariffs and nontariff measures will, however, remain a major issue in future multilateral market access negotiations, as will the elimination of such barriers in the context of the FTAA.

In his chapter Sam Laird presents a comprehensive overview of the different approaches to negotiating the reduction of tariff and nontariff barriers, taking as his point of departure the techniques employed during the Uruguay Round. He explains the benefits and challenges of each type of approach and its applicability to developing countries. His chapter sets out the important tariff and nontariff issues that will be on the market access agenda of the FTAA negotiations.

Laird emphasizes the importance for developing countries of participating actively in multilateral negotiations, as the improved security of access through increased tariff bindings may offer more advantages to developing countries than unilaterally granted but unbound preferential access. The advantage of their making their own commitments is that they can provide themselves with stable and credible trade regimes to attract investment and the associated technology needed for their further development. Laird also emphasizes the need for developing countries to develop technical expertise to deal with the depth and complexity of the negotiating issues.

The next chapter, by Francisco Javier Prieto and Sherry M. Stephenson, deals with trade in services, an issue that only recently has been brought under multilateral or regional disciplines. The General Agreement on Trade in Services (GATS) was a main result of the Uruguay Round. It provided a legal framework for the continued liberalization of trade in the services sector—as witnessed by the agreements on basic telecommunications and financial services concluded in the last two years—and is structured along the principles of most favored nation treatment, national treatment, and transparency. These same principles guide the agreements on services concluded by countries in the Americas: the North American Free Trade Agreement (NAFTA), the Mercosur, and a number of recent bilateral free trade agreements entered into by Mexico and Canada with other Latin American countries.

A key difference between these agreements, however, is the approach they take to promoting trade liberalization. As Prieto and Stephenson point out, "liberalizing trade in services involves a different approach than the reduction of price-based measures; it requires the removal, modification, or nondiscriminatory application of national regulatory mechanisms." To accomplish this the GATS and the Mercosur take a "positive list" or "bottom-up" approach whereby countries open only the services sectors they expressly include in their commitments under the agreements. The NAFTA and most of the existing trade agreements in the Americas—many of which are NAFTA-inspired—follow a "negative list" or "top-down" approach whereby all services sectors except those totally or partially excluded are covered by the agreements.

Although a debate is going on as to which of these two approaches is more conducive to trade liberalization, neither seems to guarantee full liberalization of trade in services. They do not, as a general rule, include obligations to achieve a certain level of openness by a given period of time. Their end result essentially depends on the will of countries to move the process forward. This is an important consideration for the FTAA negotiations. Equally important would be for the FTAA participants to craft their agreement in such a way as to take into account a variety of concerns that derive from existing asymmetries within the region. The FTAA participants vary widely in terms of size, level of development, and availability of resources. These factors influence the industry composition of their services sectors, their degree of openness to foreign competition, and their readiness to confront a more open and competitive environment.

Luis Jorge Garay and Rafael Cornejo address rules of origin in preferential trade agreements. Rules of origin are a key component of free trade agreements and one of the most complex issues in trade negotiations. In free trade areas they are used to avoid or control trade deflection or trans-shipment, whereby goods from a third country are imported into a free trade area through a low-tariff member country and moved duty-free to higher-tariff members. Because trade agreements are intended to benefit traded goods originating in the participating countries, such trans-shipment is prevented by requiring that goods meet minimum levels of regional content as a condition of benefiting from preferences. Such rules could be a very sensitive tool. The stricter the rules of origin, the more likely they are to distort trade (and investment).

Several regimes for rules of origin exist in the Americas. The oldest, the system used by the Latin American Integration Association (Aladi), is based on a shift in tariff classification and alternatively on regional content requirements. The newer NAFTA regime mixes various criteria—change in tariff classification, regional content, use of certain technical processes, or a combination of these—and applies them on an item-by-item basis. Most recently the Central American countries have designed a new system that falls between the more permissive Aladi arrangement and the stricter NAFTA regime. The FTAA negotiations will draw on these different approaches.

Garay and Cornejo argue that the FTAA negotiations should aim at facilitating trade by agreeing to a system of rules of origin that is "transparent, objective, and predictable." As in other areas of the negotiations, account should also be taken of developments within the WTO with regard to rules of origin for nonpreferential trade, as these may help negotiators in designing the FTAA rules. However, the FTAA participants should not wait until the end of the negotiations to start harmonizing their various rules of origin, as their simultaneous application at present is a significant source of inefficiency in terms of resource allocation and specialization patterns.

Another important market access issue is that of standards and technical barriers to trade, which is taken up in the next chapter by Sherry M. Stephenson. The role of standards and the importance they may have as potential nontariff barriers within the Western Hemisphere is increasingly being recognized, as is the ability of harmonization or mutual recognition of standards to facilitate trade. The nucleus of a common Western Hemisphere approach to the treatment of standards already exists. As Stephenson points out, common disciplines are included in the WTO Agreement on Technical Barriers to Trade (TBT Agreement) negotiated during the Uruguay Round. Common guidelines for standardization activities, including conformity assessment and quality control, have been elaborated under the International Organization for Standardization (ISO) and the International Electrical Commission (IEC). At the regional level, most countries are members of the Pan American Commission on Technical Standards (COPANT), the regional standardizing body for the Americas. Many regional arrangements include explicit provisions on standards and conformity assessment procedures and are developing harmonized standards as well as common policies in this respect.

The difficulty in this area is to distinguish the legitimate use of technical regulations for the purpose of protecting consumer health and safety, as well as the environment, from those put in place for protectionist purposes. The challenge is to ensure that legitimate standards and technical regulations are enforced with minimal adverse effects on trade. These difficulties are underscored by the lack of objective information and quantitative estimates of the impact of technical barriers on trade flows and consumer welfare.

As well as examining these commonalities, Stephenson's chapter considers whether establishing common disciplines and approaches to the elaboration of standards and mutual recognition of conformity assessment procedures that do not yet exist for the majority of FTAA participants is feasible. The task for negotiators in the standards area is not only to determine the shape of an ultimate agreement, but also to devise incentives and policies that will permit countries to implement existing disciplines and to participate in multilateral and regional standards-related activities. The FTAA negotiators will have to consider to what degree and in what areas it might be desirable to go beyond the existing multilateral disciplines that were included in the WTO TBT Agreement. Full compliance with the provisions of the TBT Agreement will certainly be one of the objectives of the negotiations. However, to what extent additional (WTO-plus) disciplines are felt to be appropriate will depend upon the political decisions of participating governments.

Murray G. Smith proposes that an alternative to antidumping and countervailing duties, especially for smaller economies, could be safeguards. The procedural requirements of the WTO Antidumping Agreement, he argues, could be cumbersome and challenging to smaller economies, which lack the administrative and legal traditions of larger economies. Also, imposing special import duties will impose net economic costs on small, open economies. The least costly alternative for a small country that wishes to have resort to import-relief laws is the development of safeguards legislation. Administration of such laws is less costly and the procedural requirements in the WTO are less burdensome than those for the Antidumping Agreement.

As border barriers have been eliminated and as tariffs have become increasingly less effective as instruments of protection, trade-remedy law has grown in importance. As developing countries have participated more in the international trading system, their use of trade-remedy procedures has increased. Brian Russell examines antidumping and countervailing duty law from a net welfare perspective. He points out that the trend toward using antidumping measures is accelerating: between 1990 and 1995 the number of active antidumping measures of which the GATT/WTO were notified increased by over 1,000 percent. This trend, which is mirrored in the developing countries, also held in the Western Hemisphere: from 1991 to 1995 the number of Mexico's antidumping measures increased from eighteen to sixty-seven; meanwhile, Brazil's jumped from four in 1990 to twenty-three in 1995, and Argentina's increased from four to twenty from 1994 through 1995 alone.

This trend is not justified by a correspondent increase in the volume of trade. Instead, says Russell, there is "troubling evidence that antidumping measures are becoming preferred tools for protection of domestic industry as more traditional forms of trade barriers are reduced or eliminated." Although trade remedy law is often justified by intuitively appealing arguments, Russell finds that these arguments do not hold water. In fact, he argues, both antidumping and countervailing duties are economically unnecessary: "Based on the net national welfare of the importing country, the economic effects that they are designed to correct would best be left uncorrected or could be more efficiently addressed by other policies."

In their contribution Gary N. Horlick and Steven A. Sugarman examine the underlying rationales offered to explain dumping and antidumping law from a legal perspective. The basic argument that imperfect trade conditions create dumping by foreigners that harms domestic producers and consumers is, they claim, at best overstated. Often-used rationales include protected home markets, government subsidies, nonmarket economies, cross-subsidization, dumping to export unemployment, national defense, and overproduction. In reality, these authors assert, antidumping laws often fall far short of responding coherently to their purported justifications. The authors argue that "If open competition between companies based in different countries is the optimal system of trade, antidumping laws must be tailored directly to their purposes such that they do not become so broad as to deter acts of beneficial competition." Therefore, they propose a system to close this gap, asking that all petitioners who claim harm to prove their stated rationales.

In the last chapter of this section Rosine M. Plank-Brumback addresses dispute settlement issues. As the frontiers of trade policy have expanded to deal with a variety of policies and regulations, an effective dispute settlement mechanism has become an increasingly important ingredient of successful trade agreements. Plank-Brumback argues that the experience of the GATT/WTO shows how initial reliance on "diplomatic jurisprudence" has been re-placed by greater institutional and legal discipline in handling disputes in order to accommodate the recent evolution of the multilateral trading system itself. As trade negotiations have evolved from an initial concern with border mea-sures toward greater preoccupation with what governments do within borders, "the substantive rules and obligations of trade, and in parallel the system to enforce them, have become more intrusive over national autonomy."

Making rules on dispute settlement is no longer confined to the fringes of trade negotiations. This is a principal task of negotiations, because designing an effective and efficient dispute settlement mechanism will help to guarantee that the commit-ments undertaken in trade agreements are fulfilled. The GATT/WTO system provides some practical lessons for the FTAA negotiations and some guiding principles or features that the FTAA negotiators need to consider. Some of these include mandatory consultations, adjudication by ad hoc panels or impartial ex-perts, a negative consensus rule for panel establishment, adoption of rulings or recommendations, and authorization for retaliation, a standing appellate body, and restraints on unilateral determinations and retaliation. However, the WTO dispute settlement system remains a work in progress, and the future may bring new ideas and experiences that need to be closely monitored.

Part IV: The Newest Trade Policy Issues

The completion of the Uruguay Round and the creation of the WTO broad-ened and deepened the scope of the multilateral trading system. Issues that previously had been deemed too sensitive or had not been considered part of the trade agenda have been brought into the WTO framework. Services, trade-related intellectual property rights, and trade-related investment measures showed up on the agenda. Competition policy, not yet part of the WTO framework but the subject of a working group, is the focus of an FTAA negotiating group. Other issues that have traditionally been considered as outside the scope of trade policy—labor and the environment—are increasingly entering trade policy discussions.

Investment is a prime candidate for multilateral negotiations and is already an integral part of the FTAA negotiations. In this area a sea change has taken place in Latin American countries. As pointed out by Maryse Robert and Theresa Wetter in the first chapter of this section, there is a new consensus throughout the region on issues that just a few years ago were highly controversial. Most countries now grant national treatment to foreign investors in all phases of an investment, have eliminated or significantly reduced restrictions on capital and profit transfers, and are ready to accept international arbitration as a means of solving disputes. This new approach to foreign investment is reflected in national policies as well as a series of regional and bilateral agreements. The latter are the focus of the chapter by Robert and Wetter.

Countries in the Americas have entered into a variety of binding obligations aimed at promoting and protecting foreign investment. Many of these obligations have been incorporated in trade and integration agreements, such as the NAFTA and the agreements of the Mercosur and the Andean Community. Others have been worked out in bilateral investment treaties, of which more than sixty have been concluded between countries of the region in recent years. These agreements provide a basis for the participation of these countries in the upcoming FTAA and WTO negotiations on investment. The latter negotiations, however, would pose additional challenges. They might need to address issues not yet included in existing agreements, such as investment incentives, which many countries would probably resist. The extent to which the FTAA and any eventual WTO negotiations on investment would provide for progressive liberalization of nonconforming measures or the opening of specific sectors will also be a critical issue.

Competition policy is perhaps the newest of all trade issues being considered for inclusion within the WTO framework. As Edward M. Graham points out in his chapter, a few years ago there was little or no perceived need to pursue competition policy goals in multilateral negotiations. This perception has changed recently as a consequence of the global extension of markets and the fact that the activities of enterprises spill across international frontiers. There is now an increasing need to make competition policy, once largely the domain of domestic law and local enforcement, more responsive to international concerns.

Competition policy includes, but is not restricted to, traditional antitrust and antimonopoly policies, such as policies related to the regulation and control of restrictive business practices that have the effect of restricting entry into a market. It also encompasses government laws, policies, and regulations that protect the enterprises established in a given market. Therefore, Graham points out, trade and investment liberalization measures are inextricably linked to competition policy as they seek to open markets and promote greater competition: "The gains from an open trade policy are increased if barriers to domestic market contestability are reduced via effective competition policy, whereas competition policy works best if the economy is open to imports and foreign direct investment."

At the international level, some of the relevant issues regarding competition policy include conflicts and overlaps among national policies; market access— that is, the extent to which domestic regulations that prevent further competition could be the subject of a multilateral agreement; and the relationship between competition policy and antidumping procedures. In none of these areas will progress be easy or fast. However, as Graham suggests, difficulties should not deter developing countries, including Latin American countries, from moving forward in this area.

Competition policy is important for developing countries for at least two reasons: it allows them to increase the contestability of their domestic markets and strengthen the trade and investment policies they have already implemented, and it allows them to open noncontestable markets by removing existing barriers and thus promoting export interests. In general, international action in the area of competition policy would be facilitated by lack of conflict between different national regulations. Unfortunately, the two sets of competition laws that countries could look to as models to eventually follow—those of the United States and the European Union—share some commonalities but also important differences, which Graham examines at some length. Graham thinks the Latin American countries should take into account their own experience in enforcing competition policies and should "add their voice—and their growing weight—to the international discussions that are now ongoing" as they "have a substantive and significant contribution to make that is in the collective interests of everyone."

For José Tavares de Araujo, Jr., and Luis Tineo, competition policy is a priority concern of the Latin American countries. These countries are focusing on the establishment of an appropriate institutional and legal framework to deal with competition issues. However, only ten Latin American countries have competition policy laws and institutions at present, and of these just a few— Brazil, Mexico, Peru, and Venezuela among them—have set up strong competition policy agencies that are autonomous and strong enough to question other public policies when necessary. Even for those countries, experience with competition policy is recent, as it has been only in the 1990s that competition policies have been implemented or updated in the region.

After reviewing competition policies at the regional level—in the NAFTA, the Andean Community, and the Mercosur—and at the national level, the authors conclude that the FTAA negotiations will need to address a variety of issues. Prominent among them are the coexistence of different policies and approaches, the fact that many countries lack competition laws and institutions, and the relationship between competition policy and other public policies as they affect trade (and investment) flows. In this sense the goals of multilateral and hemispheric negotiations on competition policy do not seem to diverge much.

Together with investment and competition policies, government procurement is gaining prominence in multilateral and regional trade negotiations, as described by Simeon A. Sahaydachny and Don Wallace, Jr., in their chapter. Until relatively recently most government procurement activities remained on the fringes of trade liberalization efforts. In the late 1970s the Tokyo Round Government Procurement Agreement (GPA) began to change this situation. The agreement, however, was accepted by just a few countries—all of them industrialized—and was limited in scope. It applied only to procurement of goods by expressly listed national or federal entities, and it had fairly high monetary thresholds. The Uruguay Round resulted in a substantial expansion of the scope of the agreement, which now covers construction and services, applies to subnational entities, and has lower thresholds, and it has become a WTO plurilateral trade agreement. The number of countries that are members of the agreement is still very limited.

At the regional level progress has also been made. The European Union is perhaps where common rules on government procurement have gone further, as this area has been singled out as a large and essential element for the construction of the European market. In the Americas the NAFTA inaugurated a new approach to government procurement—along the lines of the GPA—that is being replicated in various trade agreements concluded by Mexico with a number of Latin American countries. In the Mercosur and the Andean Community consideration is also being given to setting up rules in this area. Negotiations have also begun within the FTAA with the aim of expanding access to government procurement markets.

As Sahaydachny and Wallace indicate, "Although the future extent and velocity of procurement market opening may be unclear from today's vantage point, what is increasingly beyond question is that the trade liberalization process in the procurement field—pioneered by the [GPA] and the regional efforts in the European Union—will continue to expand." This trend certainly is present in the WTO, as the work under way on "transparency" in government procurement—initiated after the Singapore Ministerial Conference—may lead to the first truly multilateral understanding in this area, limited though it is to this particular aspect of procurement markets. This trend is also present in the Americas, as seen in the negotiations for the FTAA and other subregional initiatives under way.

Much less support is forthcoming for the inclusion in trade negotiations of issues related to civil society. These include, for the moment, labor rights and environmental concerns. Differences have evolved around the specific standards that the term *labor rights* would encompass, as well as the merits of linking trade and labor considerations. Beyond agreement that there is a need to proscribe the most egregious practices, such as slave, prison, and child labor and discrimination in its various forms, little common ground can be found in the debate on this issue. Most countries take the conventional view that poor working conditions—low wages, for instance—are a function of development and will go away as countries grow richer and more efficient, so there is no need to introduce artificial incentives or apply undue pressure to alter this natural evolution.

Others disagree, especially in the United States, where labor (and environmental) issues have been at the forefront of the trade policy debate. This debate cuts across the executive and legislative branches of the U.S. government, business and union leaders, nongovernmental organizations, and academics. Differences over this issue have so far prevented the United States from developing a consensual trade policy and clarifying its trade negotiation objectives. As noted by Craig VanGrasstek in his chapter, "The controversy surrounding labor rights and the environment continue to complicate the politics of trade liberalization in the United States and to delay or block a new extension of fast-track negotiating authority."

No agreement is in sight either at the multilateral level or at the regional level as to how to link labor issues and trade negotiations. The situation is not much different in the case of trade and the environment, although in this area a committee was established in the latter stages of the Uruguay Round to look at the relationship between GATT/WTO disciplines and regional and multilateral environmental agreements. This relationship is important, as many environmental concerns have been addressed by regional or multilateral agreements, of which some 200 are currently enforced. The problem arises when enforcement of these agreements is pursued through trade restrictions. Although the measures can be mandated by the agreements themselves and imposed on their signatories, in many instances they could be applied to nonparties. In the latter case they may violate one key WTO principle, that of nondiscrimination.

WTO members are free to protect the environment by imposing conditions on the production and consumption of products within their national borders. This freedom also extends to imported products and domestic production processes, but it does not extend to production processes in other countries. Therefore, imposing trade restrictions on third countries to induce changes in the way a given good is produced leads to the extraterritorial application of national regulations. This practice is a source of tension in the multilateral trading system, as exemplified by the two GATT "tuna-dolphin" cases.

The WTO should be supportive of action at the multilateral and regional levels for the protection of the environment, but the WTO should not be called upon to legitimize trade restrictions ex post facto. As noted by Gary P. Sampson in his chapter on trade and the environment, "[Changing] WTO rules to accommodate . . . measures that are inconsistent with WTO rules constitutes an unbalanced and isolated approach." Whatever constraints countries may face with respect to their policy choices for protecting the environment, the "key requirement from the WTO point of view is that trade-related environmental measures not discriminate between home-produced goods and imports or between imports from or exports to different trading partners."

Part One

REGIONALISM AND MULTILATERAL RULES

CHAPTER ONE

Regionalism, Multilateralism, and Deeper Integration: Changing Paradigms for Developing Countries

Robert Z. Lawrence

There is a profound tension in our world. Increasingly the economy is global, but the world is organized politically into nation-states. This process of globalization has raised two fundamental questions about how we should be governed. First, to what degree should policies be decided by nations independently, and to what degree should they be subject to international agreement? And second, if international agreement is required, should it be regional or multilateral? This chapter addresses the relevance of these questions to trade policy, adopting the perspective of developing countries. The first part describes the historical shifts in the focus of trade policies in global systems during the period after World War II and then explores specifically how these shifts have given regionalism today its distinctive characteristics. The second part considers several strategic trade policy questions from the perspective of developing countries. In particular, what are the merits of regional and multilateral agreements in achieving liberalization and to what extent should coverage of these agreements deal with more than border barriers?

This chapter draws in part on Lawrence (1996).

The Changing Approaches to International Trade Policy

When barriers at nations' borders were high, as they were in the immediate postwar period, governments and citizens could sharply differentiate international policies from domestic policies. International policies dealt with at-the-border barriers, but nations were sovereign over domestic policies without regard to the impact on other nations. In its original form, the General Agreement on Tariffs and Trade (GATT), which was signed in the 1940s, emphasized this approach. Tariffs were to be reduced on a most favored nation basis, and discrimination against foreign goods was to be avoided by according them with national treatment. But the rules of the trading system, by and large, left nations free to pursue domestic policies in other areas such as competition, environment, taxation, intellectual property, and regulatory standards.[1] To the degree that there were international agreements in other policy areas—indeed there were international multilateral agreements on business practices, labor standards, intellectual property, and the environment—these were made outside the GATT, and compliance was typically voluntary. This was the case, for example, when nations signed the conventions on international labor standards of the International Labor Organization (ILO) or the codes of conduct for multinational corporations of the United Nations.

In the 1950s and 1960s there was also a widely held view that in order to develop, developing countries should separate themselves from the world economy. In part this view was a response to the disastrous international environment that had prevailed in the 1930s. In part it reflected a skepticism regarding the potential of market forces and a faith in the capacity of governments to plan development and allocate resources. There was a view that political factors, such as neocolonialism, had created a system biased against developing countries, particularly producers of primary products. As a result, for the most part developing countries adopted import substitution policies and maintained high tariff barriers and restrictive quotas.

For developing countries the GATT approach of reducing tariffs on a most favored nation basis was attractive, particularly when it was amended to provide for special and differential treatment of countries. In principle, developing countries had considerable freedom to pursue whatever policies they chose.

---

1. Originally the charter for the International Trade Organization covered a broader range of issues, including restrictive business practices and labor standards, but it was never adopted.

Specifically, developing countries were granted leniency in the use of infant industry protection and trade restrictions for purposes of balancing payments, and they were given special market access under the Generalized System of Preferences (GSP). They were also able to receive most favored nation treatment from other member nations without undertaking much liberalization at home.[2]

In sum, there were three widely accepted principles in the period immediately after World War II that help explain the overall thrust of the policies developed. First, trade agreements should concentrate on lowering border barriers; second, developing countries should try to develop with only limited engagement in the world economy; and third, when they do engage, they should be given special treatment. Over time, however, these principles have been increasingly challenged.

In the first place, starting in relationships among developed countries, pressures began building for deeper international integration—that is, for the harmonization and reconciliation of domestic policies. A host of new issues emerged as part of the international negotiating agenda. These included such issues as services trade, intellectual property, rules for foreign investors, product standards, competition policies, and labor and environmental standards. The increased scope of international trade agreements could be seen in bilateral agreements such as the Structural Impediments Initiative (SII) between Japan and the United States, which emphasized issues such as Japan's spending on infrastructure, its distribution system, and its antitrust policy; in regional arrangements such as the single-market initiative EC92 in Europe, which emphasized increased harmonization and mutual recognition of national standards and social dimensions; and in multilateral agreements such as the Uruguay Round, which resulted in the formation of the World Trade Organization (WTO), the adoption of rules on intellectual property rights, the liberalization of services and agriculture, the adoption of trade-related investment measures, and the development of a more powerful dispute resolution system. The new emphasis is also clear in discussions on the post–Uruguay Round agenda, with some nations calling for agreements to cover issues such as competition policy, labor standards, and the environment.

---

2. To be sure, these principles were not always fulfilled, as exemplified by the failures to liberalize agricultural trade and the discriminatory treatment of exports of textiles by developing countries in the Multi-Fiber Arrangement.

Why This Shift to Deeper Integration?

There are both political and functional forces driving this trend. When nations were separated by high border barriers and had little trade with each other, they could overlook each other's domestic affairs. As the barriers have come down, however, the impact of different domestic policies has become apparent. Improvements in communications and increased travel have made countries increasingly aware of foreign practices. In addition, as international competition has intensified, firms, workers, and citizens have become increasingly aware that different national policies have international effects. Increasingly, therefore, the call is for a level playing field.

The major political actors in society are business, labor, and environmentalists. When these groups see national rules affecting trade that are different from those of their countries, they are moved to cry foul. Pejorative terms are used to describe abhorrent foreign practices. For business the problem is dumping; for labor it is "social dumping"; and for environmentalists it is "ecodumping." All three groups are therefore seeking to achieve their goals, either by directly changing the trading rules or by using trade as a weapon to enforce agreements achieved elsewhere. In some cases groups put forward these arguments as a pretext for protectionism. Their real goals are not an integrated international system based on rules, but a world economy fragmented on the pretext that national differences preclude fair competition. In other cases, however, there are more widely held social concerns about the impact of unfair competition, low labor standards, and lax environmental standards. One argument is that once markets and competition are global there is a strong case for the rules defining fair competition to be global. Similarly, as the world becomes increasingly aware of shared environmental problems such as global warming and the depletion of the ozone layer, the case for international coordination of environmental policies becomes stronger. Likewise, as labor markets become linked through immigration and trade and international humanitarian concerns are raised because of improved publicity and communications—the CNN effect—the call for basic standards becomes stronger.

In addition to these political forces, there are even more powerful functional reasons behind the trend toward deeper integration. Foreign trade and foreign investment have become increasingly complementary. Access to foreign markets has become vital for competitive success not only for products, but also for foreign investment. To sell sophisticated products requires a significant domestic presence to provide marketing, sales, and service. The ability to follow market trends, respond to customer needs, and acquire innovative small foreign firms in all major markets has become vital for competitive success. These factors all lead companies to pay increasing attention not only to trade barriers, but also to foreign domestic practices that hinder their operation. This, in turn, leads to frictions resulting from different systems of corporate governance and rules of operation. Even absent trade barriers, other factors—for example, the weak enforcement of antitrust policies—can lead to collusion by domestic firms that limits new firms' entry into the market. International investment in services industries stimulated in part by deregulation, privatization, and liberalization has contributed to these trends. Once foreign firms operate in regulated sectors, they become increasingly interested in the rules that govern their behavior.

From Closed to Open Domestic Markets

The second basic premise of the early postwar system—that developing countries should develop behind high trade barriers—has also been questioned. In the 1980s developing nations responded both to success and to failure by moving toward liberalization and outward orientation. In Asia success led to external pressures on Taiwan and Korea to liberalize; elsewhere shifts toward an outward orientation were induced by debt problems, the Asian example, the encouragement of the International Monetary Fund (IMF) and the World Bank, and the need to attract new capital in new forms. The collapse of communism brought a large new group of nations into the international marketplace. China, the world's largest developing country and also its most rapidly growing, is only the most visible of these nations. Although complete removal of border barriers has not been achieved, the leaders of most nations can agree in principle that free trade is desirable, and many are prepared to commit their countries to achieving it in the foreseeable future. In late 1994, for example, thirty-four nations in the Western Hemisphere and eighteen members of the Asia Pacific Economic Cooperation (APEC) Forum committed themselves to eventual full regional free trade and investment.

From Special to Reciprocal Treatment

As developing countries have sought to liberalize and attract foreign investment, the pressures driving deeper integration have led to erosion of another part of the postwar consensus about how developing countries should be treated. In particular, there has been a turn away from the idea of preferential treatment. This is the logical implication of the shift toward deeper integration. It is straightforward to provide special treatment when an agreement relates to barriers at the border. The developed countries simply adopt lower tariffs than developing countries. But often when the agreement relates to adherence to a common rule—whether the rule is adopted or it is not—it is more difficult to have an agreement that does not involve reciprocal obligations. In addition, developing countries have increasingly seen the adoption of such commitments to be in their interest, as their efforts have been directed toward internal reforms that can be reinforced by international agreements.

Again, this development is evident in both multilateral and regional arrangements. In the Uruguay Round, although developing countries were given longer periods of time in which to adopt new disciplines such as those related to intellectual property, they were generally not exempted to anywhere near the same degree as they had been earlier. Likewise, in traditional regional arrangements such as the Lomé Convention between the European Union (EU) and developing nations in Africa and the Caribbean, manufactured goods from developing countries were granted duty-free access, but these countries were not expected to reciprocate. By contrast, the more recent agreements signed by the EU with eastern European nations and those from the Middle East and North Africa are markedly different. These agreements envisage much more complete reciprocity. Similarly, in the North American Free Trade Agreement (NAFTA), after the transition period the obligations assumed by Mexico and the more developed NAFTA partners are reciprocal. Likewise, in the APEC agreements, although developing countries are given an additional ten years (until 2020) to adopt complete free trade and investment, their obligations are similar to those of their developed counterparts.

As countries have turned toward global markets, a paradoxical consequence has been the development of pressures toward increased regional integration. Increased global competition has led multinational firms to develop regional strategies to compete globally. To be internationally competitive, firms must have access to key inputs at the lowest prices. This leads to sourcing from nearby trading partners whose comparative advantage lies in such inputs. Similarly, firms seek to enjoy scale economies by selling to large regional trading partners.

In North America, for example, outwardly oriented policies by one of the "natural" trading partners of the United States, Canada, led to free trade arrangements to secure market access and lure foreign investment with the prospect of servicing a rich regional market. Meanwhile, U.S. manufacturing firms were attracted by the possibility of escaping restrictions on investment in Canada, which would allow them to rationalize their North American strategies. In Europe the initiative to establish a single market by 1992 was led by Eurocrats who were motivated by the goals of political union and stimulating growth. However, it was also supported by European firms whose executives felt that even fairly large domestic markets such as those of Germany, France, and the United Kingdom were inadequate home bases for global competition. The EC92 initiative was successful not simply in removing barriers, but also in reorienting the strategies of European firms that now treat Europe as a single market and as a single production base from which to service global markets. These strategies have been reflected in decisions regarding investment, plant location, and mergers and acquisitions. The changed emphasis in policies on trade liberalization and deeper integration provides an important context for evaluating current regional trading arrangements and comparing them to those that emerged earlier.

In the 1950s and 1960s developing countries concluded preferential trading agreements among themselves as part of their trade policy strategies, but these agreements often failed miserably.[3] This might have been expected given their motivation; many of these agreements were driven by purely political rather than economic considerations. To the degree that economic objectives were involved, the agreements were usually an extension to the regional level of domestic import substitution and planning policies that were proposed to achieve scale economies for protectionist policies. The theory was that participating countries would become more specialized and by relying on regional markets could develop international competitiveness. In practice, however, given the general philosophy of trying to produce everything at home, members tended to give each other access to their markets only for those products they imported from the rest of the world. In other words, the region as a whole became more self-sufficient, but in a most inefficient manner—by maximizing trade diversion.

Under these circumstances it was no surprise that preferential trading agreements among developing countries often failed. This was especially true when countries had similar patterns of specialization so that there were few opportunities for avoiding competition. However, even where there was scope for such specialization, once the extraregional trade was diverted the impact of the agreements was exhausted. It is difficult, if not impossible, to plan resource

3. Hazlewood (1979).

allocation in a single economy. It is even more complicated, if not impossible, to do so when there are several countries and resource allocation decisions are highly politicized.[4]

The forces driving these developments differ radically from those driving previous waves of regionalization in this century. Unlike those of the 1930s, most of the current initiatives represent efforts to facilitate their members' participation in the world economy rather than their withdrawal from it. Unlike those of the 1950s and 1960s, the initiatives involving developing countries are part of a strategy to liberalize the economies of such countries in general and to open their economies to implement policies driven by exports and foreign investment rather than to promote import substitution. The current moves toward regionalization are, by and large, not meant to thwart the allocative process of the market, but to strengthen its operation. They represent efforts to fill the functional needs of international trade and investment and the requirements of international governance and cooperation to which globalization gives rise. In addition, many important regional initiatives are not developing as arrangements with exclusive memberships in which insiders limit their contacts with outsiders. On the contrary, they are developing as inclusive arrangements in which members either allow outsiders to join or independently join them in developing similar arrangements.

Some major aspects of the new regionalism are listed in table 1-1. It is striking that recent regional agreements have been strongly supported by corporate leaders. In Europe the initiative to establish a single market was promoted by large European firms that argued that a fragmented Europe deprived them of the scale economies they needed to be competitive. Similarly, the NAFTA was boosted by U.S. businesses both large (represented by the Business Round Table) and small (represented by the U.S. Chamber of Commerce).[5] Major supporters of a free trade agreement in Canada were the Business Council on National Issues and the Canadian Manufacturers Association (CMA), and large Mexican industrial groups strongly backed the NAFTA. Private foreign investors have led the informal regional integration in Asia. In addition, in the APEC political leaders have explicitly institutionalized the role of business by creating an advisory Pacific Business Forum, which was established in June 1994. Both large and small firms from the eighteen member countries are represented in this forum, which is charged with providing proposals for facilitating trade and investment within the region.

4. Langhammer (1992).
5. Fishlow and Haggard (1992).

Table 1-1. Regionalsim: Old and New

Old	New
Import substitution—withdraw from world economy.	Export orientation—integrate into world economy.
Planned and political allocation of resources.	Market allocation of resources.
Driven by governments.	Driven by private firms.
Mainly industrial products.	All goods and services, as well as investment.
Deal with border barriers.	Aimed at deeper integration.
Preferential treatment for less-developed nations.	Equal rules (different adjustment periods) for all nations.

Clearly many multinational corporations view these regional arrangements as promoting their interests. This view reflects the role of these arrangements as responses to the functional demands of multinational firms in the current economic environment. In particular it is noteworthy that these initiatives are concerned with services and foreign direct investment (FDI), as well as goods trade. Also, for reasons outlined earlier, they focus on internal rules and regulations and on institutional mechanisms to ensure implementation and enforcement as well as removal of border barriers.

As they seek to attract capital and at the same time pursue programs based on export-driven growth, foreign firms become increasingly attractive to developing countries. They bring knowledge about the latest technologies and ready-made access to major markets. Moreover, in many developing countries, accompanying the shift toward more open trade policies has been a reduction in the role of the state through privatization. In this context foreign investors have become increasingly attractive as providers of capital, technology, and operational skills.

The demand for foreign investment emanating from the developing countries has corresponded with an increased supply from multinational corporations. As international competition intensifies, small cost advantages may have large consequences. Particular national locations are not necessarily well suited to the complete manufacture of complex products. With improvements in communications and transportation, firms are increasingly able to produce products by sourcing from multiple locations. Raw materials might best be sourced in one country, labor-intensive processes performed in a second, and technologically sophisticated processes performed in a third. Multinationals from many nations are therefore expanding their foreign investments.

Traditionally, FDI in developing countries was made to gain access to raw materials. Later, in countries following protectionist import-substitution policies, it was attracted by the prospects of selling behind trade barriers in a large internal market.[6] Although the motive of an attractive domestic market persists, as developing countries have lowered their trade barriers, investment has increasingly been motivated toward providing service to export markets.[7] Those able to offer export platforms have become most successful in attracting FDI.[8]

Implications

The increased importance of international investment naturally shifts attention from trade to investment barriers and focuses attention on national differences in the degree of ease with which foreign firms can enter new markets through both acquisition and new establishment, and on the effects of domestic regulations and taxes on the conditions under which such firms can operate. Similarly, firms that plan to source in one country and sell in others need security about the rules and mechanisms governing trade. Such firms also prefer secure intellectual property rights as well as technical standards and regulations that are compatible.

For developing countries, particularly those that were previously inhospitable toward foreign investment, establishing the credibility of new policies to attract investment and securing access to markets for exports has come to be of major importance. In addition, for some developing countries it may be easier to "import" new institutions and regulatory systems than to develop them independently. Although such institutions may not have the virtue of matching domestic

---

6. In the 1970s, therefore, the developing countries receiving the largest foreign investment flows were Brazil ($1.3 billion annual average inflow), Mexico ($600 million), Egypt ($300 million), Malaysia ($300 million), Nigeria ($300 million), and Singapore ($300 million). See United Nations Center on Transnational Corporations (1992: 317). Of these only Singapore was an open export-oriented economy.

7. Wells (1992).

8. Between 1980 and 1990 the list of developing countries receiving the largest annual average inflows of FDI was headed by Singapore ($2.3 billion), followed by Mexico ($1.9 billion), Brazil ($1.8 billion), China ($1.7 billion), Hong Kong ($1.1 billion), and Malaysia ($1.1 billion). Of these only Brazil has not emphasized export-oriented investment.

conditions precisely, they offer the advantages of having been pretested and of providing international compatibility. For nations in eastern Europe, for example, adopting policies that conform to EU norms is particularly attractive because they can be seen as the first steps toward full membership in the EU. Finally, entering international negotiations can affect an internal debate, tilting it in favor of one side and against another. In many cases domestic forces interested in liberalization will find their hands strengthened if they can present their policies as part of an international liberalization agreement.[9]

Given these developments, the reasons for the distinctive character of the emerging regional arrangements become clearer. They are motivated by the desire to facilitate international investment and the operations of multinational firms as much as by the desire to promote trade. Although liberalization to permit trade requires the removal of border barriers—a relatively shallow form of integration—the development of regional production systems and the promotion of investment in services require deeper forms of international integration of national regulatory systems and policies. One example is eliminating differences in national production and product standards that make regionally integrated production costly. Investment also requires credible and secure governance mechanisms, and it requires secure access to large foreign markets that is unhindered either by customs officials or by domestic actions such as the adoption of antidumping policies. Since much of the investment relates to the provision of services, the regulatory regimes governing establishment and operation become the focus of attention. In sum, regionalism is a natural outgrowth of the shift toward globalization in developing countries.

Strategic Challenges

Almost all developing countries today are committed in principle to policies of increased trade and financial liberalization. But there remain important questions about the appropriate approaches to achieving these goals. One set of issues must be faced by countries individually. One key question is at what pace and in what order should liberalization be pursued? In particular, what kinds of institutional and competitive capacity need to be in place prior to full liberalization? This issue, which will not be explored in depth in this chapter, has been the

9. Haggard (1995).

subject of considerable debate, and there appears to be an emerging consensus that trade liberalization and domestic financial reform should precede liberalization of the capital account. A second question is what are the appropriate means for achieving liberalization? In particular, to what degree should countries act unilaterally and independently in setting their trade policies, to what degree should they pursue regional free trade agreements, and to what degree should they act only multilaterally? A third question relates to the nature of agreements that are signed. Should they cover only border barriers, or should they deal with the issues of deeper integration? Each of these issues is covered in turn.

International Agreements

Why do countries sign international trade agreements that constrain their behavior? If free trade is in a nation's interest, why not simply move unilaterally to remove border barriers? In particular, why would a sovereign state want to constrain its own behavior and subject itself to the possibilities of international sanction?

First, even though a nation may benefit from removing its own trade barriers, it can do even better if its trading partners also remove theirs, raising the demand for the nation's exports and improving its international buying power. Developing countries that sign agreements such as the GATT or regional agreements may gain improved access to foreign markets for their exports.

Second, international negotiations can strengthen the influence of the parties that gain from free trade. Although trade may benefit the nation, it may create losers in industries that compete with imports. If these losers are politically powerful, they may prevent a unilateral reduction in barriers. Trade negotiations help mobilize one group of domestic producers—exporters who gain from liberalization abroad—to offset the influence of producers and workers who compete with imports and thus make it politically easier for national leaders to adopt policies in the nation's interest.

Third, international agreements may make a nation's liberal trade policies more credible. Before firms will undertake the investments necessary to serve foreign markets, they need to be confident that access to these markets will be forthcoming. When countries, particularly those with a long history of protection, proclaim their newfound allegiance to policies of open trade and investment, foreign investors often react quite skeptically. By accepting commitments that could lead to international sanctions if broken, countries can persuade others of the permanence of their changes. Therefore, even small countries that are unable to change the behavior of their trading partners may gain from the lock-in effects of signing international trade agreements.

Fourth, international agreements and constraints can also prove useful where there is compelling evidence that international markets deviate markedly from the competitive model. One such type of market failure occurs when firms have monopoly or market power. Market failures may result if countries adopt policies that enhance the market power of their firms—so-called strategic trade policies—or raise their export prices by imposing the so-called optimal tariff. International oversight or rules that inhibit such behavior could, in principle, improve global welfare. Externalities or spillovers are a second source of market failure. As in a single nation's economy, some activities, such as pollution, may lead to inefficient outcomes when the polluters fail to take account of the social costs of their behavior. In an international economy there may be international environmental problems such as acid rain and depletion of the ozone layer that would not be countered efficiently if countries acted only independently.

Finally, agreements may allow for exploitation of economies of scale. One route calls for harmonization; another could entail mutual recognition. Where these benefits are great they may involve a trade-off. On the one hand, specific local regulations may match preferences more closely; on the other hand, international norms may yield benefits from scale economies.

These considerations all create the need for international agreements. Nations that are members of the WTO have agreed to bargain multilaterally to negotiate reductions in trade barriers. To ensure that these negotiations are credible, members have agreed to permit sanctions in the event they renege. To ensure that reductions are not undermined by domestic policies, they have also agreed not to harmonize policies, but to avoid measures that discriminate against foreign goods and to achieve their goals in the least trade-restricting way possible. In addition, efforts have been made to prevent firms from gaining monopoly power through predatory practices by means of rules against dumping and against nations' applying subsidies that may nullify their tariff reductions and inflict harm on their trading partners through the codes for subsidies. It is noteworthy, however, that although the GATT is based on nondiscrimination between its members (the principle of most favored nation treatment) and nondiscrimination between domestic and imported goods (the principle of national treatment), it does not require nations to have tariffs at similar levels or to adopt the same policies. Even with respect to border barriers, there is no level playing field. Aside from export subsidies, the GATT allows nations to respond to foreign subsidies and dumping only when these are seen to cause injury. It is not the goal of harmonization to create a level playing field that lies behind the trade rules; the goal is to make markets internationally contestable so that the benefits of international specialization can be most fully realized.

Given the existence of a forum for multilateral trade agreements and the ability to join the WTO, why might countries want to sign regional trade agreements? In particular, trade theory indicates that such agreements do not necessarily enhance welfare, since they may both divert and create trade, and indeed it has been argued that this effect could be quite powerful in the case of some Latin American countries that have high trade barriers.

However, those who point to the dangers of trade diversion generally compare liberalization with a preferential arrangement that entails complete multilateral liberalization. A more realistic comparison is between multilateral liberalization that is only partial and preferential trade liberalization, which could be much more complete. Under these circumstances, both measures are "second best," and we know that partial multilateral liberalization could actually reduce the efficiency of resource allocation. This can be seen easily in terms of the theory of effective protection, in which the reduction of tariffs on primary commodity inputs can actually increase effective protection on final products. In fact, during the postwar period, the world has moved toward free trade through two means. One, the multilateral, in which there has been full participation but partial liberalization and the other, preferential arrangements, in which there has been (almost) full liberalization but partial participation. In practice the two approaches have not been incompatible.

One reason for the coexistence of these approaches is that from a political standpoint it might be easier to persuade a government to liberalize with respect to neighbors than to do so multilaterally. Political feasibility may channel liberalization toward regional initiatives. This might particularly be the case in instances such as that of the European Common Market, in which political motivations made a European Customs Union feasible, whereas complete multilateral liberalization was not. Free trade opponents of preferential trading agreements assume that in the absence of regional free trade agreements multilateral liberalization will take place. However, there may be cases in which it is possible to liberalize in a free trade area when it is not possible to do so unilaterally or multilaterally.

It is generally agreed that because firms can act collectively more easily than consumers, firms are more powerful politically than consumers. This makes import liberalization politically difficult, because even in cases where the country as a whole will gain, the benefits will be enjoyed by consumers in the form of lower prices, while the costs will be born by firms that compete with imports. If consumers are poorly organized, import-competing firms lobbying for protection might have the upper hand. To offset this advantage, it might be necessary to have another group of producers—namely exporters—also supporting liberalization.

Indeed, we should generally expect exporting firms to support liberalization, but liberalization by participating in multilateral negotiations is not particularly attractive for exporting interests originating in small countries.[10] The offers of other nations are not likely to be influenced by the liberalization in a single country. Therefore, particularly in a system such as that imposed by the GATT in which all members are given most favored nation treatment unconditionally, it will be hard for exporters to see it as worth their while to lobby for domestic liberalization. Moreover, since the GATT has operated on the principle of special and differential treatment for developing countries, exporters from small developing countries have even less reason to promote domestic liberalization. This tendency toward free riding creates problems for exporters from large countries. These considerations are different in preferential trading agreements. Exporters will see gains in the form of more open foreign markets that are contingent on domestic liberalization, and are therefore likely to lobby more enthusiastically for such agreements.[11] If scale economies are important, the benefits from liberalization may be greater for small countries than for large countries. Accordingly, the bargaining power of large countries may be greater in regional negotiations. Indeed, Bhagwati and others argue that this can lead to placing undesirable demands on small countries under these circumstances.[12]

10. Economic theory tells us that letting in more imports will tend to stimulate exports through various channels. First, increased imports could lower the exchange rate and promote exports. Second, cheap imported inputs could improve export competitiveness. Third, if resources are freed from import activities, they can be used in export industries. These arguments are very subtle, and effects operate through indirect channels that are not readily appreciated. This makes unilateral liberalization politically difficult even when it is economically beneficial.

11. The same would be true for multilateral liberalization if it was made conditional rather than unconditional.

12. Bhagwati and Kreuger (1995).

Countries may also join regional arrangements for defensive reasons. For example, once Mexico joined the NAFTA the Caribbean economies that are highly dependent on the U.S. market felt a disadvantage, and they have been driven to seek mitigation. Therefore, countries that suffer from trade diversion could be better off joining such an agreement than staying out. Countries excluded from a preferential agreement may have incentives to join it. If the agreement is open to newcomers, there could be an expanding preferential arrangement that will eventually encompass the world. The incentive to join may increase as an agreement grows and becomes more effective. Richard Baldwin describes this as the domino effect.[13] He shows how the trade diversion (and the increased efficiency) of countries forming an agreement can raise the costs for other competitors of not joining. This can increase the interest of export firms in the excluded country in joining the agreement, thereby spreading the process of liberalization. Key issues under these circumstances are the conditions under which accession is granted.

The domino effect Baldwin has identified may well be combined with another that may lead liberalization to proliferate—the incentives for a country that is prepared to liberalize to do so in a piecemeal fashion by joining a number of free trade agreements. Countries benefit from being the hub of a network of free trade agreements. Israel has free trade agreements with both the United States and the EU. Firms exporting from Israel, for example, receive preferential access to both the United States and the EU. By contrast, firms in the United States and the EU receive preferences only in the Israeli market. At the same time, by being open to more than one trading partner Israel experiences less trade diversion than it would have had it joined just one such agreement. Ultimately, in fact, the best situation for a single small country is to enjoy preferential access to all markets in the world while having open borders. If these incentives are present for every country, the system could move to free trade.

Countries trying to achieve this state face complicated timing decisions. It is necessary to have some preferences remaining to bargain away for access to each new partner, and as countries conclude these agreements the value of the preferences they confer diminishes. One of the advantages of simultaneous multilateral liberalization is that it reduces the incentive to hold back, since a country can keep track of all the concessions it receives in return for its own.

13. Baldwin (1993).

If full free trade is the outcome, why do the countries not get together and coordinate their actions? This may eventually happen, but particularly at the start there is a temporary advantage to the first movers from the preferential access they achieve. Indeed, a noteworthy aspect of liberalization, particularly in Latin America, has been the tendency of countries to join several free trade agreements simultaneously.[14] In the Western Hemisphere it appears that these will now be consolidated into a single Free Trade Area of the Americas.

Another fear is that in a customs union insiders with a stake in higher protection will capture the decisionmaking process of a more powerful entity and thus have increased power to thwart liberalization. This will particularly be the case for customs unions in which trade policy decisions require unanimity. For example, assume Spain and Poland compete in producing product A. If both are outside the EU they will lobby the EU to lower its tariffs on A. Once Spain achieves access, however, its incentives will change, and to preserve its preferential access it might oppose lower tariffs for Poland.

Moreover, a multilateral system with a few large players could be more susceptible to such foot-draggers. For a long time France opposed agricultural liberalization during the Uruguay Round. Since France was able to affect the position of the European Community (EC) as a whole, reaching agreement proved difficult. By contrast, had France been isolated an arrangement that simply bypassed or excluded it might have been possible.

However, larger customs union arrangements may be more difficult to capture than arrangements between single nations, because they are more likely to contain countervailing interests. It is true that France might have been opposed to agricultural liberalization, but other nations within the EU were not. Indeed, in the end France was forced to compromise, partly because of pressures from other members of the EU with an interest in agricultural liberalization. Moreover, a customs union such as the EU has relatively low external tariffs, and accession by more protectionist countries

14. Between 1990 and 1994 Chile signed free trade agreements with Mexico, Argentina, Bolivia, Venezuela, Colombia, and Ecuador; Mexico signed NAFTA and free trade agreements with Chile, the Caribbean Community (CARICOM), Costa Rica, Bolivia, Colombia, and Venezuela; Argentina signed agreements with Brazil, Chile, Bolivia, Venezuela, Ecuador, and the Mercosur; and Bolivia signed agreements with Uruguay, Argentina, Peru, Chile, and Brazil. See Inter-American Development Bank (1995: 217).

makes them more liberal. This was the case for Spain and Portugal, for example, in most industrial products.[15]

A third concern is the diversion of scarce political capital. Trade policymakers involved in negotiating and operating regional agreements will have less time and fewer resources available for multilateral negotiations. A related worry is that advocates for free trade with particular interests may be satisfied by liberalization with a few key countries and therefore not support multilateral liberalization. The United States is the market Mexican exporters most care about. If the only way the Mexican glass industry could sell in this market were for the United States to lower its tariffs multilaterally in accordance with the GATT, Mexican glass exporters might work hard for a GATT agreement. In a coalition with other exporters, they might tilt Mexican support for the GATT. If they gained access to the U.S. market through the NAFTA, however, their interest in the GATT might subside, and the lobby for multilateral liberalization would be weakened.

However, a regional arrangement might actually build up the political support for liberalization by doing it gradually rather than all at once. A regional arrangement might reduce the number of import-competing sectors and increase the number of exporters. This could, in turn, tilt the internal domestic political debate in favor of full liberalization.

It is of course not necessarily the case that countries are forced to choose between regional and multilateral liberalization. Indeed, both types of liberalization can be achieved simultaneously, and they could be complementary strategies. Nonetheless, there is also a danger that countries could join customs unions in particular, and thus retard the pace of their multilateral liberalization because of the opposition of such liberalization by other members of the union.

Deeper Integration

Should these issues of deeper integration become part of the regional or multilateral trading agenda? Consider first the multilateral agenda. For developing countries the stakes in how these new issues of deeper integration are handled in the international system are exceptionally high. Many in developing countries resisted the idea that the rules of the GATT should be extended to cover services and intellectual property and were willing to agree only in return

15. In the case of some agricultural products, the United States and other nations demanded compensation.

for concessions in areas such agriculture and textiles. Likewise, many are understandably wary that adopting measures on the environment or labor could actually retard their development.

A second concern is that these issues could become a pretext for protectionism that denies developing countries access to international markets. This could be the result unless sufficient recognition is given to the limited capacities of many developing countries to implement standards, regulations, and other policies in these areas. As a result of these concerns, a common response by developing countries has been to resist the introduction of these issues into the multilateral trade agenda. It is common, for example, on issues of both environmental and labor standards for developing countries to point out that when they were poor, the developed countries of today did not adhere to the standards they are trying to require of others. Similarly, others feel that in a world dominated by developed-country multinationals the adoption of tough competition rules and international investment standards could preclude government assistance for firms headquartered in developing countries.

However, there are problems with these rejection responses because, as countries without much international power, developing countries have an interest in seeing these issues decided in a multilateral setting with their participation. The absence of clear international rules could well provide opportunities for protectionists to influence their domestic policies. In addition, developing countries themselves have interests in a more competitive international market, a cleaner world, and labor standards that enhance welfare. Therefore, there appears to be a need for compromise in this area that is not easy to attain.

A second arena for deeper integration is regionalism. Traditional theorizing about regionalism considers these arrangements in the context of a paradigm in which trade policy is characterized by changes to border barriers. Regional arrangements are modeled either as customs unions (in which members have free trade internally and a common external tariff) or as free trade areas (internal barriers are eliminated, while external tariffs differ). In the view of traditional analysis, therefore, the dominant goal is the maximization of global welfare, and this will be achieved in a competitive international economy by multilateral free trade. Against this paradigm, preferential free trade arrangements are judged to be "second best" and therefore inferior to multilateral free trade.

Although the removal of internal border barriers is certainly an important feature of these arrangements, focusing only on these barriers overlooks much of what regional arrangements are about. The traditional perspective is at best incomplete and at worst misleading. A more comprehensive view of these emerging arrangements acknowledges that they are also about achieving deeper integration of international competition and investment. Once tariffs are removed there remain complex problems between nations relating to different regulatory policies. In a national context there is an extensive theory dealing with the question of how to assign authority over different aspects of fiscal policy to different levels of government—the literature on fiscal federalism.

No single answer seems to result from a general consideration of the factors that will affect this choice. There will inevitably be tensions between, on the one hand, realizing scale economies and internalization by increasing the scope of governance and, on the other hand, realizing more precise matching of tastes and choices by reducing that scope. What does seem clear, however, is that the answer will not always be the nation-state or the world. It is bound to differ, depending on the nature of the activity to be regulated. In some cases—for example, reducing global warming or establishing global financial networks—the appropriate level may be the world; in other cases, it could be the local community. The answers to this question are ambiguous, and they will not be independent of technology, history, incomes, and tastes. Indeed, there is no reason, a priori, to assume that the provision of regulatory regimes and other public goods should be the sole responsibility of the nation-state. Some goods and rules are better provided locally, although bilateral and plurilateral international arrangements may be more appropriate for providing others.

Recognizing the deeper nature of these agreements also provides challenges for appraising their effects on welfare. The nature of policy changes under these arrangements suggests that the normal presumptions about trade creation and diversion may not hold. It is generally presumed, for example, that preferential trading arrangements will reduce exports from outside the region. However, deeper internal agreements could actually stimulate such trade. For example, if members were to agree on tougher pollution controls or labor standards, their imports of products from nations with more lenient standards could rise. Similarly, the adoption of a common standard in a regional arrangement might make it less costly not only for domestic producers, but also for producers outside the region to sell their products. Likewise, the adoption of constraints on national state aids would provide benefits for both internal and external producers that compete with firms that might once have received such subsidies. Tougher enforcement of antitrust policies could provide improved market access for both internal and external producers.

In empirical studies a reduction of external trade is generally an indication of trade diversion—that is, that a member of an agreement is buying products from a less efficient internal source. However, deeper agreements could actually make regional firms more efficient. This might lead to a reduction of external trade, but it would not represent trade diversion that would reduce welfare. For example, changes in domestic regulations could give internal firms cost advantages over outsiders that would result both in fewer imports from outside the region and in lower internal costs. This concept has important implications for proposals that outsiders be compensated for their loss of trading opportunities when preferential trading arrangements are formed.

It is also possible, however, that even without raising border barriers or increasing internal trade, deeper regional agreements could become more closed to outsiders. One example would be the adoption of a common standard discriminating against external imports and raising internal costs. Another might be the adoption of common cartel-like industrial policies in the region as a whole, which would limit external producer access.

As these examples indicate, from an efficiency standpoint deeper international agreements could be better or worse than the domestic policies they replace or discipline. Deeper does not necessarily mean better or more efficient. First, the choice of the level of government is a matter of judgment and of balancing the costs and benefits of more centralized government. Mistakes could be made, and policies implemented by international agreement could violate the principle of subsidiarity. Second, much depends on the specific policies adopted. It could be much worse to harmonize on the wrong policy than to retain national policies that are not linked.

The European example is illustrative of the argument that deep integration— that is, the achievement of harmonized regional policies—could lead to either more or less protection depending on the specific nature of the policies. In particular, the EC's choice of trying to thwart market pressures in sectors such as agriculture, steel, and coal led to a Europe that was more protectionist to the outside world. In addition, the efforts by the EC to wrest control of external voluntary restraint arrangement (VRA) policies away from individual countries have probably also led to more protection for the EC as a whole. Similarly, the availability of antidumping rules has permitted producers to enjoy one-stop shopping for protection that might have been more difficult to achieve in markets that were more fragmented. There is therefore ample evidence of contamination.

On the other hand, market-conforming measures have had the opposite effect, leading to increased trade opportunities both internally and externally.

European disciplines regarding state aids and other measures, which favor domestic producers, provide benefits for all who compete within Europe. Similarly, the achievement of common standards reduces costs for all who wish to sell in the market.

In sum, although traditional trade theory provides us with interesting insights into both the benefits and the costs of regional arrangements and their dynamics, the deeper aspects of these agreements suggest that they need to be viewed through more than the narrow prism of conventional trade theory. Some emerging regional arrangements are moving to deal with measures that have not been dealt with by the GATT. Some opponents of these regional arrangements actually see the "deeper" integrative aspects of these arrangements as pernicious and undesirable. They view these as mechanisms for foisting inappropriate rules and restraints on weaker, smaller—and, in particular, developing—countries. Jagdish Bhagwati, a free trade opponent of regional arrangements, views them as "a process by which a hegemonic power seeks (and often manages) to satisfy its multiple trade-unrelated demands on other weaker trading nations more easily than through Multilateralism." Free trade arrangements seriously damage the multilateral trade liberalization process by facilitating the capture of it by extraneous demands that aim not to reduce trade barriers, but to increase them (as when countries seek to deny market access on grounds such as ecodumping and social dumping).[16]

It is indeed likely that in negotiations between countries of differing market sizes an asymmetrical power relationship will exist. However, this does not mean that poor, small countries will lose in these associations. Indeed the power asymmetries reflect the fact that the gains, particularly those from realizing scale economies, are likely to be relatively larger for the smaller countries. Similarly, economic integration generally leads to convergence, with poorer economies growing more rapidly than richer economies. Moreover, small countries join these agreements voluntarily.

Indeed, if the NAFTA or the Canada-U.S. Free Trade Agreement (CUSTA) had been seen as U.S. initiatives, they would have been doomed politically from the start. In both cases the governments and firms of these countries saw these agreements as in their own interests, and not simply because they feared American protectionism. The same is true of the eastern European nations that are voluntarily seeking to join the EU and those in Latin America that are seeking a hemispheric arrangement with the United States. Finally, particularly in agreements with the EU, aid has been made part of the package.

16. Perroni and Whalley (1994); Bhagwati and Krueger (1995).

Moreover, although countries seeking to join these arrangements may have to make "concessions" by adopting some rules and institutions that may not suit their needs perfectly, they also enjoy benefits from adopting institutions without having to incur the costs of developing them. Just as several European countries have sought to import the anti-inflation credibility enjoyed by the Bundesbank by pegging their exchange rates to the German mark, so countries can make their regulatory policies more credible through international cooperation.

The strong role played by corporations in promoting regional integration has been noted. Recognizing this role provides insight into both the promise of and the problems with the current regional initiatives. The promise is represented by moves toward deeper economic integration than is currently feasible under the GATT. Regional agreements can make progress in harmonizing domestic policies and providing more credible and more effective supranational governance mechanisms than the WTO. On the other hand, there is the concern of regulatory capture: that under the influence of companies new systems of rules will be set to help insiders and hurt outsiders. Skeptics such as Bernard Hoekman, Anne Kreuger, and Raymond Vernon are particularly concerned that although they masquerade as free trade agreements, the new arrangements have been severely compromised by intricate rules of origin and other loopholes that may actually represent a retreat from freer trade rather than a movement toward it.[17]

In addition to the traditional problem of trade diversion, there are two other major risks with regional agreements. The first is that they could implement new forms of protection not by erecting new tariffs, but by implementing rules of origin and administering antidumping and countervailing duties that have protectionist effects. The second is that some countries may join regional arrangements even when the rules they provide are inappropriate for their levels of development.

References

Baldwin, Richard. 1993. "A Domino Theory of Regionalism." Working Paper 4465. Cambridge, Mass.: National Bureau of Economic Research.

Bhagwati, Jagdish, and Anne O. Kreuger. 1995. *The Dangerous Drift to Preferential Trade Agreements*. Washington, D.C.: American Enterprise Institute.

---

17. Hoekman (1992); Kreuger (1993); Vernon (1994).

Fishlow, Albert, and Stephan Haggard. 1992. "The United States and the Regionalization of the World Economy." Paris: Organization for Economic Cooperation and
Development Development Center.

Haggard, Stephan. 1995. *Developing Nations and the Politics of Global Integration.*
Washington, D.C.: Brookings.

Hazlewood, Arthur. 1979. "The End of the East African Community: What Are the
Lessons for Regional Integration Schemes?" *Journal of Common Market Studies*
(Sept.): 40–58.

Hoekman, Bernard M. 1992. "Regional Versus Multilateral Liberalization of Trade in
Services." Discussion Paper 749. London: Centre for Economic Policy Research.

Inter-American Development Bank. 1995. *Economic Integration in the Americas.*
Washington, D.C.

Kreuger, Anne O. 1993. "Free Trade Agreements as Protectionist Devices: Rules of
Origin." Working Paper 4352. Cambridge, Mass.: National Bureau of Economic
Research.

Langhammer, Rolf J. 1992. "The Developing Countries and Regionalism." *Journal of
Common Market Studies* 30 (July): 211–31.

Lawrence, Robert Z. 1996. *Regionalism, Multilateralism, and Deeper Integration.*
Washington, D.C.: Brookings.

Perroni, Carlo, and John Whalley. 1994. "The New Regionalism: Trade Liberalization
or Insurance?" Working Paper 4626. Cambridge, Mass.: National Bureau of Economic
Research.

United Nations Center on Transnational Corporations. 1992. *World Investment Report
1992.* New York: United Nations.

Vernon, Raymond. 1994. "Multinationals and Governments: Key Actors in NAFTA." In
Multinationals in North America, edited by Lorraine Eden, pp. 25–52. Ottawa:
Investment Canada.

Wells, Louis T. 1992. "Mobile Exporters: The New Investors in East Asia." Paper
presented at National Bureau of Economic Research Conference on Foreign Direct
Investment.

CHAPTER TWO

Regionalism and WTO Rules: Problems in the Fine Art of Discriminating Fairly

Robert E. Hudec and James D. Southwick

Regional trade agreements (RTAs) among members of the World Trade Organization (WTO) have proliferated at an astonishing pace since the WTO Agreement took effect in 1995. The WTO Committee on Regional Trade Agreements (RTA Committee) indicated that it had received notification of forty-five RTAs in the first two years of the WTO.[1] A 1998 paper by the WTO Secretariat stated that 80 out of the WTO's 131 member countries are party to an RTA.[2] The rapidly proliferating RTAs include numerous agreements by the members of the European Community (EC) with Eastern Europe and other regions of the world, along with a rapidly expanding web of agreements in the Americas. No region, however, is exempt from the trend.

In at least one respect, this trend may seem surprising. A principal benefit of these arrangements is a tariff advantage for trade among the members as opposed to trade with third countries. The successive rounds of multilateral tariff-reduction negotiations under the General Agreement on Tariffs and Trade (GATT) have reduced global tariffs substantially. In theory, therefore, the relative advantage of joining an RTA would appear to be substantially reduced

1. WT/REG/3 (November 28, 1997). All WTO documents cited in this chapter are available at the WTO web site, http://www.wto.org.

2. WTO, "Regionalism and the Multilateral Trading System," http://www.wto.org/wto/develop/regional.htm.

as well. Yet the accelerating proliferation of these agreements suggests that WTO members continue to see significant advantages. The relative tariff benefit still might be important in sectors or countries where duties remain high or where an incremental tariff advantage is competitively significant. Also, some countries may benefit from the elimination by their regional trading partners of nontariff measures such as quotas or from exemption from their regional partners' application of trade protection measures such as safeguards or antidumping and countervailing duties. Finally, some regional trade partners may seek a fuller degree of economic integration, including harmonization or unification of legal regimes governing or affecting commerce among them.

The negotiators of the original 1947 GATT recognized that RTAs could bring benefits to the global trading system, or at least that the desire of member governments to enter into such agreements could not be resisted completely.[3] At the same time, the negotiators were concerned with avoiding the proliferation of preferential trading blocks that were widespread before World War II, and they wished to prevent RTAs from being used to divert trade to members of the RTAs from nonmembers.[4] Therefore, Article XXIV of GATT 1947 was a compromise to allow for RTAs, but subject them to some important disciplines.

In the 1986–94 Uruguay Round of multilateral trade negotiations, the GATT members reviewed problems that had arisen in the operation of Article XXIV and reached an understanding on some improvements.[5] This understanding was included as part of GATT 1994, the successor to GATT 1947, which was brought into the WTO structure at the end of the Uruguay Round. In addition, the General Agreement on Trade in Services (GATS), which was negotiated under the Uruguay Round to complement the GATT's coverage of trade in goods, includes an article on regional integration in services trade, Article V, similar in concept to GATT Article XXIV.

The Uruguay Round discussions of GATT Article XXIV solved some of the problems, but failed to solve many of the problems that have plagued its

3. GATT Article XXIV:4 states, in its first sentence, "The contracting parties recognize the desirability of increasing freedom of trade by the development, through voluntary agreements, of closer integration between the economies of the countries party to such agreements."

4. Article XXIV:4 states, in its second sentence, "[The contracting parties also recognize] that the purpose of a customs union or of a free trade area should be to facilitate trade between the constituent territories and not to raise barriers to trade of other contracting parties."

5. "Understanding on the Interpretation of Article XXIV of the GATT 1994."

application to RTAs over the decades. These problems continue to surface and perhaps intensify with the proliferation of regional agreements. Similarly, although the negotiators of GATS Article V avoided some of the pitfalls plaguing GATT Article XXIV, some of the issues arising under GATT Article XXIV appear under GATS Article V as well. In this chapter we review the significant problems that have arisen with GATT Article XXIV, the extent to which they were addressed in the Uruguay Round Understanding on Article XXIV, and how several continue after the Uruguay Round. We then compare these with Article V of GATS and offer our thoughts on these problems.

Basic Rules and Principles of GATT Article XXIV

GATT Article XXIV should be understood as first and foremost an exception to one of the fundamental principles of the GATT, namely nondiscrimination. GATT Article I embodies the nondiscrimination principle in the rule of most favored nation (MFN) treatment. It provides, in essence, that a WTO member must extend to each other WTO member the most favorable duties and charges on products, rules and formalities of importation and exportation, and treatment under its internal domestic regulation that it extends to any other country.[6] GATT Article XXIV is an exception to this principle, because it allows members of an RTA to treat each other more favorably than they treat other WTO members.

Specifically, Article XXIV allows WTO members to depart from the nondiscrimination principle through the formation of one of two types of RTAs: a customs union (CU) or a free trade area (FTA). In basic terms, under both a CU and an FTA the parties to the agreement eliminate substantially all barriers to trade between or among themselves. In an FTA, however, each party to the agreement maintains its own regime for trade with third countries. Under a CU the parties apply a common regime to trade with third countries; specifically, "substantially the same duties and other regulations of commerce are applied by

---

6. Article II of the "Marrakesh Agreement Establishing the World Trade Organization" states that all WTO Members are bound by, inter alia, the GATT 1994 and the GATS. The nondiscrimination principle appears in other GATT articles as well. For example, Article XIII provides for the nondiscriminatory application of quotas among WTO members.

each of the members of the union to the trade of territories not included in the union."

GATT Article XXIV includes two fundamental rules governing FTAs and CUs. The first rule, in paragraph 5, restricts the CU or FTA parties from raising barriers with third countries. In the case of an FTA, the article specifies that "the duties and other regulations of commerce" applied by each country to trade with WTO members not party to the FTA "shall not be higher or more restrictive" after the implementation of the FTA than before. In the case of a CU, the article specifies that the duties and other regulations of commerce applicable to nonparties "shall not *on the whole* be higher or more restrictive" after the agreement than before.

The difference in the rule for FTAs and CUs was created for practical reasons. A CU by definition involves elimination of each party's individual schedule of duties and other regulations of commerce and substitution of a regime of duties and other regulations of commerce common to all. Unless the parties to a CU have identical tariff schedules to begin with, the harmonization of their schedules inevitably will mean that the rates for each of the RTA parties will go up for some products and down for other products. Article XXIV:5 indicates that the common regime resulting from this harmonization may not "on the whole" impose higher duties or more restrictive regulations of commerce on third countries. In contrast, because formation of an FTA by definition does not involve creating a common external regime for the members to apply to third countries, there is no process of adjusting each party's external regime upward and downward to reach a common target. Instead, each party to the FTA keeps in place its own regime for trade with third countries, and under Article XXIV:5 the duties and other regulations of commerce in each of those individual regimes may not be higher or more restrictive after the agreement than before.

The second basic principle of GATT Article XXIV is found in paragraph 8 of that provision. It provides that parties to a CU or FTA must eliminate duties and restrictive regulations of commerce on "substantially all trade" between or among them. An exceptions clause in the rule provides that, "where necessary," parties to an FTA or a CU are not required to eliminate those duties and restrictive regulations "permitted under Articles XI, XII, XIII, XIV, XV, and XX" of the GATT. As discussed further below, these articles include some, but not all, exceptions that allow GATT members to impose trade-restricting measures in certain situations.

At first glance the "substantially all trade" rule might seem incongruous. It suggests that in order for RTA members to qualify under Article XXIV to deviate from the principle of nondiscrimination, they must in fact discriminate to a substantial degree. A nation giving its RTA partners more beneficial treatment than third parties for only some products or to a partial extent will not do: the nation must give its partners more beneficial treatment on substantially all trade between or among them.

The explanation of this rule lies in the basic policy tension underlying Article XXIV, reflecting the drafters' need to both allow and control RTAs. Commentators have cited several reasons why requiring elimination of barriers with respect to substantially all trade between or among RTA members helps discipline regional agreements and improve the likelihood that such agreements will increase trade both among members and between members and nonmembers.

First, elimination of barriers with respect to substantially all trade imposes a high threshold for countries to surmount to enter into RTAs. Countries might find it easy to set up preferential arrangements if they could exclude the most politically sensitive sectors. Having to include those sensitive sectors could limit some countries' enthusiasm for such agreements and thus reduce their number. A closely related point is that countries allowed to pick and choose sectors to include in an RTA would be politically more likely to include sectors diverting as opposed to creating trade, because the politically easiest sectors to include for both sides would be the ones in which producers could gain most at the expense of nonmember producers and least at the expense of each other's producers. Therefore, an agreement encompassing substantially all trade would be more likely to result in a balance of trade creation and trade diversion. Also, fuller integration would be more likely to lead to "dynamic" gains—that is, stronger overall economic growth in the region and thus trade gains for members as well as nonmembers.[7]

Problems in the Interpretation and Application of Article XXIV

Problems have arisen in the interpretation and application of both paragraph 5 and paragraph 8 of GATT Article XXIV.[8] Typically these problems emerge in

---

7. For a discussion of these different arguments see, for example, Roessler (1993); see also Bhagwati (1993).

8. It is worth mentioning that Article XXIV does not apply to RTAs among developing countries that are WTO members. The 1979 GATT "Enabling Clause" allows developing countries to discriminate in favor of other developing countries outside the

the review of the agreements by GATT—or, now, WTO—working parties.[9] In theory the working party review process may lead to a conclusion that an RTA is inconsistent with Article XXIV and recommendations from the appropriate WTO body (before 1994, the GATT Contracting Parties) to revise the agreement. The agreement may not take effect consistent with Article XXIV unless the recommendations are implemented. Observers have noted that in practice the review process has generated claims of noncompliance, but has never led to the conclusion that an RTA was inconsistent with Article XXIV. In only rare cases has the process resulted in any definitive conclusion at all.[10] However, the scrutiny of the process has helped bring indirect pressure on RTA members not to go too far in abusing Article XXIV rules and has brought sharp focus on the problem issues.[11]

The Uruguay Round Understanding on Article XXIV (UR Understanding) strengthened the working party review process and also made it clear that the WTO dispute settlement procedures are applicable "with respect to any matters arising from the application of those provisions of Article XXIV relating to customs unions, free-trade areas, or interim agreements leading to the formation of a customs union or free-trade area."[12] The application of dispute settle-

---

disciplines of Article XXIV. See paragraph 2(c) of the Enabling Clause, "GATT," *Basic Instruments and Selected Documents* (BISD), 26th supp., p. 203. The WTO Committee on Trade and Development reviews RTAs under the Enabling Clause. A controversy arose as to whether the Mercosur agreement among Argentina, Brazil, Paraguay, and Uruguay should be subject to Article XXIV or the Enabling Clause. An understanding worked out by the chairman of the Committee on Trade and Development provided that the Mercosur agreement would be examined "in light of the relevant provisions of the Enabling Clause and of the GATT 1994, including Article XXIV." WT/COMTD/5/rev. 1 (October 25, 1995).

9. Paragraph 7 of Article XXIV requires parties entering into a CU or an FTA to give notification and to submit to an examination of the agreement. Normally a working party is established to review the agreement based on information provided by the parties and on questions and answers from other WTO Members to the RTA partners. Before 1994 the GATT Contracting Parties set up the working parties. See "General Agreement on Tariffs and Trade, Analytical Index" (1994). Under the WTO working parties are established under the WTO Committee on Regional Trade Agreements.

10. See WTO (1995), pp. 16–17.

11. For a discussion of the effectiveness of the review process and indirect pressure, see Hudec (1993).

12. "Uruguay Round Understanding," para. 12.

ment procedures could help resolve some of the outstanding issues in Article XXIV, and indeed the first such dispute is now under way between India and Turkey, arising out of the CU agreement between Turkey and the members of the EC.[13]

The following discussion does not attempt to catalogue all the issues under Article XXIV, but to focus on those that seem to have come up most often or proven most vexing, and to propose an approach to these issues most consistent with the principles of the GATT and Article XXIV. We begin with the good news: progress on the methodology for evaluating the common external tariff of a CU. We then turn to the persisting problems regarding rules of origin, the "substantially all trade" rule, its exceptions, and a CU's common application to third parties of protective measures such as safeguards and antidumping and countervailing duties.

Duties "Not on the Whole Higher or More Restrictive . . ."

Before the Uruguay Round, working parties reviewing CUs encountered several problems deciding, under paragraph 5(a) of Article XXIV, whether the overall level of duties applied by a CU was "not on the whole higher or more restrictive" than the levels applied before. Among other issues, working parties wrestled with whether the calculation should be based on the "bound" or "applied" tariff rates—that is, the maximum rates that the CU members were allowed to apply to other GATT members or the lower rates they actually in some cases applied; whether the calculation should involve a straight or a trade-weighted average of duties; and whether "the general incidence of duties" should be examined on a product-by-product basis—in other words, whether the general incidence of duties for each product category after implementation of the CU should be no higher than the incidence of duties applied by each of the CU parties to that product category before the agreement or whether an increase in one sector (for example, agriculture) could be offset by a decrease in another sector.[14]

The UR Understanding addressed these questions as follows:

> The evaluation . . . of the general incidence of the duties . . . [shall] be based upon an overall assessment of weighted average tariff rates and of customs duties

13. See WT/DS34/1 and 2.

14. See MTN.GNG/NG7/W/13 (discussing the question of bound versus applied rates) and MTN.GNG/NG7/W/13/add. 1, p. 6.

collected. This assessment shall be based on import statistics for a previous representative period to be supplied by the customs union, on a tariff-line basis and in values and quantities, broken down by WTO country of origin. The Secretariat shall compute the weighted average tariff rates and customs duties collected in accordance with the methodology used in the assessment of tariff offers in the Uruguay Round of Multilateral Trade Negotiations. For this purpose, the duties and charges taken into account shall be the applied rates of duty.[15]

Accordingly, weighted tariffs will be used, along with customs duties collected. The rates will be those applied by the members. The data will allow the WTO Secretariat to calculate the incidence based on the value and volume of each product by country of origin. The assessment, however, will look to the impact of the duties as a whole, allowing for the averaging of increases and decreases.[16]

This understanding probably has not solved all problems in evaluating the general incidence of duties in a CU.[17] However, it has improved the review of CUs since 1995, including the enlargement of the European Union to include Austria, Finland, and Sweden.[18] One might be cautiously optimistic that remaining issues may be addressed through experience in applying methodologies derived from the UR Understanding.

Rules of Origin

Similar progress cannot be reported regarding the issue of rules of origin. In an FTA and some CUs the parties apply rules of origin to determine which

15. "UR Understanding," para. 2.

16. If in order to achieve the common rate on a particular product a party to the CU must raise its tariff above the level it has "bound" in the GATT tariff negotiations, the CU must enter into negotiations with other WTO members to provide "compensation," that is, tariff cuts on other items. See GATT Article XXIV:6 and "UR Understanding," paras. 4–6.

17. A 1997 "checklist" of systemic issues under Article XXIV prepared by the WTO Committee on Regional Arrangements reports that problems of interpretation persist, since in the "before versus after" tariff test the assessment is based on averages and therefore ignores "the fact that exports of third parties might be concentrated in a few sectors." WT/REG/W/16 (May 26, 1997), p. 3. Also, some issues appear to have come up in application of the Understanding to the enlargement of the European Union to include Austria, Finland, and Sweden. See WT/REG3/M/1–4.

18. See WT/REG3/M/1–5.

products imported from another FTA or CU party have undergone sufficient processing within the FTA or CU to benefit from the agreement's tariff preferences.[19] Problems have arisen in CUs and FTAs when the agreement imposes strict requirements, demanding unusually high levels of regional content, to qualify for the intraregional tariff preferences. The strict rules can cause manufacturers within the region to shift the sourcing of inputs from outside the region to within the region to ensure that their finished products will qualify for the preferential intraregional duties.

The tendency of RTAs to adopt demanding rules of origin sometimes appears even when one RTA is replacing another. For example, in the review of the North American Free Trade Agreement (NAFTA) some countries complained that the NAFTA rules of origin for certain products were stricter than the rules under the Canada-U.S. Free Trade Agreement (CUSTA), which the NAFTA in effect replaced for most trade between the United States and Canada. Therefore, for example, a product manufactured in Canada using third-country inputs might qualify for duty-free entry into the United States under the CUSTA, but not qualify under the tougher NAFTA rules.[20]

In some working parties GATT or WTO members have argued that rules of origin should be considered "regulations of commerce" for the purposes of paragraph 5 of GATT Article XXIV.[21] Others have strongly asserted the opposite view. For example, in the working party review of the NAFTA a representative of the NAFTA made the following statement:

> A free trade agreement provided for preferential rates, and a rules of origin regime represented one of the operational features of a free trade agreement. Article XXIV:5(b) stated that tariffs and other regulations of commerce of a free trade area could not be raised or made more restrictive vis-à-vis imports from outside the area. Nothing in the NAFTA raised a tariff or imposed a new quota or anything else on imports, be they from outside the NAFTA or from within. Furthermore,

---

19. Some CUs do not include rules of origin for products in intraregional trade. Instead any product may circulate freely within the union once it has crossed into any country of the union. GATT Article XXIV allows for CUs with or without rules of origin. Article XXIV:8 states that in a CU duties and other restrictive regulations of commerce are eliminated "with respect to substantially all the trade between the constituent territories of the union or at least with respect to substantially all the trade in products originating in such territories."

20. See WT/REG4/M/2, p. 9.

21. See the discussion in the "GATT Analytical Index," pp. 746–47.

any product trans-shipped from outside the NAFTA through a NAFTA Party would continue to face the same tariff rates and regulations as before the NAFTA had come into effect. The only difference was that, in order to qualify for a tariff preference, goods traded among the Parties were required to meet the rules of origin.[22]

The Uruguay Round negotiators considered the question of rules of origin under Article XXIV, and they appear to have specifically considered whether rules of origin were "other regulations of commerce" for purposes of Article XXIV:5.[23] However, they were unable to agree to any language clarifying the treatment of rules of origin under Article XXIV or to any new substantive disciplines governing rules of origin in regional trade arrangements.[24] Instead, the Uruguay Round Agreement on Rules of Origin includes only transparency and procedural requirements for rules of origin in RTAs.[25] Therefore, the question of whether and how to deal with restrictive rules of origin under Article XXIV:5 remains.

There can be no doubt that some rules of origin in some FTAs are quite onerous and may lead manufacturers in an FTA to source more inputs from within the region after the FTA than before in order to gain the tariff preference. One need only look at the NAFTA rules of origin for textiles and apparel, color televisions, and automobiles to see mastery in engineering rules of origin. The NAFTA parties made no secret of the fact that they wanted only textile and apparel manufacturers that use a high degree of NAFTA content to benefit from the tariff reductions and removal of quotas under the NAFTA. Of course the NAFTA is far from the only RTA with highly engineered rules of origin for some products. It is also clear, however, that rules of origin themselves do not raise or lower tariffs or quantitative restrictions. They determine only who may benefit from the reductions in barriers introduced in an RTA.

The fact that rules of origin exist in an RTA only to decide who gets the RTA preferences poses conceptual problems with respect to including rules of origin within the meaning of "other regulations of commerce" in Article XXIV:5. If

22. WT/REG4/M/2 (February 21, 1997), p. 10.

23. See "Background Note by the Secretariat, Systemic Issues Related to 'Other Regulations of Commerce,'" WT/REG/W/17 (October 31, 1997).

24. See MTN.GNG/NG7/W/13 (August 11, 1987), p. 5 (mentioning rules of origin as one of the problems in the application of Article XXIV).

25. See "Agreement on Rules of Origin," Annex 2, "Common Declaration with Respect to Preferential Rules of Origin."

rules of origin are "regulations of commerce" for the purposes of Article XXIV:5, then in the case of an FTA the rules may not be "higher or more restrictive" after the FTA than before. In the case of a CU that has rules of origin, the rules may not be "on the whole higher or more restrictive" after the CU than before. But what is the "before" to which we compare the "after"?

Before creation of an RTA there obviously are no rules of origin for the preferential regional trade tariffs of that agreement, because those preferential tariffs do not yet exist. A variety of trade regimes might exist, including a unilateral preference program (for example, the United States applied its Generalized System of Preferences to Mexico before the NAFTA), another RTA (the CUSTA preceded the NAFTA for U.S.-Canada trade), a protective measure for a particular product category (for example, antidumping or countervailing duties or textile restraints), or simply MFN duties. Each of these regimes likely includes some form of rules of origin. In each case, however, those rules are directed at deciding eligibility for or subjection to a different program with a different purpose or scope than the RTA.

It is difficult to understand why the rule of origin for determining if a product may receive a preferential RTA tariff should have to be no more restrictive than the rule of origin for determining if that product is subject to an antidumping duty order, a unilateral preference program, or a requirement to be marked as a good of a particular country. The rules of paragraph 5 of Article XXIV are not aimed at achieving global uniformity of the regulations used in these different types of regimes. Rather they aim to ensure that members of an RTA do not raise barriers to trade from third countries. That aim is logical when it focuses on the substantive barriers themselves—for example, the duties and quantitative restrictions applied by RTA members to goods from nonmembers. It is strained, to say the least, when it focuses on the rules of origin used to determine the applicability of different types of barriers or trade programs.

There are good policy reasons to use more or less demanding rules of origin for different types of trade programs. In the case of preferential rules of origin unilaterally offered by a developed country to a developing country, the developed country wants to ensure that the rules are not so strict as to deny the developing country the benefits encouraging the economic development that the program seeks. On the other hand, both the developed country and the developing country wish to avoid a result by which third-country products would in essence be shipped through the developing country in order to gain the tariff preference with little local value added. Also, the developed country might have in mind that what is unilaterally given might be unilaterally taken away if imports under the program grow to levels that cause political pain at home. This "out" might lead the developed country to offer more generous rules of origin than might be the case under an RTA, where the options to back out of a preferential tariff system would be far more limited. These different considerations lead countries to strike a particular balance in the rules of origin they apply in a unilateral preference program. In other types of trade programs, the policy balance is different. One should carefully consider these different policy uses for rules of origin before determining if a uniform set of rules should have to apply for different programs. It seems unwise to require this outcome as a price for entering into an RTA.

Along with these policy issues there are some practical concerns that would arise from including rules of origin in the meaning of "regulations of commerce" under Article XXIV:5. Paragraph 5(b) of Article XXIV states an absolute rule against imposing "higher or more restrictive" duties and regulations of commerce on nonparties to an FTA, which in the context of tariffs in essence means that no higher duty may be imposed on products from third countries. If rules of origin were "regulations of commerce" under this provision, it could mean that no rule of origin for any product could be higher or more restrictive under the FTA than before. This conclusion would cause significant practical problems not only because many WTO members apply more or less demanding rules of origin to different trade programs, but also because they use several different methodologies for applying rules of origin.

In some cases a country or an RTA will use the "change in tariff classification" methodology. Under this method country B compares the tariff classification of a product imported from country A with the tariff classifications of all the inputs for the product imported into country A from third countries. If the change in tariff classification from the inputs to the product is of sufficient degree, the product is considered to originate in country A.[26] Some rules of origin apply a value added standard. Under this approach a good is considered to originate in a country or region if a certain percentage of its value is added in that country or region. Still another approach is to require the completion of

---

26. In an RTA the question may be whether inputs from third countries have undergone the requisite changes of tariff classification in any of the RTA parties. For example, in the NAFTA, for a good imported into the United States from Mexico the question would be whether inputs for that good from countries outside the NAFTA have undergone the necessary changes in tariff classification in any of the three NAFTA parties.

certain steps in the manufacturing process in a country or region in order for the product to be considered to originate there. Finally, the United States and some other countries or agreements have applied a case-by-case analysis, attributing the origin of a product to the place where its last "substantial transformation" occurred.

A given country or RTA might simultaneously employ several of these different types of rules of origin for different trade programs. For example, the NAFTA for the most part uses a change in tariff classification methodology to determine which products "originate" in a country or countries that are subject to the NAFTA.[27] However, to decide which tariff reduction schedule to apply to a NAFTA-originating good, each party applies its own "marking" rules. For example, in the case of an import into the United States with content from Canada, Mexico, and third countries, NAFTA rules of origin would be used to determine if the changes in tariff headings for inputs incorporated in Canada or Mexico sufficed to make the product a NAFTA-originating good. But then the United States would have to decide which country, Canada or Mexico, the product was from. The answer matters during the phase-out of intraregional tariffs under the NAFTA, because the United States applies a different tariff reduction schedule to products from Canada and Mexico. To determine the answer the United States uses its marking rules, which have traditionally been based on the case-by-case "substantial transformation" approach.

Although the United States uses change in tariff classification rules for NAFTA origin determinations and "substantial transformation" rules for marking, in some other circumstances it also uses value added rules of origin. Examples include the U.S.-Israel Free Trade Agreement and the U.S. unilateral preference programs (the Andean Trade Preference Act, Caribbean Basin Initiative, and Generalized System of Preferences).

If GATT Article XXIV:5(b) required an FTA member to apply a no more restrictive rule of origin to each product after the FTA than before, the member could face a very difficult task evaluating the relative restrictiveness of each product's rule of origin in the event the FTA employed a different methodology from that the member used in other contexts. Although the UR Understanding on Article XXIV makes it clear that difficulty in assessing the relative restrictiveness of a particular measure does not excuse a member from the requirements of Article XXIV:5, one still has to gasp at the implications of having to

---

27. In some cases the products must meet a value added requirement in addition to or as an alternative to a change of tariff classification rule.

compare the relative treatment of each product under a value added methodology as compared to a "substantial transformation" methodology or a change in tariff classification approach.[28]

The situation becomes even more muddled in comparing the requirements for CUs. For CUs with rules of origin,[29] paragraph 5(a) of GATT Article XXIV would require, "assuming rules of origin were 'regulations of commerce,'" only that the rules of origin not be "on the whole" higher or more restrictive. This standard might allow the rules on some products to be stricter after the CU than before, provided that they were offset by less stringent rules elsewhere. In such a case, analysis of the rules under a CU could look at the overall impact of the rules before and after the CU, which would seem an easier task than a rule-by-rule comparison (once one had solved the conceptual problem of which sets of rules to compare). However, there is no logical reason to allow this approach in a CU but not an FTA. In both FTAs and CUs that have origin rules, the parties adopt a common rules of origin regime (unlike for tariffs, where FTA parties retain separate regimes). It serves no policy purpose to give that regime stricter scrutiny in an FTA than in a CU.

For all these reasons, rules of origin do not fit with the purpose and meaning of "regulations of commerce" under GATT Article XXIV:5. The potential for misuse of rules of origin in an RTA to shift sourcing from outside the region to within is real; however, attempting to fit rules of origin into Article XXIV:5 is not a good solution to the problem. Rather, this problem should be approached through further WTO negotiations on disciplines to address RTA rules of origin.

Paragraph 8 and "Substantially All Trade"

Working parties reviewing RTAs have repeatedly debated whether the "substantially all trade" phrase allows the exclusion of particular sectors from liberalization under the RTAs. Most often the excluded sector is agriculture.[30] Some insist that the test is not met if any major sector is excluded. Others argue that as long as the agreement covers a substantial percentage of intraregional trade, it meets the requirements of paragraph 8.

The GATT Secretariat summed up the debate as follows for the benefit of the Uruguay Round negotiators in 1987:

28. See "UR Understanding," para. 2.

29. As explained in note 19, GATT Article XXIV:8 provides for CUs both with rules of origin and without.

30. See "GATT Analytical Index," pp. 766–69.

No agreed criteria exist to determine what is to be understood by the term "substantially all the trade. . . ." . . . Past discussions in GATT on the interpretation of this term in particular cases indicate that this term has both a qualitative and a quantitative dimension. Regarding the quantitative aspect, it has been suggested that a general figure could be fixed for the percentage of the volume of liberalized trade within a free trade area which should be considered as meeting the "substantially all the trade . . ." requirement. However, against this approach it has been argued that each case should be considered on its merits and that it would be inappropriate to fix such a general figure. Regarding the qualitative aspect . . . , a view which has been expressed on many occasions is that where a particular product sector, such as agriculture, is not subject to the liberalization process within the customs union or free trade area the "substantially all trade" requirement cannot be considered as having been satisfied.[31]

The Uruguay Round negotiators essentially made no progress on this issue. The only reference to the issue in the UR Understanding is a recognition in the preamble that an RTA's contribution to the expansion of world trade "is increased if the elimination between constituent territories of duties and other restrictive regulation of commerce extends to all trade, and diminished if any major sector of trade is excluded."[32] Despite this recognition, the WTO Committee on Regional Trade Agreements noted in 1997 that in reviews of RTAs since the Uruguay Round the question of how to interpret the "substantially all trade" requirement "has been repeatedly raised, within virtually the same parameters as before [the Uruguay Round]."[33]

On its face, the phrase *substantially all trade* would seem to permit a quantitative or a qualitative approach, since *substantially all* is susceptible to being interpreted as meaning either most of the sectors or most of the volume or value of trade. The drafters of the "substantially all trade" rule must have known it would engender debate about how much trade was "substantially all" trade. Presumably, the drafters could have left off the qualifier and chosen to require an RTA to eliminate barriers on "all" intraregional trade. Such a tough standard probably would have been very difficult to achieve for many countries contemplating RTAs. It might therefore have served too well the policy objec-

31. MTN.GNG/NG7/W/13, p. 6.

32. It is not clear whether the gist of this statement is that no sector should be excluded or that in some cases some sectors may have to be excluded and that those cases should be kept to a minimum.

33. WT/REG/W/16 (May 26, 1997), p. 9.

tives of discouraging too many RTAs. Inclusion of the qualifier *substantially* suggests a compromise on how far to go in allowing versus disciplining RTAs, as well as an intention to allow some flexibility in the application of the rule.[34]

Establishing a rough compromise of competing policy objectives through use of an imprecise term is bound to create difficulties of interpretation. The vested interests of different WTO members in the different interpretations of the phrase apparently have made it impossible to reach a solution through negotiations. What remains is for a country aggrieved by the exclusion of a sector from an RTA to bring dispute resolution on the question in order to force a decision by a panel. The irony, however, is that it might be against the immediate interest of a third country to complain that members of an RTA have

34. The drafting history permits an argument that the "substantially all trade" requirement allows for the exclusion from the RTA of particular sectors. The first draft of what became Article XXIV used the formulation "all tariffs and other restrictive regulations of commerce are substantially eliminated" with respect to trade among the member countries. See MTN.GNG/NG7/W/13 and MTN.GNG/NG7/W/13/add. 1 (setting forth the drafting history of "substantially all trade"). A later drafting session reworked this language to its current form—that is, that "duties and other restrictive regulations of commerce . . . are eliminated with respect to substantially all the trade" among the parties. Arguably, the first version covers all sectors when it says "all tariffs and restrictive regulations of commerce," but allows for something less than full elimination of tariffs and restrictive regulations in those sectors. The final version arguably is more ambiguous, leaving open whether all sectors must be covered, as well as whether the barriers in covered sectors must be wholly or partly reduced.

It is noteworthy that the change from the first to the final version was made in the same drafting session that added the list of exceptions to the "substantially all trade" rule in paragraph 8. See MTN.GNG/NG7/W/13 and MTN.GNG/NG7/W/13/add. 1. The negotiators might have seen the need to rework the rule's formulation to account for the fact that under the exceptions particular sectors might be exempted from any reduction of barriers at all. Therefore, all barriers would not be substantially reduced. But if full barriers remained in some limited areas under the exceptions, the net result would be a reduction of barriers to substantially all trade. For example, one of the exceptions, Article XI:2, allowed GATT contracting parties to apply certain agricultural trade restraints to each other. The full restraints against RTA partners might not have been allowed if Article XXIV had required all barriers to be substantially reduced. These arguments, however, are not conclusive, and they do not seem a good basis on which to resolve a debate so prominently and repeatedly engaged in, but not resolved, among GATT and WTO members over several decades.

excluded from their agreement a sector of importance. The case would charge in effect that the parties to the RTA failed to offer each other preferential advantages in a sector of interest to the complaining party. Still, a case might arise if (1) a WTO member with little or no participation in regional agreements or only a minor export interest in the excluded sector were to take a systemic interest in upholding tough standards for RTAs or (2) a WTO member were to calculate that increasing the competitive pressure within the region in the excluded sector—through forcing RTA partners to bring that sector into the agreement—could help break down a protective regime in that sector to the eventual benefit of nonparties.

The potential for such a case, along with continued close scrutiny of RTAs by the WTO Committee on Regional Trade Agreements, at the very least ought to keep in check any worsening of the trend among RTA parties of excluding significant sectors from their agreements.

Application of the Exceptions List

The "exceptions list" to the "substantially all trade" rule for FTAs and CUs in GATT Article XXIV:8 allows members of a CU or an FTA, "where necessary," to apply to their intraregional trade "duties and other restrictive regulations of commerce" that are "permitted under Articles XI, XII, XIII, XIV, XV and XX" of the GATT. These articles provide for quantitative import restrictions, tariffs, and other measures to address certain policy objectives, as outlined in the box that follows.

Article	Description of exception
XI	Prohibits quotas and other restrictions on imports and exports other than duties and charges, except for certain import and export restrictions in the agricultural sector, such as those to support domestic supply management regimes.
XII	Permits import restrictions in the event of balance of payments emergencies.
XIII	Requires that in those areas where quotas are allowed (for instance, agriculture) quotas be applied on a nondiscriminatory basis.
XIV	Allows deviations from the nondiscriminatory application of quotas under Article XIII if necessary for balance of payments reasons.
XV	Allows deviation from GATT rules to comply with commitments to the International Monetary Fund.
XX	Allows qualified deviation from GATT rules for measures to protect health, safety, the environment, and so on.

Two principal questions have emerged regarding the exceptions list: first, whether a party to an RTA merely may or rather must apply the excepted measures to its RTA partners when it applies them to any third countries, and second, how to deal with other possible "exceptions" not included in the list. The exceptions language of Article XXIV:8 requires parties to an RTA to eliminate substantially all barriers to intraregional trade "except, where necessary, those permitted" in the articles of the exceptions list. The phrase *where necessary* would appear to have two possible meanings, with opposite implications for the "may versus must" debate.

First, it could mean that an RTA member country may apply those restrictions listed to other RTA members, notwithstanding the general requirement to eliminate substantially all barriers to intraregional trade, where the RTA member deems it necessary in order to address the policy concerns underlying each restriction. For example, an RTA member could apply Article XII balance of payments (BOP) safeguards to other RTA members if necessary to address a severe situation regarding its monetary reserves. This reading makes intraregional application of the exceptions measures permissive rather than mandatory.

The second possible reading is that an RTA member is permitted to apply the restrictions to other RTA members where necessary to act in conformance with the terms and principles of the exceptions measures themselves. For example, Article XII provides that in applying BOP safeguards a WTO member is to "avoid unnecessary damage to the commercial or economic interests of any other [WTO member]." As argued below, excluding RTA members from the application of BOP restrictions at least in some circumstances might damage the interests of non-RTA members. Therefore, in order to apply BOP restrictions consistent with the requirements of Article XII, it might be "necessary" for an RTA member also to apply those restrictions to other RTA members.

Most of the other articles in the exceptions list also include criteria limiting the extent to which they can be applied in a manner prejudicial to the interests of particular WTO members. This second reading of the "where necessary" language suggests that they too must be applied to RTA members as well as nonmembers where necessary to meet those criteria. Policy considerations support this reading for each of the listed exceptions as well. In each case, excluding imports of other RTA members from application of the exceptions increases the burden on imports from non-RTA members or discriminates against them without sound policy justification.

ARTICLE XI. Article XI:2(c) authorizes trade restrictions on the ground that disproportional growth in imports undermines a national government's ability to operate a domestic price support program (for agricultural products, for example). In theory, imports as a whole are to blame regardless of the source. If imports from regional partners are excluded from restriction, the necessary amount of import reduction will have to be achieved solely by reducing trade with outsiders, which will require a greater reduction in their exports than would be the case if the restriction were distributed among all responsible suppliers. Worse, unrestrained imports from other RTA members could increase to fill the gap in excluded third-country imports, requiring even greater restrictions on the third countries to meet the targets for the restrictions. The only case in which regional partners should be exempted would be the case in which the price support program was regionwide.

ARTICLES XII–XV. In a BOP crisis paying for imports is a problem without regard to the source of imports. If the BOP restrictions exclude RTA members, the restrictions will have to be more severe or of longer duration to accomplish their objective. Nonmembers should not have to accept these "emergency" restrictions while members are allowed to continue and expand, at nonmembers' expense, exports to the country in crisis. As with Article XI, the only exception to this approach should be if the RTA has adopted a regional currency scheme and therefore the BOP problem justifying the restriction is likewise regionwide.[35]

ARTICLE XX. Article XX restrictions are justified as necessary to protect public health, safety, law enforcement, and the like. They can be justified only if they are "necessary" to accomplish these ends. If a product is excluded on grounds of public health, safety, or morality when imported from a non–RTA member, it must by definition be equally unhealthy, unsafe, or immoral when imported from a regional partner.

The Uruguay Round negotiators appear not to have made progress on the "may versus must" question, at least as it applies to the articles specifically listed as

35. Although the developed countries subject to Article XII generally have abandoned the use of trade restrictions to deal with BOP concerns, the interpretation of these provisions is quite relevant to the similar interpretative problem that exists with regard to Article XVIII-B, the developing-country BOP measure, which is discussed separately a bit later.

exceptions to Article XXIV:8. However, as discussed next, they did take some limited steps regarding the exceptions not listed in Article XXIV:8, which partially reflect the policy considerations just discussed for the exceptions listed.

Discussion has focused on at least four articles not in the Article XXIV:8 exemptions list: Article XXI (national security exceptions), Article XVIII-B (BOP restrictions by developing countries), Article XIX (emergency safeguards), and Article VI (antidumping and countervailing duties). The latter two have proven the most controversial.

Although the GATT Article XXIV:8 exceptions list does not mention the national security safeguard of Article XXI, few would doubt that members of an RTA maintain the right to restrict trade with each other for national security reasons. Article XXI states: "Nothing in this Agreement . . . shall prevent any contracting party from taking any action which it considers necessary for the protection of its essential security interests." It seems a strong case that "nothing in this Agreement" includes the "substantially all trade" rule of GATT Article XXIV:8 so that, notwithstanding that rule and its failure to specifically except Article XXI measures, a member of an RTA may apply national security exceptions to its RTA partners. Given the seriousness with which any GATT member is likely to view threats to its security, it is difficult to believe that the drafters of Article XXIV would have intended to prevent members of an RTA from applying national security exceptions to each other, solely for the economic policy objectives underlying the "substantially all trade" rule.

The wording of Article XVIII-B is not as unqualified as the "nothing in this Agreement shall prevent" wording of Article XXI. Rather, Article XVIII-B permits less economically developed WTO members to impose BOP restrictions, subject to several conditions, including the condition that the restrictions "avoid unnecessary damage to the commercial or economic interests of any other contracting party" and that the party imposing the restrictions relax the restrictions as its economic conditions improve. These qualifications make the operation of Article XVIII-B more similar to the operation of the other GATT articles mentioned in the Article XXIV:8 exemptions list than to that of Article XXI. One cannot so easily conclude with regard to Article XVIII-B, as one can with regard to Article XXI, that its wording and purpose stand it apart from the other articles for which the drafters of Article XXIV:8 considered it necessary to establish specific exemptions from the "substantially all trade" rule.

To the contrary, Article XVIII-B serves a very similar purpose to the BOP exceptions listed in Article XXIV:8 (that is, Articles XII, XIV, and XV). No logical purpose appears for excluding Article XVIII-B while including these others. The best one can say is that the BOP provisions of Article XVIII-B were added to the GATT in the 1955 Review Session amendments, seven years after the formal text of Article XXIV was adopted.[36] It is entirely possible that the drafters of Article XVIII-B simply overlooked amending the Article XXIV:8 exemptions list to include Article XVIII. As a policy matter, Article XVIII-B BOP restrictions should be applied to RTA members as well as nonmembers for the same reasons as the Article XII-XV BOP restrictions already discussed.

In the case of Article XIX one can point to neither unqualified wording of exemptions as in Article XXI nor potential oversight as in a later amendment to GATT. Article XIX was part of the original GATT agreement. A note from the GATT Secretariat for the benefit of the Uruguay Round negotiators states: "There is no indication in the drafting history or the records of the Secretariat why . . . Article XIX was not included in the list of exceptions in . . . Article XXIV:8. . . . It cannot be assumed that the failure to include Article XIX in the list of exceptions contained in Article XXIV:8 was an oversight on the part of the drafters of the General Agreement, but rather that this was a deliberate omission."[37]

Article XIX allows a WTO member to raise tariffs or impose quantitative restrictions on imports if unforeseen developments lead to increases in imports of a product so as to cause or threaten serious injury to the domestic industry. Article XIX includes procedural and substantive limits on the use of these "safeguards," and the WTO Agreement on Safeguards further elaborates these limits.

The issue of how to deal with safeguards in an RTA arose in several working party reviews of RTAs before the Uruguay Round. Members of the working parties objected to RTAs in which the members exempted each other from the application of safeguards.[38] Parties to RTAs have defended exemption of their RTA partners from safeguards on the grounds that Article XIX is not on the list of exceptions to the "substantially all trade" rule, and therefore the "substantially all trade" rule permits or indeed requires RTA members to exclude each other from the application of safeguards restrictions.

36. See "GATT Analytical Index," p. 460.
37. MTN.GNG/NG7/W/13/add. 1, p. 3.
38. MTN.GNG/NG7/W/13/add. 1, p. 3.

It is not hard to understand the reasons why nonmembers of an RTA would object to the exclusion of RTA members from the application of safeguards. As is the case with BOP restrictions, the source of imports should not matter under Article XIX. The question under Article XIX is whether imports as a whole, not just those from a particular source, are causing injury to an industry to the point that it needs emergency safeguard protection. If imports as a whole are the problem, imports as a whole should bear the brunt of the duties needed to effect a solution.[39] If a safeguard imposed by an RTA member excludes other RTA members, nonmembers must bear a disproportionate burden of the effects of the safeguard. The restrictions on imports may need to be more severe or to last longer to make up for the fact that imports from other RTA members will continue to flow in, and producers in the other RTA member countries may gain a share in the market at the expense of nonmember producers restricted by the safeguard.

On the other hand, those in favor of excluding RTA members from the application of safeguards point out that the aim of Article XXIV is to create deep economic integration among RTA partners, leading toward a single regional market. Because the continued application of safeguards among RTA members undermines the creation of an integrated market, it makes sense to exclude Article XIX from the exceptions to Article XXIV:8.

A policy answer to this debate is that only when an RTA has achieved sufficient integration as to conduct its injury determinations based on conditions of a single RTA-wide industry and to impose safeguards on behalf of the region as a whole should safeguards by RTA members be allowed to exclude trade from RTA members.[40]

The Uruguay Round negotiators considered the relationship between Articles XIX and XXIV. A draft decision on Article XXIV circulated among negotiators on September 24, 1990, proposed to address this relationship as follows:

> It is recognized that when an Article XIX action is taken by a member of a customs union or free trade area, or by the customs union on behalf of a member, it need not

---

39. See "Agreement on Safeguards," Article 2:2 (safeguard measures should be applied to imports regardless of source).

40. The NAFTA safeguards provision largely follows this policy while nodding to the textualist argument that Article XIX does not appear on the list of permitted exceptions to Article XXIV:8. The NAFTA safeguards provisions require NAFTA members to exclude each other from application of the safeguards except when imports from other members are a significant cause of injury. See NAFTA Article 802.

be applied to other members of the customs union or free trade area. However, when taking such action, it should be demonstrated that the serious injury giving rise to invocation of Article XIX is caused by imports from non-members; any injury deriving from imports from other members of the customs union or free trade area cannot be taken into account in justifying Article XIX action.[41]

A 1997 note by the WTO Secretariat explains that this wording was rejected because "the language in the first sentence was found too permissive by delegations which held the view that Article XIX action should not be applied to other members of the customs union and that the absence of any reference to Article XIX in paragraph 8 [of Article XXIV] supported this view."[42]

Although the Uruguay Round negotiations did not resolve this central question in the relationship between Articles XXIV and XIX, they did make some progress. Footnote 1 to the Uruguay Round Agreement on Safeguards provides that a CU may apply a safeguard as a single unit or on behalf of an individual member state. When it applies a safeguard on behalf of the CU as a single unit, the criteria for determining injury or the threat of injury must be based on the conditions in the CU as a whole. When it applies a safeguard on behalf of a member state, the injury determination must be based on conditions only within that member state. In the latter case, "the [safeguard] measure shall be limited to that member State." The footnote concludes, "Nothing in this Agreement prejudges the interpretation of the relationship between Article XIX and paragraph 8 of Article XXIV of GATT."

This footnote is helpful in that it draws a connection between the geographic scope of the injury determination and the geographic scope of the safeguard. However, it goes only part way in that connection. Although it says that a CU may apply a safeguard on a regionwide basis if injury is determined on a regionwide basis and on an individual-country basis if injury is determined by country, it fails to further state whether in the latter case the safeguard must or may be applied as between that member and other members. For the wording "the measure shall be limited to that member State" to mean that safeguards must or may apply among members of the CU would require "prejudgment" of the debate on the relationship between Articles XIX and XXIV, precisely what the footnote professes not to do. The only reading of "the measures shall be limited to that member State" that is consistent with not prejudging the Ar-

41. See "Background Note by the Secretariat, Systemic Issues Related to 'Other Regulations of Commerce,'" WT/REG/W/17 (October 31, 1997), p. 3.
42. See "Background Note," WT/REG/W/17 (October 31, 1997), p. 3.

ticle XIX–Article XXIV debate is that this phrase simply means that imports from third countries into the injured member state are subject to the safeguard, but imports from third countries into other members of the CU are not.

Presumably the CU would face a choice in this situation. It could allow the member concerned to impose safeguards against other members, thereby relinquishing any orthodoxy on the subject of not applying safeguards among RTA members, or it could not allow the injured member to impose safeguards on imports from other members, thereby opening up the floodgates to imports from third countries brought in via other members of the customs union as well as imports that "originate" in the other CU members.

The CU might consider a third choice as well: applying the safeguards to imports brought in via other CU members, but not to those that originate in such members. To execute this approach CUs would have to put in place internal border formalities to check origin, although they might have long since dismantled such formalities for the sake of "free circulation" of goods in the internal CU market. However, this approach might allow a CU to maintain orthodoxy on the question of whether Article XXIV excludes application of safeguards among RTA members.[43] On the other hand, this approach might induce a CU nonmember that was unhappy about the application of the internal safeguards to products not originating in CU member countries to seek dispute resolution to settle whether an approach so disadvantageous to third countries was consistent with the GATT rules.

Therefore, to a certain degree the footnote "corners" CUs on the issue of applying safeguards among members. It makes it far more palatable for a CU to apply a safeguard on a regionwide basis only after a regionwide determination of injury. In this way the footnote may help reduce the Article XIX–Article XXIV debate without resolving the underlying legal question by inducing CUs to "do the right thing" with regard to regional safeguards. Of course, since the footnote does not mention FTAs, it does not resolve the questions related to them. One might hope, though, that the policy connection between the scope of

43. The "substantially all trade" rule of Article XXIV provides CUs the option to eliminate barriers to substantially all trade in originating products only, as opposed to all products. By applying the safeguard only to products imported from other CU members that originate in third countries, the CU could still claim to have eliminated barriers to substantially all trade among members in originating products, with no exception for the Article XIX safeguards.

the injury determination and the scope of the safeguard will influence how FTA partners look at the question of safeguards.

The issues regarding Article VI are somewhat similar to those regarding Article XIX. Article VI allows a WTO member to apply "antidumping" duties to imported products sold at less than fair value and "countervailing" duties to imported products that have benefited from unfair subsidies by foreign governments. A government imposing either type of duty must find injury to its domestic industry. Duties may be imposed only on imports from countries where the producers have been found to be dumping or the governments are subsidizing the products.

As with Article XIX, the absence of Article VI from the list of exceptions to the "substantially all trade" rule could be read to suggest that members of an RTA may not apply Article VI measures to each other. In practice, however, several RTAs maintain antidumping (AD) and countervailing duty (CVD) regimes that are applicable between RTA members.

In theory it should make little difference to third parties whether RTAs allow or do not allow members to apply AD and CVD regimes to each other. In contrast with safeguard or BOP measures, the source of the imports is relevant for AD and CVD measures. The premise of AD and CVD measures is that certain producers or governments are acting unfairly, causing injury to domestic industry. Therefore, the protective measures should apply only to those countries that are the sources of the problem. If only nonmembers of an RTA are causing the problem, they should face no prejudice if the protective measures exclude RTA members.

The problem with this thesis, however, is that if an RTA excludes its members from investigating each other under AD and CVD laws, an RTA member will not know if the same unfair practices exist among its RTA partners as it has found among nonmembers. Therefore, it could end up giving an advantage to its RTA partners that pursue the same subsidy or dumping practices as the third countries whose imports it restricts. In contrast, third countries should face no prejudice if RTA members apply AD and CVD measures to each other (other than the general Article XXIV policy concern that excluding members from AD and CVD measures could raise the political threshold for negotiating RTAs and therefore might reduce their number).

Discussions of this issue in the Uruguay Round negotiations did not bring a resolution, and the issue continues to arise in working party reviews of RTAs.[44]

44. See "Note by the Secretariat, Annotated Checklist of Systemic Issues," WT/REG/W/16 (May 26, 1997), pp. 7–8.

However, the UR negotiators reached agreement that when parties to a CU "have reached . . . such a level of integration that they have the characteristics of a single, unified market, the industry in the entire area of integration shall be taken to be the domestic industry [for purposes of determining the existence of material injury to a domestic industry]."[45] Therefore, similarly to the application of safeguards, a CU avoids the debate over the Article XXIV:8 exceptions list through applying AD or CVD measures to third countries based on an analysis of industry conditions in the union as a whole. The question of how to treat RTA members in other circumstances remains an issue. Dispute settlement may provide a chance in these other circumstances for nonparties to an RTA to challenge the exclusion of RTA members from application of these measures. However, a complaining party may have to demonstrate that RTA member companies or governments are dumping or subsidizing their products and that their exclusion from an AD or CVD order is prejudicial to the nonmember.

Extension of Existing Protective Measures to New RTA Members

The CU formed between the EC and Turkey has brought into focus another long-standing problem in the application of protective measures in the context of a CU: how to treat a regional partner under existing protective measures. The 1995 CU agreement between the EC and Turkey prohibited the application of safeguard measures between the parties and required Turkey to implement "substantially the same commercial policy as the Community in the textile sector."[46] In accordance with these provisions, Turkey put in place new quantitative restrictions on textile and apparel imports from non-EC countries in order to align itself with existing EC restrictions.[47]

Regarding AD and CVDs, the parties maintained their existing regimes with respect to each other and did not extend existing AD and CVD duties to third countries. The agreement provided, however, that the parties will no longer

45. "Agreement on Subsidies and Countervailing Measures," Article 16.4; "Agreement on Implementation of Article VI of the General Agreement on Tariffs and Trade 1994," Article 4.3.

46. The agreement is reproduced in WT/REG22/1 (February 13, 1996). See Article 5 (elimination of quantitative restrictions) and Article 12.2 (common policy for textiles and clothing).

47. See "Customs Union between Turkey and the European Community, Communication from the Parties to the Customs Union," WT/REG22/5, p. 5.

apply such measures to each other once Turkey "has implemented competition, state aids controls, and other relevant [measures] . . . providing a guarantee against unfair competition comparable to that existing inside the [EC] internal market."[48]

In the working party review of the agreement several WTO members complained of the extension to Turkey of textiles and apparel restrictions that originally encompassed only the EC. They pointed out that the union had not conducted a new investigation to determine if the conditions in the union as a whole (the EC plus Turkey) justified the import restrictions.[49] They argued that the imposition of new quantitative restrictions by Turkey was inconsistent with the requirement under Article XXIV:5 that duties and other regulations of commerce under a CU be on the whole not higher or more restrictive than before the union was put in place.[50]

The EC and Turkey argued that Turkey's application of EC textiles and apparel restrictions was appropriate under the terms of paragraph 8 of Article XXIV, which required each member of the CU to apply "substantially the same duties and other regulations of commerce" to trade with third parties. They also argued that the combined quota had not actually restricted trade, since the level of the quota for the EC plus Turkey was much higher than the prevailing level of imports into the combined region. They also pointed out that Turkey had lowered its duties in the textiles and apparel sector as a result of aligning its tariffs with the EC. As a result, they argued, the duties and other regulations of commerce were not on the whole higher or more restrictive under the CU than before.[51]

Some delegations noticed an inconsistency with the EC approach to textiles and apparel measures on the one hand and with antidumping duties and other trade-protective measures on the other. These delegations pointed out that with regard to AD and CVD measures the EC and Turkey had not found it necessary under Article XXIV:8 to put in place a common external regime or to eliminate

48. See "Customs Union between Turkey and the European Community, Communication from the Parties to the Customs Union," WT/REG22/5, Art. 44.

49. See "Examination of the Customs Union between the European Union and Turkey, Note on the Meeting of 23 October 1996," WT/REG22/M/1 (March 6, 1997), para. 43.

50. See, for example, "Examination of the Customs Union between the European Union and Turkey, Note on the Meeting of 1 October 1997," WT/REG22/M/2 (December 4, 1997), para. 20.

51. See WT/REG22/M/2, para. 17; and WT/REG22/M/1, para. 11.

the application of AD and CVD measures between the parties. Yet in the case of textiles and apparel measures and safeguards, the parties maintained the need to establish a common external regime and eliminate intraregional application of the measures. One delegate asserted:

> This appeared to be a case of the EC's "having its cake and eating it, too," where the EC was asserting that there needed to be a single market, but that common policies needed to be introduced only with respect to those measures that were easiest to apply in that market. The Parties had seemingly applied this rationale only in those cases where it benefited them and disadvantaged third parties, and they had chosen not to apply the rationale when it was not convenient or advantageous.[52]

India invoked the WTO dispute settlement provisions to address these issues. In March 1996 it requested consultations with Turkey,[53] and in February 1998 it requested the establishment of a panel.[54] The panel was established in March 1998.[55] The outcome of this panel proceeding is likely to shed new light on key provisions of paragraphs 5 and 8 of Article XXIV, including the "not on the whole higher or more restrictive" rule of paragraph 5 and perhaps also the relationship between Article XXIV and other articles not on the paragraph 8 exceptions list. It could therefore advance thinking on issues that countless working parties and eight years of Uruguay Round negotiation could not resolve.

GATS Article V

Nondiscrimination is a basic principle of the General Agreement on Trade in Services, as of the GATT. For members of a regional trade arrangement to provide each other more favorable treatment than they provide third countries, they need an exception to the nondiscrimination rule. GATS Article V provides that exception, subject to two basic rules that parallel the two basic rules of GATT Article XXIV. First, the regional agreement must substantially eliminate barriers to intraregional trade, subject to a list of specific exceptions. Second, the agreement may not raise barriers to third parties.

52. See WT/REG22/M/2, para. 12.
53. See WT/DS34/1 (March 25, 1996).
54. WT/DS34/2 (February 2, 1998).
55. WT/DSB/M/43 (April 8, 1998), p. 6.

In crafting these rules the GATS negotiators avoided some of the problems that had arisen under GATT Article XXIV. Their choices in this regard are informative for some of the debates that continue under Article XXIV. At the same time, GATS Article V shares some problems with GATT Article XXIV that the negotiators were not able to overcome.

Substantial Elimination of Barriers

The requirement of GATS Article V that regional trade partners eliminate substantially all services barriers among them appears to be borne of the same philosophy that supported its GATT analog: that permitting partial departure from the nondiscrimination principle would insufficiently restrain regional arrangements and would too easily lead regional trading partners into temptation to pick and choose sectors for liberalization at the expense of third parties. Like its GATT analog, GATS Article V matches these less than perfectly precise policy objectives with a less than perfectly precise rule.

Article V(1) states that a regional arrangement in services trade must have "substantial sectoral coverage" and must "provide for the absence or elimination of substantially all discrimination, in the sense of [national treatment]," between or among the parties in the sectors covered. Providing for the absence or elimination of discrimination means eliminating existing discriminatory measures or prohibiting new or more discriminatory measures. A footnote states that "substantial sectoral coverage" is to be "understood in terms of number of sectors, volume of trade affected and modes of supply." It further states, "In order to meet this condition, agreements should not provide for the a priori exclusion of any mode of supply."

One observes several things in this rule. For one thing, it is more precise than GATT Article XXIV in defining substantial coverage of trade. Whereas the GATT working parties debated a qualitative versus a quantitative approach (that is, sectoral exclusions versus quantities of trade), GATS Article V makes it clear that all sectors need not be included. It does so by separating the concept of sectoral coverage from the concept of eliminating barriers within the sectors covered, thereby suggesting that breadth and depth of coverage are two different issues. On the first issue it says that the agreement must have "substantial sectoral coverage," which by its own logic suggests that some sectors might not be covered. Then the footnote makes it clear that substantial sectoral coverage should be judged both by the number of sectors covered and by the volume of trade affected, along with the different modes of supply. It states that no mode of supply may be excluded, but fails to make the same point regarding exclusion of sectors. The only possible conclusion is that all sectors need not be covered.

Yet although GATS Article V is more precise than GATT Article XXIV in allowing for sectoral exclusions, it offers little or no help in judging how many sectoral exclusions may be allowed before an agreement no longer has "substantial sectoral coverage." Since few regional agreements are likely to have 100 percent sectoral coverage, this question is likely to come up repeatedly in working party reviews. For example, members of the NAFTA working party questioned whether the NAFTA's exclusion of aviation and maritime services and its grandfathering of state and local measures meant that it had less than "substantial" sectoral coverage.[56]

A second observation is that GATS Article V strives to be more precise than the GATT in terms of what barriers to trade must be eliminated. Rather than the "duties and other restrictive regulations of commerce" vaguely defined under GATT Article XXIV:8, the GATS requires elimination of "substantially all discrimination in the sense of Article XVII [national treatment]." This formulation emerged from a much less precise version in earlier draft texts of the GATS, which called for "a high degree of liberalization."[57] Although the meaning of the national treatment obligations stated in Article XVII will continue to develop with dialogue and dispute settlement over that article, the nature of the barriers to be eliminated under GATS Article V will develop with this Article XVII jurisprudence and will not require separate jurisprudence, as does the meaning of the "other restrictive regulations of commerce" referred to in GATT Article XXIV:8.

56. See "Examination of the North American Free Trade Agreement, Note on the Meeting of 24 February 1997," WT/REG4/M/4 (April 16, 1997). In this meeting the United States and the European Community debated the meaning of the "substantially all discrimination" rule of Article V:1. The United States took the view that parties had the choice of either eliminating all discriminatory measures or prohibiting new or more restrictive measures. The EC took the view that the requirement was to eliminate existing discriminatory measures and prohibit new ones. Mexico pointed out that this debate was academic, since in fact the NAFTA eliminated discriminatory measures and prohibited new discrimination with respect to substantially all sectors. See WT/DSB/M/43 (April 8, 1998), p. 6.

57. See Stewart (1993) (showing negotiating drafts of GATS).

Exceptions Clause

The requirement of GATS Article V to eliminate substantially all discrimination in substantially all sectors is qualified by the phrase "except for measures permitted under Articles XI, XII, XIV and XIV *bis*." Articles XI and XII address the kinds of monetary and BOP concerns addressed in GATT Articles XII, XIV, XV, and XVIII-B. Article XIV provides general exceptions to protect health, safety, morals, and the like, similar to those provided by GATT Article XX. Article XIV *bis* provides a national security exception similar to that provided by GATT Article XXI.

It is noteworthy that all the key analogs to the GATT articles not listed in the Article XXIV:8 exemptions list are accounted for in the GATS list. Specifically, all articles relating to payments emergencies are included, as is the national security exception. The list does not include safeguard measures or AD and CVD measures, but that is because the GATS has no equivalents to the safeguards or AD and CVD provisions of GATT Articles XIX and VI, respectively. An observer of GATT Article XXIV might posit that this treatment of the exceptions under GATS Article V indicates substantial support among WTO members of the precept that national security as well all BOP measures may apply among members of RTAs.[58]

"The Overall Level of Barriers to Trade"

The rule that regional trade partners must not raise "the overall level of barriers to trade in services" vis-à-vis third parties is of course similar to the GATT Article XXIV:5 rule for CUs. One may ask what are the circumstances requiring any raising of barriers so one has to worry about whether the "overall" level is higher? Why not follow the approach for FTAs under GATT Article XXIV:5 and simply impose an absolute prohibition against higher barriers in any sector?

To wrestle with this concept requires focusing on the nature of the barriers addressed by GATS Article V. This article requires elimination among the regional partners of discrimination in the sense of national treatment. There-

---

58. As a counterpoint one might ask why the Uruguay Round negotiators did not then resolve these issues under the GATT. The answer might be that it is more difficult to amend or qualify an issue in an existing text in which various WTO members have divergent vested interests than it is to start with a fresh approach on a "clean slate" under the GATS.

fore, in a covered services sector one regional partner must treat services and service suppliers from another regional partner no less favorably than services or services suppliers from its own territory. The regional trade partners might accomplish this result simply by removing or avoiding discriminatory requirements under each of their domestic regimes, or they might, in a closer integration, harmonize or impose a common regulatory regime in that sector. In either way the regime could be made to comply with the national treatment principle. However, in the case of a harmonized or common regime the specific regulatory requirements might be different in one or more parties after the agreement from what they were before. For example, the harmonized or common regime might have different licensing requirements or prudential exceptions than were applied by one or more of the parties before the agreement.

To third parties these requirements might appear more restrictive than the preexisting regime in one or more parties. Yet to achieve a harmonized or common regime, by definition the regime of one or more parties might have to be changed. The question in that case is what standards will protect third parties from the construction of an unduly restrictive regime?

The GATS negotiators considered a formulation that would have steered regional trade partners toward adopting the least restrictive regime in any of the members in the event that the regional agreement included common measures. The 1990 draft text of what became GATS Article V stated: "[Regional arrangements] shall not in respect to other Parties raise overall levels of barriers to trade in services within the respective sectors/sub-sectors. Parties to an agreement should seek to implement any common measures with respect to other Parties at the least restrictive level existing prior to entering into such an agreement."[59]

The rejection of this language in drafting the final text of Article V might suggest that the negotiators saw difficulties with applying a "least restrictive" rule in every case. Indeed, one can imagine disagreement over, for example, which regulatory methodology in a particular sector is in fact more restrictive. In the case of a harmonized or common regime, therefore, the assessment might need to proceed case by case, looking at the nature of the regulatory regime and its effects on third parties.[60] However, when the parties do not adopt

---

59. See Stewart (1993, supra note 61, Annex 1) (reproducing draft texts of GATS).

60. This issue came up in the working party review of the EC enlargement to include Austria, Finland, and Sweden. The United States mentioned concerns about whether the regime in the data processing, space transport, and legal services sectors was consistent with GATS Article V:4. "Examination of the Enlargement of the European Com-

a harmonized or common regime, it should be easier to determine if the measures imposed by a regional trade partner are more restrictive with respect to third parties after the agreement than before.

Therefore, it appears likely that problems will emerge in reviewing agreements under GATS Article V, as they have in reviewing agreements under GATT Article XXIV. The scrutiny of the review process will be important in bringing peer pressure and focus to specific issues in order to keep pressure on WTO members to follow the most trade-creating as opposed to the most trade-diverting path in their regional arrangements. With respect to particularly egregious departures from these principles, the WTO dispute resolution procedure may be able to bring the discipline that the regional trade partners failed to self-impose.

Conclusion

The jury is probably still out on whether the proliferation of RTAs advances global trade liberalization or allows for an increasingly tangled web of trade-distorting preferential regimes. It seems clear, however, that the GATT and GATS rules governing such regimes have taken on significant importance. The integrity of those rules and the principles underlying them must be watched with care. Dispute resolution may bring clarification of some of the difficult areas. However, in some cases it simply will be necessary to continue the "peer pressure" scrutiny of the working party process to ensure that rules drafted as a compromise between the competing objectives of allowing and restraining RTAs continue to maintain the appropriate balance between these objectives.

References

Bhagwati, J. 1993. "Regionalism and Multilateralism: An Overview." In *New Dimensions in Regional Integration,* edited by J. de Melo and A. Panagariya, 22–51. Cambridge, Mass.: Center for Economic Policy Research.

---

munities: Accession of Austria, Finland and Sweden, Note on the Meeting of 14 July 1997," WT/REG3/M/5 (August 12, 1997). Several working party members also strongly emphasized concerns that the EC had extended its MFN exemptions to the new members. See Stewart (1993).

"General Agreement on Tariffs and Trade, Analytical Index." 1994. *Guide to GATT Law and Practice,* 6th ed. Geneva: GATT Secretariat.

Hudec R. 1993. "Discussion on the Paper by J. M. Finger, GATT's Influence on Regional Arrangements." In *New Dimensions in Regional Integration,* edited by J. de Melo and A. Panagariya, 151–55. Cambridge, Mass.: Center for Economic Policy Research.

Roessler, F. 1993. "The Relationship between Regional Integration Agreements and The Multilateral Trade Order." *In Regional Integration and the Global Trading System,* edited by K. Anderson and R. Blackhurst. New York: St. Martin's Press.

Stewart, T. P., ed. 1993. *The GATT Uruguay Round: A Negotiating History (1986–1992),* vol. 2, Annex 1. Boston: Kluwer Law and Taxation.

World Trade Organization. 1995. *Regionalism and the World Trading System.* Geneva.

CHAPTER THREE

Dealing with Latin America's New Regionalism

Miguel Rodríguez Mendoza

A re regional arrangements really bad for the world economy? Many analysts think they are. Most notably among them, Jagdish Bhagwati and Arvind Panagariya believe that regional arrangements, particularly those that include the larger trading partners, divert countries from the ultimate goal of global free trade.[1] Others emphasize the negative economic impact of the arrangements for both the member countries and the rest of the world, as Alexander Yeats did in a polemical analysis of the Southern Common Market (Mercosur).[2] Some take a more pragmatic approach, accepting regional groups as an unavoidable trend in today's world, as do John McMillan, Robert Lawrence, and Jeffrey Frankel.[3] They advance proposals whose aim is to make regional arrangements supportive of, rather than detrimental to, overall trade liberalization. In the course of these discussions regional arrangements have been conceptualized as "building blocks" and "stumbling blocks" in terms of their effects on the multilateral trading system, and partners to these agreements have been characterized as "natural" or "unnatural" trading partners to justify the agreements themselves. In this pragmatic vein, some specific provisions of the General Agreement on Tariffs and Trade (GATT)/World Trade Organization (WTO) have been designed to accommodate regional trade arrangements.

1. Bhagwati and Panagariya (1996).
2. Yeats (1997).
3. McMillan (1993), Lawrence (1996), and Frankel (1997).

Although the debate on regionalism is an old one, recent interest in the subject has been prompted by the growing number of arrangements now in place or under negotiation.[4] According to the WTO, practically all countries belong to one or more trade agreements—the most notable exception being Japan.[5] The appropriate GATT/WTO bodies have been formally notified of more than one hundred agreements, and many others have never been subjected to these procedures. The European countries have traditionally taken the lead in the negotiation of regional agreements. Recently they have been joined by the Latin American countries, which have put in place a significant number of trade agreements in the last few years. A study prepared by the Organization of American States (OAS) identified sixteen trade and integration agreements now in existence throughout Latin America.[6] There is more to it, however, as the study left out dozens of preferential trade agreements concluded under the umbrella of the Latin American Integration Association (Aladi).

This chapter focuses on two of the most dynamic Latin American agreements, those that established the Mercosur and the Andean Community (formerly the Andean Group). It points out that these agreements have had a positive impact on trade liberalization and trade growth among their member countries and that trade with the rest of the world has not suffered as the agreements have moved forward in accomplishing their objectives. This positive impact is mainly the result of the unilateral trade liberalization reforms undertaken by the Latin American countries during the second half of the 1980s. The Mercosur and the Andean Community, with varying degrees of success, have helped their participating countries consolidate those reforms, thus ensuring that the elimination of barriers to intrasubregional trade takes place under lower levels of protection vis-à-vis trade with the rest of the world.

The Mercosur and the Andean Community belong to a new generation of regional arrangements that differ significantly from the array of agreements negotiated by the Latin American countries from the early 1960s to the late

4. As Jackson (1969, p. 576) said many years ago, "more legal literature exists concerning the GATT regional exception than for any other provision of the GATT." Since then the legal, and in particular the economic, analysis of regional arrangements has expanded considerably, with authors like Krugman (1991), Anderson and Norheim (1993), Bhagwati (1993), Bhagwati and Panagariya (1996), and Frankel (1997), among many others, making important contributions to our understanding of the functioning of the arrangements and their effects.

5. World Trade Organization (WTO) (1995).

6. Organization of American States (1996).

1980s. As examined in the next section, the Mercosur countries have in a short period of time largely fulfilled their initial goals regarding the establishment of a free trade area and the implementation of a common external tariff. The Andean Community has made comparable progress during the last decade, although not without some tensions among its members. The trade impact of the agreements and their consistency with multilateral rules is also examined, and this analysis has recourse to the analytical tools provided by a number of authors to evaluate the economic consequences of regional arrangements. The criteria included in GATT Article XXIV are also used as a reference point in evaluating the agreements, and conclusions are drawn.

The Mercosur and the Andean Community

Both the Mercosur and the Andean Group in its new incarnation, the Andean Community, operate, albeit imperfectly, as customs unions. Trade among their members has been significantly liberalized and has expanded considerably, as has trade with third countries. A common external tariff (CET) has been implemented in the two groups. Each group has a scheduled time line for further implementation and for phasing in items that are currently exempted— either from the free trade area or from the CET. The CET levels are in general lower than the national tariffs at the time of the establishment of the arrangements.

These developments have taken place in a relatively short period of time— the first part of the 1990s—and they are reviewed in this section by looking at the recent evolution of the Mercosur and the Andean Community. This review touches upon some institutional issues, but focuses on the progress achieved in these two agreements with regard to trade liberalization and expansion, as well as the establishment of the CET, so as to provide a framework for the empirical analysis included in the next section of this chapter.

The Mercosur

The Mercosur came into being on March 26, 1991, when Argentina, Brazil, Paraguay, and Uruguay signed the Treaty of Asunción, which formalized the commitment to establish a common market among these four countries.[7] The treaty provided for a five-year transition phase for the countries to move to free trade and to implement a CET. The October 17, 1994, Protocol of Ouro Preto

7. The treaty entered into force on November 29, 1991.

gave the Mercosur a juridical personality and defined an institutional structure for carrying out the agreement.

The Mercosur was built upon an already substantial trade relationship among its member countries and upon the economic reforms undertaken by these countries in the late 1980s. The objective of the Mercosur agreement was to reinforce and consolidate these economic reforms and to expedite the competitive insertion of its members into the world economy. The arrangement was preceded by several bilateral trade agreements within the Aladi framework, in particular between Argentina and Brazil, as well as by the 1979 tripartite agreement among Argentina, Brazil, and Paraguay on the use of the hydroelectric resources of the Paraná River.

Mercosur institutions are intergovernmental in nature and follow principles of flexibility and simplicity. The Mercosur countries explicitly refrained from creating supranational institutions to guide the process; rather, the structure was to consist of intergovernmental bodies whose meetings would be attended by representatives from each member country. Biannual meetings of all four presidents are held to ratify decisions made by the Mercosur bodies and to set the future agenda. The Ouro Preto agreement set out the Common Market Council of Ministers (CMC), which is made up of the ministers of foreign affairs and ministers of economy, to oversee the integration process. The CMC has negotiating authority to conclude agreements. The Common Market Group (GMC) was also created as the executive and decisionmaking body and oversees the various working groups.[8] Meetings of the GMC are attended by representatives of these same ministers and of the central banks. The Ouro Preto agreement also created a Trade Commission (CCM) to monitor the application of the common trade policy and an Administrative Secretariat to offer operational and administrative support. Each member country has one vote, and the decisions regarding Mercosur regulations require consensus. A dispute settlement mechanism was established by the Protocol of Brasilia, which was signed on December 17, 1991.

During the transition period from 1991 to 1994, countries eliminated most restrictions to intra-Mercosur trade. The Mercosur liberalization schedule was structured as a progressive across-the-board tariff reduction that started on July 1, 1991, and ended on December 31, 1994. Since then each member has

8. The Free Trade Area of the Americas (FTAA) working groups address the following issues: communications, mining, standards and regulations, financial issues, transport and infrastructure, environment, industry, agriculture, energy, and labor.

been allowed a list of sensitive products to be temporarily exempted from the free trade area.[9] Tariffs on these products are being gradually phased out through a process known as a *régimen de adecuación* (compatibility regime). According to this mechanism, exceptions to intra-Mercosur free trade are scheduled to disappear by December 31, 1998, for the two largest countries and by the following year for Paraguay and Uruguay, thus completing the establishment of the Mercosur free trade area.

The *régimen de adecuación* seems to have worked smoothly. Tariffs applied to intra-Mercosur trade in the excepted products are just a fraction of most favored nation (MFN) rates.[10] However, it is yet unclear what treatment will be accorded to two sectors of trade that so far have remained outside of Mercosur rules: automobiles and sugar. The automotive sector has been subject to special arrangements, particularly between Argentina and Brazil, and there are ongoing discussions on a common auto pact among the four Mercosur countries.[11] Trade in the sugar sector is still subject to national tariffs, although a commission has been established to design the gradual move toward free trade. Finally, it should be pointed out that a number of nontariff measures continue to distort and affect intra-Mercosur trade. Although the elimination or harmonization of these measures has been a priority goal since late 1994, very little progress has been achieved. According to the Inter-American Development Bank (IDB) the Mercosur countries have identified 368 nontariff measures on which no action has been taken so far.[12]

---

9. The lists of exceptions have included steel products, textiles and footwear, paper, tires, coffee, and furniture in the case of Argentina. Brazil has excluded textile products, rubber products, wine, and preserves. In the case of Uruguay and Paraguay, the exceptions have included textiles and footwear, machinery and equipment, steel products, pharmaceutical products, glass products, toys, and other products. See Inter-American Development Bank (IDB) (1996, p. 18).

10. IDB (1997, p. 19).

11. In late 1994 the Mercosur countries made the commitment to define a common automobile regime by December 31, 1997, and to implement it no later than January 1, 2000. This common regime was to be made up of three main elements: intra-Mercosur free trade in the sector, a CET, and the elimination of investment incentives. At the December 1998 Mercosur Summit, which took place in Rio de Janeiro, Argentina and Brazil agreed on a common framework for trade in the automotive sector.

12. IDB (1997).

Figure 3-1. Tariff Liberalization in the Mercosur, 1985–95

Average trade-weighted national tariff rate, percent

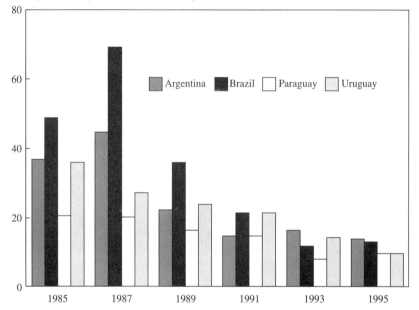

Source: Organization of American States (OAS) Trade Unit calculations based on Aladi Secretariat data.

The Mercosur CET was implemented on January 1, 1995. It consists of eleven tariff levels ranging from 0 to 20 percent at intervals of 2 percent. The CET, which covers 8,500 tariff items, was adopted for all items, but was initially put into place for 85 percent of these items, with the remaining 15 percent included on lists of temporary exceptions. Originally these lists were not to exceed 300 items for Argentina, Brazil, and Uruguay and 399 for Paraguay. Brazil was later authorized to expand its list by 50 percent. National tariffs were maintained on capital goods and are scheduled to converge to a CET of 14 percent by 2000 for Argentina and Brazil and by 2006 for Paraguay and Uruguay. In the informatics and telecommunications sectors the products will have a maximum protection of 16 percent in the year 2006 with automatic and linear convergence of national tariffs.

Following the trends at the domestic level, the tariff levels agreed upon for the Mercosur CET were in general lower than the prevailing national tariffs in place in 1990 for all countries but Paraguay. This was so even taking into

Table 3-1. Mercosur Exports, 1970–97

Billions of 1990 U.S. dollars (except where noted)

Category	1970	1975	1980	1985	1990	1991	1992	1993	1994	1995	1996	1997
Total exports	16.3	29.8	47.2	42.1	46.5	44.0	48.2	49.2	55.6	60.6	62.7	68.3
Intra-Mercosur exports	1.5	2.5	5.5	2.4	4.1	4.9	6.7	9.1	10.7	12.4	14.3	16.2
Exports to rest of world	14.7	27.3	41.7	39.8	42.3	39.1	41.5	40.1	45.0	48.2	48.4	52.2
Intra-Mercosur exports as percentage of total exports	9	8	12	6	9	11	14	19	19	20	23	24

Source: International Monetary Fund (IMF) (1997).

consideration the three-point increase in the levels of the CET decided on by the Mercosur countries in December 1997.[13] Figure 3-1 shows the average trade-weighted tariff levels in each of the Mercosur countries from 1985, before the unilateral liberalization programs were undertaken in each of the members, to 1995, the year in which the transition period of the Mercosur was completed. Argentina and Brazil achieved significant tariff reductions between 1987 and 1991. Argentina's average tariff of 44 percent in 1987 fell to about 16 percent in 1993 and was further lowered to 14 percent in 1995. Brazil's 1987 average tariff of 69 percent fell to 20 percent in 1991 and was brought down to 13 percent in 1995.

Largely spurred by this reduction of trade barriers, intra-Mercosur trade grew quickly in the 1990s, with exports expanding at an average annual rate of 25 percent between 1990 and 1997. As mentioned, the Mercosur built upon a relationship of strong trade ties already in place among these geographical neighbors, particularly between the two largest members, Argentina and Brazil. As shown in table 3-1, in 1970 trade among the Mercosur countries already made up about 10 percent of their total trade. This relationship weakened over the course of the 1980s, mainly as a consequence of the international debt crisis, in which Argentina and Brazil were particularly affected. Although in 1980—the year in which trade among the countries reached its pre-1990 peak—intra-Mercosur exports were $5.5 billion, by 1985 this level had fallen

13. This decision followed a WTO panel ruling on the *tasa estadística* (statistical tax) of 3 percent that Argentina had implemented a few years before. The Mercosur decision is of a temporary nature and will be reversed not later than December 31, 2000. The Mercosur countries were given considerable flexibility in implementing this decision, as the tariff increase could be made lower and for a shorter period if countries so desired (something that Paraguay and Uruguay both did).

Table 3-2. Mercosur Imports from Various Sources, 1990–97
Billions of 1990 U.S. dollars (except where noted)

Source	1990	1991	1992	1993	1994	1995	1996	1997	Average annual growth (percent)
Total	29.3	32.9	36.1	44.2	53.8	66.6	74.6	85.5	17
Mercosur	4.2	5.0	6.8	8.5	10.6	12.6	14.9	17.3	22
United States	5.7	6.9	8.1	9.9	10.8	13.7	15.6	19.0	19
Other Latin American/ Caribbean Countries[a]	2.2	2.9	3.3	3.5	3.8	4.9	5.8	6.3	14
Japan	2.0	2.1	2.0	2.4	2.9	3.7	3.3	3.8	10
European Union	6.9	7.8	8.6	10.4	14.9	17.8	19.5	14.3	11

Source: IMF (1997).

a. South and Central America and the Caribbean, minus the four Mercosur members.

to $2.4 billion. However, in 1990 intra-Mercosur exports had recovered to $4.1 billion. From there, intra-Mercosur exports continued to expand as shown by the 1997 level of $16.2 billion, about four times their 1990 levels and a fourth of the Mercosur members' total trade.

As the members of the Mercosur have discovered each other's markets, so has the rest of the world discovered the growing market of the Mercosur. As seen in table 3-2, both U.S. and European exporters are taking advantage of the openness of the 1990s and its resultant market expansion. European firms increased their sales to the region by 21 percent per year over the first five years of the decade—a growth rate that has dropped off somewhat in the latter part of the 1990s to average a healthy 11 percent per year for the decade. U.S. exports to the Mercosur countries for the 1990s have averaged an annual growth rate of 19 percent, and Asian exports have moved to take advantage of the falling barriers. In 1995 Japan sold over $3.7 billion worth of goods to the Mercosur countries—almost double its sales in 1990. The Latin American and Caribbean countries, considered apart from the Mercosur countries, have increased their sales to the Mercosur at a rate of 14 percent per year.

In addition to consolidating their regional market and completing the customs union, the Mercosur countries have been pursuing outside links. The Treaty of Asunción allowed for accession by other countries at the end of the transition period.[14] New members could join the Mercosur only through negotiations, and countries that were members of other Latin American integration

14. Although a sectoral waiver was included that could allow for the eventual membership of Chile.

schemes had to wait until the treaty had been in force for five years. In 1996, a year after this requirement was fulfilled, the Mercosur countries negotiated associative memberships for both Bolivia and Chile. They are currently engaged in negotiations with the Andean Community countries and with Mexico.

Therefore, the Mercosur is coming into its own as a trade entity and as one of the main actors on the trading landscape of the Americas. It has accomplished several key goals: trade is mostly free among the members, and a CET is in place. As well, the Mercosur participates as an entity both in bilateral or plurilateral negotiations and in regional forums such as the FTAA. Notwithstanding these achievements, the Mercosur as a unit and its member countries face several important challenges. The customs union is not yet fully in place. Rules of origin—a characteristic of free trade areas that should be obviated by the implementation of common tariffs—continue to be in force, as a unitary Mercosur schedule has yet to be formalized. These rules lead to further complications, such as collection of multiple taxes. Also, internal fiscal conditions have periodically caused member countries to deviate from their Mercosur commitments, and some trade frictions among countries have spilled over into the Mercosur. Most notable were Brazil's investment incentives in the automobile sector and its restrictions on import financing—from which it initially neglected to exempt its Mercosur partners—and Argentina's frequent use of antidumping procedures against Brazilian exports. So far these disturbances have not damaged the Mercosur, as members have generally worked out solutions through bilateral or quadrilateral consultations.

The Andean Community

The Andean Group metamorphosed into the Andean Community in June 1997 when the Cartagena Agreement, signed in 1969, was modified by a new protocol—the Trujillo Declaration.[15] The new protocol introduced some changes in the already strong institutional framework of the Andean Group. It created a Presidential Council and a Council of Ministers of Foreign Affairs to

---

15. As the Trujillo Protocol came into force, a new protocol was adopted by the Andean countries in June 1997—the Sucre Protocol—whereby a number of commitments were made by the Andean countries regarding their common external relations and the liberalization of trade in services. The Cartagena Agreement had gone through another major change in the late 1980s when its member countries adopted the Quito Protocol.

provide political guidance to the integration process, and it replaced a tripartite body in charge of the technical secretariat—the junta or board—with a General Secretariat. The protocol did not address the difficulties that the Andean countries had been facing in trying to deepen their integration efforts. These difficulties had resulted from the uneven application by the Andean countries of some critical decisions regarding the functioning of the customs union. That was in particular the case of Peru, which remained outside the Andean free trade area and did not implement the CET agreed to by the group. However, as the Trujillo Protocol went into effect an agreement was reached between Peru and its Andean partners that, as discussed next, put an end to this situation.

The Trujillo Protocol built upon the already strong institutional framework of the Andean Group. Modeled on those of the European Economic Community, the Andean Community's institutions are highly developed. The Andean Commission is the policymaking body. It is made up of plenipotentiary representatives from each member country, and it has legislative powers, as its decisions are directly enforceable in all member countries. As a result of the changes introduced by the Trujillo Protocol, when dealing with sectoral issues the Andean Commission should include government representatives from those sectors, including the foreign ministers as appropriate. The General Secretariat has the capacity to develop and formulate policy proposals to the Commission, and there is a judicial framework to deal with disputes, the Andean Court of Justice, to which both member countries and their citizens can have access. There is also a development fund, administered by the Andean Development Corporation (CAF), which finances projects to strengthen the integration process and whose operations have been expanded considerably in recent years.

On the trade front, a number of decisions regarding the free trade area and the CET were adopted by the Andean countries at a presidential meeting in Cartagena, Colombia, in December 1991. These decisions provided for the establishment of the free trade area and the adoption of a CET by January 1, 1992. However, this deadline was not met. Instead the Andean countries have implemented these decisions in a sequential order. With respect to the free trade area, Colombia and Venezuela moved ahead independently and eliminated tariffs and other restrictions to their reciprocal trade in February 1992. Bolivia joined them in September 1992, and Ecuador did so in January 1993. Therefore, a free trade area—with no goods exempted—went into effect in 1993 between Bolivia, Colombia, Ecuador, and Venezuela. Peru did not at that time join the free trade area. Instead it negotiated a number of bilateral trade arrangements with each of its Andean neighbors that helped to partially liberalize the reciprocal trade flows between Peru and its neighbors.[16] These bilateral agreements were in force until mid-1997, when a compromise was reached whereby Peru would gradually join the Andean free trade area by completing its trade liberalization process vis-à-vis the other countries by the year 2000 for most tariff lines and by 2005 for a few remaining sensitive products.[17]

Implementing the CET proved even more difficult. The Andean CET is determined by the level of processing of goods, with a 5 percent tariff rate applied to raw materials and industrial inputs; rates of 10 and 15 percent applied to intermediate inputs and capital goods, respectively; and 20 percent applied to final goods. There are exemptions to the CET, which will be eliminated by 1999, and higher rates apply to trade in automobiles. At the time the decisions regarding the establishment of the CET were made, Bolivia was excused from implementing it and allowed to maintain its flat national tariff schedule. Peru, which had already adopted a flat, two-level tariff rate of 15 and 25 percent for most of its tariff schedule, was not prepared to immediately implement the four-level agreed-upon CET. Therefore, it was Colombia and Venezuela that first adopted the Andean CET (also in February 1992, as the two countries liberalized their reciprocal trade), and then Ecuador did (in 1995).[18] This situation will remain unchanged for the foreseeable future. At the time Peru decided to join the free trade area it was also agreed that it would not participate in the Andean CET.[19] The Andean customs union is thus made up of three countries, whereas all the Andean Community countries participate in the Andean free trade area—with Peru doing so gradually.

The levels of the CET reflect the policy changes that had previously been made in the Andean countries' trade regimes. These countries began to unilaterally liberalize their trade in the late 1980s, bringing tariffs to new lower levels. In 1985 tariffs ranged from Bolivia's relatively low average level of

16. These bilateral trade agreements were part of an understanding reached in August 1992 that, in fact, "suspended" Peru from its obligations regarding the Andean customs union its neighbors were then trying to establish.

17. Decision 414 of the Andean Commission set out the terms for the participation of Peru in the Andean free trade area. According to this decision, approximately 85 percent of items would be liberalized by the year 2000. The phasing out of tariffs on the remaining items would be completed by the year 2005.

18. The CET formally went into effect on February 1, 1995.

19. See Andean Commission Decision 414.

Figure 3-2. Andean Community Tariff Reduction, 1985–97

Average trade-weighted national tariff rate, percent

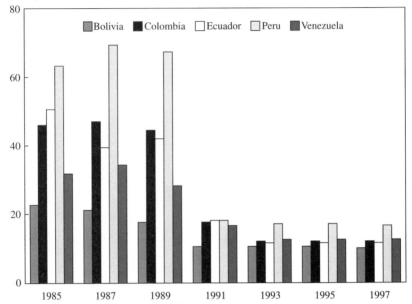

Source: OAS Trade Unit calculations based on Aladi Secretariat data.

20 percent to Peru's higher average rate of 63 percent. Bolivia began its trade liberalization process as early as 1985, adopting a more simplified flat-rate tariff and eliminating nontariff barriers. Starting in the late 1980s Colombia, Ecuador, and Venezuela also reduced and simplified their tariffs. Peru followed later, adopting a two-tiered tariff. As a result of these developments, by 1990–91 tariffs in all the Andean Community countries had been lowered, as shown in figure 3-2. By 1993 considerable MFN tariff reduction had been carried out in all of the countries: Bolivia had lowered its average tariff to 9.7; the average levels in Colombia, Ecuador, and Venezuela were 11.4, 11.2, and 11.8 percent, respectively; and Peru's average tariff stood at 16.3. These tariff levels have remained largely unchanged since then.

As in the case of the Mercosur, the trade liberalization measures of the Andean Community have had an important effect on trade among its members. After a decade of flat or declining growth in the 1980s, intra-Andean trade picked up in the late 1980s and began to grow steadily after 1990, as shown in table 3-3. Intraregional trade has grown—both in magnitude and as a percent of

Table 3-3. Andean Community Total and Intra-Community Trade, 1970–97

Billions of 1990 U.S. dollars (except where noted)

Trade category	1970	1975	1980	1985	1990	1991	1992	1993	1994	1995	1996	1997
Exports												
Total exports	18.33	31.75	45.73	29.60	34.10	29.21	26.82	26.48	30.92	34.57	38.25	41.28
Andean Community exports	0.33	1.17	1.85	0.90	1.31	1.70	2.07	2.62	3.30	4.08	4.00	4.43
Exports to rest of world	18.00	30.58	43.88	28.70	32.79	27.51	24.75	23.86	27.63	30.49	34.24	36.85
Intraregional exports as percentage of total exports	2	4	4	3	4	6	8	10	11	12	10	11
Imports												
Total imports	12.43	26.32	34.38	18.41	17.16	20.02	24.71	26.17	27.53	32.79	32.38	36.42
Andean Community imports	0.35	1.22	1.47	0.88	1.10	1.50	1.95	2.37	3.30	4.14	4.09	4.52
Imports to rest of world	12.08	25.10	32.91	17.53	16.06	18.52	22.75	23.80	24.23	28.66	28.29	31.90
Intraregional imports as percentage of total imports	3	5	4	5	6	7	8	9	12	13	13	12

Source: IMF (1997).

total trade—and is at the highest level in the history of this regional arrangement. Intra-Andean import growth has been especially strong, with imports among members more than quadrupling since 1990, from U.S.$1.1 billion to U.S.$4.5 billion in 1997. In 1970 only 3 percent of Andean Community imports came from the Andean countries; in 1997, however, 12 percent of the Andean countries' imports originated in other Andean Community members. Although trade among the member countries has grown, the Andean Community represents a relatively small although increasing portion of each country's trade.

The Andean Community has also addressed many of the newer trade issues. A common investment regime is in place, mandated by Andean Commission Decision 291, which replaced the old, restrictive Decision 24, which included mandatory registration and authorization of foreign direct investment (FDI), off-limits economic sectors, ownership restrictions, limits to local finance, technology transfer provisions, and profit remittance limits, among other provisions. The new regime grants national treatment for regional investors and eliminates all restrictions on capital and profit remittances. A common regime is also in place for intellectual property protection. Decision 344 granted patent rights to some pharmaceutical products that had been excluded before, and

Decision 351 deals with copyrights and extends protection to software and computer programs. In order to increase the feasibility of extending integration, new regulations were adopted allowing for the free movement of passenger and commercial vehicles. The harmonization of economic and social policies, long an objective of the Andean Community, continues to be on the work agenda.

The Andean Community has moved well beyond what had been accomplished in agreements previously established by the Latin American countries. The main success of the Andean Community has been to effect a significant reduction of barriers to trade among its members. Although there are still exceptions to the Mercosur and the Andean Community free trade areas, they are of a temporary nature and do not cover a significant amount of the current trade of their member countries. The implementation of the CET has been a more complex exercise, particularly in the case of the Andean Community, but considerable progress in this regard can also be registered. The fact that in both cases the CET has been set at levels comparable to those achieved by the countries through their unilateral trade liberalization measures has played a crucial role in keeping the agreements in line with the market-oriented strategies of their members. Most important, trade among the member countries and with the rest of the world has expanded—and in some cases reached unprecedented levels—as examined in the next section.

Testing the Agreements

It is now time to turn to the questions asked at the beginning of the chapter. Has the establishment of the Mercosur and the Andean Community had any undesirable economic impact on their member countries? Have third countries been affected? Have the agreements diverted their members from their multilateral obligations? The answers to these questions are not easy. Any attempt in this regard is subject to criticism, as views on regional arrangements are based not only on the observed facts, but also on ideological—or theological—considerations. Those in favor of regional arrangements will see positive signs in any of them, irrespective of their actual functioning. Those who oppose them will see only evil in their very existence. Ideas, more than realities, normally impose themselves.

From an economic point of view, the question is whether a regional trade agreement causes trade from countries outside of the arrangement to be displaced. Jacob Viner is credited as being the first to explain this issue clearly and to label the potential effects of trade arrangements as either "trade creating" or "trade diverting."[20] A preferential trade arrangement has the potential to create trade provided that the lowering of barriers will induce a shift in the purchase of certain goods from a less competitive domestic industry to more efficient producers in another member country. This result is net welfare enhancing. On the other hand, preferential trade arrangements can lower welfare. If the lowering of tariffs and other barriers among countries within a trade arrangement results in the purchase of goods from a member country that produces them less efficiently than does a third country not party to the arrangement (and therefore not privy to the lower barriers), trade diversion will have occurred.

It is not easy to definitively proclaim whether arrangements are trade creating or trade diverting, especially in the case of the Mercosur and the Andean Community, as these agreements are still evolving. Still, it is worth examining the economics and particularly the trade effects of these two agreements. To do so, a number of tests are used in this chapter, as not a single one will capture the full dynamics of trade within the agreements and with the outside world. The tests are all aggregate rather than sector oriented, and their results are illustrative rather than definitive. The tests fall into two categories: the first three aim to assess whether third countries (the rest of the world) have been adversely affected by the entry into force of the agreements binding the Mercosur and the Andean Community. The latter two tests use the criteria set forth by Article XXIV of the GATT and look into whether these two arrangements are in compliance with this requirement of the multilateral trading system.

Intraregional Shares

Perhaps the most widely used indicator of such compliance is intraregional shares. It is used to determine the importance of trade among the members of an agreement with respect to their total trade; therefore, it could measure the effects of the agreements being considered on internal trade. It is taken that a regional agreement is of some consequence if the level of intraregional trade rises after the agreement is put into place. Conversely, the effectiveness of an agreement is questioned if the level of intraregional trade remains the same or rises only marginally. The results of application of this indicator to the Mercosur and the Andean Community are included in table 3-4.

---

20. Viner (1950).

Table 3-4. Intraregional Trade as a Share of Total Trade, 1970–97
Aggregate of intragroup imports and exports divided by total trade

Country	1970	1975	1980	1985	1990	1995	1996	1997
Mercosur countries								
Argentina	0.11	0.10	0.13	0.11	0.16	0.28	0.29	0.29
Brazil	0.07	0.04	0.07	0.04	0.07	0.14	0.15	0.16
Paraguay	0.29	0.37	0.46	0.43	0.35	0.40	0.49	0.52
Uruguay	0.19	0.23	0.31	0.29	0.30	0.46	0.45	0.42
Total for Mercosur	0.10	0.07	0.10	0.07	0.11	0.20	0.21	0.22
Andean Community countries								
Bolivia	0.02	0.04	0.05	0.02	0.06	0.13	0.14	0.13
Colombia	0.04	0.08	0.12	0.08	0.07	0.16	0.15	0.16
Ecuador	0.07	0.10	0.06	0.02	0.07	0.12	0.13	0.12
Peru	0.03	0.08	0.05	0.06	0.07	0.12	0.12	0.13
Venezuela	0.01	0.02	0.02	0.02	0.03	0.09	0.08	0.08
Total for Andean Community	0.02	0.04	0.04	0.04	0.05	0.12	0.11	0.12

Source: IMF (1997).

The data show that for both the Mercosur and the Andean Community intraregional ratios have increased considerably throughout the 1990s, the period in which the agreements were established or reactivated. In the case of the Mercosur, internal trade represented 22 percent of the total trade of its member countries in 1997, up from 11 percent in 1990 and 7 percent in 1985. The intraregional trade of the Andean Community more than doubled between 1990 and 1997. These results also point out that for some individual countries trade with their partners in the agreement represents a large percentage of their total trade (30 percent or more for Argentina, Paraguay, and Uruguay). For others the share of trade with their partners is a much smaller percentage of their total trade (for example, 8 percent for Venezuela). However, the trade of *all* these countries with countries participating in their agreements has increased significantly, particularly during the 1980s.

The Simple Concentration Index

Although the intraregional trade shares of the Mercosur and the Andean Community are larger than ever, they are still low if compared with the corresponding share of, for example, the European Union, which is about

65 percent. Does it mean that the Mercosur and the Andean Community trade less than should be expected of them? Not necessarily, says Jeffrey Frankel. The reason is that an arrangement such as the European Union includes a number of very large trading countries, whereas the Mercosur and the Andean Community each involves fewer countries that are also relatively small traders on a global scale. As Frankel says, "It is a necessary property of the intra-regional share measure that the bigger the set of countries around which one throws the lasso, the higher will be the apparent concentration of trade within."[21]

To deal with this potentially distorting factor, Frankel proposes a measure of regional trade concentration, the simple concentration index, which can be used to indicate whether trade is unduly concentrated within a regional agreement. To apply this measure he proposes to divide the intra-regional trade shares of each group by the share of the group in world trade. If this adjustment is made, the results may give some measure of the impact of the agreements—and of geography—on their member countries' trade. Frankel is basically concerned with the role of geography—or rather geographical proximity—in trade patterns and regional arrangements. According to this index, a ratio above 1 would mean that trade is more concentrated within the group than would be expected of countries not linked by a regional arrangement—or distant geographically. The results of applying this index to the Mercosur and the Andean Community are presented in table 3-5.

For each of the two agreements the simple concentration index is well above 1, which may be interpreted as showing that the member countries trade more among themselves than could be expected from a similar group of unrelated countries. The fact that the index has risen significantly in the 1990s indicates that the existence of the agreements—rather than geography—may be the leading factor in explaining the trade expansion of the last few years. This is not to say that geographical proximity has not played any role. As table 3-5 shows, the concentration index for each agreement is positive in all the years considered, including those in which the agreements did not exist or were irrelevant, thus supporting the views of Paul Krugman, Larry Summers, and of course Jeffrey Frankel, who see geography as a "natural" determinant of trade.[22]

---

21. Frankel (1997, p. 21).
22. Krugman (1991), Summers (1991), and Frankel (1997).

Table 3-5. Simple Concentration Indexes for the Mercosur and the Andean Community, 1970–97

	1970	1975	1980	1985	1990	1995	1996	1997
Mercosur								
Intraregional trade[a]	0.10	0.07	0.10	0.07	0.11	0.20	0.21	0.22
Share of world trade	0.02	0.02	0.02	0.01	0.01	0.01	0.02	0.02
Simple intraregional trade concentration ratio[b]	6.00	3.72	5.72	4.78	10.02	13.77	13.60	12.96
Andean Community								
Intraregional trade[a]	0.02	0.04	0.04	0.04	0.05	0.12	0.11	0.12
Share of world trade	0.01	0.01	0.01	0.01	0.01	0.01	0.01	0.01
Simple intraregional trade concentration ratio[b]	1.57	2.80	3.18	3.46	6.34	15.87	14.43	13.42

Source: IMF (1997).

a. Aggregate of intragroup imports and exports divided by total trade.

b. Intraregional trade shares divided by the group share in world trade.

The Adjusted Admissibility Test

A different approach is taken by John McMillan, who proposes a test that is probably the most telling illustration of welfare effects. McMillan is concerned with the consistency of regional agreements with the existing multilateral rules as well as their impact on world trade. Recognizing the difficulties encountered in applying the criteria of GATT Article XXIV, McMillan suggests a more straightforward criterion to determine whether the agreements should be deemed acceptable from the standpoint of the multilateral trading system—the admissibility test. He proposes that the appropriate rule should be to require that the preexisting external trade volumes of the member countries not be lowered as a result of a regional arrangement. This would "make countries better off without making any of the non-member countries worse off."[23]

As the admissibility test is constructed along a high level of aggregation—total trade volumes—McMillan goes on to propose that it be adjusted by, for example, extrapolating into the first years of an agreement the rate of growth of imports achieved before the agreement entered into force. That is what is done in figure 3-3. For the Mercosur and the Andean Community the rate of growth

23. McMillan (1993, p. 293).

Figure 3-3. Adjusted Admissibility Test, 1970–97

Millions of U.S. dollars

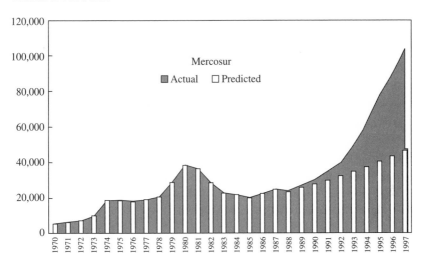

Millions of U.S. dollars

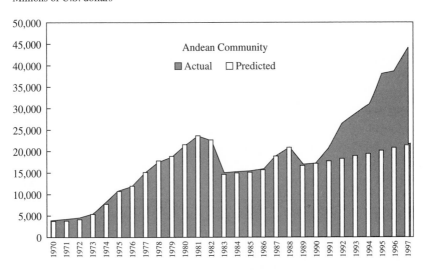

Source: IMF *Direction of Trade Statistics* and author's estimates.

of imports from the rest of the world has been estimated for 1986 to 1990, then extrapolated for 1990 to 1997.

It is clear from the figure that rather than suffering as a consequence of the two subregional agreements, the outside world has continued to enjoy its market access to both the Mercosur and the Andean Community. Moreover, had imports from third countries maintained their preagreement rates of growth, the actual sales of these countries to the Mercosur and the Andean Community would have been much lower than they actually were. This does not say that third countries' imports have grown because of the agreements, as they may have been influenced by the unilateral liberalization measures and the renewed economic growth that the Mercosur and the Andean countries have effected in these years. However, the data show that, far from adversely affecting other countries, the Mercosur and the Andean Community have been consolidating their integration efforts in a context of greater participation in and opening to the world economy.

The Trade Barriers Test

As useful as McMillan's approach could be, the fact remains that the admissibility criteria regarding the compatibility of regional agreements with the multilateral trading system are those included in Article XXIV, as interpreted—and somehow complemented—during the negotiations of the Uruguay Round.[24] One of these requirements is that countries entering into a customs union or a free trade area not raise their trade barriers higher than they were before the agreement. A proper test of this requirement may be too ambitious an undertaking, as it would involve acquiring a great amount of information on trade weighted by tariff line for a large sample of years. As this information is not easily available, an alternative route is taken here.

Since the Mercosur and the Andean Community have each implemented a CET, a comparison is made between the average level of the CET and the average level of the tariff schedules of each member country in 1989, the year preceding the implementation of the agreements. The fact that some products—or even sectors—are excluded from the CET as discussed earlier

---

24. Although Article XXIV was not changed, an understanding was reached during the Uruguay Round of trade negotiations to clarify some of its provisions. The understanding also provides a methodology to evaluate the trade effects of the agreements. See World Trade Organization (1995, pp. 31–34).

Figure 3-4. Trade Barriers Test

Average trade-weighted national tariff rate, percent

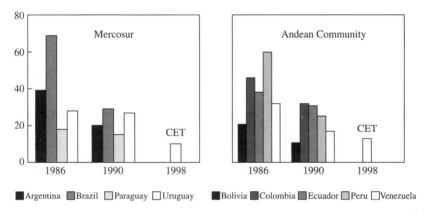

Source: Aladi Secretariat data.

should not affect the analysis as these exceptions are scheduled to be phased out within the next few years. The comparison is valid, as it will give some measure of the extent to which the agreements have affected the level of protection vis-à-vis third countries—and thus whether they comply with this requirement of Article XXIV. The results are shown in figure 3-4.

The "Substantially All Trade" Test

The other main requirement of Article XXIV is that to be consistent with multilateral rules, regional arrangements have to cover all or *substantially all* the trade of the participating countries. In this case the analysis could be more easily done, as all it requires is information on the weight of the sectors or products excluded from total trade that is conducted free of restrictions within the agreements. Figure 3-5 shows that so far the Mercosur covers a lower percentage of its internal trade than does the Andean Community. This is due to the temporary exclusion from the Mercosur free trade area of trade in automobiles and sugar products, which weighs heavily in intraregional trade. The results in the case of the Andean Community are somehow better notwithstanding the fact that all the trade of Peru within the agreement was excluded from the calculations—although this was making

Figure 3-5. "Substantially All Trade" Test

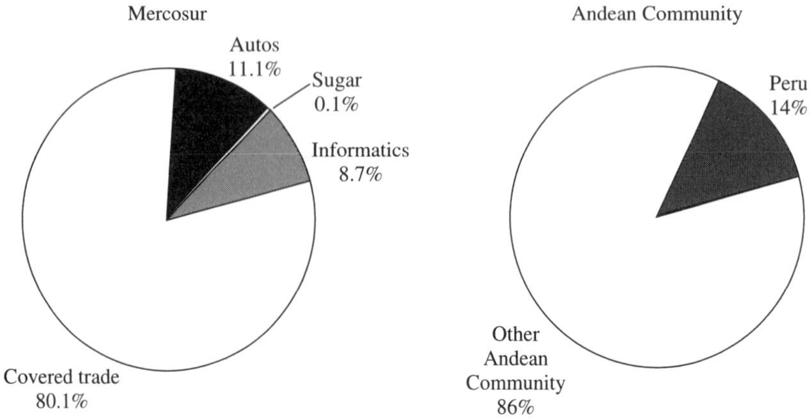

Mercosur

Autos
11.1%
Sugar
0.1%
Informatics
8.7%
Covered trade
80.1%

Andean Community

Peru
14%
Other
Andean
Community
86%

Source: DATAINTAL.

too strong an assumption, as a large part of this trade has been liberalized vis-à-vis the other Andean Community members.

Conclusions

The preceding analysis demonstrates that the Mercosur and the Andean Community are representative of a new approach to trade and economic integration throughout the Latin American region. Rooted in and expanding upon the market-oriented reforms of the 1980s—which included tariff reductions, elimination of most nontariff measures, and implementation of more stable exchange rate systems—the various Latin American regional arrangements are achieving a great deal of success in eliminating most restrictions to trade and investment among the participating countries. As a result, trade flows among the Latin American countries have reached unprecedented levels, are freer than ever before, and have grown faster than has trade with the rest of the world.

Both the Mercosur and the Andean Community are driven by the market reforms of the 1980s rather than by the import-substitution strategies that influenced past arrangements. This has had important consequences for the functioning of the agreements and the degree of trade liberalization that they have effected. When applied at the regional level, import-substitution policies obstructed rather than facilitated trade liberalization, as countries resisted opening their protected sensitive sectors. As much domestic production was considered sensitive and consequently was protected in the context of national import-substitution strategies, the end result was the exclusion of entire economic sectors from the agreements' trade liberalization schedules. This is no longer the case. Under the current policy framework, the exception of sectors or products in the Mercosur and the Andean Community has been minimal and in general of a temporary nature. Exceptions are normally subject to a pre-established phaseout schedule. This has been facilitated by the two agreements' implementation of their liberalization programs through formula approaches—automatic reduction of tariffs and elimination of nontariff barriers that apply to the entire tariff schedule—rather than by time-consuming and less effective product-by-product negotiations.

The trade expansion effects of the Mercosur and the Andean Community have been quite remarkable. A significant increase in trade flows has taken place among the countries participating in the two agreements. Intrasubregional trade in the Mercosur and the Andean Community has reached new, unprecedented peaks, as trade flows have responded positively to the trade liberalization measures implemented within the agreements. Equally important, the level of trade of the Mercosur and Andean countries with the outside world has also risen, and imports to these countries from third countries have consistently increased since the agreements were put into operation. As pointed out in the discussion of the adjusted admissibility test in the previous section, non-members have continued to enjoy their access to the markets of the Mercosur and the Andean Community; in fact, they have considerably increased their exports to the two groups.

Although both the Mercosur and the Andean Community face some difficulties in moving their integration efforts forward—difficulties of a different nature in each case—an encouraging fact is that the set of trade and trade-related issues dealt with by the two agreements has considerably widened. As the frontiers of trade policy have moved beyond the traditional focus on border protection measures (that is, tariffs and nontariff measures) to embrace a variety of new issues such as investment, competition policy, services, and intellectual property rights, so have the areas addressed by the new arrangements. This represents a major departure from the first Latin American agreements, which only incidentally touched upon those issues, concentrating rather on the reduction or elimination of tariffs. It is becoming increasingly clear that market access depends only partially on tariff commitments, as countries—and enterprises—could restrict or distort trade through a variety of devices and practices, including internal regulations and policies that have mostly been outside the scope of trade negotiations. That the new agreements negotiated by the countries of the Americas include provisions to deal with these issues bodes well for their ultimate success in trade and investment liberalization.

Finally, it seems evident from examining the evolution of both the Mercosur and the Andean Community that the mechanisms put in place to carry out their integration goals have been successful in effecting a great deal of internal trade liberalization while keeping the agreements open to the outside world. Although further analysis needs to be done to test the consistency of the agreements with the multilateral rules on regionalism, the preliminary calculations presented in this chapter suggest that, rather than deviating from those rules or harming third countries, the Mercosur and the Andean Community are structuring themselves so as to abide by the multilateral commitments of their member countries.

References

Anderson, K., and H. Norheim. 1993. "History, Geography and Regional Economic Integration." In *Regional Integration and the Global Trading System,* edited by K. Anderson and R. Blackhurst. New York: St. Martin's Press.

Bhagwati, J. 1993. "Regionalism and Multilateralism: An Overview." In *New Dimensions in Regional Integration,* edited by J. de Melo and A. Panagariya. Cambridge University Press.

Bhagwati, J., and A. Panagariya. 1996. *The Economics of Preferential Trade Agreements.* Washington, D.C.: AEI Press.

Frankel, J. A. 1997. *Regional Trading Blocks in the World Economic System.* Washington, D.C.: Institute for International Economics.

Inter-American Development Bank. 1996. *Mercosur,* vol. 1 (July–December). Department of Regional Integration and Programs.

———. 1997. *Mercosur,* vol. 3 (July–December). Department of Regional Integration and Programs.

———. 1998. *DATAINTAL Sistema de Estadisticas de Comercio de América.* Buenos Aires, Argentina: INTAL.

International Monetary Fund. 1997. *Direction of Trade Statistics and International Finance Statistics.* Washington, D.C.

Jackson, J. H. 1969. *World Trade and the Law of GATT.* Charlottesville, Va.: Michie.

Krugman, P. 1991. *Geography and Trade*. Cambridge, Mass.: MIT Press.

———. 1993. "Regionalism vs. Multilateralism: Analytical Notes." In *New Dimensions in Regional Integration,* edited by J. de Melo and A. Panagariya. Cambridge University Press.

Lawrence, R. Z. 1996. *Regionalism, Multilateralism and Deeper Integration*. Washington, D.C.: Brookings.

McMillan, J. 1993. "Does Regional Integration Foster Trade? Economic Theory and GATT's Article XXIV." In *Regional Integration and the Global Trading System,* edited by K. Anderson and R. Blackhurst. New York: St. Martin's Press.

Organization of American States. 1996. *Towards Free Trade in the Americas*. Trade Unit. Washington, D.C.

Summers, L. 1991. "Regionalism and the World Trading System." In *Policy Implications of Trade and Currency Zones*. Jackson Hole, Wyo.: Federal Reserve Bank of Kansas City.

Viner, J. 1950. *The Customs Union Issue*. New York: Carnegie Endowment for International Peace.

World Trade Organization. 1995. *Regionalism and the World Trading System*. Geneva.

Yeats, A. J. 1997. "Does Mercosur's Trade Performance Raise Concerns about the Effects of Regional Trading Arrangements?" Bank Policy Research Working Paper. Washington, D.C.: World Bank.

Part Two

PREFERENTIAL TRADE AND
REGIONAL AGREEMENTS

CHAPTER FOUR

Developing Countries and Trade Preferences

Bonapas Francis Onguglo

The granting of nonreciprocal trade preferences to developing countries by developed countries on a unilateral basis has been a traditional mechanism for conducting trade relationships between developed and developing countries. Such preferential trading schemes include the Caribbean Basin Initiative (CBI), the Canadian Trade, Investment, and Industrial Cooperation program (CARIBCAN), and the Andean Trade Preference Act (ATPA) in the Western Hemisphere; the South Pacific Regional Trade and Economic Cooperation Agreement (SPARTECA) in Oceania; the cross-regional Lomé Convention; and the Generalized System of Preferences (GSP) with global coverage. This chapter examines the continuing relevance of these schemes for developing countries and territories in the emerging international trading environment of the 1990s characterized by increasing trade liberalization and greater reciprocity in trade relations. The new situation calls for the adaptation of unilateral trade preferences with a view to their survival in safeguarding the legitimate trade and development interests of beneficiary developing countries.

Trade Preferences and Development

An important aspect of international cooperation for development has been the unilateral promulgation and implementation of nonreciprocal preferential trading schemes by developed countries in favor of the exports of developing countries and territories. The concept had its origin in the broader principle of special and differential treatment for developing countries. It was argued, primarily within the United Nations Conference on Trade and Development (UNCTAD), that trade on a most favored nation (MFN) basis ignored unequal economic realities among trading nations, especially between developing and developed ones, in terms of stages of development, factor endowments, size of markets, and efficiency and diversification of production structures. As part of global policy responses to imbalances in global economic relations, special and differential treatment needed to be provided to developing countries. This treatment was to include the elimination by developed countries of tariff barriers to exports of developing countries without requiring reciprocal treatment by the latter.[1]

The concept of nonreciprocal trade preferences was not widely supported. A number of developed countries argued against trade preferences and any trade arrangement not compatible with nondiscriminatory trade under MFN conditions. These divergences in views were captured in the final compromise that was adopted in 1968 by the international community at the second UNCTAD conference. The compromise stated that "the objectives of the generalized non-reciprocal, non-discriminatory system of preferences in favor of developing countries, should be: (a) to increase their export earnings; (b) to promote their industrialization; and (c) to accelerate their rates of economic growth."[2] This laid the foundation for the launching of the GSP. Individual GSP schemes are applied by industrialized countries and some countries of eastern Europe and made available to most developing countries. GSP schemes are determined unilaterally by the preference-giving countries, which also unilaterally modify the preferences, product coverage, and beneficiary countries. The preference-receiving countries play no part in the determination or modification of GSP schemes.

Other unilaterally determined nonreciprocal preferential trade schemes include the Caribbean Basin Economic Recovery Act (CBERA), often referred to as the Caribbean Basin Initiative, which was promulgated by the United States

1. This was the thesis posited by Dr. Raul Prebisch, the first secretary general of UNCTAD, who was among the authors of the concept of special and differential treatment in general and nonreciprocal preferences in particular. See, for example, Prebisch (1964).

2. See UNCTAD (1985).

in favor of twenty-four (among twenty-eight eligible) Central American and Caribbean countries and territories washed by the Caribbean Sea; the ATPA, which was promulgated by the United States in favor of Bolivia, Colombia, Ecuador, and Peru; and the CARIBCAN, which was enacted in favor of eighteen Commonwealth Caribbean countries and territories.[3] These schemes, like the GSP, have as their primary objective the promotion of economic development in the beneficiary countries by means of improved trade performance. The ATPA, for example, aims to assist the Andean countries in developing sources of income and livelihood that are alternatives to drug production and trafficking. Responding to the same objective, the revised GSP scheme of the European Union (EU), in force since 1995, included special incentives for member countries of the Andean Community and the Central American Common Market.

Several nonreciprocal preferential schemes have been negotiated and agreed upon jointly by the preference-giving and preference-receiving countries. These have included the four successive Lomé Conventions between the fifteen EU countries and the seventy-one countries in the African, Caribbean, and Pacific (ACP) Group.[4] (Lomé I was promulgated on February 28, 1975, for a period of five years. It was subsequently renewed and followed by Lomé II

3. The 24 CBI beneficiaries are Antigua and Barbuda, Aruba, the Bahamas, Barbados, Belize, the British Virgin Islands, Costa Rica, Dominica, the Dominican Republic, El Salvador, Grenada, Guatemala, Guyana, Haiti, Honduras, Jamaica, Montserrat, the Netherlands Antilles, Nicaragua, Panama, St. Kitts-Nevis, St. Lucia, St. Vincent and the Grenadines, and Trinidad and Tobago. Anguilla, the Cayman Islands, Suriname, and the Turks and Caicos Islands are eligible for the CBI, but they have not formally requested designation. The CARIBCAN members are Anguilla, Antigua and Barbuda, the Bahamas, Bermuda, Barbados, Belize, the British Virgin Islands, the Cayman Islands, Dominica, Grenada, Guyana, Jamaica, Montserrat, St. Kitts-Nevis, St. Lucia, St. Vincent and the Grenadines, Trinidad and Tobago, and the Turks and Caicos Islands.

4. The ACP Group membership comprises forty-eight African countries, namely Angola, Benin, Botswana, Burkina Faso, Burundi, Cameroon, Cape Verde, the Central African Republic, Chad, Comoros, Congo, Côte d' Ivoire, the Democratic Republic of the Congo, Djibouti, Equatorial Guinea, Eritrea, Ethiopia, Gabon, the Gambia, Ghana, Guinea, Guinea-Bissau, Kenya, Lesotho, Liberia, Madagascar, Malawi, Mali, Mauritania, Mauritius, Mozambique, Namibia, Niger, Nigeria, Rwanda, São Tomé and Príncipe, Senegal, the Seychelles, Sierra Leone, Somalia, South Africa (with qualified membership excluding it from Lomé trade provisions), Sudan, Swaziland, Togo, Uganda, the United Republic of Tanzania, Zambia, and Zimbabwe; fifteen Caribbean countries, namely Antigua, the

(1980–85), Lomé III (1985–90), and Lomé IV (1990–2000). The Lomé Conventions and their agreed-upon preferences have become contractual obligations that cannot be unilaterally modified by one of the parties. Another nonreciprocal preferential scheme is the SPARTECA between Australia and New Zealand and thirteen island country members of the South Pacific Forum.[5] The contractual nature of these agreements does not, however, obviate the fact that as recipients of preferences the beneficiary developing countries more often than not occupy a weaker negotiating position during the determination of the instruments of cooperation.

The nonreciprocal schemes confer preferential market access in the form of duty-free entry (a zero tariff) or a duty substantially lower than the normal MFN rate to merchandise originating in the beneficiary countries. This reduction or elimination of the MFN tariffs renders the exports of beneficiaries more competitive in terms of price than other similar products entering under MFN duties. The origin requirement ensures that only the goods produced in a beneficiary country benefit from the preferences, and not ones that are simply shipped through these countries or have undergone minimal industrial processing in them. The rules of origin include requirements related to origin criteria, local content, consignment conditions, and documentary evidence. The origin criteria normally require that goods be wholly produced and manufactured in a beneficiary country or be sufficiently worked and processed as to be transformed into a new and different article in a beneficiary country. The local content requirement can go as high as 60 percent in the CARIBCAN, 50 percent in the SPARTECA, or a lower 35 percent under the CBI or ATPA. Many schemes allow for the local content benchmark to be met cumulatively by content from various beneficiary countries or the preference-giving country alone. The main consignment condition is that products originating in the beneficiary country must be directly imported from that country into the preference-giving country. The main documentary evidence is an originating

---

Bahamas, Barbados, Belize, Dominica, the Dominican Republic, Grenada, Guyana, Haiti, Jamaica, St. Kitts-Nevis, St. Vincent, St. Lucia, Suriname, and Trinidad and Tobago; and eight Pacific island countries, namely, Fiji, Kiribati, Papua New Guinea, Samoa, the Solomon Islands, Tonga, Tuvalu, and Vanuatu.

5. These are the Cook Islands, Fiji, the Federated States of Micronesia, Kiribati, the Marshall Islands, Nauru, Niue, Papua New Guinea, Samoa, the Solomon Islands, Tonga, Tuvalu, and Vanuatu.

certificate such as form A for the GSP or the EUR.1 form for the Lomé Conventions.

The products covered include most agricultural and industrial exports, with a few but often notable exceptions. The exceptions established by the United States in the ATPA and CBI include textiles and apparel, certain types of footwear, certain leather products (handbags and luggage), certain watches and watch parts, canned tuna, and petroleum and petroleum products. Under the CARIBCAN the products excluded by Canada include textiles, clothing, footwear, luggage (other than leather luggage, which benefits from duty-free entry), handbags, leather garments, certain vegetable fiber products (other than vegetable fiber baskets), lubricating oils, and methanol. Product coverage under the Lomé Conventions is quite favorable, with all industrial and almost all agricultural products originating in the ACP states entering duty free into the EU. The exceptions include some (not all) agricultural products covered by the EU's Common Agricultural Policy, which carry a reduced duty or reduced variable levy.

The beneficiaries of nonreciprocal preferential schemes have to meet certain conditions, often noneconomic, to be designated as such and to maintain their beneficiary status. For example, the conditions demanded by the United States for designation as CBI and ATPA countries provide that a country will not be designated as a beneficiary if it is a communist country; has allowed the expropriation or nationalization of the property of a citizen of the United States or a corporation owned by the United States; provides preferential treatment to the products of another developed country that could negatively affect trade with the United States; lacks adequate and effective protection of intellectual property rights and government broadcast of copyrighted material; and does not provide internationally recognized workers' rights. The latter is also a standard of eligibility for the GSP, which includes the right to associate, the right to organize and bargain collectively, a prohibition against any form of coerced or compulsory labor, a minimum wage for the employment of children, and acceptable conditions of work in relation to minimum wages, hours of work, and work safety and health.

In May 1998 the EU introduced a special incentive scheme providing additional preferential GSP margins (between 10 and 35 percent) for beneficiaries that voluntarily comply with the International Labor Office conventions on the right to organize and to bargain collectively and on the minimum age for admission to employment, as well as the environmental standards of the International Tropical Timber Organization with respect to the importation of wood, wood manufactured items, and furniture made of tropical wood. Many developing countries have roundly criticized these conditions as being inconsistent with the development objective pursued by the preferential schemes.

Also under the GSP (unlike the other unilateral preferential schemes), a country's eligibility is affected by the application of product or full country "graduation" to preference-receiving countries that are no longer assessed as needing preferential treatment to be competitive. Graduation or the withdrawal of GSP preferences rests on the argument by preference-giving countries that preferences comprise special treatment that should be reserved only for the most needy developing countries and that developing countries that have attained a sufficient degree of competitiveness in the production of a particular product or sector should have their GSP benefits terminated for that product or sector. Full country graduation is applied to developing countries that have become economically more advanced. For example, as of March 1, 1998, Switzerland has withdrawn the GSP benefits previously offered to the Bahamas, Bermuda, Brunei Darussalam, the Cayman Islands, Cyprus, the Falkland Islands, Hong Kong, Kuwait, Mexico, Qatar, the Republic of Korea, Singapore, and the United Arab Emirates. In the case of the United States, the countries that were graduated from its GSP scheme included Hong Kong, the Republic of Korea, Singapore, and the Taiwan Province of China in 1989 and Mexico in January 1994.

The Success of Preferential Schemes

Nonreciprocal preferential schemes have proved to be resilient and durable instruments of development cooperation. Most of them have had over a decade or two of operational experience. The GSP, probably the oldest scheme, has been in operation for over twenty-seven years, the Lomé Conventions for twenty-five years, the SPARTECA for seventeen years, the CBI for fourteen years, the CARIBCAN for twelve years, and the ATPA for fewer than seven years. Most GSP schemes, the Lomé Conventions, and the CBI have been revised and renewed at least twice, and at each revision the preferential margins, product coverage, and related features have been improved by the preference-giving countries. For example, in the latest revision of the GSP scheme of the United States about 1,783 agricultural and industrial products were added to the scheme from August 1997 for beneficiaries that are least-developed countries (LDCs).[6] The stability and predictability of trade preferences, an important incentive for investors, was strengthened under the Lomé Conventions when the fourth convention was concluded in December 1989 for a period of ten years (instead of the usual five years). The ATPA and CARIBCAN have also been legislated for ten years, whereas the CBI was made a permanent scheme in August 1990.

In addition, at the request of the preference-giving countries most of the preferential trade schemes have been endorsed by the General Agreement on Tariffs and Trade (GATT) or the World Trade Organization (WTO) as legal exceptions to the basic GATT MFN principle of nondiscrimination.[7] The GSP and SPARTECA are permanent exceptions under the Enabling Clause of 1979. The others have been granted multiyear waivers, albeit subject to annual reviews, under GATT Article XXV and, after the formation of the WTO, in accordance with the Understanding in Respect of Waivers and Article IX of the WTO Agreement. The waiver duration for the Fourth Lomé Convention is to extend from December 9, 1994, to February 29, 2000 (the date of expiration of the convention); for the CBI from November 15, 1995, to December 31, 2005; for the ATPA from March 19, 1992, to December 4, 2001 (the date of its expiration); and for the CARIBCAN from November 26, 1986, to June 15, 1998, which was subsequently extended in October 1996 to December 31, 2006.

Furthermore, nonreciprocal preferences have created more favorable market access conditions and progressively stimulated trade growth in some preference-receiving countries (although the extent and dispersion of these benefits has been limited, as discussed in the following section). In 1996 the aggregated dutiable imports of the United States from its GSP beneficiaries

6. UNCTAD (1997). The following forty-eight countries are defined by the United Nations as among the most poorest of the developing countries: Afghanistan, Angola, Bangladesh, Benin, Bhutan, Burkina Faso, Burundi, Cambodia, Cape Verde, the Central African Republic, Chad, Comoros, the Democratic Republic of the Congo, Djibouti, Equatorial Guinea, Eritrea, Ethiopia, the Gambia, Guinea, Guinea-Bissau, Haiti, Kiribati, Lao People's Democratic Republic, Lesotho, Liberia, Madagascar, Malawi, Maldives, Mali, Mauritania, Mozambique, Myanmar, Nepal, Niger, Rwanda, Samoa, São Tomé and Príncipe, Sierra Leone, the Solomon Islands, Somalia, Sudan, Togo, Tuvalu, Uganda, the United Republic of Tanzania, Vanuatu, Yemen, and Zambia. With the exception of Maldives and Vanuatu, all LDCs have a gross domestic product (GDP) per capita that is below U.S.$1,000.

7. General Agreement on Tariffs and Trade (GATT), Article I. See WTO (1995).

amounted to U.S.$69.5 billion in terms of current value.[8] About 24 percent of that amount (U.S.$16.8 billion) received GSP preferences. The total dutiable imports of the EU from its GSP beneficiaries in 1996 amounted to U.S.$169.6 billion. About 37 percent of that amount (U.S.$62.5 billion) received GSP preferences. Trade under GSP preferences is therefore substantial; however, it does not yet appear to have achieved its full potential. The ratio between imports that have actually received GSP treatment under a scheme and imports covered by the scheme—that is, the GSP scheme utilization rates—have been well below 100 percent.[9] For example, the use rates for non-LDCs that are beneficiaries of the U.S. and EU schemes averaged about 60 percent in 1996.

Reports on the operations of the CBI by the Office of the U.S. Trade Representative in 1996 and of the ATPA in 1997 indicate that the level of trade under nonreciprocal preferences is rising. The main products from the Caribbean region benefiting from CBI preferences are agricultural products and commodities as well as light manufactured goods such as leather footwear uppers, finished footwear (made entirely from components made in the United States), medical instruments, jewelry made of precious metals, bars and rods of iron or nonalloy steel, higher-priced cigars, raw sugar, pineapples, beef, ethyl alcohol, guavas, and mangoes. In 1996 a record 18.9 percent of total U.S. imports from CBI countries, valued at about U.S.$2.8 billion, was generated under the CBI. This level represented a major increase over the previous year's performance (17.7 percent), and it is significantly higher than the level of 6.7 percent in 1984, when the CBI took effect. The share of global U.S. imports under the CBI preferences is about 0.1 percent. So the full potential of the CBI is yet to be fully exploited, and the displacement of competitive domestic products in the United States is for the most part negligible. Although apparel (trousers and shorts, shirts and blouses, underwear, and coats and jackets) does not benefit from CBI preferences, it has been one of the fastest-growing sectors of exports from the Caribbean to the United States. In 1995 it represented about 43 percent of the region's total exports to the United States, compared to 6 percent in 1984.

Under the ATPA, in 1996 the total U.S. imports from the four ATPA beneficiaries were valued at U.S.$7.87 billion. About 15.8 percent of that total, representing in value about U.S.$1.25 billion, entered the United States under

8. UNCTAD (1998).
9. UNCTAD (1998).

ATPA provisions; this share was 13.7 percent in 1995 and 11.3 percent in 1994. Therefore, the use of the ATPA preferences by the beneficiaries is on the rise. The remaining imports to the United States from ATPA beneficiaries in 1996 entered under other duty-free instruments, in particular under MFN duties (36.4 percent of the total) and GSP preferences (1.7 percent) or under applied duties (42.9 percent). The main products benefiting from ATPA preferences have been flower products (chrysanthemums, carnations, anthuriums, orchids, and freshly cut roses). Other items have included certain jewelry articles, refined unwrought lead, cathodes of refined copper, tuna and skipjack not in airtight containers, unwrought metal products, and raw sugar.

Fiji, Jamaica, Kenya, Mauritius, and Zimbabwe have taken advantage of the preferences under the Lomé Conventions to diversify from traditional raw materials and their derivatives (coffee, cocoa, banana, and sugar) into nontraditional exports such as clothing, processed fish, and horticultural and floricultural products.[10] Trade under the convention's commodity protocols is important for the generation of export revenue, creation of employment, and stimulation of agro-based industrial activities. This is the case for sugar in Mauritius and Fiji; bananas in the Windward Islands of the Caribbean, such as Dominica, St. Lucia, and St. Vincent and the Grenadines; beef and veal in southern African countries like Botswana; and rum in Trinidad and Tobago. Mauritius has developed from a single-crop economy into a diversified one owing to major structural reforms, including the development of export-oriented operations to produce items for the EU market using Lomé Convention preferences for textiles and clothing. The commodity stabilization funds of the Lomé Conventions have also helped states in the ACP Group to stabilize their export earnings (with respect to international price fluctuations) for major agricultural raw material exports and mineral products.

The experience of the few preference-receiving countries that have taken advantage of preferences indicates that there is a positive correlation between nonreciprocal preferences, especially in those product sectors and for those articles for which import protection in preference-giving countries is already high, and the application of a host of supportive policies affecting the competitiveness of production. These include policies regarding export processing zones, trade promotion measures, use of skilled manpower, development of a skilled entrepreneurial class, a predictable and transparent policy and political

10. Commission of the European Communities (1996).

environment, and an appropriate real exchange rate. The latter can be particularly important, as demonstrated by the experience of Fiji. The Fiji garment industry grew substantially under the SPARTECA in the early 1990s following the liberalization of the Australian garment market and a 50 percent effective devaluation of the Fijian currency, among other measures.[11] The crux of the matter has to be real market liberalization on the part of preference-giving countries, as well as deliberate macro- and microeconomic policy actions by preference-receiving countries to exploit the liberalized markets.

Deficiencies of Preferential Schemes

Generally the preferential access to major markets accorded by nonreciprocal preferential schemes has been a sufficient stimulus for export growth and diversification in only a few of the preference-receiving beneficiaries, not in the majority. The Dominican Republic is the major beneficiary of the CBI, with the main exports including sugar, leather footwear uppers, higher-priced cigars, and medical, surgical, and dental instruments; Jamaica and Guyana of the CARIBCAN, with the main exports including rock lobster, other sea crawfish, and lighting fixtures; Colombia of the ATPA, with flower products comprising the main exports; Fiji of the SPARTECA, with the main exports including garments; and some ACP Group states of the Lomé Conventions. The benefits of privileged market access have been concentrated in a few countries and a few products.[12]

Also, the use of preferences by the beneficiaries has been declining in some cases and minimal on the whole in others. It has been declining in the case of the Lomé Conventions, for example. For the eighteen years from 1976 to 1994, which are most of the years of operation of the Lomé Conventions, the share of the EU's total imports represented by non-oil imports from the ACP Group declined substantially, from 6.7 to 2.8 percent.[13] At the same time the share of non-preference-receiving, non-ACP imports expanded. The latter case applies, for example, to the CARIBCAN and the GSP. Trade in goods receiving CARIBCAN preferences amounted to Canadian$25 million in 1996, compared to C$482 million under zero MFN duties and C$14 million under the General Preferential Tariff or the British Preferential Tariff in the same year. However,

11. Grynberg and Powell (1995).
12. WTO (1997) and Grynberg and Powell (1995).
13. Commission of the European Communities (1996).

as noted previously, the level of trade under the CBI preferences is rising, which indicates a growing use of the instruments (even if by only a few countries and for a few products). The rate of use of GSP preferences by most developing countries is below 100 percent, as already mentioned.

A combination of factors accounts for the mixed results of nonreciprocal trade preferences. The nonreciprocal schemes involve too many restrictive, complex, and varying rules of origin, quotas, and designation criteria and need to be simplified and harmonized where appropriate. Other deficiencies include the exclusion of sensitive products that are of export interest to developing countries, the mismatch between exports of beneficiaries and coverage of preferences, and noneconomic conditionalities. A limited awareness in the business communities of preference-receiving countries of the preferences and their operations is another deficiency. This information lacuna, combined with the complex procedural requirements of preferences, poses a major barrier to the exploitation of preferences by the economic operators in preference-receiving countries.

Supply-side constraints have been another source of difficulty, with most developing countries' export profiles dominated by a few commodities and minerals. These products, moreover, are often subject to high price volatility and declining terms of trade. An additional barrier arises from poor infrastructure facilities, adverse climatic conditions, geographical remoteness or being landlocked, and in some cases political instability, with frequent policy changes introducing distortions into the economy. The effective exploitation of trade preferences, therefore, requires the preference-receiving countries to carry out policy reform to stimulate competitiveness and productivity in export-oriented sectors.

The system of nonreciprocal preferences also has often been criticized as a form of neocolonialism that perpetuates the production of and trade in products not compatible with their long-term comparative advantage in preference-receiving countries. It has been argued that the commodity protocols of the Lomé Conventions, such as those related to bananas in the Windward Islands, have perpetuated the one-product economy of these islands and discouraged them from undertaking more fundamental reforms for product and market diversification. The preferences have also been criticized as contributing to the creation of a dual economy in preference-receiving countries, with one part involving production of products under export processing zones that are directly exported to preference-giving countries (with few linkages to the local economy), and another involving production of products for MFN trade. Another general argument is that, far from helping developing countries, the non-reciprocal preferences (together with other forms of assistance) have led to a form of dependency that has muted the participation of these countries in the GATT or the WTO for better MFN treatment related to their main exports. The preferences for subgroups of developing countries (under the Lomé Conventions, CBI, ATPA, and so on) have created lobbies for a status quo that have led the member nations to oppose general trade liberalization efforts and hindered the developing countries from acting as an effective block in obtaining improved MFN liberalization.

Trade Preferences in the New Trading Environment

The pace of international competition has intensified with widespread economic liberalization, including the removal of political and legal barriers to the free movement of goods and services, as well as investment and capital flows between countries on unilateral, regional, and multilateral levels. The conclusion of the most ambitious GATT negotiations, the Uruguay Round, established the WTO, consolidated and accelerated the liberalization of global trade in goods and services, and set disciplines affecting investment, competition, and intellectual property rights. An important feature of tariff commitments made by developed preference-giving countries is a substantial increase in bound duty-free treatment that will cover almost 40 percent of the imports of the United States, 38 percent of the imports of the EU, and 71 percent of the imports of Japan. Further liberalization is expected in sectors agreed upon recently under the WTO, including information technology products and financial services. Also, new rounds of negotiation to further open up global trade in agriculture and services are to commence in the year 2000 under the built-in agenda of the WTO. Opening the market in trade in goods would further reduce the import protection in industrialized countries in the medium term and add to the erosion of preferential margins under nonreciprocal preferences.

Improvements in MFN market access conditions in the preference-giving countries will certainly add to the erosion of preferential margins and thus gradually undermine the competitive edge enjoyed by preference-receiving countries in these markets vis-à-vis other suppliers. With respect to the GSP, for example, the loss of preferential margins in terms of pre– and post–Uruguay Round situations in three major markets for all GSP-receiving imports from beneficiaries (other than LDCs) is estimated to be about 2.9 percentage points

(1.4 for LDCs) in the EU, 2.6 percentage points (4.1 for LDCs) in Japan, and 2.8 percentage points (2.7 for LDCs) in the United States.[14]

The deepening multilateral liberalization process has not totally eliminated one of the necessary conditions for meaningful preferences, namely high tariff barriers. Even after all Uruguay Round concessions have been fully implemented by the industrialized countries, significant tariff barriers in the form of high tariff peaks (exceeding 12 percent) continue to affect an important percentage of agricultural and industrial products of export interest to developing countries that have established or nascent manufacturing industries.[15] Over 10 percent of the tariff universe of Canada, the EU, Japan, and the United States exceeds 12 percent ad valorem in such sectors as agricultural staples; fruit, vegetables, and fish; processed (especially canned) food; textiles and clothing; footwear, leather, and leather goods; automobiles; other transport equipment; and electronics. Also, the tarrification of quotas and other nontariff measures under the WTO Agreement on Agriculture resulted in the establishment of high tariffs rather than genuinely reducing protection. Quantitative barriers maintained under the Multi-Fiber Arrangement continue to limit textiles and clothing exports to major developed countries, as their removal is to be undertaken gradually in stages in accordance with the WTO Textiles and Clothing Agreement. In industrial countries the high level of import protection accorded sensitive agricultural and industrial products, which also happen to be among the main exports of developing countries and territories and have often been excluded from nonreciprocal preferences, provides a case for maintaining the preferences and for extending the coverage to include these products.

Furthermore, tariff escalation decreased after the Uruguay Round. However, rapidly rising tariffs, from low duties for raw materials to higher duties for intermediate products and sometimes peak tariffs for finished industrial products, continue in such sectors as metals, textiles and clothing, leather and rubber products, and to some extent wood products and furniture.[16] Many of these are products of export interest to many developing countries and are important parts of the development of processed and manufactured products. Hence, the provision of preferences for these products and their effective use by developing countries could overcome the tariff escalation barrier and support the development of export capacities in these products.

14. UNCTAD (1998).
15. UNCTAD/WTO (1998).
16. UNCTAD/WTO (1998).

In industrialized preference-giving countries the continued existence of tariff peaks and tariff escalation for products exported by developing countries and territories enhances rather than diminishes the importance of providing these products with special market access treatment. The preferential market access provisions should be extended to previously excluded products such as apparel, leather products, and processed food items. The relevance of preferences is reinforced by the continued dependence of many developing countries and territories on markets in the industrialized countries for a large proportion of their exports. In recognition of this fact, some preference-giving countries such as Canada, Norway, Switzerland, and the United States have amended their GSP schemes, for example, to increase product coverage and mitigate preference erosion arising from their tariff liberalization commitments under the Uruguay Round.[17] New improvements of the preferential schemes (discussed below) have also been effected in favor of LDCs.

The preponderant majority of preference-giving industrialized countries have exhibited a certain enthusiasm for their reciprocal and nonreciprocal trade agreements with developing countries and others to be WTO-compatible. This new enthusiasm followed the Uruguay Round and has been manifested in two trends. First, trade agreements encompassing nonreciprocal preferences have been confined to LDCs. This has always been a concern of preference-giving countries in respect to the GSP, as is evident from the exemption of LDCs from the policy of product, sector, or country graduation (referred to previously). However, it has received new stimulus. Second, trade agreements with other developing countries have been subjected to greater reciprocity, mostly in the form of regional trade agreements. Thus nonreciprocal preferences are being increasingly confined to LDCs, whereas other developing countries and territories will be increasingly subjected to full reciprocity in trade relations.

The focusing of nonreciprocal preferences on LDCs was sanctioned by the GATT in the Enabling Clause of 1979. The WTO increased this focus with the decision of the First WTO Ministerial Conference in 1996 and the results of the WTO-sponsored High-Level Meeting on LDCs' Trade Development in 1997. Consequent recent revisions in several GSP schemes have substantially improved the benefits for LDCs. These include, in Canada, the EU, Japan, and the United States, duty-free access for those products that are covered by their respective schemes. In addition, the range of GSP-eligible products from LDCs has been extended—for example, by 1,783 products—by the United States.

17. UNCTAD (1997).

The EU has extended the preferential treatment enjoyed by the ACP states within the Lomé Conventions to all other LDCs, effective January 1, 1998. These preferences include zero duties on a large number of industrial products (previously excluded from the EU's GSP schemes) and tariff reductions on agricultural products. Mention could be made of the African Growth and Opportunity Act, currently under consideration by the U.S. Senate, which envisages an improvement in the GSP scheme for sub-Saharan African countries, the large majority of which are LDCs. The improvement includes allowances for regional and donor-country content (up to an amount not in excess of 15 percent of the value of the final product imported into the United States), which are not available under the GSP scheme.

In October 1997 several developing countries announced offers of nonreciprocal trade preferences to LDCs, including in the context of the Global System of Trade Preferences among Developing Countries (GSTP). Egypt, Malaysia, the Republic of Korea, Singapore, and Thailand made announcements regarding the introduction of a type of GSP for LDCs. Morocco proposed the same, but only for African LDCs, whereas India and South Africa intend to provide preferences to LDCs that are members of their respective integration groupings, namely the Southern African Development Community (SADC) and the South Asian Association for Regional Cooperation (SAARC). The effective promulgation of these nonreciprocal preferences for LDCs and their implementation would herald an innovation in the system of trade preferences, namely South-South preferences. The process has started, as Turkey announced that as of January 1, 1998, selective preferences (duty-free entry for 556 products) would be implemented in favor of LDCs. So even at the level of South-South cooperation, nonreciprocal preferences are being contemplated in favor of LDCs.

In parallel, preference-giving countries increasingly seek to have developing countries other than LDCs accept full reciprocity in their mutual trade relations in the context of regional trade agreements. Enthusiasm for regional trade agreements has grown strongly among industrialized countries in various directions, including their trade relations with developing countries. The resultant trade agreements would be cast in conformity with WTO provisions on the formation of free trade areas and customs unions so as to provide additional impetus to the process of commercial liberalization. In particular, such agreements would provide exporters from preference-giving countries enhanced market access to the expanded trading areas with developing countries. They would also ensure the survival of the special trading relations between the preference-giving and preference-receiving countries, though not in terms of nonreciprocity.

These concerns regarding reciprocity override the possible drawback for the preference-giving countries that would arise from the loss of the unilateral aspect of decisionmaking on preferential schemes. Accordingly, the pursuit of regional trade agreements by developed (preference-giving) countries with developing countries and others (countries in transition), a novelty in international trade relations, has intensified. These new regional trade agreements have been widened, often to cover an entire continent or hemisphere. This has given rise to a proliferation of regional trade agreements and concerns over their impact on world trade. By the end of 1997 the WTO had been notified of forty-five such agreements, which were under various stages of examination by the WTO Committee on Regional Trade Agreements.

One such North-South regional trade agreement is the North American Free Trade Agreement (NAFTA). In NAFTA Mexico, which was previously a GSP beneficiary of Canada and United States, accepted roughly the same reciprocal free trade obligations as the two developed countries. In addition, the NAFTA members, together with other developing countries in the Americas, have proposed the establishment of a Free Trade Area of the Americas (FTAA), which will involve reciprocal free trade between the developed North American countries and developing countries in the hemisphere from the year 2005 (as was agreed to by the second summit of the participating countries in April 1998), which may include certain support measures for smaller economies. Furthermore, the United States' African Growth and Opportunity Act proposes to radically revise U.S. trade relations with sub-Saharan African countries, and one of the instruments is the formation of free trade agreements with agreeable African countries.

Another category of agreements relates to the Europe Agreements between the EU and the Baltic, central European, and eastern European countries. Most of these agreements aim to establish free trade and to eventually integrate the latter countries into the EU as full-fledged members. The EU is also engaged in negotiations on the formation of free trade agreements with South Africa and with Middle Eastern and North African countries under the Euro-Mediterranean Association framework of cooperation. In the Pacific Rim countries the Asia Pacific Economic Cooperation (APEC) proposes to establish WTO-compatible free trade and investment regimes by the year 2020 among the participating developed and developing economies.[18]

18. APEC liberalization is implemented essentially on a voluntary basis by member economies; however, peer pressure is brought to bear to ensure compliance.

Most of the regional trade agreements between developed and developing countries attempt deeper integration, including deeper liberalization. These agreements also have extended the scope of cooperation beyond the traditional liberalization of trade in goods to include elements such as trade in services, factor (labor and capital) movements, harmonization of regulatory regimes as well as environment and labor standards, and in fact many elements of domestic policy perceived as affecting international competitiveness. Also significantly, the new agreements endeavor to embrace disciplines intended to ensure compatibility with and built on the more stringent WTO disciplines, creating a sort of WTO-plus regionalism. The NAFTA, proposed FTAA, and APEC provide for the preservation of all the GATT or WTO rights and obligations of members.

The participation of developing countries in regional trade agreements with developed countries is a result of both deliberate policy choice and the lack of viable alternatives. In the former case, many developing countries hold the view that the regional trade agreements could probably offer more favorable and even completely free access to their major markets. The alternative of being outside the liberalization trend under regional trade agreements, especially in the case of sensitive articles with higher tariffs, increases the competition they would face in the major markets. NAFTA parity has been requested by Caribbean countries, and the fact that this issue remains to be resolved is illustrative of the point being made. The Caribbean countries that are beneficiaries of the U.S. (and Canadian) preferences (under the GSP, CBI, and CARIBCAN) are requesting a deepening of the nonreciprocal concessions. This is seen as necessary to ensure that they could remain competitive vis-à-vis Mexican producers and maintain the market share in the United States and Canada they had prior to the formation of the NAFTA. This situation could arise for other preference-receiving countries that for one reason or another remain outside of regional trade agreements formed by preference-giving countries. The parity requests are being considered seriously by the United States, as they would imply providing to the Caribbean countries market access equivalent to that accorded to Mexico, but without requiring the Caribbean countries to implement Mexican obligations.

In the latter case, the regional trade agreements in the long term would render irrelevant the preferences under nonreciprocal trade arrangements. The FTAA, which would enter into force in the year 2005, could effectively supersede all nonreciprocal preferences such as those of the CBI, CARIBCAN (which expires in December 2006), ATPA (which expires in December 2001), and GSP. The CBI and GSP are permanent schemes; however, as with the other two schemes their preferences would become worthless in a free trade agreement. A similar process would take place in other regions where North-South regional trade agreements are being formulated.

Another element strengthening the trend toward reciprocity is the rule of a number of preferential schemes such as the CBI, ATPA, and Lomé Conventions regarding reverse preference conditionality. This rule stipulates that a beneficiary country will be removed from the list of preference-receiving countries if it grants preferential treatment to another developed country that could have an adverse effect on the trade of the preference-giving country. So far, in most preferential schemes the rule has not had to be invoked. However, the tremendous growth and expansion of regional trade agreements in recent years with the involvement of many preference-giving countries could create potential cases for violation of the reverse preference provision. For example, the Caribbean countries in the ACP Group entering into a free trade agreement with the EU could be required to offer equivalent compensatory market access conditions to the United States to maintain the CBI. The same countries, by virtue of their eventual participation in the FTAA, might have to provide similar treatment to the EU in order to maintain the preferences of the first Lomé Convention (or its successors). The Caribbean countries would be confronted with the dilemma of offering similar market access conditions to both the United States and the EU or to face possible retaliatory actions, including their exclusion from one of the schemes.

A significant illustration of the change toward greater reciprocity in North-South trade relations could be garnered from the intensive and extensive negotiations between the EU and the ACP Group for a successor agreement to the fourth Lomé Convention in view of its expiration on February 29, 2000. This could be a precedent-setting case, especially in view of the difficulties faced by the participants in justifying the Lomé Convention preferences and the provisions in the GATT or the WTO. The official negotiations on a new EU-ACP dispensation in the twenty-first century started in September 1998 and will continue until February 2000, after which date a new agreement must be instituted. In January 1988 the European Commission proposed a negotiating mandate for a new cooperative partnership based on a green paper released in November 1996. The European Council subsequently adopted the negotiating mandate as the official EU mandate.

The EU's basic proposal with respect to economic and trade cooperation is a continuation, under WTO waiver, of the Lomé Convention preferences for a period of five years from the year 2000. Subsequently, the nonreciprocal preferences would be maintained only for LDCs, and the EU would conclude regional economic partnership agreements with non-LDCs and also with agreeable LDCs. The regional economic partnership agreements would, among other things, include reciprocal free trade agreements in the sense of Article XXIV of the 1994 GATT and the Uruguay Round understanding on that article. An option for non-LDCs that for whatever reason do not participate in the regional economic partnership agreements is graduation to the EU's GSP scheme, which would be strengthened with enhanced preferences. The regional economic partnership agreements would be negotiated over the transitional period from the year 2000 to 2005 (while continuing the Lomé Convention preferences) and implemented from the year 2005 over a period of ten years or more to allow for gradual and progressive liberalization by the ACP Group states, taking into account their special needs and adjustment difficulties.

The ACP Group as a whole is opposed to a radical change in the system of nonreciprocal preferences within a short period. It has argued for maintaining the Lomé Convention preferences for a period of ten years, during which the fundamental supply-side and competitiveness constraints in these countries would be addressed. However, the ACP Group recognizes the need for a change in the system of trade preferences and has proposed that alternative trade arrangements be elaborated and effected after the ten-year transitional period. Both the EU and the ACP Group states have accepted that a successor agreement to the fourth Lomé Convention in terms of trade cooperation must be WTO-compatible.

The alternative trade arrangements could include an option for the ACP countries to negotiate with the EU jointly as a subregional group rather than individually. Individual bilateral agreements result in "hub and spoke" relationships that work primarily to the benefit of the more developed partner, in this case the EU. The option requires in the first place a consolidation within the ACP Group of the subregional or regional free trade areas and customs union arrangements. However, this is a formidable task. Progress in most ACP regions toward the formation of fully integrated groupings has been slow or moribund, after a decline in the 1980s. Some groupings that have achieved important advances have been seen in Southeast Asia, such as the Association of Southeast Asian Nations (ASEAN), and in the Americas, such as the Mercosur (Southern Common Market). Some groupings that have progressed further in the liberalization of the ACP Group regional market include the

Caribbean Community (CARICOM) and the Common Market for Eastern and Southern Africa (COMESA).

These advances, however, remain to be fully consummated, and new problems have emerged that could derail and undermine the regional trade liberalization processes. In this light, industrialized countries could provide greater financial and technical support to the integration groupings to assist them and their member states in implementing their liberalization programs in an expeditious and transparent manner and notifying the WTO. Such assistance is contemplated in the EU's proposal of a successor to the Lomé Conventions. In the meantime, nonreciprocal preferences could be improved to achieve the same purpose—that is, promote South-South regional integration. The EU, for example, has allowed for regional cumulation in its GSP rules of origin for products from the ASEAN and SAARC.

The issue of WTO compatibility remains prominent in the EU-ACP negotiations. It arises in the context of the continuation of the current Lomé Convention preferences for a period of five or ten years under WTO waiver. As indicated previously, the Lomé Conventions and most nonreciprocal preferences have received a multiyear waiver under GATT Article XXV (except for the GSP, which enjoys a permanent exception under the Enabling Clause). This waiver avenue remains an option, albeit a difficult one in view of the constraints posed by the rules of the WTO (in contrast to the former GATT). The recourse to the use of waiver for nonreciprocal preferences is limited by the Understanding in Respect of Waivers of Obligation under the 1994 GATT and the relevant provisions of Article IX of the WTO Agreement. These provisions require that a WTO member or a group of members requesting a waiver mobilize support from the majority—that is, three-fourths of the WTO membership—for the request to be granted. Once a waiver is granted, it is reviewed annually to ascertain if the conditions validating the waiver persist. The annual review acts as a built-in disincentive as it introduces an element of uncertainty on the longevity of the waiver.

The WTO compatibility issue also arises in the context of the proposed free trade agreements between the EU and the ACP Group states. These agreements will have to conform closely to Article XXIV of the 1994 GATT and the relevant understanding, which were accepted by the EU. This means that fairly strict conditions will have to be met by the parties (the EU and the ACP Group states) in terms of "substantially all trade" coverage, the erection of no new barriers against third countries, and observance of a maximum period of ten years for the formation of fully fledged agreements (that can be extended only exceptionally).

It is not clear that these conditions can be fully satisfied by proposed EU-ACP regional free trade agreements or by any North-South reciprocal free trade agreement. For one thing, the conditions of fairly strict reciprocity presuppose that the participating economy or economies have already acquired a high level of international competitiveness and maturity in their production and administrative structures in order to be able to face the intraregional competition, forego some development policy instruments, and in general be able to absorb reciprocal arrangements and commitments. These conditions do not yet exist in many ACP Group states and, moreover, are difficult to develop in the short run. For another thing, the ten-year transitional period can be considered too short for adjustment and economic transformation by the ACP Group states to reciprocal trade with the EU. This may lead the participants to seek derogation from such conditions that could be confusing if many agreements are involved and may face resistance in the WTO.

Another problem is that the extensive WTO review process for the many agreements would represent a major administrative and financial burden for both the EU and the ACP Group states. Such review, in contrast to past GATT practice, is conducted by the WTO Committee on Regional Trade Agreements and includes initial WTO notification of an agreement and increasingly tougher examination of WTO compatibility, followed by biennial reporting on the operation of the agreement under GATT Article XXIV.

The Way Forward

The use of nonreciprocal trade preferences such as those of the GSP, CBI, CARIBCAN, ATPA, SPARTECA, and Lomé Conventions has declined in the liberalizing world economy of the 1990s. The erosion of the utility of nonreciprocal preferences is further accentuated by the emerging practice among preference-giving countries of increasingly seeking to confine nonreciprocal preferences to LDCs and full reciprocity to other developing countries, mainly in the context of regional trade agreements. So nonreciprocal preferential schemes that expire in a few years' time can either be renewed only for LDCs or be replaced by new trade agreements based on reciprocity for medium- and high-income developing countries, or can even be superseded by wider regional free trade agreements.

Nonetheless, until such as time as their commercial value is totally eliminated, nonreciprocal preferences remain valid options for promoting trade
expansion and industrial transformation in developing countries and territories.
Nonreciprocal preferences can play a major role in those export sectors of
current and potential interest to developing countries where they have been
applied on a limited scale or barred and where the level of import protection is
high, even after the implementation of concessions under the Uruguay Round.
These sectors include in particular certain agricultural products, processed
food, and textiles and clothing.

Also, the international community recognizes that nonreciprocal preferences
will have to be preserved and improved for LDCs. The same will be necessary
for developing countries that by deliberate choice or other reasons remain
outside of the regional trade agreements formed by major preference-giving
countries. Preferences (among other measures) will provide the nonparticipants
with the tools with which to overcome the tougher market access conditions
(higher tariff levels and nontariff barriers) they will be subjected to in penetrat-
ing regional markets and will counteract potential trade and investment diversion effects. Therefore, the continuation of nonreciprocal preferences appears
inevitable in the short term.

Another consideration is that many developing countries cannot yet participate effectively in reciprocal free trade areas. They have yet to achieve a
high level of international competitiveness and maturity in the production and
administrative structures necessary to enhance their capacity and readiness to
participate effectively in reciprocal trade agreements with industrialized countries. These conditions do not yet exist in many developing countries and
moreover are difficult to develop in the short run. In this light the notion of
reciprocity appears premature at present. The developing countries and
territories need first to facilitate, strengthen, and consolidate the process of
structural adjustment at the national level as well as within their respective
subregional or regional integration groupings as the basis for becoming competitive and developing the supply capacity necessary for entry into global
markets and reciprocal trade relations with developed countries.

In the interim period prior to full reciprocity, therefore, the continuation of
nonreciprocal preferences and further improvement of the schemes should be
implemented to ensure that the market access conditions for developing economies, the most vulnerable of them in particular, are not adversely affected.
Conditionalities attached to preferences need to be openly discussed to

ascertain if the criteria and objectives are legitimate and proportionate to the economic objectives that preference-giving countries are pursuing through the application of these development measures. Policies regarding country and product graduation under GSP schemes could be revised to cater to deeper multilateral trade liberalization, as is being done with regard to the erosion of preferences. Furthermore, the coexistence of various scattered trade preference systems begs the question of whether it would be possible to develop common basic guidelines regarding such things as preferences accorded, product coverage, and rules of origin. Equally important, the improvement of the schemes must be accompanied by effective use of the preferences by the beneficiary countries and territories.

The main challenge to nonreciprocal preferences will arise from the WTO in terms of the granting of waivers. This is likely to be a difficult but not impossible challenge. It will require, among other things, a joint and coordinated effort among the preference-giving and preference-receiving countries, along with active and intensive negotiations with other WTO members in Geneva. A major effort will be required to mobilize broad-based support from WTO members for the continuation of preferential schemes under waiver. A multiyear waiver is preferable, as most nonreciprocal preferences have multiyear durations, indicating a long-term obligation on the part of preference-giving countries. The important point is the need to establish a reasonable duration that will alleviate uncertainty and apprehension among beneficiaries and their businesses about the security of the preferential access and enable them to undertake more long-term investment decisions regarding the development of export-oriented activities.

Conclusion

The role of nonreciprocal preferences in the twenty-first century has been called into question and positioned at a difficult juncture by the juxtaposition of its mixed performance so far against deepening multilateral liberalization and growing reciprocity in North-South trade relations. A careful analysis indicates, however, that nonreciprocal preferences continue to constitute an important aspect of such trade and investment strategies for the integration of developing countries and territories into the global trading system. The existing trade preferences should be maintained, improved, and effectively used by developing countries and their enterprises to enhance the process of indus-trialization and development. Preferences should be combined with other policy measures to improve productivity, the quality of products, and horizontal and vertical diversification in exports. In this process it should be noted that just as nonreciprocal preferences originated as an aspect of the wider concept of special and differential treatment for developing countries, the maintenance and improve-ment of preferences in the new trading environment should be underpinned by this concept rather than being viewed as a unilateral concession.

In the long term developing countries and territories must prepare for the fact that the trade environment in which unilaterally determined nonreciprocal preferences have been a paramount factor in the competitiveness of their exporters is gradually being succeeded by one in which global competition will prevail. More than ever before, they will need to compete on the basis of economic factors rather than special treatment.

References

Commission of the European Communities. 1996. "Green Paper on Relations be-tween the European Union and the ACP Countries on the Eve of the 21st Century: Challenges and Options for a New Partnership." COM(96) 570 final. Brussels. November 20.

Grynberg, R., and M. Powell. 1995. "A Review of the SPARTECA Trade Agreement." Canberra, Australia: Research School of Pacific and Asian Studies.

Office of the U.S. Trade Representative. 1997. "Report to Congress on the Opera-tion of the Andean Trade Preference Act" (www.ustr.gov/reports/andean.pdf). December.

Prebisch, P. 1964. "Towards a New Trade Policy for Development." In *Proceedings of the United Nations Conference on Trade and Development,* vol. 2, March 23–June 16. Geneva: United Nations. UN publication sales no. 64.II.B.12.

United Nations Conference on Trade and Development. 1985. *The History of UNCTAD 1964–1984.* New York: United Nations. UN publication sales no. E.85.II.D.6.

———. 1997. *GSP Newsletter,* no. 1 (December). Geneva.

———. 1998. "Ways and Means of Enhancing the Utilization of Trade Preferences by Developing Countries, in Particular LDCs, as Well as Further Ways of Expanding Preferences" (TD/B/COM.1/20 and Add.1). Geneva. July 21.

United Nations Conference on Trade and Development/World Trade Organization. 1998. "Market Access Developments since the Uruguay Round: Implications, Oppor-tunities and Challenges, in Particular for Developing Countries and Least Developed

Countries among Them, in the Context of Globalization and Liberalization"
(E/1998/55). New York. May 22.

World Trade Organization. 1997. "Canada-CARIBCAN: Report of the Government of
Canada under Decision of 14 October 1996" (WT/L/185)/(WT/L/236). Geneva.
October 10.

CHAPTER FIVE

Small Countries and the Free Trade Area of the Americas

Barbara Kotschwar

As the issues on the international trade agenda become increasingly complex and far-reaching and as more countries of all sizes and levels of development participate in international trade negotiations, economic size is once again emerging as an issue of significance. The role and concerns of "smaller economies" are at present a topic of discussion in the multilateral and regional trade arena and is an issue of priority in the Free Trade Area of the Americas (FTAA) negotiations, in which a significant number of participant countries consider themselves small.

This is not a new subject. A half century ago a group of scholars came together to explore the "economic consequences of the size of nations."[1] With the underlying assumption that the size of a country affects its subsequent economic growth, their objective was to examine the "practical arguments for the establishment of common markets and free trade areas . . . based on the premises that there are economies of scale which are not exhausted within the limits of the size of nations as we know them today."[2] The questions posed by these analysts remain as relevant now as they were in the 1950s. Indeed the question of what impact size has on economic performance is becoming even more compelling as more countries enter into

1. This resulted in an edited volume, Robinson (1960, p. vii).
2. Robinson (1960, p. xiii).

economic integration arrangements and as smaller countries incorporate reciprocal trade agreements with larger countries into their economic developmentstrategies.

Leaving aside for the moment the question of what criteria define a small country, it is generally agreed that smaller economies gain from economic integration. According to classical theory, opening to international trade is especially favorable for countries that are smaller in size. Real-world conditions, however, tend to diverge from the assumptions underlying economic theory, and some of the very elements that make trade especially beneficial for small countries also make it especially difficult for them to achieve these benefits. This chapter examines a number of the characteristics that are inherent to or associated with smallness and analyzes their potential effect on small countries' ability to build—and maintain—reciprocal trade relationships. The aim of the chapter is neither to demonstrate causality nor to establish absolute relationships. It is rather to identify and describe these factors, then examine them in the context of the current FTAA initiative.

Trade Policy and Small Economies

Classical trade theory tells us that free trade is good—and especially so for smaller countries. Under a two country–two good model, if a small country and a large country agree to eliminate barriers to trade with one another, the smaller one will benefit more from the relationship than its larger partner due to gains of scale and efficiency. The smaller member's increased access to the larger country's market enables it to take advantage of previously unexploitable economies of scale. As the larger country's price structure will determine that of the entire free trade area, the large country's incentive structure will remain basically unchanged, but that of the smaller member will adjust. For that reason the free trade agreement will allow the small country to fully specialize while the larger country continues to produce its previous bundle of goods. The smaller country will receive additional efficiency gains, as it will now specialize in the production of the good in which it has a comparative advantage, with a resultant reallocation of production and consumption patterns. Small countries tend to be highly reliant on trade, and a small country will therefore benefit greatly from the less costly imports and the greater demand for its exports resulting from opening to trade with a larger partner. In addition to the static effects captured in this model, countries can also, over time, expect dynamic gains in the form of technology transfer, investment, and learning.[3]

Therefore, free trade is good and, all other things being equal, small countries will gain even more than larger ones from opening up to trade. In reality, however, not all things are equal, and it is this fact that complicates the analysis. A wide body of literature exists that questions, or at least relaxes, some classical assumptions and cautions that the real-world case facing countries may not be quite so tidy as the theoretical scenario. The very same flexibility that allows a smaller country to adjust its prices and concentrate its resources on producing on the basis of its comparative advantage also makes its economy extremely dependent upon external factors.

The essence of smallness and the associated factors that influence small countries' economic maneuverability derive from both relative and absolute aspects of size. As Kuznets points out in a seminal work on the effect of economic size on growth, "The dividing line is relative to the distribution of nations by size at a given historical epoch, so it is relative to differences in the economic and social potentials that we wish to emphasize."[4] Therefore, according to Kuznets, "Contrast in size makes it all the more important to consider some distinctive problems of economic growth of small nations."[5] This contrast is certainly exhibited in the countries of the FTAA, where thirty-four countries of the Americas will be joined together with the objective of eliminating all barriers to trade and investment.[6] These countries vary widely in terms of size, territory, population, natural resource endowments, and level of economic development. The FTAA encompasses countries that are among the richest and the largest in the world, as well as countries that are among the smallest and the poorest. One illustration of the disparity in size is the fact that Jamaica, which is not the smallest of the FTAA countries, can fit over 200 times into the territory of Argentina, which is not by any stretch the largest.

Smallness also has an absolute component—although this concept may be more intuitive than empirical. As Paul Streeten says, "We know a small country

3. For further discussion of such effects see, for example, Srinivasan (1986).
4. Kuznets (1958, p. 14).
5. Kuznets (1958, p. 15) (emphasis added).
6. For the moment, all countries of the Americas, excluding Cuba.

when we see one."[7] The defining factors attributed to small countries are all related to two elements: vulnerability and dependence. They are highly vulnerable not only to the economic policies and taste and preference shifts of their larger neighbors and trade partners, but also to hurricanes, floods, and diseases. They depend upon other countries for their imports, exports, and the foreign exchange with which to buy basic goods. It is this dependency and vulnerability that define countries as small. Although smaller size may net unequivocal gains in the simple classical trade model, this same factor of smallness is associated with market and resource constraints that can incur short- or medium-term difficulties not considered in the traditional model assumed earlier. These short- and medium-term considerations may weigh quite heavily on the consciousness of policymakers while deciding whether to engage in trade and integration arrangements.

First on this list of considerations is the cost to a country's economy of adjusting to new price structures. When relative prices change, so do the incentives to consume imports versus domestic importables, as does the producer's cost structure. Small economies tend to be heavily concentrated in a small number of activities, which makes it more difficult for them to absorb this cost of adjustment. Dislocation in one sector has a proportionately larger impact on a small economy than on a larger, more diversified market. Small firms unaccustomed to competition may flounder when faced with an inflow of lower-cost, more efficiently produced imports. Additionally, the smaller economy will be relatively more dependent on its existing export firms, as it is through their export activities that the small country gains the foreign exchange needed to purchase necessary imports. These factors suggest that transition costs of trade liberalization will be higher for smaller economies than for larger ones.[8]

Second, although successful exporting companies often build upon experience they have gained in the domestic market, in smaller markets this experience is more limited, making the export learning curve larger for exporters in smaller countries than for those in countries that themselves have a larger, more competitive internal market. As exports tend to be more heavily concentrated in one industry or in a small number of industries in a

7. Streeten (1993, p. 197).

8. This element and the sustainability of trade liberalization are discussed in the context of the Latin American and Caribbean experience in Michaely and Papageorgiou (1995).

small country, this adjustment will have a much further-reaching impact on such a country than on a large, diversified economy.

Third, human resource constraints also figure prominently. Small countries may simply not have a large enough number of people trained to effect a successful transition to competitiveness. In addition, costs are relatively greater: the cost of supporting a trade ministry or an intellectual property enforcement mechanism, for example, is higher per capita in a small country than in a larger one. Yet all small countries may have to have in place the basic institutions of governance.

Yet another factor, mentioned by G. K. Helleiner and also referred to in the preceding chapter by Bonapas Onguglo, is the vulnerability of smaller countries to coercion on nontrade issues by their larger trade partners in return for trade commitments. If, asks Helleiner, the traditional trade model is correct and smaller countries net all the gains from integration, why would the larger countries wish to negotiate free trade agreements with them? In the pure world of economics large countries would do so, as this would enhance the overall welfare of the system. Although they might not gain, neither would they lose welfare. In fact, the motivation to act to enhance the welfare of the system is low if countries themselves do not perceive tangible gains. The real world in which policymakers must operate is cluttered with rent seekers and domestic interest groups and works more along the lines of profit maximizing than overall welfare enhancing. Thus, adds Helleiner, the incentive for large countries to negotiate trade arrangements with smaller countries is often agreement on ancillary issues of importance to them. While this is not necessarily negative—cooperation in issues such as banning land mines or combating the flow of drugs may be very good—such ties complicate trade arrangements for smaller countries, especially when they require costly implementation.[9]

One more concern is that small countries, which are often highly vulnerable to exogenous fluctuations—be they financial crises, weather patterns such as the El Niño current and hurricanes, or political decisions by larger countries—face major constraints on their economic integration activities. In the Americas the unfortunate truth is that many of the small, and therefore more vulnerable, countries lie directly in the path of potentially dangerous weather systems. If a crop on which a nation depends for a

9. Helleiner (1996).

significant portion of its income is destroyed—as in some of the Central American and Caribbean countries that were devastated by Hurricanes Mitch and George in 1998—the entire country is affected.

All these issues can influence the negotiating positions of policymakers from smaller economies. Moreover, these are the issues that should be taken into account while crafting trade agreements in which smaller countries are expected to participate fully.

Small Countries and the FTAA

The FTAA negotiations are undergirded by a number of fundamental principles. These include the principle of consensus in decisionmaking, that the FTAA will be balanced and comprehensive in scope—and that the FTAA will be a *single undertaking*. These have important implications for the negotiations—and for the final shape of the FTAA. In the FTAA endeavor St. Lucia and Honduras sit at the same table with their American and Brazilian partners to flesh out the text of the agreement. All countries—large and small, rich and poor, more or less open to trade—have the same vote, and all will take on the same obligations. Therefore, the FTAA must be constructed in a way that considers the needs of all countries. The concept of smallness has been embodied in the process, with a Working Group—which has evolved into a Consultative Group—on Smaller Economies that is comprised of all participating countries set up to "take into consideration the needs, economic conditions and opportunities of the smaller economies."[10]

Recognizing that smaller countries tend to reap benefits from trade integration and acknowledging that there are some particular difficulties in attaining these benefits that are associated with being small, the aspects that characterize these challenges will be examined more deeply. To address this issue it is necessary to look at some of the factors that may influence the effective participation of smaller economies in trade negotiations. These factors vary in their nature. Some of them can be considered as structural, as they result from the physical size of the countries. Others are policy related. Structural constraints correspond to factor endowments—amount of land, labor, and capital—and they are referred to in this section as natural resource constraints.

10. Ministerial Declaration of San José (1998, para. 9).

Among the most important policy constraints is the high reliance of many smaller countries on import taxes, a policy which, if left unaddressed, will severely compromise their participation in trade-liberalizing efforts at both the regional and the multilateral level.

Natural Resource Constraints

Although it can result from war or politics, smallness—especially in the case of small island economies—is often an accident of geography. In *The Wealth and Poverty of Nations* David Landes points out the importance—and the inevitability —of geography, stating, "Whatever one may say about the weakening of geographical constraints today in an age of tropical medicine and higher technology, they have not vanished. . . . The world has never been a level playing field, and everything costs."[11] Even dramatic declines in transport and communications costs and the fluidity of investment capital have not fully overcome the barriers of size and of political geography, and the costs of being a nation-state remain.

Therefore, a commonly used indicator of size is territorial surface area. As well as serving as an indicator of physical size, landmass may be used as a proxy for both the amount and potential diversity of the country's natural resources. A limited amount of land generally implies a relatively undiversified economic structure. Most small countries that are considered small are small in area and therefore offer less diversity of raw materials. This is well illustrated by the countries of the Americas, as seen in table 5-1, which ranks these countries in terms of ascending size and economic diversity.[12]

The territorial size differential among the countries of the Americas is immense: the four largest countries cover over three-quarters of the land of the Western Hemisphere, and Canada alone comprises a quarter. There are twenty-three countries, each of which fails to make up even 1 percent of the Western Hemisphere's territory. The correlation between size and lack of economic diversity is apparent: of these twenty-three countries only two (Antigua and Barbuda, and Panama) are classified as diversified economies.[13] The rest depend on bananas (five countries), coffee (five), sugar (five), petroleum or fuels

11. Landes (1998, p. 5).

12. A diverse economy is one that does not depend on one particular commodity for more than 15 percent of its exports.

13. The economies of Antigua and Barbuda and Panama are highly concentrated in services, but this sector is not included in the table. No single commodity dominates either country's bundle of goods exports.

(three), metal ores (three), wool (one), and undergarments (one). Four of the five largest economies—Argentina, Brazil, Canada, and the United States—are classified as diversified in terms of the distribution of their merchandise exports. The fifth, Mexico, depends on oil for a third of its wealth. It must be noted that this table does not take into account trade in services.

A characteristic of small countries—in the Americas and elsewhere—is that their economic structures tend to be undiversified. Although this does not necessarily have negative implications for economic growth or wealth—as some of the least diversified economies, the Middle Eastern oil exporters, are among the world's wealthiest—it does mean that small countries are generally unable to produce domestically the full range of goods that can be produced in a larger economy, and they must generally rely on trade with the rest of the world to obtain all the goods they desire. Therefore, a corollary to small territory is that international trade is more important for small countries than for large ones. Smaller economies tend to rely heavily on external trade as a means of overcoming their own inherent scale limitations. Table 5-1 reflects that in general the countries of the Americas that have limited natural resources and small markets are highly dependent on international trade. An outlier is Canada, which has vast abundant natural resources and a relatively large population and yet is highly reliant on external commerce.

These facts, however, do not spell doom for small countries that are undiversified in terms of natural resources. In fact, as small countries tend to specialize more intensely in the production of the goods that are in their comparative advantage than would larger countries, they tend to gain more from this trade. Small scale and limited resources may constrain some activities, but certainly not all of them. Therefore, although it is highly unlikely that a small island economy will develop a national auto industry or move into the production of aircraft or machine power tools, such a country may well specialize in tourism or high technology or finance. Its comparative advantage does not lie in heavy machinery, but rather lies in a skilled labor force or a reliable, pleasant climate—be it for tourism or for other types of investment. As Peter Evans puts it, "Constructing comparative advantage is no less plausible than taking it as given."[14] Some encouraging examples are Switzerland's development of high technology and a financial services industry and Norway's exploitation of its comparative advantage in fishing and shipping.

14. Evans (1995).

Table 5-1. Territorial Size: Landmass and Export Diversity in the Western Hemisphere[a]

Area rank	Country	Area (square miles)	Percentage of Western Hemisphere export market	Share of major commodities (15 percent and above) in total merchandise exports (1990–91)[b]	Year	Exports of goods and services as a percentage of GDP	Imports of goods and services as a percentage of GDP	Trade as a percentage of GDP	Openness rank
34	Grenada	340	<0.5	Bananas: 15 percent	1995	20	27	47	16
33	St. Kitts-Nevis	360	<0.5	Sugar: 41 percent	1996	48	74	123	27
32	St. Vincent and the Grenadines	390	<0.5	Bananas: 48 percent	1995	48	61	109	29
31	Barbados	430	<0.5	Sugar: 20.3 percent; petroleum product: 18.6 percent	1992	50	42	92	4
30	Antigua and Barbuda	440	<0.5	Diversified	1994	106	104	210	1
29	St. Lucia	620	<0.5	Bananas: 56 percent	1996	68	70	138	28
28	Dominica	750	<0.5	Bananas: 55.2 percent; soap: 20.7 percent	1996	45	68	113	12
27	Trinidad and Tobago	5,130	<0.5	Crude petroleum and petroleum products: 80 percent	1996	53	42	95	31
26	Jamaica	10,990	<0.5	Metal ores: 65.7 percent (alumina: 47.6 percent; bauxite: 9.9 percent)	1996	55	68	123	21
25	The Bahamas	13,880	<0.5	Fuels: 16.8 percent	1996	44	56	100	3
24	El Salvador	21,040	<0.5	Coffee: 26.1 percent	1996	21	33	54	15
23	Belize	22,960	<0.5	Sugar: 32.4 percent; fruits: 15.1 percent (bananas: 7.3 percent)	1996	45	49	94	5
22	Haiti	27,750	<0.5	Undergarments: 25.5 percent	1996	7	28	35	19
21	Dominican Republic	48,730	<0.5	Metal ores: 42 percent; sugar: 28 percent	1996	29	34	63	13
20	Costa Rica	51,100	<0.5	Bananas: 28.4 percent; coffee: 15 percent	1996	45	46	91	11
19	Panama	75,520	<0.5	Diversified	1996	94	91	185	24

18	Guatemala	108,890	<0.5	Coffee: 15.5 percent	1996	18	23	40	17
17	Honduras	112,090	<0.5	Bananas: 24.4 percent; coffee: 17.9 percent	1996	48	52	100	20
16	Nicaragua	130,000	<0.5	Coffee: 19.8 percent; meat 17.6 percent	1996	41	66	106	23
15	Suriname	163,270	<0.5	Alumina: 94 percent	1996	27	98	125	30
14	Uruguay	177,410	<0.5	Wool: 15.9 percent	1996	18	20	38	33
13	Guyana	214,970	0.5	Bauxite: 23.8 percent; sugar: 20.1 percent	1996	101	106	207	18
12	Ecuador	283,560	0.7	Crude petroleum: 38.5 percent; bananas: 21.8 percent	1996	31	26	57	14
11	Paraguay	406,750	1.0	Cotton: 29.8 percent; seeds for oil: 20 percent	1996	21	26	46	25
10	Chile	756,950	1.9	Metal ores: 32 percent	1996	27	29	55	9
9	Venezuela	912,050	2.3	Crude petroleum: 78.6 percent	1996	37	24	61	34
8	Bolivia	1,098,580	2.8	Gas, natural and manufactured: 37.8 percent; tin: 16.6 percent; zinc: 28.4 percent	1994	20	27	47	6
7	Colombia	1,138,910	2.9	Coffee: 19.8 percent; crude petroleum: 18.4 percent	1996	17	20	37	10
6	Peru	1,285,220	3.2	Copper: 19.6 percent; metal ores: 15.4 percent	1996	12	16	29	26
5	Mexico	1,958,200	4.9	Crude petroleum: 30 percent	1996	22	20	42	22
4	Argentina	2,766,890	7.0	Diversified	1996	9	9	19	2
3	Brazil	8,511,970	21.5	Diversified	1996	7	8	15	7
2	United States	9,363,500	23.6	Diversified	1995	11	13	24	32
1	Canada	9,976,140	25.5	Diversified	1995	38	35	73	8
	Western Hemisphere total	39,645,440							

Source: Organization of American States (1998).
a. Figures are for 1996, except where indicated.
b. Based on data found in OAS Trade Unit.

Market Size

Domestic market size, though naturally overlapping somewhat with the previous category, provides a proxy for production possibilities within the confines of the domestic economy. One of the characteristics widely associated with economic smallness is a limited domestic market with relatively low consumer potential. Market size is measured by the number and wealth of domestic consumers, which have implications for firms' ability to sell their goods at a particular price. Small territorial size will limit the scope of the domestic market, constraining the type of economic activity that can be undertaken both for reasons of obtaining inputs and for reasons of scale. The optimum-scale plant for many industries, especially highly capital-intensive ones, is simply too large to be supported by the limited capacity of the domestic market. In some industries comparative advantage in terms of the transport cost advantage of relying on domestic suppliers is diminished, as smaller producers have the same conditions as larger ones. The country is therefore more open to competition from imports. This is especially so for small island states, as the cost of sea transport has fallen more rapidly than for land transport.[15]

The most often-used indicator of country size is population. A small population implies a small potential market.[16] Using an arbitrary cutoff point of 10 million inhabitants, there are twenty-one small countries in the Americas, as seen in table 5-2, which ranks the countries of the Western Hemisphere by three indicators of market size.[17] This table shows that over three-quarters of the population of the Western Hemisphere lives in five countries, and nine countries comprise nearly 90 percent of the hemisphere's population. The largest economy in terms of population is more than 6,000 times more populous than the smallest. Small population size is also related to a small domestic economy, as there are fewer consumers to purchase goods. An additional constraint is the smaller pool of people from which to draw policymakers and administrators.

15. As pointed out by Streeten, this is of course an even bigger issue for small, landlocked economies, which depend on their neighbors for access to sea transport.

16. Kuznets used a population of 10 million to demarcate a small country, but also allowed for flexibility, predicting that as populations grew the population criterion for smallness would also change.

17. Interpretation of the term *inhabitants*—indeed of the term *population*—is fluid due to immigration. Many of the countries that are considered small or relatively less developed may have overstated population figures due to migration.

Another main indicator of market size is the level of gross domestic product (GDP), the aggregate wealth produced in an economy. This serves as a proxy for the magnitude of a country's domestic market, thereby offering some indications as to the possible limitations to specialization of production and exploitation of economies of scale. Table 5-2 shows that the two largest countries (identified by GDP rank, column 5) are responsible for 85 percent of the Western Hemisphere's GDP; the five largest countries account for 96 percent of the hemisphere's GDP; and 99 percent of the hemisphere's GDP is generated in nine countries. In the case of this indicator, each of twenty-nine countries makes up less than 1 percent of hemispheric GDP.

Administrative Capacity

An essential component of successful policy is adequate human resources. Small countries face constraints in administrative and financial resources that will undoubtedly affect their capacity to negotiate and to implement trade agreements. Policymakers also face certain policy challenges to the trade reforms that will necessarily accompany integration. The population indicator that was seen above also figures into this constraint: a small population means fewer people to draw from to staff a country's trade ministry—or to design the fiscal budget. The statistical probability of finding a sufficient number of talented and capable people who are able and willing to perform these necessary tasks in the public sector will be lower than in a larger market, and resources will need to be more thinly distributed.

In a small country there is less opportunity for specialized training: as bureaucracies diminish in size, there is more responsibility per person and it is more difficult for individuals to specialize. Instead, a small number of generalists must tackle—and master—all issues and address them in all forums. This limitation can be especially daunting when these individuals are facing a large team of negotiators and technical specialists from a larger country at the negotiating table. This is becoming increasingly significant as the trade agenda incorporates increasingly complex issues with which smaller countries may have had less experience and as trade frictions and disputes become more complex and costly to manage.[18]

18. The cost factor of trade litigation and the difficulties small countries face in addressing this factor are detailed in the report by the Independent Group of Experts on Smaller Economies and Hemispheric Integration (1997).

Table 5-2. Market Size in the Western Hemisphere

Country	Population rank	Population (thousands)	Percentage of Western Hemisphere export market	GDP rank	1996 GDP (millions of U.S. dollars)	Percentage of Western Hemisphere export market	GDP per capita rank	GDP per capita (U.S. dollars)
St. Kitts-Nevis	34	41.0	<0.5	28	247	<0.5	7	6,039
Antigua and Barbuda	33	65.2	<0.5	29	502	<0.5	5	7,641
Dominica	32	73.0	<0.5	34	178	<0.5	20	2,418
Grenada	31	91.0	<0.5	31	295	<0.5	16	2,980
St. Vincent and the Grenadines	30	111.0	<0.5	32	260	<0.5	21	2,328
St. Lucia	29	158.0	<0.5	28	298	<0.5	12	3,787
Belize	28	216.0	<0.5	27	640	<0.5	17	2,878
Barbados	27	266.0	<0.5	25	1,742	<0.5	6	6,591
The Bahamas	26	276.0	<0.5	22	3,459	<0.5	3	12,180
Suriname	25	410.0	<0.5	30	334	<0.5	31	773
Guyana	24	835.0	<0.5	26	717	<0.5	29	855
Trinidad and Tobago	23	1,287.0	<0.5	19	5,464	<0.5	11	4,213
Jamaica	22	2,522.1	<0.5	20	4,426	<0.5	25	1,738
Panama	21	2,631.0	<0.5	17	8,244	<0.5	14	3,083

Uruguay	20	3,184.0	<0.5	11	18,180	<0.5	8	5,676
Costa Rica	19	3,399.0	<0.5	16	9,015	<0.5	18	2,619
Nicaragua	18	4,375.0	0.6	24	1,971	<0.5	33	438
Paraguay	17	4,828.0	0.6	15	9,673	<0.5	23	1,952
El Salvador	16	5,623.0	0.7	14	10,469	<0.5	24	1,802
Honduras	15	5,924.0	0.8	21	4,011	<0.5	32	657
Haiti	14	7,168.0	0.9	23	2,617	<0.5	34	357
Bolivia	13	7,414.0	1.0	18	6,131	<0.5	30	808
Dominican Republic	12	7,822.0	1.0	13	13,169	<0.5	26	1,654
Guatemala	11	10,621.2	1.4	12	15,817	<0.5	28	1,447
Ecuador	10	11,477.0	1.5	10	19,040	<0.5	27	1,628
Chile	9	14,225.0	1.9	7	74,292	0.8	9	5,152
Venezuela	8	21,671.0	2.9	8	67,311	0.7	15	3,017
Peru	7	23,819.0	3.2	9	60,926	0.6	19	2,509
Canada	6	29,606.0	3.9	3	579,300	6.0	2	19,333
Argentina	5	34,665.0	4.6	5	294,687	3.0	4	8,367
Colombia	4	36,813.0	4.9	6	85,202	0.9	22	2,275
Mexico	3	91,831.0	12.2	4	334,792	3.4	13	3,593
Brazil	2	159,222.0	21.1	2	748,916	7.7	10	4,641
United States	1	263,119.0	34.8	1	7,341,900	75.5	1	27,676
Western Hemisphere		755,788.5			9,726,521			12,869

Source: Organization of American States (1998).

**Table 5-3. Human Development Indicator Ranking for Countries of
the Western Hemisphere**

Countries are listed in ascending order

Country	HDI index
Western Hemisphere average	0.780
Haiti	0.338
Nicaragua	0.530
Guatemala	0.571
Honduras	0.575
Bolivia	0.589
El Salvador	0.592
Guyana	0.649
Paraguay	0.706
Peru	0.717
Dominican Republic	0.718
Jamica	0.736
Ecuador	0.775
Brazil	0.783
Suriname	0.792
Mexico	0.804
Belize	0.806
St. Lucia	0.834
St. Vincent and the Grenadines	0.836
Grenada	0.843
Colombia	0.848
St. Kitts-Nevis	0.853
Venezuela	0.861
Panama	0.864
Dominica	0.873
Trinidad and Tobago	0.880
Uruguay	0.883
Argentina	0.884
Costa Rica	0.889
Chile	0.891
Antigua and Barbuda	0.892
The Bahamas	0.894
Barbados	0.907
United States	0.942
Canada	0.960

Source: United Nations Development Program (1997).

The good news is that small countries can specialize in dynamic people. One indicator in which a significant number of the small countries of the Americas rate high is shown in table 5-3, which reproduces the UN Development Program (UNDP) Human Development Indicator (HDI) for the year 1997. It is an index of each country's health, wealth, and education. A skilled, educated work force may go far in compensating for the lack of other resources. Although this is not true of all small countries, several of the small island economies ranked high, reflecting the potential of these countries for high levels of education, health, and wealth—all of which may contribute to successful environments for nurturing human capital. One challenge for the smaller economies will be to learn how to optimize the distribution of their human resources. In order to make the most efficient and effective use of these resources, some smaller economies could be well served to pool their human capital on the basis of technical expertise and capability rather than along national lines.

Countries that do not rank high according to the HDI—those that tend to be classified as less-developed countries—exhibit characteristics similar to those of small economies and face many of the same challenges. This indicator captures the poverty effect: countries that are not necessarily the smallest in terms of territorial or population size exhibit characteristics of smallness due to their low per capita income. A country with a relatively large population may look attractive in terms of market strength—unless the average purse per consumer is prohibitively small. Countries such as Bolivia and Guatemala, for example, that are not small in territorial or population terms, are quite small in terms of per capita wealth. Although population and GDP results tend to be highly correlated, with countries generally close to the same placement on the two indicators, this is not true of the results for per capita GDP. Many countries that are small in land, wealth, or population rank near the top of this distribution. This will have implications for future recommendations.

Policy Issues

One factor that is of great significance to countries' success in implementing free trade commitments is how much work must be done to dismantle barriers. Higher tariffs cause greater changes in an economy when reduced than do lower ones. A high degree of tariff dependency makes liberalization difficult—fiscally and politically.

Table 5-4. Trade Taxes as a Percentage of Government Revenue in the Western Hemisphere, 1994[a]

Country	Trade taxes as a percentage of government revenue	Country	Trade taxes as a percentage of government revenue
St. Lucia	55.1	Haiti	17.7
Belize	51.0	Barbados	15.7
The Bahamas	50.6	Ecuador	14.3
Guatemala	37.3	Paraguay	12.5
Dominican Republic	33.6	Guyana	11.6
St. Kitts-Nevis	29.5	Peru	11.4
Honduras	27.7	Panama	9.8
Suriname	24.3	Venezuela	9.1
Jamaica	23.6	Chile	8.4
Colombia	23.2	Trinidad and Tobago	8.1
Antigua and Barbuda	22.0	Bolivia	7.0
Grenada	21.6	Uruguay	6.9
Costa Rica	21.3	Argentina[b]	6.0
Nicaragua	20.4	Mexico[b]	5.9
Dominica	20.1	Brazil	2.0
El Salvador	17.9	Canada	1.6
St. Vincent and the Grenadines	17.7	United States	1.5

Source: International Monetary Fund (1997) and OECS data.

a. Data are for the central government.

b. For Argentina and Mexico data are for the federal governments.

A high reliance on tariff revenues is a policy-driven factor that is often found in smaller economies. This fact can certainly constrain the ability of these countries to effectively participate in international trade negotiations. Although being small does not cause high tariff barriers, small, trade-dependent countries are more likely to be reliant on tariffs for government revenue. This revenue is easier to collect and less politically risky than income or value-added taxes. Some small island economies have implemented zero-income tax policies to stimulate foreign investment, and they compensate by funding their public programs almost exclusively with trade taxes. As seen in table 5-4, nineteen countries in the Americas rely on trade tariffs for over 15 percent of their government revenue. Seven countries depend on tariffs for over half of their government revenue—five of them Organization of Eastern Caribbean States (OECS) microstates, the smallest economies in the hemisphere as measured by any indicator.

Therefore, the revenue effect of liberalization is of great concern to the small economies. Although a high degree of reliance on tariff revenues is not a natural consequence of being small, small economies tend to have a small base for fiscal revenue and a greater reliance on trade taxes for government revenue. The lowering of tariff barriers to major trading partners, as will happen in the FTAA, implies a loss of revenue. This is especially so in countries that are net demanders of foreign exchange, in which exchange rate policy could not be used easily as a mitigating mechanism. For this reason, policymakers will be faced with the difficult challenge of finding replacement sources of revenue for essential services such as education, health care, and police services.[19]

In a very real sense, failing to address the revenue effect of liberalization could darken the bright picture of participation in the FTAA that has been painted for some of the small economies of the Americas. Measures to mitigate these effects should be phased in well before the tariff cuts are made in the FTAA to allow the economy—and especially the polity—to adjust.

Addressing Asymmetry in the FTAA

As many small countries in the Western Hemisphere may face constraints on their participation in the FTAA, this section addresses the question of how FTAA negotiators will be able to "take into account differences in the levels of development and size of the economies in our Hemisphere, to create opportunities for the full participation of the smaller economies and to increase their level of development."[20] As discussed earlier, small countries are both vulnerable to external fluctuations and highly dependent on trade. A number of their challenges for integrating in the FTAA process stem from the immutable physical condition of being small. Other challenges are policy related.

19. Thomas, Nash, et al. (1991) elaborate on the fiscal issues related to lowering tariff and nontariff barriers in chapter 5 of their book.

20. Ministerial Declaration of San José (1998).

Although there has been discussion of according some type of special and differential treatment to small countries in the FTAA or of establishing redistributive mechanisms such as those that were implemented in the European Union, these approaches are not likely to come to fruition.[21] Such measures are, at the moment, politically or economically feasible. The first reason is that EU-type redistributive mechanisms are generally seen only in economic arrangements that strive to be much more than free trade agreements. Second, the political will for such mechanisms has not been manifested within the context of the FTAA. In addition, the age of special and differential treatment is coming to an end.[22] The FTAA is specifically designed to be a single undertaking—a fully reciprocal trade-liberalizing agreement in which all parties accept all parts of the agreement. This is but part of a larger trend in international trade relations. At both the multilateral and the regional level, smaller countries are increasingly taking on reciprocal trade-liberalizing commitments with larger countries. At the multilateral level the number of members has mushroomed since the establishment of the World Trade Organization (WTO), mostly fed by developing countries, which had previously spurned its predecessor, the General Agreement on Tariffs and Trade (GATT), as being a "rich man's club." The Western Hemisphere includes various examples of reciprocal trade arrangements between smaller and larger countries.[23]

As many countries in Latin America and the Caribbean have substantially unilaterally liberalized their trade regimes, the cost of concluding reciprocal trade agreements with larger countries has diminished—and the cost of being left out has increased. Previously the removal of high protective tariff walls in

21. For a full discussion of the redistributive mechanisms employed in the European Union, see Griffith-Jones, Stevens, and Georgiadis (1993).

22. Different types of treatment of smaller economies of the Americas are discussed in depth in Organization of American States Trade Unit (1996).

23. The North American Free Trade Agreement (NAFTA) is the first example of a thoroughly reciprocal free trade agreement between countries of such disparate levels of development: an agreement in which all parties agree to the same commitments and the same disciplines with the same end goal—trade and investment liberalization. This is not the only example. Another recent case is the free trade agreement concluded in 1997 between Canada and Chile. In the same vein, Bolivia has negotiated a free trade area and associative membership with the Mercosur, a customs union whose key player, Brazil, alone has a GDP fifty times the size of the Bolivian economy. Costa Rica and Nicaragua have both formed a free trade area with Mexico, and the agreements made by Colombia and Venezuela with the Caribbean include clauses for eventual reciprocity.

order to form trade integration arrangements with the larger partners would have caused intense short-term pain in the economy. At present the cost of tariff elimination is often dominated by the benefits of greater access to a large partner market. Regional trade arrangements are often used to allow countries to "lock in" their economic reforms by increasing the price of noncompliance with these obligations. In addition, smaller countries have begun to perceive that the days of unilateral preferences and of "free riding" in the multilateral arena are numbered and that they must soon participate reciprocally in trade agreements in order to participate at all. Therefore, reciprocal arrangements at the regional level offer good practice for multilateral reciprocity.

Although reciprocity has been gaining ground in trade arrangements among developed and developing countries, the underlying disparities remain. One of the most significant challenges that will be posed by the FTAA objective of liberalizing trade among the thirty-four participating countries is how to design rules that apply both to large and highly developed economies and to the smaller developing countries in the region. The fact that the FTAA will be a single undertaking of mutual rights and obligations will simply not allow any subset of countries to pursue obligations that are less demanding than those set out in the final agreement. All countries must implement all parts of the agreement. This, however, does not rule out the possibility for specific, temporary transition measures to be negotiated on a case-by-case basis.

Two types of measures could be developed to ensure that all countries will be able to fully participate in the negotiations and to implement the rules and disciplines of the FTAA. One is structural measures built into the agreement that will address the problems stemming from the asymmetry among the participant countries. The other is technical cooperation measures that will ease individual countries' transition into the FTAA. When considering these mechanisms, policymakers from smaller countries should look toward measures that will bring them the benefits of integration while addressing the constraints they face as a result of being small. Within the FTAA framework, negotiated provisions should be considered that will allow industries adequate time to adjust while building up a comparative advantage that will be enhanced by trade. Domestically, fiscal reform will be necessary in many countries. This should be initiated at the beginning of the process. Another essential issue is for smaller countries to design mechanisms through which they can most effectively use their scarce human resources and for the FTAA process to offer opportunities for the optimal development of this human capital. Therefore, technical support will be necessary for smaller economies to strengthen their participation in the FTAA negotiations and in the implementation of the subsequent agreements.

Built-in Measures

In recognition of the heightened vulnerability of their economies to exogenous fluctuations, smaller economies may make the case that certain industries or firms will need more time to adjust to new conditions. Given their resource constraints—both human and financial—they may seek assistance in implementing certain disciplines, especially in new areas that are as yet uncharted territory. Within the framework of the FTAA, smaller countries can thus negotiate differentiated time frames for the implementation of certain commitments, as well as differentiated application of the rules in specific areas. In addition, to save time and money it would be prudent for these countries to call for regional or group implementation of certain commitments, along with technical assistance to bolster their scarce resources and to enable them to use those they have to their full potential. Rather than seeking special treatment a priori, they should consider in which industries differentiated treatment may not be necessary or desirable—and where accelerated liberalization may be desirable.

Differentiated time frames or schedules could apply to market access commitments. Indeed, a traditionally used mechanism in trade negotiations—for both small countries and large—is extended time frames for the phasing out of tariffs and nontariff measures. Such differentiation would allow additional time for smaller countries' firms to adjust to greater competition and to wean the government from tariff revenues. Therefore, nonlinear schedules with "backloaded" tariff tables would allow for a more gentle transition to free trade while ensuring that countries would respect the single undertaking. In the same spirit, larger countries could start the process of market opening by accelerating their tariff reduction on goods that are important to the small countries. This could boost the welfare of countries in the Americas that are receiving preferences under the Generalized System of Preferences (GSP)—and would demonstrate "concrete progress" in the FTAA.[24]

24. For further elaboration of this idea, see Organization of American States Trade Unit (1997).

Flexibility could also be a key word for smaller economies in the FTAA—flexibility in the implementation of certain rules and disciplines. Many smaller countries may currently lack the legislative, administrative, and human resource capacity to implement FTAA commitments, especially in complex areas such as rules of origin and antidumping and countervailing duties and in new areas such as government procurement. These are the same areas in which the smaller countries may face challenges in meeting their WTO commitments. The steps that countries take in the FTAA may thus help them to move toward greater fulfillment of their multilateral obligations. In the FTAA countries may negotiate and implement the agreement individually or as members of a subregional trading bloc. A number of countries have already begun to do so. The members of the Caribbean Community (CARICOM), for example, have taken steps toward doing so through the creation of the Regional Negotiating Machinery (RNM). The RNM aims to optimize Caribbean resources in the negotiations by assigning technical trade experts from the region to follow all of the negotiating groups. These experts will inform the region of the discussions through RNM mechanisms, and positions will be coordinated jointly.

Regional cooperation should be urged and joint implementation of commitments encouraged, especially in complex areas such as intellectual property rights and in areas in which infrastructure and administration are costly and cumbersome. Immediate cooperation and implementation of rules in the areas of customs procedures and sanitary and phytosanitary measures and standards could greatly benefit smaller countries, where few customs facilities are fully automated, complex sanitary measures may not be fully understood, and staff may have difficulties with the preparation and application of technical regulations, standards, and conformity assessment procedures and with their eventual participation in mutual recognition agreements.

Not everything need be the result of negotiations. Countries could begin to implement at the subregional level, ahead of the negotiations, some of the measures that will be required under the FTAA. For example, subregional integration arrangements could begin to establish common investment policies or to implement and jointly monitor the enforcement of a collective intellectual property rights regime or common standards bodies. Such steps would reduce the cost of transition for individual countries by allowing them to take the actions jointly, and they would give the countries a head start on implementing that will be required in the FTAA—and they would also lengthen the time frame for the amortization of the costs of transition.

Technical Support

A main focus of the smaller economies should be to ensure that adequate and effective technical assistance exists in the Western Hemisphere. Sources of trade-related technical assistance abound at both the regional and the multilateral level, and the will to help the smaller countries in the FTAA process is almost overwhelming. The challenge is to ensure that this assistance is targeted to the specific needs of the recipient country. This is a tangible area in which smaller countries can urge that the supply be tailored to their needs. In order for this to happen, small countries will need to target their specific needs and prioritize them. Once these needs are identified, they should be expressed throughout the negotiating and implementation process.

Technical assistance can help smaller countries to overcome serious material as well as human and technical resource constraints. In other words, providing technical assistance is one low-cost way to extend the markets and the administrative and human capacity scales of smaller countries. Providing FTAA technical assistance may also have a multiplier effect. A "state-of-the-art" agreement, the FTAA will cover all of the issues on the multilateral agenda— and more. Already the architects of the process have included negotiating groups on government procurement and competition policy, as well as an advisory group on electronic commerce, an issue that is growing in importance. In addition, the FTAA will evolve along with the WTO discussions should a new round of multilateral talks be launched in 2000, as expected. The smaller countries may require technical assistance in dealing with a variety of issues, especially "new issues" such as competition policy and government procurement, but also much more basic issues such as customs valuations, tariff quantification, and standards. In areas such as customs procedures and standards, assistance can be given to smaller countries to garner human and financial resources so that these economies can jointly implement the agreements. In complying with the regulations that will be decided upon in the area of standards, smaller economies may need direct technical assistance in the preparation of technical regulations, the establishment of national standardizing bodies and participation in international standardizing bodies, and the establishment of regulatory bodies or bodies for the assessment of conformity with technical regulations and the training of personnel.

Administrative and human resource capacity will also be necessary for countries to prepare appropriately for the negotiation and implementation of the FTAA agreements. Some countries will need to strengthen their capacity in the areas of trade policy formulation, negotiation, and institutional adaptation. A well-coordinated mechanism for adopting and expressing joint positions during the negotiating process will enable countries to pool their financial, material, and human resources and to participate more fully in the entire process. In addition, according to the principles of specialization and exchange, it will allow the best and brightest negotiators from the small countries, regardless of nationality, to work for the best interest of the smaller countries. A complicated and growing area of interest to all countries is that of dispute settlement. Considering that the number of cases brought in front of the WTO dispute settlement body is growing yearly, countries may wish to concentrate on developing a support structure for the smaller members of the FTAA. One mechanism that could be envisaged is a pool of legal staff and consultants formed to provide impartial advice and technical support to the smaller members.

Conclusions

Although some smaller economies of the Western Hemisphere may be anxious about their ability to effectively compete with the larger, more developed countries of the region, it must be recognized that the costs of non-participation in trade agreements would be much higher than the costs of participation. Not playing the FTAA game would isolate the smaller economies of the region from markets that now constitute a significant and growing proportion of their trade, and they would not be able to gain from the trade—and particularly the investment liberalization dynamics—that will occur with the implementation of the FTAA. Although there will be costs for adjustment, these costs will pay the entry fee to global economic integration. By participating fully in the FTAA, the Caribbean and Central American countries will be legally entitled to enter their most important markets—those of the United States and Canada—by means of a binding multilateral agreement rather than by relying on the fragile, unilateral preferential arrangements now in place. As Thucydides cautioned, "Large nations do what they wish, while small nations accept what they must." The FTAA process, through its participatory, consensual principles, will give the small countries the opportunity to shape the framework in which they will conduct trade with their hemispheric partners.

References

Evans, P. 1995. *Embedded Autonomy: States and Industrial Transformation*. Princeton University Press.

Griffith-Jones, S., C. Stevens, and N. Georgiadis. 1993. *Regional Trade Liberalization Schemes: The Experience of the EC*. Washington D.C.: Inter-American Development Bank and United Nations Economic Commission for Latin America.

Helleiner, G. K. 1996. "Why Small Countries Worry: Neglected Issues in Current Analyses of the Benefits and Costs for Small Countries in Integrating with Large Ones." Note prepared for the University of the West Indies (UWI) Independent Group of Experts on Smaller Economies and Hemispheric Integration. Mona, Jamaica: UWI.

Independent Group of Experts on Smaller Economies and Hemispheric Integration. 1997. *Overcoming Obstacles and Maximizing Opportunities: Smaller Economies and Western Hemispheric Integration*. Mona, Jamaica: UWI.

International Monetary Fund. 1997. *Government Finance Statistics*. Washington, D.C.

Kuznets, S. 1958. "Economic Growth of Small Nations." In *The Economic Consequences of the Size of Nations,* edited by E. A. G. Robinson. London: Macmillan.

Landes, David S. 1998. *The Wealth and Poverty of Nations: Why Some Are So Rich and Some So Poor*. New York: W. W. Norton.

Michaely, M., and D. Papageorgiou. 1995. *Small Economies: Trade Liberalization, Trade Preferences and Growth*. Washington, D.C.: World Bank.

Ministerial Declaration of San José. 1998. Summit of the Americas, Fourth Trade Ministerial Meeting. San José, Costa Rica (March 19) (http:/www.sice.oas.org/ ftaa/costa).

Organization of American States. 1998. *Small and Relatively Less Developed Economies and Western Hemisphere Integration*. Washington, D.C.

Organization of American States Trade Unit. 1996. *Special and Differential Treatment in International Trade*. Washington, D.C.

———. 1997. *Mechanisms and Measures to Facilitate the Participation of the Smaller Economies in the FTAA: An Update*. Washington, D.C.

Robinson, E. A. G. 1960. *The Economic Consequences of the Size of Nations*. London: Macmillan.

Srinivasan, T. N. 1986. "The Costs and Benefits of Being a Small, Remote, Island, Landlocked or Ministate Economy." *World Bank Research Observer* 1(2): 205–18.

Streeten, P. 1993. "The Special Problems of Small Countries." *World Development* 21(2): 197–202.

Thomas, V., J. Nash, et al. 1991. *Best Practices in Trade Policy Reform*. Washington, D.C.: World Bank.

United Nations Development Program. 1997. *Human Development Report 1997*. New York.

CHAPTER SIX

Preferential and Nonpreferential Trade Flows in World Trade

Jean-Marie Grether and Marcelo Olarreaga

A rticle I of the General Agreement on Tariffs and Trade (GATT), which was originally concluded in 1947, clearly forbids preferential trade among GATT members. The Most Favored Nation (MFN) Clause states that "any advantage, favor, privilege or immunity granted by any contracting party to any product originating in or destined for any other country shall be accorded immediately and unconditionally to the like product originating in or destined for the territories of all other contracting parties." It was only twenty-three articles later that, at the insistence of the future members of the European Community (EC), the original GATT members accommodated the existence of preferential trade agreements (PTAs) on the condition that internal barriers to trade be eliminated on "substantially all trade."

The importance of considering the needs of developing countries, which were turning away from the GATT to the United Nations Conference on Trade and Development (UNCTAD), and a "pragmatic approach" to GATT's decision-making, as it was recently called by Baldwin, led to an extension of the provisions for PTAs in 1965 by the introduction of Part IV of the GATT, which dealt with trade and development and led to the introduction of the Generalized System of Preferences (GSP).[1] The GSP allows developing countries to benefit from preferential tariff reductions in developed countries' markets. The inter-

---

1. As opposed to a rules-based approach. See Baldwin (1998).

ests of developing countries were further acknowledged in 1979 by the introduction of the Enabling Clause, which allows PTAs to be formed among developing countries without having to fulfill all the conditions of Article XXIV.[2]

Partly because of the loopholes in Article I and because of the fears that the Uruguay Round of multilateral trade negotiations might never be concluded, PTAs spread throughout the world. Although the European Union (EU) is involved in more than 75 percent of the total number of agreements of which the World Trade Organization (WTO) is notified, a growing number of agreements are being signed in other regions of the world. For example, between 1990 and 1994 twenty-six agreements were signed in the Western Hemisphere alone.[3]

The literature on preferential trade has also widened enormously, and our understanding of PTAs and their consequences is much better today than a decade ago. Fears that the proliferation of PTAs might undermine the multilateral process led to the creation of a WTO Committee on Regional Trade Agreements in February 1996. Whether regionalism can stimulate or jeopardize the multilateral trading system remains an open question, and the literature generally argues that its effects depend on the institutional forms of the preferential agreements formed.[4] In general, both shallow and deeper forms of preferential agreements, such as those establishing free trade areas (FTAs) and customs unions (CUs), respectively, have advantages and disadvantages when it comes to enhancing the multilateral trading system.

The growing number of FTAs may lead to what Bhagwati has called the "spaghetti-bowl" phenomenon—a complex system of trade preferences under which products in one particular country enjoy access on widely varying terms depending on their alleged origins.[5] This is not a problem with regard to deep forms of integration such as CUs, but there are risks that this type of PTA may lead toward inward-looking trading blocks, such as has been

2. The basic requirements of Article XXIV are that external protection not be increased and that "substantially all trade" be covered. Article 5 of the General Agreement on Trade in Services (GATS) also allows for preferential treatment in trade in services.

3. The WTO had been notified of only four by the end of 1995, and it was notified of only three of these through the enabling clause. The WTO was notified of only the North American Free Trade Agreement (NAFTA) through Article XXIV.

4. For a thorough review of the literature on this issue, see Winters (1996).

5. Bhagwati (1995). Krueger (1993) also describes how rules of origin can be used to enhance protection against nonmembers in the case of FTAs.

envisioned in the so-called Fortress Europe threat.[6] The drawbacks and benefits of different types of agreements have led some authors to argue for hybrid FTA-CU agreements in the future to avoid the most trade-impeding aspects of PTAs.[7]

The importance of preferential trade has therefore been growing both in the real world and in the international trade literature. The aim of this chapter is to quantify the share of world trade under PTAs and to give an estimate of its actual importance. Note that from a theoretical perspective it is not clear whether a larger or smaller share of preferential trade leads to higher or lower levels of welfare. In other words, the figures reported in this chapter have no normative value, but should be seen as an illustration of the relative importance of PTAs in the world trading system.

A recent study by Sapir provided some quantification of preferential trade for the EU.[8] In 1995, 30 percent of total imports to the EU were brought in under extra-EU PTAs, of which 18 percent were reciprocal trade agreements such as the European Economic Area (EEA) agreement and the Europe Agreement. The rest were brought in under unilateral PTAs, such as the GSP. In his study Sapir considered as preferential imports whose MFN tariffs were above zero. The idea is that if the MFN tariff of the EU is zero, the implementation of a PTA does not provide any preference for exporting to members of the EU. When Sapir included imports at zero tariffs, the share of extra-EU imports under PTAs rose to 51 percent. Contrary to Sapir's study, which focused exclusively on the EU, our objective is to estimate the share of preferential trade at the world level.

6. The theoretical literature on the formation of PTAs that affect the terms of trade generally supports this view. See, for example, Krugman (1991); Bond, Syropoulos, and Winters (1996); and Bagwell and Staiger (1997). The line of reasoning is the following: as countries form trading blocks, their market shares increase and they have higher incentives to increase their tariffs to outside parties. This has recently been empirically verified by Winters and Chang (1997), who showed evidence for the case of Spain's accession to the EC. The literature on endogenous tariff formation through lobbying also tends to support this; Levy (1997) has shown that a move toward bilateral trade agreements may decrease incentives to participate in multilateral negotiations. Cadot, de Melo, and Olarreaga (1999) have shown that tariffs may also endogenously rise through industry lobbying after deepening of a PTA.

7. Wonnacott (1996).

8. Sapir (1998).

Serra Puche provided an estimate of the share of preferential trade at the world level by subtracting the trade of all countries that do not belong to PTAs from total world trade. Thus he assumed that all intra-PTA trade is conducted on preferential terms, and he concluded that 53 percent of world trade is conducted on preferential terms. This estimate has several biases. First, it has an upward bias since, as suggested by Sapir's study, an important share of intra-PTA trade is conducted on nonpreferential terms (that is, at zero MFN tariffs). Second, and also suggesting an upward bias, not all trade among PTA partners is conducted on a preferential basis, as rules of origin may be extremely costly (this bias was also present in Sapir's study). Third, Serra Puche's estimates do not include nonreciprocal preferential trade, such as trade under the GSP.[9]

This chapter attempts to correct these biases and also to provide comparisons across regions for two different periods (1988–92 and 1993–97). It also reports results regarding the share of preferential trade disaggregated into agricultural and industrial products.

Qualifying Preferential Trade Agreements

PTAs can be divided into two broad categories: partial PTAs (PPTAs) and full PTAs (FPTAs). A PPTA is defined as one in which trade preferences are granted only to specific products or unilaterally to a particular set of member countries by more developed members. An FPTA is defined as one in which there is full product coverage and where all members grant preferential access to other members.

Product-specific PPTAs often have some political dimension and are seen as a first step toward further interdependence among members. They generally lead toward deeper or wider forms of PTAs. As they do not satisfy the GATT Article XXIV requirement of including "substantially all trade," these agreements are more common among developing countries, which notify the WTO of them under the Enabling Clause. An early example of a sectoral PPTA is the agreement that established the European Coal and Steel Community of 1951, which was the first step toward the EC. Examples of more recent PPTAs that led toward an FPTA are the different bilateral sectoral agreements that led to the creation of the Mercosur (Southern Common Market).[10] Product-specific PPTAs do not necessarily imply

9. Sapir (1998) and Serra Puche (1998).

10. Note that all these PPTAs, both in Europe and in Latin America, also had an important political dimension.

zero tariffs among members for the specified products, but rather imply tariffs below MFN levels.

The classic example of unilateral concession in PPTAs is the GSP, whereby developing countries receive special and differential treatment for their exports to developed markets. The first concessions under the GSP schemes were introduced by the EU and Japan in 1971 and 1972. Canada and the United States introduced their schemes in 1974 and 1976, respectively. The GSP has limited product coverage, and a significant number of products included are subject to quotas and nonzero tariff preferences.

There are four categories of FPTAs: free trade agreements, CUs, common markets (CMs), and economic unions.[11] In an FTA (such as NAFTA) trade barriers between partner countries are abolished, but each member country independently determines its own external (that is, non-FTA) trade barriers. In a CU (such as the Mercosur) a common external trade policy is adopted by member countries. The next two categories of FPTAs imply a deeper form of integration in which the elimination of internal barriers to trade is not directly related to trade policy. Indeed, a CM (such as the EC) adopts additional provisions to facilitate the free movement of goods, services, and factors of production as well as the harmonization of technical standards. These clearly reduce the costs of internal trade relative to external trade. Finally, an economic union (such as the European Union) extends harmonization to fiscal and monetary policy as well as social and legal policies. This reduces uncertainty within the internal market and therefore gives further preferential access to members relative to nonmembers.

Our definition of preferential trade in this chapter includes all forms of FPTAs, but only one type of PPTA—that in which trade is subject to GSP preferences where the preferential duty is zero. This is to focus on preferential trade that is conducted duty free. We believe that this is a better indicator of economically meaningful preferential trade. PPTAs without full elimination of tariffs tend to have a political dimension only, and rules of origin often lead to nonpreferential trade.

Quantifying Preferential Trade Agreements

Ideally, to estimate the share of world trade represented by preferential trade one would need customs information that would indicate under which regimes different products enter the importing countries. Indeed the existence of a PTA does not necessarily imply that products traded among PTA members enter the

11. Winters (1991).

importing countries under the preferential regime. The reason is that the economic and administrative costs of satisfying rules of origin within the PTA may be so high that importers prefer to face the MFN tariff. Unfortunately, these types of data are not available for a large sample of countries.

The approach we have followed is to approximate the actual share of trade that receives preferential treatment by considering only imports within a PTA that are brought in under tariff lines where the MFN tariff is higher than 3 percent. The idea is that if the MFN tariff is below 3 percent, the incentives to satisfy rules of origin disappear. This figure is based on a study for the European and Free Trade Association and the EC by Herin, in which he estimated that the total cost of rules of origin for firms is at least 2 percent of the value of the imported goods.[12] Therefore, it seems reasonable to assume that any product for which the MFN tariff is below 3 percent will enter the importing country on an MFN basis rather than a preferential basis. Note that by using this as a proxy for preferential trade, we exclude all trade conducted on an MFN duty-free basis (as did Sapir), as by definition this should not be considered preferential trade.[13]

FPTAs are identified using notifications made under GATT Article XXIV and the Enabling Clause by WTO members and countries that are in the process of acceding to the GATT (China, for example). Import data are also based on notifications by WTO members. Regarding imports under GSP schemes, we have included only imports from GSP beneficiaries where there are full preferences (that is, goods are imported duty free) and no quantitative limitations.

Our sample includes fifty-three countries (counting the EU as one country), which are listed in the appendix to this chapter. For thirty-three countries we have data for two different periods: the first between 1988 and 1992 and the second between 1993 and 1997. For the remaining twenty countries we have information for only one of the two periods. The sample represents 85 percent of world trade for the first period and 86 percent of world trade for the second period.[14] Table 6-1 gives the sample's representation of different regions.

---

12. Herin (1986) also provides a "conservative" estimate of 5 percent of the value of the product as the total economic costs of applying rules of origin, that is including the administrative cost of border formalities needed to determine the origin of a product.

13. Sapir (1998).

14. To calculate the share of world trade in our sample, we applied the following method. First we obtained data from the UN COMTRADE database on total trade by region from 1988 to 1997. For each period (1988–92 and 1993–97) we calculated each

Table 6-1. Percentage of Trade Represented in the Sample by Region, 1988–97

Region	1988–92	1993–97
Western Hemisphere	87	87
Mercosur	100	100
NAFTA	100	100
Western Europe		
EU 15	95	96
Asia and Oceania	95	84
Rest of the world	16	20

Source: Authors' calculations.

The sample includes around 95 percent of western Europe's total trade, 87 percent of the Western Hemisphere's total trade, and between 84 and 95 percent of the total trade for Asia and Oceania. The trade for the rest of the world is relatively poorly represented, as we have information for only 16 to 20 percent of the rest of the world's trade. This bias is due to the lack of notification of the WTO by African countries and the fact that some eastern European countries are still in the process of acceding to the agreements. Therefore, our results for the rest of the world should be interpreted with caution. On the other hand, the representation of other regions in our sample is relatively high; therefore, our results can be seen as reasonably significant.

We calculated the share of total world trade and regional trade represented by preferential trade using two different methods. The first involved calculating an import-weighted average of each country's share of preferential trade, and the second involved calculating an unweighted average of these shares. These two averages have different economic meanings. The weighted average indicates the total share of regional or world trade represented by preferential trade, and therefore is heavily influenced by countries with large trade volumes. The unweighted average gives more

---

year's total trade. For example, in the first period 67 percent of total trade within our sample for the period 1988–92 is seen for the year 1988. In other words, there is an overrepresentation of the year 1988 in the first period of our sample. In the second period 67 percent of total trade for 1993–1997 is seen for the year 1995. We used these weights to calculate average trade at the world level and by region. The percent of trade is given by the sum of total trade for one period divided by the average trade for the period.

Table 6-2. Share of Total World Trade Represented by Preferential Trade, 1988–97

Percent

Sector	Import-weighted average 1988–92	Import-weighted average 1993–97	Unweighted average 1988–92	Unweighted average 1993–97
Agriculture	39[a] (40)[b] [4][c]	45 (46) [2]	23 (26)	34 (35)
Industry	40 (41) [8]	41 (41) [3]	19 (21)	26 (26)
Total	40 (41) [7]	42 (42) [3]	19 (21)	27 (27)

Source: Authors' calculations.
a. Open-sample shares.
b. Closed-sample shares.
c. Import-weighted share of GSP trade represented by preferential trade.

importance to countries with small trading volumes and indicates the average share of regional or world trade represented by preferential trade. Using each of these methods we computed two different shares. One is for the entire sample, and we call that the "open-sample share." The second is only for countries for which we had observations in the two periods, and we call it the "closed-sample share." This is because, when comparing trade over time, we do not want to introduce a bias by adding or deleting countries from the sample.

Table 6-2 gives the values of both preferential trade share averages at the world level (import-weighted and unweighted). Open-sample shares are given in italics, whereas closed-sample shares are reported in parentheses. Note that the values are relatively similar. The figures in brackets indicate the import-weighted share of GSP trade represented by preferential trade. Table 6-2 suggests that the share of world trade represented by preferential trade has remained relatively constant if one focuses on import-weighted averages. Using the closed-sample shares, which are more accurate for time comparisons, one observes that preferential trade has modestly increased from 41 to 42 percent despite the spread of regional integration agreements throughout the world. However, if one focuses on the unweighted average, which indicates the share of preferential trade of a representative country, the change is relatively important, as there has been a 29 percent increase in the share of a representative country's preferential trade (from 21 to 27 percent). Therefore, as regionalism spread it seems that smaller trading partners were more involved in this wave and that world trade experienced a significant increase in the share of preferential trade.

Table 6-3. Share of Preferential Trade by Region, 1988–97
Percent

Region	Import-weighted average 1988–92			Import-weighted average 1993–97			Unweighted average 1988–92			Unweighted average 1993–97		
	Agr^a	Ind^a	Total	Agr	Ind	Total	Agr	Ind	Total	Agr	Ind	Total
Western Hemisphere	15	19	19	30	26	27	30	18	19	42	26	28
Mercosur	56	14	18	51	14	18	47	16	19	59	27	31
NAFTA	11	19	19	26	28	28	11	22	21	41	47	47
Western Europe	65	69	69	71	70	70	40	48	48	42	43	43
EU 15	66	72	72	72	73	73	47	61	73	72	73	73
Asia and Oceania	3	5	4	2	3	3	10	8	8	7	5	5
Rest of the world	9	4	4	43	46	46	11	8	8	50	52	52

Source: Authors' calculations.

a. Agr = agriculture; Ind = industry.

Table 6-2 also includes a breakdown for agricultural and industrial products.[15] These averages indicate that there was a large relative increase of preferential trade in agriculture, which suggests that the PTAs of which the WTO was notified during the period 1993–97 played a relatively important role in stimulating trade in agricultural products.

The GSP's share of total preferential trade has significantly declined from 7 to 3 percent during these two periods, which could indicate that countries no longer see the GSP as an efficient instrument for development. Erosion of GSP preferences as countries opened up to trade during the Uruguay Round and entered into FPTAs may also explain the decline in the share of trade under the GSP worldwide. This is true for both agricultural and industrial products, which have declined from 4 to 2 percent and from 8 to 3 percent, respectively.

General trends at the world level cannot necessarily be transposed to different regions. Table 6-3 reports the shares computed for the four main regions of the world (the Western Hemisphere, western Europe, Asia and Oceania, and the rest of the world, essentially eastern Europe and Africa).[16] The Western Hemisphere and the rest of the world have been, by far, the regions with the most dramatic increases in their shares of preferential trade. (One must be

15. Agriculture is defined as the first twenty-four tariff lines of the two-digit Harmonized System classification.

16. The numbers reported are for open-sample shares, but the closed-sample figures are almost identical.

careful in interpreting the share for the rest of the world given its low representation in our sample.)

The large increase in preferential trade in the Western Hemisphere is valid for countries with both large and small trading volumes, as both import-weighted and unweighted shares have experienced an important increase. Closed-sample shares of preferential trade increased by 40 percent. The comparable figure for open-sample shares was 45 percent, regardless of whether the average share was import weighted or unweighted. The rise in preferential trade is seen for both agricultural and industrial products. Note, however, that countries with small trading volumes seem to have had a significantly larger share of agricultural products traded preferentially (as the unweighted shares for agriculture were 100 and 40 percent higher in the first and second periods, respectively).

The two major trading blocks that were created at the end of the first period (the Mercosur and the NAFTA countries) evolved differently. The NAFTA members significantly increased their shares of preferential trade in both agricultural and industrial products. (Note that these do not correspond to intra-block shares: Mexico also trades preferentially with the G-3, the United States with Israel, and Canada with Chile.) On the other hand, Mercosur members have had different results depending on whether they have large or small trading volumes. This is indicated by the relatively stable shares of preferential trade for the Mercosur countries seen when these are computed using import-weighted figures and by the significant increase seen when using unweighted shares. This suggests that if Argentina and Brazil have had a relatively stable share of preferential trade, Paraguay and Uruguay have dramatically shifted toward preferential trade. Note again that these shares do not correspond to intrablock shares, as all Mercosur members have PTAs signed with other Latin American countries within the Latin American Integration Association (LAIA/Aladi). Therefore, if the Mercosur as a region has not increased its share of preferential trade, the representative Mercosur country has experienced a two-fold increase in its share of preferential trade.

Western Europe has experienced a slight increase in its share of preferential trade. This is also true for the EU (whose shares include intra-EU trade). Although both import-weighted and unweighted shares have similar values in the case of the EU, this is not true for the whole of western Europe, where it seems that countries with small trading volumes have had a smaller share of preferential trade, as the unweighted shares are smaller than the import-weighted shares.

Table 6-4. Share of Preferential Trade Represented by GSP Trade, 1988–97

Percent

Region	1988–92			1993–97		
	Agri-culture	Industry	Total	Agri-culture	Industry	Total
Western Hemisphere	33	18	19	8	9	9
Mercosur	0	0	0	0	0	0
NAFTA	49	19	21	13	10	10
Western Europe	2	4	4	0	0	0
EU 15	1	4	4	0	0	0
Asia and Oceania	28	64	62	42	62	60
Rest of the world	71	8	22	18	0	2

Source: Authors' calculations.

Asia and Oceania have had extremely low shares of preferential trade, generally below 10 percent, and there seems to have been a slight decline between the two periods. Moreover, as reported in table 6-4, more than 60 percent of the preferential trade of Asia and Oceania was under the GSP. On the other hand, the rest of the world (Africa and eastern Europe) has experienced a dramatic increase in its share of preferential trade from the first period to the second. As these countries tend to have relatively small trading volumes, this partly explains why at the world level their share of preferential trade is seen to have increased from 21 to 27 percent when computing unweighted shares, whereas it is seen to have remained stable when using import-weighted shares to calculate average shares.

Table 6-4 reports share of preferential trade represented by GSP trade using an open-sample and import-weighted technique for different regions. The decline in the share of GSP trade observed at the world level and reported in table 6-2 can be transposed to all regions except Asia and Oceania, where it seems to have remained relatively stable. The more dramatic decline was in the rest of the world, where the share of preferential trade represented by GSP trade fell from 22 to 2 percent. In the Western Hemisphere and western Europe there has been a 50 percent decline, which roughly corresponds to the decline at the world level.

One may be tempted to attribute the erosion in the share of preferential trade represented by GSP trade to the important increase in other forms of preferential trade (for instance, FPTAs). This is obviously part of the story, but not all.[17] The share of total trade represented by GSP trade has also declined in all regions. By multiplying the shares in table 6-4 by the shares in table 6-2, one obtains the share of total trade represented by GSP trade. This indicates that, even for Asia and Oceania where the share of preferential trade represented by GSP trade has remained relatively constant, there has been a fall in the share of total trade represented by GSP trade from 2.5 to 1.8 percent.

The figures in table 6-4 tend to confirm what was suggested by the aggregate figures in table 6-2. There has been a move away from GSP trade and toward other forms of preferential trade as a means for developing countries to integrate into the world market. North-South FPTAs, such as NAFTA or the Europe Agreements, may be seen as a more efficient way of achieving this objective.

Characteristics of Countries That Trade on a Preferential Basis

The computation of import-weighted and unweighted shares of preferential trade in the previous section has suggested that countries with large trading volumes may behave differently than countries with small trading volumes when it comes to participating in PTAs. After comparing the figures reported in table 6-3 it appears that countries with small trading volumes tend to have smaller shares of preferential trade, as the import-weighted values computed are generally larger than the values of unweighted shares. However, this tendency does not seem to extend to all regions, as the opposite is true for the Western Hemisphere. This section discusses whether preferential trade is conducted by relatively open or closed countries and whether regionalism works hand in hand with the multilateral trading system.

Size and GDP per Capita

In our research we have focused on the relationship between the share of preferential trade and country size. The idea behind this is that small countries

17. This conclusion should be taken cautiously, as there may be a composition effect within GSP trade, and our proxy for GSP trade includes only trade conducted in tariff lines where there is a full GSP preference (that is, GSP duty free) and no quantitative limitations.

may have relatively little to gain from a bilateral (or preferential) approach to trade negotiations, as their bargaining power is relatively weak.[18] It has often been suggested that the MFN clause of the GATT significantly increased the incentive for small countries to participate in multilateral negotiations, as they can more easily "free ride" on concessions among large trading partners. This incentive obviously does not extend to bilateral agreements. From a perspective of bargaining power, the only case in which potential gains for a small country might be larger in a bilateral agreement is one in which the partner is also a small country. However, in this case the share of preferential trade will remain relatively small, as the PTA partner is, by definition, a country with a small volume of trade. One should expect small countries to have a relatively small share of preferential trade. Recall that this was also suggested by the comparison of import-weighted and unweighted shares in table 6-3.

We captured the notion of country size by using two proxies: population and gross domestic product (GDP). We tested for both log-linear and "U-shaped" relationships. As we have suggested earlier, we expected a positive correlation between volume and share of preferential trade, but by allowing for U-shaped curves we could capture the fact that extremely large countries may also have incentives to negotiate multilateral rather than bilateral agreements. The idea behind this approach was that very large countries have little to gain from bilateral agreements with smaller members and may prefer to focus on multilateral negotiations that open the world market rather than some particular country's market.[19] We tested for these relationships by running the following ordinary least square (OLS) regressions in double-log form:

$$\log(s_{i,t}) = \beta_0 + \beta_1 \log(\text{size}_{i,t}) + \mu_{i,t}, \tag{6-1}$$

$$\log(s_{i,t}) = \alpha_0 + \alpha_1 \log(\text{size}_{i,t}) + \alpha_2 \log(\text{size}_{i,t})^2 + \varepsilon_{i,t} \tag{6-2}$$

where $s_{i,t}$ is the share of preferential trade of country i in period t; $\text{size}_{i,t}$ is the proxy for size (that is, population or GDP); $\varepsilon_{i,t}$ and $\mu_{i,t}$ are the error terms; and α and β are the estimated coefficients. We ran regressions for agriculture and industry and for the first and second periods separately, but the coefficients

18. Schiff (1997) argues, however, that small countries gain more than large countries in PTAs, but abstracts from bargaining power issues.

19. Until the late 1980s, the attitude of the United States toward bilateral agreements, as described by Panagariya (1998), may be seen as an example of large countries' preferring the multilateral approach.

Table 6-5. Share of Preferential Trade and Relationship to Size of Country, 1988–97[a]

Parameter	Population		GDP	
	Equation 6-1	Equation 6-2	Equation 6-1	Equation 6-2
Constant	−1.2	−3.1	−1.5	10.2
	(−2.1)**	(−3.2)**	(−0.9)	(1.3)
GDP	...	...	−0.1	−2.2
			(−0.7)	(−1.5)
GDP^2	...	...	...	0.1
				(1.5)
Pop	−0.4	0.9	...	...
	(−2.7)**	(1.7)*	...	...
Pop^2		−0.2	...	...
		(−2.4)**		
R^2, adjusted	0.08	0.13	−0.01	0.01
F-value	7.1**	6.6**	0.4	1.3
Number of observations	75	75	75	75

Source: Authors' calculations.
*Significant at the 90 percent level.
**Significant at the 95 percent level.
a. All regressions are double-log. Figures in parentheses are t-statistics.

were not statistically different, and therefore the results reported in table 6-5 are those for pooled regressions on total shares.

Table 6-5 suggests that there is no clear relationship between the share of preferential trade and GDP. However, it appears that there is an inverted U-shaped relationship between the share of preferential trade and population. This may seem surprising, as the negotiating power of a country would seem to be better represented by its GDP than by its population. One should therefore interpret this statistical relationship cautiously. Nevertheless, it seems to indicate that very large and very small countries, in terms of population, tend to have a smaller share of preferential trade.

Using the estimates of equation 6-2 in the second column of table 6-5, we calculated the size of a country in terms of population that maximizes its share of preferential trade.[20] Using the nonrounded estimated coefficients yielded the

20. To this end we differentiated the right-hand side of equation 6-2 with respect to $size_{i,t}$ (population in this case), equalized the result to zero, and solved for size. It yielded:

Table 6-6. Share of Preferential Trade and GDP per Capita, 1988–97[a]

Parameter	Equation 6-1	Equation 6-2
Constant	−6.4	−29.7
	(−3.8)**	(−2.3)**
GDP per capita	0.5	6.3
	(2.3)**	(2.0)**
(GDP per capita)^2	...	−0.4
		(−1.9)**
R^2, adjusted	0.06	0.09
F-value	5.5**	4.6**
Number of observations	75	75

Source: Authors' calculations.
**Significant at the 95 percent level.
a. All regressions are double-log regressions. Figures in parentheses are t-statistics.

conclusion that countries with a population of 12 million should be the ones most inclined to trade preferentially. Note that a country like Chile, which is heavily involved in preferential trade, has a population of 14 million.

We then turned to the relationship between GDP per capita and share of preferential trade. The idea behind this approach was that to engage in both bilateral and multilateral negotiations countries need a certain negotiating capacity, which in turn requires financial resources. Therefore, we expected poor countries to have a small share of preferential trade given their financial constraints. We also tested for U-shaped relationships, thinking it might turn out that at certain levels of GDP per capita the financial resources necessary to negotiate both bilateral and multilateral become negligible and therefore the financial constraint becomes irrelevant. Therefore, the equations we used are given by:

$$\log(s_{i,t}) = \delta_0 + \delta_1 \log(\text{GDP per capita}_{i,t}) + \mu_{i,t}, \tag{6-3}$$

$$\log(s_{i,t}) = \gamma_0 + \gamma_1 \log(\text{GDP per capita}_{i,t}) + \gamma_2 \log(\text{GDP per capita}_{i,t})^2 + \varepsilon_{i,t} \tag{6-4}$$

Again we tested for differences in the coefficients for agriculture and industrial products and between the first and second periods, but these were not

---

$\text{Pop}^* = e^{-a_1/(2a_2)}$,

where Pop* is the population size that maximizes the share of preferential trade and e is the exponential function.

statistically different than the ones for the pooled regression on total shares. The results reported in table 6-6 confirm the existence of an inverted U-shaped relationship between GDP per capita and the share of preferential trade.

Given the inverted U-shaped relationship, we calculated the value of GDP per capita that maximizes the share of preferential trade by differentiating.[21] The calculated value was close to $7,200, which again is similar to the GDP per capita of a country like Chile.

In concluding this section we should note that the move toward preferential trade seems to depend on the size of the country and its level of GDP per capita. Very poor and small countries and very rich and large countries seem to prefer the multilateral GATT and its MFN clause to the bilateral approach. Our results may capture both bargaining power incentives and financial constraints.

Degree of Trade Openness

An important question in the preferential trade literature is whether regionalism is a complement or a substitute to multilateralism.[22] A way of exploring this issue is to test whether more open countries tend to have a larger or smaller share of preferential trade. If relatively open countries tend to have large shares of preferential trade, one would tend to conclude that regionalism does not seem to jeopardize the multilateral trading system, but that it can be seen to complement it in moving toward a similar objective: global free trade.

Our objective was to look into the relationship between overall trade openness and share of preferential trade at the country level. The overall trade openness indicators we used were the ones developed by Low.[23] These are essentially ratios of trade to GDP that have been corrected to account for the size of the country, differences in domestic prices, and share of nontraded sector in the economy. We used the openness ranking obtained by Low for the countries in our sample and checked for changes between the two periods in Spearman rank correlation coefficients with a ranking of countries according to their shares of preferential trade.

21. To this end we differentiated the right-hand side of equation 6-5 with respect to GDP per capita, equalizing the result to zero and solving for GDP per capita. It yielded GDP per capita$^* = e^{-\gamma_1/(2\gamma_2)}$.

22. Foroutan (1998) explored this issue and concluded that there is no systematic relationship between preferential trade and overall levels of protection. Our study differs from Foroutan's in its time-comparison dimension.

23. They were extracted from table 5 of Low, Olarreaga, and Suarez (1998).

However, as we suggested earlier, there seems to be some inherent bias when comparing shares of preferential trade across countries. Indeed it appears that the share of preferential trade of any country will depend on both its size and on its GDP per capita, which can be seen as proxies for bargaining power and financial constraints, respectively. Therefore, we needed to correct our shares of preferential trade for these two biases before ranking countries.[24]

The Spearman rank correlation between the corrected share of preferential trade, $\hat{s}_{i,t}$, and the overall trade openness indicator, t^*, suggested a change in the types of countries that tend to trade preferentially between the first and second periods.[25] Indeed, the Spearman rank correlation for the first period was negative ($s = -0.28$) and statistically significant ($z = -1.8$), suggesting that countries that tend to trade preferentially are more likely to be closed economies. However, in the second period the Spearman rank correlation became positive ($s = 0.11$) and also statistically significant ($z = 0.62$), which indicates that countries that tend to have a large share of preferential trade are open countries.[26]

Therefore, it appears that in the late 1980s and early 1990s countries that engaged in PTAs were relatively closed economies. However, there was a shift in the mid-1990s, and countries that had a large share of preferential trade became relatively more open. This, in turn, tends to suggest that if the regionalism of the late 1980s jeopardized the multilateral trading system, the new

24. This was done by running the following OLS unconstrained regression (to avoid multicollinearity problems) in double-log form:

$$\log(s_{i,t}) = \varphi_0 + \varphi_1 \log(\text{GDP}) + \varphi_2 \log(\text{GDP})^2 + \varphi_3 \log(\text{Pop}) + \varphi_4 \log(\text{Pop})^2 + \varepsilon_{i,t}.$$

The fitted value from this regression, denoted by $\hat{s}_{i,t}$, told us the "normal" share of preferential trade of a country with a given population and GDP per capita. This was given by $\hat{s}_{i,t} = e^{[\log(s_{i,t} - \hat{\varepsilon}_{i,t})]}$. Then our corrected indicator of share of preferential trade was computed by taking the actual deviation from its normal value for a particular country. That is, $S_{i,t}^* = S_{i,t}/\hat{S}_{i,t}$.

25. The Spearman rank correlation is given by $s = 1 - 6\sum_i D_i^2/[n(n^2 - 1)]$, where n is the number of observations and D_i is the difference in ranking for a given country with respect to trade openness and share of preferential trade. Its z-value follows a normal distribution and is given by $z = s\sqrt{(n - 1)}$.

26. Note that these qualitative results are also obtained when computing the Spearman rank correlation for the uncorrected indicator of share of preferential trade and overall trade openness. The Spearman rank correlation between the ranking of countries according to the uncorrected indicator of share of preferential trade and the corrected indicator was 0.84 and 0.69 for the first and second periods, respectively.

wave of regionalism that started in the early 1990s is working hand in hand with the multilateral trading system.[27]

Conclusions

The quantification of the share of total trade represented by preferential trade may be seen as an indicator of the importance of the move toward PTAs worldwide. As shown in this chapter, we have estimated the share of preferential trade in the world at around 42 percent for the period 1993–97 and 40 percent for the period 1988–92. This estimate of 42 percent at the regional level and the small 5 percent increase at the world level cannot be generalized to all regions of the world. Indeed, in western Europe the share of preferential trade was close to 70 percent, whereas the increase was below world levels. In the Western Hemisphere the share of preferential trade was around 25 percent for the second period, whereas the increase during the two periods was around 40 percent. Asia and Oceania have had stable shares, but they are still well below the world average (that is, between 3 and 4 percent), whereas the rest of the world (eastern Europe and Africa) has shares close to the world average, but with a tenfold increase between the two periods.

The share of preferential trade represented by GSP trade significantly declined between the two periods (from 7 to 3 percent), and this has been observed in all regions of the world except Asia and Oceania. This is due not only to the important increase in other forms of preferential trade at the world level, but also to an absolute decline in GSP trade. This, in turn, may suggest that countries may now see the GSP as a less efficient means of integration into the world economy and move toward other forms of PTAs, such as North-South agreements.

This move toward preferential trade seems to depend on the size of the country and its GDP per capita. This result may capture both bargaining power incentives and financial constraints when governments compare the potential gains between a multilateral (nonpreferential) and a bilateral (preferential) approach. A country with a GDP per capita of $7,200 and a population of 12 million would tend to have the largest share of total trade represented by preferential trade. This is roughly the case in a country like Chile.

27. Note that this is consistent with Baldwin's (1997) domino theory of regionalism, which suggests that "regionalism is half of the trade liberalization 'wheel' that has been rolling towards global free-trade."

Finally, it seems that if in the late 1980s and early 1990s countries with large shares of preferential trade tended to be relatively closed countries in terms of overall trade openness, this changed in the mid-1990s, when relatively open countries tended to have larger shares of preferential trade. This may be interpreted as showing that the rise in PTAs in the early 1990s was an engine for the multilateral trading system rather than a jeopardizing force.

Appendix: Countries Included in the Sample

The table below gives the list of countries included in the sample and the year for which we have information in the two different periods.

Country	1988– 92	1993– 97	Country	1988– 92	1993– 97
Countries with data			Switzerland	1988	1994
for two periods			Thailand	1988	1995
Argentina	1988	1994	Turkey	1989	1995
Australia	1988	1995	United States	1989	1994
Brazil	1989	1995	Uruguay	1989	1996
Canada	1988	1996	Venezuela	1990	1994
Chile	1988	1994	*Countries with data*		
China	1992	1996	*for one period*		
Colombia	1991	1995	Austria	1988	...
Costa Rica	1988	1995	Bolivia	...	1995
Czech Republic	1990	1997	Bulgaria	1992	...
Ecuador	1992	1995	Cyprus	...	1993
El Salvador	1989	1994	Finland	1988	...
European Union	1988	1995	Guatemala	...	1995
Hong Kong	1992	1995	Honduras	...	1995
Hungary	1991	1995	Jamaica	1991	...
Iceland	1988	1994	Madagascar	...	1996
India	1988	1995	Malaysia	1988	...
Indonesia	1989	1994	Morocco	...	1995
Japan	1988	1995	Nicaragua	...	1995
Korea	1988	1996	The Philippines	1991	...
Macao	1991	1995	Romania	1991	...
Mexico	1988	1996	Senegal	1989	...
New Zealand	1991	1996	Slovakia	1990	...
Norway	1988	1996	Sri Lanka	1991	...
Paraguay	1989	1996	Sweden	1988	...
Peru	1988	1994	Tunisia	1989	...
Poland	1989	1995	Zimbabwe	1987	...
Singapore	1989	1995			

References

Bagwell, K., and R. Staiger. 1997. "Multilateral Cooperation during the Formation of a Free-Trade Area." *International Economic Review* 38: 291–319.

Baldwin, Richard. 1997. "The Causes of Regionalism." *World Economy* 20: 865–88.

Baldwin, Robert. 1998. "Pragmatism versus Principle in GATT Decision-Making: A Brief Historical Perspective." Paper presented at the WTO Symposium, *50 Years: Looking Back, Looking Forward,* Geneva, April 30.

Bhagwati, Jagdish. 1995. "U.S. Trade Policy: The Infatuation with Free Trade Areas." In *The Dangerous Drift to Preferential Trade Agreements,* edited by Jagdish Bhagwati and Anne O. Krueger. Washington, D.C.: AEI Press.

Bond, Eric, Constantinos Syropoulos, and Alan Winters. 1996. "Deepening of Regional Integration and Multilateral Agreements." Discussion Paper 1320. London: Centre for Economic Policy Research.

Cadot, Olivier, Jaime de Melo, and Marcelo Olarreaga. 1999. "Regional Integration and Lobbying for Tariffs against Non-members." *International Economic Review* (forthcoming).

Foroutan, Faezeh. 1998. "Does Membership in a Regional Preferential Trade Arrangement Make a Country More or Less Protectionist?" Working Paper 1898. Washington, D.C.: World Bank.

Herin, Jan. 1986. "Rules of Origin and Differences between Tariff Levels in EFTA and the EC." Occasion Paper 13. Geneva: European Free Trade Association.

Krueger, Anne O. 1993. "Rules of Origin as Protectionist Devices." Working Paper 4352. Cambridge, Mass.: National Bureau of Economic Research.

Krugman, Paul. 1991. "Is Bilateralism Bad?" In *International Trade and Trade Policy,* edited by E. Helpman and A. Razin. Boston: MIT Press.

Levy, Philip. 1997. "A Political-Economy Analysis of Free Trade Agreements." *American Economic Review* 87: 513–26.

Low, Patrick, Marcelo Olarreaga, and Javier Suarez. 1998. "Does Globalization Cause a Higher Concentration of International Trade and Investment Flows?" Discussion Paper ERAD-98-08. Geneva: World Trade Organization.

Panagariya, Arvind. 1998. "The Regionalism Debate: An overview." Mimeo. Geneva: WTO, Economic Research Division.

Sapir, André. 1998. "The Political Economy of EC Regionalism." *European Economic Review* 42: 717–32.

Serra Puche, Jaime. 1998. "Regionalism and the WTO." Paper presented at the WTO Symposium, *50 Years: Looking Back, Looking Forward.* Geneva, April 30.

Schiff, Maurice. 1997. "Small Is Beautiful: Preferential Trade Agreements and the Impact of Country Size, Market Share and Smuggling." *Journal of Economic Integration* 12: 359–87.

Winters, Alan. 1991. *International Economics,* 4th ed. London: Routledge.

————. 1996. "Regionalism versus Multilateralism." Discussion Paper 1525. London: Centre for Economic Policy Research.

Winters, Alan, and Won Chang. 1997. "Regional Integration and the Prices of Imports." Working Paper 1782. Washington, D.C.: World Bank.

Wonnacott, Paul. 1996. "Beyond NAFTA: The Design of a Free Trade Agreement of the Americas." In *The Economics of Preferential Trade Agreements,* edited by Jagdish Bhagwati and Arvind Panagariya. Washington, D.C.: AEI Press.

CHAPTER SEVEN

Regional Trade Arrangements: Lessons from Past Experiences

Roberto Bouzas

During the period after World War II the major vehicles for liberalization were multilateral trade negotiations (MTNs) through successive rounds of the General Agreement on Tariffs and Trade (GATT) and the unilateral lowering of trade barriers. Preferential trade arrangements (PTAs) played a secondary role, but interest in them peaked in the 1950s and 1960s and again in the late 1980s and 1990s. In both periods developments in Europe set the pace. The two waves of PTAs differ in content, coverage, and membership, with the latter displaying a broader coverage of issues and disciplines and a more active role of the United States, traditionally the champion of the most favored nation (MFN) principle.

When their accomplishments are held up to their stated aims, PTAs have rarely been successful. In most cases commitments have not translated into policies and achievements have fallen short of goals. The European experience (particularly that of the European Community) has been the most auspicious. With less ambitious objectives and a shorter record, the Canada-U.S. Free Trade Agreement (CUSFTA) and the Australia–New Zealand Closer Economic Relations Trade Agreement (ANZCERTA) have also made significant progress toward their stated aims. However, the vast majority of PTAs have failed to meet their goals for reasons of both design and implementation.

Past experience can suggest some lessons for the future, but care must be taken in drawing general conclusions. First, the success or failure of a PTA can be measured either against the stated objectives or against alternative scenarios, but the latter case requires speculation about counterfactual information. Second, PTAs differ in structure, as suggested by the existence of several types of PTAs—preferences, free trade agreements, customs unions, and common markets. Finally, countries engage in PTAs for very different reasons.

This chapter examines past experience to draw some policy lessons for the future, but cautions against easy generalizations and focuses on policy outcomes rather than on the theoretical debate. It also sidesteps the difficult issue of whether PTAs are helpful or detrimental to the multilateral trading system, taking instead the line that the coexistence of regional and multilateral approaches to trade negotiations suggests that they are complementary rather than mutually exclusive. The chapter provides a brief overview of the various motives for forging PTAs and summarizes the record of PTAs in Europe, the Western Hemisphere, the Asia-Pacific region, and Africa, pointing out common threads and peculiarities.[1] Finally, some lessons and conclusions are drawn from the preceding discussion.

What Do Member Countries Look for in PTAs?

The incentives to enter into PTAs are diverse and may go well beyond economic considerations.[2] In effect, political and security concerns can play a decisive role in binding two or more countries together through a PTA. Yet if such an arrangement brings about persistent net losses in economic welfare to member countries, it is unlikely to survive as a voluntary one. Therefore, economic considerations play an important role in any case.

Narrow trade considerations are often seen as the objective behind participation in a PTA. However, the strongest case against PTAs comes from standard trade theory, which places PTAs in the realm of second-best outcomes.[3] In effect, Viner's discussion of static allocative effects reached the key conclusion that the welfare of countries taking part in PTAs may be reduced if trade diversion (when lower-cost suppliers are replaced by higher-cost suppliers from within the region) outweighs trade creation (when higher-cost domestic

1. Not all PTAs are between contiguous countries (as evidenced by the U.S.-Israel and EC-Israel free trade agreements), but the vast majority of them are.
2. For a discussion see Whalley (1998).
3. For the classic presentation see Viner (1950).

suppliers are replaced by lower-cost suppliers from within the region). Based on this framework, the Cooper-Massell-Johnson proposition concluded that discriminatory trade liberalization cannot improve the welfare of member countries beyond what would otherwise result from unilateral liberalization on an MFN basis. PTAs may increase members' welfare at the expense of the rest of the world (worsening the latter's terms of trade). However, this would be a recipe for conflict and retaliation and might eventually reduce aggregate welfare.[4] The ambiguous conclusions reached by standard trade theory do not get better when dynamic considerations are taken into account. Even the direction of effects over the rest of the world may change.

Another motivation to participate in a PTA is to gain insurance against future increases in trade protection. This motivation may be relevant for small countries that are vulnerable to trade policy changes made by large and important trade partners. Small countries especially may find that effective multilateral rules and enforcement capabilities are the best insurance against undue exercise of market power by larger partners. But policy choice by small economies is generally of little relevance to the performance and health of the multilateral system. Therefore, under certain circumstances buying insurance through a PTA may be an attractive option—depending upon the price to be paid for this insurance.

Governments may also find PTA membership useful to gain credibility for their domestic policies. This raises the question of whether the same credibility could not be gained from multilateral commitments. Political economy may offer an answer. Domestic groups (particularly exporters) may mobilize more readily to support a more open trade regime in the context of a PTA (in which gains from market access are more clearly identifiable) than in the context of unilateral or multilateral liberalization.[5] Regional agreements (particularly among asymmetric partners, as in North-South PTAs) may offer more effective constraints on reluctant enforcement or policy reversals than do multilateral commitments.

International bargaining considerations may also play a role. Countries may find that their bargaining stance strengthens if they act together in trade negotiations. Similarly, frustration over slow progress in multilateral negotiations

4. The Vanek-Kemp-Wan proposition challenged this, showing that a customs union can unambiguously enhance welfare if a common external tariff that prevents trade diversion is implemented. See Pomfret (1986) and Bhagwati and Panagariya (1996).

5. See Oye (1992).

may stimulate countries that share interests to come together in a PTA. Stream-lining differences between countries through PTAs may be an effective way to eventually reach a multilateral deal.

The European Experience as a Yardstick

Although PTAs have proliferated in Europe, not all have been equally successful. The most far-reaching was that of the European Community (EC), which became the centripetal force of European economic integration.[6] The European experience has been so dynamic and pathbreaking that the EC is seen as the paradigmatic example of a successful PTA and is frequently used as the yardstick against which the success and failure of PTAs is measured. In contrast, the competing European Free Trade Area (EFTA) has found it difficult to maintain its original membership: countries have gradually left to join the EC. Moreover, by the early 1990s those western European countries that remained in the EFTA had undertaken part of the EC's deepest integration commitments through the formation of the European Economic Area (EEA). At last the EC turned into a key reference for PTAs in central and eastern Europe (CEE) as well.

The European Community

The foundations of European regionalism were laid during the reconstruction that followed World War II. European regionalism benefited from the financial and political support of a security-driven U.S. policy, and it went much further than envisaged in U.S. plans. The first truly European (or rather French) initiative was the Schuman Plan of May 1950, which led the "original six" countries (Belgium, France, Germany, Italy, Luxembourg, and the Nether-lands) to sign the Treaty of Paris and establish the European Coal and Steel Community (ECSC) one year later. Although the main objective was to elimi-nate barriers and promote competition in the coal and steel industries, many specific provisions of the agreement were hardly compatible with economic liberalism.[7] The Treaty of Paris also established a supranational organ (the High Authority) that was empowered to levy taxes, influence investment de-

6. The EC superseded the European Economic Community (EEC) through the Euro-pean Union Treaty. For further analysis see Torrent (1997).

7. See Tsoukalis (1997, p. 9).

cisions, and even impose minimum prices and production quotas under certain conditions.

The signing of the Treaty of Rome in 1957 created two new institutions: the European Atomic Energy Community (EAEC) and the European Economic Community (EEC). The purpose of the EEC was to establish "the foundations for an ever-closer union among the European peoples" through the creation of a common market and, more specifically, a customs union and a limited number of sector policies. The Treaty of Rome established, among other things, the elimination of customs duties and quantitative restrictions; the adoption of a common customs tariff and of a common commercial policy toward third countries; the abolition of obstacles to freedom of movement for persons, services, and capital between member states; the adoption of common policies in the sphere of agriculture and transport; and the promotion of competition in the common market.[8] Following the precedent set by the Treaty of Paris, the Treaty of Rome established an elaborate governance structure composed of a Commission (the administrative and technical body), a Council of Ministers (the decisionmaking authority), a Court of Justice, and a Parliament. Since member states accepted the supremacy of ECC law over national law in the community's areas of competence, the traditional boundaries of national sovereignty were broken.

In 1968, one and a half years in advance of schedule, the EEC concluded the implementation of a common external tariff and the elimination of customs duties and quantitative restrictions on intra-EEC trade. But implementing policies on freedom of movement for goods, services, labor, and capital on the basis of the principle of national treatment required a painful process of harmonization. In a precedent-setting decision, in 1979 the European Court of Justice set in motion the application of the principle of mutual recognition by ruling that Germany could not prevent the French alcoholic beverage *Cassis de Dijon* from being sold in Germany because it did not meet the German standard for liquor.[9] The application of mutual recognition left behind the exhausting phase of detailed harmonization and was probably the single most important step (after the elimination of tariffs) toward the free circulation of goods.

In 1986 the Single European Act (SEA) amended the Treaty of Rome and instituted the principles of qualified majority voting and of mutual recognition in areas where there were no communitywide standards. The SEA also

8. See European Economic Community (1987).
9. See Wallace (1994, p. 76).

launched the EC92 program to complete the single market. In March 1992 a new Treaty on Closer Economic Union was signed in Maastricht. The treaty rested on three uneven pillars: the three old communities (now renamed the European Community), a Common Foreign and Security Policy (CFSP), and cooperation in the fields of justice and home affairs. The provisions for the creation of the European Monetary Union (EMU) were by far the most specific and far-reaching of the treaty.[10]

Deepening in the EC went hand in hand with widening. In effect, in 1973 the community broadened its membership to include Britain, Denmark, and Ireland, followed by Greece in 1979 and by Spain and Portugal in 1986. In 1995 the inclusion of Austria, Finland, and Sweden raised the total number of member states to fifteen. The community is projected to include at least five additional central and eastern European members by the year 2010.

The European Free Trade Association

Shortly after the Treaty of Rome was signed a group of European countries outside the EC (Austria, Denmark, Norway, Portugal, Sweden, Switzerland, and the United Kingdom) created the European Free Trade Association (EFTA).[11] In contrast to the objectives of the EC, the objectives of the EFTA were purely economic and more limited in terms of product coverage (restricted to industrial goods), potential further development, and political engagement.[12] In effect, the EFTA process was wholly intergovernmental, with no common court or system of law.

The centripetal forces unveiled by the EC could not be resisted by the EFTA. In the early 1970s the members of the EFTA negotiated bilateral industrial free trade agreements with the EC, to be followed shortly by the accession of Denmark and the United Kingdom to the EC. Portugal followed suit in 1986, and Austria, Finland, and Sweden adhered to the EC in 1995. As a result, by the late 1990s only Iceland, Liechtenstein, Norway (where a plebiscite to join the EC was defeated in 1995), and Switzerland remained EFTA members.

In 1992, building upon the bilateral free trade agreements concluded in the early 1970s, the EC and EFTA member states created a European Economic

10. Tsoukalis (1997, p. 52).

11. The EFTA was created in 1960. Iceland joined in 1970. Finland became an associate member in 1961 and a full member in 1986. Liechtenstein joined in 1992.

12. Wallace (1994, pp. 31–32).

Area (EEA). The agreement incorporated many facets of the EC (such as the free circulation of persons, goods, services, and capital; competition rules; and EC law as a common base of reference), but did not provide for participation of the EFTA countries in EC decisionmaking, the Common Agricultural Policy (CAP), or the common external tariff. That the EEA agreement did not satisfy all EFTA member states was demonstrated by the fact that Austria, Finland, Norway, and Sweden negotiated accession agreements immediately after the EEA was established.

Trade Discrimination in Central and Eastern Europe

Before the collapse of centrally planned economies in the late 1980s, most central and eastern European (CEE) economies were members of the Council for Mutual Economic Assistance (CMEA), which was founded in 1949 under the coordination of the Soviet Union. The disintegration of the CMEA was followed by the signature of regional and bilateral PTAs throughout the region (including some former Soviet republics). The two major agreements were the Europe Agreements between the EU and six CEE countries (Bulgaria, the Czech Republic, Hungary, Poland, Romania, and Slovakia) signed in 1992–93 and the Central European Free Trade Agreement (CEFTA) signed in March 1993 between the Czech Republic, Hungary, Poland, and Slovakia (joined by Slovenia in 1996).[13]

The trade component of the Europe Agreements provides for the establishment of a free trade area for industrial products among the EU and the CEE economies over a period of ten years. The agreements cover not only trade in merchandise (except agricultural merchandise), but also trade in services, foreign investment, payments systems, capital markets regulations, and broader economic cooperation. The Europe Agreements are generally regarded as having played a positive role in the transition of CEE countries to a market economy by improving market access to the EU, stimulating mutual trade and foreign investment, and reducing uncertainty in the context of far-reaching structural change.

The original CEFTA called for the complete elimination of trade barriers to industrial products by the year 2001, with exceptions for agricultural and

13. Other agreements have included bilateral FTAs with EFTA countries, an FTA among the Baltic countries, and a set of other bilateral agreements, including an agreement to establish a customs union between the Czech Republic and Slovakia. See Drábek (1997).

"sensitive" products, with each member country negotiating separate bilateral protocols on the speed and extent of concessions. The rationale for the CEFTA was based on "natural" partnership and cultural and historical commonality. The impediments have been sizable: recurrent problems of implementation (aggravated by a highly unstable macroeconomic environment) and modest political incentives. The scope of the CEFTA has been more limited than that of the Europe Agreements between the CEE economies and the EU.

Preferential Trade Arrangements in the Western Hemisphere

The history of PTAs in the Western Hemisphere is one of contrasts.[14] Discrimination was largely absent in North America for most of the period after World War II until the mid-1980s, when the United States embraced PTAs as a complement to its traditional multilateral stance, unexpectedly spurring the establishment of the first PTA between developed and developing countries.[15] In contrast, PTAs flourished in Latin America and the Caribbean. Although the early PTAs in Latin America and the Caribbean were largely paper commitments, by the late 1980s a new, more outward-looking trade policy environment brought about new incentives to establish PTAs in the late 1990s.

Despite the evident predominance of a multilateral approach, during the period after World War II discrimination was not completely absent from U.S. trade policies. Prominent examples of discrimination were the exclusion of communist countries from the benefits of the MFN principle, the U.S.-Canada Auto Pact, the Generalized System of Preferences (GSP), the Caribbean Basin Initiative, and the U.S.-Israel Free Trade Agreement. However, throughout the period discrimination was subordinate to MFN liberalization under the auspices of the GATT. Moreover, discriminatory arrangements made up a relatively minor share of total U.S. foreign trade, and they were basically driven by security or foreign policy considerations.

This stance has changed since the mid-1980s. Neither the CUSFTA nor NAFTA can be adequately understood on purely foreign policy or strategic grounds. International bargaining considerations provided the basic thrust for the U.S. drift toward PTAs with Canada and Mexico in the late 1980s. From the

14. Bouzas and Ros (1994).

15. The CUSFTA and NAFTA were outgrowths of this. The United States also joined the move to establish the APEC and FTAA, both of which are in their early stages.

U.S. standpoint, establishment of the CUSFTA was stimulated by growing dissatisfaction (particularly in Congress) with the evolution of the multilateral trading regime. To a significant extent the NAFTA was an outgrowth of this as well. The modest results—from a U.S. standpoint—achieved in the Tokyo Round and the failure to make substantial progress in the early years of the Uruguay Round stimulated a bilateral emphasis on advancing U.S. trade interests. Approval of the Single European Act in 1986 and growing fears of a "Fortress Europe" were also influential. Growing congressional participation in trade policymaking also supported discrimination and a bilateral approach: since the mid-1970s each new piece of trade legislation has emphasized the use of unilateral and bilateral mechanisms (including PTAs) to promote U.S. trade objectives. On balance, both the CUSFTA and NAFTA served to advance the "new issues" of trade in services, protection of intellectual property rights, and foreign investment. Moreover, the NAFTA included two side agreements on labor and the environment, which allowed for the possibility of lifting trade concessions when governments fail to meet national standards.

The Canadian and Mexican incentives to enter into an FTA with the United States varied. For Canada the dominant objective was to guarantee more stable access to the U.S. market by limiting U.S. discretion in the implementation of trade remedy laws and by protecting Canadian exporters from future increases in U.S. protection. Mexico was also interested in increasing its attractiveness to foreign investors, as well as in buying credibility for and locking in domestic reform policies.

Both the CUSFTA and the NAFTA were less ambitious than the EC. PTAs in North America did not consider the creation of a common market (with full mobility of labor) or even a customs union. However, both agreements (and particularly the NAFTA) are outstanding examples of a new generation of GATT-plus PTAs that include commitments to "deeper integration."[16] The CUSFTA eliminated tariff and nontariff barriers on goods, but maintained certain exceptions (such as for beer) or covered certain goods only partially (such as agricultural products or textiles).[17] The provisions on services were innovative, as no multilateral agreement was yet in place, but many important sectors were excluded. Moreover, prevailing discrimination was grandfathered. Canadian restrictions on foreign investment were relaxed, but not eliminated, whereas

16. Lawrence (1996, p. 62).
17. Waverman (1991).

contingent protection remained untouched except for the substitution of internal judicial review procedures for binational panels.

The NAFTA differed from the CUSFTA in a number of ways. First, it was the first PTA to bring together developed and developing countries. Second, in some areas the NAFTA went beyond the CUSFTA, expanding the GATT-plus features of the latter. The NAFTA provisions on trade in services, protection of intellectual property rights, and rules against distortions to investment are more comprehensive.[18] The NAFTA's major shortcoming is a complex and detailed system of rules of origin for products such as automobiles, electronic goods, textiles, and apparel. The unfinished business includes sector exceptions (Mexican energy and Canadian "cultural" industries), harmonization of contingent protection, and creation of subsidies (particularly in agriculture). There is agreement that the CUSFTA has contributed to the expansion of the U.S.-Canada bilateral trade and investment flows. The assessment is more mixed in regard to the effects that the CUSFTA may have had on contingent protection: although harassment of Canadian exporters may have diminished, discretion in the implementation of U.S. "trade remedy legislation" is still an issue.[19]

The NAFTA is younger than the CUSFTA, which makes any assessment tentative. Since the enforcement of the trilateral agreement, trade and foreign investment have increased (probably contributing to Mexico's recovery from the sharp 1995 recession), while inter- and intraindustry specialization has proceeded along the expected lines. The NAFTA also contributed to locking in policy reforms in Mexico, although countries such as Chile have been equally capable of sustaining reforms without bilateral commitments such as those of the NAFTA. Similarly, as may be expected, most of the burden of adjusting to the NAFTA has been borne by the smaller and most heavily protected economy. This has coincided with a worsening of the regional and functional distribution of income in Mexico. However, it is uncertain what the role of the NAFTA in this process has been.

In contrast to the North American experience, during most of the period after World War II Latin American and Caribbean countries engaged actively in PTAs. In 1960, under the inspiration of the United Nations Economic Commission for Latin America (ECLAC), Mexico and six South American countries established the Latin American Free Trade Association (LAFTA) with the objective of eliminating all barriers to intraregional trade in twelve years. By

18. Hufbauer and Schott (1993, p. 2).
19. Weston (1996). For a more critical assessment see Wilkinson (1997).

the mid-1960s the LAFTA had increased its membership to eleven countries, but each annual round of tariff-cutting negotiations rendered decreasing returns. Special financial arrangements (such as the Agreement on Multilateral Settlements and Reciprocal Credits) and new mechanisms (such as complementation agreements enabling two or more countries to liberalize trade on a sectoral basis) contributed to intraregional trade. However, the initial objective of establishing a free trade area in twelve years was not met.

In 1969 a subset of LAFTA member countries (Bolivia, Chile, Colombia, Ecuador, and Peru) signed the Cartagena Agreement and established a more ambitious Andean Common Market. The member countries expected that the new institutional arrangements embodied in the agreement would overcome many of the shortcomings of the LAFTA. An executive body with "supranational" powers was established, and a schedule for trade liberalization and gradual implementation of a common external tariff to be completed in 1980 was agreed upon. The agreement also included mechanisms to promote an equitable distribution of benefits.[20]

PTAs were not restricted to South America. In 1960 Costa Rica, El Salvador, Guatemala, Honduras, and Nicaragua set the more ambitious objective of creating a Central American Common Market (CACM), superseding a 1958 free trade agreement. The aim was to develop a free trade area (in industrial goods) in a period of five years and to implement a common external tariff. Although not all objectives were fully met, the CACM was regarded as one of the few successful agreements among developing countries. Intraregional liberalization proceeded swiftly, and trade expanded rapidly, especially in industrial products.

To complete the regional chessboard a Caribbean Free Trade Agreement (CARIFTA) was signed in 1967, to be superseded six years later by the agreement establishing the Caribbean Community (CARICOM), the objective of which was to create a customs union and a common market. In the initial years of the CARIFTA intraregional trade increased, but it stalled as of the mid-1970s.

This first generation of Latin American and Caribbean PTAs shared a number of common features. First, all agreements were targeted at strengthening weak trade relations rather than at providing a more positive framework for already existing economic ties. Second, PTAs were regarded as a complement to import substitution industrialization: broader regional markets would remove the constraints posed by small domestic markets. Third, pragmatism was

20. Ffrench-Davis (1995, p. 94).

dominant, and many original commitments (for instance, to regional planning and coordination of direct foreign investment) were overly ambitious and were never met.

Despite these common threads, the performance of these PTAs was not completely similar: in particular, and in contrast to the LAFTA and CARIFTA, the CACM made significant progress during its first decade. The reasons for the CACM's relative success were both political and economic. One factor was a tradition of colonial administrative unity and repeated attempts at political unification. Economic factors included the favorable contribution of emerging industrial interests and the limited opposition posed by established producers (industrialization in the CACM proceeded at the same rate as the implementation of trade preferences).

By the 1970s it was apparent that economic integration had failed to fulfill its promise. Contributing factors were protectionist trade regimes, conflicting interests, weak economic ties, chronic macroeconomic instability, and overly ambitious targets. Lack of progress in the 1970s was followed by a collapse in the 1980s. The Montevideo Treaty of 1980 created the Latin American Integration Association (LAIA) in substitution for the LAFTA. The LAIA included more flexible mechanisms, such as a wider scope for bilateral agreements, the benefits of which may not be extended to the rest of the LAIA members on an MFN basis. Despite Venezuela's accession in 1973, the Andean Pact waned in the 1970s, with Chile withdrawing in 1976 after a new government departed radically from prevailing economic policies. The CACM and the CARICOM also stalled, the former seriously challenged by growing political tensions.

The turning point for PTAs was in the 1980s, when the debt crisis led to an increase in import barriers and a sharp contraction of intraregional trade. By the end of the decade most Latin American and Caribbean PTAs were largely paper commitments, with a remarkable gap between reality and objectives. After the NAFTA negotiations and the launching of the Enterprise for the Americas Initiative in 1990, PTAs gained new life throughout the region. Since the late 1980s trade policy reform and more outward-oriented trade regimes have also spurred the establishment of PTAs.

The result of this revival has been a "spaghetti bowl" of PTAs linking pairs or groups of countries. In contrast to the previous goal of expanding protected domestic markets, the new focus of trade liberalization in Latin America and the Caribbean has been on improving and securing market access, facilitating industrial restructuring, and enhancing the economies' attractiveness for foreign investment. International bargaining considerations have also played a role, particularly after the swift change in the U.S. trade policy stance.[21]

The revival of trade discrimination in the region materialized in two stylized approaches. One was multiple FTA negotiations. The second was the creation of customs unions. The first approach was characteristic of Chile and Mexico, which have signed bilateral or trilateral FTAs with Latin American and Caribbean partners. The second approach was best exemplified by the establishment of the Southern Common Market (Mercosur) comprising Argentina, Brazil, Paraguay, and Uruguay. The Mercosur made significant progress toward a free trade area in a brief period of time, and intraregional trade flows experienced a significant rise.[22] Although nontariff barriers and nonborder measures still pose market access problems, preferences have reached 100 percent over MFN tariff rates for nearly all products, with the remainder subject to an automatic schedule for liberalization to be concluded in 1999.

The major question regarding PTAs in the Western Hemisphere is whether negotiations to create a Free Trade Area of the Americas (FTAA) will succeed in bringing together these multiple strands of trade discrimination. Negotiations were launched in April 1998, but differences remain as to the shape of the agreement and its mode of implementation.

Preferential Trade Arrangements in Asia and the Pacific

PTAs have been neither popular nor successful in the Asia-Pacific area. The major initiatives have been the establishment of the Association of Southeast Asian Nations (ASEAN) in 1977 (transformed into the ASEAN Free Trade Area in the early 1990s), the Australia–New Zealand Closer Economic Relations Trade Agreement (ANZCERTA) in 1983, and the South Asian Preferential Trade Area (SAPTA), which was created in 1993 by the South Asian Association for Regional Cooperation (SAARC). The Asia Pacific Economic Cooperation (APEC) forum launched in 1989 has a Pacific rather than an Asian scope (it includes Canada, Chile, Mexico, and the United States), but so far it

21. Bouzas (1995).

22. Some have argued that the rapid increase in intra-Mercosur trade (the ratio of intraregional exports to total exports rose from 11 percent in 1991 to 24 percent in 1997) is largely explained by trade diversion. However, this is unlikely to be the case, because Mercosur liberalization occurred at the same rate as a significant unilateral trade opening. See Bouzas (1997).

has established only loose commitments and has failed to come up with a blueprint for trade liberalization.

The ANZCERTA brought together two countries with similar political institutions and cultural traditions at a time when both were undergoing a process of far-reaching economic reform. In practice, it is the only agreement that can be called a success in the region. The ASEAN's record with the ASEAN Preferential Trade Area (APTA) and AFTA has been poor: preferential liberalization has advanced slowly, and intraregional trade flows have remained modest. The record in South Asia is gloomier.

Various reasons have been offered to explain the comparatively short experience with PTAs in the Asia-Pacific area and their limited success. One is the region's reliance on world rather than regional or domestic markets. Moreover, in the past the GATT regime gave ample room to domestic trade policy autonomy, enabling the survival of local institutions and trade policy regimes. Despite these features, intraregional trade has expanded fast, mainly as a result of the region's high rates of economic growth rather than of PTAs.

The AFTA was the outgrowth of the APTA launched in 1977 by the ASEAN. The ASEAN was established in 1967 by Brunei, Indonesia, Malaysia, the Philippines, Singapore, and Thailand to address security and strategic concerns, but with no economic objectives at the onset.[23] In 1977 the member countries launched the APTA, but it remained essentially dormant until the early 1990s. In 1992 it was superseded by an agreement to establish an ASEAN Free Trade Area (AFTA) within a period of fifteen years.[24]

The APTA, based on a "positive" list strategy, took a piecemeal approach to PTAs. A decade after inception only a handful of products had been covered by preferences, with a very modest impact on bilateral trade flows. One reason for slow progress was the prevailing differences in trade protection and the anticipated asymmetric effects of trade liberalization on member countries. Trade within the region was very modest and increased little after the agreement.

The AFTA agreement established the removal of all quantitative restrictions and the reduction of tariffs to the 0 to 5 percent range by the year 2007, which was later advanced to 2003. The tariff-cutting mechanism, or Common Effective Preferential Tariff (CEPT), excluded unprocessed agricultural products,

23. Vietnam joined the ASEAN in 1995, and Burma and Laos joined in 1997.
24. Panagariya (1997).

natural resources, and services. Preliminary evidence suggests that the effects of the AFTA on intraregional trade flows have been very modest, partly due to the slow pace of implementation, multiple exceptions, and the limited industrial complementation among member countries.

The predecessor to the ANZCERTA was a 1965 bilateral free trade agreement that provided for the establishment of a free trade area by 1977 for forest products and selected manufactured products, but left untouched nontariff barriers. In contrast, the ANZCERTA covered trade in all merchandise and included tariff and nontariff barriers, providing external support to far-reaching domestic economic liberalization programs.[25] The 1988 and 1992 reviews went beyond the original commitments to include, among other issues, nonborder barriers, services, antidumping procedures, business law and regulatory practices, and government procurement.

The ANZCERTA has been the only successful PTA in the Asia-Pacific region, and it and its members display several peculiarities that are worth noting. The first is its relatively low degree of institutionalization: the ANZCERTA rests on a continuous review process that has gradually extended its agenda, imposed requirements for increased transparency, and fostered consultations when required by any government.[26] The second feature is the weak economic interdependence among the member countries. Finally, New Zealand and Australia have similar institutions and preferences, and both undertook far-reaching economic liberalization.

In 1993 the members of the SAARC created a South Asian Preferential Trade Area (SAPTA).[27] The agreement aimed at periodic negotiations to exchange trade concessions on a sector or product-by-product basis. In the first round of negotiations, held in 1995, concessions—mainly tariff concessions—were minimal. During the second round, in 1996, the member countries decided to establish a free trade area by 2005, a deadline that was advanced to 2000 in 1997. However, these commitments seem beyond reach considering the relatively high level of protection that prevails in the region, the low volumes of intraregional trade, and the tradition of political and even military conflict among member countries.

25. See World Trade Organization (1995, p. 36).
26. Khaler (1995, p. 109).
27. The SAARC includes Bangladesh, Bhutan, India, the Maldives, Nepal, Pakistan, and Sri Lanka.

Finally, the Asian-Pacific Economic Co-operation (APEC) forum was established in 1989. Its first four years were devoted to issues of organization, membership, and process. At the 1993 Seattle summit the intention to promote a free trade area in the region was first mentioned. One year later in Bogor (Indonesia) a commitment was made to establish free trade by the year 2010, with an extension to 2020 for developing countries that were members.[28]

How the APEC will progress toward free trade is still unknown. There are at least two conflicting visions as to how it should proceed. Although many Asian members prefer the so-called concerted unilateral approach (unilateral liberalization on an MFN basis), the United States and others are inclined toward negotiated liberalization on a reciprocal basis. Internal differences go beyond the formal means toward trade liberalization. Trade regimes, development levels, and cultural and political traditions also differ widely among members.

Preferential Trade Arrangements in Africa and the Middle East

Regional integration in sub-Saharan Africa has a long history, with the Southern Africa Customs Union (SACU) created in 1910 and the East African Community (EAC) established in 1919. The SACU still survives, but the EAC was dissolved in 1978.[29] Most PTAs established in the 1970s were an integral component of the African postcolonial development strategy. This fact explains the large number of arrangements and their different objectives. However, PTAs in Africa and the Middle East have shown little progress either in implementation or in fostering closer economic ties. Indeed the vast majority of the agreements have failed to materialize and have experienced a high degree of noncompliance.

There are several reasons for these failures, among others the prevailing development pattern (largely inward oriented and led by the public sector), similar production structures, slow economic growth, divergent regulatory frameworks, and poor infrastructure. Diverse political and governance systems also limited the effectiveness of regional economic integration.

Most African PTAs have been made among sub-Saharan countries. The Economic Commission for Africa promoted three subregional arrangements,

28. Dieter (1997, p. 157).
29. Lyakurwa (1996, p. 116).

two of which, the Economic Commission for West African States (ECOWAS) and the Common Market for Eastern and Southern Africa (COMESA), have been in place for a number of years.[30] Each of these includes, in turn, several subregional arrangements.

The ECOWAS was established in 1975 with sixteen member countries, seven of which were already part of the French-speaking West African Economic Community (CEAO). Three other countries were members of the Mano River Union. The ECOWAS failed to establish free trade among its members. Some of the smaller groupings, such as the West African Economic and Monetary Union (UEMOA)—which arose upon the demise of the CEAO—survived. The UEMOA has a parallel central African organization, the Central African Economic and Monetary Union (UDEAC), with six members. Overall, intraregional trade is modest and largely concentrated in livestock and in agricultural and petroleum products.

The COMESA embraces twenty-two countries and began in 1981 as the Preferential Trade Area for Eastern and Southern Africa (PTA). Its original aim was to establish a common market by the year 2000. The PTA was best known for its institutional development.[31] Smaller subregional arrangements in southern Africa include the Southern African Development Community (SADC) and the SACU. The SADC replaced the Southern African Development Coordination Conference (SADCC), which was made up of the participants in a set of loose economic cooperative and development arrangements aimed at ending economic dependence on South Africa. In contrast to its predecessor, the SADC has adopted measures that involve tariff reductions and the removal of nontariff barriers. The longevity of the SACU has been explained by side payments made by its dominant partner, South Africa.

PTAs in northern Africa and the Middle East date back to the 1957 Agreement for Economic Unity among Arab League States, which comprised twenty-one Arab member countries and provided for the creation of an Arab Common Market. Yet the agreement's achievements fell short of its members' stated commitments.

The most serious attempt by a North African group of countries to establish a PTA was the Arab Maghreb Union (AMU), which was formed in September 1989, but its success has been limited. Intraregional trade was limited by its

30. Aryeetey and Oduro (1996, p. 20).
31. Aryeetey and Oduro (1996, p. 25).

members' similar resource endowments, limited potential for internal specialization, and proximity to European markets.[32]

The leading regional arrangement in the Middle East has been the Gulf-
Cooperation Council (GCC), which was formed in 1981 by the Arabic gulf
states. Its success was slightly greater than that of the AMU, with some
preferences exchanged and some progress made in coordinating monetary
policy and enabling the free movement of people between member countries.[33]

Lessons from Past Experiences

Drawing clear-cut lessons from past experience is not easy: PTAs differ
widely in motivations, objectives, and scope. Successful PTAs usually share
some of the following attributes: they increase members' trade interdependence, display a high correlation between commitments and achievements, and
include a broadening coverage of issues.[34] The EC is the classic example, but
the CUSFTA and ANZCERTA may also qualify as success stories. Failure, in
contrast, can be postulated when there is no perceived effect on economic
interdependence or there is a large gap between commitments and achievements. In such cases the agreements tend to remain largely symbolic. As in the
case of other international institutions, they rarely die.

The EC is generally taken as the yardstick for measuring success or failure
in regional integration. But for many reasons (including historical and political
reasons) the European experience is highly specific and probably nonreplicable.
Yet a number of conclusions can be drawn from it. Their relevance and
applicability need to be assessed in the specific circumstances concerned.

THE NEED FOR POLITICAL COMMITMENT. Political motivations have
been frequently cited as motivating factors for PTAs, but they are neither
necessary nor sufficient for success. A large number of PTAs (particularly
among developing countries) had strong political motivations at their origin,

32. Dent (1997, p. 55).
33. Dent (1997, p. 55).
34. These criteria are inconclusive. A PTA may increase members' interdependence,
meet its stated goals, and deepen, but at the same time hurt the rest of the world. If a
cosmopolitan yardstick is used, such an arrangement can hardly be qualified as a
success.

but fell rapidly into lethargy. Political motivations played a relatively unimportant role in successful agreements such as the CUSFTA. Past experience suggests that rather than political motivation, a key condition for a success is political commitment. Although the basis of and motivations for such a commitment may differ, a PTA will most likely fail in its absence.

THE ROLE OF AN ENABLING ENVIRONMENT.   The strength of PTA members' political commitment will be dependent upon the broader governance and economic policy environment. All success stories involve developed countries with mature governance institutions, stable macroeconomic environments, and a relatively high degree of commonality of values and objectives. These environmental factors provide a shared and stable background for implementing commitments.

When governance institutions are subject to abrupt change, commitments rarely translate into implementation. Similarly, in a highly unstable macroeconomic environment the sustainability of trade policy reforms (unilateral or preferential) is highly uncertain. Finally, shared values and objectives provide a common framework from which to build.

The trade policy environment is a particularly relevant factor, as suggested by the experience of the EC, CUSFTA, and ANZCERTA. Relatively low protection in member countries will contribute to the success of a PTA because it will result in less resistance to lowering tariffs. A shift toward trade liberalization is also likely to dissolve opposition to a PTA. The latter may also (but not necessarily) turn into a supporting factor for overall trade liberalization.

INSTITUTIONS AND PTAS.   The kind of institutionalization adopted by the EC is often referred to as a key to its success. But conventional stories about supranational authorities and the role of the European Court of Justice (ECJ) have been exaggerated. In reality, the EC institutions have been the result of an uneasy, evolving mix of intergovernmental and supranational competence and decisionmaking. The level of compliance with EC regulations or ECJ decisions has been high, but lower than implied by conventional stories about the EC. Moreover, after almost two decades of painful harmonization the EC abandoned centralized regulations and adopted the principle of mutual recognition.

The existence of a bureaucratic locus representing the "common interest" has also been highlighted as a reason for the EC's success. But neither the

CUSFTA nor the ANZCERTA has such a locus. Moreover, both have rather slim institutions. Although not all share the view that the EC bureaucracy was a key to its progress in economic integration, there is widespread agreement that it played an important role at times of stagnation.

DISTRIBUTION OF COSTS AND BENEFITS. The issue of the distribution of costs and benefits occupied a central role in the EC experience. The existence of institutions and mechanisms addressing distributive considerations is generally regarded as having prevented the latter from becoming a barrier to more integration. Occasionally distributive considerations have been addressed at the expense of more liberal trade policies (such as the Common Agricultural Policy). In the case of the EC, "variable geometry" arrangements have also been used as a means to circumvent the dilemmas posed by distributive issues or by disparate preferences or policy priorities.

Other PTAs, such as the CUSFTA and ANZCERTA, have placed more trust in market mechanisms. Whether this is a viable option for PTAs involving countries with large differences in per capita incomes or levels of development may be clarified by the NAFTA's record.

In PTAs among developed countries the distribution of costs and benefits has been facilitated by intraindustry specialization. Intraindustry trade involves less income redistribution and less dislocation of factors of production, thus limiting the extent of domestic opposition to trade liberalization.

DEEPENING AND LEVELING OF THE PLAYING FIELD. Functional interpretations of the EC experience underline the fact that successful economic integration calls for continuous deepening. As market integration develops the demand for a more stable and predictable environment increases, thus stimulating a deepening of the scope of regional agreements. Similarly, as market integration grows, demands for a level playing field mount.

Yet for the issue of policy harmonization to be effectively addressed from the start, a dominant partner is necessary. If this is not the case, harmonization is unlikely to be fully dealt with from the beginning. Eventually, as demands mount, policy harmonization and deepening initiatives may be negotiated and enforced. During the initial phases of an agreement the issue of market access must be an absolute priority. If market access cannot be guaranteed, harmonization and deepening initiatives will remain paper commitments.

Conclusions

PTAs are the result of a variety of motives, which include political, strategic, bargaining, and trade policy considerations. PTAs have rarely resulted from a careful, objective examination of economic costs and benefits. But the existence of net economic benefits and the issue of their distribution among member countries have turned into important factors as agreements have been implemented.

Political motivations may not be necessary to launch an agreement, but political commitment is necessary for success. This makes mature institutions, a stable macroeconomic environment, and a relatively high degree of commonality of values and objectives important preconditions. Liberal trade regimes (or a shift toward liberalization) are also necessary for a PTA to succeed in preferential liberalization.

The institutional design of successful PTAs differs. At one extreme is the EC, with highly structured institutions and supranational decisionmaking. Other successful initiatives have adopted alternative frameworks. Considering the multitude of failed regional integration experiences, institutional design does not appear to be a major explanatory factor.

The revival of PTAs in the last decade has been accompanied by two major novelties. The first has been the broad coverage of issues concomitant to the extension of the international trade agenda. The other has been the adoption by the United States of PTAs as a complement to its traditional multilateral stance. The latter deserves close attention, as its evolution will influence whether the present regionalist drive will complement or conflict with the multilateral system. In the end, the question of whether PTAs will be building or stumbling blocks to an effective multilateral system must be answered empirically.

References

Aryeetey, E., and A. D. Oduro. 1996. "Regional Integration Efforts in Africa: An Overview." In *Regionalism and the Global Economy: The Case of Africa*, edited by J. J. Teunissen. The Hague: Fund on Debt and Development.

Bhagwati, J., and A. Panagariya. 1996. *The Economics of Preferential Trade Agreements*. Washington, D.C.: AEI Press.

Bouzas, R. 1995. "Preferential Trade Liberalization in the Western Hemisphere: NAFTA and Beyond." In *Regionalism and the Global Economy: The Case of Latin*

America and the Caribbean, edited by J. J. Teunissen. The Hague: Fund on Debt and Development.

———. 1997. "El Mercosur: Una Evaluación sobre Su Desarrollo y Desafíos Actuales." In *Regionalización e Integración Económica: Instituciones y Procesos Comparados*, edited by R. Bouzas. Buenos Aires: Nuevohacer.

Bouzas, R., and J. Ros. 1994. "The North-South Variety of Economic Integration. Issues and Prospects for Latin America." In *Economic Integration in the Western Hemisphere*, edited by R. Bouzas and J. Ros. University of Notre Dame Press.

Dent, C. 1997. *The European Economy: The Global Context*. London: Routledge.

Dieter, H. 1997. "El Regionalismo en la Región Asia-Pacífico." In *Regionalización e Integración Económica: Instituciones y Procesos Comparados,* edited by R. Bouzas. Buenos Aires: Nuevohacer.

Drábek, Z. 1997. "Regional and Sub-Regional Integration in Central and Eastern Europe: An Overview." In *Regionalism and the Global Economy: The Case of Central and Eastern Europe,* edited by J. J. Teunissen. The Hague: Fund on Debt and Development.

European Economic Community. 1987. *Treaties Establishing the European Community*. Luxembourg: Office for Official Publications of the European Community.

Ffrench-Davis, R. 1995. "Trends in Regional Cooperation in Latin America: The Crucial Role of Intra-Regional Trade." In *Regionalism and the Global Economy: The Case of Latin America and the Caribbean,* edited by J. J. Teunissen. The Hague: Fund on Debt and Development.

Hufbauer, G. C., and J. J. Schott. 1993. *NAFTA: An Assessment*. Washington, D.C.: Institute for International Economics.

Khaler, M. 1995. *International Institutions and the Political Economy of Integration*. Washington, D.C.: Brookings.

Lawrence, R. 1996. *Regionalism, Multilateralism, and Deeper Integration*. Washington, D.C.: Brookings.

Lyakurwa, W. M. 1996. "Trade and Investment Integration in Sub-Saharan Africa." In *Regionalism and the Global Economy: The Case of Africa,* edited by J. J. Teunissen. The Hague: Fund on Debt and Development.

Oye, K. 1992. *Economic Discrimination and Political Exchange*. Princeton University Press.

Panagariya, A. 1997. "Preferential Trading and Asia." Discussion paper for FONDAD's concluding Conference on Regionalism and the Global Economy, The Hague, November.

Pomfret, R. 1986. "The Theory of Preferential Trading Arrangements." *Weltwirtschaftliches Archiv* 122: 3.

Torrent, R. 1997. "La Union Europea: Naturaleza Institucional, Dilemas Actuales y Perspectivas." In *Regionalización e Integración Económica: Instituciones y Procesos Comparados,* edited by R. Bouzas. Buenos Aires: Nuevohacer.

Tsoukalis, L. 1997. *The New European Economy Revisited.* Oxford: Oxford University Press.

Viner, J. 1950. *The Customs Union Issue.* New York: Carnegie Endowment for International Peace.

Wallace, W. 1994. *Regional Integration: The West European Experience.* Washington, D.C.: Brookings.

Waverman, L. 1991. "A Canadian Vision of North American Economic Integration." In *Continental Accord: North American Economic Integration,* edited by S. Globerman. Vancouver: Fraser Institute.

Weston, A. 1996. "Los Tratados de Libre Comercio de América del Norte: Una Perspectiva." *Integración y Comercio* (Enero–Abril).

Whalley, J. 1998. "Why Do Countries Seek Regional Trade Agreements?" In *The Regionalization of the World Economy,* edited by J. A. Frankel. Chicago: University of Chicago Press.

Wilkinson, B. W. 1997. "NAFTA in the World Economy: Lessons and Issues for Latin America." In *Western Hemisphere Trade Integration,* edited by R. G. Lipsey and P. Meller. Houndmills, U.K.: Macmillan.

World Trade Organization. 1995. *Regionalism and the World Trading System.* Geneva.

Part Three

ENHANCING TRADE RULES

CHAPTER EIGHT

Multilateral Approaches to Market Access Negotiations

Sam Laird

This chapter addresses multilateral negotiating techniques in the areas of most favored nation (MFN) tariffs and certain nontariff measures (NTMs). It does not cover market access in the sector of services, nor does it contain any detailed discussion of issues covered by other authors such as government procurement, safeguards, trade remedy laws, and trade-related investment measures (TRIMs). Export restrictions are not discussed. Although the objective is not to review the results of the Uruguay Round, it is inevitably necessary to make some reference to the procedures used in earlier rounds, since these provide the base for future market access negotiations.[1]

Tariffs

The main idea behind the tariff negotiations of the General Agreement on Tariffs and Trade (GATT) was to reduce and "bind" (or fix) MFN tariff rates, creating enhanced and more secure access to the markets of GATT contracting parties. Whatever is negotiated between particular trading partners is a "concession" available to all other members of the World Trade Organization

---

1. Those who wish to reexamine the results of the round are directed to Croome (1995), GATT (1993, 1994), Martin and Winters (1995) and articles therein, and Organization for Economic Cooperation and Development (OECD) (1993), among others.

(WTO) by application of the MFN principle. WTO members agree to bind their MFN tariff rates at negotiated levels so that such rates may not be increased except through the renegotiation of bindings under Article XXVIII of the GATT. Such renegotiation is done with the member with which the concession was first negotiated as well as any other member with a "principal supplying interest."[2]

Many developing countries have applied MFN rates that are substantially below their bound levels ("ceiling" bindings) as a result of unilateral rate reductions in the last ten to twenty years. In the Uruguay Round they sought "credit" for these reductions, but there is little evidence that they received tariff cuts on exports of interest to them for such reductions. The higher bound levels persist because individually their markets are often small and their offer to bind the applied rates is a reciprocal concession that is of little interest to developed members, a weakness of the approach under which bilateral negotiations initially are conducted on an item-by-item basis that is later to be applied on an MFN basis. The absence of such bindings leaves some uncertainty that may be discouraging to foreign investment and therefore to technology transfer and development.

Increasing the extent of bindings was one of the main objectives of the Uruguay Round, and the major result was the substantial increase in bindings by developing countries (see table 8-1). Although there was no specific target for industrial goods, it was agreed that all rates for agricultural products would be bound. Overall, the percentage of developed countries' imports of industrial goods under bound rates rose from 94 to 99 percent. However, developing economies increased their share of bound rates from 14 to 59 percent, and transition economies increased theirs from 74 to 96 percent. Most Latin American countries bound close to 100 percent of their tariff rates. Asia as a region has the lowest level: only 67 percent of industrial tariff rates are now bound.

Over the course of the eight GATT rounds since 1949, the industrial countries' import-weighted average tariffs on industrial products have been reduced from some 40 percent to 3.9 percent. Tariff reductions were also a key objective of the Uruguay Round, where the goal was to reduce average tariff levels by at least as much as in the Tokyo Round (that is, by a third) for industrial products

2. The Uruguay Round gave such additional rights to the country for which exports of a certain product represented the highest proportion of its total exports, even though it might not be the largest supplier to the country raising the duty.

Table 8-1. Pre– and Post–Uruguay Round Scope of Bindings for Industrial Products (Excluding Petroleum)

Country group or region	Number of lines	Import value[a]	Percentage of tariff lines bound		Percentage of imports under bound rates	
			Pre-UR	Post-UR	Pre-UR	Post-UR
By major country group						
Developed economies	86,968	737.2	78	99	94	99
Developing economies[b]	157,805	306.2	22	72	14	59
Transition economies	18,962	34.7	73	98	74	96
By selected region						
North America	14,138	325.7	99	100	99	100
Latin America	64,136	40.4	38	100	57	100
Western Europe	57,851	239.9	79	82	98	98
Central Europe	23,565	38.1	63	98	68	97
Asia	82,545	415.4	17	67	36	70

Source: GATT (1994).

a. Billions of U.S. dollars.

b. The data on developing countries were based on twenty-six out of ninety-three developing country participants in the Uruguay Round, representing 80 percent of merchandise trade and 30 percent of tariff lines.

(including manufactured goods, tropical products, and natural resource–based products, but not petroleum products). In the end, the average trade-weighted tariff rate on all industrial products from all sources was reduced by 38 percent, whereas the average reduction on imports from developing countries was 34 percent.[3] Overall, at the end of the implementation period in 2005, the industrial countries' import-weighted average bound tariff rate on industrial products from developing countries will be 4.5 percent, compared with 3.9 percent on imports from all sources.

In a number of industrial sectors of export interest to developing countries, tariff reductions by the industrial countries exceed the overall target. For example, duties on imports of metal products from developing countries are to be cut by an average of 67 percent (from 2.7 to 0.9 percent), whereas the rates on wood, pulp, paper, and furniture products from developing countries are being cut by 63 percent (from 4.6 to 1.7 percent). For tropical and natural resource–based products, tariff reductions by developed countries on imports from all sources also exceed the overall target: on a trade-weighted average, the cuts affecting developing countries' exports to developed countries will be 57 percent (from 4.2 to 1.8 percent) and 35 percent (from 4.0 to 2.6 percent),

3. GATT (1994).

respectively. Tariff rates are being lowered in five equal annual increments that began in 1995.

NTMs for agricultural products were to be eliminated or converted into their tariff equivalents, often amounting to reductions of hundreds of percentage points in the first instance.[4] Subsequent to this "tariffication," developed countries' tariffs were to be reduced by an average of 36 percent over six years from their 1986–88 base, and developing countries' tariffs were to be reduced 24 percent over ten years (subject to the condition that each tariff line will be affected by a 15 percent minimum reduction).[5] Rice and other staple foods are exempt from the general reduction guidelines, but are subject to the general minimum access guarantee, which is equivalent to 4 percent of domestic consumption in the 1986–88 base period and is to increase by 0.8 percent annually to reach 8 percent at the end of the implementation period. The minimum access amounts are subject to reduced tariffs, whereas amounts above that level are subject to the higher rates, which are to be progressively reduced during the implementation period. Special safeguards may be triggered by volume increases or price reductions. Average duties affecting trade in tropical agricultural products, which are of key interest to developing countries, are subject to a reduction of 43 percent, with duties on spices, flowers, and plants being reduced by 52 percent.

Abreu estimates that developing countries have cut their trade-weighted average bound MFN rates against imports from industrial countries from 14.9 to 10.7 percent.[6] These figures mainly reflect cuts by Latin America, from 22.1 to 18.2 percent; by Asia, from 12.4 to 8.4 percent; and by developing Europe, from 26.4 to 15.5 percent. Africa has made no measurable cuts, retaining average bound rates at 23 percent. Developing countries have cut their trade-weighted average bound MFN rates on imports from other developing countries from 10.1 to 7.1 percent. A sectoral breakdown of applied and bound tariffs in developed and developing countries is shown in table 8-2.

4. NTMs that were specifically covered include quantitative import restrictions, variable import levies, minimum import prices, discretionary licensing, NTMs maintained through state trading enterprises, and voluntary export restraints (VERs).

5. In the base period many agricultural prices were relatively low, so there was a wide gap between world prices and protected or supported domestic prices; the implication was that the agreed-upon tariff reductions would still provide "high levels of protection in normal times." See Hathaway and Ingco (1995).

6. Abreu (1995).

Table 8-2. Post–Uruguay Round Applied and Bound Tariff Rates of Developed and Developing Countries by Major Product Group
Percent (weighted averages, excluding trade within free trade areas)

Product group	Developed		Developing	
	Applied	Bound	Applied	Bound
Agricultural products except fish	5.2	7.2	18.6	19.9
Fish and fish products	4.2	4.9	8.6	25.9
Petroleum	0.7	0.9	7.9	8.4
Wood, pulp, paper, and furniture	0.5	0.9	8.9	10.3
Textiles and clothing	8.4	11.0	21.2	25.5
Leather, rubber, and footwear	5.5	6.5	14.9	15.4
Metals	0.9	1.6	10.8	10.4
Chemical and photo supplies	2.2	3.6	12.4	16.8
Transport equipment	4.2	5.6	19.9	13.2
Nonelectric machinery	1.1	1.9	13.5	14.5
Electric machinery	2.3	3.7	14.6	17.2
Mineral products, precious stones, and metals	0.7	1.0	7.8	8.1
Other manufactured products	1.4	2.0	12.1	9.2
Industrial goods (rows 4–13)	2.5	3.5	13.3	13.3
All merchandise trade	2.6	3.7	13.3	13.0

Source: Finger, Ingco, and Reincke (1996).

Note: The applied rates are those for the base period, whereas the bound rates are those applying after the implementation; in some instances this means that the applied rates are higher than the bound rates.

In the Uruguay Round there was some discussion of the base period from which tariff reductions would be implemented as well as the period over which implementation was to be accomplished. The discussion about the base period was most intense in the case of agricultural products, since periods in which world prices were relatively high would imply low tariff rates and allow little scope for increasing protection when world prices fell. There was therefore interest in choosing periods when protection (and other forms of support) was relatively high so that reduction commitments would be lessened, as indeed happened. In the end the base rates chosen were existing bound levels, where they existed, or for unbound products, the applied rates in 1986. Given the success of the Uruguay Round in extending binding coverage, including coverage for agricultural products, it would seem that the base period for a new round could be fixed as the final year for implementation of the Uruguay Round results.

With certain variations, Uruguay Round rate cuts are being implemented from 1995 in equal annual stages over five years for manufactured goods and six years for agricultural products, and developing countries have ten years to implement cuts for agricultural products. (For textiles and clothing the progressive opening of quotas has been back-loaded so that the more profound liberalization will only occur toward the end of the implementation period.) However, at the midterm review of the round held in Montreal in December 1988, it was decided to advance to mid-1989 at the latest the implementation of agreed-upon tariff cuts on a number of tropical products of particular interest to developing countries.

In past rounds targets for the reduction of tariffs on industrial products had been set in terms of import-weighted averages. This was to give greater weight to the more important products in trade, although petroleum products, on which tariffs are mainly set for revenue or excise purposes, were excluded. However, in the Uruguay Round negotiations on agricultural products simple averages were used to determine the depth of cuts, since in many products there was no trade, whether due to lack of demand or because of the restrictiveness of tariffs and other measures on imports. Since imports are adversely affected by duties and NTMs (acutely so in agricultural products, textiles, and clothing), there is a downward bias in import-weighted averages. Moreover, in order to achieve an overall reduction of a given amount, there would be no need to cut rates in sectors where trade was prohibited by the high rates of protection, since such items would have no weight in the calculation. This factor was partly overcome in the Uruguay Round by requiring a minimum cut of 15 percent in each tariff line (10 percent for developing countries) within the context of the overall target.

Another objective of the Uruguay Round was to reduce tariff peaks and tariff escalation. Tariff peaks are not explicitly defined in the WTO, but the reference is to rates that are substantially higher than average rates.[7] Tariff escalation refers to the practice of imposing higher rates on products of later stages of processing. This structuring of tariffs, which is common in developing and developed countries, provides greater effective protection or assistance to processing than is evident from nominal rates alone. In developing countries, tariff escalation is associated with the import-substitution industrialization (ISI) strategy, which is designed to foster the manufacture or further processing

7. OECD (1997) refers to "tariff spikes," which it defines as rates that are at least three times the average for a country.

of natural resource–based products previously exported in primary form, although it has also been identified as causing an antiagricultural bias in developing countries. Tariff escalation by developed countries works against these efforts to increase domestic processing in developing countries.

Despite eight rounds of tariff negotiations, there are still substantial tariff peaks in some sectors, and it has been estimated that a 50 percent reduction in remaining industrial tariffs would yield approximately U.S.$270 billion in global income (welfare) gains per year.[8] These gains derive in the first instance from the combination of the preexisting level of trade, the amount of the rate cuts, and the elasticities of import demand. Typically a large share of the expansion of welfare gains would derive from the textiles and clothing sector, where there is already substantial trade, the tariffs are much higher than average, and the level of responsiveness of imports to rate cuts (the import demand elasticity) is also high. However, in global general equilibrium models such as that used by Francois and McDonald, there are also complex interindustry relationships.

It has been pointed out that the abandonment of tariff-cutting formulas (discussed later) has shifted the focus of tariff cutting to less sensitive areas, and as a consequence tariff peaks persist on sensitive products.[9] This is most evident in the cases of textiles and clothing, leather, rubber footwear, and travel goods, major exports of the developing countries, for which the Uruguay Round rate cuts of 21 and 19 percent, respectively, were substantially less than the average.[10] Lesser commitments were also made for transport equipment, for which the reductions will average 18 percent. Altogether, trade in these three product groups accounts for 31 percent of developed countries' total imports from developing countries by value in 1993. However, as is discussed later, these cuts will be supplemented by the removal of nontariff barriers (NTBs) resulting from the phase-out of the Multi-Fiber Arrangement (MFA) and the elimination of VERs, especially on footwear, electronics, and travel goods.

GATT 1994 provides information on percentages and absolute changes in tariff escalation in the Uruguay Round.[11] The results, set out in table 8-3, reveal

8. Francois and McDonald (1996).

9. Blackhurst, Enders, and Francois (1995).

10. GATT (1994).

11. The definition is based on the work of a technical group of experts on the GATT tariff study that divided traded products into three stages of processing (raw materials, semimanufactured products, and finished products). See GATT (1994).

Table 8-3. Changes in Tariff Escalation since the Uruguay Round on Products Imported by Developed Economies from Developing Economies

Percentages except where noted

Product	Imports[a]	Share of each stage	Tariff			Absolute change in tariff escalation
			Pre-UR	Post-UR	Change	
All industrial products (except petroleum)	169,690	100	6.8	4.3	37	n.a.
Raw materials	36,692	22	2.1	0.8	62	n.a.
Semimanufactured products	36,464	21	5.3	2.8	47	3.2 to 2.0
Finished products	96,535	57	9.1	6.2	32	3.8 to 3.4
All tropical products	14,354	100	4.2	1.9	55	n.a.
Raw materials	5,069	35	0.1	0.0	100	n.a.
Semimanufactured products	4,340	30	6.3	3.5	44	6.2 to 3.5
Finished products	4,945	34	6.6	2.6	61	0.3 to –0.9
Natural resource–based products	33,426	100	4.0	2..7	33	n.a.
Raw materials	14,558	44	3.1	2.0	35	n.a.
Semimanufactured products	13,332	40	3.5	2.0	43	0.4 to 0
Finished products	5,535	17	7.9	5.9	25	4.4 to 3.9

Source: Based on GATT (1994), except that in the final column the absolute change shows the extent to which the difference in rates from the previous processing stage, measured in percentage points, has been reduced.

a. Millions of U.S. dollars.

that the percentage reductions were generally greater in the earlier stages of processing, except that cuts were greater for finished tropical products and semimanufactured natural resource–based products than in the preceding stages of processing. The general implication of higher percentage reductions on material or semiprocessed inputs is that effective protection on the next stage of processing does not decrease in proportion to the nominal tariff cuts on the finished goods, a strategy that has been used explicitly by some developed countries to increase effective protection while meeting overall tariff reductions.[12] Since escalation is used by developed and developing countries alike, it produces a trade bias against processed goods due to the higher import duties imposed on these items. An overview of the

12. Yeats (1994) argues that the absolute change in tariffs is more relevant for an analysis of tariff escalation. By this measure tariff escalation has been reduced in all product categories, eliminated in the first stage of processing of natural resource–based products, and reversed in the final stage of processing of tropical products.

Table 8-4. Structure of Applied Tariffs in Canada, the EC, Japan, and the United States, 1989 and 1996

Percent

Indicator	Canada		EC		Japan		United States	
	1989	1996	1989	1996	1989	1996	1989	1996
Bound tariff lines	98.4	99.6	91.8	100.0	89.8	98.8	98.1	100.0
Duty-free lines	25.7	31.6	10.5	11.4	21.9	34.8	17.4	17.8
Specific and compound, all rates	8.6	9.1	10.6	12.1	7.4	10.6	17.6	17.7
Tariff quotas, all rates	0.0	1.5	1.0	2.3	1.0	2.2	0.1	2.3
Rates with no ad valorem equivalent	0.5	2.5	8.4	2.0	1.0	4.0	1.3	5.7
Simple average bound rate	9.3	5.1[a]	7.5	7.2[a]	8.2	4.7[a]	6.3	3.9[a]
Simple average applied rate	9.1	9.2	7.4	9.5	6.9	6.7	6.2	6.2
Import-weighted average rate	6.9	5.7	6.0	6.6	3.8	3.5	4.0	3.7
Production-weighted average rate	8.7	12.1	8.2	7.7	4.2	3.4	4.4	5.2
Tariff peaks, all rates	0.5	1.4	2.2	4.8	5.3	6.8	4.5	3.8
Standard deviation	8.8	27.5	6.1	20.7	8.9	11.8	7.7	14.2

Source: OECD (1997). See OECD (1997) for further details of methodology.

Notes: Tariff peaks (called spikes by the OECD) are rates that are three times the national average.

a. Bound rates after full implementation of the Uruguay Round agreements. Ad valorem equivalents (AVEs) are used where possible.

tariff regimes of Canada, the European Communities, Japan, and the United States is given in table 8-4. This illustrates some of the issues discussed in the preceding paragraphs.

In some countries different tariff rates abound (a number of countries have hundreds of distinct rates of duty), causing a lack of transparency in the protection regime as well as making it practically impossible to compute the effects of resource allocation and welfare. The existence of multiple rates can arise from the adoption of several approaches to tariff policy, including tariff escalation. Other approaches involve setting higher rates on consumer goods and luxury goods, on the same basis used for indirect taxes, as a revenue-collecting device or to divert resources to what is perceived as more socially valued production. Under this strategy lower rates are set on intermediate goods and the lowest rates on capital goods and raw materials. However, WTO experience shows that in practice this strategy can lead to an inversion of rates at different stages of processing (for example, deescalation between inter-mediate and final stages). Although zero rates are usually used in an escalation strategy, they may be rejected in favor of minimum rates of, say, 5 percent in a strategy to increase tariff revenues. This also has the advantage of compressing dispersion and reducing the associated misallocation of resources.

Another strategy that leads to the proliferation of tariff rates is the notion of structuring made-to-measure protection, providing industries with what is said to be just the amount of protection they need to compete against imports. Such an approach takes little account of the social costs of the protection or of the social benefits, if any, of individual industries. There is no consideration of the efficiency of the industries, and the protection afforded in this way is reflected in the value of the capital and land involved in production, providing windfall gains for the owners. This approach results from the exercise of political power—for example, by entrepreneurs in certain regions of a country—as is described in a series of studies of the political economy of protection that was commissioned by the World Bank in the early 1980s.

An alternative strategy whereby tariffs are required for revenue purposes is the uniform tariff, such as that of Chile. In many developing countries the domestic taxation systems are poorly developed and trade taxes remain an important source of revenue. Uniform taxes cause less distortion in the allocation of resources than nonuniform rates (still being biased against nontradable goods and services). However, they retain an anti-import bias by reducing the demand for imports and hence foreign currency, causing an appreciation of the domestic currency and increasing the foreign prices of national exports. However, in practice the proliferation of free trade agreements (FTAs) and tariff preferences means that uniform applied rates are practically nonexistent.

In general, simplification of tariff regimes should be an objective of future negotiations (and for domestic policy purposes). Even if escalation is maintained for ISI reasons or some variation in rates were used for revenue purposes, a few broad bands might meet the objective while increasing transparency and facilitating an appreciation of the transfers associated with each strategy. Another objective would be to reduce the complexity of customs tariffs, perhaps cutting national classifications back to the basic six digits of the Harmonized Commodity Coding and Classification System (HS); at present most countries use up to ten digits, but others use as many as fourteen digits, inviting the proliferation of tailor-made rates.[13] In general, customs tariffs have around 8,000 to 12,000 lines, but there are cases in which there are some 20,000 tariff lines. In many countries a third or more of the lines attract zero rates of duty and are retained largely for statistical purposes.

13. In the Uruguay Round Canada proposed to minimize the number of items at the eight-digit level and to aim for the eventual elimination of dutiable items beyond the eight-digit level.

In any tariff negotiation there may be opposition by some trading partners to any reduction of MFN rates. Therefore, although a reduction of MFN tariff rates should increase imports from trading partners that benefit from such treatment, there may also be some diversion of trade away from suppliers that suffer an erosion of preference margins, whether in FTAs or giving unilaterally granted preferences such as those under the Generalized System of Preferences (GSP). By and large, the overall dynamism imparted to the world economy through the implementation of the Uruguay Round results should benefit all countries; indeed it is estimated that it will increase global welfare by as much as \$500 billion.[14] However, partial-equilibrium comparative static analysis shows that small net negative effects may be experienced by FTA members; African, Caribbean, and Pacific (ACP) Group countries; and least-developed countries, in that order.[15] On the other hand, developing countries may be expected to gain from the erosion of preferences among industrial countries— for instance, trade among the countries of the European Union (EU), between the EU and the European Free Trade Area (EFTA), between Canada and the United States, and so on.

It is important to note that preferential treatment under unilaterally granted schemes such as the GSP may be inferior on average to MFN treatment. For example, Laird and Yeats show that on the basis of import-weighted averages average GSP rates in some sectors can be higher than MFN rates. This is because MFN sources do not supply products such as textiles and clothing, which have very high MFN and GSP rates, whereas developing countries are minor suppliers of other products for which MFN rates are relatively low.[16]

Apart from tariff preferences for certain trading partners, applied tariff rates may also be reduced for certain products on a unilateral basis by importers. For example, there are provisions in some countries for duty-free entry of imports for which there are no domestic substitutes; for imports for government ministries, agencies, or state-owned enterprises; or for capital goods or materials for use in certain types of activities, in certain regions, or in export-processing zones. The latter may be linked to offshore or outward processing operations (for instance, the export of materials or components for processing or assembly abroad and the reimportation of the final goods, including through international subcontracting) by enterprises in industrial countries, or tariffs may be applied

14. Francois and McDonald (1996).
15. Safadi and Laird (1996).
16. Laird and Yeats (1987).

only to the value added abroad (for example, the value of the processing or assembly operations). Concessional entry may also be linked to local content or export-balancing requirements and as such may be prohibited under the WTO Agreement on Trade-Related Investment Measures (TRIMs). As in the case of trade covered by tariff preferences, trade under various concessional entry regimes can be adversely affected by MFN tariff cuts.

Tariff Types

The simplest and most frequently used tariff type is the ad valorem tariff, under which the rate is expressed as a percentage of the value of the goods. Tariff surcharges, such as those added for balance of payments reasons, are usually set in ad valorem terms. However, there are a number of other types of tariffs that are more complex and much less transparent.

Two other types of tariffs have been very common in the past, mainly for agricultural products and chemicals. These are specific duties and variable levies. A *specific duty* is a duty that has a fixed value for a physical unit—for example, U.S.$6.00 per pound or SFr10.50 per dozen. Specific duties are still allowed, and they are very common in agriculture in most countries.[17] A *variable levy* is a duty typically fixed to bring the price of an imported commodity up to a domestic support price for the commodity. Under the Uruguay Round agreement variable levies in agriculture are prohibited, but a number of countries interpret this as being effective only where the application of a variable levy would cause the charge to exceed the binding commitment. To avoid the use of variable levies but achieve a similar effect, some countries split tariff lines for the same product, charging higher rates for lower-priced imports.

Specific duties and variable levies lack transparency, since it is difficult to know their percentage or ad valorem equivalents. The ad valorem equivalent to a specific rate can be computed directly from an item's import price, but this is usually known only to customs officers and the enterprise concerned. Alternatively, the ad valorem equivalent may be approximated by the unit value if quantity and value data are published at a sufficiently detailed level or by calculating the ratio of the value of the duty collected to the import value, which is not usually published. To compute the ad valorem equivalent to a variable levy, it is necessary to know the import and domestic support prices.

17. Switzerland uses specific duties for all products.

The ad valorem equivalent to both a specific duty and a variable levy varies inversely with international prices, and it may be necessary to compute some average across a representative period. Since the ad valorem incidence of an imported product is inversely related to its price, specific rates and variable levies tend to fall more heavily on developing countries and low-cost suppliers. They also serve as a form of built-in contingency protection, discouraging importers from lowering prices to capture a larger share of a market, since any price reduction would be offset by higher duties. In this situation, the usual strategy for an exporter is to switch to higher-value products, as in the case of quantitative restrictions.

Other types of duties less frequently used are mixed rates, alternative rates, and seasonal rates. Mixed (or "composite") rates can combine specific and ad valorem rates—for example, U.S.$6.00 a pound plus 15 percent. An alternative rate might be 15 percent or, if higher, U.S.$3.00 a pound. A seasonal rate is a rate that is increased or decreased at a certain time of the year, which is usually related to the growing season in the importing country.

Antidumping (AD) duties and countervailing (CV) measures are usually, but not always, set in ad valorem terms. They are not strictly tariffs, although they are sometimes called para-tariff measures. They are applied at the firm level in the exporting country. Many actions related to AD duties or CV measures terminate in price undertakings by the exporter. Since they are, or should be, WTO-consistent contingency measures taken against the so-called unfair trade practices of a third country, they are not subject to market access negotiations, but the terms of their use are covered by negotiations on rules.

Some agricultural products are subject to tariff quotas or tariff rate quotas, attracting lower in-quota and higher out-of-quota rates. These are often set in terms of specific or mixed rates, and they may also vary seasonally. An issue is how to compute tariff averages where tariff quotas are applied: governments often average in-quota and out-of-quota rates, but economists would argue that the out-of-quota rate is more appropriate, representing the marginal, binding constraint on additional trade. This issue has not been settled in past negotiations. Another issue for future negotiations might be whether to continue to allow the use of specific rates or other more complex formulations. Given the lack of transparency associated with the use of such rates, this has an inherent appeal. However, if the use of such rates were banned, there might be even greater resort to the use of other devices such as AD duties, which are subject to abuse. One solution would be to require a justification for the use of specific or formula-type rates, perhaps including variable levies, on a case-by-case basis—for example, by waiver. Where allowed, the ad valorem equivalent of such rates should not be allowed to exceed the bound rate on any imported item (as opposed to meeting the ad valorem equivalent of the bound rate on average over a reporting period of twelve months). In addition, users could be required to provide sufficient information to other WTO members to allow them to compute the ad valorem incidence of such rates and assure themselves that binding commitments were being met.

The Valuation Base

The value for duty of a good for customs purposes is typically the FOB (free on board) value, but in some cases the CIF (cost, insurance, and freight) value is used, increasing the incidence of the tariff on an FOB basis and providing greater protection against exporters with higher transport costs. Most countries use one system or the other, but Mexico, which normally values imports on a CIF basis, values non-duty-free imports from North American Free Trade Agreement (NAFTA) partners on an FOB basis during the phase-in period of the agreement.

In many developing countries the value for duty is not the transaction value, but some kind of constructed or reference price (to compensate for under-invoicing or simply to provide surer protection for goods with fluctuating world prices or to counter AD duties). However, under the single undertaking of the Uruguay Round all countries, subject to a phase-in period, will in the future be subject to the GATT customs valuation code, which places greater emphasis on the use of transaction values as the basis for customs valuation.

Preferential rules of origin (ROOs) are used to determine the value for duty of imports from a country or countries that benefit from preferential treatment in the importing country, either under unilateral schemes such as the GSP or under mutually negotiated arrangements such as FTAs or customs unions. An import from a preferential partner using materials or components from a third country that does not benefit from preferences or receives preferences at a different level will usually qualify for the preference if enough processing is done on the product in the partner country to achieve a fixed level of value added or to cause a shift in tariff classification (substantial transformation) of the product. However, the rules vary between arrangements and even product categories. There are also a variety of treatments for cumulation of value added across several trading partners where processing is done or material and components are sourced. Apart from the resulting lack of transparency, it is difficult to assess the extent to which current ROOs affect trade diversion and the allocation of resources associated with preferential regimes. The current review of ROOs by the WTO concerns only nonpreferential rules, so any discussion of preferential rules might usefully be taken up in a future round, but would most likely occur in the context of rules negotiations rather than negotiations about market access per se.

The precise classification of items is not usually perceived as an issue for a multilateral negotiating round, but it can make a difference in the rate of duty to be applied. For example, the EU's classification of certain LAN equipment as telecommunications equipment meant it was dutiable at a different rate from that applied to information equipment, which was covered by the zero-for-zero agreement in that field. Reclassification usually occurs when there is a shift in classification either at the international level, as when the Customs Cooperation Council Nomenclature (CCCN) changed to the HS or from HS92 to HS96. However, it can also occur with the formation of a customs union or with the adherence of a new member to a customs union. The issue is that a change in the classification may imply a change of a bound rate and set in motion renegotiations of schedules under GATT Article XXVIII.

Other Charges, Including Discriminatory Application of Indirect Taxes

A number of other charges are applied to imports. Some are merely fees for services such as stevedoring, warehousing, port or airport handling, customs agent services, and so on. There are also sometimes additional charges such as customs processing fees, consular charges (for documentation), and statistical taxes. Under WTO rules these charges should represent the costs of the services provided, but some countries set these as a percentage of the value of imports. For instance, the paperwork for processing a Barbie doll and a tanker of petroleum might be the same, but charging a percentage of the value of each would yield vastly different revenues.

Although it is not a common practice today, some countries impose additional charges on imports for a variety of reasons—for instance, to support lighthouses or the merchant marine. In principle, these charges can be negotiated and bound within the overall WTO tariff binding, but this appears to be ill defined. Argentina's statistical tax was specifically covered by such a binding, which has not prevented the charge from being challenged as being unrelated to the cost of service.

Under GATT Article III, paragraph 2, indirect taxes (such as value added taxes, sales taxes, or excise duties) applied to imports should be at the same level as those applied to domestically produced items. There are few instances of differential rates today, but sometimes different rates are applied to imports that are close substitutes ("like products"), such as different liquors, but various panels have ruled that this amounts to discrimination.[18] There are also instances of imposition of high indirect taxes on goods that are not produced domestically— for instance, fuels, alcoholic beverages, perfumes, and luxury goods— effectively in the form of excise duties.

Negotiating Techniques

The basic approach to tariff negotiation used in the five rounds of the GATT negotiations that preceded the Kennedy Round was the request and offer approach, in which participants would try to balance or more than balance the "concessions" they were offering against those they sought. Tariff cut offers (concessions) were seen as negotiating "coin" with which to pay for concessions by other parties. Such negotiations were essentially bilateral, between principal suppliers in each country's markets; the results were then extended to other GATT contracting parties by virtue of the MFN principle.

The request and offer approach was also used in the Uruguay Round, subject to the overall target of an average rate reduction of 30 percent, as agreed to at the midterm review in December 1988. Despite widespread support from other participants, including other members of the Quad (Canada, the EU, Japan, and the United States), for a formula-based approach, the United States insisted that it would only negotiate item by item, dealing with tariff measures and NTMs at the same time. It implemented the request and offer approach by putting forward extensive product-specific request lists to each of its main trading partners starting in October 1989. However, other countries were not precluded from the use of formulas, to be followed by specific requests for adjustments of offers.

In request and offer negotiations computation of the equivalence of offers is usually done in terms of the percentage increase in trade to be expected from implementation. In essence, this means that one multiplies the trade flow for the base year by the percentage of tariff reduction to obtain the expected increment in trade. This is given by the formula $M_0[(t_1 - t_0)/t_0]$, where M_0

18. WTO (1995).

represents imports in the base year and t_0 and t_1 represent the tariff rates in the base year and after implementation of the reduction, respectively. Therefore, if base year imports were \$100,000 and the tariff were to be cut from 20 to 10 percent, the expected increment would be \$100,000 times $[(0.2 - 0.1)/0.2]$, or \$8,333.33.

Negotiators would argue that this simple approach avoids the use of complex simulations with estimated elasticities. However, the computation is in fact a simplified partial-equilibrium comparative static approach with an implicit assumption of an infinite elasticity of supply and a (tariff) price elasticity of import demand equal to unity for all goods. This is given by the standard formula for trade creation: $M_0[(t_1 - t_0)/t_0]e_m[1 - (e_m/e_x)]$, where e_m and e_x are the elasticities of import demand and export supply, respectively. As can be seen, when e_x is very large the expression e_m/e_x approaches zero and $[1 - (e_m/e_x)]$ approaches unity. If e_m is also unity, this formula becomes equal to $M_0[(t_1 - t_0)/t_0]$, as in the version used by negotiators. No account is taken of any possible trade diversion. Apart from the lack of realism under this limited approach, it is open to the criticism that it focuses attention only on changes in trade flows and ignores the welfare effects, which derive principally from an offer a country makes rather than from the concessions offered by its trading partners.

The request and offer approach has a disadvantage for small countries in that they are rarely principal suppliers to foreign markets, nor are their markets of great interest to other countries. This is one of the reasons developing countries took little part in early rounds of negotiations and why they made so few binding commitments prior to the Uruguay Round.

Other approaches used are formula approaches. In the Kennedy Round an across-the-board cut in rates of 50 percent for industrial goods was agreed to, and exceptions to this general formula were specifically negotiated (leaving an overall average reduction of 30 percent).[19] This can be expressed as $T_1 = aT_0$, where T_0 is the tariff rate in the initial period, T_1 is the rate after the cut, and $(1 - a)$ is the percentage reduction. The effect of the 50 percent reduction is shown in figure 8-1 by a straight line through the origin.

A number of alternative tariff-cutting formulas were considered in the Tokyo Round. One harmonization formula (intended to achieve the deepest cuts in the highest rates) is given by $T_1 = T_0 + b$, where b is a fixed percentage and the parameters a and b were to be negotiated. Another harmonization formula designed to achieve even deeper cuts in higher rates is given by

19. This section is partly based on Laird and Yeats (1987).

Figure 8-1. Implications of Various Tariff-Cutting Formulas

New rate

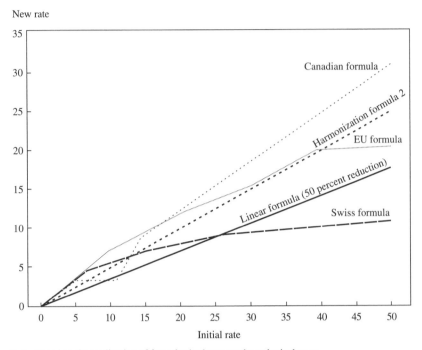

Initial rate

Note: Based on the application of formulas in the text to hypothetical rates.

$T_1 = T_0 - (T_0 \times 2)/100$, and it was suggested that this formula be reapplied three times. The effects of applying the second of these formulas are also shown in figure 8-1 as harmonization formula 2.

In the end the Swiss formula was generally applied in the Tokyo Round. This was designed to achieve deeper cuts in higher tariff rates, thereby specifically addressing the problem of tariff peaks. It is given by $T_1 = aT_0/(a + T_0)$, where the value of 14 was proposed and used for the coefficient a, although some countries used a value of 16, giving lesser reductions. The Swiss formula with a coefficient of 14 is illustrated in figure 8-1, where it is clear that it does more for reducing tariff peaks than the other formulas shown. However, exceptions to the general application of the formula carved out a number of products of export interest to the developing countries. The result was as follows:

> An examination of initial offers indicated that less than the formula reductions, or no reductions, were offered for a good number of items for which developing

countries were major suppliers. . . . The total or partial exceptions covered textile items for which the developing countries were significant suppliers as well as other sectors such as footwear, leather goods, cutlery, porcelain, wood or wood products, certain types of non-ferrous metals, etc.[20]

The Canadians and the members of the European Communities in the Uruguay Round also proposed formulas. The Canadian formula is given by $T_1 = T_0 - (T_0 a)$, where $a = 32(T_0/5)$. The EC proposed that base rates of 40 percent or more be reduced to a maximum of 20 percent, rates between 30 and 40 percent be reduced by a linear 50 percent ($T_1 = 0.5T_0$), and rates below 30 percent be reduced using the formula $T_1 = T_0(1 - a)$, where $a = (T_0 + 20)$. The results for both formulas are shown in figure 8-1. The formula approach was rejected by the United States, in particular in the Uruguay Round, as mentioned earlier.

The zero for zero approach describes a situation in which a critical mass of countries agrees to reduce tariff rates to zero in a sector, however defined. In the Uruguay Round zero for zero reductions were made in the areas of agricultural equipment, beer, certain chemicals, construction equipment, distilled spirits (brown), furniture, medical equipment, paper, pharmaceuticals, steel, and toys. It has been estimated that these reductions will increase the share of developed countries' duty-free imports from 20 to 43 percent.[21] This approach was also used in the area of informatics when the WTO Ministerial Declaration on Trade in Information Technology Products (ITA) was agreed to at the close of the first WTO ministerial conference on December 13, 1996, in Singapore. Customs duties and other duties and charges on these products are to be eliminated by twenty-nine developed and developing countries by the year 2000 on an MFN basis.[22] It is sometimes argued that many low rates of duty constitute "nuisance" rates and should therefore be reduced to zero. However, zero rates do not by themselves reduce the amount of paperwork required in a normal trade situation: normal customs procedures and ancillary inspections have to be carried out, and any additional charges and indirect taxes have to be collected. Moreover, even small rates on large cargoes—for instance, 100,000 tonnes of crude oil—can provide substantial tax revenues. Zero rates are attractive to the users of products, including consumers of final goods so

20. GATT (1979).
21. GATT (1994).
22. See *WTO Focus* newsletter, 17 (March 1997).

affected. However, if they are applied to inputs to other productive processes, they tend to increase effective protection on later stages of processing, increasing the misallocation of resources. As noted earlier, in a number of World Bank lending programs low or zero rates were often increased to 5 percent or so, while NTBs were eliminated and prohibitively high rates were reduced; this had the effect of increasing revenues while improving the allocation of resources.

A mixed approach provides for a combination of approaches such as those described above. For example, it might involve a basic formula approach on which further constraints are imposed. Such constraints might take various forms. For example, individual countries might be allowed to negotiate exceptions to the formula, permitting them to retain higher rates in certain sensitive sectors. It might be decided that in addition to using the formula, all rates below a certain level would be reduced to zero or that all rates above a certain level, say 20 percent, would be reduced to that level. In addition to using the formula results, where these have been applied, it has usually been agreed to round off the resulting ad valorem rate to some degree, such as to the next lowest half percentage point. The Uruguay Round used a mixed approach of request and offer negotiation, subject to certain constraints, as well as zero for zero negotiation, as noted above.

In past rounds of negotiations developing countries were marginalized in part because of negotiating techniques, especially the request and offer approach. However, in a sense they also opted out by sheltering themselves under the provisions of Part IV of the GATT, as elaborated in the Enabling Clause, and provisions in the terms of reference for recent negotiating rounds.[23] In particular they claimed not to be required to make reciprocal offers, but the result was that many products in which they had an export interest were excluded or the cuts were less deep than in areas where the developed countries had a mutual interest in tariff reductions. The more active approach taken in the Uruguay Round seems to have had some benefits, as the market access gains achieved by the developing countries fell only a little short of those achieved by the developed countries and, more important, they achieved welfare gains from their own liberalization.

---

23. The Enabling Clause is formally known as the Decision of 28 November 1979 of the GATT Contracting Parties on Differential and More Favorable Treatment, Reciprocity, and Fuller Participation of Developing Countries.

Nontariff Measures

In the context of market access negotiations, NTMs mainly refer to import restraints as well as production and export subsidies.[24] Within these broad categories there are a large variety of NTMs that have many different effects, including price and quantity effects on trade and production, as well as on consumption, revenue, employment, and welfare.[25] These effects occur both in the country applying the measures and in other countries directly and indirectly affected by them. NTMs may overlap with tariffs and are often used with other reinforcing NTMs; for instance, domestic price support schemes need to be supported with import measures, and any resulting surpluses need subsidies to be exported.

NTMs are difficult to quantify and costly to administer. They are costly to consumers and costly to exporters (in terms of lost trade). They are inefficient ways of creating jobs, lack transparency, are inherently discriminatory, and are most intensively used against developing countries and transition economies. They also drive a wedge between world prices and domestic prices, so domestic firms are relatively unaffected by price trends on world markets and have little incentive to adopt new technologies or modern business practices. Domestic prices are often determined by the degree of competition or the lack thereof in the home market.

The Uruguay Round made considerable headway toward eliminating or reducing the use of NTMs, as well as toward setting guidelines for the use of those that are still allowed. An overview of pre– and post–Uruguay Round NTMs by broad type and sectoral coverage in Canada, the European Communities, Japan, and the United States is given in tables 8-5 and 8-6. The two outstanding features reflected by these tables are the elimination of NTMs in agriculture, principally through tariffication, and the continued application of export restraints in the area of textiles and clothing. However, the tables reflect import measures only and do not capture the importance of domestic supports and export subsidies in the area of agriculture.

For developing countries the most important areas in which changes took place in relation to market access were the use of VERs, the start of the phase-out of restraints under the WTO Agreement on Textiles and Clothing, and the breakthroughs reflected in the WTO Agreement on Agriculture. These

24. Export restraints, also NTMs, are not discussed here.
25. For a detailed discussion, see Laird and Yeats (1990). The United Nations Conference on Trade and Development (UNCTAD) uses a classification of over 100 such measures, including tariffs with discretionary or variable components.

Table 8-5. Import Coverage of Major Nontariff Barriers in Canada, the EC, Japan, and the United States, 1989 and 1996
Percent

	Canada		EC		Japan		United States	
Indicator	1989	1996	1989	1996	1989	1996	1989	1996
All nontariff barriers (NTBs)	11.1	10.4	26.6	19.1	13.1	10.7	25.5	16.8
Core NTBs[a]	8.9	7.2	25.2	15.1	12.5	10.0	25.5	16.7
Quantitative restrictions (QRs)	6.6	5.9	19.5	13.1	11.7	9.2	20.4	10.9
Export restraints	4.8	5.9	15.5	11.4	0.3	0.0	19.5	10.8
Nonauto licensing	2.6	0.0	4.4	1.5	8.9	8.6	0.0	0.0
Other QRs	0.8	0.0	0.2	0.2	2.8	0.6	6.6	0.6
Price control measures (PCMs)	2.4	1.3	12.4	3.2	0.8	0.7	17.8	7.6
Variable levies	0.0	0.0	6.3	1.4	0.8	0.6	0.1	0.1
Antidumping duties, counter-vailing measures, and voluntary export price restraints	2.4	1.3	2.6	0.9	0.0	0.0	17.8	7.6
Other PCMs	0.0	0.0	4.3	1.0	0.0	0.0	0.0	0.1

Source: OECD (1997). See OECD (1997) for further details of methodology.

a. Core NTBs are QRs and PCMs shown in the table imposed "with the specific intent of modifying or restricting international trade" (OECD, 1997). Noncore NTBs include automatic licensing and monitoring measures.

approaches are indicative of the techniques of negotiation for improved market access for products covered by NTMs.

For example, negotiators decided to explicitly prohibit the use of quantitative VERs in industry (other than textiles and clothing) and agriculture and to eliminate the remaining VERs by the end of 1999. Apart from the fact that they covered more trade than other measures, VERs—which were used instead of GATT Article XIX on safeguards—had become a threat to the credibility of the GATT system, as the prohibition under Article XI was being ignored by all major GATT contracting parties. This prohibition of VERs was achieved at the expense of introducing some "flexibility" into the application of safeguards, which allowed discrimination among suppliers in exceptional circumstances. However, even when VERs are eliminated there will remain voluntary export price restraints (VEPRs), which often occur as negotiated outcomes of AD cases. Given the equivalence between these measures (with exporters capturing the rents in both cases), it is inconsistent economically that one be banned while the other is condoned. Similar measures also seem to be reemerging, for example, in autos and aluminum. This issue could usefully be addressed in future negotiations.

For more than forty years the developing countries' single most important export sector, textiles and clothing, was restricted on a discriminatory basis

Table 8-6. Sectoral Production Coverage of Nontariff Barriers in Canada, the EC, Japan, and the United States, 1989 and 1996

Percent

		Canada		EC		Japan		United States	
ISIC	Description	1989	1996	1989	1996	1989	1996	1989	1996
1	Agriculture, forestry, and fishing	5.0	2.1	18.8	7.2	11.3	7.0	5.5	2.8
2	Mining and quarrying	0.4	4.3	0.0	6.7	3.5	0.4	0.3	0.4
21	Coal mining	8.3	0.0	0.0	42.9	n.a.	n.a.	0.0	0.0
22	Crude petroleum	0.0	9.1	n.a.	0.0	n.a.	n.a.	0.0	0.0
23	Metal ores	0.0	0.0	n.a.	4.4	n.a.	n.a.	0.0	4.0
29	Other	0.0	0.0	0.0	3.6	n.a.	n.a.	3.4	2.3
3	Manufacturing	8.3	3.9	12.6	5.4	3.9	2.5	16.0	8.1
31	Food, beverages, and tobacco	23.0	1.5	48.5	11.1	24.3	8.6	16.4	1.2
32	Textiles and apparel	42.4	45.8	74.9	75.4	28.8	28.7	84.1	68.3
33	Wood and wood products	2.1	3.7	0.0	0.0	0.0	0.0	3.9	0.8
34	Paper and paper products	1.9	0.2	1.2	1.9	0.0	0.0	1.5	1.3
35	Chemical and petroleum products	2.4	1.3	3.5	1.6	1.4	1.4	8.6	3.2
36	Nonmetallic mineral products	0.7	0.0	4.4	0.0	0.0	0.0	10.7	6.1
37	Basic metal industries	16.5	1.7	37.7	0.6	2.5	2.6	53.2	30.4
38	Fabricated metals	1.1	1.4	4.6	0.0	0.0	0.0	13.0	6.1
39	Other	0.5	0.8	1.3	0.0	0.0	0.0	4.2	1.7
	Total	7.1	3.8	12.7	5.6	4.4	2.8	17.2	7.2

Source: OECD (1997). See OECD (1997) for details of methodology.

under the MFA and the earlier Short- and Long-Term Cotton Textiles Agreements. These restraints are now being progressively phased out under the WTO Agreement on Textiles and Clothing. There are mixed feelings among developing countries about the elimination of the MFA restrictions. Constrained exporters must be expected to lose some quota rents afforded by the MFA, but the country-specific quota system also provided a form of protection for less efficient exporters against the more efficient, to which quotas could not be transferred. (There have already been reports that Bangladesh is losing out to China in some areas.)

Subject to special safeguards, the phase-out of the MFA and the gradual integration of the textiles and clothing sector into the normal WTO rules is being effected over a ten-year period under the supervision of a Textiles Monitoring Body (TMB). A minimum of 16 percent of the total 1990 volume of imports covered by the MFA were due to be integrated into the WTO in 1995. At least another 17 percent of the value of 1990 imports will be integrated following the third year of the phase-out period. An additional minimum of 18 percent will follow after the seventh year, and the remaining 41 percent will be brought under WTO rules at the very end of the phase-out period. Each phase-out is intended to include products from four different groups: tops and yarn, fabrics, made-up textiles, and clothing.

Quota restrictions are being expanded by the amount of the prevailing quota growth rates plus 16 percent annually for the first three years. A further expansion of 25 percent will take place in the subsequent four years, and an additional 27 percent in the final three years. These rates may be adjusted if it is found that members are not complying with their obligations.

In the major review of the implementation of the Agreement on Textiles and Clothing in the first stage of the integration process, held in February 1998, a number of concerns were raised. These included the back-loading of the integration process (holding off the more difficult adjustments until the end), the exceptionally large number of safeguard measures in use, the more restrictive use of ROOs by the United States, tariff increases, the introduction of specific rates, minimum import pricing regimes, labeling and certification requirements, the maintenance of balance of payments provisions affecting textiles and clothing, export visa requirements, and the double jeopardy arising from the application of AD measures to products covered by the agreement.

The WTO Agreement on Agriculture, one of the main achievements of the Uruguay Round, brought the agricultural sector under more transparent rules and set the stage for a progressive liberalization of trade in the sector. Among its main achievements were tariffication (or elimination) of NTMs based on 1986–88 prices, the full binding of the new tariffs by developed and developing countries, and phased tariff reductions; reductions in the level of domestic support measures (except for permitted or "green box" supports and supports below a certain level, that is, "de minimis" amounts); and reductions in outlays on export subsidies and the volume of subsidized exports. The main exceptions to tariffication were rice and, for developing countries, some staple foods, to which minimum access commitments apply. Special safeguards (increased duties) can be triggered by increased import volumes or price reductions (by comparison with average 1986–88 prices expressed in terms of domestic currency). There is also a "peace" clause to constrain the use of antisubsidy actions until 2003.

Apart from these specific areas covered by the market access negotiations in the Uruguay Round, a number of important NTMs were covered in rules negotiations. These include contingency protection (safeguards, AD duties, and CV measures), technical barriers (including sanitary and phytosanitary measures), trade-related aspects of intellectual property rights (TRIPs), TRIMs, import licensing, state trading, and ROOs. These are covered by other chapters in this volume.

One important area of rules relates to the use of subsidies, which are covered by the WTO Agreement on Subsidies and Countervailing Measures (SCM) and the Agreement on Agriculture. These rules distinguish between domestic and export subsidies and provide for differential treatment of agricultural products and manufactured products. Some subsidies, notably export subsidies, are prohibited, whereas others are "actionable" or "nonactionable," either in the WTO or through CV actions. There are notification requirements for all specific subsidies—those targeted to particular enterprises, industries, or regions —as well as for export subsidies and import-substitution subsidies. The WTO Agreement on Agriculture also prohibits the use of export subsidies except in conjunction with product-specific reduction commitments, and it defines the conditions under which certain types of domestic subsidies ("green box" subsidies, or permitted subsidies; "blue box" subsidies, or subsidies that are partially delinked from production; or "S&D box" subsidies, subsidies used under the provisions of Article XV of the agreement for special and differential treatment of developing countries) are exempt from reduction commitments. In this area the emphasis on delinking supports from production was an important new approach to rural incomes.

WTO rules on NTMs were extended in the Uruguay Round to cover trade-related investment measures. In particular, the TRIMs Agreement prohibits measures that require particular levels of local sourcing by an enterprise (that is, local content requirements); restricts the volume or value of imports that an enterprise can buy or use to the volume or value of products it exports (that is, trade-balancing requirements); restricts the volume of imports to the amount of foreign exchange inflows attributable to an enterprise; and restricts the export by an enterprise of products, specified in terms of the particular type, volume, or value of the products or of a proportion of the volume or value of local production.

Among the most important TRIMs in practice are the local content and trade-balancing requirements, which are extensively used in developing countries' automotive industries. Developing countries that notified the WTO of their TRIMs are allowed to maintain them until the end of 1999, when they are to be dismantled. The abolition of TRIMs will promote a more neutral trading and investment environment in those countries and a more efficient allocation of scarce resources. The automotive industries in a number of countries are pressing their governments to seek an extension of the period in which to adjust to the new trading environment, but since the Uruguay Round the WTO members have been much more reluctant to grant waivers to the main rules.

Following the previous discussion it is clearly necessary to distinguish those NTMs that are to be eliminated from those that are to be subject to agreed-upon disciplines or to rules that set out the conditions under which they may be used. Improved market access would require the elimination or relaxation of NTMs such as remaining quantitative restrictions, domestic supports, and export subsidies (and taxes). Others will simply be the subjects of improved disciplines, such as AD or CV investigations, technical barriers, TRIPS, ROOs, standards, and so on. In some cases, such as those of subsidies and perhaps government procurement, there is scope for further work on the rules as well as improved market access commitments.

It is possible that new negotiations could lead to prohibition of further NTMs and that the options will be immediate elimination or phasing out of the measures. For those NTMs that are to be phased out, there are several possibilities: phasing out the NTMs by relaxing the provisions—for example, expanding quotas or reducing subsidies; progressively reducing the range of products affected; or converting NTMs to tariffs to then be included in the scheduled tariff reductions.

For immediate or phased elimination, there may be a case for differential treatment for developing countries as users of the measures, giving developing countries longer periods to adapt. However, given the negative effects that NTMs tend to have on domestic welfare, such differential treatment is unlikely to confer an advantage. On the other hand, even when developing countries wish to liberalize as quickly as possible to capture such welfare gains, their negotiators face the dilemma that they would wish to retain such measures to offer as concessions in negotiations and hence, one might hope, gain reciprocal concessions or expanded access to foreign markets for their exports. The expectation of obtaining enhanced access to foreign markets is also seen as being useful to persuade domestic industry to accept the liberalization of the home market. It is sometimes argued in relation to tariff offers that the key to obtaining reciprocity is not the offer to make a tariff reduction, but the offer to bind the reduced rate. A parallel might be the offer to bind the elimination of an NTM, although there is no specific WTO provision for such negotiations.

Another issue is the treatment of countries affected by the measures, particularly any quantitative measures. Normally one would expect a measure to be scaled back in proportion to the market share, but some countries may argue that they should be given differential treatment—for instance, more rapid liberalization for least-developed exporters (as provided in the Agreement on Textiles and Clothing) under a market-opening measure or less rapid phasing out of export subsidies for poor food-importing countries.

In the case of phased elimination, decisions would need to be made on the base period, the period over which the elimination was to be accomplished, and whether the percentage changes were to be equally applied or whether there were to be front- or back-loading of the elimination. In the case of conversion of tariffs, some technical work might be required on how this should be done (an agreed-upon methodology) and whether such work should be carried out by the members themselves (the approach in the Uruguay Round agricultural negotiations) or by the WTO Secretariat, ensuring more consistent treatment. Decisions might also be made on minimum cuts in each tariff line. Another issue might be whether to allow backsliding in certain areas provided average reductions are achieved.

In the case of products covered by multiple measures it might be useful to examine some technical issues, such as the coordinated phasing of changes. For example, one issue to consider is how to coordinate import liberalization with phased reductions in domestic supports and export subsidies to achieve a smooth transition to a more open regime. A technical matter is that import liberalization is usually carried out in relation to products under the tariff classification, whereas subsidies are affected in terms of different product or industrial classifications. In principle this could be resolved by means of a concordance, but this would require a change from traditional approaches. Delinking domestic supports from production partly resolves this issue.

The Agenda for Future Negotiations

Although average tariffs have fallen considerably over the last fifty years, they will rightly be a major issue in future market access negotiations. From the perspective of developing countries and good economics, the use of the Swiss formula approach would avoid the exclusion or minimalist treatment of products in which these countries have strong export interest. If necessary, developing countries should form a coalition, perhaps with interested developed countries that share such a goal. There is also a need to increase transparency by limiting the use of tariff rates that are not expressed in ad valorem terms; exceptions should be subject to detailed periodic public notifications, which would allow the trading community to assess the conformity of the ad valorem incidence of such rates with binding commitments.

It is important for developing countries to participate actively in a new round of negotiations by seeking and offering rate cuts and binding commitments, since in the long run the improved security of access through increased tariff bindings may offer more advantages to developing countries than unilaterally granted but unbound preferential access. The advantage of these countries' making their own commitments is to provide stable and credible trade regimes to attract foreign direct investment (FDI) and the associated technology needed for their further development.

If participants in a new round could agree to a formula approach, this would achieve the synergy of reciprocal concessions while allowing negotiators to sell the deal to their domestic constituencies. However, if this is unattainable developing countries should not forego the welfare gains to be achieved from advancing their own liberalization while waiting for others to do the same; strategically this implies advancing on unilateral liberalization while using bindings to achieve reciprocity.

Provided that the integration of textiles and clothing is accomplished as agreed, negotiations on NTMs in a new round of negotiations will be focused on rule making. The main exception in the area of goods will be in agriculture, where we can expect a continuation of efforts to cut back on domestic supports and export subsidies (with tariff cutting on imports). Developing countries' interests in this area are extensive, including large-volume temperate-zone products; the fast-growing area of fruit, vegetable, and floricultural products, with high levels of value added; and tropical products. However, the phasing of any new commitments will raise a number of technical questions in response to which some different approaches from those in the Uruguay Round might be usefully considered.

In the Uruguay Round market access was initially covered by separate negotiating groups on tariffs, NTMs, agriculture, natural resource–based products, textiles and clothing, and tropical products, but a number of these were covered by a single market access group in the final stages of the round. There was a determined effort to consider tariffs and NTMs together in order to avoid a situation in which cuts in tariff rates would be effectively annulled by the existence of NTMs, leading to no increase in market access. One disadvantage was that, since market access was contentious in certain product areas, as were the rules for using certain measures, there was no incentive for many countries to make offers until the general shape of the package became known. The use of a formula approach or development of a critical mass in certain areas—as in the Ministerial Declaration on Trade in Information Technology Products (ITA)—might allow a more rapid advance that would serve as an encouragement to make breakthroughs in other areas.

In any new round of negotiations there will be a need to develop technical expertise in developing countries, and this effort should be made ahead of the round. However, the WTO has relatively few resources in this area, and negotiations on the conditions for establishment of an independent secretariat suggest that such constraints will continue for some years. This gap will need to be filled either with trust funds from sympathetic member states or by other organizations, perhaps with funding from the United Nations Development Program (UNDP). As to the substance of such assistance, it is highly desirable that this be directed to institution building and the development of analytical expertise; this would allow the developing countries to formulate their own judgments, appropriate to their own politicoeconomic environments, about how best to achieve their own welfare goals.

References

Abreu, M. de Paiva. 1995. "Trade in Manufactures: The Outcome of the Uruguay Round and Developing Country Interests." In *The Uruguay Round and the Developing Countries,* edited by W. Martin and L. A. Winters. Discussion Paper 307. World Bank.

Blackhurst, R., A. Enders, and J. F. Francois. 1995. "The Uruguay Round and Market Access: Opportunities and Challenges for Developing Countries." In *The Uruguay Round and the Developing Countries*, edited by W. Martin and L. A. Winters. Discussion Paper 307. World Bank.

Croome, J. 1995. *Reshaping the World Trading System.* Geneva: World Trade Organization.

Finger, J. M., M. D. Ingco, and U. Reincke. 1996. *The Uruguay Round: Statistics on Tariff Concessions Given and Received.* World Bank.

Francois, J., and B. McDonald. 1996. "The Multilateral Agenda: The Uruguay Round Implementation and Beyond." Staff Working Paper RD-96-012. Geneva: World Trade Organization.

General Agreement on Tariffs and Trade. 1979. "The Tokyo Round of Multilateral Trade Negotiations." Geneva: GATT Secretariat.

———. 1993. "An Analysis of the Prepared Uruguay Round Agreement, with Particular Emphasis on Aspects of Interest to Developing Economies." Geneva: GATT Secretariat (November).

———. 1994. "News of the Uruguay Round of Multilateral Trade Negotiations." Geneva: GATT Information and Media Relations Division (April 12).

Hathaway, D., and M. Ingco. 1995. "Agricultural Liberalization and the Uruguay Round." In *The Uruguay Round and the Developing Countries,* edited by W. Martin and L. A. Winters. Discussion Paper 307. World Bank.

Laird, S. 1995. "Trade Liberalization in Latin America." *Minnesota Journal of Global Trade* 4: 111–27.

Laird, S., and A. Yeats. 1987. "Tariff-Cutting Formulas and Complications." In *The Uruguay Round: A Handbook for the Multilateral Trade Negotiations,* edited by J. M. Finger and A. Olechowski. World Bank.

———. 1990. *Quantitative Methods for Trade Barrier Analysis.* Macmillan and New York University Press.

Martin, W., and L. A. Winters, eds. 1995. *The Uruguay Round and the Developing Countries.* Discussion Paper 307. World Bank.

Organization for Economic Cooperation and Development. 1993. "Assessing the Effects of the Uruguay Round." *Trade Policy Issues* 2. Paris.

———. 1997. *Indicators of Tariff and Non-tariff Trade Barriers.* Paris.

Safadi, R., and S. Laird. 1996. "The Uruguay Round Agreements: Impact on Developing Countries." *World Development* 24(7): 1223–42.

World Trade Organization. 1995. *GATT Analytical Index: Guide to GATT Law and Practice.* Updated 6th ed. Geneva.

Yeats, A. 1994. "A Quantitative Assessment of the Uruguay Round's Effects and Their Implications for Developing Countries." PRE Working Papers Series. World Bank.

CHAPTER NINE

Multilateral and Regional Liberalization of Trade in Services

Francisco Javier Prieto and Sherry M. Stephenson

Although trade in services comprises more than a fifth of world trade, it is only since the end of the Uruguay Round that such trade has been brought under multilateral disciplines. The General Agreement on Trade in Services (GATS) came into force in January 1995 under the new World Trade Organization (WTO), and it is now applicable to all countries of the Western Hemisphere, with the sole exception of the Bahamas. It comprises a broad framework of rules and includes lists of specific commitments set out by all WTO members for the treatment of foreign service providers. One year prior to the GATS, the North American Free Trade Agreement (NAFTA) came into effect. This agreement also set out a basis for liberalizing trade in services and in investment between its members. Since the mid-1990s several other regional and subregional integration arrangements in the Western Hemisphere have included the liberalization of trade in services within their purview.

Issues in the area of services revolve around how the key principles of most favored nation treatment, national treatment, and transparency are to be handled in the context of a contractual agreement. Other rules to be determined include those relating to the type of access for foreign service providers, the treatment of investment, the disciplines over monopoly behavior, the recognition of the equivalence of qualifications (such as diplomas or certificates) between national service providers, rules of origin, the treatment of quantitative restrictions, the possibilities of providing subsidies and of taking safeguard action, denial of benefits, and withdrawal of concessions, as well as dispute settlement provisions.

A fundamental issue related to the treatment of trade in services concerns the mechanism adopted to liberalize this trade. Services do not face trade barriers in the form of border tariffs or taxes; markets are restricted through various types of regulatory measures including national laws, decrees, norms, and regulations. Therefore, liberalizing trade in services involves a different approach than the reduction of price-based measures; it requires the removal, modification, or nondiscriminatory application of national regulatory mechanisms.

One approach to the liberalization of trade in services is through what is termed a "positive list" or "bottom-up" approach (such as that under the GATS), whereby countries open their service markets to foreign providers only through commitments that are drafted in terms of specific sectors and regulatory measures. A second approach is termed a "negative list" or "top-down" approach (such as that under the NAFTA or the various bilateral free trade agreements in the Western Hemisphere), whereby no specific commitments are established and all types of service transactions are considered to be free of restraint unless there are indications to the contrary in lists of reservations and nonconforming measures.

Discussions on liberalizing trade in services are being conducted in the context of the Free Trade Area of the Americas (FTAA) process, and the objective, as agreed upon by the trade ministers of the hemisphere in Costa Rica in March 1998, is to "establish disciplines to progressively liberalize trade in services, so as to permit the achievement of a hemispheric free trade area under conditions of certainty and transparency."[1]

Along with the negotiations related to the FTAA, negotiations will also be conducted at the multilateral level as of the year 2000 to liberalize trade in services under the GATS framework of the WTO. This activity is part of the built-in agenda of the Uruguay Round. The FTAA negotiations must therefore not only be compatible with the GATS rules on regional arrangements, but must seek to go beyond what is agreed upon in multilateral negotiations. Accomplishing this will be one of the major challenges of hemispheric services.

The aim of this chapter is to provide an overview of the importance of trade in services for the world and for countries of the Western Hemisphere and to review the various approaches that have been adopted within the existing

1. Ministerial Declaration of San José (1998).

subregional trade and integration arrangements of the hemisphere, including more specifically the points of convergence and divergence between these agreements. A matrix of elements that could be considered for the construction of a regional agreement in the area of services is also presented and discussed.

The Importance of Trade in Services

In spite of considerable flaws in the measurement of international trade in services, partial and incomplete data indicate that for the last several years services have become a growing component of international trade.[2] They are also a significant and growing part of the trade of the countries of the Western Hemisphere.

According to WTO figures, exports of commercial services amounted to U.S.$1.2 trillion in 1996, whereas merchandise exports totaled U.S.$5.1 trillion. Therefore, services account for over a fifth of world trade in goods. It should be noted that the WTO figures reflect only cross-border trade in services; therefore, they exclude an important component of such trade, which is composed of sales through foreign affiliates. Even though complete records of such trade do not exist, in the case of the United States the U.S. International Trade Commission (ITC) has estimated that cross-border exports of services amounted to U.S.$151 billion in 1994, whereas sales through U.S. majority-owned affiliates amounted to nearly the same amount, U.S.$143 billion, that same year. Furthermore, fully 60 percent of all foreign investment flows in the world economy are now directed to the services sector.[3]

Country concentration is somewhat lower in services than in merchandise trade. Although the world's thirty leading exporters of commercial services accounted for 88.8 percent of total exports in 1996, the thirty leading exporters

2. Statistics on the various traded service categories included in the International Monetary Fund (IMF) *Balance of Payments Manual,* such as shipping, tourism, and remittances, comprise what is known as "commercial services" and do not include sales in the domestic markets of foreign affiliates that are established there, although this is the most important mode of supply for many services. Therefore, the value of trade in services is underestimated because of both underreporting of various transactions and failure to indicate the origin and destination of trade, as well as the lack of inclusion of service transactions resulting from foreign direct investment. In many cases data are stated in terms of net rather than gross values (exports minus imports).

3. World Trade Organization (WTO) Secretariat (1996).

of merchandise accounted for 92.2 percent of total goods exports. The relative importance of service trade varies substantially among countries. Although service exports represent 132 percent of domestic merchandise exports for Hong Kong (according to the WTO Secretariat), 66 percent for Turkey, and 55 percent for Austria, they represent only 15 percent for Japan, 12 percent for the People's Republic of China, and 8.8 percent for Mexico. Furthermore, although countries such as Egypt, Greece, the Philippines, Poland, and Portugal appear among the thirty leading exporters of services, they are not on the list of the thirty leading exporters of goods.[4]

The distribution of exports of services by region reveals the overwhelming importance of the European Union, which, according to the WTO Secretariat, accounts for 40 percent of total world exports of services and includes three out of the five largest exporters in the world (France, Italy, and the United Kingdom). The Western Hemisphere (Canada, the United States, Latin America, and the Caribbean) accounts for almost 24 percent of total world exports of services, and the United States alone accounts for 16 percent of these. Asia is the region that has shown the fastest rate of growth of both exports and imports of services over the past decade. It also accounts for the largest number of developing countries included in the thirty leading exporters of commercial services in the world—Hong Kong, Singapore, the Republic of Korea, the People's Republic of China, Taiwan, Thailand, and the Philippines. Asia now represents 23 percent of world exports of services.[5]

Turning now to the Western Hemisphere, in 1994 the thirty-four countries participating in the FTAA development process accounted for 23.5 percent of total world exports of services and 22.8 percent of world trade in merchandise goods. Much as was observed at the global level, trade concentration is less acute in services than in merchandise. Although the ten leading service exporters in the region account for 94.8 percent of total hemispheric service exports, the ten leading merchandise exporters account for 98.1 percent of the hemispheric total. Furthermore, the list of countries included among the ten leading service exporters has seven countries in common with those on the list of leading merchandise exporters.

Although the ratio of hemispheric service exports to merchandise exports is roughly the same as the world average (27 versus 26 percent), this ratio varies substantially among the countries that are part of the FTAA development

4. WTO Secretariat (1997).
5. WTO Secretariat (1997).

Table 9-1. Countries with High Levels of Specialization in Service Exports, 1994

Country	Service exports (value, millions of U.S. dollars)	Service to merchandise ratio (percent)
Antigua and Barbuda	395	705
Grenada	101	481
Barbados	631	353
St. Kitts-Nevis	91	303
Dominican Republic	1,887	298
St. Lucia	225	214
Panama	1,153	198
Paraguay	1,252	153
Curaçao	1,382	111
The Bahamas	1,466	109
Jamaica	1,271	107
St. Vincent	45	105

Source: Comisión Económica para América Latina y el Caribe (1998).

process. Tables 9-1, 9-2, and 9-3 rank the countries of the hemisphere on the basis of the importance of their service exports in relation to their merchandise exports. A note of warning should be sounded regarding the ranking criteria, the relative positions of countries in this ranking, and the quality of the data. For example, the United States ranks close to average in the Western Hemisphere in terms of its specialization in service exports. Yet if sales through affiliates were to be included in these statistics, both the United States and Canada would probably rank higher. The same may be said about countries such as Mexico and Chile, both or which have evidenced rather important investment in service industries abroad in recent years. Underestimation and underrecording of service exports are even greater for the developing countries of the region, which may compensate to a certain extent for the insufficiencies referred to in the cases of Canada and the United States.

Three groups of countries can be identified in terms of their relative specialization in service exports. The first group comprises countries with a revealed high level of specialization in services in their external trade. These are countries for which exports of services are equal to or greater than their merchandise exports. In the Western Hemisphere there are twelve countries for which service exports figure more prominently than merchandise exports. At the top of the list are countries like Antigua and Barbuda, Barbados, and

Table 9-2. Countries with Moderate to Average Levels of Specialization in Service Exports, 1994

Country	Service exports (value, millions of U.S. dollars)	Service to merchandise ratio (percent)
Belize	116	97
Uruguay	1,237	64
Costa Rica	1,142	52
Guatemala	659	43
El Salvador	337	40
United States	195,500	34

Source: Comisión Económica para América Latina y el Caribe (1998).

Table 9-3. Countries with Low Levels of Specialization in Service Exports, 1994

Country	Service exports (value, millions of U.S. dollars)	Service to merchandise ratio (percent)
Honduras	198	24
Colombia	2,005	24
Chile	2,770	24
Nicaragua	80	23
Suriname	69	23
Peru	1,016	22
Ecuador	709	19
Argentina	2,375	18
Bolivia	173	17
Trinidad and Tobago	317	16
Mexico	8,687	14
Guyana	59	13
Brazil	4,817	11
Canada	18,999	10
Venezuela	1,192	8

Source: Comisión Económica para América Latina y el Caribe (1998).

Figure 9-1. Trade in Services as a Percentage of Total GDP in the Western Hemisphere, 1985 and 1995

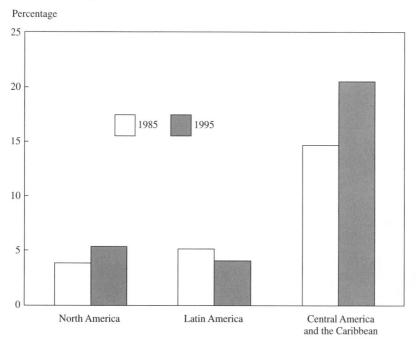

Percentage

Source: International Monetary Fund (1997) and World Bank (1997).

Grenada, whose service exports in 1994 amounted to 705 percent, 481 percent, and 353 percent of their merchandise exports, respectively (see table 9-1).

A second group comprises countries with moderate to average levels of specialization in service exports. The ratios of service exports to merchandise exports for these countries range from 27 percent to 97 percent. Six countries fall in this category: Belize, Costa Rica, Guatemala, El Salvador, the United States, and Uruguay (see table 9-2). The third group of countries, those with low or below-average levels of specialization in services in their foreign trade, have ratios of service to merchandise exports below 27 percent. At the lower end of this list are Brazil, Canada, and Venezuela, with 11 percent, 10 percent, and 8 percent, respectively (see table 9-3).

All countries with high to moderate and average levels of specialization in services—with the exceptions of Panama, Paraguay, and the United States—rely on tourism (and in a few cases "maquiladora" operations) as their single most important service export. Also, with the exemption of Paraguay and the United States, all of the top exporters are found in the Caribbean and Central America and are relatively smaller economies. Although in absolute terms the value of trade in services ranks highest for the larger countries (United States, Canada, Mexico, Brazil, Chile, and Argentina) in terms of its proportion of the gross domestic product (GDP), trade in services is actually most important for the smaller countries of Central America and the Caribbean. Figure 9-1 shows that for the latter group trade in services constituted an average of 21 percent of their GDP (in 1995), whereas the figure was around 5 percent for the larger countries of North America and Latin America. Moreover, the increase in importance of services for the Central American and Caribbean regions has been much more pronounced over the past decade than for the other two regions of the Western Hemisphere. Therefore, the smaller countries would seem to have a greater stake in the liberalization of service markets.

Somewhat perplexing is the relative stagnation of growth (or rather lack of it) in trade in services on the part of countries of the Western Hemisphere, as shown in figure 9-2. Although trade in goods increased in value by more than two and a half times from 1986 to 1995, trade in services showed only a very modest increase. This phenomenon could be due to several factors, including the dramatic response of trade in merchandise following the unilateral reduction in tariff barriers by countries of Latin America since the mid-1980s, whereas service markets have not been the object of equivalent liberalizing zeal. Therefore, these markets remain fairly closed for most countries of the region compared to the markets for goods. Some of the difference in growth rates may also have resulted from the fact that many services are embodied in the export of goods and are not captured on their own, thus artificially increasing the value of the traded goods category and lowering the value of the traded services category. Finally, service statistics are notoriously poor, and much of what is traded is not recorded, which also imparts a downward bias to the statistics. However, clearly the market for service exports is one that holds considerable potential for the countries of the Western Hemisphere.

Negotiating Trade in Services in the Western Hemisphere

Within the Western Hemisphere interest in the liberalization of trade in services is widespread and growing. Already eight subregional arrangements have incorporated formal disciplines and obligations of a comprehensive,

Figure 9-2. Growth of Trade in Goods and Services in the Western Hemisphere, 1985–95

Millions of U.S. dollars

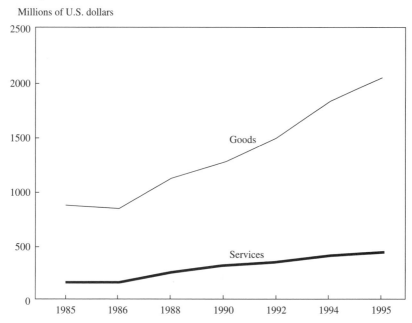

Source: International Monetary Fund (1995, 1997).

liberalizing nature with respect to services, and several other subregional arrangements are in the process of negotiating these.

Two Approaches to Liberalization

An examination of the integration arrangements that contain formal provisions on services reveals that two broad approaches exist within the region. The first is the "top-down" approach adopted first by Canada, Mexico, and the United States in January 1994 in the NAFTA. Since the implementation of that agreement Mexico has played a pivotal role in extending similar types of disciplines and liberalization to other countries in South and Central America. Service provisions have been included in the Group of Three (G-3) agreement negotiated between Colombia, Mexico, and Venezuela (January 1995), and bilateral free trade agreements have been concluded by Mexico with Bolivia and Costa Rica (also in January 1995), with Nicaragua (in December 1997), and with Chile (in April 1998). Additionally, in July 1997 Chile and Canada finalized a free trade agreement including similar provisions on services, as did the Dominican Republic with Central America (scheduled to come into effect in January 1999). In June 1998 the members of the Andean Community adopted a decision to fully liberalize intraregional trade in services over a period of five years, starting in the year 2000.

The Mercosur members have opted for a second approach to the liberalization of trade in services, a "bottom-up" approach similar to that applied at the multilateral level under the GATS. A Framework Agreement along the lines of the GATS was agreed to among the Mercosur members in December 1997, extending liberalization to the area of trade in services. This agreement provides for a gradual approach to liberalization based on the negotiation of sector-specific commitments that will progressively open members' services markets. Unlike the GATS, the Mercosur agreement specifies the full liberalization of this trade within a period of ten years.

Within the Western Hemisphere agreements relating to services exist in several different forms and constitute a complex set of overlapping understandings, cooperation agreements, and treaties. The various forums in which agreements that include disciplines on trade in services have been signed are depicted in figure 9-3.[6] At the multilateral level all countries in the hemisphere are members of the WTO GATS with the exception of the Bahamas. The majority of the countries in the Western Hemisphere have submitted GATS schedules and have improved upon their initial GATS schedules of commitments through subsequent negotiations on basic telecommunications (in February 1997) and financial services (in December 1997). The rules and disciplines of the GATS thus provide the least common denominator for trade in services in the Western Hemisphere.

At the regional level several countries have signed free trade and integration agreements that include extensive provisions covering services, as described in the preceding section.[7] In contrast to these comprehensive trade agreements, sectoral agreements on services have also been signed either as formal treaties

6. The figure is meant to serve as a useful organizational tool, but is not meant to indicate any hierarchy in the levels of obligation or degree of liberalization in the various agreements.

7. The content of these various agreements is summarized in a document prepared by the Organization of American States (OAS) Trade Unit (1997), which is currently being updated. This document, entitled *Provisions on Trade in Services in Trade and Integration Agreements of the Western Hemisphere,* can also be found at the official web site of the FTAA, www.alca-ftaa.org.

Figure 9-3. Agreements on Services in the Western Hemisphere at the Multilateral, Regional, and Bilateral Levels

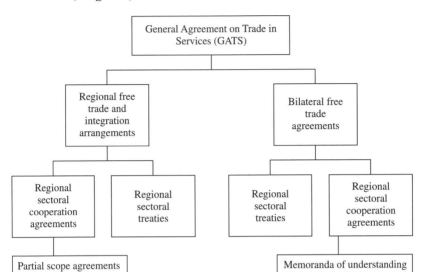

or as informal cooperation agreements. The number of such stand-alone sectoral agreements is quite high, with information presently available on some ninety of these.[8] Some of these subregional and bilateral sectoral agreements on services carry with them extensive rules and disciplines, whereas others are limited to specifying good intentions or cooperative action. Such sectoral agreements cannot be considered in the same way as integration arrangements that include comprehensive provisions and rules on all services.

Convergence and Divergence of Approaches

The convergence and divergence apparent in the approaches to liberalization of trade in services that can be found in the trade and integration agreements of the Western Hemisphere are examined in this section with respect to five

---

8. Sectoral agreements on services (including those in the area of civil aviation) are surveyed in a study by the OAS Trade Unit (1998) entitled *Sectoral Agreements on Services in the Western Hemisphere.*

Table 9-4. Principles on Trade in Services

Agreement	MFN treatment[a]	National treatment	No local presence requirement
GATS	Yes	Yes	No
Mercosur	Yes	Yes	No
NAFTA	Yes	Yes	Yes
Group of Three	Yes	Yes	Yes
Mexico-Bolivia	Yes	Yes	Yes
Mexico–Costa Rica	Yes	Yes	Yes
Chile-Canada	Yes	Yes	Yes
Mexico-Chile	Yes	Yes	Yes
Dominican Republic– Central America	Yes	Yes	Yes
Andean Community	Yes	Yes	No

Source: Comisión Económica para América Latina y el Caribe (1998).

a. With exemptions to MFN treatment allowed under the annex to the GATS and subject to a list of nonconforming measures for the other arrangements.

criteria: principles, provisions and disciplines, market access coverage, negotiating modality, and exceptions.

In the top-down type of integration arrangement the basic principles governing liberalization of trade in services are the following: unconditional most favored nation (MFN) treatment, national treatment, and the absence of local presence requirements. These three basic principles are set out in a general manner, as summarized in table 9-4, though in each of the arrangements existing nonconforming measures (with regard to MFN, national treatment, or local presence requirements) can be specified at the federal, state, or provincial level either at the time the agreement comes into force or within a certain specified period of time thereafter.

Under the bottom-up approach two types of basic principles apply to trade in services. One type is of a general nature, in the form of MFN treatment as described in Article II of the GATS. However, this principle can be the object of temporary exceptions with respect to specific service sectors.[9] In this sense

9. An annex on Article II is attached to the GATS and specifies the procedures by which such exemptions may be sought and the time period for such exemptions (in principle, not more than ten years). The annex subjects exemptions to periodic review and future negotiation.

MFN treatment does not necessarily imply liberal or restrictive conditions of market access; it simply requires that the most favorable treatment be accorded to all foreign service suppliers in all sectors and for all modes of supply.

The other principles in the bottom-up type of agreements are of a specific nature and are the result of the negotiation process. They apply only to those sectors and modes of supply that participants specifically incorporate into their schedules, and they include obligations with respect to market access and national treatment. The Mercosur Framework Agreement on Services includes an obligation to achieve full liberalization for all services (elimination of any conditional limitation to market access and national treatment) within the period of ten years.

With respect to the provisions and disciplines included in the various subregional integration arrangements, the areas in which the top-down and the bottom-up approaches are similar include, among others: definitions, domestic regulation, recognition (of licenses or certifications obtained in a particular country), general exceptions, denial of benefits, and dispute settlement.[10] The areas in which the two approaches differ are set out in table 9-5. One important difference relates to the interplay between services and investment. The top-down type of integration agreement includes separate chapters on investment that set out basic disciplines governing investment and guaranteeing right of establishment. Under the bottom-up type of agreement investment is incorporated as one of the four modes of service delivery. The GATS does not include a comprehensive body of disciplines to protect investment. Prior to its Framework Agreement on Services the Mercosur elaborated a Protocol on Investment, signed in 1994, that included comprehensive disciplines.

Under the bottom-up approach (see table 9-6) market access, like national treatment, is listed under the heading "Specific Commitments" and is binding only when specified for each individual sector or mode of supply and included in the schedule of commitments. Article XVI of the GATS lists the measures that are not to be adopted for those sectors where market access commitments are undertaken unless limitations or restrictions are specified with respect to these commitments. The bottom-up approach allows market access only for those sectors and modes of supply to which members are bound in the schedule of commitments. Under the top-down approach the concept of market access is addressed under disciplines related to nondiscriminatory quantitative restric-

10. The GATS includes references to avoidance of double taxation that the regional integration arrangements do not include.

Table 9-5. Provisions and Disciplines on Trade in Services in Various Agreements

Agreement	Right of nonestablishment	Investment disciplines (comprehensive)	Mutual recognition	Quantitative restrictions
GATS	No	No	Yes	Standstill for scheduled sectors
Mercosur	No	Yes	. . .	Standstill for scheduled sectors
NAFTA	Yes	Yes	Yes	
Group of Three	Yes	Yes	Yes	Standstill for all sectors; future liberalization
Mexico-Bolivia	Yes	Yes	Yes	Standstill for all sectors; future liberalization
Mexico-Chile	Yes	Yes	Yes	Standstill for all sectors; future liberalization
Mexico–Costa Rica	Yes	Yes	Yes	Same
Chile-Canada	Yes	Yes	Yes	Same
Dominican Republic–Central America	Yes	Yes	Yes	Same
Andean Community	Yes	No	Yes	Same

Agreement	Monopoly disciplines	Subsidy disciplines	Safeguard action	Modification of schedules
GATS	Yes	(Future)	Maybe	Possible
Mercosur	No	Yes	Yes	Possible
NAFTA	Yes	No	No	No
Group of Three	Yes	No	No	No
Mexico-Bolivia	Yes[a]	No	Yes	No
Mexico-Chile	Yes[a]	No	No	No
Mexico–Costa Rica	No	No	Yes	No
Chile-Canada	Yes[a]	No	No	No
Dominican Republic–Central America	No	No	Yes	No
Andean Community	Separate decision	No	Yes	No

Source: Comisión Económica para América Latina y el Caribe (1998).

a. Mexico-Bolivia, Mexico-Chile, and Chile-Canada treaties specify monopoly disciplines for telecommunications.

tions as well as through a guaranteed national treatment provision. With respect to nondiscriminatory quantitative restrictions the obligation is to list these measures (the "list or lose" approach), thus ensuring transparency.

The negotiating modality adopted under the bottom-up approach is based on a "positive list" approach that obliges signatories to list national treatment and market access commitments for liberalized access or for a given level of restriction in scheduled sectors. The top-down type of integration arrangement (as shown in table 9-7) is based upon a "negative list" approach, whereby

Table 9-6. Market Access for Service Providers in Various Agreements

Agreement	Coverage of sectors	Coverage of measures	Government procurement
GATS	Selective	Selective	Not covered
Mercosur[a]	Universal	Universal	Not covered
NAFTA	Universal	Universal	Covered
Group of Three	Universal	Universal	Covered
Mexico-Bolivia	Universal	Universal	Covered
Mexico–Costa Rica[b]	Universal	Universal	Covered[b]
Mexico-Chile	Universal	Universal	Not covered
Chile-Canada	Universal	Universal	Universal
Dominican Republic–Central America	Universal	Universal	Universal
Andean Community	Universal	Universal	Universal

a. The Mercosur Framework Agreement specifies the full liberalization of services with respect to all sectors and measures within a ten-year period. The Andean Community Decision 439 sets out the same objective, to be achieved over a five-year period, beginning in the year 2000.

b. In the case of the Mexico–Costa Rica agreement, government procurement will be covered once the list of reservations to Chapter IX (General Principles on Trade in Services) is finalized.

Table 9-7. Negotiating Modality for Services in Various Agreements

Agreement	Modality	Focus of negotiations
GATS	Positive list	Equivalency of commitments
Mercosur	Positive list	Equivalency of commitments
NAFTA	Negative list	List of exceptions
Group of Three	Negative list	List of exceptions
Mexico-Bolivia	Negative list	List of exceptions
Mexico-Chile	Negative list	List of exceptions
Mexico–Costa Rica	Negative list	List of exceptions
Chile-Canada	Negative list	List of exceptions
Dominican Republic–Central America	Negative list	List of exceptions
Andean Community	Negative list	Removal of exceptions

virtually all sectors are included for liberalization along with the obligation to list those nonconforming measures in place (on a "list or lose" basis). The only exceptions to sectoral coverage are specified in the annexes.

In any negotiation the traditional focus of the exchange of concessions has been on the need to broadly determine their equivalency for the purpose of "reciprocity." In the case of services this is much more difficult than it is for goods, since barriers to foreign service providers are present not in the form of border measures such as tariffs and quotas, but in the form of regulatory controls. Also, deregulation and liberalization are not necessarily synonymous in the services area, as they are for goods.

In reality neither of the two negotiating modalities guarantees full liberalization of trade in services. The top-down type of agreement provides a great deal of information in a transparent form on the existing barriers to trade (nonconforming measures). In some cases commitments exist to phase out certain specified nonconforming measures (see, for example, Annex I to the NAFTA) and to negotiate remaining nondiscriminatory quantitative restrictions. In the bottom-up type of agreement the sectoral coverage of commitments may vary significantly between the parties, and the relative importance of the types of conditions and limitations to market access and national treatment does not necessarily reflect existing access conditions (which are often subject to ceiling bindings). Neither type of agreement, as a general rule, includes an obligation to reach a certain level of liberalization within a given period of time. It is worthy of note that the Mercosur Protocol on Services demonstrates an important difference to this practice to the extent that it establishes a time period of ten years within which to achieve total liberalization of trade in services. This is similar to the more recent Decision 439 of the Andean Community, which sets the goal of eliminating all restrictions on trade in services within a five-year period, beginning in the year 2000. If these goals are realized as stated, it would imply the elimination of all conditions and limitations to market access and national treatment within these two subregional groupings.

Finally, certain service sectors have been excluded from the GATS and from the coverage of the subregional arrangements. Table 9-8 shows these sectors. Commercial landing rights or air transport routing agreements have been excluded from the GATS as well as from all the subregional arrangements. Cross-border financial services are also excluded from the Canada-Chile Free Trade Agreement. In the annexes to the NAFTA the following

Table 9-8. Exclusions from Coverage of Service Liberalization in Various Agreements

Agreement	Sector
GATS	Air transport
NAFTA	Air transport and basic government social services
Group of Three	Air transport and basic government social services
Mexico-Bolivia	Air transport and basic government social services
Mexico–Costa Rica	Air transport and financial services
Mexico-Chile	Air transport and cross-border financial services
Canada-Chile	Air transport and cross-border financial services

Agreement	Sectors excluded with reservations
GATS	n.a.
NAFTA	Maritime transport
	Basic telecommunications
	Government social services
	Sectoral others
Group of Three	Not finalized
Mexico-Bolivia	Not finalized
Mexico-Chile	Not finalized
Mexico–Costa Rica	Not finalized
Canada-Chile	Maritime transport
	Basic telecommunications
	Professional services

service sectors are listed as having reservations: basic telecommunications, air transport, and government social services. In the Canada-Chile free trade agreement the following service sectors are listed as exceptions or as having reservations: basic telecommunications, land and water transport, and social and professional services. The Group of Three has recently completed negotiations on its list of excluded service sectors as well as on the list of reservations and nonconforming measures to be set out in the annexes, but these have not yet been made publicly available. Such lists appear to be still under negotiation for the bilateral free trade agreements signed by Mexico with Bolivia and Costa Rica. The service sectors to be excluded from liberalization coverage under the Mercosur during its ten-year implementation period are not yet known.

Toward Negotiations on Services for the FTAA

In the context of the FTAA, the issue of exploring possible options to tackle the liberalization efforts is a crucial one, particularly in light of the thirty-four highly heterogeneous economies that are participating in the FTAA negotiations. Identifying the main elements included in the various existing integration agreements may be helpful to facilitate the understanding and evaluation of alternative possibilities for the FTAA countries in the design and implementation of the arrangements leading to the liberalization of trade in services. In order to make the different alternative schemes used in trade agreements on services more understandable, this section of the chapter discusses the elements most frequently encountered in trade agreements on services. Options regarding the structure and contents of agreements can be most readily visualized in terms of a three-vector matrix comprising coverage, liberalization principles, and depth of commitments (see figure 9-4).

Coverage of Commitments

The first element that needs to be defined in any agreement on services is the coverage of the liberalizing commitments. Given the particularities of trade in services, coverage basically refers to two main issues: the modes of supply (cross-border trade and cross-border trade plus investment) and the number of service sectors included under the trade disciplines. Cross-border trade includes trade from the territory of one party to the territory of the other party; trade in the territory of one party, by a person of that party, to a person of the other party; and trade by a national of one party in the territory of the other party. Cross-border trade plus investment includes all of the previous types of trade plus one party's commercial presence in the other through foreign direct or portfolio investment.

With regard to the number of sectors included in service agreements, the traditional approach has been the sectoral approach. Commitments to liberalize are limited to specific sectors or subsectors of an industry as mutually agreed upon by countries that are party to the agreement. Sectoral agreements with regard to air, land, and sea transportation are typical examples.[11] When the

---

11. It should be noted that agreements on specific service sectors would not meet the conditions set out in Article V of the GATS, particularly with respect to the need for any preferential agreement to include "substantially all sectors," and therefore probably would not be deemed compatible with the WTO requirements.

Figure 9-4. Matrix of Possible Elements of Agreements on Trade in Services

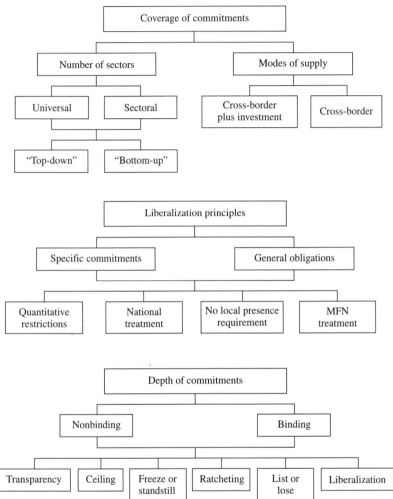

option of universal sectoral coverage is adopted, there are essentially two mechanisms by which the liberalization commitments may be met: the bottom-up or positive list approach and the top-down or negative list approach, which have already been referred to.

Liberalization Principles

Regarding the liberalization principles included in service agreements, efforts to open foreign markets are usually guided by one or several trade principles, most of which have been legitimized in international trade relations for a long time. These principles essentially have the purpose of reducing or eliminating the use of discriminatory practices in international trade in the form of differentiated treatment granted, as between different trade partners or as between national and foreign services and service providers.

However, once again it is important to make a further distinction regarding the applicability of such principles. Two basic approaches can be adopted: establishing the liberalization principles as general obligations, as is the case in the NAFTA-type agreements, or as part of the specific commitments. In the case of the GATS, some of the obligations are of a general nature, such as MFN treatment, whereas others are part of the specific commitments, such as national treatment. The choice of one approach instead of the other will have different implications, particularly with regard to the depth of the agreed-upon commitments and their trade impact.

Four principles of liberalization of border trade in services are usually taken into consideration.

MOST FAVORED NATION TREATMENT.   This is one of the fundamental principles used to secure nondiscrimination in international trade. This principle obliges member countries to give the most favorable treatment accorded to any of their trading partners to all the other members immediately and unconditionally. Many countries accord preferential treatment to some of their commercial partners in certain sectors such as transportation, telecommunications, recognition of professional qualifications, and other services. Exemptions to the requirement of MFN treatment may be included within the provisions of an agreement. However, a strong commitment to comply with this principle will reduce discriminatory treatment in international trade and will strengthen transparency in trade.

ABSENCE OF A LOCAL PRESENCE REQUIREMENT. Countries frequently require a local presence (that is, an established trade presence) as a condition for foreign individuals or juridical persons who wish to provide services within their territory. This is usually the case when services require close supervision to guarantee consumer protection. In fact, this requirement may hinder international trade, as it may impose higher costs on foreign service suppliers who are not allowed to use the other modes of supply. The alternative is to allow the service providers to choose the modes of supply.

NATIONAL TREATMENT. Services and service providers from another country are to be accorded treatment no less favorable than that accorded to similar services and service providers that originate in the nation where services are being provided. Violations of the principle of national treatment in the area of trade in services include a wide variety of practices ranging from imposition of nationality or permanent residence requirements to discriminatory practices with regard to fiscal measures, access to local credit and foreign exchange services, limitation of the types of services that may be rendered by foreign suppliers, and many others.

ABSENCE OF TECHNICAL OR QUANTITATIVE RESTRICTIONS. Technical considerations or market size may induce governments to establish quantitative nondiscriminatory restrictions on the rendering of certain services. Such is the case in the allocation of radio and television frequencies, the number of banks allowed to operate in a given market, or the number of telecommunication companies authorized to provide cellular and basic telephone services in a given region within the country. These restrictions may also be associated with unfair business practices, which may limit competition and allow for open discrimination in favor of a limited number of suppliers. Technology and other technical considerations permitting, a gradual elimination of these measures is a desirable goal when seeking full liberalization of trade in services.

Depth of Commitments

The depth of the commitments may vary. Going from lower to higher levels of commitment, we can identify the most commonly used instruments to foster freer trade.

TRANSPARENCY. This is normally the most basic or minimal level of commitment within an agreement on trade in services. It requires all members of the agreement to either directly inform the other parties or set up national "inquiry points"—at the levels of the central or federal government and of state, provincial, or local governments—to facilitate access to all the existing measures that may affect trade in services with respect to the disciplines developed for purposes of liberalization.

CEILING BINDING. A long-established practice in merchandise trade agreements, the setting of a ceiling binding is also used for the adoption of commitments regarding trade in services. For instance, in the GATS schedule of commitments a country may set up or indicate conditions and limitations to market access and national treatment that are not parts of the existing legal or regulatory measures of that respective country. An example could be setting up maximum screening quotas for foreign audiovisual programs, which could be expressed as a cap on the daily percentage of programs, and the country involved might reserve the freedom to operate below the quota.

A "FREEZE" OR "STANDSTILL" ON EXISTING NONCONFORMING MEASURES. This involves freezing the existing regime and measures up to a given date and making a commitment not to make such measures more non-conforming in the future. This type of commitment, known as a "grandfather clause," is used in agreements on trade in goods and in some agreements on trade in services (as in the NAFTA, in agreements at federal and provincial levels, and in the GATS with regard to MFN treatment).

RATCHETING. In addition to making a commitment to freeze existing measures, a country can establish a moving floor of commitments. No back-sliding is thus allowed for any unilateral liberalization implemented after the effective date of the freeze. If a given sector has been liberalized after the freeze date, any country party to the agreement cannot revert to a less liberal state of trade in the respective sector. This type of commitment is present in NAFTA-type agreements at federal and provincial levels.

"LIST OR LOSE." This type of commitment supplements a transparency commitment and speeds up the process of liberalization. In the identification of nonconforming measures with regard to a given sector or subsector, the parties undertake the obligation to list all measures that do not conform to the agreed-upon provisions of the agreement. Failure to include any nonconforming measure in the list is understood to eliminate the measure in question with respect to the other parties to the agreement. This is the approach adopted by NAFTA members with regard to the existing nonconforming measures at the federal or national level. However, such an approach failed to be implemented at the state or provincial level for those same countries.

Based on the elements included in the three vectors developed above, however, different sets of combinations can be considered by the FTAA participants as they negotiate a hemispheric agreement on services. The various components with regard to coverage, liberalization principles, and depth of commitments may be mixed, and the final combination of elements will depend on the specific commercial interests of each of the countries participating in the agreement and their individual views on the advantages that more open and liberalized service markets can afford. A customized method of negotiation can therefore be designed, and a series of commitments can be envisaged for a given group of countries that wish to advance in the preferential liberalization of their trade in services.

Conclusions and Policy Issues

The countries of the Western Hemisphere comprise a wide variety of developed and developing countries with important differences in terms of area, size of population, and availability of natural, human, and technological resources. They also vary substantially with regard to the stages of their institutional development as well as the status of their market and financial incentives, their regulatory systems, and their organizational arrangements. As noted earlier in this chapter, such differences are clearly illustrated by the fact that the gross national product (GNP) of the largest service exporter in the hemisphere (the United States) is 4,344 times larger than that of the smallest exporter (St. Vincent and the Grenadines). Also, there are wide differences in the quality and pricing of services available throughout the various countries. Furthermore, important differences exist with regard to the industry composition of their service sectors, their degree of openness to foreign competition, and their readiness to confront a more open and competitive environment. Countries also differ in their social and political perceptions of the strategic importance of certain service industries and the role of the state as the sole provider of key services.

As a result, one of the greatest challenges facing the countries of the Western Hemisphere in the area of services is the development of disciplines capable of providing for greater transparency, higher degrees of legal certainty, and a more open environment for trade in services for all countries of the hemisphere. When examining the existing service agreements in the hemisphere as well as the GATS, it is quite apparent that all of them present some important limitations. At this stage it already seems unlikely that a hemispheric trade agreement on services could mirror any of the existing arrays. Presumably a new arrangement will require the development of disciplines that are structured on an ad hoc basis and take into account the various concerns of all participating countries. Most of these concerns derive from the asymmetries and important differences among the countries of the hemisphere that were sketched in the previous paragraph.

Among the main limitations of the existing agreements, the lack of disciplines in key areas such as safeguards, subsidies, government procurement, and competition policy are usually noted. Likewise, all of these agreements rely on rather weak provisions for achieving free and open trade in services within a given time frame. Commitments and disciplines with regard to transparency as well as the movement of natural persons are either lacking or insufficient. With the exception of high-level personnel or intrafirm transferees, very little progress has been achieved with regard to the movement of natural persons of more direct commercial interest to the vast majority of countries (such as persons in lower skill categories or migrant laborers).

Following is a list of concerns that will have to be addressed with particular emphasis in the upcoming process of developing an FTAA agreement on services. This list is by no means exhaustive, nor does it imply any kind of ranking of priorities among the points discussed. As already noted, an important concern arises from the fact that there are significant asymmetries in the existing regulatory regimes throughout the Western Hemisphere. Many countries have expressed their legitimate concern with the absence or incompleteness of regulations in many of their key service industries. These regulations are in sharp contrast with the heavy, highly sophisticated, and on occasion protectionist regulatory systems in existence in the most advanced countries of the hemisphere. The lack of regulations in many countries has been the result of rapid privatization and deregulation and the introduction of very deep policies oriented toward a free market that have taken place in recent years in many developing countries in the region. Areas such as consumer protection, national security, market stability, and cultural and environmental preservation have all been affected by this fast deregulation trend. As a result, many of these areas may have been left dangerously unprotected. This lack of protection, coupled with the insufficient historical perspective, has made it very difficult to duly assess the merits as well as the social and economic gains of such important transformation.

A second point of concern relates to the handling of unfair commercial practices and the role of the state as guarantor of competition. Many service industries operate under monopolistic or oligopolistic conditions, often imposed for technical reasons. This often makes it necessary to introduce regulations that will mimic competition. However, adequate competition policies and appropriate legislation in this area are lacking in many of the countries of the Western Hemisphere. As a result, the full potential benefit of liberalization is not always realized in many of these countries. Anticompetitive practices employed by domestic or foreign service providers have sometimes nullified the benefits expected. Furthermore, results in terms of costs, quality, and accessibility of services have been disappointing due to the inadequacy of institutional development (for instance, the development of supervisory agencies) or insufficient legislation regarding competition.

Important technological innovations are affecting traditional modes of supplying services internationally. In particular, the potential for growth of traded services has been dramatically expanded with the irruption of electronic commerce. This important development remains largely unexplored vis-à-vis the critical need to assess its potential impact on domestic service industries, employment, balance of payments, government revenues, tax treatment of the same services provided by other means, consumer protection, and many other factors. In this regard, there is also legitimate concern regarding those countries with limited or nonexistent possibilities for using this new trade channel for the expansion of their own service exports.

The well-known inadequacy of the existing statistical information on the flow of trade in services puts an additional pressure on the FTAA governments and negotiators alike. This may explain a certain reluctance on the part of some countries to undertake substantial commitments in an area in which it is impossible at present to carry out a quantitative evaluation of the trade impact of such liberalization.

Finally, the concerns of the smaller economies of the hemisphere must not be overlooked. For many of these countries service export receipts largely exceed their merchandise export earnings. Particular attention should be given to the issue of minimizing the social and economic impacts deriving from the structural changes required to achieve a more open service regime while at the same time creating the conditions necessary for these countries to expand and diversify their own service exports to the markets of the hemisphere.

These are not minor challenges. The framework of rules and disciplines that needs to be developed must be capable of fully addressing these concerns as the only way to secure an equitable result of the negotiations, with clear gains for all of the participating countries.

References

Comisión Económica para América Latina y el Caribe. 1998. *América Latina y el Caribe: Series Estadísticas sobre Comercio de Servicios 1980–1997*. Document LC/G.2023. Santiago, Chile (July).

———. *A Bibliographical Note on Trade in Services: Concepts and Liberalization Principles*. Document CEPAL/ALCA/GTS/001. Santiago, Chile.

General Agreement on Trade in Services. 1994. "General Agreement on Trade in Services and Related Instruments." In *Uruguay Round Legal Texts*. Geneva: GATT Secretariat (April).

International Monetary Fund. 1995. *Yearbook*. Washington, D.C.

———. 1997. *International Financial Statistics*. Washington, D.C.

Ministerial Declaration of San José. 1998. Summit of the Americas, Fourth Trade Ministerial Meeting. San José, Costa Rica (March 19).

North American Free Trade Agreement. 1992. Vols. 1 and 2. Washington, D.C.: U.S. Government Printing Office.

———. 1994. Washington, D.C.: U.S. Government Printing Office.

Organization of American States Trade Unit. 1997. *Provisions on Trade in Services in Trade and Integration Agreements of the Western Hemisphere*. Washington, D.C. (May).

———. 1998. *Sectoral Agreements on Services in the Western Hemisphere*. Washington, D.C. (March).

Ministerio de Relaciones Exteriores—República de Chile. 1997. *Tratado de Libre Comercio Chile-Canada*. Tercera Parte: *Inversión, Servicios y Asuntos Relacionados: Dirección General de Relaciones Económicas Internacionales*.

World Bank. 1997. *World Development Report*. Washington, D.C.

World Trade Organization. 1996. *Trade and Foreign Direct Investment*. Geneva: WTO Secretariat.

———. 1997. *Annual Report*, vol. 1. Geneva: WTO Secretariat.

CHAPTER TEN

Rules of Origin in Free Trade Agreements in the Americas

Luis Jorge Garay S. and Rafael Cornejo

The objective of this chapter is to examine the role of rules of origin in free trade areas (FTAs) and to explore the criteria applied to determine origin. More specifically, the chapter analyzes the basic features of rules of origin that exist in the Americas and the importance of current trade in the Americas, and finally it offers some guidelines for increasing the compatibility and harmonization of the different origin regimes.

The Role of Rules of Origin

Trade agreements are the means through which countries grant each other different forms of preferential trade treatment. To ensure these preferences there must be guidelines to enable the origin of goods to be defined and to guarantee that the negotiated preferences benefit only those products originating in the member countries. Trade agreement terms, therefore, include origin regimes that stipulate the provisions and procedures for determining countries of origin.

Commercial exchanges in an FTA involve goods wholly obtained or produced in an exporting member nation, as well as a range of goods containing components from third countries outside the FTA. For this latter type of merchandise it is necessary to define the conditions, types, or amounts of imported components that these goods can contain and still be considered as originating inside the FTA. In accordance with this need, origin regimes are essentially based on the idea of substantial transformation, which determines the minimum level of processing and modification that components from third countries must undergo for the merchandise to be considered as originating in an exporting FTA member nation.

Rules of origin exist to prevent what is technically known as trade deflection or trans-shipment—a phenomenon in which goods from third countries receive the benefits granted by the trade agreement. Trade deflection occurs when FTA member countries impose different tariff levels on goods from third countries and when these third countries exploit this difference in order to bring merchandise into the FTA through the member country with the lowest tariffs. Requiring a minimum level of substantial transformation of goods aims to prevent such distortions by strictly limiting the applicability of the tariff advantages to those goods that meet the FTA's rules of origin.

If the aim of rules of origin is to prevent trade deflection, their stringency should be correlated to the difference between the national tariffs applicable to third countries: the greater the differential, the more demanding the requirements goods must meet in order to qualify. Similarly, when national third-country tariff rates are similar—or, alternatively, when they are relatively low—the need for rules of origin should be reassessed, particularly since the costs of administering and overseeing them can actually exceed the difference in individual tariffs.

If the goal of rules of origin is strategic—related to industrial development or trade policy, for example—origin requirements can be set independently of third-country tariff differentials. A series of factors affect the restrictiveness of an origin regime—and, in addition to other effects, in practice hinder its predictability. These include component substitution within domestic production, depending on the components' geographical origin; technological change; the supply from domestic industries that produce intermediate goods; the structure of the market for intermediate goods in the integrated zone; and the protection or promotion of output vis-à-vis third countries.

In turn, the origin regime can have a number of restrictive effects, including inefficiencies if components are imperfect substitutes or if oligopolistic competition prevails; discrimination between productive sectors and types of producers, favoring those companies that are better able to adapt to and satisfy the requirements imposed by the origin regime; greater restrictions on regional trade in downstream activities or later stages of productive processes; and unequal distribution of benefits among factors of production, activities, and countries.[1]

One of the clearest discriminatory effects occurs in the field of investment, particularly when the requirements for qualifying as originating are more stringent. Since multinational foreign investors frequently use inputs from outside the region or from their home countries, the existence of demanding rules about incorporating regional content or about technical requirements can severely restrict the implementation of their normal productive processes within an FTA. Such a situation would, at least in principle, favor investors from the region's member countries and could even lead to a true diversion of investment. Moreover, the modifications required of extraregional companies' productive processes to operate in the region in compliance with the origin demands would negatively affect their efficiency and competitiveness.[2] It should be noted, however, that in subregional economies that are sufficiently large and dynamic and offer potential for economies of scale, the existence of relatively demanding rules of origin can act as an incentive for extraregional investments with the capacity to benefit from the FTA's preferential access.

In recent years the importance of rules of origin within integration processes has risen as a result of the growing internationalization of production —and, consequently, of the increased number of countries supplying components for productive processes. Their importance has also increased due to the notable increase in trade agreements established during the 1990s and the strategic nature of the preferential lifting of tariffs that has been part of some of the FTA agreements negotiated by countries in the Americas in recent years.[3]

In addition, it is important to mention the potential magnitude of the operational and administrative costs of certifying and verifying the specific rules of origin and regimes for both domestic customs and the manufacturing firms themselves. This would heighten the losses in efficiency that the system as a whole could suffer. In theory, net operating costs can be expected to rise with increased administrative complexity, lack of transparency, multiple qualification criteria, and the proliferation of "rules of origin families" becoming more critical. This is all the more likely given the growing international integration of production. As an example, in Europe the costs of collecting, managing, and

1. For a more detailed treatment of these issues, see Garay and Estevadeordal (1996).
2. Barfield (1996, p. 42) and Winters (1997, p. 35).
3. Garay and Quintero (1997).

storing the information needed for origin verification and administration have been calculated at around 3 percent of product prices.[4]

Given these potentially restrictive effects on intraregional trade, origin regimes should be designed to be transparent, objective, and predictable and to be easily administered. Rules that are so complex or so costly to implement that they prevent economic agents from enjoying the commercial advantages introduced by an FTA should be avoided.

Given the dimensions and the diversity of the problems with applying rules of origin, the question arises whether it would be better to opt for a common external tariff (CET) within the framework of a customs union (CU) instead of for an FTA wherein member nations have different national tariffs. However, as pointed out by Garay and Quintero:

> If one of the reasons for establishing an FTA rather than a CU is the existence of substantial differences in third-country tariff policies between member nations, rules of origin will clearly be used to enable those tariff differentials to coexist alongside a preferential liberalization of intra-regional trade. [In such a case,] were it decided to reconcile those different policies in order to fix a CET, a compromise policy from among the policies deemed "desirable" by each of the members would have to be reached. . . . It is not possible to offer an a priori opinion on the general superiority of one such option in terms of social well being.[5]

Criteria for Origin Qualification

Origin regimes define a good as originating inside an FTA when it is produced or obtained entirely within the member nations.[6] If it uses imported components from third countries, compliance with the required levels of substantial transformation is determined by applying criteria from among the following:

CHANGE OR SHIFT IN TARIFF CLASSIFICATION. This involves meeting a minimum requirement for changes in the tariff classification between a finished good and the foreign components or materials (from third countries

4. Garay and Quintero (1997, pp. 4–5).
5. Garay and Quintero (1997, p. 5).
6. See, among others, Garay and Estevadeordal (1996) and Garay and Quintero (1997).

outside the integrated area) used in the production process. For example, a change in the tariff heading—that is, in the first four digits of the tariff classification determined by the Harmonized Commodity Coding and Classification System (HS)—is the basis for the preferential rules of origin system used by such organizations as the Latin American Integration Association (Aladi).

Among the main problems with the application of this criterion is the difficulty in determining those specific changes in tariff classification that guarantee equivalent substantial transformation in the production of all goods covered by tariffs. This is basically because the HS was designed not to serve as the sole instrument for determining the origin of goods, but rather to be used in classifying merchandise in terms of other criteria.

NATIONAL OR REGIONAL VALUE ADDED. This is defined as the maximum level of components and raw materials from third countries a good can have and still be considered as originating inside the integrated area or, alternatively, as the minimum value that must be added during intraregional processing for the good to qualify as originating in the FTA.

This criterion suffers from several shortcomings, including the following: it tends to penalize the use of more efficient, cost-saving techniques; it is highly sensitive to changes in the factors that determine countries' production costs, such as relative exchange rates, inflation rates, interest rates, commodity prices, wages, and workers' benefits; it can increase the cost of administering compliance in light of the need for laborious and demanding accounting, operational, and financial procedures both at domestic customs stations and within manufacturing companies themselves; and it tends to sustain imbalances in the distribution of benefits among countries, not only by favoring those with more vertically integrated and complex productive apparatuses (such as those of industrialized nations), but also by penalizing, in relative terms, those with low wages and salaries, such as countries with lower relative levels of development.[7]

There is also a problem with reliably classifying, by specific origin, the intermediate materials and components used in the production process and exactly calculating their corresponding values within a finished good's regional content value, and also with classifying all components as of either regional or extraregional origin—concepts known as roll-up and roll-down.

7. Garay and Estevadeordal (1996).

Roll-down applies when a manufactured good contains imported parts from third countries that do not satisfy the origin requirements, thus preventing the end product from being classified as originating in the exporting country. In contrast, roll-up occurs when a manufactured good contains parts imported from third countries that satisfy the requirements of origin. In this case, the product is considered to have originated from the region. In such circumstances the problem is identifying the ultimate country of origin of the good. This issue assumes even greater importance if the good is later used as a component in the manufacture of other merchandise. Only with the application of a strict classification of the origins of the various raw materials and processed components used at the different stages of the production process can the generation of differing impacts on producers with different levels of vertical integration be avoided.

USE OF GIVEN TECHNICAL PROCESSES OR COMPONENTS IN MANU-FACTURING.   Under this criterion specific technical operations must be carried out or specific components or raw materials must be used in production for a good to be classified as originating inside a region. In addition to the technical difficulties of keeping an updated, comprehensive inventory of the productive processes available at any given time—arising, among other things, from the fact that they are constantly changing—specifications are still discretionary because of the absence of classification elements that objectively guarantee the equivalence of different degrees of transformation in the production of different goods.

Types of Regimes in Force in the Americas

Origin regimes in force in the Americas are found not only in regional framework schemes such as those of the Aladi, the Central American Common Market (CACM), the Andean Community, the Southern Common Market (Mercosur), the Caribbean Community (CARICOM), and the North American Free Trade Agreement (NAFTA), but also in other trade agreements signed in recent years. In a few of the more recently signed agreements the origin clauses differ markedly from those in force in other framework agreements entered into by the same signatory nations. This is the case in Mexico's agreement with Bolivia, as well as in its FTA agreement with Colombia and Venezuela (the agreement known as the Group of Three or G-3).

These regimes can be classified into two large groups by their content, scope, and salient features. On the one side is the Aladi type of regime, which has served as a model for the Mercosur, the Andean Community, and the CARICOM. On the other is the NAFTA type of regime, which has been used as a model for Mexico's agreements with Bolivia, Colombia, Costa Rica, and Venezuela and for Chile's agreements with Canada and Mexico. Finally, the recently established CACM regime stands at an intermediate point between these extremes.

This division coincides with the specialized literature's classification of trade agreements into "first-generation" (the Aladi agreement and similar pacts) and "new-generation" (the NAFTA and G-3 and Mexico's bilateral treaties) agreements. New-generation agreements are generally more comprehensive than those of the first generation in that they cover issues such as investment, government procurement, and services, and they include more specific and detailed origin regimes.

It should be noted that these classifications have nothing to do with the dates on which the agreements came into force. This needs to be stated to avoid the false idea that first-generation origin rules are anachronistic or outdated and that those of the new generation are modern and up-to-date.

Each generic origin regime is characterized by different features that can be amended and adapted in accordance with the basic trade policy goals pursued, with different degrees of selectivity or uniformity, strictness, transparency, predictability, and so on. Some of the traditional Latin America integration schemes have in recent years modified their regimes. This indicates those countries' resolve to apply rules that are more selective and less uniform than those of Aladi Resolution 78 (described a bit later) while preserving the tariff shift as the basic qualification criterion and rejecting a multiplicity of "rules families" at the tariff item level, which occur under new-generation regimes. Of particular interest is the CACM regime, which combines greater selectivity (nonuniformity) among types of goods, much as in new-generation regimes, while preserving the change in tariff classification as the basic criterion for origin qualification (and including the option of exceptions for tariff classification shifts).

One way of analyzing the different regimes in force is by comparing the principal features of three regimes, which are used as reference frameworks: the Aladi, NAFTA, and CACM regimes.

The Aladi Regime

Aladi Resolution 78 establishes the general origin regime for the Aladi member nations, which applies to regional and partial agreements signed by those countries before 1994. Although some of the latter pacts have individual rules, they are not substantially different from those of the general regime. These rules govern partial agreements for renegotiations of traditional agreements of economic complementation and those signed by Aladi members with other countries or regions under Article 25 of the Montevideo Treaty.

Resolution 78 establishes the basic criterion for origin qualification as a change in the tariff classification in terms of HS heading number (four digits) or, alternatively, as a regional content value equal to or greater than 50 percent of the free on board (FOB) cost of the merchandise. This applies to practically all tariff classifications with the exception of a group of goods specifically negotiated by the member countries, for which certain specific origin requirements (SORs) must be fulfilled. The specific requirements take precedence over the general criteria and can be less stringent than the general rules, except for goods originating from relatively less-developed countries. Resolution 78 allows differential treatment for relatively less-developed countries (Bolivia, Ecuador, and Paraguay), whose exports are permitted to have less national or regional content. One requirement of Resolution 78 involves obtaining an obligatory certificate of origin that is created using a special form and issued by a public or private agency authorized for this purpose by the member states. Unfortunately, the Aladi regime's lack of precision in enforcing compliance with the qualification criteria and for certifying and administering the rules of origin has, in practice, hindered the strict observance of these.[8]

Although the main elements of the origin regimes of the Mercosur and the Andean Community are similar to those of Resolution 78, there are also some noteworthy differences. For some goods the Mercosur regime demands 60 percent added value and also a change in tariff heading. When substantial transformation cannot be measured by a shift in tariff classification, the regime states that the cost, insurance, and freight (CIF) price of the third-country inputs is not to exceed 40 percent of the FOB cost of the merchandise. Furthermore, Mercosur Decision 16/97 sets SORs for a list of goods from the chemical, iron and steel, data processing, and communications sectors. These requirements are applied as exceptional rules and take precedence over the

8. Devlin, Estevadeordal, and Garay (1997).

general criteria. The Mercosur regime has no provisions for differential treatment. However, the Mercosur's agreements with Bolivia and Chile provide for differential treatment in that they set less stringent requirements for goods from Paraguay and Bolivia.

The Andean Community, in turn, has an origin regime similar to that of Resolution 78, which admits special requirements in exceptional cases. In addition, it grants Bolivia and Ecuador preferential treatment. The Andean Community used some special requirements in the 1970s as part of its import substitution and industrial sector planning strategies.

It should be noted that the Andean Community's origin regime, established by Decisions 416 and 417 of July 1997, introduced important provisions regarding origin administration. Some of these were novel even in comparison to those of new-generation regimes, particularly those dealing with the dispute resolution system, which stipulated in detail the functions and obligations of the member countries' competent government authorities in this area and specified procedures for requesting the General Secretariat's intervention and guidelines for its decisions. They also detailed the sanctions applicable to certification agencies and officers for issuing irregular origin certificates and specified the requirements to be met by nongovernmental agencies empowered to certify the origin of merchandise. Finally, they regulated the criteria and procedures for setting SORs.

The NAFTA Regime

With the launch of the NAFTA in January 1994, a new type of regime for origin rules came into force. It is characterized, among others, by the following elements:

—It is a system of specific rules at the tariff item level, which are arrived at by combining some or even all of the three types of qualification criteria described earlier. Frequently more than one rule exists for determining a good's origin.

—It applies changes of tariff classifications in a much more versatile fashion than the other regimes. Classification shifts are not unique for all tariff classifications, but are rather defined according to the merchandise type broken down by chapter, heading, and subheading, and in some cases even by the tariff item (described by the eight digits of the HS classification). The different levels of tariff liberalization are used both to define the required changes of classification and to limit their scope by providing for the option of excluding certain tariff levels from the main requirements. For somewhat more than 40 percent of the existing tariff items a movable classification shift is used to determine their origin, with the additional feature that a good number of these goods also have more than one alternate qualification rule.

—It uses the regional content criterion for around a third of all items, either on its own or, more frequently, in combination with one of the other criteria. It establishes a minimum regional content value of 50 percent or 60 percent, depending on the method used for calculations (the net cost or transaction value method).

—It includes concepts not used in earlier regimes, such as a "de minimis" clause, accumulation, and self-certification by exporting companies.[9]

One of the major differences between the basic NAFTA regime and the general regimes of the Aladi and the Generalized System of Preferences (GSP) is its greater selectivity, specificity, and detail. This regime's level of detail can be seen in the official Mexican bulletin called *General Rules for the Application of the Customs Provisions of the North American Free Trade Agreement,* whose Chapter 4, dealing with rules of origin, runs to almost 100 pages.

The CACM Regime

The CACM regime is a combination of the regimes already described. The main criterion is tariff classification change, albeit it is applied more flexibly than in the Aladi regime in that it is measured in terms of changes in chapter, heading, and subheading, and in a number of cases it allows exceptions to be made to the main change. Only with regard to some specific goods does it set additional specific criteria, such as regional content and technical requirements, which to date have not been practically applied. This regime uses concepts found in new-generation agreements, such as a de minimis clause. In addition, it does not provide for differential treatment of countries with lower relative levels of development.

The CACM regime is without doubt a novelty in Latin America, since it also introduces a series of rules and procedures to ensure correct administration of and due compliance with the rules of origin. The use of tariff shifts as the basic

---

9. The "de minimis" clause is a clause under which a good can be classified as being of regional origin provided that the value of the raw materials that fail to meet the tariff classification change requirement does not exceed a given percentage of the good's value.

criterion, but applying them differently across the full range of tariff classifications, appears to be an attempt to combine administrative simplicity with greater
detail and selectivity in the rules of origin applied to different types of goods.

Differences between Alternative Regimes

The origin regimes in force in the Americas use some or all of the criteria
described above. Some of the differences between them arise from whether
they follow uniform or differentiated application of the rules, from their having
multiple criteria, and from the methods they use to calculate the value of
regional or national content.

Diversity

The three types of qualification criteria used to determine origin can be used
uniformly or selectively. The chief difference between the origin regimes is in
which way the criterion or criteria are applied among goods: uniformly for all
merchandise or selectively between types of merchandise. This difference can
be seen, for example, in the ways the tariff classification change criterion is
applied by the regimes: the Aladi regime defines it uniformly as a change in
classification at the heading level, regardless of the type of merchandise. In
contrast, under regimes like those of the NAFTA and G-3 the required tariff
change varies according to the good in question, and in different cases a change
in chapter, heading, subheading, or even tariff item can be required.

Multiplicity

Although the regimes in force in the Americas include more than one
criterion for classifying origin, they differ in the relative weight they assign to
each. The origin regimes of the Mercosur, CACM, Andean Community, and
Aladi are basically defined in terms of the tariff classification change criterion
or, alternatively, by a given level of regional content. In some exceptional
cases, however, a combination of criteria is used for specific lists of goods. In
contrast, the NAFTA and G-3 regimes and those of some of Mexico's bilateral
agreements are based on a multiplicity of criteria, which prevents any particular criterion from being singled out as the guiding principle for determining
origin. In part, this multiplicity applies to specific origin rules with the high
degree of detail and selectivity seen in new-generation agreements.

Alternation

The regimes also differ in their application of the qualification criteria at the level of individual goods. *Alternation* is to be understood as the application of more than one rule to classify the origin of a given good. In the regimes of the Aladi, Mercosur, CACM, and Andean Community, alternation is uniform across all tariff classifications, with the additional feature that each alternate rule is exclusively based on a single qualification criterion. The first criterion is based on a change in tariff heading, and the alternate one on a specific regional content value. In contrast, the regimes of the NAFTA, the G-3, and the Mexican and Chilean bilateral agreements frequently offer a variety of alternate rules for determining a good's origin, and each rule is not necessarily based on a single qualification criterion.

The set of alternate rules applicable at the individual item level is defined as a *rules of origin family,* and, at least in principle, all alternate rules of origin applicable to an individual item should stipulate equivalent demands in terms of substantial transformation. In practice, however, their levels of stringency differ as a result of the requirements of each of the criteria used to determine origin. If there are goods for which the implied degree of transformation varies between the alternate applicable rules, de facto inconsistencies and inequalities can arise among different types of companies in the FTA and its member countries.

Similar consequences tend to arise when different rules of origin families are applied to goods that, in terms of their production techniques or economic nature, are strictly similar or when a single rules of origin family is used to qualify goods produced by means of different productive processes.

Calculation Method

The methods used for calculating regional content value vary among regimes. The Aladi, Mercosur, and Andean Community regimes require the FOB or CIF transaction value of the merchandise to be used in calculating its regional or national content. These values are well known, clear, and are published, and they require neither the exporter nor the customs authorities to keep special records or maintain additional controls. The regimes of the NAFTA and some of Mexico's bilateral agreements use two alternate methods for calculating regional content: net cost and transaction value. Estimating the value of regional content using the net cost method requires detailed records of and information on merchandise promotion and sale costs. The CACM regime is midway between the other two regimes in that it uses two methods to determine regional content: transaction value, defined in accordance with the World Trade Organization's (WTO's) customs valuation code, and normal price, calculated from the FOB price of the exported goods and the CIF price of third-country components.

The new-generation agreements include novel concepts aimed at, among other things, increasing the flexibility of the tariff classification change criteria by introducing de minimis clauses, facilitating the regional integration of production processes by allowing the accumulation of regional components in calculating regional content values, and streamlining the origin certification process by enabling exporting companies to issue their own certificates. They also specify with greater detail and precision the procedures and activities for verification, control, and sanction—issues that an origin regime must address but that were not dealt with adequately in some first-generation agreements. It should be noted that some of these stipulations or innovations can increase the cost of administering the rules of origin for both the public and private sectors, but they guarantee adequate rigor in the application of the regime.

The FTAA and Origin Regimes

During the Summit of the Americas held in Miami in December 1994, the participating nations agreed to begin working toward the creation of a Free Trade Area of the Americas (FTAA), with negotiations due to conclude in the year 2005. The FTAA agreement essentially resembles a new-generation agreement, covering issues beyond the traditional trade and investment arenas. To address these issues, twelve working groups were set up to analyze different problems commonly associated with an integration project of this size. One of these groups was charged with studying customs procedures and rules of origin.

The country representatives in this working group identified a series of issues to be borne in mind vis-à-vis an origin regime for the FTAA. Two of these are worthy of particular note: the need to develop an efficient origin regime that facilitates the exchange of goods without creating unnecessary obstacles to trade and the need for both the drafting and the administration of the rules to be objective, transparent, consistent, and predictable. The representatives also decided that the regime to be negotiated must be consistent with the commitments acquired within the framework of the WTO and that in drawing up the regime the HS would be followed.[10] One of the main guidelines adopted, at least in principle, was the acceptance of changes in tariff classification —with the inclusion of exceptions to tariff classification shifts—as a basic criterion for determining origin, supplemented, as appropriate, by regional content value.

In this regard it should be noted that one of the ways to improve a qualification system based on changes in tariff classification is to define a relatively consistent regime across all tariff items that allows exceptions to be made to the main change according to the level of transformation demanded by the good's production process. In other words, consistent equivalencies should be established between levels of change in tariff classification (for example, tariff chapter, heading, or subheading) and degrees of productive transformation implemented.

Specifying a consistent regime that would substantially facilitate the administration of rules of origin would go a long way toward ensuring that compliance with origin requirements was less sensitive to fluctuations in external variables, and it would additionally favor transparency and simplicity within the origin regime. It would also allow the selection and application of nonuniform origin requirements for different types of goods, such as is appropriate within the context of a strategic trade policy. It is for these and similar reasons that such proposals for defining origin classification methods for nonpreferential trade are being so warmly welcomed.

Analysis of the advantages and disadvantages of the methods for defining origin has been going on for some time. For example, in 1987 a seminal document submitted by the U.S. International Trade Commission to the House of Representatives was published. It identified some of the failings of the criteria used to determine origin and offered four basic principles to be used in developing rules of origin: uniformity, simplicity, predictability, and ease of administration.[11] It also recommended adopting an approach based on requiring a specific productive process to be executed for a good to qualify as

10. The agreements reached to date on this matter by the WTO are found in Annex 1 of the final report, including the results of the Uruguay Round of multilateral trade negotiations (held in Marrakesh on April 15, 1994). The member nations are currently negotiating a nonpreferential origin regime to be applied to antidumping and countervailing duties, safeguard clauses, most favored nation status, and quantitative restrictions or discriminatory tariff contingencies.

11. U.S. International Trade Commission (1987).

originating. Unfortunately, as stated earlier, this has the disadvantage of requiring a detailed and updated inventory of all the processes available for manufacturing all possible goods.

The chief U.S. negotiator for rules of origin in the FTA between Canada and the United States and in the NAFTA recently recommended the following: eliminating the regional content value requirement, because it is the main reason for the NAFTA's exaggerated demands for information storage, processing, and auditing, which makes it "Byzantine in its complexity"; using simple rules of origin based on tariff classification changes as a transition toward creation of a CU and avoiding changes at a level of detail beyond six digits of the HS classification; and creating sectoral CUs to bring about the elimination of rules of origin in the corresponding sectors and to allow progress toward a "true" CU.[12]

In any event, as pointed out by Garay and Estevadeordal, emphasis should be placed on choosing principles aimed at specifying the goal sought by the origin regime; keeping the number of criteria for determining origin as low as possible; ensuring adequate consistency between alternate rules of origin and the levels of productive transformation demanded; maximizing the simplicity and transparency of procedures for overseeing compliance with these rules; duly assessing the advantages of adopting alternate transparent policy measures other than restrictive rules of origin, such as prolonging the period over which the market is extended or reducing differentials between the national tariffs imposed on third countries; and ensuring, to the extent possible, adequate consistency with the origin regime to be adopted by the WTO.[13]

The adoption of basic principles notwithstanding, given the uncertainty associated with a transition between origin regimes in a process of integration involving such diverse countries and regional arrangements (in terms of size, levels of development, geographic proximity, patterns of productive complementation and specialization, and so on), questions arise regarding the appropriate moment and timing for harmonizing the regimes prevailing in the Western Hemisphere and bringing them together.

In this regard it would not be wrong to argue that for certain countries and regions (particularly those not located on the central axes of the hemisphere's

12. The presentation was made by J. P. Simpson (from the U.S. Department of the Treasury) in Washington, D.C., at the Conference on NAFTA Rules of Origin in March 1997. It was partially reproduced in *Inside NAFTA* 4(6).

13. Garay and Estevadeordal (1996).

integration dynamics) it would be appropriate to begin the task of increasing the harmonization between the different regimes in force in their established FTAs with other countries and regions in advance of FTAA negotiations. This could not only reduce current costs in efficiency, resource allocation, and administration of the existing regimes, it could also better prepare them for new competitive conditions. The benefits of this harmonization of regimes would obviously depend on several determining factors, such as the actual origin regime adopted as the reference framework for the harmonization process and the level of consistency between that regime and the one ultimately chosen for the FTAA.

One of the problems in selecting a reference regime is that there are currently at least four basic origin regimes in operation in the hemisphere: that of the NAFTA and the new-generation FTAs entered into by Mexico and Canada with other countries of the continent; that of the Aladi, which serves as a first-generation reference regime for all the partial agreements between the signatories of the Montevideo Treaty, for Chile's FTAs with Colombia and Venezuela, and, even considering the major adaptations and amendments made in the field of origin regime administration, for the Andean Community; that of the Mercosur, providing the frame of reference for its FTAs with Chile and Bolivia, and possibly for the FTA agreement to be signed with the Andean Community; and that of the CACM regime, which stands midway between the first- and new-generation agreements and the agreements signed by Central American nations to establish FTAs with Panama and the Dominican Republic.

The question therefore arises as to which would be the most appropriate origin regime(s) to follow in order to make preliminary progress with harmonization prior to designing the FTAA, considering transition costs and the costs of changing a regime that plays such an important role in preferential trade.

Conclusions

The creation of regional trade agreements is a characteristic trend in the current phase of the economic globalization process. Economic integration is taking place within a framework of "open regionalism" following liberalization and economic reforms in the developing world and the expansion of the international market through the progressive freeing of flows of goods, services, and capital. The prevailing model for economic integration in the Western

Hemisphere continues to be, at least to date, the creation of FTAs, but with a tendency toward the progressive incorporation of issues other than trade in goods, such as investment, government procurement, and so on.

In this context the question of rules of origin is of particular relevance in both theoretical and planning terms for the design of trade and integration policies. In light of the economic impact of rules of origin and the problems in predicting their restrictiveness, it is essential that clear-cut principles and criteria for determining the origin of goods be adopted in order to ensure that they are applied as transparently and objectively as possible and that they do not pose barriers to extending preferences under the FTAA. As some degree of selectivity in trade liberalization policy is decided upon, there is a need to specify rules of origin that, in addition to preserving the advantages of transparency and simplicity that distinguish uniform regimes, can make good use of the effectiveness and detail of selective origin regimes.

To date the FTAs established between countries of the Western Hemisphere have not tended to use rules of origin to compensate for the differences in member countries' national tariffs vis-à-vis third countries in order to prevent trade deflection; instead, their design appears to have been more in response to different strategic goals.[14] It is therefore to be expected that rules of origin will tend to vary between FTAs in accordance with their degrees of "sensitivity" to intraregional competition and with the member countries' strategic goals.

Therefore, the construction of the FTAA faces the problem of the multiple regimes and specific rules of origin that exist in the hemisphere's current FTAs and of their impact on the costs of origin regime administration. These costs can be seen in terms of both financial costs—both for governments and for individual manufacturing and exporting companies—and inefficiencies in resource location, specialization patterns, and decreased well-being caused by the simultaneous application of rules of origin that differ according to the orientation of trade and are not necessarily mutually consistent. It is therefore obviously appropriate to establish basic principles for adequate harmonization between the rules of the hemisphere's existing subregional FTAs and those to be agreed to for the FTAA and by the WTO. Difficulties in this harmonization process can be expected to arise, at least initially, with the involvement of a wider variety of countries with varying levels of economic development,

14. For further details related to the Aladi, NAFTA, and G-3, see Garay and Quintero (1997).

national tariff policies, degrees of economic complementarity, geographical proximity, and other characteristics.

In any event, although not ignoring the complexity of this task, it is worth mentioning the possible usefulness of some basic transparent principles for the harmonization process. For example, the stringency of preferential rules of origin should be determined using the corresponding level of nonpreferential rules as a reference point, and the rules should be as consistent as possible with regard to the classification criterion used. As far as possible, rules of origin should not be used when the differences between members' third-country tariffs are minimal or when their tariff levels are low. Emphasis should be placed on establishing a partial CU in those sectors or industries in which the nature of the production processes and the internationalization of production make administering rules of origin sufficiently complex.

It is clear, therefore, that defining the origin regime for the FTAA is a particularly important challenge in light of the wide range of rules for determining origin in use in the hemisphere and the different characteristics of intracontinental trade seen today in first-generation and new-generation regimes.[15] There can be little doubt that rules of origin will be one of the most delicate issues in constructing a hemispheric market based on criteria of productive efficiency and equality among the region's countries.

References

Barfield, C. E. 1996. "Regionalism and U.S. Trade Policy." In *The Economics of Preferential Trade Agreements,* edited by J. Bhagwati and A. Panagariya. Washington D.C.: AEI Press.

Devlin, R., A. Estevadeordal, and L. J. Garay. 1997. "Normas en Acuerdos Preferenciales de Comercio en las Américas." Unpublished mimeograph. Washington, D.C.: Inter-American Development Bank, Division of Integration, Trade, and Hemispheric Issues.

Garay, L. J., and A. Estevadeordal. 1996. "Protección, Desgravación Preferencial y Normas de Origen." *Integración y Comercio* 0 (January–April): 2–29.

Garay, L. J., and L. F. Quintero. 1997. "Caracterización, Estructura y Racionalidad de las Normas de Origen del G3 y de la Aladi: Su Relevancia en el Caso de Colombia." Unpublished mimeograph. Washington, D.C.: Inter-American Development Bank, Division of Integration, Trade, and Hemispheric Issues.

---

15. We will analyze this issue in a forthcoming article.

Simpson, J. P. 1997. Paper prepared for the conference on NAFTA Rules of Origin, Washington, D.C.

U.S. International Trade Commission. 1987. "Standardization of Rules of Origin." Report to the Commission on Ways and Means of the U.S. House of Representatives. Washington, D.C.

Winters, A. L. 1997. *Assessing Regional Integration Agreements.* Washington D.C.: World Bank (June).

CHAPTER ELEVEN

Standards and Technical Barriers to Trade in the Free Trade Area of the Americas

Sherry M. Stephenson

Although the most popular understanding of trade negotiations revolves around market access issues, particularly the lowering of tariff barriers to trade, modern negotiations focus on the lowering or removal of nontariff barriers and the strengthening of trade disciplines. This should also be the case for the Free Trade Area of the Americas (FTAA) negotiations. The role of standards and the importance they may have as potential nontariff barriers within the Western Hemisphere is increasingly being recognized, as is the ability of harmonization or mutual recognition of standards to facilitate trade. This area may well be one of the keys to a successful hemispheric trade liberalization agreement. Standards and technical barriers to trade were the focus of one of the twelve working groups formed to undertake work during the nearly three-year preparatory phase of the FTAA process, and this area has been included in the Market Access Group for the purpose of the FTAA negotiations.

The nucleus of a common Western Hemisphere approach to the treatment of standards already exists. Common disciplines are included in the World Trade Organization (WTO) Agreement on Technical Barriers to Trade (TBT Agreement) negotiated during the Uruguay Round. Common guidelines for standardization activities, including conformity assessment and quality control, have been elaborated under the International Organization for Standardization (ISO) and the International Electrical Commission (IEC). At the regional level most countries are members of the Pan American Commission on Technical Standards (COPANT), the regional standardizing body for the Americas.

Provisions and activities of regional integration arrangements with respect to standards, technical regulations, and conformity assessment may also help toward the development of a common hemispheric approach in this area. Many of these arrangements include explicit provisions on standards and conformity assessment procedures and are developing harmonized standards as well as common policies in this respect.

The Role of Standards in Economic Development and Trade

At the national level standardization is a key element in promoting industrial and economic development and trade that covers nearly the entire spectrum of the economy. Standards and conformity assessment may either facilitate trade or impede its expansion by acting as hidden or nontariff barriers. The difficulty in the area of standards is to distinguish the legitimate use of technical regulations for the purpose of protecting consumer health and safety, as well as the environment, from those put in place for protectionist purposes. The challenge is also to ensure that legitimate standards and technical regulations are enforced with minimal adverse effects on trade. These difficulties are underscored by the lack of objective information and quantitative estimates of the impact of technical barriers on trade flows and consumer welfare.

Negotiating in the area of standards is quite a different proposition from negotiating traditional market access measures. Standards and conformity assessment as technical barriers to trade are essentially problems of economic regulations. As such, they are far less clear-cut for the purpose of negotiations than, for example, tariffs or quotas, and their liberalization is necessarily of a different nature. Standards and technical regulations cannot be reduced or eliminated through reciprocal concessions, but must be made subject to agreed-upon rules and disciplines for their development and application. Therefore, both the Tokyo Round and the Uruguay Rounds of multilateral trade negotiations established through agreed-upon principles a framework for economic regulation in the area of standards.

To facilitate trade flows, standards and technical regulations may be either harmonized or recognized as being compatible. This issue, however, is independent of the need to apply basic rules and disciplines to the standardization process. The more that standards are designed according to internationally harmonized principles and procedures, the greater will be the degree of basic compatibility between national exporters and the more smoothly will products flow between countries. As standards will likely continue to increase both in number and in their impact on trade flows in the future, the challenge for the Western Hemisphere is both to ensure that national standards are not used in trade-distorting ways and to determine how it may be possible to go beyond existing WTO rules and disciplines to facilitate trade.

The Role of Standards in Promoting Economic Development

A standard can be defined as a specification that relates to a characteristic of a product or its manufacture. Standards and technical regulations are similar types of specifications, with the major difference that compliance with standards is voluntary, whereas compliance with technical regulations is mandatory.[1] Although standards are largely the result of industry action and may arise either de facto or through a coordinated, voluntary process involving various actors in a given product market (producers, consumers, government purchasing officials, and so on), technical regulations are always laid down by regulatory authorities. Firms cannot sell their products without compliance with these regulations, which have the objective of protecting or ensuring a given level of public health and safety. Conformity assessment procedures are those testing and certification requirements that are fulfilled in order to ensure that products or processes from different national producers (exporters) comply with standards or technical regulations in the domestic (importer's) market.[2]

1. Annex 1 of the WTO TBT Agreement defines a standard and a technical regulation in an identical manner, as a "document approved by a recognized body, that provides, for common and repeated use, rules, guidelines or characteristics for products or related processes and production methods." The WTO definition adds that compliance with a standard is not mandatory, whereas compliance with a technical regulation is mandatory. Both mandatory and nonmandatory standards may also "include or deal exclusively with terminology, symbols, packaging, marking or labeling requirements as they apply to a product, process or production method." See General Agreement on Tariffs and Trade (1994a).

2. As national standards and technical regulations often differ from country to country (or producer to producer, within a country), the need to demonstrate compliance with either standards or technical regulations through conformity assessment procedures to be able to sell in a given market is critical. It does no good for a producer to comply

In terms of promotion of economic development, standards play various roles that reduce costs and enhance welfare for both consumers and producers.[3] For consumers standards serve to convey information about a product in a manner that lowers the cost to buyers. This allows consumers to compare products directly (particularly those produced abroad with those produced domestically), and they are assured through labeling and testing that such products conform to one basic standard of performance or quality. It also allows consumers to mix and match products from different producers, which is especially important for those products that are organized into networks, such as electronic items. Standards also can promote social welfare when they are designed to maintain certain levels of consumer health and safety protection and of environmental cleanliness. In this role standards can have characteristics of public goods; that is, their consumption by one party does not diminish their value for another (and often enhances it).

For producers standards embody technology and help in the process of technological diffusion, particularly in international trade. Therefore, without the direct purchase of a patent, the purchase of a product with embodied technology and a specific, traceable standard can help a firm to develop a similarly sophisticated product. This contributes to raising productive efficiency and industrial competitiveness, as firms are able to adopt standardized approaches to production, which facilitates the development of economies of scale. Standards also help organize the manufacturing process itself when specified common procedures are used for the purpose of quality control in output. This is indeed the whole point of the development of the ISO 9000 and ISO 14000 series of standards, which do not represent standards for products themselves, but rather represent standards of quality control for carrying out the production of products (or services) in the first case and of environmental control measures in the second case.[4]

---

with a standard if a seller cannot demonstrate this to the satisfaction of the purchaser, and it is equally useless to comply with a regulation if the regulatory authorities cannot be persuaded of this at a reasonable cost.

3. See National Research Council (1995) for a discussion of the contribution of standards to economic development.

4. The ISO 9000 series of standards on quality management and quality assurance was established in 1987 by the ISO Technical Committee (TC) 176. The first standard was ISO 9000 itself, which sets out the fundamental concepts of quality management and control (and was revised in 1994). ISO 9001, 9002, and 9003, published sub-

Standards and Conformity Assessment as Nontariff Barriers

Barriers to trade in the area of standards can arise in several different ways, as products falling under mandatory standards (or technical regulations) face several levels of testing and acceptance before they can be sold in foreign markets on an equal footing with domestic products. Foreign products can be refused market entry through lack of recognition of either the equivalency of the products or that of the testing procedures used to evaluate the products' characteristics. They can also face barriers at the stage of certification or accreditation when the testing entities in one country are not recognized for their technical competence to confer stamps of approval in that country for the sale of products to third markets.

Heterogeneity across national markets in product and process standards, technical regulations, or conformity assessment procedures creates impediments to trade. Even voluntary standards may constitute trade barriers through, for example, product incompatibility created by the differences between the metric and the imperial system of weights and measures or between different voltage standards for electrical appliances.

With respect to mandatory standards or technical regulations, technical barriers to trade can arise due to differing national interpretations of the reasonableness of the regulations in question, such as the scientific interpretation of tolerable health and safety risks to consumers for various products or disagreement over labeling requirements. Most government-to-government disputes over technical barriers concern the interpretation and application of mandatory government requirements for standards.

However, the most widespread and possibly more costly type of nontariff barrier to trade in the area of standards is that posed by conformity assessment procedures or the need to demonstrate compliance with standards or technical regulations in another market. Such procedures are carried out either by the

---

sequently, set out standards for conformity assessment procedures for certifications and registrations. ISO 9004 is a standard with guidelines for companies to use in establishing their quality systems. Again, the ISO 9000 series is not a product standard, but rather a standard to address the quality of management of an organization. The ISO 14000 series was developed beginning in 1993 by ISO TC 207 to develop standards on the measures a firm must follow to ensure a high level of performance in its environmental management system. The ISO 14000 series was published in draft form in June 1995 and is in the process of finalization. See United Nations Industrial Development Organization (1995).

regulatory authority of the country importing the product (government) or by quasi-public or private bodies operating on their behalf. As such, they constitute a significant additional cost to firms selling in multiple markets. Although separate certification is needed in cases where mandatory product specifications differ from country to country, even where countries rely on internationally harmonized rules or accept as equivalent other countries' standards, reliance on the exporting countries' tests and conformity certificates is rarely practiced.[5] In this situation barriers result from the duplication of effort represented by separate conformity assessment procedures in differing national markets due to unnecessarily costly testing requirements. Thus conformity assessment requirements, to the extent that they are redundant and excessively costly, partially negate and reduce the benefits from international trade.

The type of nontariff barrier that standards and technical regulations may create can be very costly. A study by the Organization for Economic Cooperation and Development (OECD) has found that differing standards and technical regulations in different markets, combined with the costs of testing and certifying compliance with those requirements, can constitute between 2 and 10 percent of a firm's overall production costs.[6] Both industry representatives and economic studies cite conformity assessment and certification requirements at the top of their list of impediments to trade.

Disputes over the possible use of standards as nontariff barriers have meant that standards are increasingly becoming the object of dispute settlement in the multilateral arena. Indeed over the first two years of operation of the new integrated dispute settlement procedures under the WTO, in around a fourth of these cases (eleven out of forty-four complaints) the complainants invoked the TBT Agreement.[7] Two developing countries from the Western Hemisphere (Brazil and Venezuela) have been involved in these standards-related disputes.

Is There a Common Base for Standards in the Hemisphere?

With respect to standards and conformity assessment, a common basis for negotiating policies would already appear to exist for countries in the Western

5. See Clarke (1996).

6. Organization for Economic Cooperation and Development (1996).

7. See General Agreement on Tariffs and Trade (1994b). This understanding applies to the entire 1994 GATT and its subagreements.

Hemisphere in the form of disciplines and guidelines set out in the WTO TBT
Agreement and in the various guidelines elaborated by the ISO and the IEC.
The main question for the FTAA negotiators on standards will therefore be how
and to what extent hemispheric disciplines should go beyond those already in
place.

Disciplines of the WTO TBT Agreement

The WTO TBT Agreement retains the original obligations of the Tokyo
Round Standards Code, but refines or adds to them in important respects. It is
important that the membership of the TBT Agreement is universal; all WTO
members participate in the agreement and are consequently bound by its
disciplines. For the Western Hemisphere this means that although only six of
the thirty-four FTAA participants were signatories to the Tokyo Round Standards Code at the end of 1993 when the Uruguay Round was concluded
(namely Argentina, Brazil, Canada, Chile, Mexico, and the United States), now
all thirty-four FTAA participants (except the Bahamas) are members of the
WTO TBT Agreement.

Disciplines in the WTO TBT Agreement that were strengthened or are new
compared with those in the earlier Tokyo Round Standards Code include the
following:

—Disciplines on standards are to be applied to process and production
methods as well as to manufactured products (Annex 1, Definitions).

—Multilateral rules are extended to nongovernmental or private standards
organizations, whereas the central government is required to be responsible for
good-faith implementation of the agreement and application of its principles at
any level of government or for any private-sector body involved in the standards system (Article 3).

—Obligations of national treatment and nondiscrimination are extended to
all forms of conformity assessment, including laboratory accreditation, recognition, and quality system registration programs (Articles 5 through 9).

—General principles for the development and application of standards by
nongovernmental organizations or private standardizing bodies are set out in a
Code of Good Practices for the Preparation, Adoption and Application of
Standards, which forms an integral part of the TBT Agreement (Article 4 and
Annex 3).

—Governments must ensure that technical regulations will not be more trade
restrictive than necessary to fulfill a legitimate objective and must ensure that

they are not "prepared, adopted or applied with a view to . . . creating unnecessary obstacles to international trade" (Article 2).

—Governments subscribe to the commitment (nonbinding) to harmonize national standards with international standards (Article 2).

—Governments are required to strive for reciprocity in conformity assessment procedures through the acceptance of results from such testing procedures in third countries, provided they are satisfied with the equivalency of such testing procedures (Article 6).

—Disputes arising from differing technical regulations are to be settled under the binding framework of the WTO Integrated Dispute Settlement Procedures, so noncompliance with provisions of the TBT Agreement (as found by a panel in its legal proceedings) will require modification of the practice in question, and if a country fails to modify the practice retaliatory tariffs can be imposed (Article 14).

Of these disciplines, several are important for the FTAA objective of trade liberalization, as they help generate common government practices and hemispheric disciplines for standards-related activities. The obligation of transparency is critical, as many problems arising in this area spring from a lack of information or from transparency in standards adoption and application. Under the WTO TBT Agreement all of these procedures are to be notified in view of possible comment by third parties, and all enquiries regarding national standards, technical regulations, or conformity assessment procedures are to be answered by an information center within each member country, or an "enquiry point."

The commitment of governments to attempt to harmonize national standards with international ones establishes a hierarchy for standardization that makes international standards the basic norm for the elaboration of national standards.[8] The existence for the first time of a Code of Good Practice for the Preparation, Adoption and Application of Standards should represent a considerable step forward toward establishing a common hemispheric basis by extending (to those

---

8. The language used in the article of the TBT Agreement relative to the adoption of international standards is unfortunately not very strong. Article 2.4 includes a form of "escape clause"; international standards are not required to be used as the basis for technical regulations when they would be "an ineffective or inappropriate means for the fulfillment of the legitimate objectives pursued." However, what is considered ineffective or inappropriate is not defined. See General Agreement on Tariffs and Trade (1994b).

private standardizing bodies that accept it) a common approach to carrying out standardizing activities. The Code of Good Practice outlines general principles for the development and application of standards for:

—National treatment of products from foreign suppliers.

—Treatment no less favorable for foreign products than that accorded to domestic products or other imports. Publication and dissemination of work on standards in progress.

—Institution of a sixty-day comment period prior to adoption of standards.

—Refraining from applying standards that could act as barriers to trade.

The existence of this code represents a significant achievement, though its adoption is not compulsory for nongovernmental standardizing bodies, as it is for central government standardizing bodies. However, WTO members are to take such reasonable measures as may be available to them to ensure that these bodies also accept and comply with the code.[9]

Finally, the WTO TBT Agreement admonishes member countries to recognize the equivalency of test results from other members through conformity assessment procedures. Article 6.3 "encourages" members to be "willing to enter into negotiations for the conclusion of agreements for the mutual recognition of results of each other's conformity assessment procedures." However, members are required to accept these only if they are satisfied that those procedures "offer an assurance of conformity . . . equivalent to their own procedures" (Article 6.1). Although the language is nonbinding, the agreement nonetheless establishes the precedent for mutual recognition to be promoted as a means of facilitating trade.

Table 11-1 lists those countries in the Western Hemisphere that had complied with the three basic obligations of the WTO TBT Agreement as of mid-1998. Of the thirty-four FTAA participants, only eleven had submitted the required statement of implementation (under Article 15.2), eighteen had established an enquiry point, and nineteen had standardizing bodies that had accepted the Code of Good Practice for the Preparation, Adoption and Application of Standards. The statement of implementation is a one-time notification by each member of the legislative, regulatory, and administrative actions it has taken to ensure that the provisions of the agreement are applied. The establishment of an enquiry point and the acceptance of the Code of Good Practice are obligatory notifications that must be updated as relevant.

9. To present, the Code of Good Practice for the Preparation, Adoption and Application of *Standards* has been accepted by some 80 standardizing bodies. There are estimated to be somewhat more than 600 standardizing bodies worldwide.

Table 11-1. Compliance with the Obligations of the WTO TBT Agreement by Participants in the FTAA Negotiation Process

A. Submission of a statement of implementation and administration of the agreement	B. Establishment of a national enquiry point	C. Acceptance of the Code of Good Practice for the Preparation, Adoption and Application of Standards
Argentina	Argentina	Argentina
Bolivia	Belize	Barbados
Brazil	Bolivia	Brazil
Canada	Brazil	Chile
Chile	Canada	Colombia
Colombia	Chile	Costa Rica
Mexico	Colombia	Dominican Republic
Panama	Costa Rica	Ecuador
Peru	Dominican Republic	El Salvador
St. Lucia	El Salvador	Grenada
United States	Honduras	Guyana
	Jamaica	Jamaica
	Mexico	Mexico
	Peru	Panama
	St. Lucia	Peru
	Trinidad and Tobago	Trinidad and Tobago
	United States	United States
	Uruguay	Uruguay
		Venezuela

Source: Notifications to the WTO Committee on Technical Barriers to Trade.

Note: The total numbers of countries of the Western Hemisphere listed in each of the above categories are as follows: A: 11; B: 18; C: 19.

The majority of international standards are developed by three major international bodies, which together issue nearly 1,000 new or revised standards each year. These bodies are the ISO, the IEC, and the International Telecommunications Union (ITU). Although the IEC and the ITU are specialized organizations developing standards for electrotechnology and telecommunications, respectively, the scope of activity of the ISO is unlimited. It is therefore the most important standardizing body, counting 115 member countries at present.[10] Both the ISO and the IEC are private, nongovernmental organiza-

10. In practice the ISO defers to specialized standardizing bodies when these exist for the development of standards in their respective areas, such as the IEC, the ITU, and the

tions, which distinguishes them from most other international bodies. The membership of both the ISO and the IEC is composed of the main national standardizing bodies from each member country, either government agencies or private-sector standards entities. The ISO membership of standardizing bodies of countries of the Western Hemisphere is set out in table 11-2, which shows that twenty-six FTAA participants are members of the ISO.

The standardizing bodies cited develop international standards through a lengthy consultative process. Such standards are the product of consensus, and a proposed a new standard can be adopted only after 75 percent of the ISO members accept it. Although standards remain "voluntary" in the sense that member nations are not obliged to adopt them in their national markets, their approval nonetheless suggests that broad-based compliance should follow. The standards developed by the ISO, the IEC, and the ITU provide a common basis for the adoption and use of standards throughout the Western Hemisphere to the extent that FTAA participants consider these appropriate to domestic needs. However, the number of standards that have been internationally approved is still quite limited, as this process is lengthy and complex.

At present the ISO has developed around 9,800 voluntary standards.[11] No standardizing body touches upon the aspect of technical regulations, which lie solely within the government domain, although many times the internationally developed voluntary standards are made mandatory by national governments. One of the major contributions of the two largest international standardizing

---

Codex Alimentarius Commission, whose purpose is to develop standards for food safety and labeling. In total, some twenty-eight international bodies are involved in setting standards on a global level. Bodies with important standardization activities include the International Conference on Weights and Measures, the International Bureau for Standardization of Man-Made Fibres, the International Commission on Illumination, the International Air Transport Association, the International Institute of Refrigeration, and the International Institute of Welding, among others. See Sykes (1995).

11. Though this number may sound impressive, to put it into perspective it should be remembered that the ISO has been at work developing standards for half a century. Therefore, standards have been developed at a rate of only around 280 per year. Also compare the 10,000 or so internationally agreed-upon standards with the more than 50,000 standards that exist at present in the U.S. market and a similar number in Western Europe. However, for smaller domestic markets such as many of those in developing countries, international standards may well be the only standards that apply to the majority of those product areas covered by standardization.

Table 11-2. Participation of National Standardizing Bodies of FTAA Members in International and Regional Standards Organizations (the ISO and COPANT) at the end of 1996

Countries and national standards bodies[a]	*Membership in* ISO	*Membership in* COPANT
Antigua-Barbuda (ABBS or Antigua-Barbuda Bureau of Standards)	Yes	No
Argentina (IRAM or Instituto Argentino de Racionalizacion de Materiales)	Yes	Yes
Barbados (BNSI or Barbados National Standards Institution)	Yes	Yes
Bolivia (IBNORCA or Instituto Boligivano de Normalizacion y Calidad)	Yes	Yes
Brazil (ABNT or Asociacion Brasileira de Normas Tecnicas)	Yes	Yes
Canada (SCC or Standards Council of Canada)	Yes	Yes
Chile (INN or Instituto Nacional de Normalizacion)	Yes	Yes
Colombia (ICONTEC or Instituto Colombiano de Normas Tecnicas)	Yes	Yes
Costa Rica (INTECO or Instituto de Normas Tecnicas de Costa Rica)	Yes	Yes
Dominican Republic (DIGENOR or Dirección General De Normas y Sistemas de Calidad)	Yes	Yes
Ecuador (INEN or Instituto Ecuatoriano de Normalizacion)	Yes	Yes
El Salvador (CONYACYT or Consejo Nacional de Ciencia y Tecnología)	Yes	No
Grenada (GDBS or Grenada Bureau of Standards)	Yes	Yes
Guatemala (COGUANOR or Comisión Guatemalteca de Normas)	Yes	No
Guyana (GNBS or Guyana National Bureau of Standards)	Yes	Yes
Jamaica (JBS or Jamaican Bureau of Standards)	Yes	Yes
Mexico (DGN or Direccion General de Normas)	Yes	Yes
Nicaragua (DGCYT or Dirección General de Ciencia y Tecnología Ministeria de Economía y Desarrollo)	Yes	No
Panama (COPANIT or Comision Panamena de Normas Industriales y Tecnicas)	Yes	Yes
Paraguay (INTN or Instituto Nacional de Tecnologia y Normalizacion)	Yes	Yes
Peru (INDECOPI or Instituto Nacional de Defensa de la Competencia y de la Proteccion de la Propiedad Intelectual)	Yes	Yes
St. Lucia (SLBS or St. Lucia Bureau of Standards)	Yes	No
Trinidad and Tobago (TTBS or Trinidad and Tobago Bureau of Standards)	Yes	Yes
United States (ANSI or American National Standards Institute)	Yes	Yes
Uruguay (UNIT or Instituto Uruguayo de Normas Tecnicas)	Yes	Yes
Venezuela (COVENIN or Comision Venezolana de Normas Industriales)	Yes	Yes

Source: Information contained in Organization of American States (1997).

a. The ICAITI or Instituto Centroamericano de Investigaciones y Technologia in Central America holds membership in the COPANT on behalf of Costa Rica, El Salvador, Guatemala, Honduras, and Nicaragua, although a separate membership body also represents Costa Rica.

bodies has been the elaboration of internationally agreed-upon guides to serve as the basis for the work and activities of national standards bodies and bodies involved in conformity assessment procedures. These guides provide the second major element constituting a common basis for the approach to standards and technical barriers in the Western Hemisphere.

It is in the area of elaborating quality system standards that the ISO has received the most attention in the past decade. These standards consist of a series of five international standards for quality assurance management systems.[12] Although the standards in the ISO 9000 series do not in themselves constitute standards (as is often mistakenly assumed), they provide consistency and reliability for the production process in terms of management practices and quality control. Certification by private firms using these ISO 9000 standards is voluntary. Relatively few firms in the Western Hemisphere, with the exception of those in Brazil, Canada, Mexico, and the United States, have been certified for their use of the ISO 9000 quality management systems. The ISO is currently finalizing a new series in the area of environmental quality management in the form of the ISO 14000. Although the ISO 14000 is still in its final stages, some certification or registration organizations have already issued certificates of conformance to the ISO 14001 draft standard.

Regional Standardizing Activity

To complete the standards panorama, an additional level of standardizing activity must be added—the regional or hemispheric level. Within the Western Hemisphere the only regional standardizing body whose membership is open to all national bodies is the Pan American Commission on Technical Standards (COPANT), a joint initiative of Argentina, Brazil, Chile, Colombia, Mexico, the United States, Uruguay, and Venezuela, which became operational in 1956 in the form of a Pan-American Committee on Standards. The functions of the COPANT were set out to be the following: to promote the establishment of national standardizing bodies and to improve the activities of existing ones in the hemisphere, to promote the establishment of national testing laboratories and to encourage coordination of activities between existing ones, to encourage the development and adoption of national standards at the national level or at the Latin American regional level, and to satisfy the need of national standardizing bodies for technical assistance.

12. See note 4.

Financed largely by the OAS during its first twenty years, the COPANT's activities were concentrated along the lines just described. However, a change of funding priorities in the 1980s and the lack of a permanent infrastructure or secretariat for the organization has meant that the COPANT has not been very active in recent years in pushing forward with hemispherewide standardizing activities, though there are signs that this may be changing. Although the COPANT is open to standardizing bodies from all countries of the hemisphere, in actual practice only twenty-four of the thirty-one FTAA countries are members of the COPANT (see table 11-2).

Besides the COPANT, two other hemispherewide organizations exist that are involved in the coordination of national activities in the area of standards. One is the Inter-American Metrology System (or SIM, Sistema Interamericano de Metrologia), which is carrying out efforts in the area of metrology to establish national systems of weights and measures in metrology laboratories and centers that are both accountable and traceable to international standards. SIM activities have been ongoing for many years in the hemisphere and have been actively supported by funds from the OAS and by the U.S. National Institute for Standardization and Technology (NIST). SIM membership is divided into four subregional groupings of the countries of the hemisphere, namely North America, Central America, South America, and the Caribbean.

The more recently developed Inter-American Accreditation Cooperation (IAAC) group, established in 1995, is the product of an effort to set up a system of coordination and recognition among the various accreditation bodies of countries in the Western Hemisphere. At its most recent meeting of November 1996 the IAAC group drew up a memorandum of understanding for formal establishment of the group, which was signed by nine countries of the hemisphere as full members and by two countries and three standardizing bodies as associates.[13] The IAAC group's stated goal is to promote acceptance of certificates of conformity granted by certification bodies, as well as the results of product testing and calibration by accredited bodies in each country. This is to

13. See the most recent *Memorandum de Entendimiento* of the Cooperacion Interamericana de Organismos de Acreditacion, which was signed on November 22, 1996, in Montevideo, Uruguay. The nine full members that signed the memorandum are Argentina, Brazil, Canada, Chile, Colombia, Cuba, Peru, the United States, and Venezuela. The five associate members are the COPANT, Relat, Trinidad and Tobago, Uruguay, and the Comité Nacional de Calidad. Brazil was elected chair of the IAAC, and Venezuela was elected vice chair.

be done through the development of mutual recognition agreements (MRAs) among members on either a bilateral or a subregional basis. This is a positive sign for the promotion of trade facilitation within the hemisphere, and it should contribute to the objectives of the FTAA in the area of standards.

Mutual Recognition Arrangements in the Western Hemisphere

Mutual recognition in the Western Hemisphere is in a very early stage. It would appear that no MRA has yet been signed between governments involving national regulatory authorities responsible for mandatory product standards or for health and safety or environmental regulations.[14]

In the area of voluntary standards as well, very few such agreements have been concluded. This is due to a number of factors, including the differences in levels of economic development between countries of the Western Hemisphere, which impact the ability of national laboratories to carry out testing and certifications of equivalent quality and therefore reduce the possibility of elaborating common approaches with respect to policy objectives. There has also been a historical tendency for many of the larger countries of South America to look toward western Europe for the development of national standards, which has led to a situation in which many more different standards are in effect within large countries of South America than is probably the case between Central America and North America or between the Caribbean region and North America, thus increasing the complexity of conformity assessment procedures for the larger countries of the hemisphere. Besides, it is only recently that policymakers have begun to appreciate the importance of standards as nontariff barriers to trade and thus to realize the potential for trade facilitation that could be brought about through the elaboration of MRAs.

Table 11-3 sets forth data on the types and coverage of MRAs in effect for standards, technical regulations, and conformity assessment activities for coun-

14. In the area of services, a few MRAs have been concluded under the North American Free Trade Agreement (NAFTA) Tripartite Framework since 1994. These include MRAs between Canada and the United States for the recognition of the diplomas of architects and foreign providers of legal consulting services. MRAs for recognition of the qualification of accountants and other professional service providers are under study. Canada and Mexico have agreed to an MRA for the reciprocal recognition of the qualification of commercial drivers. However, negotiation of parallel-type MRAs for regulated products has been slower.

Table 11-3. MRA-Type Arrangements on Product Testing by Members of the Western Hemisphere

Nations involved	Type of agreement
Canada and United States	MRA between SCC and NIST for accreditation in the area of laboratory testing
Canada and United States	MRA between SCC and A2LA for accreditation in the area of laboratory testing
Mexico and United States	MRA to allow U.S. firms to participate in Mexico's certification system for the testing of tires
Colombia and Venezuela	MRA between government ministries for reciprocal recognition of quality labels
Colombia and Ecuador	MRA between government ministries for reciprocal recognition of testing certificates and quality labels once evaluation of conformity assessment procedures is harmonized
Argentina and Uruguay	MRA between IRAM and UNIT for the certification of electrical equipment Letters of intent for MRA elaboration
Brazil and Argentina	Intention stated by UCIEE and IRAM to reciprocally recognize certification of electrical and electronic products once agreement is concluded
Uruguay and Argentina	Intention stated by UNIT and IRAM to establish a work program and timetable in order to achieve mutual recognition of certification activities

Source: Organization of American States (1997).

tries in the Western Hemisphere.[15] In the area of conformity assessment procedures, a few bilateral MRAs exist that cover the accreditation of laboratory testing or certification activities. These agreements have been elaborated between governments, between national standardizing bodies, or between a combination of the two.[16] No multilateral MRA has been concluded in the hemisphere.

One of the difficulties involved with promoting MRAs bilaterally or multilaterally between countries in the Western Hemisphere is that several countries

15. Drawn from Organization of American States (OAS) (1997).

16. A number of bilateral cooperation agreements and memorandums of understanding have also been concluded by countries of the Western Hemisphere in the area of metrology.

have not yet enacted legislation in the area of certification and consequently do not yet appear to have the capacity or procedures in place to carry out government certification of testing bodies. From the information available it would appear that only twelve countries in the Western Hemisphere had approved certification bodies and a certification system by mid-1998.[17] Of those that have them, only a few countries base their approval on internationally approved ISO guidelines. Negotiating formal MRAs, however, requires that countries have in place a system of national recognition for the conduct of laboratory accreditation, since an MRA between laboratory accreditation bodies implies that each national body is effectively accepting some responsibility for the actions of the other body. Even a less formal approach to MRA-type arrangements is difficult to promote beyond agreements on testing equivalency in the absence of functioning systems for certification or accreditation, as well as knowledge of the scope and operations of existing bodies.

Mutual recognition can also be promoted through more limited agreements covering the mutual accreditation of testing facilities. In this regard two relevant arrangements have been identified within the Western Hemisphere. The first arrangement is a reciprocal one between the Canadian Standards Association (CSA), the major standardizing body in Canada, and the U.S. Occupational Safety and Health Administration (OSHA), a government regulatory agency. The second is between Underwriters Laboratories (UL) in the United States and the SCC. These arrangements were signed between government bodies (OSHA and the SCC) on the one hand and between private certifiers (the CSA and UL) on the other, and they allow for the certified testing providers in one national market to be recognized in the other. The CSA is the first and only non-U.S. entity that has been accredited to test and certify products to U.S. standards. UL has been accredited to do the same for products with respect to Canadian standards. Regulatory acceptance throughout the United States and Canada, including acceptance by OSHA and the SCC, means that manufacturers can now have products certified at one testing site and under one set of procedures for sale in both markets.

A second arrangement, between the U.S. Department of Transportation (DOT) and the IRAM of Argentina, also would appear to be relevant in this regard. Concluded in 1984, the agreement authorizes the IRAM to carry out inspections, testing, and verification on cylinders manufactured under the

17. For the Caribbean Community (CARICOM) members an agreement exists to accept certification marks of the Bureau of Standards without further internal tests.

provisions of the DOT. The agreement was concluded following an application by the IRAM to be authorized by the U.S. DOT to carry out these functions so that such products would be considered acceptable for sale on the U.S. market without further testing or inspection. In this agreement the DOT appears to play a double role and to carry out functions of both recognition and acceptance of a regulated product. This MRA-type arrangement, of a more narrow scope than those already described, was concluded on the basis of unilateral acceptance of the equivalency of the applicant for the functions specified rather than through formal negotiations.

Commonalities and Divergences in Subregional Arrangements

Along with multilateral and regional standards-related activity, many regional trade and integration arrangements in the Western Hemisphere deal in some manner with standards and conformity assessment. Similarities between the major provisions of or activities related to standards as set out in the treaties or legal decisions of these arrangements may provide further elements for a hemispheric approach to standards in the future FTAA agreement.

In an analysis of the policy objectives and provisions on standards and standards-related activities contained in the various trade and integration arrangements of the Western Hemisphere it is important to make a distinction between objectives and disciplines. With respect to the latter, it is encouraging to note that basic disciplines regarding standards are shared by the majority of existing trade and integration arrangements in the hemisphere.

Provisions and disciplines similar to those of the WTO TBT Agreement are set out in legal treaty form in Andean Community Decision 376, in the NAFTA treaty, in the Group of Three (G-3), in the two bilateral free trade agreements between Mexico and Bolivia and between Mexico and Costa Rica, and in the more recent bilateral agreement between Chile and Canada, as well as the free trade agreement between Chile and the Mercosur. Although there is no legal text on standards in the Mercosur treaty, the member countries appear to be actively implementing the disciplines of the WTO Agreement as a common basis for their integration arrangement. Therefore, a common multilateral basis with respect to rules and disciplines is apparently being reinforced.

With respect to policy objectives in the area of standards, however, the picture is different. Two distinct approaches toward the treatment of standards can be identified in the Western Hemisphere. On the one hand, the objective of harmonization is the central policy approach for the Andean Group and the Mercosur, both of which have been actively pursuing efforts aimed at harmonization of both standards and technical regulations. Harmonization is also the stated goal of the Central American Common Market and the Caribbean Common Market, though these subregional arrangements have not been as actively at work on pursuing a common approach in this area. The objective of harmonization is the approach that is shared therefore by all of those arrangements whose stated objective is the creation of a common market.

On the other hand, compatibility is the major policy goal of all of those integration agreements whose objective is the creation of free trade areas, namely the NAFTA, the G-3, and the bilateral free trade agreements signed by Mexico and Chile. Although compatibility is not always a clearly defined objective, a goal of compatibility would seem to imply that national standards should be recognized as compatible in the sense of their interchangeability from a quality or user point of view, though they are not necessarily identical.

Although it is perhaps a fine point, the difference between the two approaches is fundamental. Harmonization requires the elaboration of not only identical policies, but also common physical standards and technical regulations. It also requires the creation of a permanent institutional mechanism, with a physical seat and secretariat, in order to oversee the implementation of such common standards in coordination with national standardizing bodies. Compatibility requires only that national standards be used in trade between member countries without creating barriers to such trade. This can be achieved through efforts to make standards more identical, to ensure their interface, or to recognize their equivalency, so that goods and services can be used interchangeably in the member countries to fulfil the same purpose. Efforts to recognize the equivalency of the qualifications of the testing and certification bodies in the member countries also play a big role in this approach. These may include the development of MRAs or less formal types of arrangements with similar effects.

Toward the FTAA Negotiations on Standards

It would appear from what has been said that a considerable amount of common background already exists in the area of standards in terms of multilaterally agreed-upon, legally binding rules and disciplines under the WTO and that there has been a large amount of voluntary activity toward the development of international standards and international guidelines on standardizing activities under the ISO, the IEC, and other bodies. Hemispherewide standards-related activities are already conducted under the COPANT, the SIM, and the IAAC group.

However, a note of caution must be sounded. This potentially rich common base in the Western Hemisphere is, in fact, far from universal, since many countries in the region have not been able to fully implement the disciplines of the WTO TBT Agreement and many are not members of the ISO, the IEC, or the COPANT and therefore do not participate in international or regional standardizing activities. Recent efforts to bring about greater compliance with multilateral disciplines or to adopt international standards have been slow at best.

Thus, in reality, common disciplines and approaches toward the elaboration of standards and mutual recognition of conformity assessment procedures do not yet exist for the majority of FTAA participants. Reasons include the cost of the infrastructure necessary for development of a proficient and reliable system of metrology and laboratory testing, the long-term nature of the creation of human resources necessary to carry out such functions, and the relative lack of prominence which this area has received until recently by national policy-makers. The task for negotiators in the area of standards is therefore not only to determine the shape of an ultimate agreement, but also to devise incentives and policies that will permit countries to implement already existing disciplines and to participate in multilateral and regional standards-related activities.

A great deal remains to be accomplished with respect to the development of MRAs in the Western Hemisphere. However, progress toward the elaboration of MRAs or MRA-type arrangements need not await the point of convergence of levels of economic development between all FTAA participants. Much can be envisaged and carried out to advance this objective in the short and medium terms. Obtaining and disseminating information on the certification and accreditation bodies that presently exist in the Western Hemisphere—their status, scope of activity, and other relevant data—would facilitate transparency in this area, as well as contact between standardizing and testing or certifying entities. Participation in relevant international forums, including that related to the Treaty of the Meter; the International Organization for Legal Metrology (OIML), which is dedicated to the harmonization of regulations on measurements; and the International Conference on Weights and Measures, is likewise important.

The FTAA negotiators will have to consider to what degree and in what areas it might be desirable to go beyond existing multilateral disciplines included in the WTO TBT Agreement. Full compliance with the provisions of the TBT Agreement will certainly be part of the objectives of the negotiations. However, to what extent additional (WTO-plus) disciplines are felt to be appropriate will depend upon the political decisions of participating governments.

As the FTAA agreement will create a free trade area and not a customs union, it will be difficult to imagine that negotiators would adopt an approach to harmonize standards at the hemispheric level. More realistic would be the promotion, wherever possible, of the equivalency of national standards and technical regulations. This objective could be associated with the elaboration of MRAs for the establishment of equivalency, particularly for the results of conformity assessment procedures. However, formal MRA agreements are not the only alternative to achieving this goal, and the FTAA negotiators may attempt to identify as many mechanisms as possible in this respect, particularly those that may be easier to achieve in the first instance, such as recognition of the equivalency of test results through more informal agreements, elaboration of memorandums of understanding in this regard between governments as well as between private standardizing bodies and testing laboratories, and so forth. Such mutual recognition–type arrangements will necessarily have to be elaborated within each product sector rather than through a horizontal or broad agreement.

References

Clarke, John. 1996. "Mutual Recognition Agreements." *International Trade Letter* 2. Brussels: European Community.

General Agreement on Tariffs and Trade. 1994a. Annex 2 of the Uruguay Round Agreement. "Understanding on Rules and Procedures Governing the Settlement of Disputes." In *The Results of the Uruguay Round of Multilateral Trade Negotiations: The Legal Texts.* Geneva: GATT Secretariat.

———. 1994b. *The Results of the Uruguay Round of Multilateral Trade Negotiations: The Legal Texts.* Geneva: GATT Secretariat.

National Research Council. 1995. *Standards, Conformity Assessment, and Trade.* Washington D.C.: National Academy Press.

Organization for Economic Cooperation and Development. 1996. *Proceedings from the Conference on Consumer Product Safety Standards and Conformity Assessment: Their Effect on International Trade.* Paris.

Organization of American States. 1997. *National Practices on Standards, Technical Regulations, and Conformity Assessment Procedures in the Western Hemisphere.* Washington, D.C.

Stephenson, Sherry M. 1997. "Standards and Conformity Assessment as Nontariff Barriers to Trade." Working Paper 1826. World Bank.

Sykes, Alan O. 1995. *Product Standards for Internationally Integrated Goods Markets.* Washington, D.C.: Brookings.

United Nations Industrial Development Organization. 1995. *Trade Implications of International Standards for Quality and Environmental Management Systems: Survey Results.* Vienna.

World Trade Organization Committee on Technical Barriers to Trade. 1996. Report to the Singapore Ministerial Meeting (November).

CHAPTER TWELVE

Import-Relief Laws:
The Role of Safeguards

Murray G. Smith

Although countries in the Western Hemisphere have moved toward more liberal trade and investment regimes under the auspices of regional and multilateral negotiations, many of the countries in the Western Hemisphere have also adopted import-relief laws. Reflecting the global trend, antidumping duties have become the preferred import-relief mechanisms for domestic industry, especially in the larger economies, and countervailing duties are used as well. This chapter suggests that under the new rules and procedures of the World Trade Organization (WTO) safeguards should be considered as an alternative to antidumping and countervailing duties, especially for the smaller economies. In addition, safeguards could be an important issue in the negotiations related to establishing a Free Trade Area of the Americas (FTAA).

The International Context of Import-Relief Laws

The major trading nations have increasingly used import-relief or trade-remedy laws to respond to the pressures of import competition. This was especially true in the decade prior to the completion of the Uruguay Round in December 1993. Since the implementation of the WTO many developing countries have implemented antidumping or safeguards laws and procedures. The evolution of the use of import-relief or trade-remedy laws and procedures has been shaped by broader developments in the trading system.

"Ancient History"

In the original General Agreement on Tariffs and Trade (GATT) of 1947, fundamental objectives were to bind tariffs (even if at high levels) and to eliminate quantitative restrictions.[1] However, there were a number of exceptions, including those provided under Article VI (for antidumping and countervailing duties), Article XI (for certain types of quotas), Article XII (for quota restrictions for balance of payments purposes), Article XVIII (for purposes of economic development by developing countries), Article XIX (for emergency action or safeguards), Article XX (for general exceptions), Article XXI (for national security), and Article XXV (for waivers) and the grandfathering of existing restrictions under the Protocol of Provisional Application (PPA). The pattern of use of these exceptions has varied over time. In addition, the WTO has made it more difficult to invoke many of them and has eliminated some, such as the Article XI exceptions, the Article XXV waivers, and the grandfathering under the protocol.

In the first decade of the GATT the use of antidumping and countervailing duties and safeguards measures was quite limited. For example, it was not until 1958 that the GATT Secretariat commissioned a report from the Group of Experts on Antidumping and Countervailing Duties, which could find only thirty-seven antidumping or countervailing measures in force among member countries, twenty-two of which were imposed by South Africa.[2]

Similarly, the safeguards described in Article XIX of the GATT were used on a limited basis, but the use of safeguards tended to be seen as a response to sudden import surges because the requirement that a nation negotiate compensation (or be subject to retaliation) meant that use of safeguards by GATT members was closely linked to the renegotiations of tariffs under Article XXVIII of the 1947 GATT. Since tariffs in most countries were fairly high, there was scope for renegotiation of tariffs either as compensation for the safeguards under Article XIX or as tariff renegotiation under Article XXVIII.

Countries also used various other exceptions to the GATT to restrict imports. In the 1950s, for example, a number of European countries still had quotas for

---

1. The other fundamental principles were most favored nation (MFN) treatment in restrictions on trade and national treatment for products once they had entered the domestic market.

2. General Agreement on Tariffs and Trade (1959, p. 145).

balance of payments reasons, a special waiver for agricultural trade restrictions was granted to the United States, and a number of European countries had restrictive quotas on trade with Japan that were grandfathered under Japan's protocol of accession to the GATT.

During the 1960s and 1970s the major trading countries used both safeguards and antidumping laws to provide relief from import competition. The antidumping and countervailing duty laws still were used in a very limited fashion. For example, out of about 700 antidumping complaints in the United States from 1921, when the law was enacted, until the late 1960s, duties were imposed in only about 10 percent of the cases.[3] Regarding safeguards, the concern about import disruption in the early 1960s was focused on imports of cotton textiles in the industrial countries. However, instead of using the safeguards under Article XIX of the GATT, a series of special quota arrangements were developed, initially for cotton textiles, which evolved into the Multi-Fiber Arrangement (MFA), which covered a wide range of textile and clothing products.[4]

The European Community (EC) made great efforts during the Tokyo Round in the late 1970s to negotiate the selective use of safeguards, but the EC was blocked by developing countries that feared that selective safeguards would cause more products to become subject to a discriminatory regime such as that already applied to textiles under the MFA.[5] As a result, there were no changes to the rules of Article XIX of the GATT for safeguards during the Tokyo Round, but there were new rules for antidumping and countervailing duties under the Tokyo Round Codes. The implementation of these new rules, especially the antidumping rules, in the trade legislation of the EC and the United States tended to make it easier for domestic industries to obtain relief from import competition. In particular, there were procedural changes to the antidumping laws, which imposed deadlines on the process and, especially in the United States, tended to make the process mandatory.

3. Seavy (1970, p. 26).

4. The MFA (and its predecessors) involved a type of "voluntary export restraint" whereby the exporting country restricts the volume of exports, but because the exporting country administers the quota, the quota profit is normally obtained by the exporters.

5. The term *selective safeguards* refers to safeguards targeted at a particular country. Japan was a concern in the 1950s and 1960s, whereas China is a concern today.

Developments in the 1980s

During the 1980s the United States and the EC increasingly used antidumping duties instead of safeguards measures.[6] In the United States, from 1980 through 1989 there were 398 antidumping cases and 318 countervailing duty cases that were brought by domestic petitioners.[7] In their study of the cost of protection to the U.S. economy, Hufbauer and Elliot document the shift to the use of antidumping and countervailing duty laws or voluntary export restraints in the United States by industries seeking import relief. Comparing the industries receiving protection in the United States in 1984 with those in 1990, they state: "Another striking difference between the cases documented in the 1986 study and those studied here is the virtual disappearance of the escape clause (safeguards) as an avenue for import relief. . . . Instead the unfair trade laws have become an increasingly popular path to special protection."[8]

Similarly, in a fairly recent analysis of EC antidumping law Eymann and Schuknecht state that antidumping laws are the primary instrument of protectionism in the EC.[9] Although Eymann and Schuknecht are overlooking the special and highly restrictive trade regime of the EC for agricultural products under the Common Agricultural Policy and the restrictions on textiles trade, the EC became a heavy user of antidumping laws during the 1980s. From 1980 until 1990 the EC initiated 904 antidumping actions, and in 76 percent of the cases the result was either an antidumping duty or a price undertaking by the exporter.[10]

There are several factors that contributed to this increased use of antidumping (and countervailing) duties and the reduced use of safeguards. The fact that tariffs were relatively low after the Tokyo Round made it more difficult to negotiate compensation and made retaliation more likely if safeguard measures were imposed. The United States retained considerable discretion over the use of safeguards, while the antidumping process became virtually mandatory: if an industry complained, if there was dumping and a finding of material injury, duties were imposed. In the EC the so-called 113 Committee supervised the administration of safeguards by the Commission, and it was often difficult to

6. The United States also became a heavy user of countervailing duties laws.
7. Finger (1993, table 1.1, p. 5).
8. Hufbauer and Elliot (1994, pp. 17–18).
9. Eymann and Schuknecht (1993, p. 221).
10. Eymann and Schuknecht (1993, pp. 223–25).

get the support of the Council of Ministers to take safeguards measures. Although in the EC the use of antidumping measures was more discretionary than in the United States (or Canada) and the support of the Council of Ministers was required to impose measures, in the 1980s the EC member states tended to accept the rhetoric that antidumping duties were preventing unfair trade practices and to accept the recommendation of the Commission about the imposition of antidumping duties.

In assessing this debate, it is important to recognize that the distinction between fair and unfair trade is ultimately a political judgment. I. M. Destler has analyzed how successive U.S. administrations have used the slogan of "free but fair trade" in order to build a political coalition in favor of open markets, while offering access to the trade-remedy laws or import-relief laws as a consolation to industries who are worried about import competition.[11]

Implications of the WTO

This section briefly reviews the results of the Uruguay Round with respect to the import-relief laws governed by the WTO Agreement and summarizes some recent key developments in national policies related to import-relief laws.

The Uruguay Round Bargain

As noted at the outset, the results of the Uruguay Round negotiations, which led to the creation of the WTO in January 1995, have greatly limited or eliminated the ability of countries to use various exceptions to the 1994 GATT, notably those of Articles XI (for certain quotas), Article XII (for balance of payments), Article XVIII (for developing countries), and Article XXV (for waivers) and grandfather rights under the protocol of accession. In addition, sectors such as agriculture and textiles, which had special rules that permitted trade restrictions and export subsidies, are being reintegrated into the system of normal trade rules of the WTO. Of course the WTO system also incorporates new rules for trade in services and intellectual property, as well as a strengthened, integrated dispute settlement mechanism.

---

11. Destler (1986 and 1995).

It is worth briefly reviewing the main changes in safeguards and antidumping and countervailing duties under the WTO. The concern that the use of voluntary export restraints was eroding the rules of the trading system caused a different approach to safeguards to be taken in the Uruguay Round negotiations. The use of voluntary export restraints was explicitly prohibited in the Agreement on Safeguards, and incentives were created to use safeguards only on a temporary basis. Specifically, the right of trading partners (which experience a reduction in exports when the safeguards measures are imposed) to seek compensation or to retaliate by withdrawing equivalent tariff concessions is to be suspended if the safeguard measures are genuinely temporary and are imposed only for a maximum of three years. In addition, the safeguard measures can not be reintroduced for a period equal to their application if the right of compensation and retaliation is to be suspended. The suspension of the right of compensation or retaliation (which was a deterrent to invoking safeguards measures under Article XIX) was offered as an inducement for countries to use safeguard measures under the rules of the WTO instead of using the extra-GATT measures such as voluntary export restraints.

The negotiation of the Antidumping Agreement was one of the most contentious issues in the Uruguay Round. In the United States and Europe, import-sensitive constituencies forcefully resisted any efforts to limit their resort to import relief under the antidumping and countervailing duty laws, which they recognize are the source of the threats that are used to enforce the voluntary export restraint arrangements. Reflecting these kinds of domestic constituency pressures, some of the proposals for negotiation of antidumping laws in the Uruguay Round were based on an enforcement mentality that seeks to limit recidivist dumping and circumvention. On the other hand, countries and territories such as Hong Kong, Japan, New Zealand, and Norway took an extremely liberal approach to the antidumping issues. The result of this collision of pressures was a text that includes much more procedural detail, but received the lowest grade of any of the Uruguay Round agreements in an assessment of the degree of trade liberalization resulting from the Antidumping Agreement.[12]

One of the potential liberalizing provisions in the Uruguay Round Antidumping Agreement is that investigating authorities are "normally" required to compare average prices of export transactions with normal values.[13] In the past

12. Schott (1995).

13. The full name of the Antidumping Agreement under the WTO is the Agreement on Implementation of Article VI of the General Agreement on Tariffs and Trade 1994.

14. See Horlick and Shea (1994, pp. 5–31) and Palmeter (1995, pp. 39–82).

the investigating authorities could compare individual transactions to normal values (some of which might be aberrant—for instance, if the goods were end-of-line or end-of-season goods) and disregard transactions above normal values. This practice led to an upward bias in the calculation of antidumping margins and can even lead to significant dumping margins when there would be no dumping at all if average prices were compared to normal values. However, the problem is that the "abnormal" can become the norm for the administration of antidumping laws, and it is still possible to get individual price comparisons instead of more appropriate comparisons between average prices. There is also an annex to the Antidumping Agreement that was put in place to limit the discretion of antidumping administrators in using the so-called best available information instead of accepting the data and information provided by the exporting firms.

Some other aspects of the WTO Antidumping Agreement are controversial. Some view as potentially liberalizing provisions in the Uruguay Round Antidumping Agreement that call for greater precision in making allowances for profit in determining constructed value and calculating profit from sales in the ordinary course of trade instead of applying a fixed rate of return, but others see potential for abuse of these provisions.[14] Set against these modest gains are the restrictive U.S. approach to price comparisons and the potential application of anticircumvention procedures. The major users of antidumping duty laws—the EC, the United States, and Canada—were willing to agree to detailed procedural requirements for antidumping laws and procedures, with similar provisions applied to countervailing duty proceedings.

Recent Developments

With the conclusion of the Uruguay Round and the implementation of the WTO, many developing countries have been introducing trade laws. Before 1990 about 90 percent of antidumping investigations were undertaken by Australia, the EC, Canada, and the United States, the traditional users of antidumping duties. From 1995 through 1997 these traditional users of antidumping laws launched 237 investigations out of a total of 610 investigations of which the WTO was notified.[15] More than half of antidumping

15. These data are based on antidumping investigations of which the WTO Antidumping Committee has been notified as tabulated by the Rules Division of the WTO.

investigations were launched by developing countries in the first three years of the WTO.

In the Western Hemisphere Argentina, Brazil, and Mexico have joined the United States and Canada as frequent users of antidumping actions to deal with the economic and political pressures of import competition. Also, in the last three years Chile, Colombia, Costa Rica, Guatemala, Peru, and Venezuela have initiated antidumping actions.

The proliferation of antidumping laws around the world could be a source of mounting friction in the trading system. The procedural requirements of the WTO Antidumping Agreement could prove a challenge to many developing countries and will likely lead to trade disputes, because they lack the traditions of administrative and legal due process. Already Mexico has brought a dispute to the WTO claiming that Guatemala breached the procedural obligations stated in the Antidumping Agreement when it imposed antidumping duties on cement from Mexico.

Another interesting development in the last two years is that the member states of the EC have been less disposed to accept the recommendations of the Commission regarding imposition of antidumping duties. In recent cases involving cotton fabrics and small fax machines, the imposition of duties was blocked by the Council of Ministers.[16] Although it is not clear whether this pattern will be sustained, in these cases the EC member states have been taking a more pragmatic approach in determining whether the imposition of antidumping duties is of benefit to their own economies, and the results seem to be closer to those seen in the region's earlier experience with safeguards, where the member states often blocked the imposition of duties or quotas. There are several possible explanations for this trend, including the fact that expansion of the EC to include Austria, Finland, and Sweden has introduced a more liberal approach to policy and also made the economic interests of the member states more diverse.

In the Western Hemisphere the widespread use of antidumping duties needs to be reconsidered. Only eight countries in the Western Hemisphere have revised their safeguards laws in accord with the WTO system, and the use of safeguards has been much more limited than the use of antidumping duties since implementation of the WTO.[17]

16. The Commission persisted with a "new" case on cotton fabrics, but eventually a group of member states blocked the case.

17. The source of this information is the Rules Division of the WTO.

Policy Choices for Small Economies

In the context of these international developments it is useful to consider some of the factors that shape the policy choices for small economies. What should be the role of different import-relief mechanisms in national trade policy?

Economic and Trade Policy

It is important to remember that imposing special import duties or quotas will normally impose net economic costs on relatively small and relatively open economies.[18] The nature of these costs and benefits for a small economy will vary depending on the type of product involved in a safeguards, antidumping, or countervailing duty proceeding; the structure of the industries producing the product; and the uses of the product subject to the higher duties.

A few examples might clarify the issues involved. Suppose a small economy imposes a special duty of 20 percent on imported grains. This will benefit domestic grain producers as the domestic price of grains rises. (Of course, there will be no benefit for grains that are exported.) However, producers of other products that purchase grains, such as livestock producers, flour mills, breweries, and bakeries, will lose as their costs rise. There may well be many more people employed in these downstream activities than are employed in the sector receiving the special import duty. There also will be broader effects on the economy and society, such as adverse effects on the cost of restaurant meals or on the welfare of pensioners as a result of higher food costs. Often these broader effects on the economy and society are ignored in the decisionmaking process, but the impact on downstream producers that use the product as an input can be very significant.

The structure of the industry that might receive a special duty is an important factor in determining the economic and also the political effects of the special duty. For example, a manufacturing industry that exports a high proportion of its production will not benefit from the import duties on its export sales and may worry that other countries will impose similar kinds of duties in response.

Also, in a smaller, open economy different manufacturers may produce items for different stages of an overall production cycle. For example, one

18. A more detailed survey of the economic issues involved in import-relief laws is included in Smith (1997, pp. 18–85).

manufacturer of small engines might manufacture engine blocks in the country, but import pistons and valves from Korea. At the same time, another firm might manufacture pistons and valves in the country, but import engine blocks from Brazil. In these types of situations the impact of special duties on the pistons or on the engine blocks could have negative consequences for one or the other of the manufacturers.

Economic analysis suggests that there is limited potential for predatory dumping and that—although a large surge in imports, which might trigger safeguards, can be disruptive—economic performance and economic growth are enhanced over the longer term by allowing open access to imports. In a small economy special duties or quotas restricting imports will have anti-competitive effects, impair economic efficiency, and impede innovation and economic growth.

Domestic Politics

The primary economic argument for import-relief laws is actually a political argument. The claim is that if a country has the ability to provide import duties that are compatible with WTO rules and procedures, this facilitates the acceptance of a more open trade regime. Therefore, many smaller developing economies are opening to increased international competition as a result of commitments made to the WTO. This opening of the economy will enhance economic growth prospects at least over the medium term, and the concerns of various groups about disruptive imports can be addressed by the elaboration of safeguards or of antidumping or counter-vailing duty laws.

On occasion the economics and politics of safeguards and of antidumping and countervailing duties can collide quite dramatically. For example, a special import duty on fertilizer may have only modest benefits for fertilizer producers if a large proportion of output is exported, but can have a significant impact on farmers, who experience rising costs.

Reaction of Trading Partners

For a small economy the reaction of trading partners is an important consideration in the design and application of import-relief or trade-remedy laws. Meeting all of the requirements of the WTO for the application of safeguards measures or of antidumping or countervailing duties is only a minimum requirement for obtaining the acceptance of trading partners of the application of duties or other trade restrictions.

Although they may use these measures themselves, large trading partners may take exception to the application of import duties to their exports even if the measure is fully compatible with the WTO rules and procedures. It is difficult to predict the precise reaction of major trading partners to the application of import-relief laws, apart from the obvious point that they will not like the idea. If one import-relief measure is more acceptable to major trading partners than another, this could prove to be an important policy consideration for a small economy.

Regional Economic Integration and Import-Relief Laws

A number of issues arise with respect to the development and implementation of import-relief laws in regional economic agreements. Various commentators have suggested that there are linkages between competition policy and the use of trade remedies. The suggestion is often made that as trade barriers are eliminated among partners in a regional trading arrangement, safeguards and antidumping and countervailing duties should be eliminated within the regional trading arrangement.

Replacing Antidumping Duties with Competition Policy

At least at the beginning, antidumping remedies were conceived as the international extension of the anti–price discrimination laws under national jurisdictions.[19] Over time the approaches to the implementation of these antidumping measures and domestic anti–price discrimination laws have evolved in somewhat different directions, especially in the United States.

In the United States, at least, it seems to have become somewhat easier to obtain import relief through the application of antidumping measures or other trade laws. For example, out of 371 antidumping cases processed from 1955 through 1968, only 12 resulted in application of duties and in 89 cases there was some form of price undertaking by exporters or voluntary termination.[20] The probability of success with an antidumping case increased during the

19. Grey (1968).
20. Destler (1995, p. 141).

1970s and especially during the 1980s. During the period from 1980 through 1989, Destler observes that "out of 327 antidumping petitions carried to term 173 (53 percent) resulted in duties or suspension agreements, and 111 petitions were withdrawn, largely after agreement on voluntary export restraints."[21] This pattern has continued into the 1990s, with record filings of antidumping cases in the early 1990s and success rates of about 50 percent.

Although it has become easier to obtain relief from imports through antidumping measures, it has become more difficult to obtain relief under the anti–price discrimination laws or antimonopolization laws in the United States. This shift in the application of anti–price discrimination and antimonopolization laws reflects the skepticism among economists about the viability of predatory pricing strategies and about the influential legal commentaries and analysis criticizing these laws.[22]

Several studies have suggested that antidumping laws should be replaced by anti–price discrimination laws. A study by the Joint Chambers of Commerce examined this issue in some depth.[23] This study compared Canadian and U.S. antidumping laws and their respective competition and antitrust laws, and it concluded that competition laws should replace the antidumping laws. Boddez and Trebilcock have made a similar proposal.[24]

The U.S. Council of Economic Advisors has observed that antidumping laws often restrict trade and increase prices, unlike antitrust laws, which seek increased competition and lower prices. The council argued that making sound competition policies more easily enforceable against foreign misconduct would be a more appropriate response to restrictive business practices than the imposition of antidumping duties.[25] In this connection, it is interesting to note that Australia and New Zealand have each redefined their competition laws to apply to the Trans-Tasman economic area and have eliminated antidumping from their regional trade agreement.

In advance of the Singapore Ministerial for the WTO, the EC proposed the development under the WTO of a new framework of rules for competition

21. Destler (1995, p. 154).

22. See, for example, Bork (1980) and Salop (1981), both of which include a comprehensive survey of these issues.

23. Feltham, Salen, Mathieson, and Wonnacott (1991).

24. Boddez and Trebilcock (1993).

25. United States Council of Economic Advisors (1994, p. 239).

policy. A communication from the Commission to the Council of Ministers of the EC states:

> The relation between the elaboration of a competition framework and the functioning of existing trade instruments is a key issue in the trade-competition debate. It is true that the incorporation of competition provisions into trade law and/or more comprehensive and effective enforcement of competition policies through increased international cooperation, would lessen the need to have recourse to instruments of commercial defense. However, competition instruments cannot be seen as substitutes for trade instruments. The latter only lose their *raison d'être* in the context of fully integrated markets. A framework of competition rules would, therefore, complement present trade law and create a new instrument to tackle anticompetitive behavior in markets that are not integrated. Thus the development of new instruments would complement, not supplant, present instruments.

The validity of this statement is illustrated by practice within the EC itself. Antidumping action on intra-EC trade is excluded, as this is a fully integrated market.[26] For member states this integration has led to the following: the elimination of all tariffs, the elimination of measures of equivalent effect to tariffs (which is a wider concept than the GATT's national treatment obligation), and the adoption of the four freedoms—goods, services (including establishment), capital (including investment), and labor.[27] The question remains, of course, how trade laws, such as laws governing antidumping and countervailing duties and safeguards, will be dealt with in the FTAA.

Comparing Safeguards with Antidumping Duties and Countervailing Duties

This section briefly summarizes the main elements of safeguards and of antidumping and countervailing duties under the WTO.

---

26. The following footnote is attached to the text at this point: "The EEA Agreement between the EC and EFTA countries follows the same approach: antidumping is excluded in those areas where the 'acquis communautaire' has been taken over. In trade between the Community and the countries of central and eastern Europe, however, antidumping action can still be taken, as well as between the U.S., Canada and Mexico in the NAFTA context. The same applies between the EU and Turkey: antidumping action remains a possibility despite the customs union agreement."

27. Communication submitted by Brittan and Miert (1996) to the Council of Ministers.

Safeguards

The requirements under the WTO include the following:

—An investigation and determination of whether increased imports are causing or threatening to cause serious injury to domestic producers of a like or directly competitive product.

—Specific procedural and detailed notification requirements.

—Application of remedy—either duties, duty quotas, or quotas—to all trading partners.[28]

—A requirement for compensation to be negotiated or to be subject to retaliation by trading partners if measures extend beyond three years.

Antidumping Duties

The requirements under the WTO include the following:

—An investigation and determination of whether imports are causing or threatening to cause material injury.

—An investigation and verification of dumping margins on imports on a company-by-company basis (country-by-country for nonmarket economies).

—Extensive, detailed procedural and notification requirements.

—Application of remedies—duties or price undertakings—on a company-by-company basis (country-by-country for nonmarket economies).

—No requirement for compensation, but a requirement for a five-year review of the injury determination.

Countervailing Duties

The requirements under the WTO include the following:

—An investigation and determination of whether imports are causing or threatening to cause material injury.

—An investigation and verification of subsidy margins on imports on a country-by-country basis or a jurisdiction-by-jurisdiction basis (for instance, the EC, fifteen member states, or subnational governments).

—Extensive, detailed procedural and notification requirements.

—Application of remedies—duties or price undertakings—on a country-by-country basis (or a jurisdiction-by-jurisdiction basis).

—No requirement for compensation, but a requirement for a five-year review of the injury determination.

28. There is some debate about whether safeguards measures ought to be applied to regional partners under the GATT or WTO rules.

Policy Options for Small Economies

There are a number of options for smaller economies to consider with respect to import-relief laws. This section outlines the main possibilities.

Have No Import-Relief Laws

It is a valid economic policy position for a small, open economy to have no import-relief laws. For example, for many years both Hong Kong and Singapore did not have import-relief laws because they believed that open markets and free access to imports were the best ways to enhance economic performance and to promote economic growth. However, sustaining this policy position requires a fairly broad domestic political consensus that open markets are the best economic policy. For example, Singapore has recently adopted an antidumping law, but it has not invoked any measures under this new law.

Enact and Implement Safeguards Laws and Procedures

If a small economy wishes to implement import-relief or trade-remedy laws, the least costly alternative (at least in terms of administrative and budgetary costs) is the development of safeguards legislation. Administration of safeguards is less costly than administration of antidumping or countervailing duties laws, because the only investigation that is required is investigation as to whether there is serious injury in the domestic economy. The procedural and notification requirements under the WTO are substantial, but they are less onerous than the WTO requirements for the antidumping and countervailing duties laws.

The rhetorical distinction between fair and unfair trade seems to be less important for small economies. From a pragmatic point of view, the main issues with respect to safeguards are the basic requirements under the agreement: specifically, that there should be increased imports causing serious injury; that the special duties are limited to three years or less (because the "negotiation of compensation or be subject to retaliation" is a strong disincentive to the use of safeguards for a longer period); and the MFN requirement that duties are imposed on imports from all sources.

Enact Antidumping or Countervailing Duties Laws, but Delay Implementation

One possibility is that a small economy could develop antidumping or countervailing duties legislation and pass the legislation, but not implement the procedures. The advantage of this approach is that it might deter the most predatory types of dumping, but it would limit both the budgetary costs of administering the laws and the economic costs of imposing the duties. The disadvantage of this approach is there might be domestic political pressure to use the laws in a particular case, and there could be difficulties in meeting the very detailed procedural and notification requirements under the WTO if there was inadequate preparation and training of staff for implementation of the legislation.

Implement Antidumping and Countervailing Duties Laws and Safeguards

Implementing antidumping or countervailing duties laws as well as safeguards laws and procedures would impose significant budgetary costs on a small economy and could impose economic costs on the economy if duties were imposed on a significant volume of imports. The procedural requirements for antidumping and countervailing duties procedures are more onerous than those for safeguards under the WTO, and it is expensive to analyze and verify the margins of dumping or subsidy for exporters to a small economy.

This step of implementing antidumping and countervailing duties as well as safeguards should be taken only if it is believed that safeguards will not provide an adequate response to import competition pressures or if it is believed that antidumping or countervailing duties laws will be more acceptable to a major trading partner or partners than safeguards measures.

One potential advantage of antidumping or countervailing duties over safeguards is that they can be targeted at one or two trading partners, whereas safeguards must be imposed on imports from all sources. Depending on the trading partners involved and their reaction to the use of antidumping or countervailing duties laws, this can simplify bilateral relations, but it can also be a source of friction in bilateral trade relations.

The Role of Safeguards in the FTAA Negotiations

A few key issues can be identified related to the potential role of safeguards in the FTAA negotiations. One issue is whether and how to design safeguards that could be implemented in conjunction with the FTAA process of liberalization of tariff and nontariff measures. Another issue is how to deal with safeguards laws and procedures that countries have in place under the WTO within the FTAA.

The issue of whether and how to develop a special safeguards mechanism that could operate in conjunction with FTAA liberalization should be considered in the FTAA negotiations. The simplest kind of safeguards mechanism that might be considered is one with provisions that if imports surge rapidly in a particular industry when tariff reductions are implemented according to the agreed-upon schedule, the schedule for further tariff reductions can be delayed, or even temporarily reversed in a temporary "snapback." It is important that any such special FTAA safeguards be temporary in their application; otherwise they could undermine the fundamental objective of trade liberalization. At the same time the possibility of application of such special safeguards could facilitate the participation of countries in the FTAA development process.

Such a special safeguards mechanism would not raise issues with respect to the WTO as long as the tariffs that were imposed remained within the individual country's tariff bindings under the WTO. Therefore, such a special safeguards mechanism need not correspond exactly with the requirements of the Agreement on Safeguards under the WTO.[29] However, it would be desirable to require a determination of serious injury by the domestic authorities in order to limit the extent to which countries might resort to this type of measure.

The potential imposition of safeguards measures within the FTAA might seem to be of greater interest to smaller countries that are concerned about the possible disruption of particular domestic industries as trade barriers are reduced and eliminated under the regional agreement, but the large economies might also resort to this type of measure in selected industries. For example, the United States brought a safeguard action against imports of corn brooms from Mexico under the North American Free Trade Agreement (NAFTA).

The issue of whether partners in regional trading arrangements that meet the requirements of Article XXIV of the 1994 GATT are permitted to exempt their regional partners from trade restrictions imposed as safeguards has been controversial in GATT practice.[30] However, several regional trading arrangements

29. Note that under the WTO there are "special" safeguards for agriculture and textiles products that were previously subject to quantitative restrictions if these conversions are incorporated into the schedules that were agreed to at the end of the Uruguay Round.

30. See, for example, the reports of the working parties on the agreements between the EC and Austria, Iceland, Portugal, Sweden, Switzerland, and Liechtenstein in GATT (1973, pp. 140–207).

have excluded their regional partners from the application of safeguards measures. Therefore, this is an issue that needs to be considered in the FTAA negotiations. Should FTAA partners be excluded from the application of safeguards under the WTO by FTAA member countries?

Conclusion

If a small economy enacts either safeguards or antidumping and countervailing duties laws, it must be prepared to implement the legislation. Of course there might be a gap of several months or even years before a case is brought under these import-relief laws after they have been enacted. However, the pattern in a number of countries has been that once the laws are enacted, they tend to be used. The detailed procedural and notification requirements under the WTO mean that implementation of import-relief laws must be done carefully and precisely.

It is important for a small, open economy to maintain some discretion in the application of import-relief measures. Therefore, either safeguards measures, antidumping duties, or countervailing duties should be subject to a public or national interest review before they are imposed. For any of these laws, in every case the country must make a pragmatic assessment of the impact of imposing the proposed duties on various sectors of the economy and of the implications for trade and economic relations with major trading partners.

Various countries in the Western Hemisphere that are considering the implementation of safeguards or antidumping laws and procedures—especially the smaller economies—should consider implementing only safeguards, because they are a relatively flexible instrument and have lower administrative and economic costs than antidumping (and countervailing) duties procedures. Even the larger countries in the Western Hemisphere, which are or have become frequent users of antidumping actions, should carefully consider limiting the use of antidumping duties and making somewhat greater use of safeguards procedures as an alternative to antidumping actions. Furthermore, safeguards measures taken under the WTO are likely to be temporary, because the requirement that a country negotiate compensation or be subject to retaliation applies to safeguards measures after three years. This is a potent pressure to remove any safeguards measure within three years.

Safeguards could be a significant issue in the FTAA negotiations. Should there be a special safeguards mechanism that provides for some flexibility in the timing of tariff reductions for FTAA members when these importing countries experience a surge in imports that is disruptive to particular industries? Should FTAA members exempt their partners from the application of safeguards measures under the WTO? Properly designed safeguards mechanisms can facilitate the integration process.

References

Boddez, T., and M. Trebilcock. 1993. *Unfinished Business: Reforming Trade Remedy Laws in North America.* Toronto: C. D. Howe Institute.

Bork, R. 1980. *The Antitrust Paradox: A Policy at War with Itself.* New York: Basic Books.

Brittan, L., and K. V. Miert. 1996. "Towards an International Framework of Competition Rules." Communication submitted to the Council of the European Community (June 18).

Destler, I. M. 1986. *American Trade Politics: System under Stress.* Washington, D.C.: Institute for International Economics.

———. 1995. *American Trade Politics,* 3d ed. Washington, D.C.: Institute for International Economics.

Eymann, A., and L. Schuknecht. 1993. "Antidumping Enforcement in the European Community." In *Antidumping: How It Works and Who Gets Hurt,* edited by J. M. Finger. Ann Arbor: University of Michigan Press.

Feltham, I., S. Salen, R. Mathieson, and R. Wonnacott. 1991. *Competition (Antitrust) and Antidumping Laws in the Context of the Canada-U.S. Free Trade Agreement.* Ottawa: Canadian Chamber of Commerce.

Finger, J. M., ed. 1993. *Antidumping: How It Works and Who Gets Hurt.* Ann Arbor: University of Michigan Press.

General Agreement on Tariffs and Trade. 1959. "Report of the Group of Experts on Anti-Dumping and Countervailing Duties." *Basic Instruments and Selected Documents,* 8th supp. Geneva: GATT Secretariat.

———. 1973. *Basic Instruments and Selected Documents,* 20th supp. Geneva: GATT Secretariat.

Grey, R. de C. 1968. *The Antidumping Code.* Montreal: Private Planning Association.

Horlick, G. N., and E. C. Shea. 1994. "The World Trade Organization Antidumping Agreement." *Journal of World Trade* 28: 5–31.

Hufbauer, G. C., and K. A. Elliot. 1994. *Measuring the Costs of Protection in the United States.* Washington, D.C.: Institute for International Economics.

Palmeter, D. 1995. "United States Implementation of the Uruguay Round Antidumping Code." *Journal of World Trade* 29: 39–82.

Salop, S. C. 1981. *Strategy, Predation and Antitrust Analysis.* Washington, D.C.: Federal Trade Commission.

Schott, J. 1995. *An Assessment of the Uruguay Round.* Washington, D.C.: Institute for International Economics.

Seavy, W. A. 1970. "Dumping Since the War: The GATT and National Laws." Thesis, Docteur en Sciences Politiques, Thesis No. 205, Institut Universitaire des Hautes Etudes, University of Geneva. Oakland, Calif.: Office Services.

Smith, M. G. 1997. "The Evolution of Trade Remedies in NAFTA." In *Finding Middle Ground: Reforming the Antidumping Laws in North America,* edited by M. Hart. Ottawa: Center for Trade Policy and Law.

United States Council of Economic Advisors. 1994. *Economic Report of the President.* Washington, D.C.: Government Printing Office.

CHAPTER THIRTEEN

How Long Can You Tread Water? The Anti-Economics of Trade Remedy Law

Brian R. Russell

This chapter applies an economic perspective to the issue of dumping and subsidy trade remedy laws.[1] Although there are other criteria for valuing and evaluating the usefulness of these trade remedy laws, it is economics that is most frequently advanced as an explanation of the need for these rules in the governance of global trade. The existence of "unfair" trade practices and the consequent economic harm caused to importing countries is frequently advanced as a justification for the enactment and continuation of these rules, which, it is argued, are designed to restore conditions of fair market competition. This chapter examines that argument in some detail. It is a discussion from

The author thanks Miranda Davies for her valuable research assistance.

1. *Dumping* is the sale in a foreign market of a good or service at a price below the price charged in the home market or at a price below the cost of production. *Subsidy* is defined in the Agreement on Subsidies and Countervailing Measures of the 1994 General Agreement on Tariffs and Trade (GATT) as a financial benefit conferred on a certain firm or industry by any level of government or a government agency. The term *trade remedy laws* embodies a wide variety of legal measures designed to deal with the trade practices of foreign countries and firms. As used here, it refers to antidumping and countervailing duty laws which, respectively, are the trade remedy rules enacted to address foreign dumping and subsidy practices.

first principles of the economic rationale and effects of the antidumping and antisubsidy rules that have been developed to compensate domestic producers for these practices by foreign exporters and their governments.

In discussing the issue the chapter examines the effects of these practices and rules with a view to the net national welfare of the importing country, as well as the global political economy. It is acknowledged that dumping and subsidization can have negative effects on particular firms, industries, or regions. These effects not only can occur, but do. The chapter argues that in most alleged cases of dumping these effects are the result of the normal market forces of competition increasingly inherent in a globalized and technologically sophisticated marketplace. Further, where these effects are the result of truly anticompetitive actions, remedies other than antidumping duties (ADDs) are more appropriate solutions. Even in cases of foreign subsidization it will often be the case that remedies other than countervailing duties (CVDs) are the most efficient for the national economic interest.

The chapter begins with a discussion of the international incidence of and trends in antidumping cases as an example of the increasing importance of trade remedies in international trade. A discussion of the economics of antidumping follows, much of which is also relevant to the issue of CVDs.[2] Finally, the chapter provides a discussion of some business and political-economic realities of the issues and concludes with some recommendations for public policy and future negotiations in light of the preceding discussion.

The International Use of Antidumping Measures

The United States is by far the world's most active user of antidumping remedies.[3] At the end of 1995 the United States had 294 antidumping measures in effect, over twice the number of the next most active user, the European Union (EU) (133), and triple the totals for the third- and fourth-place countries, Canada (98) and Mexico (81). This level of activity translates to about

---

2. Since both ADD and CVD statutes are designed to impose a common remedy, compensatory tariffs, for unfair dumping and subsidy practices, the economic effects of these trade remedy laws are similar. Accordingly, the discussion of the economics of CVDs is truncated to avoid repetition.

3. The data in this section are based on GATT or World Trade Organization (WTO) antidumping reports and information from the Congressional Budget Office (1998).

5 measures for every $10 billion of U.S. imports. This compares with an average of 2 active measures against the United States by foreign countries for every $10 billion of U.S. imports. From 1991 to 1995 the United States initiated over 49 cases per year, 18 percent of the world total. In the same period Australia, the next most active user of ADDs, averaged 43 case initiations annually, the EU 33, and Argentina and Mexico about 23 each.[4]

Although these figures suggest that the United States is the most active user of antidumping measures, they do not indicate the volume of imports affected by these measures. Such measures are notoriously difficult to accurately quantify, and for the present purposes all that can be said is that the United States has been a frequent and disproportionate user of the remedy. It is also important to note that other countries such as Argentina, Australia, Canada, and Mexico are initiating an even higher ratio of cases than the United States when compared to their import volumes. When this figure is adjusted to account for national gross domestic product (GDP), however, the United States is by far the largest initiator.

In considering the use of antidumping remedies it is important to determine the trend of usage. The United States maintained 80 active antidumping measures in June 1979, a number that increased in twenty-eight of the thirty-three subsequent biannual reporting periods and approached 300 by the end of 1995. This steady increase is not mirrored in most other industrialized countries, which show considerable variation over the period and little recognizable trend.[5]

The trend among developing countries, however, is far more striking. None of the twenty-two developing countries for which data are available for the period from 1978 to 1995 had fewer active measures at the end of the period than at the beginning, and ten had more. For almost all countries the trend toward an increase seemed to be accelerating at the end of the period. Mexico's measures increased from 18 to 67 from 1991 to 1995, Argentina's from 4 to 20 from 1994 to 1995 alone. Brazil jumped from 4 to 23 active measures between 1990 and 1995, and Turkey from 27 to 37 between 1993 and 1995. India, which had no active antidumping measures prior to 1994, had 12 by the end of 1995.

4. Adjusting U.S. antidumping activity to account for its large volume of imports and GDP yields even more dramatic results; by this measure the United States has an almost 50 percent larger case initiation level than the EU, the next most active user of ADDs.

5. A trend toward a modest increase can be seen in the decade of the 1990s for Australia and New Zealand.

Between 1990 and 1995 the number of active antidumping measures of which the GATT or WTO was notified in the twenty-two developing countries for which data were available rose from 16 to 197, an increase of 1,231 percent. The figures for case initiations are almost equally dramatic. In 1990 just 15 cases were initiated by a broad sample of fifty-four developing countries. By 1995 this number had increased to 157. There can be little doubt that the use of ADDs as a remedy has proliferated among the countries of the developing world to a point at which significant amounts of trade are now being affected.

The combination of aggressive and increasing use of antidumping measures by the United States, coupled with a rapid rise in the instances of use by developing countries, is not explained by corresponding increases in the volumes of trade, which are much more modest. This is troubling evidence that antidumping measures are becoming preferred tools for protection of domestic industry as more traditional forms of trade barriers are reduced or eliminated as the result of trade liberalization efforts. It is also interesting to note that among the developing countries there has been a steady rise in the number of both cases and active measures against the United States in this decade.[6] No developing country has shown a decrease in the number of measures against the United States over this period. This at least suggests that the active use of antidumping measures against developing countries by the United States may be beginning to encourage greater use of antidumping rules by the developing nations.

Trade Remedies and Economics

The world of trade remedies is an arcane one populated by a group of lawyers, economists, and policymakers who preside over a system that from the outside has a certain luster based on its intuitive appeal. The most common justification offered for trade remedy law is relatively simple to state and on first acquaintance seems attractive. In the case of antidumping law, the usual explanation is that antidumping law remedies unfair price discrimination implemented by foreign producers in order to gain market power and extract economic rents. These rents are achieved by a foreign producer through selling at prices in the domestic market that are below the price at which it sells in its home country. Such price discrimination, which is impossible in conditions of

6. Brazil, Columbia, and Mexico are particularly notable in this regard.

perfect competition since prices would equalize as a result of arbitrage between the jurisdictions, occurs frequently in reality as the result of additional costs for such things as transportation, consumer preferences, and government barriers to the free exchange of goods and services.[7]

Many proponents of antidumping laws would go on to make the argument that dumping is often done for a period of time sufficient to drive domestic competition from the market. At this point the foreign producer, now a monopolist or at least a price determiner, raises prices to levels higher than before its market entry. This is a strategy that the producer can successfully implement due to the lack of competition from local producers who have been forced out of the market—or perhaps even business—by the earlier low prices.

In this view the long-run effects of dumping are reduced competition, domestic unemployment, and higher prices to consumers. The remedy to this situation is provided by antidumping law, which, upon proof of both dumping and material injury or threat thereof, imposes a dumping duty designed to offset the difference between the price charged by the dumper in its home market with the "dumped" price that the producer charges in the domestic market.[8] This duty is levied at the border and purportedly levels the playing field for domestic producers.

The argument for the other major branch of trade remedy law, CVDs, runs along similar lines. When a foreign producer receives public funds or other benefits from its government, this inflow of public support enables the foreign firm to enjoy an unfair cost advantage that cannot be matched by domestic producers that receive no such public funds from their own governments. Absent redress, such a situation can result in artificially low prices or other competitive advantages. Since full costs need not be factored into the foreign firm's production prices, a situation similar to that in the dumping example will arise and the same long-run concerns for domestic employment and pricing will be expressed. The intuitive case for remedies of subsidies is strengthened by the seeming unfairness of domestic firms' being forced to compete not only with the foreign firm, but also the foreign public treasury. The legal remedy

---

7. For a discussion of the price discrimination issue and the appropriateness of antidumping rules in a free trade area, see Hart (1997).

8. *Material injury* is defined in U.S. antidumping statutes and those of many other countries as injury to a domestic producer or industry that is not insignificant.

here—again following proof of the subsidy and of material injury or threat thereof—is a CVD measured to offset the benefit conferred by the subsidy.[9]

The classic examination of the economics of these contentions is found in the work of Jacob Viner.[10] Viner examined dumping as a form of international price discrimination and argued that absent "predation," dumping does no harm to the importing country, and in many cases results in increasing its net welfare. Although it is true that some elements of society may be hurt by dumped imports, the net economic benefit to society is positive. Since society is obviously a net demander of the dumped goods, the economic benefits to consumers through lower prices will exceed the economic losses to import-competing firms and their employees. If one takes the point of view of the importing country only, all consumers are being discriminated in favor of. That is, the importing country as a whole benefits unambiguously from dumping to the extent that it receives access to imported goods at lower prices than it would pay if dumping were not being done.[11]

In such a situation sound economics would instruct policymakers in the importing country to encourage the dumping to continue. Certainly imposing an ADD to raise prices to domestic consumers would not be recommended. Further, it may sometimes be the case that the imposition of an ADD results in retaliation against domestic exports by the foreign country, thus causing further hardship to domestic industries.

International Price Discrimination

Price discrimination occurs when a firm sells a product in two different markets for different prices. Price discrimination departs from perfect competition in two ways: first, because a perfectly competitive firm would sell all of its output in the market with the higher price, and second, because in any event prices should equalize in both markets as the result of arbitrage by consumers. However, barriers to arbitrage, such as transportation costs and regulatory

9. National methodologies for calculating dumping margins and appropriate duties are notoriously skewed in favor of domestic producers, often resulting in duties that make the foreign imports unable to be price competitive. For an excellent discussion of the fairness claims of trade remedy law, see Cass and Boltuck (1996).

10. Viner (1923).

11. Deardorff (1989, p. 27).

barriers, make the second condition unlikely in many markets, including those within domestic economies. In practice, many firms are also unable to sell their entire output in the higher-priced market and therefore seek other outlets for their additional production. Accordingly, price discrimination is a fundamental feature of both domestic and international business.

Prices will be higher in markets in which demand is less elastic. Economic theory validates the intuitive assumption that higher prices have the net effect of reducing national welfare, but this conclusion says nothing directly about the welfare effects on markets with lower prices (that is, the markets into which products are being dumped). Eliminating price discrimination would most likely lead monopolists to reduce prices in one market while raising them in the other. The net welfare effects that this change would make inside a domestic economy are impossible to determine and could as easily be negative as positive, depending on such variables as market size and relative price changes. Only in the special case in which a dumper was a perfect competitor in one of the markets and benefiting from inelastic demand in the other would prohibition of price discrimination clearly increase welfare.[12] Price discrimination that occurs across international borders is, prima facie, dumping if the price is lower in the export market than in the home market. Generally the elimination of such price discrimination cannot be said to improve welfare.

There are many reasons why prices in the home market may be higher than prices abroad. Firms that enjoy monopoly or protected domestic markets may face increased price competition abroad. If additional costs of sales abroad are not too high, prices in foreign markets will often be lower than prices in the home market, where demand is less elastic. Even in a case in which a firm has some power to set prices in the foreign market, it is the high price in the home market, not the lower price abroad, that lowers net welfare. Although some workers and firms in import-competing industries may be hurt by the foreign dumping, it is also true that the benefits to consumers from lower prices outweigh these losses. Although it is defensible to argue that offering some form of direct assistance to the affected workers and firms may be appropriate,

12. If, for example, a firm is charging a price of $10 in Market A, where demand is completely elastic, and $20 in Market B, where demand is significantly less elastic, the prohibition of price discrimination will result in a lower price in Market B with no offsetting gain in price in Market A. Net welfare will increase as the result of the gains to consumers in Market B.

imposing ADDs that reduce net national welfare in the importing country is not economically justifiable. By focusing on the ostensible cause of the dislocation—lower prices—instead of the impacts on affected firms and workers, ADDs penalize society as a whole. Numerous economic studies have verified that the cost of this type of protection far outweighs its benefits to individual workers.[13] A 1995 study by the U.S. International Trade Commission conservatively estimated that the removal of all outstanding antidumping and CVD orders would result in a net benefit to the U.S. economy of $1.59 billion.[14]

Other rationales for antidumping and CVD laws have been advanced. Suggestions that such measures are influential in prying open protected foreign markets are substantially weakened both by the weight of experience and by the fact that most trade remedies affect sectors of the overall foreign economy that are not sufficiently significant economically or politically to result in a foreign government trade policy change. The data presented earlier would suggest that in fact the use of trade remedies results in their proliferation and in decreased market access rather than the opposite. It seems likely that most of the proponents of the view that ADDs open markets are far more concerned with protecting their domestic market shares than with liberalizing global trade.

It has also been argued that foreign dumping forces domestic industries to waste resources in adjusting to lower prices. This is a concern only in cases of temporary price adjustments, since adjustments to permanent or long-term price changes are efficient and desirable. Such a situation might occur if a firm were protected in its domestic market from changes in the world price of its product. When the world price is low, perhaps due to a surge in supply, the firm may technically be dumping in foreign markets. Imposing an ADD that will reduce the price fluctuation in the importing market may exclude the foreign firm, but since the dumping is caused by changes in the world price the ADD will have little effect on raising the price in the importing market. Even if the ADD reduces the costs of temporary adjustments to such price shocks, it is not clear that using an ADD as a tool in such a situation is more appropriate than using other policy instruments such as safeguard measures, which are specifically designed to respond to sudden fluctuations.

13. See, for example, Hufbauer, Beliner, and Elliot (1986).
14. U.S. International Trade Commission (1995).

Dumping below Cost

In recent years the definition of *dumping* as the pricing of exported products below the prices charged for the same products in the home market has been the subject of some expansion. Most notable have been suggestions that products priced below the cost of production also be included in the category of dumped goods. This expansion, it is argued, is justified if two conditions are met. First, evidence of sales below cost must indicate that the product is being sold at a higher cost in the home market, since the firm would not wish to sell all production at a loss. Second,the sale of exports below cost must indicate an intention to raise prices in the future and thus would support allegations of predation.

In examining these contentions, distinguishing between average and marginal costs is crucial. *Average costs* represent the total fixed and variable costs of production divided by the total number of units of production. *Marginal costs* represent the costs of additional units of production. Since firms bear the fixed costs regardless of production levels, these marginal or short-run variable costs are key in determining efficient output and price levels. The important question is whether the price of sale of a product exceeds the additional costs of production.

If a firm sells below average cost, it will take a loss on the transaction. However, since a portion of this cost is fixed and must be incurred regardless of production levels, it is possible that an even greater loss would be incurred with lower levels of production and sales. If the price that the firm receives for additional output exceeds the marginal cost of production, it will still be in the firm's interest to produce and sell at any price above this marginal cost.

An exporting firm might be expected to continue to sell a product at a price below its average cost in order to pay a higher percentage of fixed costs. Such behavior might continue for a short time to minimize losses incurred by the product before leaving the business or until market prices rebounded. In situations in which both foreign and domestic firms are responding to reduced demand in this way, imposing an ADD is blatant protectionism. However, foreign and domestic firms may account for their production costs in different ways. This may result in higher fixed costs for one than the other. The most common example is that in some countries with rigid labor markets labor might be regarded as a fixed cost. In others with more flexible structures it might not. In such a case firms in the latter country might leave the market, whereas firms in the former country might continue to produce and sell at lower costs in an attempt to recover a percentage of the higher fixed costs. If the latter firms are exporters, they will displace domestic production. Similar arguments have been made with respect to levels of investment in technology.

In these cases the so-called dumping appears to reflect merely cultural or structural differences in the two economies. However, if the differences result from the actions of government, a credible argument can be made for a policy response. The difficulty lies in making this determination. For example, although some would suggest that government programs of social assistance are a natural reflection of societal difference, others see such programs as unfair government manipulation of the market. Although these programs may have ample national social and political justification, they nonetheless may result in allegations of dumping if, for example, firms in countries with generous unemployment assistance programs are more willing to lay off workers than firms in countries with less generous programs, thereby reducing marginal costs.

This problem of the "interface" between cultures and institutions is an increasingly difficult one in the global economy. For purposes of dumping rules, drawing neat lines between "natural" and "unnatural" differences is a task that is at best confusing and at worst arbitrary.[15] Even if some form of policy response by an importing country is justified, it is sound economics to suggest that a more direct approach, such as imposing a wage subsidy or a layoff tax, would more effectively address the results of dumping without imposing the additional national welfare costs of a duty.

At first look it would not seem rational for a firm to sell at a price below marginal cost under any circumstances. Yet there is considerable debate about whether firms engage in this behavior nonetheless. At least three situations can be identified in which a firm might theoretically sell goods at a price below marginal cost. The first of these is the result of a miscalculation of the expected price and is not really an instance of sale below marginal cost at all. When a firm has predicted and committed to production based on a higher price than actually results in the marketplace, the production in effect has a marginal cost of zero. The original marginal cost based on the incorrect price estimate is no longer relevant. Therefore, sale at any price is rational. The "price surprise" has resulted not in production below marginal cost, but rather in a change in the relevant marginal cost.

15. For a further discussion of the interface problem, see Jackson and Davey (1986, pp. 650–52).

A second case might be one in which a firm was seeking to maximize sales rather than profits. Such behavior might be imaginable in an attempt to increase market share, for example, or to benefit from the economies of "learning by doing."[16] In this situation the net beneficiary is the consumer in the nation that achieves net gains resulting from the reduced prices. Again there will be costs to import-competing firms, but these will be offset by the consumer gains. The most economically efficient response for the importing country is to accept the inflow of cheap imports and allow the market to employ its import-competing resources more efficiently elsewhere. Alternatively, direct payments to the injured industries would be transparent and would specifically target the affected parties and therefore would be preferable to imposition of an ADD with broad economic impacts. Clearly this would be the response were the same behavior to occur domestically, unless the behavior was to fit the definition of predation set under antitrust statutes.

Predation is the third case in which a firm might produce a product below marginal cost. A predatory firm might seek to drive competitors from the marketplace through the use of low prices. Following the exit of its competitors, it could extract monopoly rents by raising prices to higher levels. In this case the firm would sacrifice short-run profit maximization for long-run excess rents. Although this would be economically rational behavior by the firm, the resulting monopoly pricing would lower the level of societal welfare more than it would raise the level of welfare of the monopolist. Many economists have argued, however, that such behavior is extremely unlikely. This is so, first, because as the monopolist caused prices to rise new competitors would be likely to appear and lower prices. Second, it is generally the case that low-price foreign imports have a number of potential sources. It would be expected that the foreign producers would compete aggressively among themselves even in a situation in which domestic competition was eliminated. Finally, other policy instruments such as the threat of a monopoly profits tax or the use of antitrust alternatives are more direct and efficient responses and could deter potential predators.

In none of these instances in which a firm might sell goods at a price below marginal cost would antidumping measures appear to be the best remedy. In most cases they would be, strictly speaking, unnecessary.[17]

---

16. Jackson and Davey (1986, note 2 at p. 38).

17. A recent review of antidumping cases in Australia, Canada, the EU, and the United States found that in 90 percent of cases activity judged unfair by antidumping standards would have been perfectly acceptable under domestic competition policy rules. See Finger (1997).

Subsidies and Countervailing Duties

Much of the earlier argument with respect to the effects of an ADD can be applied to the question of CVDs. These tariffs, which are designed to compensate for foreign subsidies such as ADDs, reduce consumer surplus. This reduction exceeds the gain in producer surplus and government revenue, thus reducing net national welfare.[18] The argument against foreign subsidies is that they represent "unfair" trade. Surely, it is contended, it is unfair for a domestic firm to have to compete not only against a foreign firm, but also against the public coffers that are supporting it. Indeed, this contention is likely to be true if the domestic firm is unsubsidized.

CVD law attempts to remedy the distortion caused by a subsidy.[19] However, CVD law provides for no offset of any subsidies that a domestic firm may also receive that reduce its costs of production, and like ADD law it does not take into consideration the positive net effect of the foreign subsidy on the importing country's economy. As in the case of dumping, it would seem that the primary economic concerns here should be national welfare and competitive conditions in the marketplace.[20] The latter would be better dealt with through antitrust concepts, and the former though no CVD at all. Although subsidization can be shown to reduce global welfare, it is extremely doubtful whether unilateral action by any one country on one product can have much effect. Further, as in the case of ADDs, it may provoke retaliation.

CVD regulators also could face the almost impossible task of determining which subsides are truly market distortive and which, for example, merely redress other government-imposed distortions.[21] Given such circumstances, it is perhaps not surprising that CVD law does not attempt to directly address the issue of market distortion, which is its supposed justification, but rather concentrates on domestic firm- and industry-level effects as defined by material injury criteria. This determination is subject to the numerous vagaries of calculation methodology, and noninjury findings are quite rare. The resulting duty calculations are also the subject of intense debate and are equally subject

18. See, for example, Sykes (1989, p. 199).

19. See, for example, Diamond (1989, p. 767).

20. For a very useful discussion of the nexus between ADD law and antitrust concepts, see Lipstein (1997, pp. 405–38).

21. For an interesting discussion of the difficulties of determining the resource allocation efficiencies of subsidies, see Schwartz and Harper (1972).

to manipulation in favor of domestic producers. Although it is possible to make a much more convincing economic argument that subsidization of foreign imports is unfair than it is in the case of dumping, it is still the case that the remedy provided by CVDs is economically inefficient and reduces net national welfare. Arguments for the use of CVDs, then, are largely confined to claims of unfairness in competitive terms, which, as will be discussed later, are far better dealt with in the context of antitrust law than in the context of trade remedies.

The Political Economy of Trade Remedies

This chapter has argued that both ADD and CVD laws are economically unnecessary. Based on the net national welfare of the importing country, the economic effects that they are designed to correct would best be left uncorrected or could be more efficiently addressed by other policies such as safeguards, antitrust laws, or direct adjustment assistance. Antidumping statutes in particular are an anachronism and not only discriminate against price discrimination behavior—which is, quite correctly, completely inoffensive when engaged in domestically—but also reflect an international business environment that no longer exists. Aside from the strong case against these measures that can be made on the basis of net national welfare, changes in the structure of international business operations are increasingly removing even a notional justification for these rules.

In a globalized business environment in which production, operation, and marketing are carried out by multinational corporations in many international locations, the borders of nation-states are not rational boundaries for efficient business decisions about pricing behavior. Regional and global production are now far more important determinants of firms' pricing decisions. Antidumping laws, which attempt to enforce arbitrary national discrimination against "foreign" firms—which in many cases are difficult to distinguish from "domestic" firms—have little place in such an environment. Their very existence contributes to economically inefficient business decisions that may have far-reaching negative "backflow" effects on firms, leading to adverse impacts on the very workers whom antidumping rules are intended to protect. At the very least, these decisions about production and investment are made in an environment in which the dictates of comparative advantage are substantially distorted.

Similarly, the effects of both ADDs and CVDs on downstream industries result in increased costs to those industries that may outweigh the benefits to the protected industry.[22] Such situations can also lead to a rolling file of antidumping claims as adversely affected industries downstream seek protection from foreign competition.[23]

The problems of dumping and subsidization, however, are much more than economic issues. The political economy of trade policy processes provides a point of concentration for the lobbying efforts of firms and industries adversely affected by imports. Economic theory tells us that in most cases this temporary pain of individual industrial groups will result in either enhanced competitiveness or more efficient use of resources elsewhere. Nonetheless, the availability of ADD and CVD processes provides a politicized environment in which highly concentrated claims for assistance can be made within an existing institutional structure. The resulting interpretation of the ADD and CVD rules by national authorities tends to favor domestic producers and to result in economically indefensible results.[24]

It is worth considering where the nexus of these complaints might move if the systems were made substantially more restrictive or even eliminated. Two outcomes are possible, one of which is desirable and the other of which is quite dangerous. First, it is possible and perhaps likely that the complaints seeking protection of a small group of industries or firms would be lost in the broader context of antitrust-type actions and would result in much more economically justifiable cases of remedy. Alternatively, however, concepts such as cumulation and other politically malleable ideas might begin to creep into competition determinations, thus reducing the overall efficiency of those proceedings. Perhaps even more ominous, a lack of trade remedy structure could result in more direct pressure on national legislatures. This could result in even broader measures, with further detrimental economic effects on the national welfare. More sanguinely, one might forecast that such entreaties would be lost or at least misplaced in the larger range of issues before lawmakers. It is certainly

22. The best-known example of this phenomenon arose in the case of an ADD that the United States imposed against imports of flat-panel displays used in laptop computers. The resulting component price increases led to movement of some computer manufacturers offshore. An analogous situation arose in Canada regarding CVDs on imported corn, which devastated the domestic corn-milling industry.

23. For a full discussion of this effect, see Hoeckman and Leidy (1992, pp. 883–92).

24. See, for example, Clarida (1996, p. 357).

likely that the number of cases judged sufficiently significant and sufficiently politically salient to receive trade-restrictive remedies would decline.

In many countries—including, but not only, the United States—trade remedy laws are widely regarded as an important instrument of national sovereignty. Any derogation of the national right to impose and interpret these laws is guarded against, and talk of some form of bilateral or multilateral system is usually rejected out of hand in the United States. Although it is no doubt a nation's right to enact and enforce laws that reduce its national welfare, it is desirable at least that some reform of these laws be pursued to bring them more in line with economic efficiency and make them less susceptible to the influence of special interests. Some limited progress has been made at least with regard to methodology in the context of the dispute settlement panels under the North American Free Trade Agreement (NAFTA) and in the Uruguay Round agreements on antidumping rules and subsidies.

Some agreements, such as the recent Canada-Chile Free Trade Agreement and the Australia–New Zealand Closer Economic Relations Trade Agreement go much further toward economic rationality, however, and eliminate dumping and subsidy rules altogether, replacing them with competition policy concepts. The EU is most advanced in this process, having no internal dumping rules and a unionwide system administered by the Commission for member states' determining acceptable "state aid" practices. This system allows the Commission to roll back offending subsidies and fine governments for excessive use. Such multilateral approaches provide some guidance for possible future developments in the Western Hemisphere, but cannot currently be said to be politically realistic, at least not without considerable incrementalism. It would appear that for the foreseeable future ADDs and CVDs are likely to continue and become even more ferocious as trade remedy systems and cases proliferate. The question is how long can policymakers allow this activity, which runs completely counter to the objectives of market-opening agreements, to continue?

Arguments explaining the negative economic consequences of the trade remedies that are the subject of this chapter are not new. Yet they have not succeeded in ending or even much altering the practices. This suggests that what is required may be a new or additional justification for change. There are grounds for hope. It is submitted that just such an opportunity may be presented by the increasingly globalized nature of international business practices. As Marx suggested, the tide of history may indeed favor the withering of the state, at least in this area. As outlined earlier, not only is it in the economic interests of nations not to utilize these policies, it is coming to be less and less in the self-interest of many companies and workers whose prosperity and even survival depend on expanding international markets.

Over the next several decades, market growth for the firms of most developed countries will be dependent on rising levels of international sales. This is true not only because of population and age demographics in the developing world, but also because of slowly growing and aging populations at home. For developing countries improved access to prosperous markets in developed countries is key to propelling development efforts in the next century. Herein, then, lies the seed of a possible virtuous bargain: for developed countries, guarantees of market access to the rapidly expanding markets of developing countries, unimpeded by a proliferation of restrictive trade remedies; for developing countries, reduction or cessation of legal maneuvers that most often restrict the very products in which their comparative advantage is greatest.

From a corporate perspective, all of this should become remarkably attractive to an increasing percentage of corporations as global production and operations make national restrictions less and less optimal and profit maximizing. For the vast majority of workers, too, these effects should become markedly more clear and attractive as international operations account for larger shares of total investment and output. Of course all of this will not happen overnight, but the writing is perhaps on the wall. Responsible and farsighted public policy should anticipate these changes and begin moving as rapidly as possible in this direction.

Recommendations and Conclusions

It has been suggested in this chapter that changing international business environments and net national and global welfare argue strongly in favor of the elimination of antidumping and antisubsidy laws in their current form. Other policy instruments could provide suitable alternatives that would address the practices for which ADDs and CVDs are currently the preferred remedies. Although it is beyond the scope of this chapter to discuss these alternatives in detail, adjustment policies, safeguards, and antitrust laws provide progressive levels of improvement. Offering one-time financial and training assistance to workers directly affected by foreign imports is a strategy that provides some promise for the more efficient medium-term allocation of resources, without the economywide negatives of an ADD. Such a system would be politically responsive to economic adjustments based on foreign competition while also providing for economic redeployment of labor.

The increased use of safeguards—a somewhat risky alternative in that these procedures might also be open to manipulation—provides for the more judicious use of trade remedies. Safeguards are limited to use in situations in which severe and sudden inflows of foreign goods cause severe economic disruption in specific industries. They are also time limited to encourage long-term adjustment. Antitrust or competition policy is the best solution for achieving the objectives that both types of trade remedies seek to address. Since the primary concern with both dumping and subsidies is unfair foreign competition, an existing legal system that is specifically designed to deal with anticompetitive practices would seem the ideal means to resolve such problems. In any event, in an increasingly multinational and globalized business environment any rationale for separate systems for determining the competitive effects of foreign and domestic production is rapidly evaporating. Antitrust policy could adequately respond to any legitimate economic detriments caused by foreign practices in the national marketplace.

Bill Cosby performs a classic comedy routine in which he imagines the conversations between God and Noah during the construction of the ark. At one point as the project is progressing, Noah is overcome by the ridicule of his friends and neighbors, the complexity of constructing such a gigantic marine vessel, and, worst of all, the unimaginable difficulty of filling the vessel with a breeding pair of every species in creation. He simply quits and refuses to go on. After unsuccessfully attempting to explain to Noah the virtues of continuing and the benefits of saving humanity from the impending flood, God plays his trump card, sternly inquiring: "Noah, how long can you tread water?" Thus motivated, Noah resumes his labors with renewed vigor.

A similar question might be asked of today's trade policymakers. Although it seems clear that ADD and CVD trade remedy laws are anachronistic and reduce the net national welfare of any country imposing them, they not only continue to exist, but are assuming an even greater importance as a tool of contingent protectionism. Trade officials and elected officials in some countries continue to resist the compelling economic arguments in favor of eliminating them altogether. We are not far from a century of experience with the effects of these laws, effects which can be measured in decreased efficiency and lost opportunity. For most of this period it has at least been possible to argue that the negative effects of these laws were relatively small and constant. But this is a dodge that is rapidly becoming untenable. The increasing use of trade remedy laws by developing countries has opened a new and dangerous front for the rapid expansion of detrimental effects. The significant rise in their use by the United States during times of economic prosperity augurs poorly for the likely outcomes when economic contractions occur. Indeed, even in other developed countries the temptation to make greater use of these measures will increase due to both global economic fluctuations and the disappearance of more traditional forms of protectionism. The paucity of use of these remedies in Asia, for example, can be quite logically supposed to be nearing an end. The proliferation of ADD cases in Latin America is quite probably a harbinger of things to come. Treading water by preserving the status quo is a recipe for increased use of these remedies and for raising barriers to the flow of trade, a result manifestly contrary to both multilateral and regional trade agendas.

In order to do the right thing, Noah only needed to be given proper incentives. These incentives to do the right thing in terms of trade remedy policy are most likely to come from the broad menu of policy changes inherent in large-scale trade negotiations such as those related to the Free Trade Area of the Americas (FTAA) or the WTO. Trade policymakers are in a delicate position. Failure to begin to deal with the anomaly of ADD and CVD laws may well result in a litigation flood of major proportions. Although treading water might be the easiest and politically safest policy for the short term, it poses a substantial threat to open trading systems for the longer term. Accordingly, the negotiation of new trade arrangements in both the FTAA and the WTO provide crucial opportunities to deal with the serious problems in this area constructively.

There are other means for dealing with the very real short-term costs that adjustment to open markets requires. What is required at this juncture is a commitment by all parties involved in trade negotiations to seriously examine these possible improvements with a view to reducing and eventually eliminating the negative economic effects of the current ADD and CVD system. Short of such a commitment, negotiators are giving liberalization with one hand and taking it back with the other. Such self-defeating behavior condemns the trading system to a debilitating and unnecessary struggle to stay afloat in a rising sea of trade remedy complaints and market-access barriers. It is time to begin the difficult process of removing these barriers.

References

Cass, R. A., and R. Boltuck. 1996. "Antidumping and Countervailing Duty Law: The Mirage of Equitable International Competition." In *Fair Trade and Harmonization:*

Prerequisites for Free Trade? edited by J. N. Bhagwati and R. E. Hudec. Cambridge: MIT Press.

Clarida, R. H. 1996. "Dumping: In Theory, in Policy and in Practice." In *Fair Trade and Harmonization: Prerequisites for Free Trade?* edited by J. N. Bhagwati and R. E. Hudec. Cambridge: MIT Press.

Congressional Budget Office. 1998. *Antidumping Action in the United States and Around the World: An Analysis of International Data.* Washington D.C.

Deardorff, A. V. 1989. "Economic Perspectives on Dumping Law." In *Antidumping Law and Practice: A Comparative Study,* edited by J. H. Jackson and E. A. Vermulst. Ann Arbor: University of Michigan Press.

Diamond, R. 1989. "Economic Foundations of Countervailing Duty Law." *Virginia Journal of International Law* 29.

Hart, M. 1997. *Finding Middle Ground: Reforming the Antidumping Laws in North America.* Ottawa: Center for Trade Policy and Law.

Hoeckman, B., and M. Leidy. 1992. "Cascading Contingent Protection." *European Economic Review* 36.

Hufbauer, G. C., D. T. Beliner, and K. A. Elliot. 1986. *Trade Protection in the United States: Thirty-one Case Studies.* Washington, D.C.: Institute for International Economics.

Finger, J. M. 1997. "GATT Experience with Safeguards: Making Economic and Political Sense of the Possibilities That GATT Allows to Restrict Imports." Mimeo. Washington, D.C.: World Bank.

Jackson, J. H., and W. Davey. 1986. *Legal Problems of International Economic Relations,* 2d ed. St. Paul: West Publishing.

Lipstein, R. A. 1997. "Using Antitrust Principles to Reform Antidumping Law." In *Global Competition Policy,* edited by E. M. Graham and J. D. Richardson. Washington, D.C.: Institute for International Economics.

Schwartz, W. F., and E. W. Harper. 1972. "The Regulation of Subsidies Affecting International Trade." *Michigan Law Review* 70.

Sykes, A. O. 1989. "Countervailing Duty Law: An Economic Perspective." *Columbia Law Review* 89: 199.

U.S. International Trade Commission. 1995. *The Economic Effects of Antidumping and Countervailing Duty Orders and Suspension Agreements.* Washington, D.C.

Viner, J. 1923. *Dumping: A Problem in International Trade.* Chicago: University of Chicago Press.

CHAPTER FOURTEEN

Antidumping Policy as a System of Law

Gary N. Horlick and Steven A. Sugarman

Numerous articles, papers, and books have been written that offer rationales for the existence of antidumping laws.[1] They argue that imperfect trade conditions create dumping by foreigners, which harms domestic producers and consumers. At least in the United States, proponents work with their allies in Congress and the executive branch to preserve and expand laws that prevent such harms.[2] However, the product of their efforts, antidumping law, lacks a correlation to the rationales that serve as their justification. Thomas Howell, a leading proponent, states that "if certain defined trade-distorting practices that cause economic harm

---

1. Garten (1994), Labor/Industry Coalition for International Trade (LICIT) (1995), Howell (1998), and Mastel (1998). The last item is a "party line" U.S. Department of Commerce speech by the individual who was then undersecretary, who, aside from his stance on antidumping policy, was one of the best to occupy that position.

2. A public example of the imbalance of lobbying efforts in the United States between proponents and opponents can be seen in the response to a request for comments by the U.S. trade representative on the seemingly unrelated topic of the 1998 World Trade Organization (WTO) review of the Dispute Settlement Understanding, in *Federal Register* 63, no. 100 (May 26, 1998). Of the nineteen comments filed, twelve were by proponents of antidumping law (apparently concerned at the prospect that WTO panels would find the portions of U.S. antidumping law that they wrote inconsistent with the WTO rules) and none by opponents (the other seven focused on nondumping issues).

exist," antidumping laws are important, since they allow "the importing country [to] employ offsetting duties."[3]

Yet there are no WTO requirements or national antidumping laws to ensure that antidumping measures are applied only when "trade-distorting practices" are found to exist; further, no burdens are placed on petitioners or national authorities before raising WTO-bound tariffs on a non–most favored nation basis to show that the alleged dumping will produce a net economic harm to the domestic economy.[4] To the extent that antidumping laws impose sanctions absent a showing of trade barriers or unfair market conditions, they can be considered traditional protectionism rather than a proportional response to an identified problem.

This chapter reviews the underlying rationales offered as explanations of the phenomena of dumping and antidumping laws and explains the extent to which antidumping rules are tailored to achieve only those goals that justify their existence. Finally, it concludes with a modest proposal to change current antidumping laws in order to better link them to their rationales.

Dumping and Antidumping Rationales

Even proponents admit that antidumping laws are a system of second best. Greg Mastel states that if "evaluated from the perspective of perfectly competitive conditions, antidumping laws and all other government efforts to influence the market are difficult to justify because they necessarily alter the optimal market outcome."[5] The stated purpose of antidumping laws is to protect domestic producers and consumers from "mercantilistic commercial strategies pursued by foreign companies from behind their home governments' trade barriers."[6] Proponents assert that protected markets and other forms of trade

---

3. Howell (1998, p. 299).

4. The European Union (EU), for example, in its analysis of "Community interest," contradictorily finds that antidumping duties should be imposed because in the absence of antidumping duties EU consumers would suffer since EU suppliers would disappear, but that the antidumping duties will not harm consumers because they have many other non-Community sources that are not subject to the antidumping duties. See, for example, the EU's statement on the "consequences for users and consumers" of the antidumping duty on microdisks, *Official Journal* L 63/9, paras. 47–48.

5. Mastel (1998, p. 67).

6. LICIT (1995, p. 21).

barriers in foreign countries make antidumping laws necessary. For this reason it is interesting that no antidumping law of which the authors are aware requires the plaintiffs or the national authorities to prove that any substantial trade barriers or unfair practices exist before measures can be imposed to remedy conduct deemed to be dumping.

In *Keeping Trade Free and Fair: A Rational Defense,* LICIT states that "the *only* instances in which dumping can be pursued as a long-term strategy involve government activity (or inactivity) through one of the following channels: (1) government subsidies, (2) a protected home market, or (3) government toleration of cartels."[7] Yet neither the WTO nor antidumping laws require any showing of government support of any of these to impose a duty—often quite high—based on a claim alleging a long-term dumping strategy.[8] In order for a dumping claim to be substantiated and a measure imposed, none of the conditions that are rationales in support of antidumping laws need even be alleged to exist. Economically, domestic consumers are advantaged in the short term by dumping, and they are harmed only if foreign companies are able to win monopoly profits from them in the long term. Hence, only if those conditions are met can domestic consumers be harmed. It is inexplicable why there is not a requirement of, at a minimum, showing that at least one of these conditions exists. In this section each rationale that has been offered in support of antidumping laws is examined and its relevance to real-life antidumping law is reviewed.

Closed Home Markets

According to Greg Mastel, director of studies and vice president of the Economic Strategy Institute and a leading advocate of antidumping laws, "A closed or restricted home market is . . . a virtual precondition to a successful dumping strategy."[9] Other proponents have pointed to closed or noncompetitive foreign markets as a rationale for antidumping laws. These problem markets take two forms: sanctuary home markets and government-supported cartels.

7. LICIT (1995, p. 17). Emphasis added.
8. In 1993–95 the mean antidumping duty in the United States was 60.6 percent. See Congressional Budget Office (1998). The average U.S. tariff on manufactured goods was only 3 percent. See "Clinton Says World Should Start New Talks to Cut Trade Barriers," *The Investors' Business Daily* (May 19, 1998, p. A6).
9. Mastel (1998, p. 43).

A government may provide a sanctuary home market for its domestic producers. This type of market is a protectionist strategy that forbids the importation of a product into the country, thereby restricting market access to domestic producers. A sanctuary market could allow producers to earn monopoly profits domestically. Even if sanctuary markets are internally competitive, however, their domestic producers are afforded protection against foreign competitors. Therefore, if a company with a sanctuary home market chooses to dump products abroad, it need not fear reciprocation. Reciprocal dumping has been demonstrated to make an otherwise successful dumping campaign a losing strategy for foreign producers.[10] Therefore, eliminating the fear of reciprocal dumping could cause foreign producers to institute an otherwise unwise dumping campaign.

Foreign markets are also deemed restricted if domestic cartels, oligopolies, or monopolies are permitted to form and dominate the market. Foreign competitors theoretically would be permitted to export products into the market, but practically they could not compete with domestic producers because of the government's sponsorship or toleration of a cartel. Hence, domestic firms would be able to capture supercompetitive profits and use the profits to offset losses incurred by dumping products abroad.

Both forms of restricted or closed markets could exist in unison, providing domestic producers a competition-free home market. Proponents of antidumping laws point to closed home markets as a root cause of dumping. They claim that foreign companies that gain monopoly profits at home have the ability to subsidize predatory dumping abroad. Recognizing this as a threat to domestic producers in the short term and to consumers in the long term, they state that they fashion antidumping laws to prevent this practice.

Interestingly, neither the WTO's Agreement on Implementation of Article VI of the General Agreement on Tariffs and Trade (GATT) 1994 (WTO Antidumping Agreement or Antidumping Agreement) or any nation's antidumping laws require domestic industries to show that the foreign companies they accuse of dumping have closed or restricted home markets in any relevant sense. It is not

10. This is best exemplified by the Michelin-Goodyear case study by Mastel (1998, p. 43). Michelin allegedly began to dump tires in the United States, thereby decreasing Goodyear's market share. However, Goodyear simply began to dump in the EU to counter Michelin. Almost immediately Michelin stopped its dumping in the United States without the use or involvement of any antidumping laws.

necessary to even allege that a competitor has a home market.[11] The administrators of the EU's antidumping rules point out the following:

> If sales on the domestic market are not representative, for instance because they have only been made in small quantities, the normal value may be established on another basis, such as the prices of other sellers on the domestic market. Subsidies consist of a financial contribution from a Government, which confers a benefit to producers or exporters (e.g., grants, tax and duty exemptions, preferential loans at below commercial rates). In the majority of cases where dumping occurs on a more than incidental basis, a certain market segregation exists where that segregation may be due to government regulation, but also to other circumstances, including consumer preferences.[12]

This seems odd given Mastel's comments with regard to the Michelin-Goodyear case. Citing Goodyear's ability to effectively counter Michelin's dumping in the U.S. market by reciprocal dumping in Michelin's home market of Europe, he admits that "dumping strategies are difficult to pursue from an open market." Mastel further notes that "if markets are open, dumping often can be countered without resorting to an antidumping complaint."[13] In open markets antidumping laws interfere with and preclude the optimal result.

The WTO not only does not require any showing of a closed home market or any home market at all, but it permits a finding of dumping based on a product's price in a third country or its constructed value. These legal dispositions are inconsistent with the closed or restricted markets rationale. When the price of a product in a third market is used, there is no requirement to show that the third market is somehow protected for the alleged nonlocal dumper. Nor does it seem sensible to assume that an unaffiliated country would give one foreign company exclusive reign over its market without any evidence to support such an assumption. Given the potential differences in demand curves, export costs, and consumer preferences, absent proof that a third market (or even a home market, for that matter) is closed, price differentials between markets are of little to no probative value in a dumping inquiry. (Of course in

11. WTO (1994, Article 2.1). See also "Notice of Final Determination of Sales at Less Than Fair Value: Fresh Atlantic Salmon from Chile," *Federal Register* 63, no. 110 (June 9, 1998): 31411 for a finding that salmon from Chile is being sold or is likely to be sold in the United States at less than fair value, although there was no finding of a home market for the salmon.

12. Commission of the European Communities (1996, p. 2).

13. Mastel (1998, p. 43).

open or closed markets price differences between markets could arise as a result of market-driven forces unrelated to dumping.)

Imposing antidumping measures based on the use of a constructed value is also inconsistent with the requirement of a closed home market. Constructed values are used when there is no home market and there are no third-country sales. Under these circumstances dumping can occur only if it is cross-subsidized by another product.[14] However, no proof of cross-subsidization by another product is required in order to prove dumping under WTO rules, as we discuss a bit later.

Finally, the "sulfur amendment" added to U.S. laws in 1974 and then to the WTO Agreement in 1994 lends further credence to the finding that the restricted home market rationale for antidumping laws is not aligned with real-life antidumping laws. This amendment greatly expanded the concept of dumping to include a situation in which the price of a product sold in the exporting country is below its production "cost."[15] This exemption allows dumping to be found when it is shown that the price of an exported good is below "cost," even when the price of the exported good is above the price of the same good in the producer's home market. Because Article VI of the GATT does not permit the export price to be compared to constructed value except when there is no home market, the 1974 U.S. amendment defined *sales below cost* as being "not in the ordinary course of trade," and thus disregardable as home market sales under GATT Article VI and Article 2.4 of the 1967 GATT Antidumping Code. Once the prices in the home market are deemed below cost and therefore disregarded as not in the ordinary course of trade, a constructed value is compared to the exported product's price. This makes clear the lack of any requirement of a sanctuary home market (and the fact that the sulfur amendment eliminated the ability to use the absence of a sanctuary market as an affirmative defense) since a company can be sanctioned for dumping even when its products are priced lower in the home (or third-country) market than in the export market.

14. Dumping could also be found artificially by relying on private cross-subsidization by the same product from a different time period, and indeed both the United States and the EU do so, but it is unclear why this is "unfair." Yet it is certainly not uncommon in U.S. and EU business practices or business school teaching.

15. Further, Article 2.2.7 of WTO (1994) requires a definition of the profit to be imputed to cost that would constitute criminal securities fraud in the United States and many other countries.

It seems plausible to require that over some reasonable period of time a business recover all its costs for each separate product. Unfortunately, in practice this logic is flawed. For a business is able to project its revenues only over the course of time, and it cannot know until the end of the "reasonable period" whether it has made money on a product (as no business can predict recessions or changes in demand that will affect a product's profitability). But only foreign producers are punished with antidumping duties (or similar penalties) for retrospective failure to meet projections.

Further, the sulfur amendment has made real-life antidumping law even more distant from normal business practice, since the 1994 WTO Antidumping Agreement has been used by antidumping enthusiasts as a pretext to require that all costs be recovered within one year preceding the investigation rather than spread out over the product's life cycle or the business cycle.[16] This requirement appears to be contrary both to the intent of the legislature and to economic reasoning in general. The Senate committee that wrote the 1974 sulfur amendment offered as an example of a business that does not recover all its costs within a year or two a large commercial aircraft company. American businesses note that for some products it can take as long as thirty years to recover all costs. When large up-front fixed costs and small marginal costs are coupled with a sharp learning curve, this effect is especially noticeable. Further, start-up companies typically must make substantial investments in plants and equipment that can be recovered only over time. However, several national antidumping laws do not provide exemptions from the one-year requirement.[17]

16. The WTO Antidumping Agreement does not limit the reasonable period to one year. Compare Commission of the European Communities (1998) ("Account has to be taken of the fact that the Agreement states that the normal period for cost recovery for a product is 12 months") and U.S. House of Representatives (1994) ("Under current law, there is no clear definition of cost recovery—the measure of cost recovery could have been based on speculative estimates of future production costs. Under the amended law, if prices which are below cost at the time of sale are above weighted-average costs for the period of investigation or review (one year), such prices shall be considered to provide for recovery of costs within a reasonable period of time") with Koulen (1994, p. 205) ("Article 2.2.1 does not specifically define the 'reasonable period of time' for recovery of costs").

17. The WTO Antidumping Agreement expressly requires allowance for start-up costs. The EU has limited start-up by defining the period of start-up as irrebuttably less than one year, on the unsupported assertion that "a start-up phase can only constitute a

Nonetheless, Mastel attempts to defend the requirement by indicating that for the long term "all costs can be said to be variable."[18] However, all costs can be said to be variable only when a company can terminate all production without suffering any financial loss. Therefore, for a one-year time horizon to be considered the long term a company would need to have the ability to stop production at the beginning of any given year and not face losses from interest, rent, equipment, employment contracts, and so on. It is difficult to see how the proponents of antidumping laws can argue in any credible way that the one-year time horizon used by the EU and the United States constitutes the long term.

In sum, not only is showing a closed or restricted home market not required, but numerous provisions of the WTO Antidumping Agreement and national antidumping law indicate that this need not even be a consideration relevant to a finding of dumping.

Government Subsidies

A second rationale for antidumping laws is based on the existence of government subsidies. Proponents argue that "dumping and subsidization are . . . closely related. By lowering the cost of production or the cost of export sale, subsidies result in commercial behavior that can be characterized as dumping—selling below price in commercial home market or below production cost. . . . [Hence] government subsidies are a major underlying cause of dumping."[19] Since foreign companies must have the financial strength or resources to offset short-term losses in order to pursue dumping, dumping requires "the help of subsidies" or a closed home market.[20]

---

part of that period of cost recovery, and this is made clear in the proposed text" (Commission of the European Communities [1998, p. 3]), although the United States has irrebuttably presumed that start-up costs could never include marketing or other nonproduction costs, withstanding the plain language of Article 2.2.1.1 of the WTO Antidumping Agreement ("cost of production *and sale*") (emphasis added). See U.S. House of Representatives (1994, p. 837) ("However, sales expenses, such as advertising costs, or other non-production costs, will not be considered startup costs because they are not directly tied to the manufacturing of the product").

18. Mastel (1998, p. 107).
19. Mastel (1998, p. 51).
20. LICIT (1995, p. 17).

Again, this rationale may or may not lend support to antidumping laws, but antidumping laws in no way require that government subsidies be shown for dumping to be found. To the contrary, Article VI and the WTO Agreement do not even permit subsidies to be considered as dumping per se. Instead, Article VI and the WTO Agreement on Subsidies and Countervailing Measures separately provide for countervailing duties to offset subsidies and preclude "double counting." Therefore, although government subsidies are alleged to give foreign companies a trade advantage over domestic producers and thereby to harm consumers, this possibility is already offset by countervailing duties. Hence this rationale for antidumping laws is often just a red herring, but in any case antidumping laws do not require any showing of subsidies to support a dumping claim based on government subsidies.

Nonmarket Economies

According to this rationale, when the state owns or operates a business it may make non-market-based decisions. To the extent that decisions are made to sacrifice profits in order to attain some nonpecuniary benefit (for example, to maintain high levels of employment or increase foreign market share), they have much the same effect as a government's subsidizing a private company's implementation of a certain policy. Therefore, the effect on dumping would be identical to that in the discussion earlier. Again, there is no requirement (outside of cases aimed at current and former communist countries) to show either that a firm is government owned or controlled or even that its decisions are based on nonpecuniary factors in order to win a dumping case.[21] For that reason, the nonmarket economy rationale cannot support most dumping cases.

21. The "nonmarket economy" area is one area in which the WTO explicitly requires proof of the stated rationale. Application of the nonmarket economy methodology (that is, application of something other than an exporter's own prices and costs) is permitted only when "*all*" prices" (emphasis added) are controlled by the state. See "Ad Note" to GATT (1994), Article VI. Most WTO users of antidumping laws—certainly including Australia, Canada, the EU, Mexico, and the United States—flout this requirement either all the time or virtually all the time. Indeed, it is hard to identify any WTO member that meets the criterion, which the Ad Note requires to be proved. Instead, the EU and the United States have offered to provide the normal treatment (which is legally required already unless all prices are controlled) only to those nonmarket economy companies that can prove that all of their costs are unaffected by state action. Certainly many European countries would have a very difficult

Cross-Subsidization of Dumping

The cross-subsidization of a dumped product is yet another rationale offered to justify the need for antidumping laws to level the playing field for domestic producers. In theory, if a company earns super-competitive profits from one product, it can utilize its excess profit pool to subsidize the dumping of another product. This rationale is based on the same assumption as the government subsidies rationale. Proponents argue that regardless of the source of funds, all that is needed for dumping is access to capital to finance short-term losses. The profits from one product are used as a private system of subsidies to finance unfair trade practices. Therefore, it is argued, antidumping laws are necessary.

Just as they can be cross-subsidized by sales of other products, dumped goods can be subsidized by profits from the same product that have been accumulated over time. By aggregating "excess" profits gained during times of prosperity a company can subsidize dumping during a recession to keep plants and equipment operating. This practice is referred to as cross-subsidization over time. Once again, there is no need to allege any form of cross-subsidization in order to "prove" dumping. It would seem logical to require a dumping action based on a claim of subsidization to prove the existence of a system of

---

time meeting that standard with respect to, for example, energy, other utilities, and much transportation.

Even if the major users could successfully delete the inconvenient words from the agreement (as they are attempting to do with China and Russia in accession talks), it would still be illogical to apply antidumping laws to nonmarket economies. If by definition the prices and costs of a nonmarket economy producer are not reliable, antidumping law cannot logically be applied. Safeguards would be better. The opponents of such proposals claim that the use of safeguards would be a "license to dump" for nonmarket economies, but it is impossible to know if a nonmarket economy exporter is dumping or not if its prices and costs are not reliable, so it is impossible for a logical person to claim that the use of safeguards would be a license to dump. By the same token, advocates for nonmarket economies claim that safeguards deprive nonmarket economy exporters of their competitive advantages. However, if the prices and costs are unreliable—and especially if exchange rates are fixed—how can one know where the nonmarket economy has true comparative advantage? In the end, the application of antidumping laws in a nonmarket economy is an application not of "interface," but of raw power. Small nonmarket economies take what they can get, and big nonmarket economies use their power where they choose to resolve cases outside of the WTO antidumping rules (for instance, those involving cartels, whether legal or not, on aluminum and steel).

subsidization, whether public or private, in order to be successful (even assuming that such ubiquitous private cross-subsidization should be attacked). However, the WTO does not make any attempt to distinguish dumping from "fair" competitive reasons for differential (including domestic) pricing.

Exporting Unemployment

Proponents of antidumping laws argue that dumping can be used to export unemployment during a recession. Again, no country's antidumping laws require any showing of such an intent or effect, and EU and U.S. antidumping laws expressly protect their local industries from imports by finding dumping when an exporter fails to raise its prices as demand drops (and unit costs rise).[22] Therefore, in a global recession all countries could raise their barriers to imports through findings of dumping based on the failure of prices to increase as demand decreases—a recipe for disaster from the 1930s.

A more sophisticated variation of the "exporting unemployment" argument is that antidumping rules serve as an "interface" between structurally different economies. The argument is that if Country A has a higher ratio of debt to equity than Country B, in a recession exporters in Country A will have to continue or increase production (because they must continue to meet their interest payments). Meanwhile producers in Country B, with low interest expenses, will cut production and dividends. The result will be a flow of exports from Country A to Country B that antidumping rules could prevent.[23]

---

22. Compare this antidumping policy to the laws of supply and demand as stated in any basic economics textbook, such as Samuelson and Nordhaus (1985).

23. Although the objective of this chapter is to illustrate the disjunction between antidumping law and its rationales, it is worth noting the basic flaws in this "interface" theory of exporting unemployment. It is true that Company A will need to increase its production or risk going bankrupt due to its high leverage; however, it is equally true that it would be in the financial interest of Company B to increase its production until the marginal costs of production are greater than marginal revenue. Hence, although it could be more important to the future viability of Company A to increase production (whereas Company B could choose to simply cut production and dividends and wait until the recession ends), it is in both companies' best interest to increase production as long as marginal revenue remains above variable costs. Further, it is in the interest of neither to produce when marginal revenue falls below variable costs. Simply put, assuming that other things are equal, a company's ratio of debt to equity should not affect its optimal production during a recession (or at any other time, for that matter). Therefore, it appears

However, no antidumping laws require that there be any showing (much less legally sufficient proof) that an exporting company in Country A has a higher ratio of debt to equity than its allegedly injured competitor in Country B.[24] In practice, dumping can be found where an exporter in Country A actually has a lower ratio of debt to equity than its competitor in Country B.

The rationales concerning the export of unemployment are in effect dependent on recessionary conditions, or at least a worldwide decline in demand for a product. However, there is no requirement to allege or prove that such a decline in demand exists. A finding of dumping to export unemployment does not need to be substantiated by evidence that there is a recession, that the price of a competitor's exported product is cheaper than the price charged in its home market, or that prices are below cost as a normal business would define it. Instead, if local producers can show that their market share decreased and foreign exports were somehow a factor in causing such decrease (that is, if they can show "material injury"), antidumping sanctions can almost always be imposed (the United States finds dumping in 95 to 99 percent of all cases). This can be extremely easy in recessionary conditions, since a recession can cause both domestic and foreign producers to lose money in the short term, as falling demand causes unit costs to rise while depressing price.

National Defense

Proponents sometimes point to national defense as a rationale for antidumping laws. In the context of technologically advanced products and other "defense"-related industries, it is argued that if foreign competitors were able to drive domestic companies out of business they could cause serious harm to a country's long-term national defense capabilities. This argument is difficult to respond to in the abstract; however, it should be noted that again there is no requirement that a relationship between a specific product and national defense be shown in order for antidumping laws to be used to call for sanctions. Although there is little debate that when national defense is truly an issue domestic production of necessary items can be protected, antidumping laws are

---

that this theory has mistaken the different levels of importance Company A and Company B give to the need to increase production with differing optimal levels of production. See Samuelson and Nordhaus (1985).

24. To the extent that the issue is differing ratios of fixed to variable costs, those ratios are more likely to vary by industry than by country.

so far removed from national defense policy that it seems unlikely that a country would tie its security to them, especially in light of the fact that these laws make no special exceptions or accommodations for petitioners alleging that national security issues are involved.[25]

Overproduction and Opportunistic Dumping

The EU has articulated a rationale for antidumping laws based on the competitive advantages a foreign company can reap from strategic dumping (the EU does not explain why the same rationale does not apply to domestic firms). This rationale is encapsulated in table 14-1.[26] The table illustrates how a foreign company can use dumping to reduce overall losses and loss margins, maintain employment, gain market share, and reduce marginal costs. In the example a company is able to successfully increase its profit margin from −34 percent to 0 percent by overproducing its demand. This table is used as evidence of the unfair nature of dumping, thereby providing a rationale for antidumping laws.

It is important to understand the unstated assumptions made by the EU in creating this table. First, the benefits realized by the imaginary producer are due to dumping only if the prices in the export market are below their "fair" value. If a foreign company is making a profit, dumping is predicated on a finding that export prices are below domestic prices for a specific product. No stated rationale for resort to antidumping law supports a finding of dumping, however, solely because a company is able to charge higher prices (8.75 in our example) in the domestic market and lower prices (6.00) in export markets. However, current antidumping law often bases the success of a dumping complaint solely on the price of a product in the company's domestic market. For example, if the company represented in the table sold its product for 4.00 in the home market and 6.00 in an export market, it would not be dumping. If that company sold its product for 6.00 in the home market and 6.00 in an export market, it would not be dumping.[27] However, if the company sold its product

25. To the contrary, the only exemptions from U.S. antidumping duties are military items, which is directly contrary to the national defense rationale. See 19 U.S.C. 1677(20).

26. Adapted from an EU handout, "Synthesis (figures)," given at a seminar in Moscow in September 1997.

27. For simplicity's sake we assume that there are no tariffs or transportation costs.

Table 14-1. Synthesis (figures)

Parameter	Example	Dumping 1	Dumping 2	Dumping 3
Domestic market				
Quantity sold	800	800	800	800
Unit price	8.75	8.75	8.75	8.75
Turnover	7,000	7,000	7,000	7,000
Export market				
Quantity sold	0	200	200	800
Unit price	0	3	6	6
Turnover	0	600	1,200	4,800
Profitability				
Fixed costs	7,000	7,000	7,000	7,000
Variable costs	2,400	3,000	3,000	4,800
Profit/loss amount	–2,400	–2,400	–1,800	0
Profit margin	–34%	–32%	–22%	0%

Source: European DG I/C3, PL/CS.

for 8.00 in the home market and 6.00 in an export market, it would be dumping.[28]

This example illustrates that current antidumping laws that categorically define *dumping* as "export price below domestic price" are often not punishing firms for dumping at all. In the example dumping would be found if prices in the home market were more than 6.00; however, no dumping would be found if they were less than or equal to 6.00. Therefore, in the EU's example it is not the price in the export market for which a foreign firm is necessarily punished; a firm is punished because it is able to charge higher prices for any reason in the home (or a third-country) market. This situation by itself has no recognizable relationship to the situations of importing (EU or U.S.) consumers or producers.

In order for this scheme to work as portrayed by the EU, the company would need to actually have a sanctuary home market (as opposed to assuming one). If the home market were open to international competition, by definition 8.75 would be the competitive price per unit on that market. In that case there would be nothing to prevent the company from selling 800 units at 8.75 in the export market and 800 units at 6.00 in the domestic market. This would benefit domestic consumers at the expense of foreign consumers, with no harm done to

28. For this example we assume that the company is able to make an overall profit under each scenario, and therefore the "sulfur amendment" does not apply.

the company (and little basis in the rationales for antidumping laws for an antidumping complaint). This scenario would be unrealistic only if 8.75 were a supercompetitive price. That, in turn, could occur only if the home market were closed or restricted.[29] Therefore, in order for the EU's example to have the harmful effects alleged to be caused by dumping, it would have to be based on an unproven assumption that the company in the example enjoyed a closed home market.

If the company's home market was not restricted or closed to imports, producers in the export market could employ the same dumping strategy as their foreign competitor. This reciprocal dumping would cause the firm depicted in the table to lose market share in the domestic market and no longer be able to sell 800 units of its product for 8.75 each. Therefore, such a strategy would backfire and cause the company to suffer greater losses than it would have experienced if it had not entered into dumping. To protect against opportunistic dumping, antidumping laws need to require a petitioner to prove a closed or restricted home market. As discussed earlier, they do not.

In the example there could be a finding of dumping even if the company charged 8.75 per unit for its goods in the export market. This is because antidumping laws calculate costs to include fixed expenditures during the past year. In this example the price would be 7,000 in fixed costs plus 3,000 in variable costs for each unit produced. If the company produced 1,000 units (as in examples 1 and 2) and charged 8.75 for all units (800 sold in the domestic market and 200 in the foreign market), it would not break even for the year. Therefore, a competitor from the export market could allege that, under the "sulfur amendment" described earlier, the price was less than the "cost." Actually the company could charge up to 15.00 per unit for 200 units in the export market (while maintaining the 8.75 per-unit price in the import market) and still not break even.[30] Therefore, dumping could be found even if prices in the export market were substantially above those in the "domestic

29. Or the product enjoys some degree of market power at home for reasons unrelated to the anticompetitive practices claimed as the rationale for antidumping.

30. The situation is even worse if one considers the requirement that export costs and tariffs be added to the price in the export market in order to avoid a finding of dumping. Garten (1994, p. 148) concedes that a finding of dumping based on an importing country's tariff is unjustifiable, but that dumping findings based on freight from a foreign producer to the customer are justifiable—even if the domestic competitor's freight cost to the customer is higher, which can easily occur (for example, if the product were shipped from Windsor, Ontario, north one mile to Detroit as opposed to a domestic competitor's shipping from Mackinac, Michigan, several hundred miles farther north of Detroit).

market."[31] All that would be required for the requisite showing of harm would be for the price in the export market to be slightly below that of an inefficient, uncompetitive producer whose domestic production was in the export market.

It should be mentioned that the EU table does not depict a case of predatory pricing (assuming that the EU industry is as efficient as the foreign one). In order to drive competition from a particular industry, as is the objective of predatory pricing, a foreign company must sell its products at prices below variable costs. Otherwise, it would be in its competitors' best interest to continue production. When sales are above variable cost but below total cost, as in the export market of the EU example, it is more profitable for the local industry to continue producing at "losses" than to discontinue production altogether and lose all sunk costs. Since there is no evidence that the objective of the company depicted in the table is predatory in nature, there is little evidence that there would be any net economic harm to the export market in the long term. Antidumping laws do not currently require a petitioner or authorities to provide any explanation as to how the alleged dumping harms the economy or consumers in general. They must show only that the local industry (in many U.S. cases, often just one or two companies) is harmed in some way. This is even true if domestic companies that use the imported product as inputs and domestic consumers who purchase the product are benefited in a more substantial way.

The EU table purports to be a numeric depiction of how opportunistic dumping could benefit foreign corporations. However, such opportunities are available only under specific conditions and assumptions.[32] Mastel articulates the importance of maintaining the proper perspective (which is counter to that of the table) by quoting William Culbertson: "The intent of foreign competitors is of secondary importance so far as national policy is concerned. The result is the thing that is to be prevented."[33] The LICIT seconds this idea, saying, "Merely because a practice might be rational for a business to undertake under

31. As long as the industry in the export market could show harm.

32. For the sake of argument, we accept the EU's definition of dumping in this case. But note that the price charged for exports may be above the product's variable cost. Some would argue that this would be dumping only if the price was below variable cost because any price over variable cost allows a company to be more profitable having made the sale than if it had not produced the unit at all.

33. Mastel (1998, p. 19).

some circumstances . . . does not mean a government should not act to counter the practice if it harms the larger national interest."[34]

In sum, assuming that the EU table accurately depicts a real-life firm, antidumping laws should not be used to sanction that firm unless harm to the domestic economy is also proven. Further, if the existence of at least one rationale was required in order to prove dumping, not only would there be protection against the EU's concern depicted in the table, but sanctions would be imposed only against firms engaging in practices that could arguably have a harmful effect on a country as a whole.

Discussion and Proposal of a New Antidumping Policy

The gap between antidumping laws and their rationales portends increasing problems for the future of international trade. If open competition between companies based in different countries is the optimal system of trade, anti-dumping laws must be tailored directly to their purposes such that they do not become so broad as to deter acts of beneficial competition. Current laws fail to achieve this objective. Garten states that dumping is often found when no "closed home markets, anti-competitive practices or predatory intentions" are found.[35] He further notes that "neither U.S. law nor our international obliga-tions require a finding of any particular market conditions—like anti-competi-tive practices—in order to impose a dumping duty."[36] Only by limiting the application of antidumping laws to dumping that has been shown to be caused by one of the stated rationales for using antidumping laws—and that has the potential to cause a net economic harm to domestic markets—can it be ensured that such laws will not be used to inhibit fair trade.

Proponents have articulated numerous rationales detailing the need for anti-dumping laws, and without dismissing the strong and passionate positions on each side of the debate over antidumping laws, all should agree with the basic premise that antidumping laws should not exceed the scope of their ratio-nales.[37] Without exposing domestic producers or consumers to the risks and dangers proponents allege can result from foreign dumping, the current system

34. LICIT (1995, p. 6).
35. Garten (1994, pp. 138–39).
36. Garten (1994, p. 139).
37. If more rationales are agreed to in the future, they could be added to this list.

of antidumping laws could be replaced with one correlated to the rationales justifying its existence. This would ensure that antidumping laws are not abused.

Currently antidumping laws are susceptible to protectionist misuse. They require a petitioner to show only that dumping occurred (within the statute's expansive—and expanding—definition of dumping) and that harm resulted for the petitioners. Although the WTO requires a causal link between these two factors, national authorities frequently rely on mere coincidence of the two factors. An inefficient company that is unable to compete in a free market can easily prove that it has been harmed by a foreign competitor's prices. Therefore, dumping should be appropriately defined such that no firms whose lower prices reflect only their competitive advantages are found to be dumping. Howell has stated: "From a policy perspective, the shape of a country's economy should be determined by the competitiveness of its industries, not maneuvering of anti-competitive business groups," and antidumping laws should seek to protect only this interest.[38] The rationales discussed earlier outline those conditions proponents have deemed necessary for a successful strategy of dumping to be undertaken. If antidumping laws can be invoked only upon showing that sufficient conditions exist for rational dumping, they may fulfill their stated purpose. Hence, we would like to propose a requirement that antidumping laws mandate such a showing.

In order to achieve consensus, our recommendation accepts the proponents' rationales for antidumping laws at face value and does not question their economic basis. With that in mind, we propose to amend current antidumping rules to require each petitioner who claims to have been harmed by dumping to (1) assert a rationale upon which to base the dumping claim that is sufficient to justify such a claim and (2) prove, or depend on the authorities to prove, the existence of such a rationale.[39] For example, if a petitioner alleged that a foreign competitor was receiving government funds to finance its dumping,

---

38. Howell (1998, p. 305).

39. Garten (1994, p. 138) asserts that antidumping laws should be designed to preserve the "natural competitive advantage" of a domestic company, and not to give it an advantage. Therefore, a company that would not be competitive in a system of perfect competition should not be allowed to use antidumping laws to become competitive. Such a company would not be allowed to file an antidumping petition unless it first showed that it was competitive with the foreign company alleged to be dumping and the authorities so proved.

this proposal would require the petitioner to prove its competitor is indeed receiving government funds and that they resulted in lower export prices than home market prices. If a petitioner alleged cross-subsidization from a closed home market, the case would require proof that those conditions that comprise a closed home market in theory in fact exist and that they result in the alleged amount of cross-subsidization.[40]

Garten uses three industry-specific examples—bearings, semiconductors, and steel—to illustrate what he depicts as the need for antidumping laws.[41] Our proposal would not compromise any of the examples he puts forward defending the use of antidumping sanctions to protect the domestic producers in these industries.

The Proposal Applied to Bearings

The U.S. antidumping investigations of antifriction bearings from numerous European and Asian countries are given as examples of antidumping complaints based on closed or sanctuary home markets. Accepting Garten's factual account of the complaints, closed home markets allowed foreign producers to earn protected monopoly profits at home and use such profits to dump excess production in U.S. markets. These claims by Garten may indeed be supported by factual evidence; however, neither the U.S. bearing manufacturers nor the authorities were required to either allege that closed markets existed or prove that the competitors were earning monopoly profits at home.

Under our proposal, antidumping procedures would be safeguarded against abuses. The U.S. bearing manufacturers would have been required to prove that its competitors benefited by sanctuary home markets where they reaped monopoly profits. Such proof would not have been difficult according to Garten's recounting of the investigations. Further, it would have been necessary to show

40. Under current antidumping rules a Monegasque company could sell one casino chip for U.S.$10.00 in Monte Carlo and each of twenty identical chips for U.S.$9.00 in the United States, thus earning an "unfair" profit of $1.00 that could be used to cross-subsidize the sales in the United States. The United States would then charge a total duty of U.S.$20.00 (20 × U.S.$1.00) to offset the total "cross-subsidization" of U.S.$1.00.

41. For a discussion of the role antidumping law played in "saving" these three industries, see Garten (1994, pp. 141–43). If the allegations were not provable, this could illustrate how enforcement of antidumping laws without having to prove the underlying rationale creates "client" pressure groups that will strongly support a continuation and extension of the existing system.

that such excess profits were being used to subsidize losses resulting from dumping. Again, Garten alleges as fact that their insulation from foreign competition in their home markets allowed foreign competitors to "afford to dump their excess production at low prices in the United States rather than disrupt the artificially high prices in their own markets."[42] Therefore, the bearing industry, after proving those allegations, would have remained protected under our proposal.

The Proposal Applied to Semiconductors

Garten alleges that "the experience of the U.S. semiconductor industry in the 1980s shows the pernicious effects of anti-competitive practices which can allow selling below the manufacturer's cost of production. A combination of a protected home market, a cartelized home market, substantial financial resources, and aggressive dumping, including selling below the cost of production, allowed Japanese companies to nearly decimate the U.S. semiconductor industry."[43] The first part of our proposed procedure (assert a rationale sufficient to justify an antidumping claim) should not have been difficult for the U.S. semiconductor industry to fulfill. The second part (prove facts sufficient to support such an assertion) would require only legally sufficient proof to support Garten's allegations. Either the petitioning company or the national authorities would need to prove that there actually was a "protected home market, a cartelized home market, substantial financial resources, and aggressive dumping." Once proven, the requirements of our proposal would be met, and the semiconductor industry would be protected. Our proposal would reject the petition only if the facts asserted by Garten were not proven facts, but unproven conjecture.

The Proposal Applied to Steel

Finally, Garten asserts that the steel industry provides a classic example of "sustained government intervention that led to excess production and dumping." He claims that European steel manufacturers have benefited from "substantial subsidies and other structural support from their government" that caused them to dump their overproduction in the United States.[44] Under our

42. Garten (1994, p. 141).
43. Garten (1994, p. 141).
44. Garten (1994, p. 143).

proposal U.S. steel manufacturers would first need to assert a rationale that would justify an antidumping claim. To do this they would need to assert that government subsidies in Europe not subject to countervailing duties and other specifically identified types of "structural support" have made it in the best interest of each of the separate European steel manufacturers to overproduce their demand and that these incentives have resulted in their dumping of excess production into U.S. markets. It would be necessary to prove such allegations, again, for each individual specified European producer (including some that received fewer subsidies than their U.S. counterparts). Assuming that Garten's discussion of the steel industry has a strong factual basis, such proof hardly would seem difficult.

Current antidumping laws, however, do not require even this minimum showing of proof. Therefore, a petitioner would need to show only that the prices of European steel companies in U.S. markets were below either the prices in European markets or the "cost" as defined in antidumping laws and below the price of U.S. steel in U.S. markets. This does not sufficiently protect U.S. consumers from findings of dumping unconnected to the rationales for antidumping law.

Antidumping rules have been incorporated into the WTO system. Therefore, all U.S. companies that export to other countries would be subjected to the same forms of treatment the United States is able to level against its importers. LICIT's paper argues that open, transparent adjudication of dumping complaints protects the interests of U.S. producers abroad.[45] However, even the most transparent and perfectly administered implementation of bad law can produce bad results.

As an example of how our proposal would eliminate some of the duties resulting from antidumping hearings, we look at the case of "Sweaters Wholly or in Chief Weight of Man-Made Fibers from Hong Kong."[46] Antidumping cases against companies based in Hong Kong provide a unique glimpse of the flaws in current law. Hong Kong is unique in its practice of free trade. It has no tariffs, no government subsidies to industry, and a general customs duty of only one-twentieth of 1 percent in most instances. Yet even a company in this haven of free trade is not safe from antidumping law. As demonstrated by the "Man-Made Sweaters" case and the twenty-seven others filed against companies

45. LICIT (1995, pp. 23–24).

46. See "Sweaters Wholly or in Chief Weight of Man-Made Fibers from Hong Kong," *Federal Register* 59, no. 35750 (July 13, 1994).

based in Hong Kong, antidumping law does not require proof of a closed or restricted home market or government subsidies. Further, in this case there was no showing of cross-subsidization of goods and, in the context of sweater making, national defense was presumably not an issue. However, even with the absence of each of these factors, authorities in the United States actually found that dumping existed and that such dumping had caused harm to domestic producers.[47] This result is not supported by any of the rationales for antidumping laws offered by proponents.

Our proposal would eliminate this undesirable result, since a rationale does not exist that can be substantiated and that would justify the imposition of duties in this case. Although the petitioner, National Knitwear and Sportswear Association, could have satisfied the first part of our proposal by showing a rationale other than a desire for protection to support its complaint, given Hong Kong's open markets and laissez-faire government policies it would be extremely difficult to substantiate such allegations.

Conclusion

The use of antidumping laws is likely to substantially increase in the future as nonmarket economies transition to capitalism.[48] Therefore, it is important to ensure that antidumping laws indeed promote the development of these nonmarket economies. In 1994 the Clinton administration proposed to change the application of antidumping laws to nonmarket economies currently transitioning to market-based economies. This implies that the current laws are providing disincentives for such countries and are not adequately promoting an international system of free and fair trade. Further evidence that implies that current antidumping law is being misused as a protectionist weapon comes from empirical research into the use of antidumping laws abroad. Currently companies from the United States and the EU, two self-declared open markets that according to their own statements do not enjoy sanctuary markets or lax antitrust policies, are among the most frequent subjects of antidumping cases. Further, Hong Kong's choice to open its markets to all trade has not prevented twenty-eight antidumping

47. See *Federal Register* 54, no. 47585 (November 15, 1989) and *Federal Register* 55, no. 20733 (July 27, 1990).
48. LICIT (1995, p. 20).

actions against its domestic firms. Finally, as barriers have disappeared under the North American Free Trade Agreement (NAFTA), antidumping actions between Canada, Mexico, and the United States should have become a thing of the past, yet such actions still exist. These facts indicate that current law is not serving the stated purposes of its designers and is unfairly restricting trade in free trade areas.

Our proposal seeks to reverse this trend. By requiring petitioners to allege with particularity a rationale justifying the need for antidumping sanctions in a particular situation, foreign firms will be protected from arbitrary duties. By requiring legally sufficient proof of such allegations, only the guilty will be punished. Our modest proposal will allow antidumping laws to maintain all the benefits proclaimed by their proponents while minimizing the possibility that they can be misused by domestic producers intent on constructing barriers to trade. At the same time the debate can continue regarding the fundamental desirability of antidumping laws themselves.

References

Commission of the European Communities. 1996. "Fifteenth Annual Report from the Commission to the Parliament on the Commission's Anti-dumping and Anti-subsidy Activities."

———. 1998. "Uruguay Round Implementing Legislation."

Congressional Budget Office. 1998. "Antidumping Action in the United States and Around the World: An Analysis of International Data." Congressional Budget Office Papers (June).

Garten, J. E. 1994. "New Challenges in the World Economy: The Antidumping Law and U.S. Trade Policy." Remarks made before the U.S. Chamber of Commerce. Washington, D.C. (April 7).

General Agreement on Tariffs and Trade. 1994.

Howell, T. R. 1998. "The Trade Remedies: A U.S. Perspective." In *Trade Strategies for a New Era: Ensuring U.S. Leadership in a Global Economy*. New York: Council on Foreign Relations.

Koulen, M. 1994. *The New Antidumping Code Through Its Negotiating History*. Bruges, Belgium: College of Europe.

Labor/Industry Coalition for International Trade. 1995. *Keeping Trade Free and Fair: A Rational Defense*. Washington, D.C. (June).

Mastel, G. 1998. *Antidumping Laws and the U.S. Economy.* Washington, D.C.: Economic Strategy Institute.

Samuelson, P. A., and W. D. Nordhaus. 1985. *Economics,* 12th ed. New York: McGraw-Hill.

U.S. House of Representatives. 1994. "Uruguay Round Agreement, Texts of Agreements, Implementing Bills, Statement of Administrative Action, and Required Supporting Statements, September 27, 1994."

World Trade Organization. 1994. "Agreement on the Application of Article VI of the General Agreement on Tariffs and Trade 1994" (Antidumping Agreement).

CHAPTER FIFTEEN

The GATT/WTO Dispute Settlement System and the Negotiations for a Free Trade Area of the Americas

Rosine M. Plank-Brumback

Not so long ago international trade negotiators would approach dispute settlement as more of an administrative than a substantive matter. Dispute settlement issues were regarded as less crucial than the trade commitments themselves and more innocuous than the objectives expressed in an agreement's preamble. Today it is recognized that an effective dispute settlement mechanism is an important guarantor that commitments undertaken in a trade agreement are fulfilled and that the benefits that parties expect to derive from these commitments are realized. Negotiations on dispute settlement are integral to the entire negotiating process and goals.

This chapter seeks to describe the general functioning of the dispute settlement system established under the General Agreement on Tariffs and Trade (GATT) and the World Trade Organization (WTO), including its current difficulties, and to draw possible lessons for the negotiators of the Free Trade Area of the Americas (FTAA) as they consider how to resolve disputes that will eventually arise under the FTAA agreement.[1] Dispute settlement as a concept

---

1. The basic rules and procedures governing the WTO dispute settlement system are set forth in the "Understanding on Rules and Procedures Governing the Settlement of Disputes" (hereinafter "DSU"), Annex 2 to the "Marrakesh Agreement Establishing the World Trade Organization" ("WTO Agreement"), signed April 15, 1994.

signifies not only a formal means to work out future differences in interpretation of and compliance with the agreement, including rulings, recommendations, and, if necessary and appropriate, concerted retaliation, but a whole framework of clear rules, transparency, common goals, and cooperation among signatories.

An examination of the GATT/WTO dispute settlement system is relevant to the FTAA for several reasons. First, it is the most comprehensive and micromanaged system for dealing with interstate trade disputes. It also has the longest track record. Although the WTO dispute settlement system is new, many of its aspects were derived from over four decades of experimentation, development, and codification under its GATT predecessor.[2]

Second, as virtually all governments participating in the FTAA negotiations are WTO members, attention must be paid to how to handle differences arising among the various subregional, regional, and multilateral instruments governing trade in and with the Western Hemisphere in the event of conflict. An examination of WTO cases reveals some of the issues or measures about which members—or important domestic interests on whose behalf governments pursue these cases—are concerned. If they fail to achieve satisfaction through this route, the issues may be raised in future negotiations, be they bilateral, subregional, regional, or multilateral. In other words, hot issues under the WTO are hot issues in the FTAA negotiations.

The Development of the WTO Dispute Settlement System

The GATT/WTO dispute settlement system developed from two provisions of the GATT that the original twenty-three contracting parties signed in 1947 to protect the value of the tariff concessions exchanged. The provisions mention

2. The principal decisions and agreements governing GATT dispute settlement include those in the "Procedures under Article XXIII," adopted on April 5, 1966 (hereinafter "1966 Procedures"), *Basic Instruments and Selected Documents* (*BISD*) 14S/18 (1966); the "Understanding Regarding Notification, Consultation, Dispute Settlement and Surveillance," adopted on November 28, 1979 (hereinafter "1979 Understanding"), *BISD* 26S/210 (1980); the "Dispute Settlement Procedures" in the "Ministerial Declaration," adopted on November 29, 1982 (hereinafter "1982 Ministerial Declaration"), *BISD* 29S/13 (1983); the "Dispute Settlement Procedures," adopted on November 30, 1984 (hereinafter "1984 Procedures"), *BISD* 31S/9 (1985); and the "Improvements to the GATT Dispute Settlement Rules and Procedures" in the "Midterm Agreement," decided on April 12, 1989 (hereinafter "1989 Midterm Agreement"), *BISD* 36S/61 (1990).

neither dispute settlement nor the ad hoc independent tribunal or panel that some herald as the GATT's finest achievement. Instead Article XXII of GATT 1947 speaks of consultations and Article XXIII speaks of nullification or impairment of a benefit. Both articles provide a bilateral track for the parties to consult directly to try to resolve a matter. If no satisfactory solution is found bilaterally, the articles provide a multilateral track for referring the matter to the collective body to consult, give rulings, or make recommendations, as appropriate. Article XXII broadly states that "any matter affecting the operation of [the General] Agreement" can be the object of consultations. As was more formally and concretely stated under Article XXIII, a complaining party has to allege nullification or impairment of a benefit accruing to it under the agreement or that the attainment of any objective of the agreement is being impeded as the result of any of three specified situations: infringement by another contracting party of an obligation under the GATT (a so-called violation case); application by another of a measure, whether or not it conflicts with the GATT (a so-called nonviolation case); or any other situation.[3]

In order to assist the contracting parties in carrying out their investigative and other responsibilities under paragraph 2 of Article XXIII, including the possibility of authorizing retaliation, a variation of the normal working party was introduced in 1952, called a panel on complaints, which was "composed of representatives of countries not directly affected by the charges to be examined." The panel was set up to prepare findings and recommendations for a decision by the contracting parties on a specific dispute on the basis of an objective assessment of the information and arguments submitted by the parties. The GATT panel process evolved through use and greater systematization of its practices. Additional procedures were adopted in 1966 under Article XXIII with the aim of promptly solving complaints raised by a developing contracting party against a developed contracting party.

3. Nullification or impairment has never been defined strictly speaking under the GATT other than by practice and case law holding that a measure applied inconsistently with the GATT "would, *prima facie,* constitute a case of nullification or impairment, and would *ipso facto* require consideration of whether the circumstances [were] serious enough to justify the authorization of suspension of concession or obligations." See "Uruguayan Recourse to Article XXIII" (adopted on November 16, 1962), *BISD* 11S/95, 100 (1963). With respect to a nonviolation case, the panel did not preclude that a prima facie case of nullification or impairment could arise even if there were no GATT infringement, but the burden of proof would lie on the invoking party. Ibid. See also "1979 Understanding," above note 2, Annex, para. 5, and "DSU," above note 1, Art. 3.8.

The first major codification of GATT dispute resolution and panel practices occurred at the conclusion of the Tokyo Round. The 1979 Understanding affirmed, among other things, that the aim of the GATT dispute settlement system "has always been to secure a positive solution to a dispute. A solution mutually acceptable to the parties to a dispute is clearly to be preferred."[4] Also concluded pursuant to the Tokyo Round were a series of multilateral trade negotiation (MTN) agreements including their own provisions for settling disputes among signatories arising from commitments under these instruments. These provisions followed traditional procedures under Articles XXII and XXIII, but were neither uniform nor consistent vis-à-vis those procedures.

The GATT members agreed to additional improvements to the dispute settlement system in 1982, 1984, and 1989.[5] The 1989 Midterm Agreement imposed time deadlines and default procedures on some of the stages of the dispute settlement process so as to minimize the possibility of procedural deadlock. Most significant, the 1989 decision introduced a right to a panel upon request by a complaining party, provided certain procedural requirements were fulfilled (for example, having made a prior request for consultation, filing a written complaint, and including the panel request as an item on the regular agenda of the GATT Council for two meetings). Unlike prior GATT practice whereby a panel was not established unless there was consensus in the council, under the negative or reverse consensus rule adopted in 1989 a panel would be established unless there were consensus not to establish a panel.

Articles XXII and XXIII remain at the heart of the WTO dispute settlement system. The main instrument in the WTO Agreement governing dispute settlement, the Dispute Settlement Understanding (DSU), applies to disputes concerning and brought under the WTO Agreement itself, the Multilateral Agreements on Trade in Goods (including the 1994 GATT), the General Agreement on Trade in Services (GATS), the Agreement on Trade-Related Aspects of Intellectual Property Rights (TRIPS), the DSU itself, and the Plurilateral Trade Agreements (PTAs). The DSU enshrines past GATT practices and also incorporates verbatim many of the dispute settlement rules or formal statements of practice previously adopted by the contracting parties. The DSU, however, has gone much further than the GATT toward dispute settlement.

The major innovations brought about by the DSU are to:

4. "1979 Understanding," above note 2, 216, para. 4.
5. "1982 Ministerial Declaration," "1984 Procedures," and "1989 Midterm Agreement," above note 2.

—Create an integrated dispute settlement system among the covered agreements.

—Establish a standing Dispute Settlement Body (DSB).

—Introduce an appellate process.

—Extend the negative or reverse consensus rule to the adoption of panel and Appellate Body (AB) reports and to the authorization of retaliatory measures.

—Provide for cross-retaliation across goods, services, and intellectual property obligations.

—Provide for arbitration specifically to determine a reasonable period of time for compliance with rulings or the proper level of retaliation.

—Commit members explicitly to redressing violations or nullification or impairment of benefits exclusively within the confines of the DSU—that is, not to allow unilateral determinations.

How a Dispute Is Handled in the WTO

What would be a typical WTO case? Some point to the complaint by Venezuela and Brazil regarding U.S. regulatory standards, which discriminated against imported gasoline. This was the second dispute ever brought to the WTO and the first to go through the entire panel, appellate review, and monitoring and compliance process as provided in the DSU. Some interest groups would also consider this case as a model that confirmed their view of the WTO's approach to concerns about national sovereignty and environmental conservation.

A more "typical" case would be the first dispute ever brought to the WTO, a dispute involving Malaysia and Singapore, which resulted in the parties' achieving a mutually satisfactory solution. Perhaps more common, but less ascertainable, are the cases in which national officials, contemplating the threat of WTO legal action and possible international opprobrium, eschew taking measures likely to be ruled contrary to their obligations.

A dispute, typical or not, begins with written notification by a WTO member government to the DSB and any other relevant WTO organ with competence on the issue requesting bilateral consultations with another member pursuant to Article XXII or XXIII of GATT 1994, the GATS, or some other corresponding provision of a covered agreement.[6] This request will be based on an action on

6. The DSB is the central authority for administering the rules and procedures, consultation, and dispute settlement provisions of all covered agreements. See "DSU," above note 1, Art. 1.1. The DSB—basically the WTO General Council meeting in

the part of the member subject to the complaint that the complaining member considers impairs a benefit accruing to it under a covered agreement. Members are committed to seeking redress for any violation or for nullification or impairment of such benefits only through recourse to the DSU and to abiding by its rules and procedures.

Who Can Request Dispute Settlement

Only WTO member governments have rights and obligations under the covered agreements, and accordingly only governments, not private parties, have standing to request formal consultation and dispute settlement. Similarly, representations and complaints are directed against member governments regarding measures they have taken. Private parties may be affected by governmental measures, but it is their governments that must advance their interests. Member federal governments are responsible (to the extent of taking all measures available to them) for measures taken by subfederal levels of government that nullify or impair benefits accruing to another member state.

A member does not necessarily have to demonstrate a legal or trade interest in a matter in order to have a right to raise a complaint. All members have a vested interest in the maintenance of competitive opportunities through the fulfillment of all obligations and in the overall balance of rights and obligations. There may be several complainants on a particular matter, which eventually may be dealt with by a single panel without prejudicing the rights all the parties would enjoy. A third-party member with a substantial trade interest in having bilateral consultations held under Article XXII:1 may ask to join the consultations or is free to request consultations on its own. Members self-elect whether to be a party bringing a complaint or an interested third party to the

---

dispute settlement mode with its own chairperson—is open to all WTO members. It establishes panels, adopts panel and AB reports, monitors implementation of rulings and recommendations, and authorizes retaliation. See "DSU," Art. 2.1. The DSB meets regularly and sometimes in special session as needed to carry out its functions. See "DSU," Art. 2.3. It decides matters by consensus, which is deemed to occur when no member present at the DSB meeting formally objects to the proposed decision. See "DSU," Art. 2.4 and note 1. The DSU does not prejudice members' rights to seek authoritative interpretation of covered agreements through decisionmaking under the WTO Agreement or a PTA. See "DSU," Art. 3.9.

dispute.[7] Interested parties have a right to be heard by a panel if they so reserve their third-party rights within the specified deadline, but they do not enjoy the same procedural rights as disputants.

A governmental measure that allegedly nullifies or impairs a benefit accruing directly or indirectly under a covered agreement is justiciable. This includes a measure that infringes an obligation under a covered agreement or one that is not necessarily illegal but erodes the anticipated value of a concession. It may include a measure not yet implemented, but legislated and mandatory for the executive to uphold; a measure no longer in effect; or in some circumstances a measure previously adjudicated. There is no consensus as to whether there may be an inquiry or ruling on the validity of invoking national security exceptions. Measures taken by regional or local authorities are justiciable, as is the issue of whether a federal government has taken all reasonable measures available to it to ensure observance by regional or local authorities.

To access the dispute settlement process, the complaining member first must try to resolve the dispute bilaterally. The request for consultations addressed to the DSB must be in writing and state the reasons, identify the measures at issue, and indicate the legal basis for the complaint. The member to which the request for consultations is addressed has ten days to reply and "thirty days to enter into consultations in good faith . . . with a view to reaching a mutually satisfactory solution." These time periods may be altered by mutual agreement. Consultations are confidential. Within ten days of a request for consultations under Article XXII:1, any other member that considers it has a substantial interest in the matter may notify the parties and the DSB that it wishes to join the consultations. This will happen only if the member to which the request for consultations was addressed agrees that the former's claim of substantial interest is well founded. Otherwise the member can request consultations of its own. Additionally, the good offices of the Director General, acting in ex officio capacity, are available to try to resolve the dispute.

Arbitration within the WTO is recognized as an alternative means of dispute settlement. Solutions mutually agreed to by the parties are preferred to litigation and are encouraged even throughout the panel process. A mutually agreed-upon solution to a dispute, including an arbitration award, must be consistent with the covered agreements. Notice of the solution must also be given to the DSB and other relevant bodies and can be questioned by any member.

7. WT/DS27/AB/R, para. 135.

The Panel Process

If bilateral consultations fail to settle a dispute within sixty days of the initial request for consultations (twenty days in case of urgency) or if the parties agree jointly that consultations have failed before then, the complaining member may request the DSB to establish a panel. Moreover, if the member to which the request for consultations was addressed does not enter into consultations within thirty days or a period otherwise mutually agreed to, the complaining member may proceed to request the establishment of a panel. The defending member is thus limited in blocking a panel request on the basis that bilateral consultations have not been exhausted.

A panel is established, at the latest at the second DSB meeting at which the panel request is an agenda item, unless the DSB decides not to establish a panel. The DSB meets at least once every month. Generally the legal claims contained in the request for a panel are specified more elaborately than in the prior request for bilateral consultations. If the requesting member seeks other than standard terms of reference for the panel, the request or complaint is to include the proposed text of the special terms of reference. Since these terms refer back to the request or complaint and the measures, product scope, and legal claims included therein, the complaint is arguably the most important document that the complaining member will submit on the case. The terms of reference are circulated to the DSB. If the parties to the dispute agree to special terms of reference within the prescribed time period, any member may raise a point relating thereto in the DSB.

A panel of three members (or five if the parties so agree within ten days) is set up to investigate a particular dispute, and it disbands after fulfilling its mandate and submitting its final report with its rulings and recommendations to the DSB. When there is more than one complainant on the same matter or one complainant against multiple parties on the same matter, a single panel (or different panels with the same panelists) is usually established. Panels are to be composed of "well-qualified" persons selected for their expertise and independence from the parties, who should not reject the nominations "except for compelling reasons." If there is no agreement on the panel's composition within twenty days, the Director General, at the request of either party, is to appoint the panelists. Panelists serve in their individual capacity, without instructions from governments on the matters before the panel. The DSB has adopted rules of conduct designed to ensure to the greatest extent possible that the system operates, and is perceived to operate, with fairness and impartiality.

The panel deliberates in camera. There is no ex parte communication on matters under consideration. The panel should issue its final report within six months (three months in case of urgency). The DSB must be notified of any anticipated delay, and the panel may not exceed nine months, as measured from the time of agreement on its composition and mandate, to issue its report.[8] Submissions to the panel are treated as confidential, but are made available to the parties. Position statements and nonconfidential summaries of the information submitted may be disclosed by the parties to the public. A panel usually holds two substantive meetings with the parties, with the complaining party leading with its case at the first meeting followed by arguments from the defending party. The latter leads with its rebuttal arguments at the second substantive meeting. Third parties attend the session of the first substantive meeting set aside for them and are given an opportunity at that time to be heard by the panel.

A panel is supposed to make an objective assessment of the facts of the case and the applicability of and conformity with the relevant covered agreements. It arrives at its findings and conclusions on the basis of written submissions and oral testimony given by the parties and any information the panel considers relevant. It may seek information and technical advice from any source. A panel may also establish a technical expert review group to assist it.

After the parties have finished with their oral arguments and written rebuttal submissions, the Secretariat drafts the descriptive section of the panel's report comprising the facts of the case and the arguments presented by the parties. The panel circulates this draft section to the parties for their written comments to ensure that the panel understands the case before it issues its finding and conclusions. The panel then circulates to the parties an interim report containing a revised descriptive section along with the panel's findings and conclusions. A party may request that a panel review aspects of the report and hold a further meeting with the disputants. At the conclusion of this interim stage the panel issues its final report to the parties to the dispute, and after a period of time set by the panel it circulates the report to all members, barring a settlement of the dispute by the parties. A panel report does not constitute a definitive interpretation of the WTO agreements, since the exclusive authority to adopt such interpretations is granted to the WTO Ministerial Conference and the

8. "DSU," Art. 12.9. If the defending party is a developing country, these deadlines may be altered to accord it sufficient time to prepare and present its arguments. See "DSU," Art. 12.10.

General Council. Panelists aim at reaching unanimous conclusions. The opinions of the panelists expressed in the panel's report are anonymous.

Except in antidumping cases in which a specific standard of review applies, a panel generally makes an objective assessment of the factual determination made by national authorities. This standard appears to occupy an area between de novo review and total deference. A panel often refers to past panel reports, adopted and unadopted, but is not necessarily bound by their reasoning. There is no rule of precedent or stare decisis rule as such. The AB has ruled that an adopted panel report is binding on the parties with respect to the particular dispute, but does not constitute a definitive interpretation of GATT 1947 for purposes of the GATT 1994. Unadopted panel reports have no legal status under the GATT or the WTO, but nevertheless can provide useful guidance to a panel.

If a panel concludes that nullification and impairment has taken place because the defending party has breached its obligations under a covered agreement, it will write in its report that the DSB should recommend that the party bring the inconsistent measure into conformity. The panel may suggest ways in which the member could do so. If the panel finds nullification and impairment of a benefit in the sense of Article XXIII:1(b) (a nonviolation case), however, it will state that the DSB should recommend that the party make a "mutually satisfactory adjustment," which might include compensation. In such a case the member country is under no obligation to withdraw the measure, as it has not been found to be illegal.

Twenty days after the panel's report has been circulated, it is considered for adoption by the DSB. All members may participate in this consideration. Within sixty days of its circulation the report will be adopted by the DSB unless it decides by consensus not to or a party to the dispute formally notifies its decision to appeal.

The Appellate Review

A party to a dispute may appeal any issue of law or any legal interpretation developed by the panel to a standing AB for review. The AB, a major innovation brought about under the DSU, is composed of seven qualified and impartial nongovernmental individuals who are broadly representative of the WTO membership.[9] They are appointed to serve for a limited time in staggered terms,

9. "The Appellate Body shall comprise persons of recognized authority, with demonstrated expertise in law, international trade and the subject matter of the covered agreements generally." See "DSU," Art. 17.3. The DSB approved the appointment of the

up to two terms of four years each.[10] AB members serve in rotation, with one division of three members hearing any one appeal.

AB members are subject to the same kinds of rules of conduct approved by the DSB to govern panelists, particularly as regards confidentiality, conflict of interest, and disclosure requirements. The AB has drawn up its own working procedures, whereby they have agreed, among other things, that they will select members to constitute a division based on rotation and regardless of nationality.

An appeal begins when a party to the dispute notifies the DSB in writing within sixty days after the circulation of the panel report and simultaneously files a notice of appeal with the Appellate Body Secretariat. The appellant has ten days from the filing of this notice to submit a written submission setting out "a precise statement of the grounds for the appeal . . . of the provisions of the covered agreements and other legal sources relied on; and the nature of the decision or ruling sought."[11] Any party to the dispute that wishes to respond to the appellant's submission may file a written appellee's submission within twenty-five days of the filing of the notice of appeal. A party to the dispute other than the original appellant may also join in the latter's appeal or may appeal on the basis of other alleged errors of law.

Within twenty-five days of the filing of the notice of appeal any third party to the dispute may file a written submission as a third participant in the appeal, including the grounds and legal arguments in support of its position. The AB may also hear third participants at the oral hearing. There is no ex parte communication between the AB and participants on matters under appeal. The AB division draws up its working schedule, generally aiming to hold its oral hearing within thirty days and to circulate its appellate report within sixty days—but in no case more than ninety days—after the date of the appeal

---

original seven members of the AB on the basis of a recommendation by a selection committee (made up of the WTO Director General as well as the chairmen of the DSB and four other WTO councils), which interviewed the thirty-two different candidates nominated by twenty-three countries and consulted fifty-four delegations on the matter. "Minutes of 1 and 25 November 1995 Meeting," WT/DSB/M/9 (February 1, 1996); "Minutes of 19 July 1995 Meeting," WT/DSB/M/6 (August 28, 1995).

10. Three of the original seven persons who were appointed to the AB served an original term of only two years. The three were determined by lot. See "DSU," Art. 17.2. They were then reappointed for another four-year term, so each of the three will serve six years altogether.

11. WT/AB/WP/3.

notice. These deadlines are shorter if a case involves prohibited subsidies under the Subsidies and Countervailing Measures (SCM) Agreement, and they may be accelerated in appeals of urgency, including those involving perishable products. The AB may uphold, modify, or reverse the panel's legal findings or conclusions.

Almost every panel report that has been issued under the WTO has been appealed to the AB. As of November 9, 1998, appeals had been filed on panel rulings with respect to sixteen out of nineteen distinct cases. The AB has basically upheld all or most of the conclusions for which it has completed appellate review, sometimes modifying certain aspects of the panel's legal reasoning or of their conclusions. One could almost say that the AB has been more critical of how panels have reached their conclusions than of the conclusions themselves. In only one case has the AB fully exonerated a defending member previously found by a panel to be in breach of its obligations.[12] The AB has in some other cases modified or reversed some of the grounds for infringements. It declined to make findings on the substantive issues on appeal in one case.[13]

Among the more significant rulings of the AB regarding WTO jurisprudence are those to do the following:

—Enshrine the rules of treaty interpretation of the Vienna Convention as guideposts for panels in interpreting the covered agreements.

—Hold that panels are entitled, when necessary, to carry out their mandate to review and assess objectively.

—Uphold the factual determinations underpinning decisions by national regulatory authorities.

—Uphold the scope of obligations undertaken by members of treaties or agreements negotiated outside the WTO framework.

—Confirm that it is the WTO members acting jointly and politically together that are the ultimate arbiters and interpreters of the WTO agreements.

An AB report is adopted by the DSB within thirty days of its circulation to members and unconditionally accepted by the parties to the dispute unless the DSB decides by consensus not to adopt the report (negative or reverse consensus).

12. The European Community with regard to customs classification of certain computer equipment.

13. An antidumping investigation regarding imports of Portland Cement from Mexico involving Guatemala.

Compliance

A basic principle of international law is that agreements should be observed. Members have committed to conform their laws, regulations, and administrative procedures to their WTO obligations. No member has ever refused to comply with an adverse ruling rendered by the WTO. Once adopted by the DSB, a panel's report, including any modifications by the AB, is considered to embody the rulings and recommendations of the collective body. A finding of nullification and impairment based on a breach of obligations under a covered agreement will generally lead to a recommendation that the inconsistent measure be withdrawn. If the measure is no longer in force, no further action is required by the member found to have infringed its obligations. Compensation is not generally awarded for past trade damage inflicted by a disinvoked illegal measure.

If the member is still applying the inconsistent measure, within thirty days after adoption of the panel or AB report it must inform the DSB how it intends to comply with the DSB recommendations within a reasonable period of time. The "reasonable period of time" is that proposed by the member and approved by the DSB, that mutually agreed to by the disputants within forty-five days of the report's adoption, or that determined through binding arbitration within ninety days of the report's adoption. The general guideline under the DSU is that the reasonable period of time for compliance should not exceed fifteen months from the time of the report's adoption.

The way an illegal measure is brought into conformity has been left largely to the member's own choice, such as withdrawal, substitution with a consistent measure, or waiver. In case there is a dispute as to whether any action taken to bring the measure into compliance is consistent with the recommendations or rulings, this matter can be decided by recourse to dispute settlement procedures including, where possible, the original panel. The infringing party may offer compensation as a temporary measure pending withdrawal of the inconsistent measure. Full implementation of a recommendation to bring a measure into conformity is preferred to compensation (or retaliation). Compensation may prove to be an expensive alternative to compliance, moreover, since compensation must be granted on a most favored nation basis.

Binding arbitration has been resorted to on four occasions to determine a reasonable implementation period. The emerging trend has been for the defending member to argue for more than fifteen months, the complainants to argue for less time, and the arbitrator to conclude that fifteen months is reasonable. The WTO spotlight remains fixed on the infringing member until it complies in full with the recommendations. Six months after the determination of the reasonable period, the implementation issue automatically goes on the agenda for every DSB meeting thereafter until the matter is resolved. Before each such meeting the member has to provide the DSB with a written status report of its progress in implementation.

As a last resort against a member that fails to comply with DSB recommendations within a reasonable period of time, the complaining party, upon request, may be authorized by the DSB to suspend concessions or other obligations to the recalcitrant member on a discriminatory basis and at a level equivalent to the level of nullification or impairment found. Such retaliation may be authorized within the same sector in which the panel or the AB found nullification or impairment, or if this is not practicable under the same agreement, under another covered agreement.

A finding of "nonviolation" nullification or impairment will usually lead to a recommendation that the parties concerned negotiate a mutually satisfactory adjustment with a view to restoring the competitive relationship found to have been nullified or impaired. There is no obligation that the defending party withdraw the noninconsistent measure concerned, but it must report how it intends to comply with the DSB recommendations within a reasonable period of time. This reasonable period may be determined by an arbitrator; however, any suggestions by the arbitrator as to "ways and means of reaching a mutually satisfactory adjustment" are not binding.

Current Difficulties of the WTO System

The WTO dispute settlement system remains a work in progress. Given its current level of activity, it may become a victim of its own success. More trade disputes, by more countries, of more varied development stages, on more kinds of measures, of more complexity, are being filed with the WTO than were ever brought under its GATT predecessor. In fact, if the number of disputes being brought under the WTO is sustained, by the end of its fourth year of operation their number may almost reach the total number of complaints brought under the GATT.

It is difficult to ascribe such dispute resolutionism or resolutionitis to any one factor. As GATT history has shown, the period immediately following the conclusion of a major trade round may witness increased activity as governments try to test the scope and effectiveness of the new multilateral disciplines and commitments undertaken. Sometimes the measures being disputed are the leftovers of the negotiations—that is, those problems on which it was not possible to achieve new multilateral understandings.

There are such things as perennial disputes that will not go away. Disputes that appeared settled by negotiation or adjudication may come back through measure shifting or measure repackaging. Under this practice new measures that replace the original measures at issue change the form of the protectionism, but may affect trade just as adversely or more so. Further recourse to dispute settlement proceedings may be required to determine the consistency of the new measures. There also exist what can be categorized as tit-for-tat disputes whereby a party on the receiving end of a complaint decides to go on the offensive with its own complaint.

An increase in trade disputes filed with the WTO is not altogether an unhealthy sign. It is a function of an increase in trade and trade players and of growing confidence that the WTO contract and its dispute settlement system stand for something. Casting one's démarche on a trade problem within the framework of Article XXII or Article XXIII or their equivalent is fast becoming routine, a way of conducting trade policy business as usual, to enhance the possibility that foreign officials will pay attention to and correct the matter.

With more disputes being adjudicated by panels, the WTO system's resources are being taxed to such a point that there is a risk of litigation implosion. Deadlines are being missed. The panel selection process is being bogged down by a lack of acceptable and available panelists. Yet members still want the control and flexibility of deciding the panel makeup for each case.

The growing number of members expressing an interest in any matter at issue or launching complaints of their own is further diminishing the panelist pool and adding to administrative woes. A certain piggybacking, especially when a panel finding against a defending member is imminent, may be motivated by the desire to be well positioned for purposes of compensation or retaliation.

The sheer volume of facts, legal arguments, and claims that panels have to wade through is growing exponentially, with one panel deluged with 20,000 pages of evidence. These must be carefully summarized by the Secretariat in the panel report to the fullest satisfaction of the parties—which can number as many as a dozen on a case—to demonstrate that the panel took note of all the relevant material presented. The panel's own findings and conclusions with respect to the several claims under its mandate must be meticulously elaborated for possible appellate review. A certain procedural legalism is creeping in—for instance, demands that the claims or arguments presented at the bilateral consultation stage be specified with as much particularity as the subsequent complaint itself or challenges as to whether claims (such as those made in response to unforeseen counterclaims) or products fall within the panel's terms of reference.

Panels are producing huge reports faster than the Secretariat can translate and distribute them to all members. As a consequence, nonparties to a dispute are at an increasing disadvantage from such delays. This is particularly acute when they themselves are parties to disputes involving similar issues (and involving members that are parties to both disputes). Panel reports of several hundred pages are being issued fortnightly faster than the trading community can understand them, let alone the general public.

The system also appears to be under heightened attack by interest groups that charge that it is esoteric and remote. There are demands heretofore addressed on an ad hoc basis for more open participation in the panel process through the possibility of submission of amicus curiae briefs by nongovernmental organizations. There is also the question of representation of parties by private lawyers. On the one hand, this might raise difficulties regarding conflicts of interest, loyalty, and the separation of public and private roles. It might also alter the customarily genteel and informal manner in which adjudicatory proceedings tend to be conducted in the WTO. The other side of this argument is that governments should be able to decide for themselves how they choose to be represented. Moreover, the use of private counsel may be the only viable way for governments of smaller economies to participate effectively in the dispute resolution process, especially given its increasingly legalistic nature. Legal assistance provided by the WTO Secretariat's technical cooperation services, including the hiring of outside counsel as consultants, has not been sufficient to meet this demand. The Secretariat also views its role as one of impartiality, which necessarily limits how far it can serve as advocate on behalf of any one member.

Lessons for the FTAA Negotiators

Among the practical lessons that can be drawn from the operation of the WTO dispute resolution mechanism is that an effective system requires the shared interests of participants and adequate resources to make it work. Not every procedural problem or impasse can be anticipated and fully addressed in an agreement. Just as Dr. Bhagwati has posited the existence of a law of constant protection, there may be a law of constant proceduralism whereby procedural obstacles seemingly redressed by new rules pop up in different form elsewhere in the process.[14] It is useful to spell out the process by which conflicts can be resolved and to leave room for developing ad hoc solutions as necessary. Also useful may be provision for regular review and stocktaking of the operation of the dispute resolution mechanism.

Deadlines imposed to minimize the opportunity for procedural delay may become prerogatives to drag matters out as long as possible up to that point. Even with the best of intentions, certain matters are so complex factually and legally that delays are inevitable. Nationality can never be discounted entirely even with respect to qualified experts, as important national interests are at stake. The selection process for the AB members and the criticism leveled against the appointees for deciding to assign cases among themselves regardless of national origin bear this out. The roster of nongovernmental individuals to serve on panels depends on nominations from member governments. In a sense they are "governmental nongovernmental" candidates, which demonstrates a degree of separation from "governmental governmental" candidates.

Distinctions between parties to a dispute and third parties are becoming increasingly blurred not only in terms of trade interest, but also in terms of procedural participation. Given the myriad subregional agreements connecting FTAA participants, the issue will arise as to who are the bona fide parties to any dispute under the FTAA and the scope of third-party participation. In an exercise involving several disparate issues and interests eventually leading to separate instruments under the FTAA umbrella, the operation of the WTO system has shown the need for an integral approach to ensure that the various instruments interconnect and serve the goals of an overall trade package or contract.

The nature of some of the disputes under the WTO has revealed areas in which countries are calling for new, substantive rules and obligations. Some of these issues already have been tagged for negotiation under the FTAA, such as competition policy, electronic commerce, and investment. The operation of an

14. Jagdish Bhagwati. 1996. "The Demands to Reduce Domestic Diversity among Trading Nations." In *Fair Trade and Harmonization*, edited by Jagdish Bhagwati and Robert E. Hudec. Cambridge, Mass.: MIT Press.

increasingly legalistic WTO dispute settlement system, in particular a certain textual literalism adopted by the AB in its interpretation of the WTO agreements, underscores the care with which rights and obligations must be formulated to ensure their enforcement. This might involve, for example, rules that clearly proscribe certain government conduct as opposed to setting hortatory limits on the trade effects of such conduct, the assignment of burden of proof between the parties, or the standard of review over factual determinations by national authorities. These factors favor the participation of lawyers on trade negotiating teams sooner rather than later in the process. Of course lawyers do not have a monopoly on writing, reading, thinking, or even arguing; but the drafting and interpretation of contracts, rules, and codes and the mastery of procedure are their particular strengths.

Transparency and accountability in the process and society's perception of openness are becoming more appreciated as desirable ingredients of a mechanism for resolving trade disputes, particularly as international rules encroach further on national action. The issue of private parties' access to the resolution of disputes concerning governmental behavior affecting trade is multifaceted. It includes whether private parties have a right in a domestic legal system to challenge a violation of a trade agreement by a foreign government or their own government. Apart from members' obligation to conform their domestic law to their WTO commitments, the direct application of these obligations in domestic law has been left to members as a matter of their respective systems of domestic law. With respect to private parties' access to the WTO dispute settlement system, it has already been noted that only member governments have rights and obligations under the WTO. Members may disclose non-confidential summaries of their briefs to the public. The electronic dissemination of information regarding actions taken pursuant to the DSU has been helpful in making the dispute settlement process somewhat more transparent, but there have been calls for even greater access by private parties.[15] Such demands for participatory rights may reflect a desire that the WTO interfere less with domestic policies, especially those undertaken to advance nontrade objectives.

There are many areas of the FTAA negotiations on dispute settlement for which no precedent exists under the GATT/WTO resolution mechanism. There is much room for the FTAA negotiators and their private partners to think

15. See "United States—Statement by Mr. William J. Clinton, President," WT/FIFTY/H/ST/8 (May 18, 1998).

creatively, for example, about more effective ways to resolve disputes between private commercial parties or between a state and a private party. This may involve proposals, building on the existing groundwork already undertaken by various bar associations and alternative dispute resolution (ADR) centers, on how to harmonize the practice of law, train and certify mediators and arbitrators, and encourage ADR in order to promote hemispheric trade.

As the FTAA negotiators embark on their own approach to constructing a dispute resolution mechanism, particularly for state-to-state disputes, there may be certain guiding principles or features of the WTO dispute settlement system that it may be useful for negotiators to consider incorporating—but not necessarily copying exactly. Some of the key elements of the DSU that have been described more fully earlier in this chapter include the following:

—An emphasis on a positive solution, mutually acceptable to the parties, that respects the rights of all other members.

—An integrated system with a central body composed of all members to coordinate and monitor dispute settlement, including under the several covered agreements.

—A ban on unilateral determinations and retaliation.

—Mandatory bilateral consultations to be undertaken in good faith.

—Availability of good offices or conciliation or binding arbitration.

—Basing causes of action on nullification or impairment of benefits accruing under the covered agreements (violation, nonviolation, and situation complaints).

—Recourse to adjudication by an ad hoc panel of impartial experts.

—Time limits and default procedures, including standard terms of reference for panels.

—A roster of eligible panelists.

—Standard working procedures for panels.

—A negative consensus rule for panel establishment, adoption of rulings or recommendations, and authorization of retaliation.

—Accelerated proceedings in case of urgency.

—Special procedures for disputes involving developing countries, especially the least-developed developing countries.

—An "objective assessment" standard of review.

—Allocation of burden of proof to the complainant to present evidence sufficient to allow a presumption of infringement and to the party invoking an exception as an affirmative defense.

Table 15-1. Features of the WTO Dispute Settlement System

Party control	Institutional limits
• Members raise complaints, self-elect to be a party or interested third party, and choose mode for settling dispute: bilateral consultations, good offices, or binding arbitration.	• Members must seek redress under the DSU, no unilateral determination or retaliation. Bilateral solutions and arbitration awards must be notified to and conform to WTO.
• If bilateral talks fail to settle dispute, complainant may request a panel to examine complaint.	• Defendant may not block DSB from establishing a panel (negative consensus rule) at its second meeting.
• Complaint serves a panel's jurisdiction. Parties may agree to special terms of reference.	• Complaint must specify measures and legal claims. Barring mutual accord, standard terms of reference apply.
• Members submit nominees for roster of eligible panelists. Parties approve panelists who will hear their case.	• Panelists are qualified individuals selected for their independence. If parties do not agree to panel composition, DG may appoint panelists.
• Parties make submissions to a panel that it must duly consider. Parties review descriptive section of panel's report and may demand an interim hearing after receiving rulings. Parties may continue to try to resolve dispute themselves and may ask panel to suspend its work.	• A panel may seek information from any source. It issues findings and conclusions on its own responsibility. If parties resolve the dispute, a panel reports that a solution was reached. Authority for panel lapses if its work is suspended for more than one year.
• Parties may appeal a panel's rulings. Members nominate and change by consensus the AB members, who serve fixed terms.	• Only parties to the dispute may appeal issues of law. The AB selects members who will hear case. A member may not block adoption by the DSB of panel and AB reports (negative consensus rule).
• A member may choose how to bring a measure found illegal into conformity with the WTO: withdrawal, new measure, waiver, or compensation. Parties may agree mutually to the period of time for compliance.	• The DSB monitors compliance by a member within a "reasonable period of time" (may be determined by binding arbitration). Consistency of compliance is decided through the DSU. WTO members must approve waiver. Compensation is temporary, pending withdrawal of the illegal measure, and granted on an MFN basis.

Table 15-1. (*continued*)

Party control	Institutional limits
• A party may refuse to remove an illegal measure or otherwise not comply with the DSB recommendations.	• Members must conform their measures to WTO obligations. If a party does not comply, DSB may authorize retaliation (possibly in another sector) at the other party's request (negative consensus rule).
• A party need not withdraw a "non-violating" measure found to nullify or impair complainant's benefits from covered agreement.	• A party should negotiate "a mutually satisfactory adjustment" to settle the dispute.
• Members remain collectively the ultimate arbiters and interpreters of WTO obligations.	• Adopted rulings are binding with respect to resolving the particular dispute between the parties to the dispute.

—A (theoretically rebuttable) presumption that breach of rules has an adverse impact.

—Panel access to outside technical expertise.

—A standing AB to review panel rulings of law or legal reasoning.

—Multilateral surveillance of implementation of rulings or recommendations.

—Multilaterally sanctioned retaliation.

—Possible suspension of benefits across different sectors or agreements.

—Member governments' acting collectively as the ultimate arbiters and interpreters of the agreements.

The GATT/WTO dispute resolution mechanism evolved slowly from an initial reliance primarily on diplomatic jurisprudence to help parties work out their differences in a mutually agreeable fashion and on practical, ad hoc negotiated solutions. The system has moved toward greater institutional discipline and control over the settlement of disputes and, in the words of a former DSB chairman, the "thickening of legality."[16] At the same time trade negotiations have evolved from an initial concern about what was being done ostensibly at the borders to affect trade toward greater preoccupation with what governments do within their borders to affect trade. Thus the substantive rules and obligations of trade, and in parallel the system to enforce them, have

16. Statement by Mr. C. Lafer (Brazil), chairman of the DSB, WT/DSB(97)/ST/1 (January 31, 1997).

become more intrusive over national autonomy, but in the mutually perceived interest of all participating countries.

Many aspects of the WTO dispute settlement system remain member driven and member controlled. It is a mix of the political model and the rules-based or adjudicatory model (see table 15-1). That balance continues to shift as members continue to fine-tune the dispute settlement system to ensure that it arrives at the right answers in a fair way. Ultimately this should be the aim of any system.

Part Four

THE NEWEST TRADE POLICY ISSUES

CHAPTER SIXTEEN

Toward an Investment Agreement in the Americas: Building on the Existing Consensus

Maryse Robert and Theresa Wetter

The 1990s have seen the emergence of a new consensus in the Americas over the rules governing foreign direct investment (FDI). On issues that seemed controversial not long ago, common approaches have been adopted in investment agreements in areas such as scope of application, treatment, transfers, and expropriation and dispute settlement mechanisms. In fact, as a result of the debt crisis in the 1980s, countries in Latin America and the Caribbean, which had relied mainly on volatile portfolio investment and import-substitution policies, undertook economic reforms liberalizing trade and adopted national investment regimes promoting, protecting, and liberalizing FDI. From the Yukon to Tierra del Fuego, FDI is now championed as a way to increase economic growth and development and to stimulate innovation, competition, and jobs.

The widespread acceptance of FDI and its implications for trade have convinced governments of the Americas to enter into binding obligations aimed at promoting, protecting, and in some cases liberalizing foreign investment. Since the early 1990s more than sixty bilateral investment treaties (BITs) have been signed between countries of the region. At the regional level specific investment commitments have been included in plurilateral free trade agreements (FTAs) such as the North American Free Trade Agreement (NAFTA) and the Group of Three (G-3) agreement between Colombia, Mexico, and

Venezuela, as well as in bilateral FTAs signed respectively by Mexico with Bolivia, Chile, Costa Rica, and Nicaragua; by Canada with Chile; and by the Central American countries with the Dominican Republic (this last agreement applies bilaterally). The Colonia Protocol for the Mercosur member countries and the Buenos Aires Protocol for nonmembers also incorporate comprehensive investment disciplines. Trade agreements under discussion, such as that between Mexico and the Northern Triangle (El Salvador, Guatemala, and Honduras), follow the trend and provide for extensive investment coverage. Other integration arrangements, the Andean Community with Decision 291 and the Caribbean Community (CARICOM) with Protocol 2, also contain investment provisions. In addition, countries of the region have been active at the multilateral level in the context of the World Trade Organization (WTO). They were instrumental in the creation of the WTO Working Group on the Relationship between Trade and Investment at the Singapore Ministerial Meeting in December 1996. Moreover, the United States, Canada, and Mexico participated from 1995 to 1998 in the negotiation of a Multilateral Agreement on Investment (MAI) at the Organization for Economic Cooperation and Development (OECD), whereas Argentina, Brazil, and Chile took part in these negotiations as observers starting in 1997.

As countries of the Americas are beginning the negotiation of an investment agreement within the process of creating the Free Trade Area of the Americas (FTAA), this chapter aims at reviewing very briefly the numerous endeavors to negotiate multilateral rules governing FDI, from the early attempts to the investment-related rules and disciplines in the WTO and the negotiations to create an MAI. It also aims at providing an overview of the main investment provisions that have been entered into between countries of the Americas and at identifying the commonalities emerging from these instruments. The chapter proposes to build on the existing consensus in the negotiations on investment in the FTAA, and it concludes by describing some of the remaining challenges facing countries of the region.

Early Efforts to Devise Multilateral Investment Rules

The first attempt at designing multilateral rules on investment was made shortly after World War II during the negotiation of the Havana Charter leading to the establishment of the International Trade Organization (ITO). However, with the exception of Articles 11 and 12 in Chapter III of the charter, these efforts were essentially timid because they addressed only restrictive business practices related to goods and services, more specifically the regulation of international cartels (Chapter V). Although proposed by the United States, the issue of protecting foreign investors in host countries was opposed by developing countries and therefore was never included in the charter. In fact, concerns of U.S.-based multinationals related to nationalization, expropriation, and lack of prompt, adequate, and effective compensation for foreign investment were also not dealt with. The Calvo Doctrine, which had been the tradition of most Latin American countries, was at the heart of these concerns. In resolving disputes between foreign investors and a host state, foreign investors had to seek local remedies and were not entitled to the protection of their home state even if under customary international law they had the right to such protection after having expended these local remedies.

The only surviving chapter of the Havana Charter, which became the General Agreement on Tariffs and Trade (GATT), did not address investment issues per se, albeit a resolution on international investment for economic development was adopted as early as 1955 asking the GATT contracting parties to adopt conditions conducive to international investment activities. Suggestions to create a "GATT for Investment" in the 1970s remained without strong support.

The 1980s offered new opportunities. Trade-related investment measures were first brought into the GATT discussions by the United States at a meeting of the Consultative Group of Eighteen in 1981. Quoting a study prepared by the International Monetary Fund (IMF) and the World Bank on the trade-distorting effects of performance requirements, the United States called for the compilation by the GATT Secretariat of an inventory of performance requirements, an idea that received very little support. More detailed proposals made in 1982 and 1985 had the same fate. However, in 1982 the United States challenged Canada over performance requirements imposed by Canada's Foreign Investment Review Agency (FIRA) on local subsidiaries of foreign-based firms. A GATT panel later ruled that the FIRA's local-content requirements violated Article III(4), the national treatment provision. As mentioned by Edward M. Graham and Paul R. Krugman, "The same panel, however, did not support a U.S. contention that export performance requirements were inconsistent with GATT Article XVII:1(c), which prohibits member governments from preventing an enterprise from behaving in a nondiscriminatory manner." In fact, developing countries found comfort in that "the panel also noted that countries could in principle invoke GATT Article XVIII:C (on government assistance to promote economic development) to justify local-content requirements."[1]

Following the panel ruling the United States renewed its efforts to address trade-related investment measures. In preparing the final declaration launching the Uruguay Round, proposals encompassing a wide variety of investment issues ranging from performance requirements to the right of establishment were put forward by the European Community, Japan, and the United States. The United States aimed at addressing these issues on a comprehensive basis. Although initially opposed by most developing countries, some investment issues were later included in the 1986 Punta del Este Ministerial Declaration, which launched the Uruguay Round of multilateral trade negotiations.

Investment-Related Rules and Disciplines in the WTO

A number of agreements resulting from the Uruguay Round negotiations include investment provisions. These are the Agreement on Trade-Related Investment Measures (TRIMS), the General Agreement on Trade in Services (GATS), the Agreement on Trade-Related Aspects of Intellectual Property Rights (TRIPS), and the Agreement on Subsidies and Countervailing Measures (ASCM).

The Agreement on Trade-Related Investment Measures

The mandate of the TRIMS negotiations reads as follows: "Following an examination of the operation of GATT articles related to the trade-restrictive and distorting effects of investment measures, negotiations should elaborate, as appropriate, further provisions that may be necessary to avoid such adverse effects on trade."[2] The debate first centered on the definition of this very mandate and, more specifically, whether performance requirements would be prohibited both as a condition of establishment and as a condition for receipt of investment incentives. The second option was not addressed directly in the TRIMS Agreement. Investment incentives were handled by the Subsidies Negotiating Group.[3]

1. Graham and Krugman (1990, pp. 150–51).
2. General Agreement on Tariffs and Trade (GATT) (1986).
3. Graham and Sauvé (1996, p. 125).

Performance requirements have been used by capital-importing countries with the intent of increasing exports, local production, or technology transfer. However, by imposing on foreign investors conditions that are not based on the market, performance requirements may distort investment decisions and affect international trade. There are two broad categories of performance requirements. The first is related to trade and local production. Local content and trade-balancing requirements, the two measures identified in the illustrative list of the TRIMS Agreement as being inconsistent with GATT Article III (on national treatment), and trade and foreign exchange–balancing restrictions and domestic sales requirements, the three measures identified in the illustrative list of the TRIMS Agreement as incompatible with GATT Article XI (on the general elimination of quantitative restrictions), are examples of this first type of measures. The second category is related to capital structure and management of an investment, and it includes measures such as local hiring targets, technology transfer, and nationality of management.[4]

Under Article 5(1) of the TRIMS Agreement, which covers goods only, member countries had within ninety days of the date of entry into force of the WTO Agreement to notify the Council for Trade in Goods of all inconsistent TRIMS. Developed countries had to phase out their performance requirements within two years of the date of entry into force of the WTO Agreement. Under Article 5(2) developing countries have a deadline of five years, whereas least-developed countries are required to undertake the same commitments within seven years. Under Article 5(3) the council may extend the transition period for developing and least-developed countries.

An illustrative list of prohibited measures—measures that "are mandatory or enforceable under domestic law or under administrative rulings, or compliance with which is necessary to obtain an advantage" and that are linked to the national treatment provision of GATT Article III(4) and to the obligation to undertake general elimination of the quantitative restrictions of GATT Article XI(1)—is annexed to the TRIMS Agreement. It has been suggested that the term *advantage* may signal an overlap with the provisions of the Agreement on Subsidies and Countervailing Measures, albeit this term may actually be broader in scope than the word *subsidies*.[5]

Member countries are also required not to modify the terms of any TRIM ["standstill clause," Article 5(4)]. However, under Article 5(5) a country may

4. See Organization for Economic Cooperation and Development (OECD) (1996, p. 38).
5. Sauvé (1994, p. 8).

choose to apply a TRIM to a new investment during the transition period in order not to disadvantage established enterprises that are already subject to such measures. Finally, under Article 9 the TRIMS Agreement provides for the Council for Trade in Goods to review this agreement no later than five years after the entry into force of the WTO Agreement and to "consider whether the Agreement should be complemented with provisions on investment policy and competition policy." Therefore, although the TRIMS Agreement has often been labeled as rather narrow in scope and substance because it does not go beyond the ruling of the 1984 GATT Panel on FIRA, the review provision leaves the door open for a more comprehensive coverage of investment issues within the purview of the WTO.

The General Agreement on Trade in Services

The GATS is not an investment agreement, but it includes several investment-related provisions. First, the definition of services incorporates four modes of supply, one of which, the third mode, "commercial presence in the territory of any other member," is essentially an investment activity and a right of establishment. *Commercial presence* means, under GATS Article XXVIII, "any type of business or professional establishment, including through (i) the constitution, acquisition or maintenance of a juridical person, or (ii) the creation or maintenance of a branch or a representative office, within the territory of a Member for the purpose of supplying a service." It is worth noting that this definition is not as comprehensive as the definition of investment found in most BITs and FTAs signed in the Americas.[6] The fourth mode, which is the supply of service "through presence of natural persons of a Member in the territory of any other Member," is also linked, albeit indirectly, to investment issues, because it implies the temporary entry of managerial and other key personnel.

The GATS is the WTO agreement with the most far-reaching implications for a multilateral investment agreement because of its all-encompassing most favored nation (MFN) provision (in Article II), which applies across the board to all members and service sectors. Although MFN exemptions are allowed if listed in an annex at the time of the entry into force of the agreement, they are temporary in nature and subject to multilateral review. The GATS also provides that preferential treatment may be granted to a foreign service supplier located

6. Sauvé (1994, p. 9).

in a party that is a member of an economic integration agreement if such agreement has substantial sectoral coverage and provides for the absence or elimination of substantially all discrimination (Article V). Other GATS provisions of a general nature that are investment related include transparency obligations, general exceptions, and security exceptions.

The GATS provisions regarding national treatment (Article XVII) as well as market access obligations (Article XVI) are, however, conditional, a clear departure from common practice in investment agreements with respect to the national treatment provision.[7] They are granted according to specific commitments listed in members' schedules indicating to which sectors and modes of supply these obligations apply. The GATS thus makes use of what is known as a "positive list" by identifying which sectors are covered by the agreement. More specifically, this means that new discriminatory measures will be allowed in sectors not included in a member's schedule. Moreover, as opposed to the provisions of the TRIMS and TRIPS Agreements, existing measures inconsistent with the agreement do not have to be eliminated as long as they are listed in a member's schedule.[8]

Nevertheless, the GATS includes commitments to further liberalize trade in services. The so-called built-in agenda for services is scheduled to be addressed by the Council for Trade in Services no later than five years after the entry into force of the WTO Agreement. Continued liberalization is also contemplated. For both market access and national treatment conditions the GATS uses a negative list approach.[9] Six conditions that are prohibited unless otherwise specified in a member's schedule may be imposed on market access. Two of these conditions are directly related to commercial presence: those that "restrict or require specific types of legal entity or joint venture through which a service supplier may supply a service" and "limitations on the participation of foreign capital in terms of maximum percentage limit on foreign shareholding or the total value of individual or aggregate foreign investment." National treatment conditions are not specified, but may be listed in a member's schedule.

The Agreement on Trade-Related Aspects of Intellectual Property Rights

The TRIPS Agreement is the first-ever comprehensive multilateral agreement to set minimum standards protecting all areas of intellectual property

7. World Trade Organization (WTO) (1996, p. 71).
8. Sauvé (1994, p. 12).
9. WTO (1996, p. 71).

rights (copyright and related rights, trademarks, geographical indications, industrial designs, patents, layout designs of integrated circuits, and trade secrets), to include domestic enforcement measures, and to be covered by a dispute settlement mechanism. Its impact on investment issues, although indirect, is nonetheless significant. The TRIPS Agreement contributes to strengthening the protection afforded to foreign investment by reinforcing the protection of intellectual property rights, one of the key elements often listed in the definition of investment found in most recent BITs and FTAs currently in force worldwide.

The Agreement on Subsidies and Countervailing Measures

The ASCM includes disciplines that cover investment-related issues. In fact, some examples of investment incentives (fiscal, financial, or indirect) fall under the meaning of *subsidy,* as defined in the ASCM. Except as provided in the Agreement on Agriculture, such investment incentives are prohibited if they are given upon export performance or use of domestic over imported goods (Article 3). Others, which may not be prohibited but are found to cause adverse effects, are subject to compensation. However, as noted by the WTO, "the underlying concepts of the ASCM are oriented toward trade in goods, and as such may not in all cases be easily applied to investment incentives." For example, an investment incentive is usually granted *before* any production begins, which means that "neither a recommendation to withdraw or modify a subsidy, nor a countervailing duty applied to the exported goods, will be able to 'undo' or to change an investment that already has been made."[10]

The WTO Working Group on the Relationship between Trade and Investment

At the Singapore Ministerial Meeting in December 1996 it was agreed to create a Working Group on the Relationship between Trade and Investment. At its first meeting held on June 2–3, 1997, the group adopted a work program that focuses on the following issues: implications of the relationship between trade and investment for development and economic growth, the economic relationship between trade and investment, and preparation of an inventory and

10. WTO (1996, pp. 72–73).

analysis of the existing international instruments and activities in the area of trade and investment. On the basis of the first three elements, the work program has also focused on identification of common features, differences, and possible gaps in existing international instruments; respective advantages and disadvantages of national autonomy and bilateral, regional, and multilateral rules on investment, in particular from a development perspective; the rights and obligations of home and host countries and of investors and host countries; and the relationship between international cooperation on investment policy and international cooperation on competition policy. The General Council will review the group's mandate after two years of operations. Should a "miniround" or "millennium round" of negotiations be launched, investment appears to be one of the candidates that might be included in the negotiations.

The Multilateral Agreement on Investment

In May 1995 the OECD ministers launched negotiations on an MAI that would be a freestanding international treaty open to nonmember countries with high standards of liberalization, investment protection, and effective dispute settlement procedures. The 1997 deadline to complete the negotiations was extended to the 1998 ministerial meeting held in Paris on April 27–28. On that occasion the OECD ministers agreed to suspend the negotiations until October 1998 and declared the following:

> Taking into account the positive results produced by the Negotiating Group, as well as the remaining difficulties and the concerns that have been expressed, Ministers decide on a period of assessment and further consultation between the negotiating parties and with interested parts of their societies, and invite the Secretary-General to assist this process. Ministers note that the next meeting of the Negotiating Group will be held in October 1998. Ministers direct the negotiators to continue their work with the aim of reaching a successful and timely conclusion of the MAI and seeking broad participation in it. In the same spirit, they support the current work program on investment in the WTO and once the work program has been completed will seek the support of all their partners for next steps towards the creation of investment rules in the WTO.[11]

11. OECD (1998b). Twenty-nine OECD member countries and the European Commission were involved in the negotiations. In addition, eight nonmembers also par-

Representatives of the twenty-nine OECD member countries met in the Executive Committee in Special Session (ECSS) in Paris on October 22, 1998, to discuss developments in the multilateral system, including trade and investment. This meeting was held eight days after the French government had announced that it was pulling out of the MAI negotiations. With respect to these negotiations, the ECSS stated that "there was a consensus among delegates on the need for and value of a multilateral framework for investment." Although it was acknowledged that this "goal should still be sought," the OECD delegates agreed on the importance of "taking stock" of the "significant concerns" that "have been raised during the consultations on the MAI," including "issues of sovereignty, protection of labor rights and environment, culture and other important matters." The OECD members also declared that "in further consultations, it will be important to broaden the participation of non-OECD member countries and to engage in further discussions with representatives of civil society." They finally noted that "these consultations should proceed with a view to deciding how best to reach the shared goal of a multilateral framework for investment and to deal effectively with the concerns that have been expressed."[12]

The OECD has been active in the investment arena for over thirty-five years. In 1961 it adopted two codes, the Code of Liberalization of Capital Movements and the Code of Liberalization of Current Invisible Operations, providing for gradual nondiscriminatory liberalization of capital movements. Provisions on the right of establishment and cross-border financial services were included, respectively, in 1986 and 1992. Although these codes are binding in nature, they were thwarted from the beginning, in part because of a number of important reservations against their main provisions. The Committee on Capital Movements and Invisible Transactions (CMIT) oversees their operations.

A draft Convention on the Protection of Foreign Property was prepared in 1967, but never adopted. However, a decade later, in 1976, the OECD countries adopted the Declaration on International Investment and Multinational Enterprises, a nonbinding instrument made up of six sections: the Guidelines for Multinational Enterprises and sections on national treatment, conflicting requirements, international investment incentives and disincentives, consultation

---

ticipated as observers of the negotiating group starting in 1997: Argentina, Brazil, Chile, Estonia, Hong Kong, Latvia, Lithuania, and the Slovak Republic.

12. OECD (1998a).

procedures, and review. The declaration is not binding and lacks enforcement provisions. In 1976 the OECD member countries also created the Committee on International Investment and Multinational Enterprises (CIME) to oversee its activities. In order to strengthen OECD investment instruments and ensure that national treatment obligations would be binding on the OECD countries, the CIME and CMIT started working in 1991 on an MAI. In 1994 five working groups of independent experts were set up to examine the different issues. They prepared a report, which led to the 1995 launching of the MAI negotiations.

Toward an Investment Agreement in the Americas

In September 1998 countries of the Americas began negotiations on hemispheric investment rules. The FTAA Negotiating Group on Investment, currently chaired by Costa Rica, which also presided over the FTAA Working Group on Investment, has been given the mandate "to establish a fair and transparent legal framework to promote investment through the creation of a stable and predictable environment that protects the investor, his investment and related flows, without creating obstacles to investments from outside the hemisphere." Work prepared for the FTAA Working Group on Investment, which met nine times between September 1995 and September 1998 and set the stage for the current negotiations, has shown that a clear consensus has emerged in the region over rules and disciplines on investment.

There has been an unprecedented growth in the number of investment agreements in the Americas. As mentioned earlier, sweeping economic reforms and trade liberalization in the 1980s and 1990s brought a substantial liberalization in the investment regime of most Latin American and Caribbean countries. Binding obligations governing the promotion and protection of foreign investment have been entered into through the negotiation of BITs, investment chapters in FTAs, and investment protocols and decisions. Although the first BITs originated in Europe in the late 1950s, it took more than thirty years before countries of the Americas started negotiating and concluding BITs among themselves. However, several countries such as Colombia, the Dominican Republic, Ecuador, El Salvador, Haiti, Honduras, and Paraguay signed BITs with the Federal Republic of Germany, France, and Switzerland during the 1960s and 1970s. The first BIT concluded within the Americas was between the United States and Panama in 1982. During the 1980s only the

United States was active in entering into BITs with other countries of the region. In addition to the treaty with Panama, the United States signed a BIT with Haiti in 1983 and one with Grenada in 1986.

An overwhelming majority of countries in the Americas have signed at least one BIT. In fact, only three countries (the Commonwealth of the Bahamas, St. Kitts and Nevis, and Suriname) have not yet done so, whereas twenty-four have concluded at least one BIT with another country of the region. With the exception of Barbados, Jamaica, and Trinidad and Tobago, most Caribbean countries have not entered into BITs with other countries of the Western Hemisphere, albeit Grenada and Haiti have each signed an investment treaty with the United States. Most BITs signed by Caribbean countries are with European countries such as France, Germany, Switzerland, and the United Kingdom. However, Trinidad and Tobago concluded a BIT with the United States in 1994 and one with Canada in 1995, Barbados concluded a treaty with Venezuela in 1994 and one with Canada in 1996, and Jamaica signed a BIT with the United States and another with Argentina, both in 1994.

The trend is also present at the regional level with the elaboration of detailed investment provisions in the NAFTA and the G-3, the liberalization of the Andean Pact's investment regime (via Decision 291), and the enactment of two Mercosur protocols for the promotion and protection of investments: the Colonia Protocol, applicable to the Mercosur's member countries, and the Buenos Aires Protocol, applicable to nonmembers. As mentioned in the introduction to this chapter, a number of FTAs including comprehensive investment provisions have also been negotiated by Mexico with Bolivia, Chile, Costa Rica, and Nicaragua; by Canada with Chile; and by Central American countries with the Dominican Republic.

This section covers essentially six elements of investment treaties: scope of application, admission, treatment, transfers, expropriation, and settlement of disputes. A detailed summary of each of these elements as they are reflected in bilateral and regional legal instruments follows. Other issues that are often covered in investment instruments are also addressed.

Scope of Application

The scope of application of an investment treaty is essentially determined by the definition of the terms *investment* and *investor* and by the period of time during which the agreement will be in force. These elements constitute the main variables explaining who will enjoy and benefit from the protection of the treaty.

Recently developed investment instruments have adopted a broad "asset-based" definition of investment that includes, for example, portfolio investment, real estate, and intangible assets such as intellectual property. Such definition goes beyond the more narrow "enterprise-based" definition of FDI. Typically modern definitions use phrases such as "every kind of asset," "any kind of asset," or "every kind of investment," accompanied by an illustrative but nonexhaustive list of examples. Such a list commonly includes the following five components: movable and immovable property and any related property rights, such as mortgages, liens, or pledges; shares, stock, bonds, or debentures or any other form of participation in a company, business enterprise, or joint venture; money, claims to money, claims to performance under contract that have a financial value, and loans directly related to a specific investment; intellectual property rights; and rights conferred by law (for example, concessions) or under contract.

Although the objective of using such a comprehensive definition is to guarantee protection of as many forms of investment as possible, there has been an attempt to avoid coverage of purely monetary or speculative flows not related to an investment. Therefore, recently concluded agreements include qualifications of their coverage. For example, the typical BIT states that a loan is covered only if directly linked to a specific investment, whereas some agreements exclude from the definition of covered investment "real estate or other property, tangible or intangible, not acquired in the expectation or used for the purpose of economic benefit or other business purposes." Moreover, in the case of the NAFTA, the G-3, and the Canada-Chile and Mexico-Nicaragua FTAs, there is also an asset-based definition that covers a broad list of assets that are expressly linked with the activities of an enterprise. This type of formulation excludes from coverage of the agreement those transactions that might occur in capital or money markets with no connection to specific investments. Finally, claims to money that arise solely from commercial contracts are excluded from the definition of investment in the FTAs signed between countries of the hemisphere.

BITs and investment chapters in trade and integration agreements define investors or nationals who are entitled to the benefits accorded by each agreement. Typically the definition of *investor* covers natural persons and juridical persons (or other legal entities). In most investment instruments citizenship is the only criterion used to determine whether a natural person should be considered an investor under the agreement. In other cases the definition is broadened to include permanent residents. Residency is sometimes used to exclude natural persons from coverage of the agreement. With respect to juridical persons, three different criteria have been commonly used to define the nationality of a company or legal entity: incorporation, seat, and control. Countries with a common law tradition use the place of incorporation of a company to determine its nationality. All BITs signed by the United States and Canada with countries of the region use the place of constitution as the sole criterion to define each company covered by the treaty.

Other investment instruments such as the NAFTA and the Canada-Chile FTA, for example, follow the same approach. Under the NAFTA, to be an "investor of a party" an enterprise (and a branch of an enterprise) must be constituted or organized under the law of a party to the agreement. There is no requirement that the enterprise be controlled by nationals of a NAFTA country. However, if the enterprise is controlled by investors of a non-NAFTA country, benefits can be denied if the enterprise has no substantial business activities in the territory of the party under whose laws it is constituted. Recently this criterion has been used in agreements between countries with civil law traditions. Under the G-3 and the Mexican FTAs with Bolivia, Chile, Costa Rica, and Nicaragua, an enterprise is considered an investor of a party if it is constituted or organized (or protected in the case of the G-3) in accordance with the laws of that party. The same applies to a branch located in the territory of that party that engages in commercial activities therein. But civil law countries have traditionally relied instead on the place where the management or seat of a company is located. In the case of investment agreements signed between Latin American countries, this criterion is often combined with the place of constitution and in some cases with the requirement that the company actually must have effective economic activities in the home country. In some cases BITs use the control of a company by nationals of a party as the sole criterion to determine its nationality. This is the case of the Colombia-Peru BIT. Finally, some agreements combine the above criteria or use them as alternatives. In general, it can be said that the combination of different criteria is used in those cases in which governments are interested in restricting the benefits of an agreement to those legal entities that effectively have ties with the home country. On the contrary, when the objective is to broaden the scope of application, agreements provide for the possibility of applying different alternative criteria.

A BIT normally includes provisions regarding the treaty's entry into force as well as its duration. With some variations, the most common formulation is to provide that the treaty enters into force one month from the date of exchange of instruments of ratification and remains in force for an initial period of ten years, usually renewable according to procedures set out in detail in the agreement. Increasingly, and departing from what was common in earlier agreements, BITs apply not only to investments made after their entry into force, but also to those made prior to that date. Although in some cases this forms part of the definition of *covered investments,* in others a separate provision to that effect is included in the section dealing with application in time of the treaty. This last approach is followed in all BITs signed by the United States with countries of the region.

Admission

The section on admission refers to the entry of investments and investors of a contracting party into the territory of another contracting party. Two different approaches have been adopted with regard to this issue. Newer instruments such as the Colonia Protocol in the Mercosur, most FTAs negotiated in the region, as well as U.S. and post-NAFTA Canadian BITs (with the exception of the Canada-Venezuela agreement) call for national treatment and MFN treatment as a condition for both the preestablishment phase (admission) and the postestablishment phase of an investment. This new approach creates a right of establishment for investors and investments of the other contracting party. In fact, these instruments have been designed with the purpose of assuring the free entry of such investments— albeit with country-specific reservations—into the territory of the host country. They require national treatment and MFN treatment, and they prohibit specific performance requirements as a condition for establishment. With the exception of the Colonia Protocol, they mention that such treatment is to be provided for investments made in "like circumstances" (or in "like situations" in the case of U.S. BITs). This phrase is not, however, defined. Other BITs require that the national treatment and MFN standards be applied to investments of investors after admission of these investments; that is, they are applied only during the postestablishment phase. The Buenos Aires Protocol, like most BITs signed between countries of the region, follows this more traditional approach.

Treatment

States have incorporated the five following standards of treatment into their investment agreements: fair and equitable treatment, full protection and security, nondiscrimination, national treatment, and MFN treatment.

Fair and equitable treatment is a general concept without a precise definition. It provides a basic standard not related to the host state's domestic law and serves as an additional element in the interpretation of treaty and trade agreement provisions on investment. Full protection and security is a principle that has its origin in the modern Friendship, Commerce, and Navigation Treaties signed mainly by the United States until the 1960s. Although this principle does not create any liability for the host state, it "serves to amplify the obligations that the parties have otherwise taken upon themselves" and provides a general standard for the host state "to exercise due diligence in the protection of foreign investment."[13]

Most investment instruments in the Americas include a fair and equitable treatment clause. This standard is generally combined with the principle of nondiscrimination or that of full protection and security. In a few cases these three principles are combined. In other cases it is clear that fair and equitable treatment is to be in accordance with the principles of international law. Most treaties also require some form of protection.

The Mercosur and almost all BITs prohibit discrimination against investments of investors of the other contracting party. The term "unreasonable," "arbitrary," or "unjustified" is used with the word "discriminatory" to prohibit measures that impair the management, maintenance, use, enjoyment, or disposal of investments of investors of the other contracting party. U.S. BITs state that "neither party shall in any way impair by unreasonable and discriminatory measures the management, conduct, operation, and sale or other disposition of covered investments." In some BITs prohibited measures have to be both unreasonable (or arbitrary or unjustified) and discriminatory; in other cases, measures can either be unreasonable (or arbitrary or unjustified) or discriminatory.

All BITs, FTAs, and the Mercosur protocols provide for both national treatment and MFN treatment. Most treaties state that each contracting party

---

13. Dolzer and Stevens (1995, p. 61). These treaties provided for "the most constant protection and security."

has to grant to investments of the other parties treatment no less favorable than that it accords to investments of its own nationals or companies or to those of third countries. Some agreements also emphasize that a contracting party has to grant MFN treatment to investors of the other contracting parties if this treatment is more favorable than that it accords to its own investors. In relation to losses due to war or to other armed conflicts and civil disturbances, most investment treaties and trade arrangements provide for national treatment and MFN treatment should there be compensation. Several treaties require the better of either national treatment or MFN treatment, whereas others emphasize that these payments are to be transferable.

Transfers

Over the years through bilateral and multilateral treaty practice, provisions for transfers have become a permanent component of investment treaties. Under customary international law, which provides for monetary sovereignty, a state has the exclusive right to regulate the transfer of foreign exchange.[14] Broad limitations on such rights were first adopted in the Articles of Agreement of the IMF. However, in practice the IMF articles provide little protection, since restrictions on only current—as opposed to capital—transactions are prohibited.[15] This has prompted states to seek protection and to negotiate provisions in investment agreements that require the host state to guarantee the right of transfer of funds related to investment.

Every BIT and trade arrangement requires the host country to guarantee to investors of the other contracting party the free transfer of funds related to investments. Although almost every treaty defines in great detail which types of payments are to be included in the transfer clause, most treaties emphasize that the guarantee of transfers of funds is not limited to this list. Three types of payments are generally always included in the definition of transfers of funds that are to be guaranteed: returns (profits, interests, dividends, and other current incomes), repayments of loans, and proceeds of the total or partial liquidation of an investment. In addition, other types of payments are often listed, such as additional contributions to capital for the maintenance or development of an

14. Dolzer and Stevens (1995, p. 85).

15. See International Monetary Fund (IMF) (1990, Article VII:3(b) and Article XIV:2).

investment, bonuses and honoraria, wages and other remuneration accruing to a citizen of the other contracting party, compensation or indemnification, and payments arising out of an investment dispute.

Most treaties also stipulate that transfers are to be effected in a convertible currency. Some treaties specify that it could be the currency in which the investment was made or any other convertible currency. U.S. BITs require that transfers be made in a freely usable currency.[16] With respect to the exchange rate, treaties generally state that transfers are to be made at the normal rate applicable on the date of the transfer. Almost all treaties stress that transfers are to be effected without delay. A few BITs, in particular all Chilean treaties, define *without delay* as the "normal time" necessary to complete the formalities with respect to the transfer. This normal time ranges from thirty days to six months.

Some treaties allow for limitations or exceptions to transfers, underlining, for instance, that transfers are to be in accordance with the laws and regulations of the contracting parties. Chile reserves the right to maintain requirements and adopt measures for the purpose of preserving the stability of its currency.[17] Moreover, in the BITs signed by Chile transfers of capital are restricted for a period of one year. Other investment instruments state that the contracting parties could establish restrictions with respect to the free transfer of payments related to investments in the case of balance of payments difficulties. These restrictions are to be exercised for a limited period of time in an equitable way, in good faith, and in a nondiscriminatory manner.

Expropriation

An important concern of foreign investors is to ensure that their interests are protected in the event of expropriation of their investments by the host country. Treaties generally refer to either expropriation or nationalization (or to both) without differentiating between these terms. In fact, the language is broad enough to allow for coverage of "indirect" or "creeping" expropriations—that is, measures with effects equivalent to those of expropriation or nationaliza-

16. The five currencies recognized by the IMF as freely usable are the U.S. dollar, German mark, Japanese yen, pound sterling, and French franc.

17. These measures are explained in Annex G-09.1 of the Canada-Chile FTA.

tion. Under customary international law states are allowed to expropriate foreign investments as long as it is done on a nondiscriminatory basis (that is, affording national treatment and MFN treatment), for a public purpose, under due process of law, and with compensation.[18] BITs signed among countries in the region, the Mercosur protocols, and all the FTAs prohibit the expropriation of investments except when these conditions are met. Regarding the standard for this compensation, most agreements use the Hull formula, according to which compensation should be "prompt, adequate, and effective." Only in a very few cases is the more general expression "just compensation" used. In relation to the value of the expropriated investment, most treaties use the term "market value" or "fair market value," whereas others speak of the investment's "genuine value" immediately before the expropriatory action was taken or became known, thus protecting the investor from the reduction in value that may result as a consequence of the expropriation. Agreements also stipulate that compensation is to include interest, and in most cases they specify that it should be calculated at a normal commercial rate from the date of expropriation. In general, payments must be fully realizable, freely transferable, and made without delay. In some instances it is also necessary that payments be transferable at the prevailing market rate of exchange on the date of expropriation. In most cases, however, exchange rates are not dealt with in the context of expropriation. Instead, general transfer provisions are applicable.

Dispute Settlement

Following traditional treaty practice, provisions for the settlement of disputes between contracting parties are included both in BITs and in regional trade arrangements with provisions for investment. In the case of all FTAs, disputes between contracting parties fall under the general dispute settlement mechanisms included in these agreements. Such a mechanism is based on consultation and, failing resolution through consultation, panel review. In the Andean Group state-to-state disputes are referred to the Andean Court of

---

18. Some treaties add expressions such as "national interest," "public use," "public interest," "public benefit," "social interest," or "national security." Notwithstanding the fact that *public purpose* is difficult to define in precise terms, there is a general consensus that a state can adopt expropriatory measures only when there is a collective interest that justifies it.

Justice. The Colonia Protocol provides for resolution of disputes concerning its interpretation or application through the dispute settlement procedures established in the Brasilia Protocol of December 17, 1991. When disputes involve a third state, the Buenos Aires Protocol refers them to ad hoc arbitration.

All BITs have provisions for disputes between states concerning the interpretation or application of the treaties to be submitted, at the request of either party, to ad hoc arbitral tribunals. Arbitration, however, has to be preceded by consultations. Typically BITs set some rules for the constitution of an ad hoc tribunal. They generally provide that each party is to appoint an arbitrator, usually within a two-month period. These arbitrators are required to select a national of a third state to serve as chairman of the tribunal within a period that varies from thirty days to two, three, or five months depending on the treaty, although a two-month period seems the most used formulation. The treaties also include procedures for those cases in which agreement regarding appointments cannot be reached or other circumstances prevent the tribunal from being constituted.

Moreover, general procedures to be followed by the arbitration tribunal are normally included in the agreements. The provisions in this regard state that decisions of the tribunal are to be made by a majority of votes, and they are to be final and binding on both parties. Apart from these basic indications, BITs leave it to the tribunal itself to determine its own procedures. BITs entered into by the United States refer to the U.N. Commission on International Trade Law (UNCITRAL) arbitration rules when agreement on procedures cannot be reached. Finally, in most cases BITs do not set time limits for an arbitration tribunal to render its decision. However, U.S. BITs do. They state that "unless otherwise agreed, all submissions shall be made and all hearings shall be completed within six months of the date of selection of the third arbitrator, and the arbitral panel shall render its decisions within two months of the date of the final submissions or the date of the closing of the hearings, whichever is later."

Almost all investment instruments include separate provisions for the settlement of investor-state disputes. This constitutes a departure from traditional treaty practice in this field, whereby no such mechanism was provided. Therefore, a foreign investor was limited to bringing claim against the host state in a domestic court or having its home state assume his claim against the host state (diplomatic protection). Investment agreements include reference to a specific institutional arbitration mechanism. They normally refer to arbitration under the International Convention on the Settlement of Investment Disputes between States and Nationals of Other States (ICSID Convention) or under the

ICSID Additional Facility Rules when either the host or the home state of the foreign investor is not an ICSID contracting party.[19] Following what is increasingly the practice in modern investment treaties, most agreements include alternative forms of arbitration such as the UNCITRAL rules.[20] These might prove particularly relevant where ICSID arbitration is unavailable due to jurisdictional constraints.

The typical treaty requires that the investor and the host state seek to solve the dispute amicably through consultations and negotiations before taking it to arbitration. In some cases a certain period of time has to elapse before a dispute can be submitted to arbitration. Evidently investors also have the right to bring disputes to local courts of the host state. However, agreements differ in the way recourse to local remedies is treated. The most common approach is to allow the investor to choose between referring the dispute to local courts or resorting to arbitration. When following this approach, a number of BITs signed between Latin American countries as well as the Colonia Protocol state that election by the investor of either international arbitration or domestic remedies "shall be final." Other agreements provide for arbitration only when a case has previously been submitted to local courts and a certain period of time (usually eighteen months) has elapsed without a final decision being made, the decision is inconsistent with the agreement, or the decision is "manifestly unjust." A different approach has been taken in recent U.S. BITs. In order to avoid inconsistent decisions in different forums, the agreements do not allow recourse to international arbitration if the investors have already submitted the disputes to local courts or administrative tribunals.

Most investment instruments cover a wide range of investment disputes. Some BITs refer to "disputes relating to investments" between an investor and a host state, whereas all the FTAs, the Colonia Protocol, and a few recently concluded BITs mention disputes relating to the provisions of the agreements themselves. It can be argued that the broad scope of these provisions allows an investor to make use of the dispute settlement mechanism for disputes relating to the denial of admission of an investment when the treaty provides for

19. The ICSID Convention came into force in 1966. On the ICSID Convention, see International Convention for the Settlement of Investment Disputes between States and Nationals of Other States (ICSID) (1985); on the ICSID Additional Facility Rules, see ICSID (1979).

20. Only in the case of the Haiti–United States BIT is a reference made to arbitration under the International Chamber of Commerce (ICC). On UNCITRAL, see U.N. Commission on International Trade Law (1976).

national and MFN treatment with respect to the establishment or acquisition of an investment in sectors other than the ones specifically excluded. However, in some cases, such as the BITs signed by Canada with countries of the region, the decisions of a party as to whether to permit the establishment of a new business enterprise or the acquisition of an existing business enterprise by investors or prospective investors of the other party have been explicitly excluded from the mechanisms for the settlement of investment disputes.

Other Issues

Other issues are also covered in some investment agreements. A few are mentioned here: general exceptions and other derogations, performance requirements, key personnel, environmental concerns, and extraterritorial application.

GENERAL EXCEPTIONS AND OTHER DEROGATIONS. General exceptions allow countries to exempt from treaty obligations all actions related to such exceptions; that is, they often—but not always—apply to all obligations and also to all parties to an agreement. They are generally invoked for reasons of maintenance of national security, international peace and security, and public order. In the Americas the FTAs, the U.S. BITs, and the Peruvian BITs with Bolivia, Paraguay, and Venezuela permit such general exceptions. Other derogations to treaty obligations include a carve-out for taxation matters found in almost all investment agreements, exceptions to the MFN principle when a contracting party is a member of a preferential trade agreement, country-specific reservations with respect to national treatment and MFN treatment when these two standards apply during all phases of an investment, temporary derogation in case of balance of payment problems, and prudential measures to protect the rights of creditors and the stability of the financial system.

PERFORMANCE REQUIREMENTS. Several investment agreements, including U.S. and Canadian BITs, the FTAs mentioned in this chapter, the Colonia Protocol, and a few BITs signed between Latin American countries (between the Dominican Republic and Ecuador and between El Salvador and Peru) prohibit specific performance requirements. For example, the NAFTA and the Chilean FTAs with Canada and Mexico require that performance requirements—requirements to achieve a particular level or percentage of local content, to purchase local goods and services, to impose trade or foreign exchange–balancing requirements, to restrict domestic sales of goods or services, to export a given level or percentage of goods or services, to transfer technology, and to act as exclusive supplier of goods and services—be prohibited as a condition of the establishment, acquisition, expansion, management, conduct, or operation of a covered investment. The first four requirements are also prohibited as a condition of receiving an advantage (that is, a subsidy). However, there is no such limitation with respect to requirements to locate production, provide a service, train or employ workers, construct or expand particular facilities, or carry out research and development.

Moreover, there are some exceptions to the performance requirement prohibition. For example, NAFTA Article 1106(6) provides that requirements to achieve given levels of domestic content or to purchase local goods and services be allowed, provided that they are not applied in an arbitrary or unjustifiable manner or do not constitute a disguised restriction, if these measures are necessary to secure compliance with laws and regulations that are not inconsistent with the provisions of the agreement; to protect human, animal, or plant life or health; or for the conservation of exhaustible natural resources. Finally, the prohibition of performance requirements does not apply to some of the requirements stated earlier with respect to export promotion and foreign aid programs, procurement to a state enterprise, or the content of goods necessary to qualify for preferential tariffs or tariff quotas in the case of an importing party. The Andean Pact, on the other hand, establishes particular provisions for the performance of contracts for the license of technology, technical assistance, and technical services and for other technological contracts under the national laws of each member.

KEY PERSONNEL. U.S. and Canadian BITs, the FTAs covered in this chapter, and a few other BITs (those between Argentina and Nicaragua, the Dominican Republic and Ecuador, and El Salvador and Peru) provide for the temporary entry of managers and other key personnel. U.S. BITs allow investors of another party to hire top managerial personnel of their choice, regardless of nationality. Most other investment instruments use a different wording. They state that a contracting party may not require that an enterprise of that contracting party appoint to senior management positions individuals of any particular nationality. They also mention that a contracting party may require that a majority of the board of directors of an enterprise that is an investment under the agreement be of a particular nationality, provided that the requirement does not materially impair the ability of the investor to exercise control over its investment. The FTAs, in the respective chapter of each on temporary entry for businesspersons, grant temporary entry to a businessperson to establish, develop, administer, or provide advice or technical services that are key to the operation of an investment as long as the businessperson or his or her enterprise has committed or is in the process of committing a substantial amount of capital. The businessperson must comply with existing immigration laws and work in a capacity that is supervisory or executive or involves essential skills. U.S. BITs have a similar provision, whereas Canadian BITs have a more general clause that refers only to a businessperson in a managerial or executive capacity. Labor certification tests or other procedures of similar effect and any numerical restriction relating to temporary entry of businesspersons are also strictly forbidden under most investment agreements covering key personnel.

ENVIRONMENTAL CONCERNS. The FTAs and most post-NAFTA BITs signed by Canada mention that nothing is to be construed so as to prevent a party from adopting, maintaining, or enforcing any measure otherwise consistent with the agreement that it considers appropriate to ensure that investment activity in its territory is undertaken in a manner sensitive to domestic health, safety, and environmental concerns.

EXTRATERRITORIAL APPLICATION. Finally, the Mexican FTAs with Bolivia, Costa Rica, and Nicaragua provide that a party may not, with respect to the investments of its investors established and organized in accordance with the legislation of another party, exercise jurisdiction or adopt any measure that has the effect of extraterritorial application of its legislation or of obstructing trade between the parties or between a party and a nonparty country.

Challenges Ahead

Considerable progress has been achieved with respect to the rules and disciplines covering investment in the Americas. Notwithstanding the existing consensus, a number of issues will need to be addressed. Without prejudging the level of priority that they should be assigned, a few of these challenges are identified in this section.

A central issue is the need to determine what role an investment agreement should have. Should it aim at only providing for nondiscrimination and investment protection with an effective dispute settlement mechanism, or should it also aim at ensuring a progressive liberalization of nonconforming measures? A first challenge is therefore to determine whether a hemispheric investment agreement would maintain or go beyond the status quo. There are obviously arguments in favor of ensuring that the liberalization that has already been achieved by countries of the Americas at the bilateral and regional levels is multilateralized. For example, most countries of the region have accepted the notion of a right of establishment accompanied by a list of reservations or country-specific exceptions. To date more than twenty countries in the Americas have signed at least one investment agreement including an obligation to accord national treatment and MFN treatment during *all* phases of an invest-ment, including the preestablishment phase. With such a framework the host country will not be pressed by foreign investors to open a particular sensitive sector listed as an exception to the rules in the agreement, and the foreign investor can rest assured that the host government will not alter the admission requirements. However, the broader the scope of the reservations, the less significant will be the results of an open framework. But again, the main issue here is whether an investment agreement would go beyond a standstill commit-ment and aim at a progressive liberalization of nonconforming measures with, for instance, a built-in agenda.

There has also been intense competition among both developed and devel-oping countries in trying to attract FDI by using investment incentives. Such measures have at times rendered obsolete the concept of comparative ad-vantage. Investment incentives—be they fiscal, financial, or of other types—are often used to subsidize investors to come and establish a plant or firm in a foreign country. Both central governments and subnational states (that is, provinces and states) make great use of these instruments to attract foreign investment. Although they have not been identified as a prime determinant of FDI, investment incentives often play a role in influencing the location of some specific investments. They may also lead countries to embark on costly "grant shopping," resulting in discrimination and distortions in the allocation of production and resources, essentially in rent-seeking behavior by investors. Countries with fewer resources may find it difficult to compete on a level playing field with other states using such instruments. Countries with federal structures have traditionally been very hesitant to tackle this issue in inter-national negotiations. They often feel they cannot or should not bind their subnational states. A discussion on investment incentives could address issues related to their scope, their codification, the prohibition of some types of incentives, the principles of transparency and nondiscrimination (national treatment and MFN treatment) as well as possible exceptions, and the obligations of standstill and rollback commitments.

But more generally, the question is this: should an investment agreement address issues of deeper integration? Rules on mergers and acquisitions and on subsidies and taxation, among other issues, may indirectly raise investment barriers and significantly reduce the benefits of the agreement. Therefore, should an investment agreement aim at leveling the playing field and at eliminating rent-seeking behavior by investors and misallocation of resources? Or should those issues be addressed elsewhere in other FTAA chapters or in other agreements?[21]

Another major concern has to do with the impact of a very broad definition of the term *investment* on the provisions of an agreement and on an eventual liberalization process. Although numerous questions can be addressed here, only a few are mentioned. How could the objective of excluding short-term speculative capital flows be reconciled with a broad definition? Should the definition be narrowed, or should it be broad enough to allow for the inclusion of new forms of investment while providing for the definition of what is not an investment? Should it include safeguards provisions? How could it be geared toward encouraging "patient capital"?[22] Finally, how would obligations related to a right of establishment, expropriation and compensation, transfers, and dispute settlement apply to a broad definition? What are the implications?

Finally, in negotiating an investment agreement within an FTAA context countries of the region will strive for a balanced framework that will ensure mutual advantage and increased benefits for all participants. In so doing they may wish to review their recent experience with their own investment instruments and draw lessons from the MAI negotiations. They will have to ensure consistency with an eventual WTO agreement should such an agreement be negotiated and completed before the end of the FTAA negotiations. They will also need to provide for compatibility between the service and

21. On issues of deeper integration, see Schwanen (1996).

22. The term *patient capital* refers to FDI. It is borrowed from an issues paper presented at an informal seminar on multilateral rules for investment held by the OECD in Paris on December 2, 1998.

investment frameworks in the FTAA. But more important, as was mentioned earlier, countries need to reflect on the role that an investment agreement should play. What is it that they want to achieve with such an agreement?

References

Dolzer, R., and M. Stevens. 1995. *Bilateral Investment Treaties.* Boston: International Center for Settlement of Investment Disputes/Martinus Nijhoff Publishers.

General Agreement on Tariffs and Trade. 1955. *Basic Instruments and Selected Documents.* Geneva: GATT Secretariat.

———. 1986. *Punta del Este Ministerial Declaration.* Geneva: GATT Secretariat.

Graham, E. M., and P. R. Krugman. 1990. "Trade-Related Investment Measures." In *Completing the Uruguay Round: A Results-Oriented Approach to the GATT Trade Negotiations,* edited by J. J. Schott. Washington, D.C.: Institute for International Economics.

Graham, E. M., P. R. Krugman, and P. Sauvé. 1996. "Toward a Rules-Based Regime for Investment: Issues and Challenges." In *Investment Rules for the Global Economy: Enhancing Access to Markets,* edited by P. Sauvé and D. Schwanen. Toronto: C. D. Howe Institute.

International Convention for the Settlement of Investment Disputes between States and Nationals of Other States. 1979. *ICSID Additional Facility for the Administration of Conciliation, Arbitration and Fact-Finding Proceedings.* Washington, D.C.

———. 1985. *ICSID Basic Documents.* Washington, D.C.

International Monetary Fund. 1990. *Articles of Agreement of the International Monetary Fund Adopted at the United Nations Monetary and Financial Conference, Bretton Woods, New Hampshire, July 22, 1944; Last Amended 28 June 1990.* Washington, D.C.

Organization for Economic Cooperation and Development. 1996. *The Multilateral Agreement on Investment: Chairman's Notes on Main Issues.* Paris.

———. 1998a. *Chairman's Statement, Under Secretary of State Stuart Eizenstat (USA), Executive Committee in Special Session.* Paris.

———. 1998b. *Ministerial Statement on the Multilateral Agreement on Investment (MAI).* Paris.

Sauvé, P. 1994. "A First Look at Investment in the Final Act of the Uruguay Round." *Journal of World Trade* 28 (October): 5–16.

Schwanen, D. 1996. "Investment and the Global Economy: Key Issues in Rulemaking." In *Investment Rules for the Global Economy: Enhancing Access to Markets,* edited by P. Sauvé and D. Schwanen. Toronto: C. D. Howe Institute.

U.N. Commission on International Trade Law. 1976. *Decision on UNCITRAL Rules*. U.N. doc. A/CN.9/IX/CRP.4/Add.1, amended by U.N. doc. A/CN.9/ SR.178.

World Trade Organization. 1996. *Annual Report, Special Topic: Trade and Foreign Investment*. Geneva.

CHAPTER SEVENTEEN

Approaches to Competition Policy

Edward M. Graham

In September 1998 an "ad hoc group of experts" met to advise the Secretary General of the United Nations Conference on Trade and Development (UNCTAD) on whether there should be a new round of international trade negotiations. The experts overwhelmingly felt that the Uruguay Round indeed had left unfinished or even untouched many issues of importance to the world trading system. Among the most important of these issues, it was agreed, was the role competition policy might play in the multilateral system. Latin America experts especially underscored that competition policy should be a centerpiece of future negotiations.

Two decades ago this last fact would have been implausible. At that time there was little or no perceived need for competition policy in Latin America, and indeed no countries in Latin America had competition laws or enforcement authorities in place. Further, no Latin nation or any other nation would have endorsed making competition policy part of the international trade agenda. Although there were some provisions for competition policy in the unratified 1947 Havana Charter for an International Trade Organization, the idea subsequently disappeared from the multilateral agenda.[1]

---

1. It did not disappear entirely, however. With the creation of the European Common Market—the precursor of today's European Union (EU)—in 1959, the European Economic Commission was granted powers to enforce certain aspects of competition policy,

Today the situation has changed substantially. A number of Latin American nations now have in place competition laws and enforcement agencies, and other nations in the region are contemplating establishing similar laws and agencies. Within the World Trade Organization (WTO) the issue of competition policy has been resurrected. A WTO Working Group on Trade and Competition Policy meets regularly, although this group has not yet put forth any recommendations.

Why has this shift occurred? In Latin America the answer certainly lies in the trend to replace inward-looking, often *dirigiste* development policies with outward-looking, market-oriented ones. The most important step to take in such a policy shift, doubtlessly, is to reform trade policies by opening domestic economies to competition from outside through the removal of restrictions on imports and foreign direct investment (FDI). This reform is itself a form of competition policy. It brings the benefits of greater competition, with effects both on the demand side (consumer welfare is enhanced) and, perhaps more important, on the supply side. The latter benefits come when domestic firms must compete with foreign firms rather than being protected from competition on dubious "infant industry" grounds.[2] Throughout Latin America impressive steps in this direction have been implemented, albeit the process is far from complete.

Such opening might be the most important single step that small nations can take to achieve the goals of competition policy. Indeed, many specialists in development have argued that for smaller economies open trade and FDI policies are sufficient to ensure that there is adequate competition in these economies. Therefore, they have often argued that formal competition policy beyond open trade and FDI policies is unnecessary. During the past five or so years, however, this thinking has been reevaluated in light of the persistence of

---

largely on the grounds that private restrictive practices should not "undo" the benefits of liberalized trade achieved via the European Common Market. Later in this chapter some aspects of European competition policy are discussed. Also, during the 1970s there was discussion of a Code on Restrictive Business Practices within the UNCTAD, but this code was never ratified.

2. This statement is not meant to imply that goals of expanding exports are not also important. Such expansion can bring about important spillover effects bearing on long-term dynamic efficiency. However, the point is that from the specific point of view of competition policy the main benefits of trade liberalization come from domestic market opening.

domestic barriers to market contestability in many Latin nations. Experience has shown that even if formal trade and investment barriers are lowered, there can remain significant barriers to entry by new firms that are created and maintained by incumbent firms. These barriers tend to be especially pervasive in certain service sectors and in the distribution sector. The latter can create significant barriers to otherwise highly competitive imports of manufactured goods.

Such incumbent firms, it should be noted, can include local affiliates of multinational enterprises in positions of domestic monopoly or oligopoly. It is not uncommon that these affiliates originally entered into Latin economies under import substitution regimes whereby the affiliates were assured of protection from competition as a condition for establishing local production, including use of local suppliers of inputs under various domestic content requirements. Often the result has been that an affiliate itself, as well as its local suppliers, has been noncompetitive relative to imports or entry by other multinational firms. Under such circumstances a local affiliate is quite likely to seek continued protection from competition, not to be a voice for more open markets.

In short, experience has shown that open trade and investment policies, although necessary to create a market-driven and efficient domestic economy, might not be sufficient. In such instances domestic competition policy can be an important complement to an open trade and investment policy: each works better in the presence of the other than standing alone. Neither policy is a substitute for the other. The gains from an open trade policy are increased if barriers to domestic market contestability are reduced via effective competition policy, whereas competition policy works best if the economy is open to imports and FDI.

At the same time it has become increasingly apparent that even if Latin nations successfully develop domestic firms that are highly competitive in the sense that these firms can meet international standards for quality, performance, and price, significant international barriers to the export of the goods and services offered by these firms might nonetheless persist. In some instances these barriers are the result of overt trade-restricting policies of importing nations. For example, in the textile and apparel sectors, even after the phase-out of the Multi-Fiber Arrangement (MFA) tariffs will be very high or, in the agricultural sector, not only do high tariffs persist, but quota and quota-like instruments are profligate. These problems must be addressed in traditional trade policy negotiations. But other less overt barriers also exist that cannot be addressed via traditional trade liberalization, such as problems of access to distribution channels in potential export markets. Latin nations, therefore, have a growing interest in how to overcome these barriers, and one potential avenue might be multilateral negotiations centering on competition policy.

There also is a third barrier to exports that is particularly vexing to Latin nations: the proliferation of the use of antidumping measures by many nations as a means of restricting import competition. Once upon a time, antidumping measures were used infrequently and by only a minority of the world's trading nations (but these were among the largest trading entities, such as Australia, Canada, the EU, and the United States). But the past decade has witnessed a proliferation both of the number of countries that use antidumping measures (over forty at the last count) and of the frequency of use. In this matter it must be noted that the Latin American nations are not themselves "clean"; many nations in the region have become frequent users of antidumping measures. Nonetheless, in net terms the Latin countries are "victims" rather than "perpetrators" of antidumping measures, and, in contrast to the United States, most would gladly give up their own antidumping regimes if others would do likewise. Therefore, reform of antidumping measures looms quite large on the agenda.

There is a split among experts as to whether reform of antidumping measures belongs on the agenda of the WTO Trade and Competition Policy Working Group. Certain nations, led by Japan and Korea, insist that it does. Predictably, the United States leads those nations that take the contrary position. The former nations argue that antidumping measures facilitate anticompetitive practices by incumbent firms in domestic markets, such as cartelization. The latter nations insist that major reform of antidumping measures is not a pragmatic political reality and that there are other important issues on the trade and competition policy agenda that might fail to be addressed if reform of antidumping measures becomes the major issue undertaken by the WTO working group.

This chapter explores some of the issues raised in the prologue in more detail. There is a detailed discussion of exactly what competition policy is and what its goals are, a discussion of substantive issues in the regulation of private business practices, a brief look at issues involving enforcement of competition law, and last, an examination of the interface between competition policy and international trade.

Competition Policy: What Is It, and What Is It Supposed to Achieve?

Formally, *competition policy* is any policy or set of policies meant to eliminate or reduce market entry barriers to new sellers in any definable market. Therefore, competition policy encompasses the domain of traditional antitrust or antimonopoly policy—that is, the regulation and control of private business practices that have the effect or potential of restricting entry into a market by new sellers. Because governmental laws, policies, and regulations can have the effect of protecting incumbent sellers within a market, policies to deregulate or offset governmentally induced market entry barriers can also legitimately be termed competition policy. By this definition, liberal trade policy is a subset of competition policy, as noted earlier.

However, even though there are substantive interlinks among private business practices and government policies, governments typically separate the regulation and control of private restrictive business practices (that is, antitrust or antimonopoly policy) from other aspects of competition policy. Therefore, in the governments of all countries international trade and investment policies are pursued by agencies other than competition agencies, and these latter agencies generally have no jurisdiction over international trade and investment policies. Likewise, most matters of governmental regulation of domestic markets are not within the domain of competition authorities. Indeed, the basic laws regarding private anticompetitive practices, domestic regulation, and international trade and investment are themselves most often separate documents and not always consistent with one another. It should be no surprise that this separation can create significant public policy conflicts.[3]

A concept closely akin to competition policy is market contestability. A market is contestable if, in the event that prices rise above competitive levels, there is no barrier to entry of new sellers into the market. Alternatively expressed, a market is contestable if there are no barriers to entry by new sellers when incumbent sellers are earning supranormal returns. Therefore, a market can be contestable even if the actual number of sellers is limited if there is no chance that these sellers can raise prices to earn supranormal profits without inducing the entry of new sellers that would tend to drive the prices down and profits back to normal levels. Likewise, a market is contestable if a potential

3. On this see Graham and Richardson (1997) and Rosenthal and Nicolaides (1997).

seller that is more efficient than incumbent sellers is in fact able to enter the market. If this entry is blocked for any reason, the market is not contestable.

Contestability, however, is not an absolute concept. Markets can be imperfectly contestable if entry barriers exist that are substantial but not insurmountable. Indeed, markets would rarely be either completely noncontestable or perfectly contestable. As has been noted, one reason markets might not be fully contestable is the existence of government regulations that prohibit or discourage new entry.

But even in the absence of such regulations, not all markets are contestable. The main reason is that sunk costs often must be incurred before market entry can be achieved. Costs are "sunk" if they are fixed (they do not vary with respect to short-term output of the relevant product or service) and they are irrecoverable (once the costs are incurred, they cannot be immediately reversed). Not all fixed costs are fully irrecoverable, because these costs might create assets that can be sold to another new entrant, but this recovery is uncertain, so potential entrants might nonetheless treat them as sunk. Sunk costs must be amortized if the entry into a market is to earn a satisfactory return, and this implies that prices must be above marginal cost.

If sunk costs are sufficiently high relative to total revenue that can be generated at any attainable combination of price and resulting quantity demanded, the market might in fact be able to support only one seller, in which case the market is termed a "natural monopoly." The classic example is the provision of a good or service that can be achieved only with a very large physical "network"; for instance, to provide electrical power there must be created, at large sunk cost, a network of cables, towers, and switching and transforming stations such that only one provider can economically operate in any given locality. The provision of local telecommunications services also is often cited as an example. Because markets for electricity and local telecommunications services indeed seem to be instances of natural monopoly, it is argued that these markets must be regulated in order to protect consumers from abusive practices by the monopoly supplier. Public ownership of the network has also been argued on this same ground.

But although sunk costs in such markets may indeed create natural monopolies and justify some regulation, the regulation itself can become easily abused via "regulatory capture." This happens most often if the regulators see their interests as coinciding with those of the incumbent supplier rather than the consumers. The worst abuses are ones that inhibit market contestability. The list of such abuses is long and includes mandated tie-ins (for example, governmental requirements that telecommunications consumers use only peripheral devices supplied by the monopolist, even if they could be supplied in a competitive market), unnecessary backward vertical foreclosure created by regulation (for example, prohibiting independent generators of electricity from being connected to the power distribution grid so that the monopoly owner of the grid also becomes a monopoly generator of the power even if there could be competition in supplying it), and similar arrangements. Often these abuses come about over time and changing circumstances when the regulation fails to adapt to the changes. Advances in technology, for example, can change the nature of the sunk costs that are required for market entry so that a natural monopoly evolves into a market where competition becomes economically feasible. But if regulations forbid or discourage new entry, the advantages enabled by these advances might not be fully realized. Indeed, operating under the cover of regulation, the incumbent monopolist might actually deliberately slow down the rate of adoption of new technology.[4] An "unholy alliance" between service providers, often state owned, and national regulatory agencies can help to explain the relative technological backwardness or the high cost structures of some telecommunications service providers in Latin America.

There is an exceptional circumstance, however, in which it might be desirable for the government to restrict market entry and hence deliberately to reduce contestability. This is the instance of protection of intellectual property. Intellectual property consists of "intangible assets" such as knowledge (including technology) and textual and visual entities where the property is the entity itself and not the medium whereby it is stored or represented. Intellectual property is generated via the creative use of the human mind, and often the initial creation of the property entails a far greater sunk cost than subsequent reproduction of the same intangible asset. The most important such case is the creation of new technology, where the sunk cost is for research and development (R&D). R&D expenditures are usually not recoverable and are subject to significant uncertainty with respect to whether commercializable results will follow. But if the result of this expenditure is in fact a commercially significant new technology, this technology might be of substantial commercial value.

---

4. Therefore, for example, it has been found that in nations where the telecommunications industry is a publicly owned monopoly or is heavily regulated, the quality of service provision is actually lower than in nations where there is private ownership that is less heavily regulated. On this see Petrazzini (1996).

Because it often is possible for rival firms to duplicate technology at much lower cost than that of its initial creation through "back-engineering" of the end product, a strong case can be made for giving the innovator exclusive rights to exploit the technology via intellectual property protection for some duration of time. Arguably, in the absence of such protection the incentive to sink resources into its initial creation will be eliminated or greatly reduced.[5] Similar (although perhaps less compelling) arguments can be made for protection of other forms of intellectual property, such as the creation of artistic products or even trade names. By allowing only the owners of the relevant property to sell it or otherwise to work it, society encourages the expenditure of resources to create the property in the first place, and without the property we ostensibly would all be the poorer.

A question that has been much debated (but has been largely resolved in recent years in scholarly circles if not entirely in application of law) is whether competition policy should protect only the competitive process or whether there also is a role for this policy to protect individual competitors. The consensus among most economists and lawyers who specialize in the area today is that the goal of competition policy is not to protect specific competitors per se, even if failure to do so might result in sellers exiting a market and leaving behind a monopolistic or oligopolistic market structure. The reason is simply that if competition policy were to see its mission as to protect specific competitors, it would run the risk of sheltering inefficient sellers from competition from more efficient ones.[6]

This implies that the ultimate goal of competition policy is to promote efficiency, and most specialists today would agree with this implication. However, this near-consensus has been reached only in relatively recent times. In the United States, for example, until the late 1970s the U.S. Department of Justice, through its Antitrust Division (ATD), clearly aimed at preventing

5. The extent to which this is true seems to vary greatly from industry to industry. See, for example, Scherer and Ross (1990).

6. There is a general exception of sorts to this, and that is the enforcement of various antifraud and consumer protection laws. In some countries such laws are enforced by competition authorities (in the United States, for example, the Federal Trade Commission, which shares authority over antitrust law enforcement, also enforces certain consumer protection laws). Such laws are meant to protect individual competitors only from fraudulent means to put them out of business (such as besmirchment of product or reputation), not from legitimate competition.

markets from becoming too concentrated, irrespective of considerations of efficiency. The main manifestation of this doctrine was in the review of mergers and acquisitions (M&A). Prior to the 1980s, if the effect of a merger or acquisition was determined to materially increase seller concentration in a market (including some instances in which the market was rather narrowly defined), the ATD often acted to block the merger even if it could be demonstrated that the merger or acquisition would result in efficiencies that would be passed to consumers.[7] Beginning in the early 1980s, however, ATD doctrine changed, and M&A became subject to an "efficiency defense" whereby even if market concentration were to increase significantly, the merger or acquisition would generally pass ATD review if a significant efficiency that would not be achieved in the absence of the merger or acquisition could be demonstrated and benefits deriving from the efficiency would be passed on to consumers. (Even now, however, a merger or acquisition that results in one seller achieving a monopoly or near-monopoly position in the market is likely to be subjected to close scrutiny and possible blockage by the ATD even if an efficiency can be identified.)[8] Also, it should be noted that certain provisions of U.S. law, most notably the still-extant Robinson Patman Act, protect competitors. The ATD has rather openly stated that it will not pursue Robinson Patman cases when the effect might be to shield an inefficient competitor from an efficient one, but this act can nonetheless be invoked in the United States in private action cases

---

7. Technically speaking, the ATD cannot on its own actually block a merger or acquisition; it can only challenge such a move in court. Such a challenge is usually tantamount to a block, however, because for most firms defending against such a challenge would be a very costly matter, and the probability of a successful defense would be low.

8. Other defenses might be allowed for such a merger, however, such as imminent failure of one of the firms in the absence of merger or acquisition (the "failing firm" defense) or even likely poor financial performance of one of the firms in this absence (the "flailing firm" defense). The latter seems to have prevailed, for example, in the decision of the ATD not to challenge the merger of McDonnell Douglas with Boeing in 1997, even though this resulted in a single domestic U.S. seller of wide-bodied commercial aircraft and only two sellers worldwide. The ATD did require certain restructuring of the defense business of the combined firms, and the merger was challenged by the EU. This latter challenge was settled when Boeing agreed to certain conditions, in particular to ending exclusive selling agreements with certain airlines. Such agreements, it might be noted, could in fact be deemed illegal in U.S. as well as European law, but the U.S. position was that they resulted in efficiencies and therefore were legal.

(see the later section in this chapter on domestic competition policy enforcement).

If the ultimate goal is to promote efficiency, does increased market contestability achieve this goal? In most situations increased market contestability does enhance efficiency, because if incumbent sellers do not operate efficiently—resulting in higher prices than might otherwise be possible or in inferior product or service attributes—if the market is contestable, some other seller is likely to enter who offers a lower price or a better product or service. In a contestable market, even if no entry actually occurs, the threat of such entry is likely to keep incumbents "on their toes" by giving them a very big incentive to be efficient themselves.

As noted, however, there are situations in which more contestability might not necessarily be compatible with the goal of enhancing efficiency, such as instances in which intellectual property protection is warranted. In particular, because the creation of new technology is known to be the most important long-run driver of efficiency (and also because the creation of artistic products enhances the quality of life), no policymaker would knowingly destroy the incentives to create intellectual property. But even so there are important questions that must be asked. Intellectual property rights do reduce market contestability, and with associated costs. Therefore, how much intellectual property protection is optimal? Can such protection become overzealous, such that marginal benefits from additional protection are dominated by the marginal costs of decreased contestability? Is the optimal set of policies the same irrespective of the category of product or service that is protected? Although specialists agree that intellectual property protection is necessary, there is little consensus that current law and policy are optimal.[9]

Intellectual property protection is not the only domain in which there are potential conflicts between enhancing market contestability and enhancing economic efficiency. The next section examines substantive issues pertaining to regulation of private anticompetitive business practices with an eye to these potential conflicts.

Substantive Issues in the Regulation of Private Business Practices

An unfortunate fact is that consensus that the basic goal of competition policy is to optimize economic efficiency by making markets as contestable as

9. Scherer and Ross (1990).

possible (but keeping in mind possible cases in which enhanced efficiency and enhanced market contestability are at cross-purposes) is of rather recent origin. One consequence is that the two most fully developed bodies of competition law and practice—those of the United States and the EU—were put into place before this consensus. Therefore, in both areas provisions in the law exist that can conflict with the goal. The conflicts might be diminishing: because competition authorities and judges on both sides of the Atlantic increasingly are guided by this common goal, there is a trend for both sets of laws to be enforced with efficiency and contestability in mind. Nonetheless, enforcement agencies and courts must work within the bounds of their legal authority, and conflicts still exist.

Bearing these considerations in mind, this section examines substantive aspects of competition law in the United States and the EU. This is of relevance to Latin America, because there is pressure worldwide for competition law to conform to either the U.S. or the European "model." Uniformity in competition law is desirable so that, to as great an extent as possible, conflicts among laws and enforcement procedures of different nations can be minimized. This also suggests that convergence of the two models themselves would be desirable, but alas, this convergence is not yet a complete fact.

With respect to cartels, U.S. law (the Sherman Act) mentions "agreements, combinations or conspiracies in restraint of trade," whereas European law mentions price fixing, control of production, discrimination among buyers, and other practices used to facilitate cartel behavior. There is little conflict between EU and U.S. law in the treatment of cartels. In both Europe and the United States most cartels are per se illegal, with few exceptions.

The differences between EU and U.S. law regarding cartels mostly concern these exceptions. In Europe there are "block exemptions" whereby whole industries or sectors are granted limited immunity from competition law. Exclusive dealings between automobile manufacturers and distributors and retailers, for example, are subject to a block exemption that has led to quasi cartelization of the auto market. The European steel sector (covered by the law of the European Iron and Steel Community and not that of the EU) operates within a sanctioned "rationalization" cartel. In general, a cartel-like arrangement can be granted an exemption under EU law under the following criteria (all four must be met): it contributes to improving the production or distribution of goods or promoting technological progress (therefore, European cartels are subject to an efficiency defense not present in U.S. law), it must allow consumers to share in the resulting benefits, it must not impose restrictions superfluous to achieving those benefits, and it must not lead to elimination of competition "in respect of a substantial part of the product in question."[10]

Under these criteria, European consortia organized by firms to conduct and disseminate R&D generally are not treated as cartels. Since the 1980s there has also been a limited exemption for R&D consortia in the United States. However, in neither Europe nor the United States can consortium members cartelize markets for products or services embodying the resulting technologies via price fixing or production-restricting agreements. Consortium members can withhold technology from nonconsortium rivals. Other exceptions in U.S. law are very few. The United States exempts major league baseball from its antitrust laws, and this sport is thus cartelized. Also exempt are cartels that are created solely for the purpose of regulating exports.

Both the United States and Europe regulate monopoly. But in this area matters are not as clear as in the area of cartels, either in theory or in practice. In practice, the issues that matter with respect to monopolization of markets can be imperfectly categorized into three subissues: regulation of monopoly per se or of "incipient monopoly" (sometimes termed regulation of horizontal restraints); regulation of vertical restraints (agreements between firms and their "upstream" suppliers of inputs or the "downstream" distributors, wholesalers, and retailers that handle their products that might have the effect of impeding entry by competing firms); and regulation of "predation." The next section examines each of these in turn, but keep in mind that these are not airtight categories; there is much overlap among them.

Regulation of Monopoly and Incipient Monopoly

It would follow from the discussion in the previous section that lack of contestability in a market and high market share by one or a few firms (termed variously high "market concentration" or high "seller concentration," the limiting case of which would be monopoly) are not necessarily the same thing, and accordingly neither U.S. nor European law actually prohibits high seller concentration or even monopoly. Rather, both bodies of law are concerned with the conduct of sellers in highly concentrated markets. But in the United States "to monopolize" a market is forbidden, whereas what is forbidden in Europe is

10. Nicholaidis and Vernon (1997).

"abuse of a dominant firm position" (see Treaty of Rome, Article 86). In both cases the law is rather imprecise in its wording. The framers of both laws clearly felt discomfiture with very high seller concentration, but also recognized that a firm might grow to be very large by pursuing meritorious means. Early legal opinions in the United States noted that it would be irrational to punish a firm for growing to be big if this had been achieved solely because the firm reduced its costs or improved its products at a faster rate than its competitors. (Therefore, the notion of an "efficiency defense" entered into pragmatic U.S. legal thinking long ago.) But somewhat different standards have prevailed at different times. Early in this century U.S. authorities undertook to break up certain large firms that had near-monopoly status in certain markets.[11] Not since that time, however, has a firm deemed a monopoly in the United States actually been involuntarily broken apart into smaller competing units.[12] Likewise, no effort has ever been made under European law to break up a firm deemed a monopoly.

It should be noted that in Europe regulation of monopoly is conditioned by the Treaty of Rome, Article 90, which in effect allows member nations of the EU to create sanctioned monopolies within their territories. These monopolies typically are state-controlled firms in telecommunications service provision, rail transport, electrical power generation and distribution, and so on. There has been some trend in recent years to deregulate these industries, privatize state-owned firms, and end sanctioned monopolies in some European nations. This process is far from complete, however.

Therefore, in both the United States and Europe most enforcement efforts in modern times have been directed toward preventing an incipient monopoly rather than remedying an extant monopoly. This has been largely exercised via regulation of M&A of ongoing firms. As noted in the previous section, in the United States there has been a significant change in policy toward M&A since

---

11. In the United States, as is developed more fully in the next section, courts of law are the final arbiters of competition cases. The competition enforcement agencies can bring cases against alleged violators, but the defendant in such a case always has recourse to a trial in a court of law. Therefore, the successful case is one in which the courts uphold the petition of the government to force the breakup of a monopoly, and the unsuccessful case is one in which the petition is not upheld.

12. Certain firms have voluntarily split themselves into multiple units, as has AT&T.

the 1970s. During the 1970s and earlier, U.S. enforcement agencies often acted to block a merger or an acquisition if the result would have been increased seller concentration in a market, even if the transaction might be improved efficiency.[13]

For example, suppose two smaller firms had proposed to merge in order to achieve efficiencies needed, in the mutual judgment of the firms' management, to compete with a larger and more efficient rival. Were the effect to have been significantly increased seller concentration, during the 1970s or earlier the U.S. enforcement agencies would likely have moved to block the merger irrespective of efficiency considerations. Since the 1980s, however, the case for increased efficiency would in most instances have been seen as overriding, and the merger consequently would have been allowed. Merging firms must demonstrate that the benefits of an efficiency gain will be passed on to consumers and that these benefits offset any loss to consumers that would result from reduced contestability. An exception is mergers that create very high market share. These are subject to special scrutiny under which an efficiency defense might not be allowed.

Also allowable can be a "failing firm" defense—that is, in the absence of a merger one of the firms would likely go out of business and the surviving firm gain market. A transaction might be allowed under this defense even if, in the absence of the transaction, both firms would survive but one would be unable to compete effectively with the other. This latter reason was apparently one reason for the U.S. approval of the Boeing Company's merger with McDonnell Douglas in 1996.

European merger policy is shaped by the Mergers Regulation of 1989, which established that effect on competition is the main criterion by which a merger or acquisition should be evaluated.[14] Transactions that create or enhance domi-

13. Again, in the United States the federal enforcement agencies do not, strictly speaking, have the power to block a merger, but rather have only the power to prosecute a court case to achieve this end. Under the Hart-Scott-Rodino Act the enforcement agencies can, however, request voluminous information from merging companies and can issue a finding that they will seek to block a merger. When the agencies have thus indicated that they would seek to block a merger, the expectation has generally been held that they would win the case if it were actually to come to court. Therefore, if challenged by the enforcement agencies, merging firms in the United States have in most instances either backed away from the merger or worked with the agencies to take steps to win agency approval (for instance, through divestiture of facilities).

14. Formally, Council Regulation 4064/89 on the Control of Concentrations among Undertakings.

nance are candidates for blockage.[15] Authority to regulate mergers is granted to the EU if and only if certain criteria regarding size of the merging parties and impact on Europe as a whole are met; smaller mergers whose effects are limited to national markets are not evaluated by EU authorities. Consideration of efficiencies and economic progress is relevant, but these must be "to consumers' advantage and not form an obstacle to competition."[16] This language stops short of defining an efficiency defense.

Authority to regulate mergers in both the United States and Europe extends to vertical mergers (for example, mergers between a firm producing an end product and a supplier of inputs to that firm or between that firm and a distributor of its product) and conglomerate mergers (mergers between sellers of unrelated products), as well as to horizontal mergers.

Regulation of Vertical Restraints

Vertical restraints are business practices among firms with seller-customer relations among themselves such that these practices reduce market contestability. Examples include (but are not limited to) exclusive dealing or selling arrangements, whereby, for example, a retail chain agrees to sell at retail level only items produced by one manufacturer of a particular type of product; resale price maintenance, whereby a producer of a product sold through retail outlets requires that each outlet maintain prices above a certain "floor"; territorial restrictions, whereby a manufacturer or service provider prohibits a retailer of the product or service to sell to customers outside of a specified geographical area (often such a restriction will be given in conjunction with a territorial exclusive dealing arrangement whereby the retailer is given exclusive rights to sell to customers within the specified geographical area); and "tie-in" sales, whereby a retailer is given the right to carry a manufacturer's or service provider's product or service only if the retailer agrees to carry (perhaps exclusively) certain related products or services. *Wholesaler* or *distributor* could be substituted for *retailer* in each of these descriptions.

Evaluation of vertical restraints largely rests on whether these restraints enable an efficiency that offsets the potential for loss of market contestability. Most often the issue comes down to prevention of "free ridership." An example of free ridership has already been offered in the discussion in the previous section on intellectual property protection. Rival firms that replicate an innova-

15. See Fox (1997).
16. Fox (1997).

tion of another firm without having to bear the sunk costs of R and D are free riders because they benefit from another firm's sunk costs without contributing to these costs. Free ridership is often countered by granting an exclusive dealing franchise or other vertical restraint. Consumers benefit, because in the absence of some such restraints free riders could destroy any incentive to invest in R and D.

The attitudes of competition law enforcement agencies (and courts) in the United States have moved in recent years to admit the validity of arguments against free ridership and hence to allow certain restraints that once were prohibited. Such thinking has been slower to be accepted in Europe. Also, in the United States not all vertical restraints are accepted. Currently U.S. authorities and courts tend to apply a "rule of reason" to most such restraints rather than to treat such restraints as per se illegal. There is one major exception to this trend: U.S. courts still generally find resale price maintenance to be per se illegal.

In Europe the rules on abuse of a dominant firm position explicitly mention that certain vertical restraints are consistent with such abuse, and hence they are illegal if the result is an increase in the dominance of one firm.[17] However, as with cartels, exemptions can be granted by the European Commission for exclusive purchasing and dealership arrangements. It is therefore argued by many legal scholars that European law as currently enforced is generally more stringent toward vertical restraints than is U.S. law. The main motivation for rather stringent European policy is that vertical restraints have historically impeded European economic integration by restricting the flow of products and services across national lines. However, the EU is currently reexamining policy on vertical restraints, and there is likely to be some relaxation of the stringency of current rules in this domain.

Predatory Pricing

Predatory pricing occurs when a firm uses low prices or perhaps price discrimination in selective market segments (that is, charging certain cus-

---

17. This standard, for example, seemed to figure heavily in the initial decision of the European Commission to block the merger of Boeing and McDonnell Douglas. This merger had already been cleared by the U.S. authorities when the Europeans announced their decision. The ultimate outcome was that Boeing agreed to give up exclusive dealing contracts—a form of vertical restraint—that it had concluded with a number of major airlines in exchange for European clearance of the merger (Boeing also agreed to a number of other less important conditions). More is said about this case in the final section of this chapter.

tomers a lower price than others) as a means to drive other firms out of business and thus to establish itself as a monopolist. If a market were intrinsically contestable, such tactics would never be effective; as soon as the "predatory" seller raised its prices, competing sellers would enter the market and bid away all rent. This has led some economists to conclude that predatory pricing is a chimera: although it might be true that sellers exit some markets because they cannot survive at prevailing prices, this must be because the exiting firms are less efficient than their rivals that can survive at these prices.

This having been said, there might be circumstances in which predation could work. Necessary conditions would be that, once having driven rivals from the market, the predatory firm would be able to deter reentry or that there would be exogenous factors that would work to deter reentry—for instance, if there were to be substantial costs to consumers from switching suppliers. Even so, in some cases this could be efficiency enhancing (for instance, if the surviving firm were then able to realize a scale economy that was not available to it at an earlier time).

For these reasons, in the United States both enforcement authorities and courts have been increasingly unwilling in recent years to pursue or find guilt in predatory pricing cases.[18] To establish price predation, most U.S. courts require evidence that the alleged predator charged prices below marginal costs (or at least below average variable costs) with an intent to put rival sellers out of business. Some courts also require demonstration that the alleged predator could reasonably expect to recoup losses incurred by such pricing. The existence of many sellers or potential sellers is deemed evidence that such an expectation did not exist.

In the EU the standard for establishing whether there is illegal predation is whether the practice constitutes abuse of dominant position. Two cases in the EU within the past seven years (involving AKZO and Tetrapak) indicate that the standards for predation there are less friendly to the alleged predators than in the United States. In the AKZO case the European Court of Justice indicated that a firm can be guilty of price predation if it sets prices below average variable costs even if rivals are not driven out of the market. In the Tetrapak case the Court did not require a demonstration of probable recoupment of costs as a condition for finding price predation.

---

18. Even this law recognizes, however, that there are circumstances under which it might be efficient for a firm to engage in price discrimination.

Control of price predation would seem to have a goal similar to that of antidumping measures, serving as a trade policy "safeguard" mechanism. However, there is concern among economists that the standards for establishing "dumping" and for establishing "predatory pricing" are extremely different, with the former favoring plaintiffs (alleged victims) to a much greater degree than the latter. Because antidumping measures are directed exclusively toward imports, there is further concern that this mechanism is used in a discriminatory manner against foreign-made goods that would not pass muster in a competition law setting, either under U.S. law or even under the relatively plaintiff-friendly standards of the EU.

Enforcement of Competition Law: Private Business Practices

Competition policy is not only about substantive issues. It also is about the enforcement of law. And, as with substantive issues, the U.S. and EU "models" differ on matters of enforcement. The main differences are as follows:

—Compared to European enforcement, U.S. enforcement is generally more stringent.[19] In Europe, for example, other than for merger review almost no cases are initiated by competitor complaints. In the United States the enforcement agencies are as a matter of practice more likely to "self-initiate" a case. One reason is that the resources available to the U.S. enforcement agencies are greater than those available to the Europeans.

—Enforcement of U.S. law is largely driven by litigation, or in some instances criminal prosecution. In Europe, by contrast, a bureaucratic process drives most enforcement, and notification and negative clearance (including individual and bloc exemptions) play a relatively greater role.

—European law is entirely civil law; there are no criminal penalties for violation, whereas in the United States certain violations can be treated as criminal acts.[20] This difference has led to problems with cooperation between

19. It is important to note that this statement applies to levels of enforcement and not to substantive standards. Therefore, there is no contradiction between this statement and the fact, as noted previously, that European substantive standards for both vertical restraints and price predation are more stringent than U.S. standards in that fewer defenses of practices are allowable.

20. Although a number of practices can be treated as criminal violations under U.S. law, in practice most criminal prosecutions are for overt price-fixing agreements or other actions taken to create an overt cartel. A rather constant U.S. complaint is that European law and practice are relatively soft on cartels. See Fox (1997).

the United States and the EU because European authorities are unwilling to see their nationals face possible criminal actions in the United States.

—Although in both Europe and the United States there is a role for "private actions," in practice these are carried out significantly differently. In Europe, as already indicated, most private actions consist of firms' approaching the Commission with complaints about behavior of competing firms alleged to be in violation of law. In the United States firms with similar complaints can go to the enforcement agencies, but also can (and do) bring cases directly to the courts, bypassing the enforcement agencies.

In the United States there are two federal-level enforcement agencies, the Antitrust Division (ATD), a unit of the U.S. (federal) Department of Justice, and the Federal Trade Commission (FTC). The authorities of these two agencies overlap, but the overlap is not total. For example, only the ATD prosecutes criminal cases, whereas only the FTC enforces consumer protection laws. In addition to the federal agencies, the governments of the individual states through their attorney generals can also enforce state statutes pertaining to competition through state courts. Private right of action is available through both state courts and federal courts.

Enforcement of European law is conducted through Directorate General IV (DGIV) of the Commission of the EU. Some but not all member nations of the EU also have in place national competition laws and enforcement agencies. In addition to enforcing competition law, DGIV also regulates the granting of state aids in the EU. Even if enforcement of competition law in the United States is generally more stringent than in Europe, DGIV generally has more discretionary power to decide competition cases than do the two American federal enforcement agencies. This is because DGIV not only is an investigative and enforcement agency, but also serves, for all practical purposes, as the final arbiter of most cases. (Therefore, DGIV's role is quasi-judicial, whereas the U.S. enforcement agencies have no statutory power to act as courts.)[21] Decisions of DGIV can be appealed to European courts (first the Court of First

---

21. Even so, the U.S. enforcement agencies at times enter into "consent decrees" with private parties, whereby it is agreed that if certain conditions are met the enforcement agencies will take no further action. Arguably these decrees grant a de facto limited judicial power to the enforcement agencies. Even so, it should be noted that although if a private party enters into and abides by a consent decree it is generally immune from further actions from the enforcement agencies, it might not necessarily be immune from court actions taken as the result of private lawsuits. Also, in one recent instance a U.S.

Instance and ultimately the European Court of Justice), but such instances are rare and must involve issues related to whether DGIV has overstepped its authority. Appeals of this sort involve only cases in which the decisions of DGIV have gone against the defendants. By contrast, in the United States if plaintiffs do not gain satisfaction from actions taken by the federal enforcement agencies, they have recourse to private action in the court system.

Effective enforcement of competition law requires that enforcement agencies have access to detailed information. Accordingly, the powers of "discovery" of both DGIV and the U.S. enforcement agencies are substantial. In both cases authorities can have access to internal records kept by firms, and there are substantial penalties if firms fail to produce records when requested.

Although the procedures for enforcement in the United States and Europe are different, neither model is clearly superior to the other. Therefore, although these procedures are more stringent in the United States than in Europe, some analysts believe that U.S. enforcement at times has been overzealous. This was especially true during the 1960s and 1970s. It has already been noted that there has since been some relaxation of per se enforcement of U.S. law because of recognition that the economic effects of certain practices largely depend upon circumstances. The alternative rule of reason standard arguably grants somewhat more discretionary powers to U.S. enforcement agencies and courts than does a per se standard. To the extent this is true, it could be argued that U.S. procedures are becoming a little more like European ones. However, there is still more effort in the United States to make as explicit and transparent as possible the circumstances and factors that are pertinent in any rule of reason situation and, in addition, the analytical procedures used to weigh these circumstances and factors. European enforcement at the end of the day still relies on discretionary "judgment calls," the outcome of which cannot be predicted in advance. Even so, there might be some additional convergence if European authorities increasingly continue to accept economics-based standards as the basis for decisionmaking.

---

federal judge threw out a consent decree entered into by the ATD with software giant Microsoft. This judicial decision itself was overturned, however, on appeal. The case at this time is somewhat moot, because at this writing the ATD is preparing a new action against Microsoft.

International Aspects of Competition Policy

It is a cliché that markets today are becoming global, but the cliché is of substance. One consequence of the globalization of markets is that the formulation and execution of competition policy is becoming more complex. As markets and the operations of sellers who serve these markets increasingly spill across international boundaries, it makes sense that competition policy should follow suit. But because the authority of any law enforcement agency stops at the boundary of the jurisdiction in which the agency operates, it is not easy to "globalize" competition policy.[22]

Three aspects of competition policy in particular argue for internationalization of this policy: conflicts and overlaps among national policies, issues of market access, and the very vexing issue of antidumping measures.

Conflicts and Overlaps among National Policies

The Boeing–McDonnell Douglas merger, which consolidated the two remaining U.S.-based manufacturers of wide-bodied commercial aircraft into one firm, perhaps best illustrates such conflicts. Following the merger there remained only one other manufacturer, the Europe-based consortium Airbus Industries. The market for wide-bodied aircraft is about as global as one can imagine. The true test of whether a market is truly global is whether price differentials for the same product can exist, net of taxes and transactions costs, in open markets in different parts of the world. The answer for wide-bodied aircraft is surely not. The product—for reasons that are very obvious—can be delivered to virtually any location in the world in a matter of hours at a cost that is a tiny fraction of the price of the product. Any significant price differential due to price discrimination by a manufacturer is likely to be arbitraged away.[23]

When Boeing and McDonnell Douglas proposed to merge, an interesting question posed itself: exactly what competition enforcement agencies had the authority to review and, if it was deemed necessary, challenge the merger? Because both firms were located in the United States (at least in terms of headquarters and assembly operations), the U.S. agencies obviously had this authority. But DGIV in Europe also claimed authority, because under European

22. See, for example, Scherer (1994), Fox (1997), and Graham and Richardson (1997).

23. However, in some areas price discrepancies exist because of closed bidding practices.

rules the merger qualified as reviewable under the Mergers Regulation of 1989. To this claim the United States had in fact little reason to object, because U.S. courts have asserted an "extraterritorial" reach of U.S. antitrust law if an event covered by the substance of this law but taking place outside the United States has "material effects" on U.S. commerce. Indeed, on a number of occasions U.S. enforcement agencies have reviewed and in some instances acted against mergers that have taken place outside of the United States but where there would be domestic effects. Under the "effects doctrine," indeed, virtually any country where there is commercial airline activity could reasonably have claimed such authority.

The United States and the European authorities reached opposite conclusions on the substance of the case. The United States was prepared to allow the merger, accepting both efficiency and "flailing firm" arguments in spite of the fact that the merger would have significantly increased seller concentration in an already very concentrated market. The EU sought, by contrast, initially to block the merger on grounds that it would substantially increase the dominant position of one firm, Boeing. For some time following the announcement there was a standoff between European and American authorities, with the Americans complaining that Europe was acting for nationalistic rather than economically rational reasons and the Europeans claiming that the Americans were prepared to condone global monopoly, but only if it served their own nationalistic interests. In the end there was a compromise: Boeing agreed to certain conditions, including termination of exclusive dealing relationships with a number of airlines, to achieve European approval of the merger. On both sides of the Atlantic there were sighs of relief. Privately some European authorities had worried that the European position had in fact been overly nationalistic. But privately some American authorities also worried that a monopolistic Boeing would not be in anyone's interests. One reason was that Boeing's own rate of technological improvement of its products had improved sharply after Airbus established itself during the 1980s as a serious competitor.[24]

The Boeing–McDonnell Douglas case is not the first instance—nor is it likely to be the last—in which competition authorities from two or more jurisdictions review the same situation and arrive at different conclusions with respect to what should be done. One solution to this dilemma would be for

---

24. These statements are based on informal interviews I have conducted with authorities who wish to remain anonymous.

there to be a common set of rules with a supranational authority to enforce them. Another less satisfactory solution would be for competition law to be "harmonized" worldwide. However, for a variety of reasons, neither of these two approaches is to be realized anytime soon.

Therefore, U.S. and European agencies have arrived at a third approach, termed "positive comity." Under positive comity two or more enforcement agencies with an interest in the same situation would agree that one and only one of these agencies would perform the necessary review and implement, if needed, the action necessary to remedy a competitive problem. The other agencies would agree to recognize this outcome. The agency that took on the review and remediation would in most instances be the one that could be identified to have the greater interest in the situation. But this agency would take into account in its analysis and remediation the legitimate concerns and interests of those agencies that had agreed to "step aside."

It is interesting that the United States and Europe already have in place a positive comity agreement. It does not apply to mergers, however, and in the case of the Boeing–McDonnell Douglas merger the principle clearly did not function very well even in spirit. European and U.S. authorities both are quick to claim that this was a very exceptional case and that no similar cases are likely to arise in the foreseeable future.[25] We shall see.

Issues of Market Access

Another argument for some sort of international rules on competition policy rests on the assertion that in many countries (certain East Asian nations are most commonly cited) private business practices serve effectively to foreclose domestic markets to imported goods (or to restrict greatly the access of imports to these markets). It is further asserted that these practices are often supplemented by governmental regulations that favor, deliberately or nondeliberately, incumbent domestic sellers over foreign sellers. Finally, it is alleged that domestic competition policy in these countries is inadequate to remedy the problems of foreclosure, or perhaps local competition enforcement agencies are simply unwilling to enforce the laws to the benefit of foreign sellers.

Such foreclosure, to the extent that it exists, cannot be satisfactorily addressed through the present WTO mechanism. The main reason lies in the fact

25. It should be noted that during the 1990s several hundred mergers have been reviewed and passed by both sets of agencies.

that the only rules in the General Agreement on Tariffs and Trade (GATT), the WTO agreement that pertains to international trade in goods, that would seem to be applicable to this type of foreclosure are those stated in Articles XXIII.1.b and XXIII.1.c. These allow a WTO member nation that believes that its realization of benefits (read exports) is "nullified or impaired" by government measures or by "any other situation" to use the WTO dispute settlement procedures to try to remedy the nullification or impairment. However, for reasons pertaining to the failure of nations to ratify the 1947 Havana Charter to Establish an International Trade Organization, the GATT Council more than thirty years ago decided that Article XXIII cannot be used against private restrictive business practices that foreclose imports. The article can be invoked only against government measures that foreclose imports.

Such foreclosure is one issue that the WTO Working Group on Trade and Competition Policy was created to consider. However, only a subset of countries represented in this working group has to date wanted this to be a focal point of the group's work. Other nations, particularly those of East Asia, have attempted to steer the group clear of this issue set and to focus instead on antidumping measures, the last issue on which this chapter will focus.

The Very Vexing Issue of Antidumping Measures

The simple fact is that antidumping measures are more a political issue than an economic one. No economist or indeed any legal scholar (other than perhaps ones employed specifically to defend antidumping measures) can find a rationale for antidumping measures other than perhaps as a means to control predatory pricing. But as noted earlier, antidumping regimes are extremely overzealous means to control predation. Nonetheless, such regimes exist in the trade laws of over forty nations and are allowed under WTO rules.

Indeed, most specialists believe that antidumping regimes are much more likely to be anticompetitive than procompetitive. The suspicion is that antidumping rules are used to some very large measure as a means to foster the functioning of de facto cartels: if an importer tries to sell below the cartel price, one sanction that the seller faces is the possibility of antidumping actions, even if under no criterion the seller is behaving as a predator.[26] Short of this,

26. The consistent finding of researchers who have examined whether antidumping cases entail predatory behavior on the part of the importers is that overwhelmingly the answer is no. The latest of these is a forthcoming study by Robert Willig to be published

antidumping measures almost surely reduce market contestability. The very essence of contestability is that if incumbent sellers raise prices above those that would prevail if there were perfect competition, new entrants will bid those prices down. But if the new entrants happen to be foreign, antidumping measures limit their ability to do so.

This having been said, the major question posed by the politics of antidumping measures is the following: is the loss of welfare brought about by the existence of antidumping regimes sufficiently great to warrant all-out war against these regimes in an effort either to replace antidumping policies with more rational competition-based policies or at least to reform the antidumping policies significantly so as to make them less plaintiff friendly? If so, those nations that might be inclined to reform (or dump) antidumping measures will have to be prepared for a very long and protracted battle given the entrenched nature of the pro-antidumping forces. At a minimum these countries must be prepared to form a coalition. On the other hand, is the loss of welfare due to antidumping measures sufficiently small to warrant moving on to other matters on the competition agenda and leaving antidumping measures as an issue for the future?

If there is to be a major reform of antidumping measures, leadership for this initiative will necessarily come from nations other than the United States or the EU, albeit that many pro-reform allies could be found within these nations. But whether an alternative leadership will emerge, only time will tell.

Conclusions

Latin American nations have a strong interest in competition policy for two reasons. The first is to improve the performance of domestic economies by making domestic markets more contestable. Domestic competition laws and policies can complement open trade and investment policies to achieve this latter goal. It is important in an increasingly "globalized" world economy, however, that domestic law and policy, to as great an extent as possible, not conflict with those of other nations. Unfortunately, because of persistent differences in U.S. and EU law and policy that can engender conflict, the Latin countries often are in a position in which they can harmonize their own laws

---

by the Brookings Institution based on a suppressed study done for the Organization for Economic Cooperation and Development (OECD).

and policies with those of either the United States or the EU, but not both. It is therefore important that Latin policymakers at least be informed with respect to these differences, even if in the end there is relatively little that can be done about them.

What model is best for Latin America, that of the United States, that of the EU, or some other, perhaps home-grown, model? At this point it is not easy to answer this question. However, a growing body of experience now exists in Latin America. One very worthwhile exercise at this time would be to conduct a comparative study of Latin national experiences with the goal of trying to determine what has and what has not been effective in achieving long-term goals of increased efficiency and consumer welfare.

Beyond purely domestic considerations, Latin nations have a strong interest in the international aspects of competition policies because there is potential for eventual removal, or at least reduction, of persistent barriers to Latin exports. Export sectors are likely to continue to lead Latin American development, and the efficiencies that are imparted to domestic economic activity via development of these sectors will in fact help to achieve the long-term goals of domestic competition policy. Therefore, Latin American nations should be enthusiastic supporters of reform (or abolishment) of antidumping measures as well as efforts within the WTO to use competition policy as a means to address private and public "behind-the-border" measures that impede market access.

Alas, progress in this area is likely to be slow for two reasons. First, efforts to reform antidumping measures and to reduce barriers to market access are likely to be opposed by strong and entrenched interest groups. Second, there is legitimate disagreement among specialists as to what exactly are the normatively correct directions for policy to follow. On both matters it is important that Latin Americans add their voice—and their growing weight—to the international discussions that are now ongoing. This voice is important so that the long-run interests of Latin America can be represented in forums such as the WTO. It is also important because Latin Americans increasingly have a substantive and significant contribution to make that is in the collective interests of everyone.

References

Fox, E. 1997. "Toward World Antitrust and Market Access." *American Journal of International Law* 91(1).

Graham, E. M., and J. D. Richardson. 1997. "Conclusions and Recommendations." In *Global Competition Policy,* edited by E. M. Graham and J. D. Richardson. Washington, D.C.: Institute for International Economics.

Nicolaidis, K., and R. Vernon. 1997. "Competition Policy and Trade Policy in the European Union." In *Global Competition Policy,* edited by E. M. Graham and J. D. Richardson. Washington, D.C.: Institute for International Economics.

Petrazzini, B. 1996. *Global Telecom Talks: A Trillion Dollar Deal.* Washington, D.C.: Institute for International Economics.

Rosenthal, D. E., and P. Nicholaides. 1997. "Harmonizing Antitrust: The Less Effective Way to Promote International Competition Policy Competition." In *Global Competition Policy,* edited by E. M. Graham and J. D. Richardson. Washington, D.C.: Institute for International Economics.

Scherer, F. M. 1994. *Competition Policies for an Integrated World Economy.* Washington, D.C.: Brookings.

Scherer, F. M., and D. Ross. 1990. *Industrial Market Structure and Economic Performance,* 3d ed. Boston: Houghton Mifflin.

CHAPTER EIGHTEEN

Competition Policy and Regional Trade Agreements

José Tavares de Araujo, Jr., and Luis Tineo

In the post–Uruguay Round period competition policy is becoming a key element in regional trade agreements for three interrelated reasons. First, mergers and acquisitions have been the dominant forms of foreign direct investment during the 1980s and 1990s. This trend has engendered a greater demand for predictable rules to simultaneously enhance the confidence of potential investors and enforce the correct mechanisms to protect the public interest. Second, domestic entry barriers facilitate the action of international cartels and can distort trade flows among the members of a regional trade agreement. The removal of such barriers may require joint efforts by competition policy agencies not only to promote equitable conditions of competition within the region, but, more important, to achieve a coherent set of policies for sustaining the process of economic integration. Third, national oligopolies often react against trade liberalization through collusion, rent seeking, and other forms of anticompetitive behavior that can offset the benefits of the enlarged market. In the absence of effective competition rules, such activities will imply a permanent source of trade disputes among member countries, adding new obstacles to the integration process.

To harmonize the conditions of competition within a free trade area, governments should first develop a common view on, or at least a converging approach to, a series of intricate subjects. In addition to analytical methods for approaching relevant markets, concentration indexes, market power, technological

444

innovations, entry, and contestability, these include a list of explicit rules for those practices to be forbidden in the region, such as price fixing, bid rigging, and predatory pricing. However, in contrast with other topics on the integration agenda, such as tariffs, quotas, and subsidies, the harmonization of competition rules is achievable not through mercantilist negotiations, but essentially through cooperation among national competition policy agencies in the enforcement of their respective domestic laws. Indeed, the most important part of this process is accomplished unilaterally when a competition policy authority is prepared to act as the regulator of last resort in the economy.

Competition policy implies a major challenge to the implementation of the Free Trade Area of the Americas (FTAA). In addition to Canada and the United States, which have a century of experience with the subject, only ten Latin American and Caribbean countries have competition policy laws and institutions.[1] Although some countries, such as Argentina and Mexico, have had competition policy laws since the beginning of this century, it was only after the wave of economic reforms that spread throughout the continent in the 1980s that the implementation of competition rules became a relevant issue in the region. Moreover, most Latin American competition policy authorities are not prepared to act as regulators of last resort. This role presupposes that a competition policy agency is autonomous and strong enough to question other public policies whenever necessary, that no sector in the economy is exempted from the competition policy law, and that there is a clear-cut division of functions between the competition policy authority and the sectoral regulatory agencies. Even in those countries that formally meet these requirements, such as Brazil, Mexico, Peru, Venezuela and others, the economic reforms are yet to be concluded and the competition policy agencies are still forging their public image.

1. These countries are Argentina (first law passed in 1919, amended in 1946 and 1980, and currently under review), Brazil (passed in 1962, amended in 1990, and revised in 1994), Chile (passed in 1959, amended in 1973, and revised in 1979), Colombia (passed in 1959, supplemented in 1992), Costa Rica (passed in 1994), Jamaica (passed in 1993), Mexico (passed in 1934, replaced in 1992), Panama (passed in 1996), Peru (passed in 1991, modified in 1994 and 1996), and Venezuela (passed in 1991). For a comparative description of these laws see Organization of American States (OAS) (1998a), which also includes an inventory of the current competition policy agreements signed by FTAA member countries. For a collection of official reports on the recent developments and enforcement of competition policy in the Western Hemisphere, see OAS (1998b).

In recent years several authors have discussed the relations between competition policy and other variables that affect international trade, such as industrial targeting, subsidies, quantitative restrictions, antidumping actions, intellectual property rights, investment rules, and government procurement.[2] Despite the importance of these interactions, they are not expected to be on the FTAA agenda in the near future for the aforementioned reasons. As the following discussion in this chapter shows, competition policy is a clear priority in the Western Hemisphere, but governments are currently focused on the establishment of the institutional framework for addressing this matter. Before completing this task, any effort to address the interplay of competition policy and other policies at a regional level would be premature.

In order to assess the likely evolution of the FTAA debate on competition policy, this chapter examines the provisions of the existing regional agreements on this topic. First it discusses the nature of the commitments made by the countries participating in the North American Free Trade Agreement (NAFTA) regarding monopolies, state enterprises, and competition policy enforcement. Next it presents a short account of two agreements, one signed by Colombia, Mexico, and Venezuela, the G-3, and the other between Canada and Chile. It reviews the norms enacted by Decision 285 of the Andean Community and comments on recent institutional developments in member countries. Finally, it provides an analysis of the Protocol for the Defense of Competition, which was signed by the countries of the Southern Common Market (Mercosur) in December 1996, followed by some concluding remarks.

The North American Free Trade Agreement

Brevity is the soul of the NAFTA approach to competition policy. Chapter 15 of the agreement covers the subject in four substantive articles. The first addresses competition law, mutual assistance, and dispute settlement in eleven lines; the second and third provide the rules for monopolies and state enterprises in two pages; and the fourth establishes a working group to examine the relevant issues concerning the relationship between competition laws and policies and trade in the free trade area. The final report of the working group

2. Guasch and Rajapatirana (1994); Hoekman and Mavoids (1994); Buigues, Jacquemin, and Sapir (1995); Graham and Richardson (1997); Vautier and Lloyd (1997); and Waverman, Comanor, and Goto (1997).

was due in December 1998, but an interim report on the results achieved from 1994 through 1996 was released in February 1997. The whole period was reviewed in three pages.

Despite the parsimony of words, the NAFTA approach may provide five important guidelines for the initial phase of the FTAA debate on competition policy, namely:

—Focus on domestic law enforcement.

—Strengthen national agencies through mutual regional assistance.

—Give priority attention to the conduct of firms instead of the attributes of industry structure.

—Gradually and pragmatically advance toward joint commitments for dealing with international competition policy cases.

—Postpone to a latter stage of the negotiations actions related to the harmonization of competition policy with other policies at a regional level.

Chapter 15 of the NAFTA offers a clear statement that there will be no regional competition policy until the Mexican competition policy agency has reached the enforcement capabilities of its American and Canadian counterparts. Article 1501 indicates that the NAFTA countries should take measures to proscribe anticompetitive business conduct, but it does not establish any standards to be incorporated into the domestic laws, as Johnson has noted.[3] Moreover, dispute settlement procedures do not apply to this chapter of the agreement, which means that when facing a competition policy case with international implications, governments should act as though the NAFTA did not exist. Article 1501 also recognizes the importance of cooperation: the parties are to cooperate on issues of competition law enforcement policy, including mutual legal assistance, notification, consultation, and exchange of information relating to the enforcement of competition laws and policies in the free trade area. However, as in the case of national legislation, it does not make any specific commitments.

Articles 1502 and 1503 comprise the most important policy commitments. At a moment when privatization and deregulation are fashionable worldwide, it is not odd that the NAFTA countries have dedicated the major part of the competition policy chapter of their agreement to stressing their right to create and regulate national monopolies and states enterprises. This only reiterates the point that from the competition policy perspective, what matters is the existence of effective mechanisms to protect the public interest, not the size and ownership of firms or the industry structure.

---

3. Johnson (1994).

The NAFTA negotiations have had a marked influence on the modernization of Mexican competition policy institutions. On December 24, 1992, one week after the signing of the trade agreement, a new law replaced the old and inoperative 1934 legislation and, among other important innovations, established the Federal Competition Commission as an autonomous agency. During 1995 and 1996 the commission examined 58 cases of anticompetitive practices and 209 cases of mergers and acquisitions, had an active role in the national process of regulatory reform—especially in the areas of energy, transportation, and telecommunications—and followed a busy international agenda that included regular meetings with NAFTA and FTAA working groups, the Asia-Pacific Economic Cooperation (APEC) group, the Organization for Economic Cooperation and Development (OECD), the United Nations Conference on Trade and Development (UNCTAD), and the European Union.[4] In March 1998 the FCC enacted a series of regulations, including guidelines for mergers and acquisitions that are similar to those of Canada and United States in all relevant aspects.

The convergence of merger guidelines among the three countries means that even without regional mechanisms the NAFTA is already prepared to deal with the most common competition policy problem engendered by trade agreements, which is the trend toward market concentration that follows the process of economic integration. These guidelines provide a set of stable and transparent rules that reduces the uncertainty of investment decisions by keeping the private sector informed about the government's surveillance instruments. They describe the methodology applied by the competition policy agency to inquire whether a merger would be harmful to the public interest. The analysis is focused on a single question, which is whether the merging firms will have market power to impose a small but significant and nontransitory increase in price. However, in the absence of Schumpeterian innovations, trade protection, and government-generated entry barriers only a few unregulated oligopolies are powerful enough to adopt that behavior. Therefore, in most cases the merging firms will know in advance that the competition policy authority will not challenge their project.

But the preparation of regional mechanisms has already been started. In 1995 Canada and the United States signed an agreement that established, among other important cooperative procedures, the following: (1) The countries are to engage in mutual notification of enforcement activities that may

---

4. OAS (1998b).

affect the interests of the other country, including both anticompetitive practices and mergers. Each notification is to be sufficiently detailed to enable the notified party to make an initial evaluation of the effect of the enforcement activity on its own important interests, and it is to include the nature of the activities under investigation and the legal provisions concerned. Where possible, notifications are to include the names and locations of the persons involved. (2) Officials of either competition policy agency may visit the other country in the course of conducting investigations. (3) Either country may request that the other initiate an investigation in its territory on anticompetitive practices that adversely affect the interests of the first country. (4) The countries are to provide mutual assistance in locating and securing evidence and witnesses in the territory of the other country. (5) Regular meetings are to be held to discuss policy changes and exchange information on economic sectors of common interest.[5]

The final report of the 1504 Working Group will conclude the set of preliminary efforts on the subject of regional competition policy instruments. The report is supposed to present evidence and recommendations on three basic topics: cross-border anticompetitive activities in the region, the scope of enforcement of either bilateral or trilateral mechanisms, and the interaction of competition and trade in specific sectors. Besides setting the stage for a second phase among NAFTA countries, such results will also be relevant to the ongoing FTAA negotiations.

The Group of Three and Canada-Chile Free Trade Agreements

The free trade treaty between Canada and Chile, which was concluded in 1996 and due to enter into force in 1998, and the free trade treaty of the Group of 3 (G-3), which was signed in 1994 and has been in force since 1995, include in Chapter J and Chapter 16, respectively, provisions governing competition, monopolies designated by each country, and practices of state enterprises. The provisions of both agreements are identical to those established in the NAFTA, and the principles discussed in the preceding paragraph therefore apply.

5. See "Agreement between the Government of the United States of America and the Government of Canada Regarding the Application of Their Competition and Deceptive Marketing Practice Laws," OAS (1998a).

As in the case of the NAFTA, the parties to these treaties have approved and actively implemented the laws governing competition in their jurisdictions. Also, both agreements provide for the establishment of working groups to consider the relationship between trade and competition policies. A working group was set up in 1995 within the framework of the G-3. It has met on two occasions to focus on comparative analysis of laws governing competition. It has not yet produced any report with recommendations for future discussions in this area. A working group under the Canada-Chile Free Trade Treaty is due to be set up once the treaty has been ratified by the parliaments of these countries. However, in light of the experiences that these countries have had with the NAFTA, the approach and dynamic of this group may be expected to show characteristics similar to those of the NAFTA working groups.

The Andean Community

Like most Latin American economies, all the Andean countries have promoted major trade policy reforms since the mid-1980s in conjunction with other programs in the areas of macroeconomic stabilization and state modernization. These initiatives have paved the way for a reevaluation of the attempts at economic integration made since 1969 within the scope of the Cartagena Accord. Therefore, in February 1989 the presidents of the five countries decided to relaunch the Andean Pact, now renamed the Andean Community, which led to the creation of a free trade area in 1992 and to other new developments. With this market-oriented vision, the Commission of the Cartagena Agreement enacted Decision 285 in 1991, establishing common rules "to prevent or correct distortions in competition resulting from practices aimed at restricting free competition."[6]

Decision 285 represents the first effort to address competition issues at a subregional level in Latin America. Its substantive provisions and enforcement mechanisms are modeled after European Union competition rules. Principles applied by community bodies govern the system. Curiously, when Decision 285 was enacted only Colombia had a competition law. Although the decision was seen as a model for policy harmonization in the region, its components and scope fall short of what was developed in each country later on. Nonetheless,

6. Decision 285 on Standards for Preventing or Correcting Market Distortions Caused by Practices That Restrict Free Competition, April 4, 1991, OAS (1998b).

due to the supranational principles applied, it prevails over domestic law in subregional cases.

Decision 285 has a limited scope. It deals with restrictive practices resulting either from collusive agreements or from abuse of dominant position so long as they affect competition in more than one country of the subregion. If the practice does not have extraterritorial implications, national law applies. Concerted actions prohibited by the decision include price fixing; imposition of restraints on output, distribution, technical development, and investment; market allocation; discrimination; and tying arrangements. Abuse of dominant position includes, besides the practices mentioned before, refusal to deal, withholding input from competing firms, and discriminatory treatment. The decision, however, does not deal with the most important practices affecting competition in integrated markets: vertical restraints and merger review.

The enforcement of Decision 285 is the responsibility of the Secretariat, which conducts investigations and proceedings at the request of countries or affected firms. To this extent the decision, in contrast with the European Union model, provides the Secretariat with a peculiar "rule of reason" standard of analysis. In what looks more like an analysis of antidumping policy than of competition policy, joint consideration must be given to evidence of the practice, threat of injury or actual injury to a subregional industry, and the cause-and-effect relationship between the practice and the injury. Proceedings must be completed within two months after investigations are initiated. If the Secretariat determines that the practice is restrictive to competition, it may issue an order to cease the practice. It may also authorize the affected country to impose corrective measures—that is, lower tariffs to the products exported by means of restrictive practices.

In spite of its framers' good intentions, Decision 285 has failed to promote competition in the Andean market. In fact, only one case has been submitted to the Secretariat for examination, and its outcome was negligible. The case involved restrictions to competition in the formerly controlled subregional sugar market. In *Imezucar v. Ciamsa* the former party, a Venezuelan sugar trading company, in 1996 requested an investigation of allegedly concerted practices in the sugar market by the latter, a sugar trading company owned by several Colombian and Venezuelan sugar producers.[7] Imezucar claimed that Ciamsa-Colombia had developed a concerted agreement with Ciamsa-Venezuela to restrict sugar production and exports, fix prices, and allocate

7. OAS (1998b).

market and quotas among its affiliates in each country. It also manifested that such collusive and monopolistic practice had injured its activities and reduced its market participation in both countries. Ciamsa, on the other hand, alleged that its affiliated companies competed on an individual basis with each other and that Ciamsa was an efficient means to import and distribute sugar to its members. After the investigation the Secretariat did not find evidence of collusive pricing, nor did it establish a relationship between the alleged injury and the concerted practices. The case was dismissed.

A number of institutional limitations have contributed to the failure of Decision 285. A first limitation is that the Secretariat cannot initiate investigations on its own. Its actions have to be requested either by the countries or by firms that have legitimate interests. This leaves the Secretariat with little power to oversee the Andean market. The ability to select cases and open investigations is the most important enforcement power. Such power guarantees the independence of the Secretariat with regard to the issues affecting the integration process, competition, and consumer welfare. Competition rules do not envisage the protection of individual competitors. To the contrary, they seek to protect the competition process. Under Decision 285 the Secretariat acts more as an arbitrator between private parties than as a protector of the competition process.

A second limitation of Decision 285 is that the Secretariat has neither punitive nor coercive powers to force firms to adopt its decisions. It simply issues a finding with an explanation setting forth its conclusions and a recommendation to cease the practice. This lack of a mechanism to dissuade countries from engaging in restrictive practices weakens the Secretariat's authority.

A third limitation of Decision 285 has to do with the unusual remedy the Secretariat may impose. It may authorize countries to grant preferential treatment to imports of the products subject to investigations from third countries. This remedy seems to work in a protected scheme, but not in an open one in which such preferences have been eliminated at the national and regional levels. Again, it is a remedy thought to address individual industry concerns and not competition itself.[8] Despite these shortcomings, Decision 285 in-

8. These limitations provide compelling reasons for reviewing Decision 285, and a draft proposal was put forward by the Venezuelan competition agency. It suggests a system of exemptions similar to the European model, whereby authorization can be granted either on an individual basis to agreements among competitors or on a global basis to sectors, depending upon their welfare impact. The proposal also suggests a pre-merger notification system along the lines of the European model.

augurated the age of competition policy enforcement among the Andean countries. In November 1991 the Peruvian government enacted the laws on foreign investment and competition that led to the creation of the Institute for the Protection of Free Competition and Intellectual Property (INDECOPI) in the following year. The INDECOPI is a multifunctional agency independent of the executive branch that is in charge of promoting and enforcing a variety of newly passed market regulations. Under this agency's jurisdiction are the laws on competition, antidumping and countervailing duties, consumer protection, unfair competition and advertising, technical barriers, and intellectual property rights. The INDECOPI also deals with the removal of entry and exit barriers and with economic deregulation. An independent commission has been established over each of these areas.

The Competition Commission started its activities in 1994. It has focused on anticompetitive practices and abuse of dominant position. Between 1994 and 1996 fifty-seven cases were investigated. Of these, fifty-two investigations were opened at the request of individuals and five on the commission's initiative. The investigations were broken down as follows: twenty-one were for restrictive practices, twenty-two for abuse of dominant position, and twenty-six for a mix of both. Nearly thirty-six cases ended with formal decisions, whereas the rest were dismissed due to lack of merit or relevance. Abuse of dominance cases centered around discriminatory treatment and refusal to deal, whereas restrictive conduct cases concentrated almost exclusively on collusive arrangements to fix prices. In seven cases the commission found merits and fined the firms involved.[9] Two cases, both initiated by the commission, have had particular implications in shaping the policy toward conduct violations. The former, decided in 1995, involved eighteen wheat flour producers charged with price-fixing. The latter case, decided in 1996, involved sixteen poultry producers also for price-fixing. In both cases the commission found the firms guilty and significant fines were imposed.

One month after the enactment of the Peruvian competition laws the government of Venezuela created the Superintendency for the Promotion and Protection of Free Competition (PROCOMPETENCIA), granting it sufficient autonomy to enforce the new competition policy law. The 1991 Venezuelan law includes provisions dealing with restrictive practices and merger control. Restrictive practices are prohibited unless expressly authorized or exempted by the competition agency. Regarding merger control, the law prohibits economic con-

9. OAS (1998b).

centrations when they create a dominant position in the market. From 1993 to 1996 PROCOMPETENCIA reviewed twenty-seven mergers and conducted fifty-four investigations on anticompetitive practices, and it has played an active role in the area of competition advocacy. For instance, successful identification and review of the compatibility of valid rules with competition goals have been conducted in the pharmaceutical, sugar, coffee, and health sectors, among others.

Competition issues have also had a role in the privatization process. The privatization law deems void privatization that may lead to high levels of market concentration. As a result, the privatization agency and the Venezuelan Congress have informally conferred with PROCOMPETENCIA in a counseling role on the potential effects on competition that would result if one of the actual rivals of the privatized company happens to procure the bid. In these areas the agency has issued sixteen reports since 1992, which have included opinions on the privatization of two state-owned airlines, a state-owned aluminum conglomerate, a state-owned milk factory, and several state-owned financial institutions. They have also included opinions on regulatory issues related to airfare tariffs and energy. Although nonbinding, these reports have earned PROCOMPETENCIA a sound reputation among the public agencies and the investors involved in the privatization bids.

Following the path initiated by Peru and Venezuela, in December 1992 the Colombian government enacted Decree 2153, which updated the provisions of the 1959 law, strengthened the powers of the competition policy agency, and reduced the degree of government discretion on competition matters. Decree 2153 charged the newly created Superintendency of Industry and Trade with the enforcement of the law. A deputy superintendent is charged with investigations and merger analysis. Concerning anticompetitive practices, Decree 2153 set out rules against horizontal practices such as price fixing; discriminatory practices; market, supply, or quota allocations; tying arrangements; output restraints; refusal to deal; and bid rigging, leaving vertical practices to a rule of reason standard of analysis. The decree also specified conduct considered abuse of dominant position under a rule of reason standard of analysis. Regarding merger review, Decree 2153 introduced exceptions for efficiencies by which mergers found to be anticompetitive may nonetheless be allowed if the merging parties demonstrate that the efficiencies are greater than the restrictive effects on the market. These improvements in enforcement and policy formulation promise a more active role for competition in the Colombian economy.

Since 1992 the Superintendency has reviewed 142 cases related to conduct violations, but most of them were closed due to lack of merit. Only 27 cases have been formally investigated, out of which 9 were dropped at the plaintiffs' request and 18 resolved by settlement before the agency. The issues at stake were price fixing, resale price maintenance, use of exclusive practices, and abuse of dominant position. The relevant investigations were carried out in the automotive, cellular phone, and health industries.

The agency's practice has been to settle the cases by reaching consent agreements with the firms involved in the investigations. This procedure has yielded a number of benefits in the Colombian transition process by minimizing the impact that sanctions could have had in the economy. It also has provided the agency and firms with a mutual understanding of the laws and markets, which, in turn, has created a competition culture among the participants as well as the conditions and expertise necessary for a stricter enforcement of the law. So far the Superintendency has reached consent agreements with powerful industries such as the cement, beer, and health services industries. The agency also has dealt with abuse of dominant position by important state-owned companies such as railroad, oil, and energy companies. In the settlements these industries have pledged to end their alleged anticompetitive practices and have been warned that further violations of the agreements will be punished.

In the area of mergers, the Superintendency has been busy due to the mandatory pre-merger notification system established by the Colombian law. Since 1992 some 212 notifications have been filed before the agency.[10] All transactions have either been approved or simply not opposed. In most cases the agency has found the merging firms to have only a small amount of market power and no need to worry about likely anticompetitive effects. In other cases notifications have targeted firms' conglomerate consolidations. One concern is the burdensome load created by the merger review that is carried out by the Colombian agency. Much of this workload is due to the excessively low thresholds set by the 1959 law. These have caused virtually every transaction to be submitted for approval. Merger analysis is the most time-consuming task in competition enforcement. So far it seems that big mergers have not occurred yet, and merger review has turned out to be a bureaucratic routine that diverts important resources from the agency. As recognized by the Superintendency itself, these thresholds need to be updated. This would allow the agency to

10. OAS (1998b).

effectively focus on transactions that are likely to impact the market and develop methodologies accordingly.

The Southern Common Market (Mercosur)

The harmonization of competition policies has been on the agenda of the Mercosur since the signing of the Asunción Treaty in March 1991. According to its first article, that treaty involves the coordination of macroeconomic and sectoral policies between the states that are parties to the agreement in the areas of foreign trade, agriculture, industry, fiscal and monetary matters, foreign exchange and capital, services, customs, transport and communications, and any other areas that may be agreed upon in order to ensure proper competition between the parties and their commitment to harmonize their legislation in the relevant areas in order to strengthen the integration process.

Within this ambitious framework, in December 1996 the Mercosur countries signed a protocol that indicates the guidelines for working toward a common competition policy in the region. The implementation of this protocol, which is pending the approval of the national parliaments, will imply, among other institutional innovations, that every member country will have an autonomous competition agency in the near future, that the national law will cover the whole economy, that the competition agency will be strong enough to challenge other public policies whenever necessary, and that the member countries will share a common view about the interplay between competition policy and other governmental actions. Following the Mercosur philosophy, the protocol does not create supranational organisms; the effectiveness of the regional disciplines will rely on the enforcement of the national agencies.

The protocol's goals are threefold. First, it provides mechanisms to control firms' anticompetitive practices within the Mercosur. Second, it calls for convergent domestic laws in order to ensure similar conditions of competition and independence among firms regarding the formation of prices and other market variables. Third, it provides an agenda for overseeing public policies that distort competition conditions and affect trade among the member countries. Therefore, the Mercosur competition policy should be an instrument for abolishing obstacles to the enlargement of the regional market. From this viewpoint the protocol cannot be seen just as a set of rules to be applied to anticompetitive practices with extraterritorial implications. It is more far-reaching. It deals with both governments' and firms' interference with the competition process. It does not expressly consider competition benefits, whether related to efficiency, consumer welfare, or deconcentration of economic power. However, these are expected to result from a larger market with more participants.

Regarding its first goal, the protocol seeks to prevent any concerted practice between competing firms as well as individual firms' abuse of dominant position with the aim of limiting competition in the Mercosur market. Its provisions apply to acts performed by any person, natural or legal, private or public, including state enterprises and natural monopolies, so long as such acts have extraterritorial effects. The list includes price fixing, imposition of restraints, reduction or destruction of input and output, market division, restriction of market access, bid rigging, exclusionary practices, tying arrangements, refusal to deal, resale price maintenance, market division, predatory practices, price discrimination, and exclusive dealing.

The protocol is enforced by the Mercosur Trade Commission (TC) and the Committee for the Defense of Competition (CDC).[11] The TC performs adjudicative functions, whereas the CDC is responsible for the investigation and evaluation of cases. Modeled after the provisions of a Brazilian law, the proceedings and adjudication of cases are conducted in three stages. Proceedings are initiated before the competition authority of each country at an interested party's request. After a preliminary determination of whether the practice has Mercosur implications, the competition agency may submit the case to the CDC for a second determination. Each body's evaluation must follow a rule of reason analysis in which a definition of the relevant market and evidence of the conduct and its economic effects must be provided. Based on its evaluation, the CDC must decide whether the practice violates the protocol and recommend that sanctions and other measures be imposed. The CDC ruling is submitted to the TC for final adjudication by means of a directive. As part of these procedures, the protocol has established provisions for preventive measures and undertakings of cessation. This mechanism allows the defendant to cease the investigated practice under certain obligations agreed upon with the CDC. The monitoring of these measures and the enforcement of the sanctions are the responsibilities of the national competition authorities.

Some problems may be anticipated with this system. Given the fact that the national agencies, the CDC, and the TC are independent in their judgments at

---

11. Both bodies are composed of representatives from each member country. However, in the case of the CDC, countries' representatives must come from the respective competition agencies.

each stage and that one can overrule the other at the following stage, the process of defining the Mercosur dimension of each case may be cumbersome under this system. At each stage the agency involved may apply a different criterion to define the relevant market. For instance, the national agencies may well use a restrictive criterion for market definition and close an investigation. The opposite scenario may occur if the criteria applied are more permissive. The same problems can be anticipated regarding the evaluation of the evidence and the economic effects of the practice. There is a large controversy about the limitations of applying economic analysis to anticompetitive practices. Nonetheless, assuming that each criterion is adequately defined by the national agencies, this does not ensure that other definitions and approaches may not be yielded by the CDC.

Likewise, although it is expected that the TC will adopt the CDC's rulings, the latter holds the power to overrule the rulings of the former based on its own criteria. Furthermore, given the limited experience of each country with such practices, the preliminary analysis and the CDC analysis may lead to inconsistent results. This may open the doors for discretion and political influence at any stage if the bodies base their decisions on considerations other than technical ones, particularly in their analysis of the effects of the practices under investigation on the market. Therefore, it remains to be seen how well the intergovernmental coordination mechanisms of the protocol will work and how sound and politically neutral will be the criteria applied to the practices investigated. These issues lead to consideration of a more preventive approach to practices of an extraterritorial dimension, since many of these practices are possible only when there is a lack of balance regarding their treatment at each national level.

To address this crucial area, the protocol includes provisions for the harmonization of domestic competition policy and law. Article 7 calls on the member countries to adopt, within two years, common rules for the control of acts and contracts of any kind that may limit or in any way cause prejudice to free trade or may result in the domination of the relevant regional market of goods and services, including those that result in economic concentration, with a view to preventing their possible anticompetitive effects in the Mercosur. It also calls on the countries to undertake, also within two years, to draft joint standards and mechanisms to govern state aid that is likely to limit, restrict, falsify, or distort competition and to affect trade between the parties. These provisions establish the basis for a comprehensive harmonization of competition policy to be completed by the end of 1998. The process, as clearly stated, goes beyond the treatment of anticompetitive practices to include structure concerns and competition advocacy. For the Mercosur countries this means that a long road of work is ahead of them.

At present competition is approached very differently by the various Mercosur countries. Paraguay and Uruguay do not have competition laws in place, leaving this process to be governed by the market following trade liberalization and deregulation. In Argentina and Brazil, although competition laws exist, their components, enforcement mechanisms, and policy goals differ greatly.[12] In Argentina the competition regime focuses only on preventing anticompetitive conduct. At present the Argentine Congress is working on a bill to improve enforcement of the current law, clarify the enforcement standards, introduce the evaluation of economic concentrations, and make the Competition Commission independent from the Ministry of Economy. In Brazil the amendments introduced to the law in 1994 made competition policy a critical complement to its trade and investment policies. They raised the Conselho Administrativo de Defesa Econômica (CADE) to a status independent of the Ministry of Justice, of which it had previously been a subordinate part. The CADE was given competition advocacy powers to ensure that conditions encouraging competition would not be affected by other provisions connected with privatization and regulatory reform of natural monopolies. Regulations were introduced to control economic concentrations, anticompetitive practices were more broadly defined, and the CADE was given more precise standards for analyzing and evaluating such practices. All this has set Brazil's policy apart from those of the rest of the Mercosur countries, as it is the only one that shows initial signs of the coherent approach conceived by the Mercosur protocol.

The protocol acknowledges these discrepancies, as Article 30 indicates. The program of cooperation described therein will allow countries to identify grounds of commonality and divergence regarding the goals and scope of competition and its implications for Mercosur integration. It will also lead to the identification of exceptions that might allow those anticompetitive practices that affect the market of another country—that is, state monopolies and

12. In Brazil, the Law for the Prevention of Practices against the Economic Order, No. 8.884, passed on June 11, 1994. Brazil enacted its first law on competition in 1962, and it was amended in 1990, 1991, and 1994. See OAS (1998a). In Argentina, the Law for the Protection of Competition, No. 22.262, passed on July 7, 1980. Argentina passed the region's first law on competition in 1919, and it was amended in 1947 and 1980. See OAS (1998a).

import and export cartels. These efforts may engender a coherent set of regulations on conduct and structure as well as common procedural rules and enforcement standards to be applied by independent agencies. The final outcome will be a common approach to the treatment of anticompetitive practices—that is, horizontal and vertical practices and abuse of dominant position, especially those of a discriminatory nature—as well as methodologies for merger evaluation.

The cooperation program described earlier is not explicit in the protocol, but the protocol seems to foresee it. This program includes four clear-cut stages of implementation at the national level, which are, by the way, similar to the NAFTA approach. The first stage is the enactment of a national law containing the provisions required by the protocol. The second is the creation of an autonomous and properly staffed competition policy agency. The third is the establishment of transparent operational routines by the competition policy agency, such as the publication of annual reports, guidelines to orient the private sector, consistent enforcement criteria, and so on. The fourth is the consolidation of competition advocacy as a priority task of the competition policy agency.

Concluding Remarks

The previous discussion suggests that the role of competition policy in the FTAA will be defined gradually through an overlapping set of commitments that includes at least four different types of interaction among the countries in the region. The first type is restricted to domestic law enforcement and the strengthening of national competition policy agencies through mutual regional assistance, as in the case of Mexico and its NAFTA partners. The second, as in the 1995 U.S.-Canada agreement, is focused on specific mechanisms for dealing with cases that have international consequences. The third, as in the Mercosur protocol, includes broader assignments toward policy harmonization, but without creating supranational institutions. The fourth, as in Decision 285 of the Andean Community, prevails over domestic law in cases of regional dimension.

This diversified set of institutional mechanisms is designed to solve three basic problems mentioned in the introduction to this chapter, namely how to engage those countries that do not have competition policy agencies, how to harmonize the conditions of competition in the hemisphere while preserving the variety of policy approaches, and how to ensure coherence between competition policy goals and other governmental actions that affect international trade. These issues will probably remain on the FTAA agenda well beyond the year 2005, when the negotiating process is set to end.

References

Buigues, P., A. Jacquemin, and A. Sapir, eds. 1995. *European Policies on Competition, Trade, and Industry: Conflict and Complementaries*. Aldershot, U.K.: Edward Elgar.

Graham, E., and J. Richardson, eds. 1997. *Global Competition Policy*. Washington, D.C.: Institute of International Economics.

Guasch, J., and S. Rajapatirana. 1994. "The Interface of Trade, Investment, and Competition Policies." Working Paper 1393. Washington, D.C.: World Bank.

Hoekman, B., and P. Mavroids. 1994. "Competition, Competition Policy, and the GATT." *World Economy* 17(2): 121–50.

Johnson, J. 1994. *The North American Free Trade Agreement: A Comprehensive Guide*. Aurora, Ontario, Canada: Law Book, Inc.

Organization of American States. 1998a. *Inventory of Domestic Laws and Regulations Relating to Competition Policy in the Western Hemisphere*. Washington, D.C.: OAS Trade Unit. Available on the Internet at http://www.ftaa-alca.org.

———. 1998b. *Report on Developments and Enforcement of Competition Policy and Laws in the Western Hemisphere*. Washington, D.C.: OAS Trade Unit. Available on the Internet at http://www.ftaa-alca.org.

Sarafian, E. 1997. "Trends in the Forms of International Business Organization." In *Competition Policy in the Global Economy: Modalities for Cooperation,* edited by L. Waverman, W. Comanor, and A. Goto. London: Routledge.

Vautier, K., and P. Lloyd. 1997. *International Trade and Competition Policy: CER, APEC, and the WTO*. Wellington, N.Z.: Institute of Policy Studies.

Waverman, L., W. Comanor, and A. Goto, eds. 1997. *Competition Policy in the Global Economy: Modalities for Cooperation*. London: Routledge.

CHAPTER NINETEEN

Opening Government Procurement Markets

Simeon A. Sahaydachny and Don Wallace, Jr.

This chapter provides an introductory overview of current multilateral and regional approaches to liberalization of government procurement markets, describing the basic techniques employed, the limitations of those efforts, and some possible future directions. This chapter also summarizes aspects of the procurement reform and modernization process that in many ways are common to both multilateral and regional procurement liberalization efforts, as well as to reform of national procurement systems.

The scope of government procurement is broad in terms of both the very wide range of goods and services that governments buy and the virtually countless numbers of public entities on the national, provincial, and municipal levels that engage in procurement activity on a daily basis throughout the world. Though by and large public purchasers buy tradable goods and services, government procurement has remained at the fringe of trade liberalization efforts. Traditionally preference for domestic suppliers has dominated the government procurement domain and more often than not insulated it from the pressures to reduce or remove national barriers to entry in commerce.

Estimates of the amount of world trade represented by government procurement vary. Minimum estimates of 10 percent or more are not uncommon. Wherever one pegs the estimate, it can be predicted that the volume will increase. Yet although moves to systematically liberalize trade policy and reduce and eliminate trade barriers have been underway in a concerted multilateral process since the end of World War II, that process has only relatively recently begun to focus on government procurement.

The traditional domestic preference is beginning to yield as a result of efforts at the multilateral and regional levels to liberalize government procurement markets and as a by-product of the general increase in international trade. The importance of government procurement as a share of world trade is bound to continue. Although the size of that market might be affected by trends toward divestiture of public holdings and privatization of functions traditionally performed by public bodies, those trends may very well be overshadowed by large-scale procurement involved in "build-operate-transfer" (BOT) projects or in other forms of privately financed infrastructure construction or rehabilitation and operation efforts. Therefore, multilateral and regional trade liberalization efforts aimed at government procurement continue and in fact are expanding.

The increased willingness to expose public procurement to market forces, including the forces and opportunities of international trade, is in line with the spreading recognition that a public purchaser is more likely to obtain value for money by using procurement procedures to mobilize the commercial marketplace to offer the best available value, the latest technology, and the most favorable contractual terms. The path to those objectives lies in erecting fewer rather than more trade barriers in the government procurement field.

Parallel to this process of greater multilateral and regional attention to government procurement, today an increasing number of countries are undertaking modernization and reform of national public procurement rules and systems. Such national efforts are inspired by domestic demands for greater economy and efficiency in procurement. There is also beginning to be a broader view of how economic development benefits can be derived from a transparent, competitive procurement system that helps to properly manage and channel public spending and investment and curb corruption and is open to rather than insulated from greater domestic as well as international competition.

With a new view of how government procurement can be harnessed in the service of economic development, decreasing emphasis is placed on the cruder tools of exclusion of foreign bidders and margins of preference in favor of domestic bidders; instead, more recognition is given to the economic development benefits of measures such as the following:

—Training and monitoring public entities to upgrade their procurement skills and to reduce faulty implementation of procedures, which results in obstacles to participation, especially by small and medium-sized enterprises (SMEs).

—Training the private sector, in particular SMEs, in the skills required for effective participation in public procurement.

—Using procurement packaging techniques that permit SMEs to "get a foot in the door" of procurement markets.

—More effectively disseminating information about procurement opportunities and distributing bid solicitation documents in a more timely fashion.

—Facilitating the availability of bid and performance securities for SMEs, or in certain cases waiving such requirements.

—Providing information to failed bidders as to the reasons for their failure so that they can improve their competitiveness in future proceedings.

—Promptly paying amounts due under procurement contracts.

There are many common elements—if not a symbiosis—between the multilateral or regional procurement liberalization process and the procurement reform process at the national level. That is because foreign suppliers of goods, works, and services require, from a trade liberalization point of view, not only mere "market access"; in order to compete effectively they also require transparent, predictable, objective, and fair procedures. And those happen to be features that procuring entities and domestic suppliers need as part of their own national procurement systems.

Multilateral Approaches

As in the case of investment transfers and trade in services, government procurement was traditionally a sector in which those negotiating the General Agreement on Tariffs and Trade (GATT) declined to get involved.[1] That position began to erode with the historic negotiation in 1979 during the Tokyo Round of the GATT Agreement on Government Procurement (referred to as the Government Procurement Agreement or GPA), to which adhesion was optional rather than mandatory for contracting parties to GATT. The limited initial scope of the GPA reflected the tentative and partial steps with which the

1. Article III of the basic GATT, which establishes the general principle of national treatment, reads as follows at paragraph 8(a): "The provisions of this Article shall not apply to laws, regulations or requirements governing the procurement by governmental agencies of products purchased for governmental purposes and not with a view to commercial resale or with a view to use in the production of goods for commercial sale." An analogous exclusion of government procurement is set forth in Article XIII of the General Agreement on Trade in Services (GATS).

multilateral trade liberalization process advanced onto the procurement field. Its scope was limited to procurement of goods (or "supplies"), it was subject to fairly high monetary thresholds, and it extended only to public entities of the national governments expressly listed in the annexes (a "positive list" approach) as a result of negotiation among the countries of their individual commitments.

Although the GPA is essentially a "market access" and "national-treatment" agreement in that it has lowered trade barriers in the government procurement field, the bulk of the GPA text concerns itself with various aspects of conducting procurement proceedings. This reflects a recognition that in order to give meaning to the market access provisions it is necessary at the same time to ensure that the national procurement systems have a requisite minimum degree of transparency, fairness, objectivity, and accountability.[2] This illustrates the point already alluded to—namely, that foreign bidders need more than mere market access and that there is therefore an extensive common ground for procurement reforms that are deemed essential, both from the standpoint of trade liberalization and from a purely national perspective of fostering competition, transparency, economy, and efficiency.

The Uruguay Round, which culminated in the 1994 Marrakesh Accords that transformed the GATT system into the World Trade Organization (WTO), also propelled the multilateral trade liberalization process further into government procurement. That round resulted in a substantial expansion of the scope of the GPA in 1994. The GPA now covers procurement of construction and services in addition to goods, subcentral authorities now fall within the ambit of the negotiated coverage of GPA, and monetary thresholds triggering applicability have been lowered.

2. Therefore, the GPA sets forth minimum procedural standards with respect to steps of the selection process, such as drafting objective, performance-based, and nondiscriminatory technical specifications (Article VI); using nondiscriminatory criteria for assessment of essential qualification (Article VIII); using open or selective tendering procedures, at the minimum, as a norm (Article VII); using the required contents in solicitations (Article IX); using competitive solicitation procedures in restricted tendering (Article X); adhering to minimum time frames for the submission of tenders (Article XI); using the required contents and forms of transmission for tender solicitation documents (Article XII); using standard procedures for the submission, receipt, and opening of tenders and awarding of contracts (Article XIII); dealing with information on outcome of procurement proceedings (Article XVIII); and adhering to standard bid challenge procedures (Article XX).

Although the scope of procurement covered by the terms of the GPA has expanded, with few exceptions the GPA remains an agreement among developed countries.[3] Furthermore, its scope of application depends not only on monetary thresholds, but also on a "scheduling" system. In that system each party lists its covered entities; all procurement of goods is covered, but only services and construction services specified in positive lists are covered.[4] Nevertheless, the GPA applies to a significant and increasing share of the global government procurement market. The WTO reports that from 1990 to 1994 the GPA applied annually to contracts with a total value of approximately U.S.$30 billion. It also reports an estimated tenfold increase in the value of procurement covered under the revised GPA.

Regional Approaches

With varying degrees of intensity, regional economic groups promote a procurement component in their agendas for economic integration and development.

The European Union

It has been estimated that yearly procurement by public authorities in the EU represents approximately 720 billion ECU, which is about 11 percent of the EU's gross domestic product.[5] With those kinds of numbers it is understandable

3. Parties to the GPA include Austria, Belgium, Canada, Denmark, Finland, France, Germany, Greece, Hong Kong, Ireland, Israel, Italy, Japan, Korea, Liechtenstein, Luxembourg, the Netherlands, Norway, Portugal, Singapore, Spain, Sweden, Switzerland, the United Kingdom, and the United States.

4. When discussing the scope of the GPA and similar arrangements, it should be noted that members are left free to take actions or to withhold information when they consider it necessary to protect essential security interests (GPA, Article XXIII(1)). They are also free to leave in place, as long as they are not applied in an arbitrary or discriminatory manner, enforcement measures linked to the protection of public morals, order, or safety; human, animal, or plant life or health; or intellectual property, as well as measures related to products or services for handicapped persons, philanthropic institutions, or prison labor (GPA, Article XXIII(2)). Similar exceptions are available under the Treaty of Rome for European Union (EU) member countries.

5. For an assessment of the progress achieved thus far in the EU and a discussion of suggested reform measures, see European Commission (1996). See also the subsequent Commission Communication (1998), which recommended a variety of developments and changes in the EU procurement regime.

that a cornerstone of the regional economic integration efforts of the EU has been the removal of trade barriers in government procurement. Over the last three decades this has resulted in the issuance of a series of directives freeing market access and establishing minimum procedural standards across the broad field of procurement.[6] The directives are predicated on the economic judgment that the government procurement market is a large and essential element in the construction of the common or "single" European market, that liberalization of government procurement markets is essential to give meaning to the basic common European economic liberties called for in the Treaty of Rome, and that a regional procurement market will bolster the global competitiveness and growth of European industries.

The EU experience illustrates the ambitious scope of liberalization to which a regional economic group can aspire. The directives cover procurement of supplies, public works, and services contracts, now also entities in the formerly excluded utilities fields. The detailed implementation measures include, for example, mechanisms for soliciting participation in procurement proceedings, reporting on and monitoring procurement proceedings, and dispute settlement and enforcement.

At the same time the EU experience illustrates difficulties that can linger in the implementation of regional aspirations. Those difficulties include, in particular, imperfect or incomplete implementation at the national level and limited economic impact compared to initial expectations.[7]

The North American Free Trade Agreement

Trade liberalization in government procurement is an integral component of the NAFTA, with an extensive chapter of the agreement devoted to the sub-

6. The public works consolidated text is Council Directive 93/37/EEC, *Official Journal* (OJ) no. L 199/54 (September 8, 1993); the public supply consolidated text is Council Directive 93/36/EEC, OJ no. L 199/1 (August 9, 1993); the public-sector remedies directive is 89/665/EEC, OJ no. L 395/33 (December 30, 1989); the public services text is EEC 92/50, OJ no. L 209 (1992); the service, supply, and public works directives have been amended by Council Directive 97/52/EC (October 13, 1997); and utilities procurement is subject to Council Directive 93/38/EEC, OJ no. L 199/84. The latter was amended by Directive 98/4/EC (February 16, 1998).

7. In November 1996 the EU Commission reported that only three member countries had fully implemented all texts into national law. See European Commission (1996, note 6, para. 2.9).

ject.[8] To achieve that objective the NAFTA includes provisions such as the following, which are typically relevant to a regional procurement liberalization agreement: scope of covered procurement (defined by monetary thresholds and an annexed "positive list" of covered authorities, envisaging eventual coverage of subcentral authorities), with a possibility of exceptions (for example, on the grounds of national security or defense or public safety); national treatment and nondiscrimination, in particular with regard to application of rules of origin, and provision of information to bidders; restriction of extraneous elements in technical descriptions and evaluation criteria (such as design or trade name–based specifications) and offsets; various aspects of the actual selection procedures (such as qualification requirements and assessment); solicitation procedures; various aspects of conducting procurement proceedings, such as required contents of tender documentation, minimum time frames for submission of tenders, negotiation techniques, and opening and evaluation of tenders and awards; use of "limited" or sole-source procedures; bid challenge procedures; technical cooperation programs aimed at providing training for procuring entities and bidders about procurement systems of member countries; and participation by SMEs.[9]

Pending Multilateral and Regional Developments

The arrangements negotiated thus far under the GPA and NAFTA umbrellas are by no means static. The GPA includes a mechanism for periodic review and negotiations aimed at improving the agreement and expanding its scope. A similar provision is included in the NAFTA.[10]

Apart from continuing to promote accession to the GPA, the WTO is exploring a possible multilateral agreement on transparency in government procurement. A Working Group on Transparency in Government Procurement has been established and is gathering information on national practices and the transparency provisions of existing international instruments, including WTO agreements.[11] The fact that this possible new convention is being pursued by

---

8. NAFTA, Chapter 10 ("Government Procurement").

9. NAFTA, Articles 1002–20.

10. GPA, Article XXIV(7)(b); NAFTA, Article 1024.

11. The working group was formed after the WTO Ministerial Conference held in Singapore in December 1996. The Secretariat's study on transparency-related provisions in existing agreements is set forth in Document WT/WGTGP/W/3. The Secretariat has

the WTO even though it would not focus on market access further highlights the importance of transparent public procurement procedures—from both the domestic and the international trade liberalization perspectives. The WTO Working Party on GATS Rules has been collecting information regarding government procurement of services under the GATS.

The fact that procurement reform is an ongoing process and that it is imperative not only in developing countries, but also in developed ones, is illustrated by the EU experience. The reform efforts being promoted include, in broad terms, making the EU legal framework simpler and more flexible, improving implementation of EU rules at the national level, and facilitating access to participation in procurement markets.[12] In Latin America, apart from the NAFTA process, to one extent or another consideration is being given in integration arrangements such as the Mercosur, the Andean Community, the Central American Common Market (CACM), and the Caribbean Community (CARICOM) to covering government procurement issues. Negotiations have begun within the Free Trade Area of the Americas (FTAA) framework with the broad aim of expanding access to the government procurement markets of the FTAA countries. More specifically, the objectives include openness and transparency in the normative framework, nondiscrimination within a negotiated scope of covered procurement, and fairness and impartiality in the review procedures.

Furthermore, an FTAA Working Group on Government Procurement has been established. The terms of reference of this FTAA working group include creating an inventory of applicable national procurement legislation and regulations and of procurement regulations in regional integration schemes and other existing agreements in the Western Hemisphere; compiling procurement-related data; identifying similarities and differences among national procurement systems in the hemisphere; recommending methods to promote understanding of the GPA; recommending methods of promoting

---

also gathered and synthesized information on transparency-related provisions in national procedures and practices (for example, Documents WT/WGTGP/W/5–9). Reports on working group meetings are found in Documents WT/WGTGP/M/1–6. Current work includes discussion of transparency-related provisions in existing international agreements and national regimes. Further steps may involve exploration of possible elements of an international convention on transparency in government procurement.

12. See European Commission (1998).

transparency; and recommending further development of the FTAA in the procurement field.[13]

Other developments in the Americas include the procurement-related provisions in the Group of Three (G-3) Accord concluded by Colombia, Mexico, and Venezuela. The relevant provisions of that agreement, in many respects substantively similar to the procurement provisions in the NAFTA, at present cover only procurement by federal government entities. As in the NAFTA, provision is made for eventual negotiation to expand the scope of the agreement to other levels of administration. On various issues the applicability of the procurement provisions varies among the three countries (for instance, regarding tendering rules and review procedures).

Procurement is also a subject of bilateral agreements that have been concluded by Mexico with Bolivia and Costa Rica. Those agreements offer procurement market access above specified thresholds that differ from country to country. Chile has concluded a series of bilateral agreements (with Bolivia, Colombia, Ecuador, Mexico, and Venezuela) that provide for the establishment of an administrative commission charged with defining the scope of regulation and the terms that will regulate government procurement between signatories. Elsewhere, in the Pacific Rim region a process has been commenced within the Asia Pacific Economic Cooperation (APEC) framework aimed at gathering and disseminating information on existing procurement regimes, with a view to enhancing transparency and ultimately leading to liberalization of procurement markets.

The principles and procedures of multilateral, regional, and national instruments designed to foster transparency, competition, fairness, and accountability all contribute to the control and reduction of corruption. This is because corruption thrives in nontransparent and noncompetitive environments. In addition to such approaches to the corruption problem, in the latter part of 1997 a major multilateral initiative was launched to combat corruption, namely the Convention on Combating Bribery of Foreign Public Officials in International Business Transactions. The convention, concluded under the auspices of the Organization for Economic Cooperation and Development (OECD), is aimed at controlling the "export" of corruption by bidders that seek to gain business in other countries by bribing foreign public officials.[14]

13. Inter-American Development Bank (1997).

14. The convention entered into force on February 15, 1999. As of February 12, 1999, the following countries had become parties to the convention: Canada, Finland, Germany, Hungary, Iceland, Japan, Korea, the United Kingdom, and the United States.

In the anticorruption area mention should also be made of the Inter-American Convention against Corruption (concluded on March 29, 1996) and the anticorruption provisions that have been introduced into the procurement guidelines and standard bidding documents of international lending agencies, including the World Bank (referred to as the International Bank for Reconstruction and Development or IBRD) and the Inter-American Development Bank (IDB).[15]

Procurement Reform at the National Level

Parallel to the multilateral and regional developments referred to earlier, in recent years there has been a growing wave of reform of procurement laws and institutions at the national level. This has been particularly evident in but certainly not confined to the transition countries of central and eastern Europe and the former Soviet Union.[16] The process in that region has been supported in particular by the World Bank as part of the institution-building assistance it gives to countries, and of course is to be distinguished from the application of the World Bank guidelines for procurement under its loan agreements.

When the Berlin Wall came down and the Soviet Union collapsed, a large number of countries were suddenly "in the market"—in particular, in the market for a modern legal and institutional framework for government procurement. Under their former systems there was no tradition of a market-based procurement system by which public authorities met their needs by going out into the marketplace and finding the best value for public expenditures. Rather the needs of public authorities were planned for and met within the central planning and command structure. That changed rather suddenly when public authorities had to turn to a commercial market to meet their needs—devoid of practical experience, an appropriate institutional and legal framework, and a private sector with the capacity to participate in public procurement.

---

15. For example, section 1.15 of the IBRD Procurement Guidelines (governing goods and works) defines corrupt and fraudulent practices and related grounds for rejection of proposed awards or cancellation of related portions of loans. Section 1.16 refers to the inclusion in bid forms for large contracts of an agreement by the bidder to observe the antifraud and anticorruption laws applicable in the borrower's country. Similar provisions are included in the guidelines for procurement of consultant services.

16. See Wallace (1995, pp. 58–62).

A Model Law on Procurement

In a case of striking historical coincidence and good fortune, just at the time that the economic and political changes were taking place in eastern Europe and the former Soviet Union, and the transition countries were beginning to think about procurement, the United Nations Commission on International Trade Law (UNCITRAL) happened to be preparing the UNCITRAL Model Law on Procurement of Goods, Construction and Services. In a sense the model law was able to come to the rescue of those countries by providing a template on which to base a modern, market-oriented procurement law. It is now being used in virtually all of those countries as they develop their procurement legislation and practices.

However, as already noted, the procurement law reform process is by no means confined to the former socialist countries. It is a spreading phenomenon that reflects economic and administrative transitions taking place across many regions. The reform process is fueled by increased budgetary limitations in the public sector. It is also being propelled by the increased recognition that an efficient, modern, and not excessively protective procurement system is not only good for the performance of public authorities and societal well-being, but is also a fertile ground for the development of a strong and competitive private sector. Therefore, public procurement law reform efforts are increasingly being pursued in diverse regions.[17] Furthermore, procurement law reform is being spurred by the need of member countries to implement into their national law and practices the principles and procedures of the multilateral and regional arrangements to which they belong (for instance, those of the EU).[18]

The UNCITRAL Model Law is therefore not relevant solely to one or the other geographic region or level of economic development; it codifies what are widely recognized as a set of minimum essential procedures for economy and efficiency, economic development, competition, fairness, transparency, and accountability. For that reason the Model Law may be used by countries throughout the world to measure the adequacy of existing procurement rules and to serve as a model for national procurement law reform that can be used to implement in national law the principles and procedures mandated by regional and multilateral procurement arrangements.

Use of the Model Law to implement in national law a country's regional and multilateral procurement obligations is made possible by the broad common-

17. See, for example, Office of the Vice President (1993).
18. D'Hooghe and Heijse (1997, pp. CS90–97) and Gutknecht (1997, p. CS121).

ality between the principles and procedures in the Model Law and those in regional and multilateral instruments.[19] It may also be noted in this context that the Model Law does not "reinvent the wheel"; it is the product of a consensus process within the United Nations General Assembly in which representatives of governments, expert institutions, and practitioners arrive at a codification of best practices that are acceptable in all legal systems.

If used widely, the Model Law can facilitate the opening of procurement markets, not only by imbuing them with transparent and competitive practices, but also by establishing a more harmonized and uniform procedural regime that is more familiar to bidders throughout the world than the presently diverse and splintered procedural environment in which rules and practices differ from country to country and even within countries.

The following pages survey some of the main principles and procedures of a modern national procurement law, most of which are addressed in the UNCITRAL Model Law. If enacted into national law, those principles and procedures would not only help to establish a modern national procurement system; they would also substantially accomplish compliance with the requirements of multilateral and regional arrangements.

Procurement Guidelines of Multilateral Lending Agencies

An important source of practical information about sound rules and practices that is helping to inform national reform efforts is the procurement guidelines of multilateral lending agencies, in particular the World Bank, as well as the regional institutions such as the IDB. The guidelines have been revised over the years to reflect the accumulated experience of those institutions, and they reflect principles and procedures that promote competition, transparency, and the other fundamental procurement policy objectives.[20]

---

19. Examples of issues on which there is substantial common ground include scope of application, broad solicitation requirements, nondiscrimination principles, qualification assessment procedures, transparency requirements, variety of procurement methods (with a preference for competitive ones), essential elements of invitations and other solicitation documents, objective description of procurement object, public bid-opening procedures, notice of contract award, record requirements, and review procedures.

20. A summary of the latest revisions to the World Bank guidelines is found in Hunja (1997).

Juridical Level of Procurement Rules: Statute or Regulation?

Some countries have a tradition of regulating public procurement with legal instruments of a "sublegislative" character (for example, administrative procedures, regulations, and practices). In a number of countries that approach has experienced some difficulty in obtaining tighter enforcement of procurement rules and proper practices in a modern context. Difficulties with a sublegislative approach have arisen in particular where there has not been a sufficiently strong auditing body or parliamentary oversight. Where this has been an increasing concern, a state may wish to upgrade its regulations to the level of statutory control using the UNCITRAL Model Law as the reference standard. From that viewpoint it is interesting to note that in states that have traditionally followed the United Kingdom in an approach based on administrative regulations rather than statutes, that traditional approach has begun to erode. That approach has begun to erode even in the United Kingdom itself as part of the process of enacting the EU procurement directives with legislative effect and subject to individual right to judicial review.

*Some Essential Features of an Open Government
Procurement System*

Though it is often neglected in discussions and writings about improvement and liberalization of public procurement, timely and effective planning of procurement activity is essential not only to achieving economy and efficiency in public procurement, but to maximizing competition and openness as well. This is because the procuring entity takes various crucial steps during the planning stage, including conducting market research to identify possible technical solutions to its needs and to assess the range of suppliers available, drafting technical descriptions and specifications, selecting technical evaluation and qualification criteria, selecting the contractual form, and choosing the procurement method. Those steps and others at the planning stage determine the level of openness and competition of procurement proceedings as well as their efficacy and ultimate success.

Providing Information about Procurement Opportunities

Transparency and competition in a public procurement system depend on making information about procurement opportunities available to the commercial community. The adequacy of this information goes to the heart of whether a system ensures adequate levels of participation and competition. It also affects the extent to which public procurement achieves a desired type of economic contribution to the development of local commerce and industry—for selling both to the domestic market and to potential foreign buyers.

Requiring publication of annual notices of planned procurement is a mechanism that may be used in regional and multilateral instruments governing market access to public procurement. This technique is intended to provide as wide a circle of bidders as possible with early notification of intended procurement requirements during the upcoming fiscal year.[21] Such early notice allows bidders themselves to engage in "procurement planning." It increases the number of bidders that can compete in procurement proceedings, thereby enhancing competition.

Chronologically, the next point of providing information about procurement opportunities is at the stage of actually inviting or soliciting the submission of bids. Legislative provisions on such invitations or solicitations—which typically are in the form of published notices—focus on the required contents of an invitation (essentially a "preview" of the forthcoming procurement) and the form of publication of the invitation (which may include, for example, publication in a periodical or journal of wide international circulation). It should be noted that the introduction of modern information and communications technology into the procurement process will be particularly helpful in achieving wider dissemination of information about procurement opportunities.

Selecting Time Frames for Preparation and Submission of Bids

The time frames for bids intended to accommodate foreign participation will be longer than those that envisage and facilitate only the participation of domestic companies. Basic considerations also include the nature and complexity of the procurement and the extent of subcontracting.[22]

A typical approach in legislation is to establish a minimum time frame for the preparation and submission of bids, beginning from the date of the invitation or perhaps from the date of availability of the solicitation document package.[23] Some sets of rules permit shortening the normal minimum time

21. See, for example, Article 11(1) of the EU public works directive.

22. See GPA, Article XI; NAFTA, Article 1012; and the EU public works directive, Articles 12 and 13.

23. See GPA, Article XI(3), and NAFTA, Article 1012(3).

frame for preparation of bids—for instance, in the case of urgent circumstances, for the procurement of commodities subject to market prices, if the procurement was the subject of an earlier indicative notice, or in the case of selective solicitation proceedings. In some cases there may be an absolute minimum time frame of ten days.[24] Beyond that, in cases of grave urgency, sole-source procurement would be available.

Assessing the Qualifications of Bidders

Multilateral and regional procurement liberalization agreements reflect a particular concern about the manner in which the qualifications of bidders to participate in procurement proceedings are assessed. A uniform approach in those instruments is to limit the qualification criteria to the technical, financial, managerial, and professional capability of a bidder to perform the procurement contract. Another area of concern is the potential anticompetitive effect of the use by procuring entities of lists of suppliers and contractors. Minimum safeguards for the use of such lists include publicizing the existence of any lists, not using discrimination in soliciting from firms on a list, keeping lists open for entry at any time, periodically renewing all requirements for inscribed bidders, and allowing interested bidders not on the list to participate in procurement.

Technical Description of the Object of Procurement

Defining procurement requirements properly is a crucial element of efforts to foster participation and competition by both domestic and foreign bidders. Therefore, this is an area of prime importance in developing both multilateral and regional instruments, as well as effective national procurement statutes. Describing procurement requirements is an art that involves several characteristics:

—Focusing on the performance characteristics of the object of procurement and the results desired in drafting technical specifications—rather than selecting a priori a particular product or design—and referring to international standards, when such exist, or to recognized national standards.

—Fostering best prices and more choices for the procuring entity—for instance, by permitting deviations within a permissible range—and disclosing to bidders the manner in which deviations will be quantified and assessed in the evaluation of bids.

24. See NAFTA, Article 1012(3)(c).

—Establishing clear channels for promptly responding to requests for clarification of solicitation documents.

Providing Information about the "Rules of the Game"

All the bidders need to be provided with all the necessary information about the rules applicable to the competition between the bidders participating in a procurement proceeding. That includes information about qualification criteria and procedures; technical requirements; evaluation criteria; in procurement of supplies and works, keeping the assessment of bidder qualifications separate from the technical assessment of bids; the procurement method to be employed, including whether any negotiation stage is planned; the deadline for submission of bids; any planned conference of bidders or site visit; requirements as to bid and performance securities; the contract form to be signed; and review and complaint ("bid challenge") procedures.

As important as is revealing the rules of the game to bidders, it is essential that public officials themselves be versed in the rules, procedures, and techniques of public procurement. This requires the establishment of adequate entry-level educational requirements and the provision of initial training as well as procedures for certification and ongoing upgrading of professional skills. Preparation and circulation of standard forms and other guidance materials can be very useful.

Such measures can be accomplished at a relatively low cost to a country vis-à-vis the potential savings and other benefits to the economy of an effectively managed procurement system (for instance, standard forms and guidance materials can be made available on line and through other applications of information technology, and training programs can be conducted at regional centers). Part of providing more detailed procedural steps, particularly for relatively young and less experienced procurement systems, may be to issue "procurement regulations" in order to implement the principles and procedures stated in the law in greater detail.

From the standpoint both of procuring entities and bidders, it is crucial that the applicable rules be set forth in as clear a manner as possible. Desirable means of achieving such clarity include avoiding the issuance of multiple overlapping instruments, which can be confusing and contradictory, preferring when possible the consolidation of procurement rules into a single text; reducing the complexity of applicable legal instruments; issuing clear statements of the scope of application of procurement rules that include broad definitions of covered procuring entities, goods, works, and services and permissible means of acquisition; including rules on valuation and aggregation of contracts (rules against artificial division of a procurement for the purpose of avoiding monetary thresholds that require the use of more competitive methods of procurement); and disclosing the applicable legal rules to bidders in advance.[25]

Establishing Objective Evaluation Criteria

Evaluation criteria basically fall into two categories: price and price-related criteria and nonprice criteria. It is essential to proper practice that bids be evaluated in accordance only with the criteria and their relative weight, as disclosed to bidders. A pitfall generally to be avoided is the mixing of qualification and technical evaluation criteria in the evaluation process. Such a mixing of criteria can put the procuring entity in the position of unnecessarily paying a premium for the highest qualifications when a less qualified though still very qualified bidder could have performed the procurement contract with full effectiveness and at a better price.

It should be noted that procurement market liberalization efforts generally tend to diminish the extent to which the tender evaluation process can continue to use criteria that are linked to socioeconomic policies or designed to favor domestic industry.[26] It should be further noted in this regard that to facilitate participation by developing countries the GPA calls on the parties to the agreement to take into account finance needs and trade factors that may affect developing countries' participation in procurement, including safeguarding their balance of payments and reserve positions so they will be able to pursue economic development programs; promoting economic development in various sectors, including the establishment of domestic industry, in particular rural and SMEs; providing support for companies that are wholly or substantially dependent on government procurement; and participating in regional or global arrangements among developing countries.

However, the GPA refers to those needs not in terms of altering the selection or evaluation criteria in procurement proceedings, but in terms of negotiating and sometimes modifying the designated scope of covered entities and procurement in favor of the needs of developing countries. The GPA establishes a

---

25. See Boyle (1994, pp. 101–13); European Commission (1996, note 6, para. 3.6); and NAFTA, Article 1010(8).

26. For a discussion of this question, see Arrowsmith (1995, pp. 235–84).

negotiation process for identifying any exclusions from a developing country's designated coverage under the agreement.

The UNCITRAL Model Law refers to the possibility of considering criteria other than price in the evaluation and comparison of tenders in Article 34(4)(c)(iii). The inclusion of this provision in the Model Law should not be interpreted as a recommendation that enacting countries necessarily apply such socioeconomic criteria. As in the case of margins of preference in favor of domestic bidders, application of socioeconomic evaluation criteria may lead the procuring entity to pay a higher price. As a result, some jurisdictions have retreated from the application of such criteria in order to avoid increased costs at a time of austerity. Furthermore, use of such criteria, which are by definition vague and difficult to quantify, may increase subjectivity and the risk of abuse and may erode the transparency and competition achieved by procedures of the type in the UNCITRAL Model Law.

What the Model Law requires is that, if an enacting country opts for socioeconomic criteria, the permitted types of criteria should be limited to those identified in the statute or regulatory instrument. Furthermore, only those criteria predisclosed in the solicitation documents may be used in any given procurement proceeding. It is also recommended that any such criteria be quantified in monetary terms to the extent possible so as to increase the predictability and objectivity of their application.

Providing Information about the Procurement Proceedings

The most obvious information about what happened in the procurement proceedings is the notice of award of contract to be given to the successful bidder. Providing information about what happened in the procurement proceedings to unsuccessful bidders—those rejected either on technical or qualifications grounds—helps them to develop their capability with a view to success in future proceedings. It also helps bidders to monitor the procuring entity's compliance with required procedures and is essential to upholding the right of bidders to obtain review of alleged noncompliance by procuring entities.

Providing information about the procurement proceedings is valuable in other situations as well. A technique for making more transparent the use of procurement methods that are less than the most competitive is to require public notice in such cases. Such a requirement may particularly be applied when restricted tendering or sole-source procurement is used for procurement of items above a certain value. In view of the risk of abuse in the cancellation of procurement proceedings or in the rejection of all bids—especially when that may lead to a sole-source procurement—in such cases some systems require the publication of a notice. Multilateral and regional procurement arrangements—and sound national laws—require procuring entities to maintain "minutes," a "record," or at least documentation of the procurement proceedings.[27]

Regional and multilateral agreements establish an obligation that countries party to the arrangements make available to other countries party to the arrangements information on procurement within their jurisdictions. Such measures allow authorities of these parties to respond to their constituents as to the conduct and outcomes of procurement proceedings in other countries.[28] Regional or multilateral agreements may also require obligatory periodic reporting by countries party to regional economic groupings of, for example, annual procurement statistics and patterns (which may have to be broken down in terms of total annual value and number of procurement contracts and assorted sectors or procuring entities) and use of restricted solicitation methods of procurement).[29] It is crucial, however, that both domestic and international reporting requirements be designed in a way that avoids imposition of excessive burdens on procuring entities and disruption of the procurement process.

Developing an Adequate Range of Procurement Methods

From the standpoint of opening up the procurement process to as much competition as possible, an adequate range of procurement methods is crucial. Without it procurement systems tend to drop down from the most competitive method (open tendering) through such methods as restricted tendering to the least competitive method (sole-source procurement, which is used in those situations in which open or restricted tendering is not appropriate or feasible).

A "procurement method" may be understood as the type of specific procedure applied to select the supplier or contractor with which the procuring entity will conclude a procurement contract. Procurement methods vary as to several aspects, including extent of competition (for example, open solicitation and

27. See GPA, Article XX(4); NAFTA, Article 1017(1)(o); and UNCITRAL Model Law, Article 11.

28. See GPA, Article XIX(2) and (3), and NAFTA, Article 1019(3).

29. See GPA, Article XIX(5), and NAFTA, Article 1019(7).

participation or restricted or sole solicitation), time required to complete the procurement selection process, whether opportunities exist for negotiation with bidders during the selection process, dominance of price as the selection criterion, and amount of procedural structure and transparency.

Showing a Preference for "Open" Tendering Methods

A characteristic of many if not most public procurement systems is a preference for use of open tendering—that is, unrestricted competition with the selection based on "lowest price" or "lowest evaluated price," as disclosed in advance to bidders. That preference is found in many national laws and is reflected in the UNCITRAL Model Law. The preference for use of open tendering proceedings is also reflected in the guidelines for procurement of goods and works of the World Bank and other international financing institutions.

The minimum requirements of the EU directives focus on the mandatory publication of a "notice" of the procurement, but fall short of insisting that countries mandate use of open tendering as the "normal method." The normal minimum method is either open or "restricted" tendering, which is like a normal tendering proceeding, but without the open solicitation of participation (instead there is direct solicitation of a limited number of bidders). For either variant the EU system requires the procuring entity to publicize the procurement. The GPA similarly leaves open the choice of using an open or restricted tendering method. At the national level, however, most countries implement this requirement by mandating the use of open tendering, allowing restricted tendering to be used only in exceptional circumstances.

Use of open tendering as a default method for procurement serves simultaneously objectives of maximizing competition and providing access to the procurement market—both for domestic bidders and for foreign bidders. Its characteristic structure, transparency, and use of price-based criteria for selection also serve to strengthen the integrity of the procurement system, deliver generally lower prices, and develop a climate of fairness, economy, and efficiency in public procurement.

Using Alternative Procurement Methods

Promoting economy and efficiency and the other objectives of procurement means that for situations in which tendering is not appropriate other methods of procurement must be available. Yet promoting those objectives also requires that the use of alternative procurement methods that are less competitive and transparent than open tendering be confined to the situations for which they are intended.

The ways in which the "conditions for use" of alternative procurement methods are formulated and implemented in a national procurement law affect the effectiveness as well as the degree of openness of a procurement system. In other words, the economy, efficiency, and competition of public procurement can be measured by the extent to which alternative methods may be used, as well as by the procedures applicable to their use.

Some typical situations in which national procurement laws, as well as multilateral and regional arrangements, authorize the use of alternative methods are set forth here. Exceptions to the requirement to use open tendering are typically available when the value of the item to be procured is low, such that the cost involved in conducting open tendering or using other relatively elaborate methods outweighs the possible cost savings available under such methods. Depending on the value of the item to be procured—and the approach used under the specific applicable legal regime—the purchase may be exempt from normal procurement procedures if its cost is within the limit of funds that can be spent on a "petty cash" type of basis without the use of any competitive procedures. Alternatively, for procurement of an item whose value is higher than that limit but not very high, procedures for a restricted tendering or request for quotation may be available for use.

A classic case of the use of alternative methods of procurement is the one in which the goods, works, or services are available only from a sole source or from a limited number of bidders known to the procuring entity. In the former case sole-source procurement would obviously be authorized. In such cases and in view of the lack of competition involved, it is crucial to scrutinize whether what is alleged to be available from only a single source is an item that truly is required and can be used only if it comes to the procuring entity in the unique configuration or scale in which it is available from the particular supplier.

Additional types of situations in which the use of an alternative method of procurement might be authorized include situations in which the procuring entity is unable to provide complete technical specifications, research contracts do not result in the production of goods in commercially recoverable quantities, commodities are purchased at public market prices, artistic works are needed, there is an urgency not due to the dilatory conduct of the procuring entity or urgency involving a threat to physical safety or property, supplemental orders are needed, or when technically necessary.

Establishing an Institutional Framework

An essential feature of procurement systems that promote transparency, competition, and fairness is an effective and swift system for review of bidder complaints about violations by procuring entities of required procedures during the procurement proceedings leading to contract award. Such a system is an important tool for making procurement rules to some extent "self-enforcing," since it allows bidders to have their complaints about transgressions of rules heard. Multilateral and regional arrangements typically require their member countries to establish such systems for review of bidder complaints.[30]

Key features of a bid challenge system include clear recognition of bidders' right to independent review of complaints; availability of review at any stage of the procurement proceedings, including the possibility, in appropriate circumstances, of initially lodging complaints directly with the procuring entity itself, which maximizes the possibility that more complaints will be resolved at an early, less detrimental stage; safeguards against excessive disruption and delay of the procurement proceedings by excluding certain limited, discretionary acts and decisions of the procuring entity and maintaining tight deadlines and time frames for the review process; and ultimate recourse to judicial-level review.

Training and Procurement Professionalism

The experience with the nascent public procurement systems in the transition countries illustrates to an extreme degree a lesson that is applicable everywhere: effective implementation of a procurement law and resultant procurement contracts—no matter how perfectly those legal instruments may be drafted—requires skilled professionals. This means in particular that whenever the volume of procurement is sufficient it is preferable that there be a core staff that devotes most if not all of its time to procurement. Without that it is unlikely that the job can be done properly and in a way that avoids unnecessary expenditures, diminished quality, and delay.

Reference has already been made to the need for training of both public officials and the private sector. The need for initial and ongoing training cannot be overemphasized. The relatively small amounts involved in funding training programs need to be spent if the procurement system is to achieve savings rather than incurring losses for the country.[31]

30. See GPA, Article XX; NAFTA, Article 1017; and EU remedies directive.
31. See NAFTA, Article 1020.

Establishing a Monitoring and Oversight Body

The operations and effectiveness of procurement operations in various countries are subject to a degree of monitoring and, to one extent or another, oversight. The exact structure and setup of monitoring and oversight bodies vary from country to country. The level, substance, and style of such activity depend upon the degree of decentralization of administrative authority, including procurement authority, across various levels of administration.

What is generally preferable is that regulatory, monitoring, oversight, and policymaking bodies be independent and report to the highest levels of government. Experience has shown that such bodies are more effective if they are not also involved in procurement decisionmaking (either by conducting procurement proceedings themselves or by having ex officio seats assigned to them on the tender committees of individual ministries or other procuring entities).

On the national level, monitoring and oversight from a central vantage point in the administrative structure can be an effective tool for promoting compliance with required procurement norms and procedures. Regionally or multilaterally, monitoring activities also play a role in implementing procurement arrangements. The degree of intrusiveness of such activities into national procurement prerogatives depends upon the ambitiousness of the economic integration arrangement in the procurement field. Therefore, in the EU the Commission is provided with fairly detailed information about procurement activities. The Commission's monitoring capability is enhanced by the publication of procurement notices in the *Official Journal*. Moreover, the Commission is given authority to review implementation and application of the procurement directives of the EU. The Commission also has standing to bring national authorities before the European Court of Justice to obtain enforcement measures.

Using Standard Forms and Documents

As an aid to the implementation and harmonization of procurement procedures, a central body may develop and promulgate general conditions of contract, sample forms of instructions to bidders for preparation and submission of bids, and standard forms of other documents to be used in implementation of procurement procedures (for instance, standard forms for bidder and bid evaluation and for keeping records of procurement proceedings). The use of such standard documentation may in particular assist newly trained procurement officials, increase transparency in the procurement system (for example, by increasing the clarity of the rights and obligations of the parties to the procurement contract), and facilitate participation by more bidders, both domestic and foreign.

Using Information Technology

It is not possible in an overview of this type to discuss information in the procurement process without mentioning the growing use of modern "information technology" in the procurement process. Application of information technology to government procurement will benefit all participants in the process, both domestic and foreign. Information technology can be used for various purposes in the procurement process. It can be a powerful tool for diffusion of information about procurement opportunities, including publication of invitations to tenders. Other uses include establishing linkages to suppliers and materials management systems; performing market research; storing and improving access to communications about procurement proceedings that have taken place; facilitating payment; circulating among procuring entities, suppliers, and contractors legal texts, standard forms, and training materials; distributing solicitation documents; and collecting statistics. The increased use of information technology is anticipated in the GPA, which calls on the parties to hold consultations to ensure that such technology is used with a view to achieving the basic objectives of public procurement procedures, including nondiscrimination and openness.[32]

Conclusion

It used to be that government procurement was a stepchild of the trade negotiation process. That is clearly no longer the case, as the subject is increasingly approaching, if not center stage, at least an important supporting role in trade liberalization.

Although the future extent and velocity of procurement market opening may be unclear from today's vantage point, what is increasingly beyond question is that the trade liberalization process in the procurement field—pioneered by the GATT Agreement on Government Procurement and the regional efforts in the EU—will continue to expand. This is already the case in the Americas with the advent of the NAFTA and in the nascent moves being made in other

32. See GPA, Article XXIV(8).

regional integration developments. That process will be significantly assisted by the fact that many of the same procurement reforms that are fueled by the imperative of national economic and administrative development also help to lay the groundwork for open government procurement markets.

References

Arrowsmith, S. 1995. "Public Procurement as an Instrument of Policy and the Impact on Market Liberalization." *Law Quarterly Review* 111.

Boyle, R. 1994. "EC Public Procurement Rules: A Purchaser Reflects on the Need for Simplification." *Public Procurement Law Review* 3.

D'Hooghe, D., and R. Heijse. 1997. "New Belgian Legislation on the Award of Public Procurement Contracts." *Public Procurement Law Review* 6.

European Commission. 1996. "Public Procurement in the European Union: Exploring the Way Forward." Green Paper (November). COM (96) 583 final, 27.11.1996.

———. 1998. "Public Procurement in the European Union." Commission Communication (March 11). COM (98) 143.

Gutknecht, B. 1997. "Amendment to the Austrian Federal Procurement Act." *Public Procurement Law Review* 6.

Hunja, R. 1997. "Recent Revisions to the World Bank's Procurement and Consultant Selection Guidelines." *Public Procurement Law Review* 6: 217–26.

Inter-American Development Bank. 1997. "Government Procurement Rules in Integration Arrangements in the Americas." Washington, D.C. (January).

Office of the Vice President. 1993. "Reinventing Federal Procurement." Report of the *National Performance Review*. Washington, D.C. (September).

Wallace, D., Jr. 1995. "The Changing World of National Procurement Systems: Global Reformation." *Public Procurement Law Review* 4.

CHAPTER TWENTY

Labor Rights

Craig VanGrasstek

More than is the case with any other topic examined in this volume, there is no consensus that the issue of labor rights is a fit subject for trade negotiations. Even the proposed link between trade and the environment is more firmly entrenched in the agenda than is labor rights, insofar as it has been the subject of numerous dispute settlement panels of the General Agreement on Tariffs and Trade (GATT) and the World Trade Organization (WTO) and is under consideration in the WTO Committee on Trade and Environment. It is nevertheless erroneous to characterize labor rights as the newest issue in trade policy. As far back as the mercantilist era, concerns over different international wage rates and standards of living have been cited as an argument for import protection. These fears, coupled in recent decades with the elevation of human rights as a legitimate topic of foreign policy, have inspired several domestic laws and a few international agreements. Rather than examining the introduction of labor rights into the international trading system, therefore, it is more correct to examine the evolution of this topic and its potential impact on trade relations in the Americas.

This chapter focuses primarily and deliberately on the laws, policies, and internal political debate of the United States. It is my thesis that the high profile of this issue has posed a great complication for the politics of trade liberalization at both at the domestic level and the international level. The prospects for achieving real progress in the negotiations for the Free Trade Area of the

Americas (FTAA) depends, first and foremost, upon reaching some accommodation in the internal U.S. debate. The lack of a domestic consensus on labor and environmental objectives has blocked a new extension of fast-track negotiating authority from Congress to the president. Unless and until Congress grants new authority to the president, the ability of the United States to reach definitive deals on any issues in the FTAA negotiations will be compromised. Even if it is ultimately decided that labor rights will not be identified as negotiating objectives in a new fast-track grant and this topic does not become a formal part of the FTAA negotiations, the United States may pursue this matter with its Latin American and Caribbean partners through other means.

What Are Labor Rights?

The term *labor rights* encompasses a wide array of standards, not all of which are of equal importance. Between 1919 and 1997 the members of the International Labor Organization (ILO) adopted 181 conventions and 188 recommendations, ranging from essential human rights to the specific needs of seafarers.[1] The diversity of labor standards has prompted several attempts to distinguish between essential and less significant standards, including that of a 1997 report prepared by the labor ministers of the member countries of the Organization of American States (OAS). The array of "key," "basic," "core," and "internationally recognized" standards, as defined by international organizations and U.S. law, is summarized in table 20-1. Examining these lists closely, one can distinguish between three broad categories of essential standards: prohibited practices, political rights, and specific standards.

One approach is to prohibit the more egregious forms of exploitation, which are generally recognized to constitute violations of essential human rights. These include slave labor, indentured servitude, prison labor, and some child labor, as well as discrimination on the basis of race, religion, or sex. The Universal Declaration of Human Rights, for example, prohibits slavery and the slave trade.[2] The identification of prohibited practices is the least controversial means of defining labor standards and is the only one to receive partial recognition in WTO law.[3] Even some economists who are otherwise leery of the

1. Data from the ILO web site (http://www.ilo.org/public/english/235press/leaflet/page5.html).
2. "The Universal Declaration of Human Rights" (1948), Article 4.
3. See the discussion that follows of GATT Article XX(e).

proposed trade-labor linkage agree that certain practices are beyond the pale and should be proscribed (albeit on a voluntary basis).

A second and more politically sensitive approach is to focus on the civic rights of workers, especially the rights to organize and bargain collectively. These rights appear in all lists of core rights, but figure most prominently in U.S. policy. Former secretary of Labor Robert Reich had this political class of labor rights in mind when he declared:

> The existence of democratic institutions—multiple parties, freedom of speech and the press, clean elections—makes it more likely that low wages and poor working conditions are caused by unfortunate but legitimate economic constraints. The less democratic is the country, conversely, the greater the grounds for suspicion that labor standards are being suppressed to serve narrow commercial interests or a misguided mercantilist impulse on the part of elites, at the expense not just of mass living standards but also of global economic efficiency.[4]

We can be thankful that this approach is less troublesome to Latin American countries today than at any time in the past four decades. All of the heads of state attending the Miami and Santiago summits were elected democratically. The stress on democratic rights is also carried over into the U.S. negotiating position within the FTAA process, where the Office of the U.S. Trade Representative (USTR) has argued that workers must not be "disenfranchised" and that labor unions should enjoy the same advisory role that is already extended to business organizations.

The third approach, and perhaps the most problematic for free traders, is to identify specific standards that must be met regarding the ages of workers, their wages, working hours, or other criteria. The OAS and Organization for Economic Cooperation and Development (OECD) lists of essential standards make no reference to these matters, but they are the subject of one key ILO convention and fall within the U.S. definition of "internationally recognized worker rights." The emphasis is most commonly on wages, where the gap between industrialized and developing countries can be quite wide. In 1996, for example, the average hourly compensation for workers in manufacturing industries was $17.70 in the United States and $1.50 in Mexico.[5] The principal fear of critics is that high-wage industrialized countries might seek to impose specific standards on low-wage developing countries and hence undercut one

4. U.S. Department of Labor (1994, p. 4).
5. U.S. Department of Labor (1997).

Table 20-1. Alternate Definitions of Principal Labor Standards

"Key conventions" (ILO)	"Basic labor standards" (OAS)	"Core labor standards" (OECD)	"Internationally recognized workers' rights" (U.S. law)
No. 87—Freedom of Association and Protection of the Right to Organize Convention (1948): Establishes the right of workers and employers to form organizations without interference.	Freedom of association and protection of the workers' right to organize.	Freedom of association and collective bargaining, i.e. the right of workers to form organizations of their own choice and to negotiate freely their working conditions with their employers.	The right of association.
No. 98—Right to Organize and Collective Bargaining Convention (1949): Provides for protection against anti-union discrimination, and for measures to promote collective bargaining.	The right to bargain collectively for the terms of employment and working conditions.		The right to organize and bargain collectively.
No. 29—Forced Labour Convention (1930): Requires suppression of forced or compulsory labor.	The prohibition of child labor and forced labor.	Elimination of *exploitive* forms of child labor, such as bonded labor and forms of child labor that put the health and safety of children at serious risk.	A prohibition on the use of any form of forced or compulsory labor.

ILO Convention	Description		
No. 105—Abolition of Forced Labour Convention (1957): Prohibits the use of any form of forced or compulsory labor as among other things a means of political coercion or education.		Prohibition of forced labor, in the form of slavery and compulsory labor.	
No. 111—Discrimination (Employment and Occupation) Convention (1958): Calls for the elimination of discrimination in access to employment, training, and working conditions.	The right to choose one's job without being subject to sexual, racial, religious, or any other form of discrimination.	Non-discrimination in employment, i.e. the right to equal respect and treatment of all workers.	
No. 100—Equal Remuneration Convention (1951): Calls for equal pay and benefits for men and women for work of equal value.			Acceptable conditions of work with respect to minimum wages, hours of work, and occupational safety and health.
No. 138—Minimum Age Convention (1973): Aims at the abolition of child labor, with the minimum age being younger than the age of completion of compulsory schooling.			A minimum age for the employment of children

Sources: ILO web site (descriptions of conventions edited for length); OAS (1997, p. 6); OECD (1996, p. 26) (emphasis in original); section 502(a)(4) of the Trade Act of 1974, as amended in 1985 (19 USC 2462(a)(4)).

of the few economic advantages that these countries enjoy. Under a nightmare scenario, importing countries might enact something like a "wage-differential tax" to impose penalty tariffs on imports from countries where low wages are deemed to confer an unfair competitive advantage. One need look no further than the antidumping laws to appreciate how such a mechanism could be captured by protectionist interests.

Although the U.S. law suggests that a country should specify a minimum age and a minimum wage, it does not require that these be set at any particular level. American policymakers have repeatedly assured their counterparts that they do not intend to seek the establishment of an international minimum wage. On at least two occasions, however, a U.S. negotiating partner made a tacit (if unspecific) bargain in this area. Although the issue was not a formal part of the negotiations, Japan announced after concluding tariff talks with the United States in 1955 that wage standards and practices would be maintained at "fair levels."[6] Similarly, the government of Mexico announced in 1993 that the country's minimum wage would from that time forward rise with overall productivity; this pledge was intended to win support for ratification of the North American Free Trade Agreement (NAFTA) in the U.S. Congress.

The specific U.S. negotiating objectives remain a matter of intense dispute between the executive and legislative branches of government. Congress first included labor rights as an approved negotiating objective in the Omnibus Trade and Competitiveness Act of 1988. This law, which is still on the statute books, stated the U.S. objectives that there be "a review of the relationship of worker rights to GATT articles, objectives, and related instruments with a view to ensuring that the benefits of the trading system are available to all workers" and that the GATT adopt the principle "that the denial of worker rights should not be a means for a country or its industries to gain competitive advantage in international trade."[7] These objectives were supplemented by section 131 of the Uruguay Round Agreements Act of 1994, which called for the establishment of a WTO working party "to examine the relationship of internationally recognized worker rights . . . to the articles, objectives, and related instruments of the GATT 1947 and of the WTO, respectively."[8] The provision proposed, among other things, that the working party consider ways to address the effects that the systematic denial of these rights have on international trade

6. Charnovitz (1986, p. 65).
7. 19 USC 2901(b)(14).
8. 19 USC 3551.

and "develop methods to coordinate the work program of the working party with the International Labor Organization." Neither the 1988 nor the 1994 objectives were achieved in the Uruguay Round or in subsequent WTO ministerial meetings. More recent efforts to define U.S. objectives in this area have failed to produce consensus, as is discussed in the next section.

The Controversy Surrounding the Issue

The issue of labor rights inevitably provokes sharp debate between its proponents and its detractors. Many members of the trading community echo the concern that "the trade-standards link could become hijacked by protectionist interests attempting to preserve activities rendered uncompetitive by cheaper imports,"[9] whereas the advocates of stricter standards express equally strong objections to the perceived threats posed by an unbridled market to the interests of working people.

The controversy lays bare a cultural and ideological divide between two strains of liberal thought. Both political liberalism and economic liberalism are based on the proposition that individuals should be free to make decisions for themselves, whether in the political sphere (democracy) or in the economic sphere (the marketplace). A dilemma arises when democratic demands call for government intervention in the market, whether in matters domestic (a minimum wage, rent control, and so on) or in matters international (for instance, trade protection). Economic liberals fear that such intervention will cause market failure, whereas the proponents of stricter labor standards fear that the poor and politically weak are vulnerable to exploitation when market forces are not tempered by the state.

Economists traditionally focus on efficiency and productivity and view labor—like land and capital—as an input in the production process. Like any other input, this commodity will fetch a lower price in places where it is abundant or of lower quality (that is, developing countries) than it will in places where it is scarce or of higher quality (that is, industrialized countries). Liberal economists argue that low wages, poor working conditions, and exploitative labor practices are inferior goods that countries will consume in decreasing quantities as they grow more efficient and prosperous. In this respect, it may be argued, violations of workers' rights will wither away in the same fashion as

9. World Bank (1995, p. 79).

protectionist trade policies, lax environmental rules, or loose enforcement of intellectual property laws. Economic optimists believe that each of these problems will solve itself as an economy grows and a society adopts middle-class values, and therefore reform need not be prodded along by state intervention. The self-correcting nature of this mechanism will be frustrated, however, if developing countries face new barriers to their exports.

For labor unions, human rights organizations, and other like-minded groups it is offensive to view labor as a commodity. They argue that considerations of equity and fairness, including the distribution of income between workers and their employers, must come before questions of productivity and efficiency. Some among them see trade not as part of the solution, but as a key component of the problem. Open markets are sometimes said to encourage a "race to the bottom" in which countries seek to attract footloose capital by repressing wages and assuring prospective investors that they will face no trouble from labor unions. The greater mobility of capital can even be a union-busting tactic: its owners can threaten to move production offshore if workers do not moderate their demands for higher wages.

Operating on a principle of enlightened self-interest, American labor unions have perennially opposed the exploitation of foreign workers. The manner in which they promote this issue has shifted markedly over the past half century. Labor unions were part of the U.S. pro-trade coalition during the 1930s through the early 1960s, and during this period they favored both the reduction of trade barriers and the promotion of labor rights. As an increasing number of industries faced competition from developing countries, and especially when firms shifted more production overseas ("exporting jobs"), the unions began to change their objectives. For a time the unions' support for liberalization could be maintained by grants of trade adjustment assistance (TAA) for workers who lost their jobs to foreign competition; the promise of TAA secured the support of the American Federation of Labor–Congress of Industrial Organizations (AFL-CIO) for the Trade Expansion Act of 1962. By the late 1970s, however, the AFL-CIO had become a core member of the anti-trade coalition, and its demands for linkage between labor rights and trade liberalization became more combative. Some critics believe that these demands are intended not so much to influence the outcome of trade negotiations as to prevent them altogether.

Unions are not alone in promoting a link between trade and labor rights. Three American presidents—each one an internationalist Democrat—put a high priority on both objectives. For President Woodrow Wilson labor rights and open markets were related components of a liberal new world order. Free trade was the third of Wilson's Fourteen Points, and the ILO was a cornerstone of the League of Nations. Wilson convinced his peers to adopt these initiatives, but not his countrymen; Congress refused to ratify the Treaty of Versailles and enacted protectionist trade laws in the 1920s. President Franklin Roosevelt renewed Wilson's internationalist policies. It is no coincidence that 1934 saw both the enactment of the Reciprocal Trade Agreements Act (the legal foundation of U.S. trade liberalization through the 1960s) and U.S. entry into the ILO. Both of these steps were facilitated by the fact that Roosevelt, unlike Wilson, enjoyed the luxury of united government (that is, his party held majorities in both houses of Congress). President Clinton shares the internationalist proclivities of Wilson and Roosevelt, but operates under the same partisan handicap that hindered Wilson.

The current fight over this issue dates to the domestic U.S. politics of the NAFTA. In the early 1990s Presidents Bush and Clinton responded to growing demands that labor rights be on the NAFTA negotiating agenda. Both presidents hoped that accommodations would neutralize or reduce the level of opposition that labor unions might mount to their trade programs: President Bush negotiated a few provisions in the NAFTA itself dealing with this topic, and President Clinton supplemented these provisions with a more explicit side agreement. Their maneuvers on this issue, as well as the inclusion of environmental issues on the agenda, were successful in the short term, but exacerbated partisan conflict in the long term.

President Clinton has sought to build upon the NAFTA precedents in new trade negotiations, but Republicans—who took control of Congress in the 1994 elections—have opposed these plans. That turnover in party control, which has greatly exacerbated the difficulties in obtaining a new grant of fast-track negotiating authority, ironically coincided with the formal start of the FTAA process at the Miami Summit of the Americas. Congress and the Clinton administration have negotiated ever since over a renewal of the president's fast-track negotiating authority. The principal stumbling block has been the disagreement between Democrats and Republicans over the objectives that the United States will pursue on labor and environmental matters. Although many Democrats insist that these issues must become an integral part of trade agreements and be backed with the power of enforcement, most Republicans insist that such matters be "off the table." The Clinton administration has been unable to devise language that would satisfy a sufficient number of legislators in both parties. The most recent failure came in September 1998, when the House of Representatives rejected a fast-track renewal bill on a vote of 180 to

243. In the absence of a politically acceptable compromise, U.S. participation in the FTAA negotiations will be conducted under a cloud of uncertainty.

Despite this internal disagreement and even sharper objections from several of its trading partners, the United States has pressed forward with proposals in several different forums. Fast track is not necessary for U.S. statesmen to participate in negotiations or to sign agreements, but this mechanism vastly facilitates congressional approval of agreements. As is reviewed in the following pages, these U.S. proposals are now pending in multilateral, bilateral, and regional negotiations. In addition, the executive is also empowered to employ unilateral measures in pursuit of these goals.

Multilateral Options

The history of multilateral efforts to promote workers' rights is much longer than is commonly believed. It stretches at least as far back as a 1906 convention on phosphorus matches, which aimed at eliminating a notorious industry that was responsible for the poisoning of workers. This agreement linked trade with labor standards: in addition to banning the production, sales, and exportation of these matches, the pact also prohibited imports of this product.[10]

Today the two key international organizations dealing with trade and labor rights—respectively, not together—are the WTO and the ILO. The institutional cultures and political histories of these two bodies are very different, as is summarized in table 20-2. One might argue that their closest similarities are geographical and architectural. Both institutions are located in Geneva, and the WTO is housed in the former headquarters of the ILO.[11] When trade negotiators ascend the staircase into the meeting rooms, they still pass by a charming 1931 mural entitled *La Dignité du Travail*.

Some argue that the ILO alone has the mandate and the means to address labor issues. This claim is reminiscent of the arguments in the early 1980s that there was no need to bring intellectual property rights within the purview of the GATT because the World Intellectual Property Organization (WIPO) already enjoyed a well-established institutional competence in this area. The U.S.

10. Shotwell (1934).

11. In another twist of architectural irony, the first formal meeting of the ILO was held at the Washington headquarters of the OAS. See ILO (1994, especially pp. 14–15).

Table 20-2. Comparison of the International Labor Organization and the World Trade Organization

Parameter	International Labor Organization	World Trade Organization
Purpose	To improve "condition of labor" through such means as "the regulation of hours of work. . . . the regulation of the labor supply, the prevention of unemployment, the provision of an adequate living wage, the protection of the worker against sickness, disease, and injury. . . . the protection of children, young persons, and women, provision for old age and injury, protection of the interests of workers when employed in countries other than their own . . . recognition of the principle of freedom of association . . . and other measures."	To "rais[e] standards of living," "ensur[e] full employment," and achieve other economic aims by "entering into reciprocal and mutually advantageous arrangements directed to the substantial reduction of tariffs and other barriers in trade and to the elimination of discriminatory treatment in international trade relations."
History	Established in 1919 as part of the Treaty of Versailles, in the aftermath of World War I.	Established in 1995 as successor to the General Agreement on Tariffs and Trade. GATT was created in 1947 in the aftermath of World War II.
Membership	173 countries. Virtually all major economies other than Taiwan are members.	134 countries; another 30 countries are currently seeking accession. major economies still in the process of accession include China, Russia, and Taiwan.
Representation	A unique "tripartite" arrangement in which states, labor organizations, and employers' organizations each have formal representation.	Governments only. Although states may at their discretion include representatives of their private sectors within a delegation, they rarely do so.
Form of agreements	Freedom of association and collective bargaining are enshrined in the ILO Convention, but other rights are incorporated in separate conventions that are open to adherence by member states on an à la carte basis.	The GATT 1994 and most of the individual codes negotiated under the auspices of the GATT and the WTO are a "single undertaking" (i.e., a package deal that members are required to accept altogether).
Means of enforce- ment	Procedures allow for the investigation of alleged violations of standards, but the ILO does not have the authority to enforce these standards by imposing or permitting sanctions. Only those rights that are (a) in the ILO Convention or (b) in codes to which a country is a signatory can be the subject of investigation.	Country B can (in the absence of reform by or compensation from Country A) request permission from the Dispute Settlement Body to take retaliatory action.

Sources: International Labour Organization and World Trade Organization.

negotiators objected that the WIPO had no power to enforce the agreements that it administered, and today they find the same fault with the ILO. The conventions negotiated in the ILO are essentially pledges of good behavior at home that are subject to review, but not to coercive enforcement, in the international body. The principal tool available to the ILO is peer pressure. Alleged violations of ILO codes and principles can be formally investigated, and the release of critical reports has sometimes resulted in rectification of national practices. The ILO's ability to conduct such investigations was reinforced in 1998, when members agreed to enhance the Secretariat's authority to investigate allegations of labor rights violations.

Another perceived shortcoming of the ILO is the à la carte nature of its conventions. Although all members are obliged to respect the core principles of the ILO charter, they can pick and choose which of the more specific codes they will ratify. For example, the United States has ratified just 9 of the 181 ILO conventions and only 1 of the 7 "fundamental" conventions (as listed in table 20-1). The Senate has consistently taken the position that it will not approve any ILO convention that would require the enactment of any substantive implementing legislation. The GATT once operated on a similar principle of "code reciprocity," by which all contracting parties had to abide by the principles in the General Agreement itself, but many other codes were optional. This problem, which encouraged some countries to act as "free riders," was rectified by the Uruguay Round rule of a "single undertaking" (that is, all but a handful of older codes are now mandatory).

In the WTO system the commitments that countries make to other member states in their accessions and in negotiating rounds are both reviewable and enforceable. Some advocates of labor rights envy the WTO Dispute Settlement Body's power to authorize sanctions, even though this authority is more a matter of theory than of practice (that is, disputes are generally resolved before an injured party seeks permission to retaliate). At present there is just one provision of WTO law that explicitly permits countries to enforce labor rights with trade sanctions. GATT Article XX provides a series of exceptions to the general rules of the GATT and now the WTO. Among the ten types of otherwise WTO-illegal measures that countries might employ (subject to the condition that they not constitute "arbitrary or unjustifiable discrimination") are those "relating to the products of prison labor." This provision—GATT Article XX(e)—thus protects the use of laws such as section 307 of the U.S. Tariff Act of 1930 (as described in a later section of this chapter). To summarize, in the ILO there are labor standards without "teeth," whereas the WTO has teeth but very limited standards related to labor. This distinction is even more true in the aftermath of the Uruguay Round, which greatly increased the enforcement power of the WTO over its GATT predecessor.

The ILO has shown much greater interest in strengthening the trade-labor link than has the WTO. In 1993 it established a Working Party on the Social Dimensions of the Liberalization of International Trade. This group presented a report the following year suggesting, among other things, that the WTO dispute settlement procedures might offer a means for the enforcement of norms that countries have agreed to under various ILO codes.[12] The ILO working party proposed that the jurisdiction of the WTO and its dispute settlement powers could be widened significantly by linking them to ILO conventions. Although the United States and France supported this proposal, other members of both the ILO and the WTO—especially developing countries—opposed the initiative. The depth of opposition was evident in the results of the WTO's 1996 ministerial meeting in Singapore, when the assembled dignitaries declared:

> We renew our commitment to the observance of internationally recognized core labour standards. The International Labour Organization (ILO) is the competent body to set and deal with these standards, and we affirm our support for its work in promoting them. We believe that economic growth and development fostered by increased trade and further trade liberalization contribute to the promotion of these standards. We reject the use of labour standards for protectionist purposes, and agree that the comparative advantage of countries, particularly low-wage developing countries, must in no way be put into question. In this regard, we note that the WTO and ILO Secretariats will continue their existing collaboration.

The reference to "existing collaboration" between the secretariats is somewhat puzzling. Apart from a brief and fruitless effort in 1960 to study labor practices in the textile industry, these two institutions have not worked together on issues of international economic policy.[13] The ILO working party suggested that it "would be interesting to explore [these options] further, in consultation with the competent services of the GATT," but to date that desire for interinstitutional collaboration has gone unrequited by the WTO.[14] It is notable that the heads of the United Nations Conference on Trade and Development (UNCTAD), the

12. ILO (1994, especially pp. 14–15).
13. Patterson (1966, pp. 306–07).
14. ILO (1994, p. 13).

OECD, and the International Monetary Fund (IMF) all spoke at the Singapore ministerial, but the head of the ILO was not extended the same courtesy. The ILO is not even an official observer in the WTO General Council, whereas seven other international organizations enjoy this status; the WTO is an official observer in the ILO Governing Body and its committees.[15]

Bilateral and Regional Options

Bilateral and regional negotiations create a subtle but potentially powerful linkage between labor rights and trade liberalization insofar as they allow for a choice of negotiating partners. Multilateral and nondiscriminatory agreements include countries at all levels of economic development, but a discriminatory regime allows for greater selectivity. The possibilities of this approach are evident in the European Union's expansion, in which the countries of southern and eastern Europe have faced greater resistance to entry and have had to undergo a process of "leveling up" their regulatory regimes. In the United States the AFL-CIO has advocated a similar approach. Although the union has opposed the expansion of the NAFTA, especially through the accession of developing countries, it has frequently stated that it would favor negotiation of a free trade agreement between the United States and the European Union. Similarly, the AFL-CIO has preferred the negotiation of a bilateral U.S.-Chile free trade agreement over Chilean accession to the NAFTA because the former approach would allow for the negotiation of stricter labor provisions than are found in the NAFTA.

The NAFTA and the North American Agreement on Labor Cooperation (commonly known as the "labor side agreement") represent tentative but important steps in the evolution of this issue. The side agreement establishes an enforcement system that stands somewhere between the principles employed by the ILO (in which a country's alleged transgressions can be investigated but not punished) and those of the WTO (in which one country can seek permission to retaliate against another's transgressions). Before any sanctions are imposed, however, any alleged violations must be subject to a lengthy series of investigations and consultations, which might then lead to the levying of fines. Sanc-

15. In addition to the United Nations, the WTO General Council extends either permanent or ad hoc observer status to the UNCTAD, the OECD, the IMF, the World Bank, the Food and Agriculture Organization, and the WIPO.

tions are nevertheless at least hypothetically possible, with Article 41 providing that, "where a Party fails to pay a monetary enforcement assessment within 180 days after it is imposed by a panel," then "any complaining Party or Parties may suspend . . . the application to the Party complained against of NAFTA benefits in an amount no greater than that sufficient to collect the monetary enforcement assessment." Such sanctions are permissible only in cases related to child labor, occupational safety and health, or minimum wages. These provisions are further qualified by Article 42, which states: "Nothing in this Agreement shall be construed to empower a Party's authorities to undertake labor law enforcement activities in the territory of another Party."

Although the NAFTA remains the foremost example of a trade agreement that is tempered by a "social clause," it is not the only regional trade agreement that deals obliquely with labor rights. In a 1994 joint statement of the presidents of the Mercosur countries, the executives emphasized the relevance for the common market of issues related to employment, migration, workers' protection, and the harmonization of the countries' labor legislation.[16]

Where will labor standards fit within the planned FTAA? The steps taken thus far suggest that the agreement might declare support for workers' rights, but it is doubtful whether the agreement will go beyond rhetorical support to provide specific standards, and even less likely that it will allow for the enforcement of such standards through trade sanctions. The first Summit of the Americas in 1994 produced a Plan of Action in which the leaders declared that they "will further secure the observance and promotion of worker rights, as defined by appropriate international conventions." This statement was softened by an avowal to "avoid disguised restrictions on trade, in accordance with the GATT/WTO and other international obligations." The leaders reiterated these sentiments at the 1998 Santiago Summit. When they noted that "overcoming poverty continues to be the greatest challenge confronted by our Hemisphere," the leaders declared that they will, among other things, "promote core labor standards recognized by the International Labor Organization (ILO)."

The Inter-American Conference of Ministers of Labor took a closer look at the issue when they met in 1997 to advise the hemispheric trade ministers. They declared: "Economic integration and free trade do promote labor rights, based on internationally recognized principles of the ILO and provided each country strictly respects those rights, *following its own laws* and in accordance

16. ILO (1995, p. 6).

with its labor situation."[17] More specifically, the ministers stated that the "design and implementation of the Free Trade Area of the Americas should" do the following:

—Recognize the vital contribution that workers make to the growth of productivity, ensuring that the benefits of economic integration will be widely distributed.

—Introduce a social dimension that guarantees, as a minimum, respect for basic labor standards: freedom of association and protection of the workers' right to organize and bargain collectively, prohibition of child labor and forced labor, and nondiscrimination by reason of gender, race, religion, or any other.

—Establish a three-way dialogue (involving the government, workers, and entrepreneurs) to build consensus and ascertain the private sector's views about integration-related matters.

—Ensure that economic integration and free trade live up to their promise to expand our economies, raise our standards of living, improve working conditions and increase markets by increasing the workers' purchasing power.[18]

Though this statement was more detailed than the declarations made in Miami and Santiago, its language was not fundamentally different. The labor ministers expressed support for the advancement of labor's interests, but left it up to the individual countries and (by implication) the ILO to deal substantively with these matters. Nor have the trade ministers taken any steps to move beyond these principles. At the Fourth Trade Ministerial in San José, Costa Rica (in 1998), the ministers declared the goal of further securing "in accordance with [their] respective laws and regulations, the observance and promotion of worker rights, renewing [their] commitment to the observance of internationally recognized core labor standards and acknowledging that the International Labor Organization is the competent body to set and deal with those core labor standards." The ministers did not establish any group to negotiate on this matter, but agreed to give labor a greater voice in the advisory process. In their joint declaration they stated:

We recognize and welcome the interests and concerns that different sectors of society have expressed in relation to the FTAA. Business and other sectors of production, labor, environmental and academic groups have been particularly active in this matter. We encourage these and other sectors of civil societies to present their views on trade matters in a constructive manner. We have, therefore,

17. OAS (1997, p. 2) (emphasis added).
18. OAS (1997, p. 6).

established a committee of government representatives, open to all member countries, who shall select a chair. The committee shall receive these inputs, analyze them and present the range of views for our consideration.

This arrangement mirrors to a certain degree the process in the United States, where the USTR is advised by a network of committees representing business, labor, environmental, and others interests. It has become a tradition in the United States for the labor advisory committees to issue dissenting reports on the plans for new reductions in trade barriers. The USTR politely and attentively receives these reports, but has not halted its plans for new negotiations.

The early experience with the FTAA negotiations suggests that the USTR may have much greater expectations for the participation of "civil society" groups and the transparency of the negotiating process than do its counterparts in the region. The U.S. negotiators take the position that regional and multilateral trade negotiations should be conducted on a more open and participatory basis so as to win greater political support from the domestic "stakeholders" (that is, firms, unions, and consumers), but this viewpoint is not universally shared.

Unilateral Options

The main objective of the United States is to conclude meaningful and enforceable agreements with its trading partners. In the absence of progress in such talks, however, the United States might act on a unilateral basis. Some policymakers believe that the use of sanctions—or even the threat of sanctions —might serve a useful purpose in promoting negotiations on this issue. The comparison with the politics of intellectual property rights is again apt. In the 1980s the United States encountered serious resistance in the GATT to the proposed inclusion of this issue in new negotiations, so it acted alone by pursuing "reciprocity" cases against some countries (that is, threatening retaliation for their failure to enforce patents, copyrights, and trademarks). It also made countries' trade preferences conditional upon their actions in this area.

This policy of "aggressive unilateralism" was widely criticized by U.S. trading partners and violated the spirit (and perhaps the letter) of U.S. obligations under the GATT, but it nevertheless achieved some success. If U.S. policymakers were to take a similar approach in the case of labor rights, they could use several existing instruments in national law. The principal difference today is that under the reformed dispute settlement procedures of the WTO it is now more difficult for the United States to act on its own with impunity. Under the new regime sanctions that are imposed without the express permission of the Dispute Settlement Body can themselves lead to the formation of a dispute-settlement panel.

For over a century it has been illegal to import into the United States the products of prison labor. This ban is currently provided under section 307 of the Tariff Act of 1930. China is by far the most frequent target of section 307, but the law has also been applied in recent years to products imported from Mexico and Japan.[19] Congress amended the law in 1997 to include within its scope the products of "forced or indentured child labor." Although the original section 307 is protected in WTO law by GATT Article XX(e), the new language does not appear to enjoy the same status.

The executive branch also has the power to treat the denial of labor rights as a violation of U.S. trade rights and to respond with retaliatory measures. Section 301 of the Trade Act of 1974 (as amended) gives the USTR the authority to investigate foreign laws, policies, and practices that are alleged to be unreasonable, unfair, or discriminatory and to negotiate with the country in question for redress. If an investigation determines that U.S. trade rights have indeed been violated and the foreign country does not take action to correct the problem, the USTR has the authority to retaliate by imposing restrictions on imports. Congress amended section 301 in 1988 to allow for the use of this mechanism in cases involving foreign countries' denial of internationally recognized labor rights. This provision has never yet been tested in an actual case. If the United States were to impose such sanctions on imports from a WTO member country, it is reasonable to expect that the target country would seek the formation of a dispute settlement panel.

The international legal constraints that might restrict use of the section 301 and 307 authorities are not as binding on preferential trade programs. Under U.S. law a beneficiary of the Generalized System of Preferences (GSP), Caribbean Basin Initiative (CBI), or Andean Trade Preferences Act (ATPA) can be threatened with the reduction or loss of duty free privileges if it fails to protect labor rights. From the U.S. perspective there is one real advantage to using preferences as leverage: although actions taken under section 301 and other reciprocity laws are subject to review and discipline by the WTO, trade prefer-

19. See 19 USC 1307, which is further backed by a statute (18 USC 1761) that establishes criminal penalties for importing prison labor products knowingly and intentionally and transporting them across state lines.

ences are not similarly protected. Within the WTO legal regime they are a privilege extended at the discretion of the sponsoring country rather than a legally protected right. If the United States were to retaliate against a country with poor labor standards by imposing sanctions under section 301 and withdrawing the country's GSP privileges, the first action could lead to the formation of a WTO panel, but the second would be immune.

The first step in linking workers' rights with trade preferences came in the CBI. The Caribbean Basin Economic Recovery Act of 1983 provided that a beneficiary country must (among other things) show that it is taking steps toward improving the rights accorded to workers. Several governments in the region, including those of El Salvador, Guatemala, Haiti, and Honduras, made pledges on labor rights in order to obtain CBI certification.[20] Congress built on this precedent in 1984 by adding a similar provision to the GSP. Since that time the workers' rights issue has been the single most frequently raised issue in GSP proceedings. It accounted for 116 out of the 184 "country practices" petitions that were filed with the USTR during 1985–98.[21] As summarized in table 20-3, thirteen countries in the region have been subject to such complaints, and eleven were investigated. Three countries lost their GSP benefits either permanently (Nicaragua) or temporarily (Chile and Paraguay), but each one of these sanctions has subsequently been vitiated.

Foreign aid programs offer another and a less confrontational means of promoting labor rights. Some U.S. assistance programs are aimed specifically at enhancing the capabilities of public and private authorities in developing countries. For example, in a 1997 meeting with her Central American counterparts, Secretary of Labor Alexis Herman announced that the United States would provide $3 million to support labor ministries in the region and another $1 million to support efforts to stop child labor. Other U.S. economic programs are conditioned on labor rights. For example, the authorizing legislation for the Overseas Private Investment Corporation (OPIC) provides that OPIC may insure, reinsure, guarantee, or finance a project "only if the country in which the project is to be undertaken is taking steps to adopt and implement laws that extend internationally recognized worker rights . . . to workers in that country (including any designated zone in that country)."[22] OPIC is also required to include in any contracts a clause providing that the investor "agrees not to take

20. See Perez-Lopez (1988) and Lyle (1991).
21. Author's calculations based on data provided by the USTR.
22. See 22 USC 2191(a).

Table 20-3. Investigations of Workers' Rights in Latin American and Caribbean Countries under the Generalized System of Preferences

Country	Years	Result
Chile	1985, 1987	Chile was suspended from the GSP in 1988. Upon petition from the government of Chile, the country was redesignated in 1991.
Colombia	1990, 1993, 1995	The U.S. Trade Representative (USTR) did not accept the petitions for review.
Costa Rica	1993	Costa Rica was found to meet the requirements of the law.
Dominican Republic	1989–90, 1993	The Dominican Republic was found to meet the requirements of the law in 1990 and again in 1993.
El Salvador	1990–93	El Salvador was found to meet the requirements of the law in 1993.
Guatemala	1992–98	Guatemala was found to meet the requirements of the law.
Haiti	1988–90	Haiti was found to meet the requirements of the law in 1990.
Mexico	1991, 1993	The USTR did not accept the petitions for review.
Nicaragua	1985–87	Nicaragua was removed from the GSP and has never been reinstated (but was later designated in 1987 for the superior benefits extended under the Caribbean Basin Initiative).
Panama	1991–92	Panama was found to meet the requirements of the law.
Paraguay	1985–87, 1993	Paraguay was suspended from the GSP in 1987. Upon petition from the government of Paraguay, the country was redesignated in 1991. Paraguay was found to meet the requirements of the law in 1993.
Peru	1992–93	Petition rejected in 1992, but accepted for investigation in 1993. Peru was found to meet the requirements of the law.
Suriname	1985–87	Suriname was found to meet the requirements of the law.

Source: Compiled from information provided by the Office of the U.S. Trade Representative.

actions to prevent employees of the foreign enterprise from lawfully exercising their right of association and their right to organize and bargain collectively."

The United States also seeks to promote labor standards through its influence on the IMF and related institutions. American law has required since 1994 that the U.S. executive directors of international financial institutions use their "voice and vote" to promote "policies to encourage borrowing countries to guarantee internationally recognized worker rights . . . and to include the status of such rights as an integral part of the institution's policy dialogue with each borrowing country."[23] In 1998 Congress conditioned its approval of a $17.9 billion contribution to the IMF upon several new criteria. Among other things, the U.S. executive director is now directed to advocate "establishing or strengthening key elements of a social safety net to cushion the effects on workers of unemployment and dislocation" and to encourage the IMF to do the following:

> Structure International Monetary Fund programs and assistance so that the maintenance and improvement of core labor standards are routinely incorporated as an integral goal in the policy dialogue with recipient countries, so that—
>
> (A) recipient governments commit to affording workers the right to exercise internationally recognized core worker rights, including the right of free association and collective bargaining through unions of their own choosing.
>
> (B) measures designed to facilitate labor market flexibility are consistent with such core worker rights.
>
> (C) the staff of the International Monetary Fund surveys the labor market policies and practices of recipient countries and recommends policy initiatives that will help to ensure the maintenance or improvement of core labor standards.[24]

Given the pivotal role of the IMF in managing the current economic crises in Asia and the former Soviet Union, these are potentially crucial reforms. They have already had an impact on U.S. economic relations with Latin American countries. In 1999 testimony before a Senate subcommittee, a Treasury Department official stressed that the United States had placed great emphasis on these matters when involved with the IMF's economic consultations with Brazil. He said the United States had "vigorously used its voice to stress the importance of insulating from fiscal cuts programs to enforce labor laws—especially prohibi-

23. See 22 USC 262p–4p.
24. Excerpt from section 610 of Public Law 105-277.

tions against child labor and forced labor—and programs to enforce laws protecting the rights of Brazil's indigenous populations."[25] Similar issues may arise in U.S.-IMF consultations with other countries in the region.

Private-Sector Options

For almost every instrument that is available to governments a comparable approach is taken by labor unions, consumer organizations, private firms, or other nongovernmental organizations. These include training and organizational assistance (equivalent to foreign aid), codes of conduct (equivalent to negotiated standards), and boycotts of products that are found to violate these codes or other principles (equivalent to trade sanctions). These options are not always "pure" private initiatives insofar as they are often coordinated with or funded by the government. In the event that labor rights are not made a formal part of the FTAA negotiations, these private alternatives may acquire greater importance.

It is not much of an exaggeration to state that the AFL-CIO has its own diplomatic corps. Like other countries' unions, it is formally represented in the ILO (which, like the AFL, was founded by Samuel Gompers). The AFL-CIO and its predecessors have sponsored programs in Latin America as far back as the Mexican Revolution. Other international arms of the AFL-CIO include the Free Trade Union Institute (FTUI) and the American Institute for Free Labor Development (AIFLD). The FTUI acts as the administrator of grants made by the National Endowment for Democracy (a U.S. government–funded agency), whereas the AIFLD and other affiliated organizations also receive funding from the Agency for International Development and the U.S. Information Agency.

The principal activity of these AFL-CIO branches is to provide educational and training programs to foreign labor unions. Although these programs focus primarily on the establishment and expansion of unions, the topics can be wide-ranging. AIFLD encourages Latin American union leaders to participate more actively in regional trade negotiations, and it worked with the Inter-American Regional Organization of Workers to organize a "Labor Summit" in Denver, Colorado, in mid-1995. This meeting was held one day before the trade ministers of the Western Hemisphere gathered, and participants urged the ministers to include labor issues on the FTAA negotiating agenda.

25. Geithner (1999).

Another private means of promoting labor rights is through business codes of conduct. The grandfather of current codes was the Sullivan Principles, named after the Reverend Leon Sullivan. In 1977 Sullivan proposed that firms trading with or investing in South Africa agree to a series of pledges regarding its treatment of workers. The Sullivan Principles inspired several comparable initiatives, such as the Slepak Principles for Western businesses dealing with the Soviet Union and the MacBride Principles for investments in Northern Ireland. Although these and other ethical codes had their origins in private-sector initiatives, they can also be promoted by the state. The Clinton administration proposed its own "Model Business Principles" in 1995, which called for, among other things, the "provision of a safe and healthy workplace" and "fair employment practices, including avoidance of child and forced labor and avoidance of discrimination based on race, gender, national origin or religious beliefs; and respect for the right of association and the right to organize and bargain effectively." It is the intention of the administration that these principles be adopted by U.S. companies on a voluntary basis. The Clinton administration has also given its backing to a proposal under which U.S. companies would voluntarily adopt a "NO SWEAT" label indicating that garments and other products had not been produced in "sweatshops" and would agree to be policed by an inspection force.

Conclusion

The proposed linkage between trade and labor rights remains tenuous except at the level of economic theory. At this juncture there is no agreement within the United States on what should be sought in the FTAA negotiations or in other negotiating arenas; the industrialized countries do not agree among themselves on what might be sought from developing countries. In this environment it is difficult to imagine when or on what terms there can be a substantive and enforceable agreement on labor rights between the United States and its trading partners in the region. This does not mean that the linkage is moot. There are already provisions of WTO and U.S. law that provide for such a connection, and it is possible that—in the absence of progress in regional or multilateral negotiations—the United States might begin to use those authorities more aggressively.

Ironically, a slowdown in negotiations on this topic might be attributable in part to the lack of consensus over this issue in the United States. The controversy surrounding labor rights and the environment continue to complicate the politics of trade liberalization in the United States and to delay or block a new extension of fast-track negotiating authority. As long as the executive and legislative branches of the U.S. government cannot agree on what the United States will seek from its trading partners on this issue, Congress may continue to deny a grant of fast-track negotiating authority to the president. That denial will make it difficult for the United States to negotiate and conclude agreements on any other issue now pending in the FTAA negotiations. Even if the FTAA does not deal substantively with this issue, the United States may employ other means to seek commitments from its Latin American and Caribbean partners.

References

Charnovitz, S. 1986. "Fair Labor Standards and International Trade." *Journal of World Trade Law* 20(1): 61–78.

Geithner, T. 1999. Testimony before the Senate Banking Committee Subcommittee on International Trade and Finance (March 9).

International Labor Organization. 1994. "The Social Dimensions of the Liberalization of World Trade." GB.261/WP/SLD/1. Geneva.

———. 1995. "Overview of the Work of Other International Organizations and Bodies Concerning the Social Aspects of the Liberalization of International Trade." GB.262/WP/SDL/Inf.4. Geneva.

Lyle, F. 1991. "Worker Rights in U.S. Policy." *Foreign Labor Trends,* FLT 91–54. Washington, D.C.: U.S. Department of Labor.

Organization for Economic Cooperation and Development. 1996. *Trade, Employment and Labour Standards.* Paris.

Organization of American States. 1997. "Declaration of the Tenth Inter-American Conference of Ministers of Labor, Presented at the Meeting of Ministers of Trade, Belo Horizonte (Brazil)." OAS/Ser.L/XIX.10. Washington, D.C.

Patterson, G. 1966. *Discrimination in International Trade: The Policy Issues.* Princeton University Press.

Perez-Lopez, J. F. 1988. "Conditioning Trade on Foreign Labor Law: The U.S. Approach." *Comparative Labor Law Journal* 9(2): 253–92.

Shotwell, J. T. 1934. *The Origins of the International Labor Organization.* Two volumes. Columbia University Press.

U.S. Department of Labor. 1994. *By the Sweat and Toil of Children: The Use of Child Labor in American Imports.* Washington, D.C.

———. 1997. *International Comparisons of Hourly Compensation Costs for Production Workers in Manufacturing—Updated Data for 1996.* Washington, D.C.

World Bank. 1995. *World Development Report 1995: Workers in An Integrating World.* Washington, D.C.

CHAPTER TWENTY-ONE

Trade and the Environment

Gary P. Sampson

The World Trade Organization (WTO) does not have as its primary objective the protection of the environment, and it places no constraints on governments' implementing within their borders whatever legitimate policy options they wish to with respect to the environment.[1] Although WTO members are free to adopt whatever national standards they wish, many environmental problems are transboundary—global or regional—in nature, and therefore call for solutions that extend outside the borders of individual countries. The importance of environmental protection is clearly acknowledged in the WTO Preamble and various agreements.

If transboundary environmental standards are agreed to on a regional basis, an attractive enforcement mechanism is discrimination against the exports of parties to the WTO Agreement that do not respect these standards. This raises a number of issues of potential importance to the WTO—particularly in instances in which individual countries or parties to a regional agreement take discriminatory trade measures to enforce environmental standards vis-à-vis WTO members that have not agreed to these standards. Unless exceptional circumstances prevail, this constitutes a violation of one of the most fundamental rights of WTO members—namely, the right to nondiscrimination in international trade.

---

1. To be consistent with the WTO obligations, trade measures must not restrict imports for protectionist purposes or discriminate unfairly between foreign suppliers.

WTO members formally acknowledged this potential problem at an early stage and established the Committee on Trade and Environment (CTE) to address this and many other issues. The purpose of this chapter is to draw on the work of the CTE—which is relevant in any examination of the relationship between regional environment agreements and the WTO—to examine the WTO rules and procedures themselves and to draw conclusions about the policy implications that follow from that examination.

Background

The WTO members recognized some time ago the complexity of the relationship between trade policy and environment policy. As a result of discussions that coincided with the latter stages of the Uruguay Round, the WTO General Council established the CTE in January 1995. The CTE mandate and terms of reference are included in the Marrakesh Ministerial Decision on Trade and Environment of April 15, 1994. They are far-reaching and indicate an early concern by WTO members for the compatibility of the WTO rules with multilateral environment agreements (MEAs). This decision also mandated that the CTE report to the first biennial meeting of the Ministerial Conference, where the work and terms of reference of the CTE were reviewed in light of CTE recommendations. The report was heavily negotiated, forwarded to ministers, and adopted at the Ministerial Conference meeting in Singapore in December 1996. The CTE has now structured its work around the ten items listed in the Decision on Trade and Environment.[2]

The CTE has a broad-based mandate covering all areas of the multilateral trading system—goods, services, and intellectual property. The mandate of the committee is first, to identify the relationships between trade and environmental measures in order to promote sustainable development, and second, to make recommendations on whether any modifications to the provisions of the WTO are required. Several items on the work program relate to the interface between the rules and disciplines of the multilateral trading system and trade-related aspects of the multilateral environmental agenda. One item is the relationship

2. For several of the items the CTE was able to build on discussions that had been conducted in 1992–93 in the GATT Group on Environmental Measures and International Trade (EMIT) and on preparatory discussions conducted in 1994 in a Subcommittee on Trade and Environment of the WTO Preparatory Committee.

between the WTO provisions and trade measures applied for environmental purposes, including those pursuant to multilateral and regional environmental agreements.

Two principal events ensured a high profile on the WTO agenda for matters relating to the environment. The first related directly to a regional trade arrangement—namely, the inclusion of environmental provisions in the North American Free Trade Agreement (NAFTA). The second event was the imposition by the United States of a ban on imports of tuna fish from a number of countries on the grounds that their tuna-fishing activities were causing the accidental death of dolphins. Two GATT "tuna-dolphin" dispute panels concluded that the United States' trade ban was inconsistent with its GATT obligations. In turn, this raised concerns about the ability of the then-GATT dispute settlement mechanism to cope with environment-related disputes. The dispute was essentially regional and—some would argue—should have been settled on a regional basis.

The WTO Rules

The WTO does not inhibit governments from protecting (as they wish) against damage to the environment resulting from the production and consumption of products produced within their national boundaries. Final products can be taxed and other charges levied for any purpose thought appropriate by national governments. If carbon dioxide emissions and energy use associated with the use of a product are considered excessive, the products can be taxed in the form and to the extent considered necessary. Similarly, there are no problems from a WTO perspective with governments' levying taxes according to the manner in which a product is produced within their territory. For example, domestic taxes can be levied on production processes that are directed toward reducing energy consumption or carbon emissions.

From an environmental perspective, an approach concentrating only on domestic goods and activities potentially has limitations. For environmentalists the manner in which a product is produced and disposed of—its "life cycle" from the cradle to the grave—is important, whether the production takes place within or outside the borders of their own country. The WTO flexibility extends to regulation of products produced domestically, imported products, and domestic production processes. It does not provide for the application of restrictive measures relating to production processes in exporting countries. In short, from a WTO perspective the manner in which a foreign product is produced is not a basis on which WTO rights and obligations are established. The underlying thesis is that should any country wish to influence the manner in which products are produced in other countries—however appropriate this practice may be thought by the importing country—this is not to be done through the application of discriminatory trade measures. Therefore, for trade measures to be WTO-consistent, products that have the same physical form are to be considered like products by the importing country, regardless of whether they have been produced abroad in an environmentally friendly manner.

Nevertheless, the possibility of imposing WTO-inconsistent measures on imports for environmental purposes is provided for by the WTO agreements. Under specific circumstances WTO members can invoke measures that normally would constitute a breach of WTO obligations to protect the environment. These circumstances are spelled out in Article XX of the GATT, which addresses general exceptions.[3] Exceptions to the WTO obligations can be sought provided that a measure is necessary to protect human, animal, or plant life or health (Article XX(b)). Exceptions are also provided for measures related to the conservation of exhaustible natural resources (Article XX(g)). This general exception provision is clearly designed to permit governments to maintain or implement laws they feel are necessary to preserve the lives of people, flora, fauna, and exhaustible natural resources.

According to Article XX, however, any measure that breaches WTO obligations for this purpose should not be used as a means for arbitrary or unjustifiable discrimination or to impose a disguised restriction on international trade. Further, that the measures must be necessary to protect the environment means that other less trade-restrictive options are not available. An additional and important consideration is that on the basis of past decisions on disputes brought to the WTO (and the GATT), exceptions apply only to the lives and resources within the territory of the country taking action. Although this limits the intrusion of countries into the practices of others, it leaves open a number of questions relating to transboundary considerations, such as the effects of greenhouse gas emissions produced outside a country's national boundaries, but with effects in that country.

Another area of importance to the WTO is the role of voluntary standards, mandatory regulations, and conformity assessment procedures used for en-

3. See GATT (1955).

vironmental purposes. Flexibility is also provided for here. The WTO Technical Barriers to Trade (TBT) Agreement establishes obligations to ensure that voluntary standards, mandatory regulations, and conformity assessment procedures do not have as their objective the restriction of trade. However, the agreement provides considerable flexibility to accommodate environmental concerns. Although it encourages the adoption of international standards and technical regulations to encourage the harmonization of regulations and therefore to facilitate trade, it specifically recognizes that priorities with respect to the environment differ between countries and formally acknowledges that this can be fully reflected in domestic regulations. The agreement therefore permits the adoption of different standards and regulations by any WTO member. A principal obligation is that standards and technical regulations not be implemented in such a way that they restrict trade more than necessary to achieve the policy objective. This is the concept of proportionality.

The WTO Subsidies Agreement has as its main purpose the prohibition of governments' providing direct assistance to their own industries to improve their competitive position. However, the agreement identifies certain nonactionable subsidies. Included in the list of such subsidies is assistance to promote the adaptation of existing facilities to comply with new environmental requirements imposed by law or regulations that result in greater constraints and financial burdens on firms. However, these subsidies are carefully circumscribed to keep them from constituting trade barriers to improve competitiveness.

Regional and Multilateral Agreements

The discussions within the CTE on environment agreements generated one clear conclusion: that the WTO is not an environmental policymaking institution and therefore that the formulation and monitoring of environmental standards should be left to those with the relevant expertise.[4] What this conclusion argues for is an approach whereby agreements (either multilateral or regional) are established to address environmental problems of international concern. If these agreements are broad based and involve a large number of WTO members (generally the same governments that have the environmental concerns), the parties to the agreements may agree to be discriminated against if certain standards are not met, and therefore willingly forgo their WTO rights. This type

4. WTO (1996, Section II, item I).

of agreement is nothing at all new, as such MEAs already exist outside the WTO.

In fact, there are already approximately 200 regional and multilateral environment agreements in place. These agreements stand as testimony to the fact that cooperation at the regional and multilateral levels on environmental standards is a practical option. Most agreements do not include provisions relating to trade and consequently do not raise any evident point of difficulty with the WTO. However, some twenty of these agreements do include trade provisions. The Basel Convention on the Movement of Hazardous Waste, the Montreal Protocol on Substances that Deplete the Ozone Layer, and the Convention on International Trade in Endangered Species (CITES) provide examples. In the case of the Montreal Protocol, after a ten-year phase-out period trade in covered products with nonparties will be banned altogether, with the aim of securing the compliance of nonparties with the protocol's environmental objectives. For a WTO member this amounts to a clear breach of GATT Articles I and III.

In regional or multilateral environmental agreements parties adopt common standards and agree on how they are to be enforced. However, environmental agreements do not all attract universal participation, and indeed some of the most recently concluded and the most important from an environmental point of view have not. This has the potential to create problems within the context of the WTO. First and foremost is the use of discriminatory trade restrictions by parties to an environment agreement against nonparties.

There are considerable differences in the kinds of trade measures that MEA parties are authorized or required to apply and the conditions pursuant to which the measures are taken. No GATT or WTO trade dispute has arisen so far over the use of trade measures applied pursuant to an MEA.[5] Nevertheless, doubts have been expressed by some WTO members about the WTO-consistency of certain trade measures applied pursuant to some MEAs, particularly discriminatory trade restrictions applied by MEA parties against nonparties involving extrajurisdictional action. The following paragraphs reflect some views expressed in the CTE.[6]

One school of thought is that no real problem exists. When account is taken of the limited number of MEAs that include trade provisions and the fact that

5. For a description of the trade provisions of the main MEAs, see *The Use of Trade Measures in Select Multilateral Environmental Agreements*, United Nations Environment Program (1995).

6. For the following views and the discussions in the CTE, see WTO (1996).

no trade dispute has arisen over the use of those measures to date, it could be argued that there is no evidence of a real conflict between the WTO and MEAs. With some limited resort to the WTO dispute settlement procedures, the existing WTO rules could be considered to be of sufficient scope to allow trade measures to be applied pursuant to MEAs, and it could be thought that it is neither necessary nor desirable to exceed that scope. According to this view the proper course of action to take to resolve any underlying conflict in this area would be for WTO members to avoid using trade measures in MEAs that are inconsistent with their WTO obligations.

The opposing view is that the real problems related to the relationship between MEAs and the WTO are on the way. International cooperation is the most environmentally effective means of tackling transboundary and global problems, and a joint effort by all countries concerned is required. It is argued that there is an increasing agenda of MEA negotiations, such as the Climate Change Convention, that are clearly of a transborder nature. Although no conflict has so far arisen regarding trade measures pursuant to MEAs and the WTO rules, it is perhaps important to adopt a preventive attitude and provide greater certainty as concern grows about the collective impact of individual countries on the global commons.

Various proposals have been advanced in the CTE with a view to establishing a framework for the relationship between MEAs and the WTO. Although these proposals differ in nature, scope, and level of ambition, they are all based on the view that the WTO should be supportive of action at the multilateral level for the protection of the environment. They develop the view that, if specific conditions are met, certain trade measures taken pursuant to MEAs should benefit from special treatment under the WTO provisions. This approach has been described as creating an "environmental window" in the WTO. In terms of the earlier discussion, for example, the test of Article XX for the "necessity" of discriminatory measures could be adjusted where a broad-based MEA already exists. It could be argued that the existence of an MEA that recognized the importance of the problem for which the exception was being sought (greenhouse gas emissions) would establish the necessity of action.

The CTE has in fact looked at the issue in terms of whether it is appropriate to provide for differentiated treatment of trade measures applied pursuant to MEAs, depending upon whether they apply between parties or against non-parties and whether they are specifically mandated in an MEA.[7] One view is that

7. WTO (1996).

specific and jointly notified trade measures applied among MEA parties would prevail over their WTO obligations to the extent of the mandated inconsistency, and WTO dispute settlement would not be available to them for trade action within the terms of the notified measures. It has been proposed in the CTE that nonconsensual measures (those applied among parties, but not specifically mandated in an MEA, and those applied against nonparties that are specifically mandated in an MEA) could be tested through the WTO dispute settlement mechanism against procedural and substantive criteria that would be set out in an understanding to be established by WTO members. The understanding would not apply to trade measures taken against nonparties to an MEA that were not specifically mandated in the MEA, nor would it apply to unilateral measures. These would continue to be subject to existing WTO provisions.

It seems reasonable to adopt the premise that trade measures—in particular discriminatory trade measures against nonparties to MEAs—are not an appropriate way to pursue international environmental objectives and should not be used to coerce countries to become signatories to an MEA. This is not the role of the WTO. Trade measures are only one alternative in the package of instruments that can be used to achieve MEA objectives. The conclusion of this line of reasoning is that making changes in WTO rules to accommodate MEA trade measures that are inconsistent with WTO rules constitutes an unbalanced and isolated approach as long as there is no parallel commitment to first use and enforce positive measures as a means to increase participation in MEAs.

The respective roles of the dispute settlement procedures in MEAs and the WTO are also an important consideration in looking at the compatibility of MEAs and the WTO. Most of the MEAs that are the focus of the CTE's work include mechanisms for resolving disputes. Like the WTO, MEAs emphasize the avoidance of disputes. They include provisions to increase transparency through the collection and exchange of information, coordination of technical and scientific research, and collective monitoring of implementing measures as well as consultation provisions. These range from nonbinding consensus-building mechanisms to binding judicial procedures of arbitration and, in certain cases, resort to the International Court of Justice.[8]

In the event of a dispute between two WTO members, one a nonparty to an MEA, over trade measures applied pursuant to the MEA, the WTO provides the only available dispute settlement mechanism, since the nonparty would

8. WTO (1996, Section II, item II).

have no rights under nor access to the MEA dispute settlement mechanism. In such a circumstance it would be important for the Dispute Settlement Body to avoid becoming involved in a purely environmental conflict, but a WTO dispute settlement panel could seek relevant environmental expertise and technical advice.

Discussions in the CTE have also considered that before using discriminatory trade measures account needs to be taken of the reasons a nonparty to an MEA would have decided not to join the MEA and who should judge the merit of that country's decision to opt out. There might be many reasons a country would not join in multilateral action to address an environmental problem. It might find the scientific evidence unpersuasive, it might not be able to afford to join or have access to the necessary technology on favorable terms, or it might believe that more pressing policy problems deserve higher priority. In this regard it is worth recalling Principle 7 of the Rio Declaration, which states that there is a "common but differentiated responsibility" of states in resolving environmental problems of a global nature.

An additional consideration from a WTO perspective is that a number of environment agreements with trade provisions provide countries with considerable scope to use trade measures to protect national environmental resources, but not to act extraterritorially or in an extrajurisdictional manner. Some regional and multilateral agreements necessarily involve provisions for extraterritorial action to protect environmental resources outside the parties' borders—for example, trade bans in the United States to protect elephants in Africa. Clarifying that extraterritorial action is legitimate in the context of the regional agreement (and only in that context) would remove the risk that any serious misunderstandings would arise over the use of trade measures among parties to the environment agreement.

Despite these considerations, the dimension of the problems in this area should not be exaggerated. None of the trade provisions in MEAs that involve a subset of WTO members has ever been subject to a legal challenge under the GATT/WTO. However, it is important to accept that environmental agreements and the WTO represent different bodies of international law. Various proposals have been advanced with a view to establishing a framework for the relationship between MEAs and the WTO. Although these proposals differ in nature, scope, and level of ambition, they are all based on the view that the WTO should be supportive of action at the multilateral level for the protection of the environment.

Exceptions

All WTO provisions are relevant to any consideration of the use of trade measures for environmental purposes. Those that are cited regularly as being of key importance are the provisions relating to nondiscrimination (most favored nation and national treatment) and to transparency. As noted earlier, however, Article XX of the GATT allows a WTO member legitimately to place its public health and safety and national environmental goals ahead of its WTO commitments if it does not go beyond what is necessary, in terms of trade restriction or discrimination, to achieve those policy goals.

An issue here is whether the provisions of GATT Article XX permit a member to impose unilateral trade restrictions that are otherwise inconsistent with its WTO obligations for the purpose of protecting environmental resources that lie outside its jurisdiction. One view is that a specific commitment needs to be made by WTO members to avoid using trade measures unilaterally for that purpose. Another view is that there is nothing in the text of Article XX that indicates that it applies only to policies to protect animal or plant resources or conserve natural resources within the territory of the country invoking the provision.

Throughout the history of the GATT there has been relatively little push for member countries to examine and interpret the provisions of GATT Article XX in the context of trade measures applied for environmental purposes. However, there has been strong criticism by the environmental communities relating to the tuna-dolphin rulings of the dispute settlement panels convened as part of the GATT dispute settlement process. These concerned the United States' embargo on imports of tuna and tuna products from Mexico, which were imposed because the tuna were being fished in a manner that caused the death of dolphins. There have been two tuna panels, and the adoption of the decisions of both has been blocked by the United States. A more recent case was the turtle-shrimp case, in which the United States announced an import ban on imports of shrimps from certain countries, claiming that their failure to use turtle-excluder devices to protect turtles in their fishing methods resulted in a high level of sea turtle mortality. Although the CITES deals with endangered species, sanctions could not be applied under this convention as the endangered species was not itself being traded. The United States was not successful in this emotionally charged case, and at the time of this writing has taken the findings of the panel that was convened to the WTO Appellate Body for its consideration. The United States is not alone in having legislation in place to use unilateral trade measures for environmental purposes: European Union legislation banning imports of furs from animals caught in leg-traps falls into a similar category.

One thing that is clear to those who are dedicated to the preservation of the rules-based multilateral trading system is that unilateral action in order to impose domestic environmental preferences on trading partners through the use of trade sanctions contradicts the basic premise of the WTO. In its report to the Singapore Ministerial Conference the CTE stated: "Unilateral actions to deal with environmental challenges outside the jurisdiction of the importing country should be avoided. Environmental measures addressing transboundary or global problems should, as far as possible, be based on an international consensus."

Another option to allow for the use of trade measures beyond what is already provided for in the regular WTO provisions is recourse to the waiver provisions of the WTO. Article IX of the WTO Agreement provides the opportunity for members to seek waivers to WTO obligations in exceptional circumstances. Such waivers need to be approved, preferably by consensus, but at a minimum by a supporting vote of three-quarters of the WTO membership. Conditions designed to protect the integrity of the WTO legal contract are attached to the granting of a waiver: among them are that the waiver is time bound and must be renewed periodically and that a legal challenge (nonviolation, nullification, and impairment) can be made by a WTO member whose trade interests are damaged.

Dispute Settlement Mechanisms

A related issue is the proper forum for the settlement of disputes that arise over the use of trade measures pursuant to regional agreements. Is it the WTO, or is it whatever dispute settlement machinery exists in the regional agreements? At the most fundamental level the answer lies in the fact that better policy coordination between trade and environmental policy officials at the national level can help prevent situations in which trade measures applied pursuant to MEAs could become subject to disputes. Problems are unlikely to arise in the WTO over trade measures agreed to and applied among parties to an MEA.

If a dispute arises between WTO members that are also parties to an MEA over the use of trade measures they are applying between themselves pursuant to the MEA, this should logically be addressed through the dispute settlement mechanisms available under the MEA. Improved compliance mechanisms and dispute settlement mechanisms available in the MEAs would encourage resolution of any such disputes within the MEAs. A dispute involving the United States' measures on reformulated gasoline was environmental in nature, as it arose in connection with measures applied under the U.S. Clean Air Act. The panel report in this case stressed that it is not the legitimacy of an environmental agreement or objective that will be questioned in a WTO dispute, but rather whether a trade-related measure is applied in a way consistent with WTO rules and disciplines.

It has been generally felt in the CTE that it is each government's responsibility to avoid entering into conflicting obligations in treaties to which it is a signatory; that is best done at the negotiating and drafting stages. Disputes can be avoided if WTO members who are parties to an MEA review the trade measures applied by other countries pursuant to the MEA in the context of the totality of their international obligations. In the event of an environmental dispute, it is important to note that Article 13 and Appendix 4 of the WTO Dispute Settlement Understanding (DSU) allow a panel to seek information and technical advice from any individual or body that it deems appropriate, to seek information from any relevant source and to consult experts on certain aspects of the matter, and to request a report in writing from an advisory review group with respect to a factual issue concerning a scientific or other technical matter raised by a party to a dispute. This facility is available to panels examining disputes that arise over the use of any environment-related trade measures, whether these have been applied pursuant to an MEA or not.

Although it is generally considered that these DSU provisions are sufficient and there are no grounds for making special provision for environmental expertise, mechanisms could be explored to inform panels of MEA provisions, including the application and interpretation of an MEA or judgments on environmental matters in MEAs. One suggestion has been that cooperation and consultation arrangements between MEAs and the WTO be established to ensure that the MEAs' environmental objectives are given appropriate consideration.

Another suggestion has been made that the role of expert groups be strengthened in WTO disputes involving environmental issues, particularly in any disputes that might arise over the use of trade measures applied pursuant to MEAs—for example, by requiring the use of such a group when there are scientific and technical points at issue in a dispute. In that connection it has been noted that under the provisions of the Annex on Financial Services of the General Agreement on Trade in Services (GATS) "panels for disputes on prudential issues and other financial matters shall have the necessary expertise relevant to the specific financial service under dispute." In this regard, it is felt that environmental expertise would be particularly important in any disputes involving the interpretation and application of an MEA for testing the necessity of an environment-related trade measure and for the assessment of scientific evidence. However, concerns have been raised that the independence of WTO panelists to judge a dispute should not be compromised; expert opinion could help inform a panel, but outside experts should not become involved in judging whether measures are consistent with the WTO.

Technical Barriers to Trade

Technical regulations and product standards applied for environmental purposes are subject to the rules and disciplines of the WTO TBT Agreement. Broadly speaking, these rules and disciplines require that the measures be made known to WTO members, be applied in a nondiscriminatory way, and not be more trade restrictive than necessary to achieve their policy objective. Where international standards exist and are suited to meeting the objectives of a member, they must be used. However, nothing prevents a country from adopting higher environmental standards as long as the agreement's basic disciplines are respected. Essentially, these disciplines have existed under the GATT for the past fifteen years. More than 350 national environmental standards have been notified under the agreement. They cover national measures applied to implement international environmental agreements, such as the Montreal Protocol and CITES; import prohibitions on products harmful to the environment; and standards and regulations on air, water, and noise pollution, energy and soil conservation, recycling requirements, and so on.

Conclusions

The WTO rules place essentially no constraints on the policy choices available to a member country to protect its own environment against damage either from domestic production or from the consumption of domestically produced or imported products. In general terms, imports and exports can be treated as are domestically produced goods. Similarly, a government can take any action to regulate its own production processes. Therefore, with respect to regional and multilateral environment agreements the key requirement from the WTO point of view is that trade-related environmental measures not discriminate between home-produced goods and imports or between imports from or exports to different trading partners. Nondiscrimination and national treatment are the cornerstone of the multilateral trading system based on the WTO rules.

In the final analysis, rather than resorting to unilateral trade restrictions to enforce environmental standards that have little to do with trade, the preferred approach should be to seek cooperative solutions at either the regional or the multilateral level among those that have the mandate and expertise to deal with environmental considerations. The more international environmental problems can be resolved regionally or multilaterally, the less risk of trade friction there will be in the WTO. Therefore, if trade provisions are to be included as an enforcement mechanism in a regional or multilateral agreement, the parties should be fully cognizant of the fact that they may be forgoing their WTO rights of nondiscrimination. Should trade measures be used outside of the environmental agreement vis-à-vis nonparties that are WTO members, this may well constitute a breach of WTO rights.

References

General Agreement on Tariffs and Trade. 1955. *Basic Instruments and Selected Documents*. Geneva: GATT Secretariat.
GATT Group on Environmental Measures and International Trade. 1992–93.
Subcommittee on Trade and Environment of the WTO Preparatory Committee. 1994. Preparatory discussions.
United Nations Environment Program. 1995. *The Use of Trade Measures in Select Multilateral Environmental Agreements*. United Nations.
World Trade Organization. 1994. Decision on trade and environment. Marrakesh (April 15).
———. 1996. General Council decision on transparency. Geneva (July).

Contributors

Roberto Bouzas, *Latin American School of Social Sciences/Argentina*

Rafael Cornejo, *Inter-American Development Bank*

Luis Jorge Garay S., *Inter-American Development Bank*

Edward M. Graham, *Institute for International Economics*

Jean-Marie Grether, *World Trade Organization*

Gary N. Horlick, *O'Melveny and Myers*

Robert E. Hudec, *University of Minnesota Law School*

Barbara Kotschwar, *Organization of American States*

Sam Laird, *World Trade Organization*

Robert Z. Lawrence, *Council of Economic Advisors*

Patrick Low, *World Trade Organization*

Marcelo Olarreaga, *World Trade Organization*

Bonapas Francis Onguglo, *United Nations Conference on Trade and Development*

Rosine M. Plank-Brumback, *Organization of American States*

Francisco Javier Prieto, *University of Chile*

Maryse Robert, *Organization of American States*

Miguel Rodríguez Mendoza, *Georgetown University*

Brian R. Russell, *Institute for International Economics*

Simeon A. Sahaydachny, *Attorney at Law*

Gary P. Sampson, *World Trade Organization*

Murray G. Smith, *International Consultant*

James D. Southwick, *Dorsey and Whitney*

Sherry M. Stephenson, *Organization of American States*

Steven A. Sugarman, *Yale Law School*

José Tavares de Araujo, Jr., *Organization of American States*

Luis Tineo, *The World Bank*

Craig VanGrasstek, *American University and the VanGrasstek Company*

Don Wallace, Jr., *Georgetown University*

Theresa Wetter, *Organization of American States*

Index